AF600095

THIS GHOSTLY POETRY

History and Memory of Exiled Spanish Republican Poets

This Ghostly Poetry

History and Memory of Exiled Spanish Republican Poets

DANIEL AGUIRRE-OTEIZA

UNIVERSITY OF TORONTO PRESS
Toronto Buffalo London

Toronto Buffalo London
utorontopress.com

ISBN 978-1-4875-0381-9 (cloth)
ISBN 978-1-4875-1885-1 (EPUB)
ISBN 978-1-4875-1884-4 (PDF)

Toronto Iberic

Library and Archives Canada Cataloguing in Publication

Title: This ghostly poetry : history and memory of exiled Spanish Republican poets / Daniel Aguirre-Oteiza.
Names: Aguirre Oteiza, Daniel, author.
Series: Toronto Iberic ; 51.
Description: Series statement: Toronto Iberic ; 51 | Includes bibliographical references and index.
Identifiers: Canadiana (print) 20190237155 | Canadiana (ebook) 20190237163 | ISBN 9781487503819 (cloth) | ISBN 9781487518851 (EPUB) | ISBN 9781487518844 (PDF)
Subjects: LCSH: Exiles' writings, Spanish – History and criticism. | LCSH: Spanish poetry – 20th century – History and criticism. | LCSH: Spain – History – Civil War, 1936-1939 – Literature and the war. | LCSH: Ghosts in literature.
Classification: LCC PQ6098.H5 A38 2020 | DDC 861.609/3526914–dc23

This book has been published with the support of the Faculty of Arts and Sciences, Harvard University and the Murray Anthony Potter Fund, Department of Romance Languages and Literatures, Harvard University.

University of Toronto Press acknowledges the financial assistance to its publishing program of the Canada Council for the Arts and the Ontario Arts Council, an agency of the Government of Ontario.

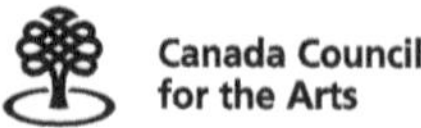

Funded by the Government of Canada
Financé par le gouvernement du Canada

Para Elisa Oteiza Álvarez y Silvia Aguirre Oteiza

This book was written in memory of:

Sixto Aguirre Roncal (Pamplona 1900–Rosario 1953)

Carlos Aguirre Oteiza (Pamplona 1966–Pamplona 1998)

Carlos Aguirre Salinas (Pamplona 1936–Pamplona 2011)

Armando López Salinas (Madrid 1925–Madrid 2014)

Contents

Illustrations

Acknowledgments

This book would not have been written without the advice, mentorship, patience, and kindness of Joe Blackmore, Luis Fernández Cifuentes, Mary Gaylord, Luis Girón, Christopher Maurer, Santiago Morales, Mariano Siskind, and Diana Sorensen. My deepest thanks to all of them.

For many different forms of collaboration, conversation, encouragement, generosity, hospitality, support, understanding or warmth during the making of this project, my gratitude to Adriana Alfaro, Palmar Álvarez-Blanco, Pablo Antoñana, Alba Aragón, Juan Arias, Antonio Arraiza, Alberto Artieda, John Ashbery, Ignacio Azcueta, Raquel Ballabriga, Magdalena Bassi, librería Bibliofilia (México DF), librería La Bola (Barcelona), Brattle Book Shop (Boston), Lia Brozgal, calle de Donceles (México DF), librería Canuda (Barcelona), Miguel Casado, Alberto Castillo, Josetxo Cerdán, librería El Cid (Santiago de Chile), Michelle Clayton, Greg Cohen, El Colegio de México, Commonwealth Books (Boston), Tom Conley, Lucía Cotarelo, Kathy Coviello, David Damrosch, Christina Davis, Anna Deeny, Benito del Pliego, Rodrigo del Río, Juan del Solar, Hernán Díaz, Eugenia Dimant, Edgardo Dobry, Cathy Downey, Paloma Duong, Marta Enrech, Sebastiaan Faber, Elvira G. Di Fabio, Matylda Figlerowicz, Celia Filipetto, Albert Freixa, Forrest Gander, Lorgia García-Peña, Anthony Geist, Francesca Giacchino, librería El Glyptodón (Buenos Aires), Merche González, José Ángel González Sainz, librería El Gran Remate (México DF), Virginie Greene, La Guadalupana (Coyoacán), Claudio Guillén, librería Gulliver (Madrid), Adriana Gutiérrez, Sylvaine Guyot, Elizabeth Habtegabriel, Mike Holmes, Walter Hryshko, Rosario Hubert, librería Huemul (Buenos Aires), John K. King Used and Rare Books (Detroit), Jim Iffland, Amalia Iglesias, librería Inframundo (México DF), librería Iratxe (Pamplona), Eduardo Iriarte, Neiel Israel, Lana Jaffe, Andreu Jaume, Julián Jiménez Heffernan, Clemence Jouët-Pastré, Annabel L. Kim, Ashford King, Ally Ladha, Lame Duck Books (Cambridge), Elizabeth Langdon-Gray, Heather Lantz, Clara Lida, Johanna Liander, Frannie Lindsay, Ernesto Livon-Grosman, Christine Legros, Juan Gabriel López Guix, Isaac Magaña, librería Maldà (Barcelona), Ricardo

Maldonado, Marta Mateo, Martín y Rosa, Jonathan Mayhew, José Antonio Mazzotti, Mercado del libro de la Cuesta de Moyano (Madrid), Mercat de Llibres de Sant Antoni (Barcelona), librería Merlín (Bogotá), Lucas Mertehikian, Eduardo Milán, Moheli (Coyoacán), Inmaculada Moliner, Cristina Moreiras, Francisco Moreno, Carmen Moreno-Nuño, librería Muntaner (Barcelona), Sandra Nadaff, José María Naharro-Calderón, Marysa Navarro-Aranguren, César Núñez, Javier Ortega, Alexandra Ortiz Wallner, María Ospina, José Ignacio Padilla, librería El Parnasillo (Pamplona), Marimar Patrón, Pepe Payà, Marcelo Pellegrini, Luis Arturo Pérez, Katharina Piechocki, Julia Piera, Claudia Pineda, Gabriela Poma, Edurne Portela, Julio Prieto, Ana Pulido, José Rabasa, Raven Used Books (Cambridge), Kathy Richman, the David Rockefeller Center for Latin American Studies, Jimena Rodríguez, Susan R. Suleiman, Pablo Ruiz, Roberto Ruiz, Ángeles Rull, Peter Sacks, Stephanie Sandler, librería Salvador Novo (México DF), Julie Salzinger, Nicolau Sevcenko, Lynn Shirey, Judith Singer, Doris Sommer, Arturo Souto Alabarce, Anthony Stanton, librería Studio (Barcelona), Christina Svendsen, librería Taifa (Barcelona), Jorge Téllez, Juan Torbidoni, librería El Tomo Suelto (México DF), librería La Torre de Viejo (Coyoacán), librería Las Tres Cruces (Coyoacán), librería Walden (Pamplona), Michael Ugarte, Felipe Valencia, Carlos Varón, Lucas Vermal, Vuelvilla, Catarina von Wedemeyer, David Yagüe, Josefina Yanguas, Ana Yáñez, Simos Zenios, and Suzanne Zepp.

I would like to gratefully acknowledge the help of all the caring people who work at the Romance Languages and Literatures Department at Harvard University. I also owe a very special debt to Erin Dougherty, Heather Dubnick, Lucas Cuatrecasas, Andy Gray, and Matthew Miller, who provided tireless and sympathetic assistance with editing, translation, and manuscript preparation. My deep appreciation to the University of Toronto Press, and particularly to Mark Thompson, Robert Davidson, Siobhan McMenemy, as well as the anonymous readers enlisted by the press. Early versions of sections of this book appear in *Wall to Wall: Spaces of Law in Latin American and Iberian Contexts* (2020), *Letras Hispanas* (2019), *Revista de Estudios Hispánicos* (2018), *Poéticas: Revista de Estudios Literarios* (2017), *Revista Hispánica Moderna* (2017) and *Hispanic Review* (2015). I thank the editors and publishers of each of these publications for permission to reprint those sections in substantially revised, updated, and expanded form. Their anonymous referees also contributed insightful criticism and valuable suggestions. My gratitude also to *Laberintos: Revista de estudios sobre los exilios culturales españoles*.

Last, but by far not least, I want to thank the Red de Bibliotecas Públicas de Navarra, the Boston Public Library, the Cambridge Public Library (Massachusetts), and anonymous members of the Phillips Room staff at Harvard's Widener Library.

El viento ha hecho invisibles los caminos
por los que vino a este lugar de espectros
[The wind has made invisible the roads
whereby he came to this place of specters]

Tomás Segovia (1982)

Vengo – digo – no vuelvo.
[I'm coming – I say – not coming back]

Max Aub (1969)

Estos días azules y este sol de la infancia.
[These blue days and this sun of childhood]

Antonio Machado (1939)

CHAPTER ONE

Introduction: On Forewords and Historical Ghosts

Present-day Spanish literary history tends to take the form of a coherent, chronological narrative based on a belief in the continuous advancement of national culture. This assumption of a teleological temporality of nation informs a recuperative rhetoric of historiographical approaches to the cultural productions of exiles. This rhetoric is, in turn, buttressed by the creation of a canon containing names and titles to be retrieved for the hypothetical reconstruction of Spanish national culture. Under this view, critics and historians often read exilic poems as claim-making narratives, full of referential meaning, that fit the national literary teleology. *This Ghostly Poetry: History and Memory of Exiled Spanish Republican Poets* critiques this conventional understanding of Spanish literary history. It argues that poems written by Republicans who left Spain as a result of the Spanish Civil War invite readers, including critics and historians, to seek continuity with the past just as they prevent their narrative articulation in every here and now of reading. This shift in critical attention – away from intentional, representational, and referential meanings and towards claim-subverting textual elements – reveals how exilic poems may run against the grain of teleological narratives of national culture.

The reading practices that *This Ghostly Poetry* explores and analyses trace the various ways in which exilic poems resist and disrupt these historical narratives. Primarily, I contend that the modes of memory identifiable in exilic poems complicate the temporality of national literary history. In its place, I posit poetic memory as a spectral form of spatiotemporal disruption that haunts and hinders narratives of Spanish national culture. Three main concerns guide this critical re-examination: first, in what ways is the production of national identity linked to poetry as the prevalent form of discourse in the specific historical context of the Spanish Civil War (1936–9) and its aftermath of repression, exile, death, and oblivion? Second, what is at issue in debates about the relation between history and memory when exilic poetry is read today? Third, what is the unique political potential available in exilic poetry in a historical period distinctly marked by narrative discourses of collective memory, such as the early decades of the twenty-first century in Spain?

In *Diario de Djelfa* [Diary of Djelfa], published in Mexico in 1944, the Spanish author Max Aub provides an instructive suggestion of such reading practices. This volume of poems revolves around the months of imprisonment that Aub spent in an Algerian concentration camp barely two years after he went into exile on the heels of the Republican defeat in the Spanish Civil War.[1] Towards the end of his foreword – datelined in Mexico on January 1944 – Aub points to the loss underlying his poems: "Esta poesía atada al recuerdo, se desdibuja, palidece y cobra virtud fantasmal según los fantasmas de cada lector, que si de lo vivo a lo pintado piérdese una dimensión, ¡qué no perderá en lo escrito!" [This poetry tied to memory, becomes blurred, turns pale and takes on a ghostly quality depending on each reader's ghosts, because if one dimension is lost from living to painting, so much more will be lost in writing!] (*Obras completas: Vol. I* 94). In apprehensively drawing the reader's attention to the spectral memory haunting the intentional and referential meanings inscribed in his poems, Aub delineated a discursive space of discontinuity between living – "lo vivo" – writing – "lo escrito" – and reading – "cada lector."

What was at stake for Aub in circumscribing his poetry so emphatically? Was some form of resistance implicit in the assertion that his poetry "se desdibuja" and "palidece" "según los fantasmas de cada lector"? Indeed, "fantasmas" may be the most arresting term in this foreword. In Aub's tropological description, the ghosts that each reader may need to invoke from their horizon of expectations in every here and now of successive readings will keep reaching through the poems, seeking in "lo escrito" some form of continuity with the unattainable, lost dimensions of "lo vivo" – here, a significantly abstract, deanimated, and spectral nominalized adjective. Conversely, "lo vivo" will keep receding into a more and more distant past, becoming more and more spectral, widening the gap with the increasingly animated ghosts reading "lo escrito." Thus, Aub's discursive space is dialectically animated and deanimated by the combined spectral forces of continuity and discontinuity. His poetry is, in this sense, haunted and haunting: it is a ghostly poetry.

The only living people traceable in Aub's foreword may be the future readers of his poetry. But Aub was not invoking the readers themselves – you, me – but their ghosts. Naturally, no fully living person is to be found in his foreword, just as no fully written poem is to be found there either. In fact, Aub's poetry has already become proleptically ghostly by virtue of the deictic indication of presence and present made possible by "esta." As a spatiotemporal demonstrative, "esta" paradoxically demonstrates that Aub's poems are somehow out of time and out of place. This poetry – "lo escrito" – reanimates the lost dimensions of "lo vivo," but only to the extent that it becomes personified – "palidece" – as a ghost, while each reader – also, presumably, "lo vivo" – reanimates the found "escrito" – this poetry – but only to the extent that he or she becomes objectified as a ghost.

"Cada lector" must become a ghost to approach the ghostly mask speaking in *Diario de Djelfa*. Consequently, ghosts are themselves a trope for the animating and deanimating power of Aub's exilic poetry.

After referring to the loss of life underlying his poems, Aub went on to conclude his foreword by suggesting yet another divergence between living, writing, and reading: "sólo mis compañeros muertos y enterrados en Djelfa, el millar de sobrevivientes, podrán, quizá, captar lo que aquí se apunta" [only my comrades dead and buried in Djelfa, the thousand survivors, will perhaps be able to grasp/capture what is pointed out here] (*Obras completas: Vol. I* 94). Only the ghosts of the now absent comrades who were imprisoned there and then, in the Djelfa concentration camp from 1941 to 1942, might be able to grasp, capture, or – to refer to spectres with a less physically charged metaphor – elucidate what is merely pointed out or recorded in Aub's foreword: presumably, the memory of "lo vivo." But this ghostly memory is, in all likelihood, entirely gone by now, as we read Aub's words. Or is it? Would readers who were not present at Djelfa then necessarily fail to capture "lo que aquí se apunta," so much so that access to memory would only be possible for us "en lo escrito"? After all, deictic markers – "esta," "aquí," "mis" – also indicate that Aub's phantasmal poetry is discursively tied to the here and now of every successive reading, since each reader must conjure up in their memory those ghosts allegedly able to approach that other ghostly memory.

Could Aub's foreword be read, then, as an implicit forewarning to each future reader – including critics and historians – against attempts to recuperate and restore in the present a past loss of exile that he deemed uncapturable in his poetry? This hermeneutic distance between the loss of "lo vivo" folded into an exilic poem and its posterity in each new reading is one of the overarching concerns that this book sets out to address. How is the memory of Aub's readers different from the memory held by the ghosts of the irretrievably dead and buried, and by the survivors – also dead and buried now and again, as we read and reread *Diario de Djelfa* – who accompanied Aub at the camp and experienced "lo vivo" of exile? How is history – as past life but also as historiography – interwoven with memory every time an exilic poem is read in the twenty-first century? As Paul Ricoeur argued in *La mémoire, l'histoire, l'oubli* [Memory, History, Forgetting] (2000), for those who remember, what memory recognizes is an "enigma": it is "doubly other: as absent (other than presence) and as earlier (other than the present)" (*Memory* 39). What memory recognizes is then uncanny both in space and in time.

In this spectral light, Aub's exilic poetry reveals a spatiotemporal tension – an unhomely and untimely dimension – inasmuch as we read his foreword as inviting us to seek continuity amid a seemingly unbridgeable spatiotemporal discontinuity, to undertake the perhaps unavoidable yet unfulfillable task of retrieving, in every here and now of reading "lo escrito" by an exiled poet, an irretrievable past loss – the lost memory of the dead in a different time and in a different place. The incommensurable anachronism and displacement created in Aub's foreword by, among other textual elements, spatiotemporal markers – "enterrados," "podrán," "aquí se apunta" – point then to an arresting, albeit potentially appealing, aporia: the textual encounter between the ghosts of the dead and the ghosts of the living, as the memory of the former's past is somehow figured and refigured in every here and now of our readerly memory. Indeed, Aub's foreword reminds us that his poems haunt and hinder our reading, inviting us to approach "lo vivo" just as they, somehow, prevent "cada lector" from grasping it and capturing it. Circumscribing *Diario de Djelfa* as a dialectical space of both continuity and discontinuity is therefore a compelling act of resistance. This act of resistance hinges on understanding memory as a spectral form of spatiotemporal disruption vis-à-vis historical narratives of national culture.[2]

Of course, among the memories of the – now dead – survivors from Djelfa are also those of Max Aub himself, who was born in France in 1903 and died in Mexico, where he arrived and lived after fleeing the Algerian concentration camp as well as several other life-threatening situations. This survivor was among the numerous writers who left Spain between 1936 and 1939, during, or right after, the Spanish Civil War (Llorens, *Estudios* 129).[3] As such, "lo vivo," for Aub, was the experience of a history of exile, repression, death, and oblivion. The sheer importance of the biographical, cultural, and sociopolitical consequences of this experience cannot be understated. Yet it is also important to reiterate, at the risk of pointing out the obvious, that Aub's memory "de lo vivo" is, for each reader of *Diario de Djelfa*, the memory "en lo escrito." It is the memory of his untimely and unhomely poetry – a memory both in and out of time and place with regard to the country he was forced to leave and to its recent history, a time and place to which he was not able to return. Readers, including critics and historians, cannot quite "return" to those times and those places either.

In this sense, the reader's position parallels Aub's. Even when Aub did visit Spain in 1969, thirty years after becoming an expatriate, he realized the impossibility of returning to the Spain he had left behind. As he wrote in the diaristic text *La gallina ciega* [The Blind Hen] (1971): "aquí estás buscando lo que no hallarás nunca. Ni tú ni nadie ... El tiempo pasado. Tu juventud" [here you are seeking what you will never find. Neither you nor anyone ... Time past. Your youth"] (*La gallina* 162). He then defiantly and dejectedly stated: "Vengo – digo – no vuelvo" [I'm coming – I say – not coming back] (220). When, shortly after, Aub returned to Mexico, he also wrote that if he died there it would be "lo justo" [appropriate, right] (*Luis Buñuel* 22). Thus, the impossibility of returning was not only linked to the sociopolitical and cultural situation that Aub witnessed in Spain and denounced in *La gallina ciega*. Indeed, the rhetoric and deictic markers in this text also dramatize the displaced and anachronistic condition characteristic of exile itself.

How, then, do we read in exilic poetry the resistant elements of anachronism and displacement to which Aub is at pains to alert us in his foreword to *Diario de Djelfa*? That is a key question in *This Ghostly Poetry*. The textual uncanniness traceable in exilic poems – i.e., poems written in exile versus poems written about the experience of exile – results not just from a terrible history of repression, exile, death, and oblivion but from what in this book I call *poetic memory*: a verbal fabric that is often self-reflexive as well as claim-subverting. Poetic memory's verbal fabric animates, and is in turn animated by, every here and now of successive readings. For poetic memory to animate and be animated, the reader of a poem must heed not only – as Aub argued – the ghosts figured into his or her horizon of expectations, but also the various threads of deictic, tonal, prosodic, rhetorical, topical, translational, and intertextual repertoires available in (and around) the poem.[4] Through these repertoires, the reader will recognize various kinds of border-crossing, non-chronological, plurivocal, and plurilingual patterns that shape the verbal texture of the poem.

In Nietzschean and Benjaminian terms, poetic memory is untimely and unhomely; it thus furnishes the reader with an uncanny experience of spatiotemporal disruption. Consequently, poems written in exile can offer a ghostly form of resistance to a teleological model of national literary history; that is, resistance to a "monumental" historicism – as Nietzsche called it – claiming and aiming to capture, recuperate, and restore the irretrievable loss threaded into poems, to bridge the hermeneutic distance, and hence to dispel the spatiotemporal "enigma" – as Paul Ricoeur had it – posed by their thickly intermeshed verbal fabric.[5] As will be seen, in the specific case of Spain, monumental literary historicism often seeks to suture the discontinuities in, and even achieve the cultural fulfillment of, an imagined national community deeply marked by a long history of exile and death (Subirats 12). Circumscribing an exilic poem as an uncanny space of both continuity and discontinuity subverts this erasure of historical strangeness and hermeneutic distance with relation to past life, particularly to past life marked by war, exile, death, and oblivion.

Poetic memory's patterns of anachronism and displacement – by which poems may be read as resisting the sequential unfolding of literary history – can also be found in non-exilic poetry. In a 2016 review of *The Cambridge History of American Poetry* (2014), Jahan Ramazani persuasively pointed to the irrepressible ways in which poetry's memory moves cross-temporally and transnationally, underscoring the tensions between poetry studies and national paradigms: "as the largely classical vocabulary of poetic form indicates ... even when you localize, nationalize, and historicize the poetry you study, your critical templates and poetry's deep memory of literary form and antecedent, its linguistic and aesthetic sedimentation, transport you willy-nilly across national and historical boundaries" ("Lines" 310–1). This exploration of poetic memory "across national and historical boundaries" is nonetheless particularly relevant in the case of poems produced by exiles. This is especially true in view of the high symbolic, cultural, and political value accorded to poetry in the historical situation of extreme national and international strife that the Spanish Civil War and its consequences represented.[6]

Moreover, the recovery of the cultural legacy of Spanish Republican exiles is of considerable importance in current public and academic debates on both sides of the Atlantic about the historical memory of the war. This constellation of historical circumstances renders examining the continuities and discontinuities between exilic poetry and national cultural and literary history all the more pertinent. Such an examination has methodological and critical implications, as it highlights the political import of reading, analysing, and conceptualizing cultural materials of a traumatic past from the standpoint of the present.[7] Resistance to the teleological temporality of national literary history goes hand in hand here with resistance to a dichotomous, monolithic understanding of the relation between memory and history.[8] *This Ghostly Poetry* is thus about how to read exilic poems as acts of textual resistance to historicist attempts at hermeneutic recovery within nationally inflected frameworks. Focusing on poems written in exile by writers who were expatriates during the dictatorship of General Francisco Franco (1939–75), it suggests reading practices that may be used to trace the discordant ways in which memory is enmeshed with history. A prominent argument in *This Ghostly Poetry* is that what renders an exilic poem a densely layered historical material (and thus a valuable form of exilic memory) hinges precisely on the resistance that its verbal fabric poses to present-day recuperative readings – in other words, readings whose intent is to recover, through narrative, the historical references and lived experiences presumably alluded to in the poetry.[9]

This book's exploration of reading practices centres on the relationship between the modes of memory made available in and by exilic poems written by Republicans and the attempts at (re-)inscribing them in teleological narratives of Spanish literary history. Poets such as Max Aub, Luis Cernuda, León Felipe, Juan Ramón Jiménez, Antonio Machado, and Tomás Segovia have been strategically selected for this purpose because they represent the kind of canonical, or potentially canonical, authors frequently mustered to buttress Spanish literary history: "Spanish men who write in Castilian" (Epps and Fernández-Cifuentes 17).[10] That is, these writers' status is precisely what makes their exilic poetry amenable to being productively read here as spatiotemporally disruptive – as ghostly – vis-à-vis conventional constructions of literary history. Combining the latest developments in memory studies, new generic theorizations of lyric poetry and poetic voice, deconstructive strategies of reading, insights from literary and cultural studies about the temporality and textuality of nation and nationalism, and cultural materials associated with the collective memory of the Spanish conflict, *This Ghostly Poetry* reveals in exilic poetry a time signature that troubles the canonical temporality of Spanish literary history. It is this dynamic conceptual framework that sets it apart from existing studies in English or Spanish that question the forms of recuperative rhetoric shaping literary historiography in Spain.

In 1993, John Guillory called into question the "hypothesis of 'exclusion'" that governed historical accounts of literary canon formation; i.e., canon understood "as representing or failing to represent particular social groups" (vii). In recasting the debate about canon formation, Guillory contended that "a given social problem should be understood in relation to the context which yields the best explanation for that problem (ix). Drawing on Guillory's premises, I propose that the context that yields the most productive answer to the question about the ways in which the production of national identity is linked to poetry as a prevalent form of discourse is the crisis of the signifier "nation" brought about by civil war and exile. It is this context, particularly that of exile, that casts into relief the tensions between the explicit or implicit nationalist claims that a poem may make and the claim-subverting textual elements traceable in it, and, consequently, between reading practices mainly focused on intentional, representational, referential elements in a poem, and reading practices also alert to the border-crossing, non-chronological, plurivocal, and plurilingual patterns that shape its textual and verbal materiality. These tensions reveal that the national canon formation is a reductive framework for elucidating the discursive complexity of exilic poems. Furthermore, the uncanny experience of spatiotemporal disruption that exilic poems make available for readers eludes the logic of exclusion/inclusion underpinning accounts of canon formation in national literary history.

This Ghostly Poetry also contributes to a larger comparatist re-examination of nation as a framework for explaining literature as a cultural phenomenon.[11] To do so, it draws on recent discussions of the contested connections between modernity, literary history, and national identity, as collected and analysed in edited volumes on transatlantic studies, Iberian studies, and transarea studies.[12] In addition, this book intervenes in three of the most dynamic fields in contemporary Hispanism: exile studies, memory studies, and identity studies.[13] Building on pioneering studies of Republican exilic literature such as Michael Ugarte's *Shifting Ground* (1989) and José María Naharro-Calderón's *Entre el exilio y el interior* (1994), *This Ghostly Poetry* participates in ongoing conversations about intellectual history in the Americas and Spain.[14] Thus, this book also engages in a re-evaluation of Hispanism as an academic field as well as to novel reappraisals of the value and function of poetry as cultural memory in twentieth- and twenty-first-century Western society.[15] Nevertheless, *This Ghostly Poetry* offers a twofold perspective that has been missing from these discussions: a plurivocal poetics, in keeping with the post-structuralist reading strategies of Barbara Johnson, Jonathan Culler, and David Nowell Smith, and a transnational poetics beyond Spain, along the lines of Jahan Ramazani's reassessment of the value of modern poetry beyond national literary paradigms in *A Transnational Poetics* (2009). As we will see, this twofold perspective provides useful tools for exploring those ghostly continuities and discontinuities of exilic poetry that Max Aub circumscribes in his foreword to *Diario de Djelfa*.[16]

A transnational – and transatlantic – perspective was put forward by Juan Marichal, a respected Harvard professor of Spanish intellectual and literary history, at a relatively early stage in the study of the cultural productions of Republican exiles. In 1967, Marichal, who was forced to go into exile from Spain in 1939, published an essay with the self-explanatory title "Apología de la literatura española, siglo XX" [Apologia for Twentieth-Century Spanish Literature] (Marichal and Paz, *Las cosas* 11–24). A few months later Octavio Paz, who at the time was among the Latin American writers with a deeper and closer knowledge of said cultural productions, penned a critical response to Marichal's nationalistic understanding of literature:

> [N]o hay una literatura española: hay una literatura europea o, más exactamente, una literatura euroamericana (desde el siglo XVI) ... [L]a literatura española no resulta inteligible sino dentro del contexto de la literatura europea ... [S]e debería substituir la noción de lengua por la de lenguaje ... [A] la visión diacrónica y nacional de la literatura ... habría que oponer una visión sincrónica, sea dentro de un periodo y entre diversas lenguas ... o dentro de una lengua y sin hacer caso de la historia. (Marichal and Paz, *Las cosas* 30–1)
>
> [There is no Spanish literature: there is a European literature or, to be more precise, a Euro-American literature (since the sixteenth century) ... Spanish literature is not intelligible except within the context of European literature ... The notion of *lengua* [tongue] should be replaced by that of *lenguaje* [language] ... To the diachronic and national view of literature ... one should oppose a synchronic vision, whether within a period and among various tongues or within one tongue and without paying attention to history]

Despite their schematically Eurocentric and structuralist premises, Paz's arguments provided a compelling early critique of the homogenizing tendencies informing the Spanish academic school of philology with regard to exile literature (Faber, "Beyond" 435). These tendencies have generally remained formative in current readings of modern cultural history in Spain.[17]

But apart from their contribution to debates about Republican exiles' cultural or political impact in Spain, Paz's arguments are also a reminder of the critical need to re-examine from a transnational perspective the specific ways in which poetic memory is spun into exilic poems.[18] Sebastiaan Faber has made the case for such critical re-examination: "any approach to cultural history that takes the nation-state as its principal organizing unit is bound to misunderstand or underestimate exiles' life, work, and genealogy" (436). This claim is also applicable to stateless nations, whether within or beyond Spain understood as a nation-state. Thus both categories – the nation-state and the nation – are bound to become reductive organizing units in any approach to the exilic cultural production of individuals born in the Iberian Peninsula in the twentieth century. Insofar as culture in the context of exile – or in any other context for that matter – can hardly be taken as essentially or originally national, the dialogue between exilic poems and other discursive forms necessarily involves cross-boundary and non-chronological textual patterns. By shifting attention to an intertextual dialogue with other discursive forms, such as translation or fiction, we can productively acknowledge the uncanny strands woven into exilic poems. Conversely, to approach the intricate relation between, for instance, Max Aub's diverse exilic writings and the spatiotemporal coordinates of Spanish history, translation and fiction need to be taken into account along with Aub's poetry. A similar case can be made for the writings produced in exile by authors such as Juan Ramón Jiménez, Luis Cernuda, and Tomás Segovia.[19]

Embracing this situatedness, the second part of *This Ghostly Poetry* is structured as a series of case studies, each set in its own micro-historical context. Four case studies explore exilic texts as modes of disruption vis-à-vis national cultural history: Juan Ramón Jiménez's unfinished project *Guerra en España* [War in Spain] is shaped by a heterogeneous *visionary* form of exilic testimony beyond nationally inflected spatiotemporal continuities; Luis Cernuda's mythopoetic figurations of (self-)exile complicate his status as an emblematic poet of Spanish historical memory; Max Aub's marginal poems of alterity, plurivocality, and opacity resist attempts to recuperate his testimonial fictions of exile for twenty-first-century Spanish culture; Tomás Segovia's rhetoric of nomadism activates a dialectic between universality and particularity on the borders of discourses of nationality. Each chapter defines and explores the particular problematics of each case study as it delves into a selection of primary materials (mostly poetry) and examines their relation to other discursive forms like autobiography, blurb, diary, epigraph, epitaph, essay, memorial, novel, obituary, photography, and translation.

The choice of authors forms a revealing constellation: with some exceptions, they wrote about each other's poetry, exiles, and relationships with Spain. Reading their exilic writings in relation to each other therefore provides a unique set of angles on the value of their current respective positions in the field of Spanish cultural productions. This is an important consideration, as the legacy of each of these writers has also been discussed, albeit in different degrees, in the ongoing debate on both sides of the Atlantic about how to recover the memory of Republican exiles. Consequently, while discursive forms and temporal settings raise the particular questions that each chapter sets out to explore, the book's argument is driven throughout by larger inquiries concerning the reading practices whereby national culture and identity are linked to poetry, and the potential cultural and political import of studying the specific verbal texture of exilic poems in the context of debates about historical memory in Spain.

The present introductory chapter lays out the critical and theoretical underpinnings of the book and re-examines conventional approaches to the construction of Spanish literary history. It also offers several readings focused on claim-subverting textual elements within the verbal fabric of exilic poems, and on the tense relationship between these elements and the historical conditions in which the poems were written. After appraising the ghost as a trope for formulating discursive disruptions between memory and history, chapter 2 continues the re-examination of the teleological temporality and canonical foundations of Spanish literary history. It then discusses some of the ways in which the production of national identity during the Spanish Civil War and its aftermath – when poetry was a prevalent form of discourse – is seen today, in a historical period marked by a strong narrativization of collective memory.

Chapter 3 applies the lens of poetic memory to four key poems in the cultural context of the Spanish conflict, understood as a poet's war. Three of the four were written around 1937: Miguel Hernández's "Vientos del pueblo" [Winds of the People], César Vallejo's "Himno a los voluntarios de la República" [Hymn to the Volunteers from the Republic], and Pablo Neruda's "Explico algunas cosas" [I Explain a Few Things]. The fourth was published in Mexico in 1939: León Felipe's apostrophe to Franco "Reparto" [Distribution] – perhaps the most emblematic poem of Spanish Republican exile. Here, the theoretical framework of *This Ghostly Poetry* is bolstered by an examination of the idea, variously proposed by Theodor W. Adorno, Jacques Rancière, and Jonathan Culler, that poetry maintains an oppositional relation to modern society. I consider in particular Barbara Johnson's and Judith Butler's claim that political debate can be premised on textual undecidability and evaluate to what extent such a claim applies to exilic poems. I then reflect on elegiac and epitaphic poetic memory, the temporality of death in exilic poems, and the discursive scope of national literary history in this regard.

Chapter 4, "'Photography Is Death Itself': Visionary Testimony, Ruins, and the Testimony of Antonio Machado," focuses on the exilic writings of the prolific poet, editor, translator, critic, and Nobel laureate Juan Ramón Jiménez (Spain, 1881–Puerto Rico, 1958). From 1936 to 1954 Jiménez assembled an archive of heterogeneous texts and documents produced by him and others: photographs, journal entries, newspaper clippings, letters, poems, translations, lectures, interviews, and aphorisms. Published in Spain in 1985 as *Guerra en España*, this corpus of materials was Jiménez's transatlantic testimony of his pro-Republican activities during the Spanish Civil War and his long exile in the U.S. and Latin America. This chapter argues that this unfinished cross-generic project also contains a visionary poetic testimony to life after death. Guided by the memory of Antonio Machado, the towering Republican poet who died in exile in 1939, Jiménez's poetics becomes an autobiographical montage of epitaphic ruins that bears witness to a symbolic near-death experience in a time of crisis while also safeguarding his own work against reductive political uses. In this light, the materials gathered in *Guerra en España* can be read as a prosopopoeia allowing the exiled poet to speak from posthumous life. As shall be seen, among the most memorable of these materials is Jiménez's extensive poem "Espacio" [Space].

Chapter 5, "'Remember Him and Remember Him to Others': Historical Memory, Self-Elegy, and Mythopoetic Figuration" delves into the exilic writings of another prominent poet, critic, essayist, and translator: Luis Cernuda (Spain, 1902–Mexico, 1963). Cernuda went into exile in 1938 and never returned to Spain. His memorable line of verse "Recuérdalo tú y recuérdalo a otros" [Remember It/Him and Remember It/Him to Others] can be read as a felicitous speech act, one that has carried out what it describes in serving as a motto for historical memory. Cernuda penned it shortly before his death in 1962 as the opening line of a poem whose title points to the year the Spanish Civil War began, "1936." The poem refers to an encounter in 1961, in Los Angeles, California, with an unnamed former soldier in the Abraham Lincoln Brigade, the group of international volunteers who went to Spain in 1937 to fight Franco's rebel forces. Self-reflexively, though, the poem relies on the contrast between the time signature of narrative and the time signature of lyric: if a story is about what happened next, Cernuda's poetic enunciation is about what happens now. This textual and contextual analysis of "1936" is set within a larger discussion of Cernuda's rhetoric of exile, as it also touches on his poetry translations, his essays on English and German Romanticism, and his intellectual legacy in Spain and Mexico. When analysed through the transnational, non-chronological lens of poetic memory, Cernuda's exilic poems can be read to rely on self-elegiac and mythopoetic figurations – they posit forms of textual posterity whereby the destruction of poetic personae warrants their phantasmal survival. These forms of textual posterity are key to considerations of Cernuda as a poet of historical memory in Spain.

The first half of chapter 6, "'Enclosed into Myself, Purblind, Mute: Margins of the Poetic 'I' and Testimonial Memory," examines Max Aub's singular place in Spanish political and cultural history. Aub was born in Paris in 1903 to a French mother and German father who were both agnostics of Jewish descent. His family moved to Spain, where Aub remained until 1939, when he returned to Paris. Aub spent more than two years in jails and concentration camps. Finally released in 1942, he escaped to Mexico, where he died thirty years later. In Mexico, Aub published *El laberinto mágico* [The Magic Labyrinth], his vast cycle of testimonial fictions about the Spanish Civil War. The first half of this chapter analyses Aub's *Antología traducida* (Mexico 1963), an idiosyncratic collection of translations of short apocryphal and semi-apocryphal poems prefaced by highly particularized biographies of real and fictional poets. The constellations of marginal and fragmentary poetic voices that emerge in this volume indirectly highlight the testimonial inadequacy of the narrator in Aub's fiction. *Antología traducida* not only dramatizes Aub's elaborate construction of the witness figure – it provides a sustained reflection on the relationship between documentary evidence and truth.

The second half of this chapter, titled "Usurping the Apocryphal: Exilic Testimony, Cosmopolitan Memory, and National Culture (The Case of Antonio Muñoz Molina)," focuses on how the renowned Spanish novelist, essayist, and public intellectual Antonio Muñoz Molina has sought to recuperate Max Aub's testimony of uprootedness in France, Algeria, and Mexico. It argues that Muñoz Molina's gesture relies on the concept of cosmopolitan memory as it has been developed in Holocaust studies. In using the Holocaust as a template for a transnational cultural history based on a supposedly shared Jewish past – as evidenced in his partially fictionalized compilation of testimonial narratives, *Sefarad* [Sepharad] (2001) – Muñoz Molina tends to generalize on two levels: he turns Aub into an exemplary witness of a historical conjuncture – the Second World War – and he subsumes that conjuncture under a general rubric of totalitarianism. In doing so, Muñoz Molina downplays Aub's main tropes of testimony, the alias and the apocryphal, and displaces Aub's rhetoric of alterity, plurivocality, and opacity with a rhetoric of equivalence, univocality, and self-evidence. This half of the chapter shows the ways in which a ghostly reading of Aub's poetry – tellingly overlooked by Muñoz Molina – can contribute to a reassessment of Aub's exilic writings. It does so by providing a highly detailed close reading of one the most notable thematizations of voice and nation in exilic poetry: Aub's poem "Tres Años." Drawing on Edward Said's reflections on exile, the chapter concludes with a discussion of Aub's eccentric position in Spanish culture today.

Chapter 7, "'In Exile from Exile': Nomadic Ethics and the Broken Language of Ghosts," explores the writings of poet, short story author, essayist, and translator Tomás Segovia (Spain, 1927 – Mexico, 2011). Segovia's rhetoric of nomadism renders his exilic poetry suggestively paradoxical. Segovia arrived in Mexico in 1940, when he was thirteen years old, and occupied a problematic position vis-à-vis the so-called *niños del exilio* [children of exile]. From 1976 until his death in Mexico in 2011, he lived alternately between Spain and Mexico. Focusing on Segovia's poetry collection "Cuaderno del nómada" [Nomad's Notebook] – published in Mexico in 1982, and admittedly revealing the poet's impressions of his first visit to Spain since childhood – this chapter shows how his rootless nomadic figures destabilize the reader's deictic orientation in their wanderings through a nameless landscape of spectres. Significantly, *Cuaderno del nómada* is also the title of Segovia's 2014 collected poems. Drawing on Kwame Anthony Appiah's definition of cosmopolitan ethics as an ethics that addresses the challenge of harmonizing universality and particularity, I read Segovia's poetry as pointing towards a universal horizon that derives from a difference that the writer cannot entirely shed: his experience or feeling of difference as an exile prompted his poetry's attempt at universality. The chapter concludes with a discussion of the ways in which the dialectic between universality and particularity activated by Segovia's aporetic notion of exile is dramatized in, and complicated by, his essays.

The coda to *This Ghostly Poetry*, "Antonio Machado's Afterlives and Memories of Spanish Literary History," discusses Machado's legacy as a site of exilic memory in order to draw some tentative conclusions about the value and function of poetic memory vis-à-vis the cultural and literary history of the Spanish Civil War and the exiles that followed. The starting point for this discussion is Tomás Segovia's 1979 essay "Antonio Machado desde otra orilla" [from another shore], a commemorative text in which the institutional value of Machado's poetry for

Hispanism and Hispanicity is critically re-examined from the perspective of a poet who spent his childhood years in Republican Spain, and then went into exile, first to France and then to Mexico. Machado's status as an exile is quite unique. He was born in Seville, Spain, in 1875, and died in Collioure, France, on 22 February 1939, shortly after going into exile. He wrote almost nothing as an expatriate, and yet his significance as the poet of the Spanish people has been considerable. Indeed, the iconic figure of Machado as the Republican poet *par excellence* accrued immense cultural capital after his death in exile. Discussing Antonio Machado's legacy as a site of memory is particularly relevant today, as the eightieth anniversary of the Republican exile is being commemorated, and numerous visitors to Machado's grave in Collioure pay tribute to the poet's memory.[20]

At the specific historical intersection of the Spanish conflict, exilic poems were shaped by the different senses of exile associated with the various cultural shifts of modernity as well as by the deep-rooted Romantic idea that poetic voice could articulate, and even embody, notions of person, people, land, and nation. Situating my discussion within the wider context of modernity, I draw from historiographical investigations by exiled literary historian Vicente Llorens, including his study of the writings produced in exile by the author of the first modern history of Spanish literature: the Spanish Romantic poet, historian, and politician Antonio Alcalá Galiano. The question of the forms of discontinuity in Spanish cultural history is then discussed with reference to the distinguished comparatist of exilic literatures, Claudio Guillén.

Segovia's criticism of the value of Machado's poetry for Hispanism was deeply moulded by his transnational poetic memory of Latin American *modernismo*. Likewise, the transnational perspective provided by the exiled literary critic Aurora de Albornoz in her comparative study of Machado's and Rubén Darío's poetry allows for a critical re-examination of the ghostly forms of poetic memory threaded into "Estos días azules y este sol de la infancia" [These blue days and this sun of childhood], the emblematic verse found in Machado's overcoat after his death in exile at the end of the war (Machado 836). Considering the shifting cultural landscape of Spanish modernity, then, helps to elucidate the spectral ways in which the memory of exile inscribed in Machado's last line harks back to contexts beyond and prior to the war. Cross-boundary and cross-temporal forms of poetic memory are similarly threaded into "Mínimo homenaje" [Minimal Homage], Max Aub's eerie tribute to Machado, published in Mexico in 1958. A discussion of the intricately memorable ways in which Aub's dramatic use of epitaphic address fashioned Machado's ghostly image brings the book to a close.

From Inside the National Canon

The construction of literary history as a coherent emplotment of events, names, and titles following a continuous, chronological line is still widespread in Spain despite the manifold theoretical problems underlying critical concepts such as nation and canon. A popular instance is *Breve historia de la literatura española* [Brief History of Spanish Literature] (1997, 2014), where Carlos Alvar, José-Carlos Mainer, and Rosa Navarro argued for an evolutionary, sequential, and canonical understanding of literary history, and offered to provide a purportedly unitary overview of "ochocientos años de quehacer literario continuo, con autores cuyo único punto en común es el empleo de la misma lengua" [800 years of continuous literary work by authors whose only common ground is the use of a single tongue] (11–13).[21] Among the consequences of this construction is, in Sebastiaan Faber's view, the sidelining of "women and texts written in languages other than Castilian," as well as a blindness to its "imperialist underpinnings" ("Review" 594–5).

Not the least among these consequences is also the neglect of transnational intertextualities in poetry. In *Spanish Poetry of the Twentieth Century: Modernity and Beyond* (1994), Andrew Debicki alluded to this problem when he remarked on the methodological quandary presented by historiographical approaches to the intricate verbal texture of poems: "traditional literary histories obscured the individuality of specific works and invited readers to reduce complex poems to simplistic examples of movements or trends" (*Spanish* 1). The retrieval and recuperation of marginalized or forgotten names and titles from the specific cultural field of the Spanish Republican exile, albeit necessary, may run the risk of reconstructing the canon of national literary history at a different level, while rewriting or writing off the spatiotemporal tensions threaded into exilic poems, irrespective of their canonical status. Instead of offering a list of names and titles in need of commemoration, *This Ghostly Poetry* critiques the historiographical underpinnings of national literary history through readings that acknowledge spatiotemporal tensions in poems written in exile by a small group of canonical authors. Considering the various ways in which poetic memory is spun into exilic texts produced by canonical authors is especially germane today: institutional interest in the cultural legacy of Republican exiles in twenty-first-century Spain continues to grow, and public and academic debates about the cultural implications of the historical memory of the Spanish Civil War and its aftermath are still very much alive.[22]

Between 2002 and 2010 the now defunct Spanish Sociedad Estatal de Conmemoraciones Culturales [State Society for Cultural Commemorations] made sustained efforts to promote, publish, publicize, commemorate, and celebrate the cultural productions of important exiled Republican poets, including Max Aub, Luis Cernuda, Juan Ramón Jiménez, Antonio Machado, and Tomás Segovia.[23] A substantial part of *This Ghostly Poetry* comprises new readings of exilic poems by these writers and of other texts related to such poems. Nevertheless, these readings are not meant to be examples of a theory of exilic poetry, let alone of poetry in general, but essayistic explorations and conjectural probings into the different temporalities of poetic memory in exilic texts, which complicate teleological national-literary temporalities. In the groundbreaking study *Shifting Ground: Spanish Civil War Exile Literature* (1989), Michael Ugarte referred to "the unknown quantity of exile" – i.e., its discursive shiftiness – in temporal terms: "exile resists theory and systematization ... The deviations from preconceived patterns create new ones, and as the literary critic, historian, or social scientist attempts to unravel the subject of exile, the more it seems to defy the order and logic of academic discourse" (3). Informed by Ugarte's caveat about the discursive complexity of exilic cultural productions, the exploratory methodologies proposed in *This Ghostly Poetry* derive from an interest not just in the likelihood, or necessity, of national literary history, but, above all, in the spectral condition of its present-day existence in Spain.

In keeping with a poststructuralist conception of discourse, Brad Epps and Luis Fernández-Cifuentes argued in *Spain Beyond Spain: Modernity, Literary History, and National Identity* (2005) that literary history seemed to share the ghostly fate of other entities, such as "the author, the subject, history, literature, humanism, or God" (14).[24] Considering the spectral condition of national literary history in Spain, *This Ghostly Poetry* shares the aim suggested by scholars of Spanish cultural studies to "pay attention to individuals, currents, and genealogies that cross cultural and linguistic borders" (Faber, "Beyond" 435). Analogously, in 2005 Leonardo Romero Tobar pointed out the critical need for tracing "the mark of multilingualism and mobility" in "the grand fabric of so-called *national literatures*" (189–90). Although Romero Tobar drew attention mostly to fictional characters, narrative texts, and prose writers, his focus on what he called "the real tension that binds writers to their native languages," and more specifically, on the various polyglot and extraterritorial forms of textuality resulting from the "peripatetic lives" of exiles, refugees, diplomats, adventurers, professionals, migrant workers, and women such as Juan Ramón Jiménez's wife Zenobia Cambrubí – as we shall see – is particularly relevant when it comes to tracing the uncanny patterns shaping the verbal texture of exilic poems (190). In brief, the critical assumption undergirding the study of a constellation of canonical exiles like the one proposed in this book is that, by tracing the tensions between continuity and discontinuity in their poems, the teleological temporality of organic national history and identity may be productively re-examined.

Even though the specificity of reading practices should justify the restricted scope of this study, it is important to point out that *This Ghostly Poetry* is neither a history nor a survey of Spanish Republican exilic poetry, understood as a historically situated cultural phenomenon. Nonetheless, an exploration focused on the claim-subverting textual elements in poems written in a historical period when the struggle over the definition of nation led to lasting tragic consequences may enrich the critical analysis of cultural productions shaped by a nationalist sense of immediacy, unity, identity, truth, and presence.[25] This exploration is, however, not necessarily meant to deflect the nationalist bias emergent in the thematics of many exilic poems. It aims, instead, to reevaluate them as historical materials – that is, as thick textual fabrics where nationalist biases are inextricably interwoven with contrasting, obscure, even contradictory, warp and weft threads. Such biases can be critically highlighted by precisely the untimely and unhomely threads that, in Barbara Johnson's words, critics and historians "have traditionally been trained to disregard, overcome, explain away, or edit out" (*A World* 18). In line with Johnson's approach to textual analysis, this re-examination of exilic poems entails reading national literary history against the grain. Following the time-honoured Aristotelian contrast between poetry and history, the value that this shift in critical attention could possess might lie in asking to what extent the national history of a canonical poetic archive can subvert itself from within.

The exploratory bent of this book extends to its title, *This Ghostly Poetry: History and Memory of Exiled Spanish Republican Poets*, in which terms such as "exile," "Spanish," "Republican," and "memory" are used only tentatively. The term "exile" does not fully describe the diverse forms of displacement experienced by the Spanish citizens who had to move to other countries as a result of the war. As Sebastiaan Faber has explained, both during and after the Spanish Civil War "groups and individuals left for different reasons, under different circumstances, enjoyed different kinds of legal status, and faced different options when it came to the possibility or desirability of return" ("Beyond" 429).[26] This terminological question becomes more involved in light of the discursive multilayeredness of a key signifier in this context: *desterrado* [dis-terred]. In addition to its more explicit sociocultural and political connotations, the key topos *tierra* – earth, land, soil, ground – took on various philosophical and religious undertones which complicate any historiographical investigation aiming to circumscribe the spatiotemporal coordinates of exilic cultural formations at this historical conjuncture.

The multiple nuances of *desterrado* and variants such as *transterrado*, *soterrado* and *conterrado* [trans-terred, sub-terred, con-terred] point not only to a specific political calamity, but also to various, often inextricably overlapping, anxieties of historical, geographic, and existential belonging.[27] More important, insofar as poetry was the prevalent discursive form during the Spanish Civil War, any approach to the meaning of exile should take into account the polysemous richness of *desterrado* in poems written by Republican expatriates.[28] In this respect, it is important to bear in mind, as the eminent exiled literary historian Vicente Llorens pointed out in 1949, that for many Republican exiled poets, "la evocación de lo comarcal, de la patria chica, es más frecuente y más íntima" [the evocation of the local/regional, of one's hometown, is more frequent and intimate] (*Estudios* 139). It is from this local experience of rootedness that *desterrados* were also banished – from their land, but also, somehow, from their native soil. As Ugarte has explained: "[t]he existential need to recover something lost (a land, an identity, a place of origin) results from the absence of an integral part of one's being – a fact which causes the exile to perceive of him or herself as something less than human, as the Spanish word, *destierro,* suggests" (*Shifting* 20). Thus the exact boundaries of land and soil and also, frequently, of the human take on a ghostly dimension to the extent that they resist precise definitions in writings by exiled poets.[29]

The case of the Catholic poet José Bergamín may illustrate this ghostliness.[30] After the Republican defeat, Bergamín went into exile in Mexico, where he and the poet Juan Larrea founded the journal *España peregrina* [Peregrine Spain], a premier venue for publications by exiled writers. In resorting to the biblical topos of a "new pilgrimage," Bergamín and Larrea redefined the Republican exile and broadened its symbolic and spatiotemporal scope (Naharro-Calderón, "Twentieth-Century" 622).[31] In 1954, when Bergamín decided to return to Spain from his exile in Uruguay, he portentously but pithily embroidered, with characteristic Baroque, ominous rhetoric, the *tierra* motif: "Prefiero ser enterrado vivo que desterrado muerto" [I would rather be buried alive than banished dead] (qtd. in Penalva 185). Bergamín also thematized the relationship between the ghost and returning to one's *tierra* in his exilic poem "Volver" [Returning], published in Madrid and Uruguay in 1957 and 1958, respectively. He shared this poem with exiled poet and philosopher María Zambrano, in a letter written in Paris in 1957: "Volver no es volver atrás. / Yo no siento la añoranza; / que lo que pasó no vuelve / y si vuelve es un fantasma." [Returning is not to return back. / I do not feel the longing; / for what passed does not return / an if it does it is a ghost] ("Volver" 59).

Later, in 1970, when Bergamín decided to return to Spain for the second time, Max Aub – always alert to the spectral comings and goings of *desterrados* after more than three decades of Francoist dictatorship – fatalistically warned in his diary: "No puedes volver, sólo puedes ir. Para volver tendrías que ser otro mundo, José, José Bergamín. Sólo somos ya fantasmas de nosotros mismos y no fantasmas a secas, ¡y tan a secas!, como quieres serlo tú y lo proclamas" [You can't return, you can only go. In order to return you would have to be a different world, José, José Bergamín. We're now simply ghosts of ourselves, not ghosts cut-and-dry. Cut-and-dry indeed! That's the sort of ghost you want be, and you proclaim it!] (*Diarios: 1939–1972*, 391–92). Aub seemed to be lingering, in characteristic self-reflective fashion, on his own return to Spain a few months earlier, in 1969, as yet another revenant.[32] Indeed, the spectral connotation of *destierro* becomes thematically dominant in many exilic poems where the workings of voice are foregrounded and sepulchral figures are variously invoked, evoked, and revoked, sometimes in vaguely defined earthy landscapes.

A sterling example of this mode of spectrality is Luis Cernuda's melancholy "Lázaro" [Lazarus], included in his 1940 volume *Las nubes* [The Clouds]. Cernuda started this collection during the war and tentatively titled it *Elegías españolas* [Spanish Elegies]. *Las nubes* was completed amidst all the disruption and uncertainty brought about by exile, as Cernuda drifted from Madrid to London, and then to Paris, Cranleigh, and Glasgow.[33] The first-person singular speaker in this self-elegiac poem sees himself retracing his steps back from *tierra*, but still as "un muerto / Andando entre los muertos" [a dead man / Walking among the dead]. The scenery is sparsely sketched as having "olivos y alcores" [olive trees and hills], and consequently may be somewhat reminiscent of Cernuda's native Andalusian landscapes. But this is only a dreamy, transient, remote impression. After sinking his forehead in the dust and feeling the "pereza de la muerte" [laziness of death], the spectre describes a different landscape, located inside his body: "un alma doliente en mis entrañas / Gritó, por las oscuras galerías / Del cuerpo, agria, desencajada, / Hasta chocar contra el muro de los huesos" [in my guts a soul in pain / screamed through the dark galleries / of the body, bitter, out of joint, / until it crashed against the wall of bones] (*Obra I* 292–3). Although sound is somehow emitted, the spectre's "alma" is violently unable to reach the mouth to become a voice, as though the grave just left behind had been internalized. "Alma" – or *ánima* – is therefore both animated and deanimated just as the first-person-singular speaker leaves *tierra* and is reanimated.[34]

Exilic poems frequently employ this basic constellation of voice, earth/land, and death, reflecting on the status of the speaker in a site of enunciation marked by a dramatic rhetoric of stark disruption. In *Romances de la voz sola* [Ballads from the Voice Alone] (1951) by Nuria Parés, another first-person male speaker addresses his own voice as other from himself and as the cause of its end or undoing: "Esta voz, que no es mi voz, / ... / y habrá de acabar conmigo" [This voice, which is not my voice, / ... / and will be the end of me] (qtd. in Rivera 73). Later the speaker addresses himself again, in self-reflective, epitaphic fashion, as a "peregrino" [pilgrim], and becomes seemingly deanimated in a ghostly in-between state between dust and border: "Desnudo te han dejado, polvo fino / ... / ¡Entre la tierra y Nada, eres frontera" [you have been left naked, fine dust / ... / between earth and Nothingness, you are the frontier!] (qtd. in Rivera 74).[35]

Likewise, the exiled Catalan poet and critic Manuel Durán included "Los perros en la noche" [Dogs in the Night] in *La paloma azul* [The Blue Dove], published in Mexico in 1959. Dogs in this poem "desentierran los huesos del silencio en un patio" [unearth the bones of silence in a yard] (qtd. in Rivera 52), as though the speaker could hear the ghost of his voice returning to the surface of earth, or its embodied silence had turned his voice into a spectral voicing.[36] As the uncanny figurative interplay between *voz* and *tierra* in these brief examples shows, sharp binary distinctions between opposite types of banishment – such as "political" versus "poetic," or "historical" versus "mythical" exiles – would fail to register the complex discursive enmeshment whereby such poems variously dramatize liminality. The philosophical and religious modes of rhetoric informing poems by Republican *desterrados* were mediated by both the intertextual memory of exilic motifs and the material determinations of the specific historical conjuncture at which the poems were produced. At play in such distinctions is, among other things, the scope of a loss that for many exiles probably became as symbolically mutable as it was sharply felt.

Rather than simply thematized, political exile is often entangled with various long-standing, cross-boundary strands of exilic topoi and rhetorical figures, like biblical themes and modes of address. The historicity of an exilic poem may then be highlighted by turning the critical focus towards the ways in which the dialectic between long-term and context-specific discourses is thickly interwoven in each text. A case in point would be *Nabí*, the outstanding poetic sequence written in Catalan by Josep Carner (Spain 1888–Belgium 1970).[37] *Nabí* pivots on Jonah's dialogue with God about his exile from, and return to, *terra*. The original text in Catalan first appeared in Buenos Aires in 1941, even though Carner started writing it before the war.[38] Carner's Spanish translation was published in 1940 by Editorial Séneca, a distinguished press run in Mexico by José Bergamín. *Nabí* is thus closely linked to the complex cultural field of Republican *transterrados* in Mexico.[39] The historical specificity of this exilic poem would risk becoming an abstraction if its critical analysis were restricted to the historiographical confines of one particular national exile.[40] The specificity of a poetic sequence like *Nabí* as a historical material is inflected by the multiple views of exile afforded by both its thickly layered verbal texture and the tortuous transnational path informing the conditions of its production.[41] As we shall see presently, one of the crucial ways in which an exilic poem acquires political potential is the dynamic, uncanny transaction it makes possible between the voices and voicings available in the text, and their utterances by each reader beyond referential and representative meanings.

Obviously, "Spanish" was also a highly charged term in the context of the civil war, where discussing the very definition of nation could and did have disastrous repercussions. In the 1930s the secular-progressive nationalism of the Second Republic was identified as the *anti-España* by a belligerently reactive Spanish conservatism, as José Álvarez Junco eloquently explained in 2001: "'Spain' was not only Catholicism, it was also the system of inherited social power – order, property, family, tradition, authority, anti-liberalism and anti-Enlightenment – while 'anti-Spain' was not only revolution but also modern civilisation, the 'godless' materialistic, secular, urban world" (373). This form of Spanish conservatism provided the ideological underpinnings for the coup d'état against the legitimate Republican government that would trigger the war. But the "myth of the nation" shaped the propaganda of both opponents, "the 'Republican' option" and "the 'National' Catholic-conservative option," so much so that between 1931 and 1939 the "nationalization of political life" in Spain was complete (Álvarez Junco 374–5).[42] Interestingly, many poetic texts by Republican exiles highlight overlapping and multilayered scales of cultural and territorial belonging and identification, sometimes without clear reference to, or claim of, national identity. Signifiers such as *país* [country], *patria* [fatherland / homeland], and *región* [region] are hard to separate from only slightly less politically overdetermined terms such as *campo* [country / countryside], *tierra* [land / soil / ground], *terruño* [native soil], and *patria chica* [home town / home area], and can have symbolic implications which would complicate institutional definitions of national and even regional identity (Caudet, "Mediterrani" 73).[43]

In relation to the refugees' lived experience in France after the internecine conflict, Scott Soo pointed out in 2013 the tensions involved in using the umbrella adjectives *Spanish Republican*, since the victory of Francoist *nacionales* and the lack of political unity among exiles complicated discourses of national identity among Republicans, while, paradoxically enough, many exiles espoused a form of nationalism which at times may not seem too different from the one fostered by Franco's dictatorship. And yet, Soo added, a certain Republican commonality could be found among exiles.[44] As for the use of the term "poetic memory," exploring the critical tools suitable for revealing the concrete ways in which memory is inscribed in the exilic writings of Spanish Republicans leads us to re-examine the poetry produced during and after the Spanish Civil War, understood as a poet's war. As we shall see later in this chapter, this re-examination involves, among other things, considering the different, sometimes conflicting, ways in which poetic voice relates to notions of person, people, land, and nation.

On Poetic Voices and Voicings

In *A World of Difference* (1987), Barbara Johnson provocatively sought to shift the deconstructive analysis of difference from the domain of linguistics to contexts in which difference was at issue in the world.[45] Political engagement, not political indifference, was, as she saw it, at the centre of deconstructive reading practices. Among the claims made by Johnson in this regard was: "the undecidable is the political. There is politics precisely because there is undecidability. And there is also poetry" (*A World* 194). *This Ghostly Poetry* draws on the critical possibilities opened by Johnson's arguments, notably that the political consequences and complexities of address are singularly highlighted in poetry, because of the ways in which poetic language can blur "the boundary between life and death" (194–5). It seems relevant to take this ghostly approach to language – especially to poetic language – into consideration when examining historical contexts in which questions of life and death become issues of pressing political import, such as that of the Spanish Civil War and the debates about historical memory that continue in Spain today. Indeed, among the issues now under discussion in this respect is how the voices of the living in the early twenty-first century may evoke the voices of poets who died long ago. This temporal interconnectedness renders the study of the tense relationship between exilic poetry and national literary history all the more necessary.

Ghostly temporalities in poetry may be traced from grammatical and rhetorical angles as well. Through what Karl Bühler called *deixis am phantasma* or imagination-based deixis, readers can rely on spatiotemporal shifters to position themselves and imagine an absent there and then different from the here and now of every successive reading (140). Simultaneously – but also transitorily – a reader can occupy the present site and time of enunciation of the first-person deictic marker, as Emile Benveniste showed (144).[46] If a reader is receptive to the disparate ways in which voices and voicings are laced into the verbal texture of the poem, shifters can reveal an uncanny tension between continuity and discontinuity (Nowell Smith 13) – that is, the enigmatic double otherness of memory "as absent (other than presence) and as earlier (other than the present)" (Ricoeur 39). This uncanny tension is foregrounded when the spatiotemporal gap between living, writing, and reading is made thematically explicit in a poem, as often happens in exilic poems.

Poetic voice also becomes rhetorically uncanny as soon as it is taken as prosopopoeia. In Paul de Man's definition, prosopopoeia is "the fiction of an apostrophe to an absent, deceased, or voiceless entity, which posits the possibility of the latter's reply and confers upon it the power of speech. Voice assumes mouth, eye, and finally face" ("Autobiography" 926). But as de Man went on to explain, the symmetrical, chiasmic structure of this trope, "crossing the conditions of death and of life with the attributes of speech and of silence," poses a threat for the reader: while prosopopoeia permits the animation of the dead or absent in the present of reading, it also deanimates and depersonalizes the reader in the very speech act of animation enabled by the voicing of the text: "the living are struck dumb, frozen in their own death" (928). This form of ghostliness becomes patent and potent in exilic poems. As we shall soon see, the verbal dynamics in a poem are vocally interactive, creating the conditions for a somatic "transaction" between text and reader (Nowell Smith 12). In this sense, the vocal interaction peculiar to prosopopoeic rhetoric lends an added ghostly dimension to exilic poems if we understand them, following Aub's foreword, as discursive spaces animated and deanimated by the combined spectral forces of continuity and discontinuity. Only if this ghostly dimension is forgotten can the symbolic return of the poet's voice to its land of origin be uncomplicatedly claimed and reclaimed. Only if the verbal and textual repertoires specifically situating each act of enunciation are neglected can exilic poetry be unproblematically read into the continuous line of national narrative.

Far from drawing on an idea of poetry as a non-committal form of discourse concerning the relation of continuity and discontinuity between and within person, people, land, nation, and voice, *This Ghostly Poetry*'s approach is predicated on the assumption that the potential for political debate hinges on acknowledging the resistant uncanniness folded into exilic poems understood as historical materials. The ghost, taken as a key trope for the undecidability between claim-making and claim-subverting elements in a poetic text, is thus a helpful tool for exploring exilic poetry as a strongly dialectical form of discourse. Person relates here, primarily, to categories of voice and address. Drawing on Emile Benveniste's theory of deixis, Barbara Johnson published in 2008 an investigation of the eerie linguistic threshold between persons and things. She argued that the notion of person had "something to do with presence at the scene of speech" and seemed "to inhere in the notion of address" (*Persons* 6).[47] Johnson went on to explore address as providing the way to achieve the act of animation consisting in turning a thing – including "a person who neither addresses nor is addressed" – into a person (6). For that purpose she studied four major rhetorical figures that enable such an act of animation: apostrophe, personification, anthropomorphism, and prosopopoeia. In Johnson's view, prosopopoeia becomes a key rhetorical figure for understanding the uncanny act of animation consisting in bringing the dead back to life and thus obfuscating the boundary between life and death, particularly in epitaphs. As such, address is indispensable among modern poets, for any attempt to provide a "living" voice in a poem (9). As we shall see, many figures of voice in exilic poems are epitaphic.

The poetic production of Spanish Republican exiles offers a privileged site for the textual exploration of figures of voice, as it was produced in a historical conjuncture when poetic voice was generally seen as a key political metaphor for the embodiment of the national people. Close analysis of exilic poems brings out the multifaceted, even undecidable, spatiotemporal ways in which figures of voice are threaded into their verbal fabric. Michael Ugarte has explained the self-reflective dimension characteristic of exilic literature in terms of the relation between dialogue and spatiotemporal divergence: "The particular nature of exilic experience (displacement, the importance of correspondences and relations, comparisons, temporal and spatial disunity, self-duplication and division) leads the writer, perhaps unwittingly, into a dialogue with him or herself on the very nature of writing" (*Shifting* 19–20).

With regard to the workings of voice and dialogic forms in poems, David Nowell Smith's contribution to recent theorizations of the lyric proves especially generative. In his 2015 *On Voice in Poetry: the Work of Animation* Nowell Smith traced the indeterminate ways in which voice works in poems, and placed into "polylogue" the various figures through which readers grasp it (2).[48] Voice can be figured as an individual (for instance, the "biographical" poet; i.e., the exiled poet as personified through the forms of textuality converging on his or her production as a public intellectual) and as a collective identity (the voice of the poet as both presenting and representing the national, or pan-national, father- or motherland). But voice can also be figured through what Nowell Smith called "the matrix of prosodic patterning, of employments of deixis and apostrophe, of ventriloquisms of different persona," as well as through "the poem's conversation with an ongoing tradition" (3–4). In this sense, poems are far from univocal (4). More important, poems are often constructed around figures designed to bring into presence a named entity, as Barbara Johnson contended. To Nowell Smith, it is the rhythmic dynamics specific to figures like interjection, apostrophe, and deixis that highlight the ways in which such figures "proffer themselves as surrogate presences" (13).

In his classic *Poetry and the Body* (1979), John Vernon studied the concrete bodily dynamics generated by poems: "the experience of all language is kinetic, at least in the sense that language is successive and exists in time" (2). Vernon explained at length how this mode of kinesis is heightened by "the resistance of form," mainly through devices such as "repetition, enjambment, the use of periodic sentences" (2). As Nowell Smith also argued, these verbal dynamics are vocally interactive: they create the conditions for a "transaction" with the reader "in the space between poem and any singular, provisional voicing of the poem" (12). Voicing is here understood as the uttering of sound that the poem demands of readers. Nowell Smith further contended that voice is produced "out of text as we share our voices with it, implicate ourselves within its vibratory articulation" (75). Thus the poetic text "opens up fissures in our breath that serve to embody the 'between' through which poem and reader address one another, trace a path towards one another" (76). Significantly, if the uncanny sense of bodily presence enabled by a poem's texture is shaped through addresses to its readers, the vocal presence becomes plural not as the voice of the poem, "but rather the voicings it releases" (Nowell Smith 13). This is an important consideration for any critical re-examination of the conventional use of dichotomies such as individual/collective in the study of modern poetry, particularly poetry that may have been – or still be – read as embodying the voice of a national people.

In *Poetry and the Fate of the Senses* (2002), Susan Stewart invited similar reflections about textual plurivocality in relation to the cross-boundary somatic elements specific to poetry: "Lyric poetry in particular as the expression and record of the image of the first-person speaker across and through historical and cultural contexts provides us with a form on the boundary among sense impressions, somatic memory, individuation of agency and social context" (41–2). But along with expressive approaches to the position of the first-person speaker such as Stewart's, the dynamic, somatic transaction between poem and reader can also be taken as a particular experience of otherness if attention is paid to verbal patterning, positional deixis, or forms of suspension like what Nowell Smith called "fissures in our breath" (76). In 2006, Mladen Dolar outlined analogous meditations on the paradoxical topology of voice with regard to the body and to language in general: "The voice ties language to the body, but the nature of this tie is paradoxical: *the voice does not belong to either*" (72). As Brandon Labelle concluded in 2014, voice operates as "an essential force that animates the other to bring him or her closer to me, while also prompting my own: it is this voice that calls me into speech ... I turn to the other, with a voice shaped by *this other one*: I speak in order to locate myself near you" (3).

This paradoxical topology can bring about a transitory suspension of representation, particularly that of expressive voices. Jonathan Culler argued in 2015 that rhythm is "an event without representation" that provides lyric poems with a somatic element largely lacking in the novel. This somatic element not only affords a reader of verse "a sense of a special otherness": it also allows him or her to articulate the text "as he or she hears it, occupying, however temporarily, the position of the speaker" (*Theory* 138). It is from this standpoint that voice in a poem can be felt kinetically as "generated by text rather than transcribed into text," as Nowell Smith averred, and the poem itself understood as creating the conditions for a "transaction" rather than being just an "object" (12). Also from this standpoint, the vocal presence in exilic poems and the tension between voices and voicings that the reader's attention to deictic positionality involves can be felt to be dramatically plural both in time and in space.[49] These tensions between voices and voicings invite us to again re-examine poems as ghostly forms of resistance to linear, even teleological, emplotments of national literary history.[50]

PART ONE

Exiles in Literary History

CHAPTER TWO

Re-engaging with Ghosts in the Poetic Machine

In her 2002 essay "Introduction: Engaging with Ghosts," cultural historian Jo Labanyi drew on Jacques Derrida's 1993 book *Specters of Marx* to reconsider the construction of identity in contemporary Spain and made a convincing case that the entirety of modern Spanish culture could be productively approached as a ghost story.[1] In Labanyi's estimation, critical writings had restricted themselves to examining high culture in modern Spain, and as a result had "systematically made invisible – ghostly – whole areas of culture which are seen as non-legitimate objects of study, because they are consumed by subaltern groups" ("Introduction" 1). Labanyi's championing of a cultural studies approach to subaltern cultures in Spain was a perceptive and pertinent one, since the study of the history and memory of the victims of the Spanish Civil War and its aftermath – the dead and the survivors, both in Spain and in exile – had started to gain traction in Spain at the turn of the twenty-first century (11–12).[2]

The considerable contributions by cultural studies to the visualization of hitherto neglected areas of culture could nonetheless be supplemented by an examination of the different ways in which Spanish literary histories have also often disregarded – and thus made invisible and, in a way, ghostly – aspects of high culture other than the canonical ones arranged along "genealogical lines of influence and inspiration" (Faber, "Beyond" 428). Among these aspects are the non-chronological, border-crossing, plurivocal, plurilingual threads of textuality inscribed in poems produced in exile: the spectral elements of anachronism and displacement that make up what I have called *poetic memory*. One of the the reasons for this invisibility – this form of ghostliness – is that exilic poems resist being primarily read for historical reference and analysed for content. Consequently, they resist being turned into claim-making narratives and even historiographical and biographical documents that fit what Labanyi elsewhere denounced as "the national frame of reference that structures so many literary histories" (*Short* 9).

This resistance is all the more critically significant in texts by canonical writers whose titles are often marshalled to bolster precisely the genealogical lines undergirding institutional literary history. The approach to reading exilic poetry focused on constative speech acts, content-based meanings, or even storytelling has sometimes been encouraged by canonical writers themselves.[3] In his foreword to *Diario de Djelfa*, Aub averred that all that was "narrado" [narrated] in his poems was "real sucedido" [real as what happened], and linked their value to the "desoladora epopeya del ejército español" [the devastating epic of the Spanish army] (*Obras completas: Vol. I* 93–4). But even when a poem eschews explicit claims of a referential and/or narrative tenor, critics often restrict their analyses to readings suitable for the teleological emplotment of national history, disregarding and silencing the deictic, prosodic, tonal, rhetorical, topical, translational, and intertextual repertoires that may have contributed to shaping the specific temporality of the text.

An early case in point is the content-based reading of León Felipe's iconic exilic poem "Reparto" proposed by Carlos Blanco Aguinaga, Julio Rodríguez Puértolas, and Iris Zavala in their popular *Historia social de la literatura española (en lengua castellana)* (1979): "No mentía León Felipe cuando refiriéndose a los poetas del exilio declaraba que se habían llevado la 'canción'; y con la canción, por mucho tiempo, la esperanza y las posibilidades de desarrollo moderno" [León Felipe did not lie when, in reference to the exiled poets, he declared that they had taken away the "song"; and with the song, for a long time, the hope and chances for modern development] (123).[4] This critical reduction of Felipe's poem to little more than a socio-historical document or statement derives from the marginalization of reading practices beyond intentional, representative, and referential meanings, constative speech acts, content analysis, and narratological frameworks: in other words, precisely the sort of reading practices that would help to trace those discordant, claim-subverting elements at odds with what Jo Labanyi has criticized, in reference to histories of modern Spanish culture, as the "seamless narratives" of chronological, monumental national history ("Introduction" 5).[5]

At stake in reading a poem for content is, of course, the old debate in literary studies about the difference between content and form. If engaging with ghosts is a suitable approach to the cultural history of modern Spain, re-engaging with the content ghost still lurking in the formal machine of a poem's text may also be a generative critical strategy in this respect. The formalist argument in cultural studies – to attend to the specificities of the text in order to elucidate in new ways the relationship between its composition and the conditions of its production – raises a key question for *This Ghostly Poetry*. As Raymond Williams posed it in 1986: "How do certain negations and absences which can be well identified by formalist methods constitute themselves in the social and historical structure?" (184). If we accept that a text can be haunted by voices from the past, as exilic poems written by Spanish Republicans tend to be, then such voices are, according to Julian Wolfreys's approach to textual spectrality, "the others of the very texts we read in any given moment": "Texts are neither dead not alive, yet they hover at the very limits between living and dying. The text thus partakes in its own haunting, it is traced by its own phantom, and it is this condition which reading must confront" (xii). Thus if reading is tantamount to heeding the ghostly voices threaded into a poem's text, attention needs to be paid to the different ways in which – as Aub suggested – a poem partakes in its own haunting or liminality: the multifaceted, even undecidable ways in which traces of voices within a text, the spectral forces of continuity and discontinuity at work in it, break down the separation of content and form.[6] In brief, attention needs to be paid to poetic memory. Otherwise, its ghosts may hardly be forthcoming.[7]

Roland Barthes's idea of the temporality of performative speech acts may shed light on the concept of poetic memory. In line with Aub's distinction between "lo vivo," "lo escrito," and "cada lector," writing no longer entirely designates, in Barthes's words, "an operation of recording, notation, representation" (*Image* 145). Also, to the extent that an author like Aub is absent from his poems, "there is no other time than that of the enunciation," and Aub's texts are again "written here and now," that is, performed anew, by each successive reader (*Image* 145). However, if Aub is present in a poem but only as a ghost, so is "cada lector," and the ghostly present/presence of every successive reading becomes dialectical vis-à-vis past living and past writing. Consequently, the temporality of reading is, as we saw earlier, that of a dialogue between ghosts in a discursive space of continuity and discontinuity.

Likewise, if the poetic text can be seen as "a multidimensional space in which a variety of writings, none of them original, blend and clash," and as "a tissue of quotations drawn from the innumerable centres of culture" (Barthes, *Image* 146), the poem becomes historical as it dialectically highlights in the present its performative difference with past lives. Such historical dialectic is possible if the poem is seen as animating – and being animated by – an intricate mesh of writings and readings, voices and voicings. However, this difference between past and present is also internal to the text. Among the textual strands threaded into the poem may also be the constative historiographical traces of recording and representing past life ("real sucedido" in Aub's words). Thus the multidimensional space of the poem also becomes historical in its dialectical difference from historiographical writing *within* its textual fabric.[8]

Ghosts can become a powerful trope of difference and otherness as embodiments of a shocking sense of discontinuity in continuity – and vice versa – in historical periods profoundly marked by violent forces of change and transition such as civil war and exile. A recent but irretrievable past can remain attached to an uncertain present as ghosts enable the imaginative articulation of a continuum between life and death. Yet, if the past is still somehow alive, its apparition in the present is always in a transformed, troubling guise (Cox and Gilbert ix). This arresting power of ghosts can be more marked when history is constructed according to developmental, progressive movement. If a ghost is defined by anachronism, its haunting implies an overlap of past and present that disrupts linear temporality (Buse and Stott 1). In this framework, memory can be, as Katharine Hodgkin and Susannah Radstone argued in 2006, "that which complicates or refuses to sit within that temporality" (15). The ghost is then a compelling trope for unpacking the temporal complication of historical continuity brought about by memory.

If Derrida's Marxian notion of hauntology has become a generative theoretical tool for thinking beyond "an historical temporality made up of the successive linking of presents identical to themselves and contemporary with themselves" (*Specters* 87), the trope of spectrality can also be used as a suitable critical device for reading the specific material modes of anachronism and displacement interwoven in exilic poems – their untimeliness and unhomeliness. Inasmuch as poems by canonical exiled writers have been, and may again be, restrictively read in a "detached" and "aesthetic" manner as presumably untroubled and untroubling objects of high culture (Labanyi, "Introduction" 3), emphasizing their disruptive textual modes of memory may encourage critics to read and voice them as densely historical materials.[9] Derrida's notion of ghosts is a historical-materialist one, as Labanyi has underscored ("Introduction" 6). Consequently, a poem's material discursivity, its texture, can also be seen, in line with Theodor W. Adorno's critical logic, as a social form where historical forces come spectrally into play. It is in this sense that the ghostly modes of memory spun into poems can be taken as historical documents.

This Ghostly Poetry explores the political resonances of this dynamic. To extrapolate from Derrida's reflections on ghosts, "this being-with specters would also be, not only but also, a politics of memory" (*Specters* xviii). In the case of canonical Spanish Republican writers, a critical reading strategy sensitive to the potential of their exilic poems for resisting and disrupting national history and identity would entail a politics of poetic memory. The documentary value of exilic poems understood as densely historical materials may conceivably lie in their potential for troubling and complicating the recuperative rhetoric that often fashions the chronological temporality of national history.

Exiles and Teleologies of National Culture

In its sheer quantity and complexity, exilic literature is bewilderingly hard to encompass in the twenty-first century, as exile seems today, despite differences between specific historical conditions, at least as widespread a phenomenon in the West as it was more than eighty years ago.[10] The case for the study of Spanish exilic literature is particularly fraught with challenges, at least to the extent that exile is still seen today by many critics and historians as foundational for the conceptualization of modern Spanish literary and cultural history.[11] After the Spanish Civil War, the historiographical question regarding the structural importance of exile in the study of culture in modern Spain was posed most notably by the prominent cultural historian, philologist, and literary critic Américo Castro, who expatriated himself from Spain in 1936 and moved to the United States. One of Castro's pivotal books about what he called the "estructura" [structure] of Spanish history is *España en su historia: cristianos, moros y judíos*, published in 1948, when he was based at Princeton University.

In the foreword, which Castro wrote in 1946, ten years after leaving his native country, he asked what "sentido de la historia y de la vida" [sense of history and of life] "hombres extraordinarios" [extraordinary men] like Cervantes, Velázquez, Goya, and Hernán Cortés shared (*España* 9). Castro was interested in knowing how "lo que hoy denominaríamos la forma hispánica de vida" [what today we would call the Hispanic way of life] was formed and developed (*España* 9). Castro sought to understand "lo español" [Spanishness], a way of life peculiar to a specific "pueblo" [people] (*España* 12–13). Insofar as it did not correspond to "lo europeo" [Europeanness] and "lo oriental" [Orientalness], he claimed, "lo español" should be defined as "hispanidad" [Hispanishness] (*España* 16). The use of categories such as "lo español" and "hispanidad" allowed Castro to typify as "irreductiblemente español" [irreducibly Spanish] not only important cultural figures from early modernity, but also, in a trans-historical perspective, twentieth-century writers, musicians, and artists like Miguel de Unamuno, Manuel de Falla, and Pablo Picasso (*España* 13). Significantly, Castro traced "lo español" back to the "Christian-Arabic-Jewish contexture" that shaped Spain from 711 on (*The Structure* 500), and took the expulsion of the Moors and the Jews in the late fifteenth century as a pivotal moment in Spanish history. Thus, in his view, the "sojourn" of the Jews in Spain during the Middle Ages and their final exile "traced indelible lines upon Iberian history" (*The Structure* 468–9).[12]

In his overview of Spanish cultural history, *The Disinherited: The Exiles Who Created Spanish Culture* (2007), British historian Henry Kamen also claimed that a key element in the construction of modern Spanish culture was the experience of exile (X). Kamen characterized exile as a trans-historical event defining Spanish culture from the crucial year of 1492 – when Spain became a "land of perpetual leave-taking" – to what he called "The Elite Diaspora of 1936–39." Not surprisingly, Kamen also resorted to the trope of the ghost when he argued that for more than four centuries "exile became the spectre that haunted Spain's cultural destiny" (4). A controversial premise for Kamen's argument is that self-inflicted exile has debilitated Spanish identity as a nation, with the corollary that Spain may "always have a defective elite culture" (X). Thus, in Kamen's understanding of modern Spain, exile is an element of both cultural continuity and discontinuity.

At issue in Kamen's arguments is the value of what he called "elite culture" for the construction of national identity following a structural long-term pattern of preservation and disruption.[13] "Elite culture" can be seen here as "defective" only if it represents an indispensable value for the continuity of national history. This appraisal of high culture can then be made to buttress an understanding of culture as following genealogical lines of national influence, whether discontinued by exile or not. In other words, high or elite culture would only make sense, in Kamen's view, within the framework of a national canon.[14] It is this nationalistic understanding of high culture that renders all the more necessary the re-examination of those ghostly areas of culture that have been seen, in Labanyi's words, "as non-legitimate objects of study" ("Introduction" 1).

Among these objects would, however, also be those productions of elite culture that do not fit easily in the construction of national identity; for instance, as mentioned earlier in the case of Republican exile, the unhomely and untimely memory made available by canonical poets in their exilic production. The question of difference between high and low culture becomes more involved as soon as the verbal texture of poems – including those supposedly popular ballads or *romances* that were seen as a key cultural production in rewritings of the Spanish nation during the civil war (Labanyi, "Introduction" 3) – is taken into account in a critical study of the various ways in which a national culture is textually constructed. It is arguably the thick textual and verbal materiality of poems that throws into relief what Labanyi called the "messy heterogeneity and discontinuity of cultural processes" edited out from histories and anthologies of modern Spanish literature intent on assuming a teleological continuity of national culture in the face of traumatic historical discontinuities such as civil war and exile ("Introduction" 3).[15] Attending to the materiality of poems may reveal that the question about the difference between opposing conceptions of national identity in times of internecine conflict remains, if not entirely undecidable, at least largely "messy" within them.[16]

Partaking of a Romantic understanding of nationality in which "land, spirit, and people are tightly tied to artistic and linguistic production," twentieth- and twenty-first century Spanish literary history is often structured as a chronological narrative linked through a set of consecutive generational periods and built on a belief in the continuing advancement of national culture (Epps and Fernández Cifuentes 11).[17] Particularly in this sense, it is necessary to critique the ways in which poetry has been accorded a solidly central position in the institutional construction of modern Spain's cultural identity as a nation. Put schematically, poetry is key to constructions of modern Spanish culture that take as canonical landmarks:

- The early twentieth-century cultural resurgence known as the "Edad de Plata" [Silver Age] – embodied by the poets of the so-called *generación del 27* [generation of 1927] – among others, Rafael Alberti, Luis Cernuda, Federico García Lorca, Jorge Guillén, Juan Larrea, Emilio Prados, and Pedro Salinas – as well as by established *modernistas* and /or members of the so-called *generación del 98* [generation of 1898] such as Antonio Machado, Juan Ramón Jiménez, and Miguel de Unamuno, all of them included by Gerardo Diego in his legendary 1932 volume *Poesía española: antología 1915–1931*.[18]

- The catastrophic setback to Spanish cultural modernity caused by the civil war and Franco's dictatorship – as notoriously epitomized by the murder of Federico García Lorca in 1936, and the death in exile of Antonio Machado in 1939.[19]
- The purported retrieval, resumption, and renewal of a culture in ruins during the second half of the twentieth century – as signalled since the 1950s by the growing interest that prominent late twentieth-century Spanish writers have publicly displayed in exiled poets such as Cernuda (Cuenca 10).[20]

The 1999 supplement to the eighth volume of the highly successful and influential *Historia y crítica de la literatura española* [History and Criticism of Spanish Literature] covered the years from 1939 to 1975 – the entire period of Franco's regime. In the introductory paragraphs about the production of Spanish poets during this period, the editor of this supplement cautiously favoured the idea of a "continuum" of lyrical tradition, despite the destruction brought about by the civil war and the death, repression, exile, and oblivion that followed (Sanz Villanueva 6–7). In the section specifically devoted to poetry, Juan José Lanz similarly questioned the idea of a presumed "ruptura regresiva" [regressive rupture] as a consequence of the rebels' devastating victory in the conflict, and made the case that the brilliant "tradición poética" [poetic tradition] of modernity that flourished in Spain during the first decades of the twentieth century – represented by the now shattered or at least scattered *generación del 27* – was not interrupted in Spain, notwithstanding the tragic consequences of the dictatorship: "pese a la dispersión del exilio y a la diferente militancia política, existe una continuidad estilística entre los dos momentos estéticos separados por la guerra" [despite the dispersal of exile and the difference in political militancy, there exists a stylistic continuity between the two aesthetic moments separated by the war] (Lanz 70).

Behind this debate about the extent of the "ruptura" – or conversely, the "continuidad" – of poetic modernity in the wake of the war is a seemingly unshakable belief in the methodological value of foregrounding overarching national styles, trends, and traditions rather than other possible critical frameworks.[21] The assumption of this teleological temporality also informs, as mentioned above, the recuperative rhetoric of historiographical approaches to the cultural production of Republican exiles.[22] Thus, at the turn of this century, exiled and non-exiled cultures could allegedly start being studied and appreciated together, but also assimilated to one other.[23] In his 1996 official speech accepting his induction into the Royal Spanish Academy, Antonio Muñoz Molina claimed that Spanish culture would not achieve its "verdadera plenitud" [true plenitude] without recovering its "tradición abolida" [abolished tradition] in 1939 ("Destierro" 117).[24] In his 2010 *A la intemperie: exilio y cultura en España* [Out in the Open: Exile and Culture in Spain], a widely informative, panoramic cultural history of the Republican exile, Jordi Gracia construed the productions of both exiled intellectuals and those who remained in Spain as part of "un solo cauce" [a single channel] defined by Spanish culture (19, 72). As a conclusion to his overview, Gracia shored up his arguments by quoting Muñoz Molina's authoritative claim about the "verdadera plenitud" of Spanish culture, within the context of public and academic debates in Spain and abroad about the historical memory of the consequences of the civil war (211).[25]

The contention that Spanish culture, whether exilic or not, should be seen as "un solo cauce" was put forward again a year later, in 2011, in a literary history of considerable institutional weight, the nine-volume *Historia de la literatura española* [History of Spanish Literature], coordinated by José-Carlos Mainer and published by the prestigious Spanish press Crítica. In the seventh volume, Domingo Ródenas and Jordi Gracia leaned on a rhetoric of convergence and progress to depict exiled and non-exiled cultures as participating, with regard to the thwarted modernity of Spain, in a "restitución en marcha" [restitution underway] (491).[26] This rhetoric, highlighted in the title *Derrota y restitución de la modernidad: 1939–2010* [Defeat and Restitution of Modernity: 1939–2010], implied that the ruptures and losses brought about by civil war and exile could be restored following a principle of national cultural development.[27] In the introduction, exile was thus coherently presented as "integrado" [integrated] within a "sistema literario complejo y muy cambiante" [complex and highly changeable literary system] (9). If exiled culture was purportedly integrated within this system without losing its specificity, it was also not treated as "una provincia marginal al núcleo central de la historia" [a marginal province to the central nucleus of history] (9). Thus, "La continuidad asimétrica" [asymmetric continuity], the title of the paragraph establishing the ties between the culture of exile and the "núcleo central de la historia" (Gracia and Ródenas 15–40), confirmed the persistence of homogenizing tendencies within the Spanish school of philology (Faber, "Beyond" 435). Ródenas and Gracia also explained that the discourse of their history was built on an "armazón expositiva y narrativa" [expository and narrative framework] (9).

In his 2014 *Historia mínima de la literatura española*, José-Carlos Mainer similarly defined exiled and non-exiled cultures as keeping a certain "continuidad natural" [natural continuity], at least as far as the 1900–36 "Edad de Plata" was concerned (182).[28] The teleological temporality undergirding Mainer's notion of literary history in both projects may be then said to suture, as cultural critic Mari Paz Balibrea argued in 2005, "the break in the continuum of time opened up by exile" by closing it "in a full circle when the presence of what was made absent realizes itself in the nation" ("Rethinking" 12). The underlying premise in such critical and historiographical language is a conception of history as an inherently ongoing process of growth in national culture whereby, despite catastrophic confrontations over the redefinition and reappropriation of nation – confrontations bringing death, persecution, and displacement to hundreds of thousands of people – past losses in the cultural field can be retroactively made up for through readings designed to foster national development.

Balibrea also turned to the trope of the ghost in her argument that the political and cultural legacy of Republican exiles holds a crucial, albeit paradoxical, position in the history and collective memory of contemporary Spain. In her view, exile is "both central and residual; it has been dismissed and ignored by many, and yet its absence is structurally indispensable to any understanding of dictatorial *and* democratic Spain. There is arguably no more resilient ghost haunting actually existing Spanish (post)modernity than that of Republican exile" ("Rethinking" 3). In Balibrea's study, Max Aub embodied the uncanniness of this position in 1969 during his visit to Spain from Mexico, after an absence of more than twenty-five years ("Rethinking" 11). Aub saw in Spain how "inoperative and out-of-synchrony" Republican modernity was vis-à-vis the "reconstitution of Spanish modernity" that Franco's dictatorship had embarked upon in 1959 ("Rethinking" 10–12).[29] Balibrea questioned not only the discourses of integration and recuperation often championed in Republican exile studies in the context of the debates about the historical memory of the war but also the category of nation as an adequate frame for the study of exilic cultural productions ("Rethinking" 12).[30] The relationship between nation and narration – let alone between nation and poetry – was, however, left unaddressed in this discussion.

War Narratives, Memory, and Poetry

In 2010, Jordi Gracia argued for the relevance of exilic culture in these debates, and dwelled on the recuperative and restorative practices fostered by a "fascinación mítica" [mythical fascination] with exile among the grandchildren of those involved in the war (*A la intemperie* 210). An early example of this sort of practice, dating from 1996 – the sixtieth anniversary of the start of the war – was Muñoz Molina's alluded-to argument for the commemoration and rehabilitation of Aub's legacy in the name of the "verdadera plenitud" of Spanish culture (211).[31] Within a discussion about the legacy of a historical setting whose prevalent form of discourse was poetry, it is telling that the cultural productions that Gracia links to the so-called memoria histórica [historical memory] of the war and its consequences are narrative forms like novels and films – some of which have become massively popular (*A la intemperie* 211–13).[32] Gracia lucidly focused on a key bestseller in this context: *Soldados de Salamina* [Soldiers of Salamis] by the Spanish novelist Javier Cercas, published in 2001 (208–13).

Gracia's choice is highly significant here, since the action of *Soldados de Salamina* is triggered by the narrator writing a necrological article about none other than Antonio Machado, sixty years after the poet's death in France. Interestingly, the narrator's necrological article is titled "Un secreto esencial" [An Essential Secret]. Indeed, for numerous readers in Spain and abroad today, the memory of Machado's exile and death is arguably mediated by the recuperative, commemorative, and investigative discourses underpinning Cercas's immensely popular novel. At the start of *Soldados de Salamina*, the narrator, prompted by a visit to Machado's grave in Collioure, speculates about the possibility of unveiling there "un secreto esencial" to Spain's tragic history. As he is quick to point out, this secret is also essential to the story he is writing.[33] History and storytelling are thus marshalled together in Cercas's narrative as interpretative, explanatory tools for approaching Spain's enigmatic, and traumatic, recent past.

An effective rhetorical gesture for the dramatic momentum driving *Soldados de Salamina* is the quotation of Machado's famous alexandrine "Estos días azules y este sol de la infancia" [These blue days and this sun of childhood]. As mentioned earlier, this line was found in the poet's overcoat after he passed away in exile, and can be considered to be among the first verses written by an exiled Republican (Albornoz, "Poesía" 18). The narrator in Cercas's novel surmises that it may be "el primer verso de su último poema" (24) [the first line of his last poem (*Soldiers* 11)]. But, as he hastens to add, "La historia no acaba aquí" (24) [the story/history doesn't end here (11)]. Indeed, as Alison Ribeiro de Menezes has argued, the overlapping of history and memory in *Soldados de Salamina* arises initially from the "fetishistic aura" of Machado's famous verse (125).[34] Given poetry's prevalent status in Spanish culture during the war and its aftermath, the study of the narrative modes of memory spun into, around, and beyond Machado's line merits close attention. Such a study would contribute to a critical re-examination of the ways in which national literary and cultural history are framed by recent debates about the relationship between history and collective memory in Spain.[35] This re-examination would be particularly germane as these debates are almost exclusively centred on narrative forms such as novels and films like the 2002 screen adaptation of *Soldados de Salamina*.[36] At stake would be the modes of memory – whether fetishistically auratic or not – specific to poems inserted in commemorative historical fictions like Cercas's novel.

Another important case in point in this regard is Almudena Grandes's novel *El corazón helado* [The Frozen Heart] (2007). Grandes holds a prominent position as a public intellectual in the cultural debates about historical memory in Spain, as evidenced by her weekly contributions to the highly influential newspaper *El País*. One of the most popular novels about the memory of the Spanish Civil War in recent years, *El corazón helado* takes its title from two famous octosyllables by Antonio Machado: "Una de las dos Españas / ha de helarte el corazón" [One of the two Spains / will freeze your heart]. Machado's lines are also inserted as an epigraph to Grandes's novel.[37] Published in the early twenty-first century, best-selling novels like *Soldados de Salamina* and *El corazón helado* are fictional investigations that aim to reveal the presumed secret of Spain's tragic history through the lens of Machado's iconic poetry. The memory of the war, preserved in narrative form, is thus presented as the key to this secret, which seems to be only available through the narrator's memory of poetry.

In his reflections on this secret and the relationship between history and story, Cercas's narrator also quotes lines from another poem: "Apología y petición"

[Apology and Plea]. This poem is a virtuoso sestina composed in 1966 by the widely respected Spanish poet Jaime Gil de Biedma (1929–90). The lines read: "De todas las historias de la Historia / sin duda la más triste es la de España, / porque termina mal" [of all the histories/stories of History / no doubt Spain's is the saddest / because it ends badly] (*Las personas* 80). Gil de Biedma's poetry was modulated by echoes from Machado's writings (Iravedra 15). Gil de Biedma, who has been labelled an "exiliado interior" [internal exile] in Franco's dictatorship, also visited Machado's grave in Collioure in 1959.[38] He wrote "Apología y petición" as a response to a fatalistic vision of Spanish history partly constructed by Machado in poetry volumes like *Campos de Castilla* [Fields of Castile] (1912) and *Nuevas canciones* [New Songs] (1924) (Walters 67).

"Apología y petición" meticulously meets the elaborate rules of the sestina verse form. In following a strict stanza sequence and constructing an intricate interlocking rhyme scheme, Gil de Biedma fashioned an eminently memorable poem in a historical period of "imposed oblivion" (Ferrán 145). After quoting the three lines from "Apología y petición" about "todas las historias de la Historia," the narrator in *Soldados de Salamina* questions their presumed conclusion about Spanish history – "¿Termina mal?" (26) [Does it end badly?] (13) – and goes on to reflect on the possibility of unveiling the secret to Spanish history and also, consequently, to the story he is writing. He does not quote the poem's open-ended last line, "que el hombre sea el dueño de su historia" [that man be the master of his story/history], nor does he linger on the hyperbolic rhetoric informing its highly stylized thematization of the relationship between story and history ("sin duda la más triste"), or on the formal interweaving of story, history, and memory particular to a tightly structured poetic composition like the sestina.

Jonathan Mayhew's insightful and instructive close reading of "Apología y petición" provides an apt preface to the study of the modes of memory specific to poems inserted in commemorative historical fictions about the war. In *The Poetics of Self-Consciousness: Twentieth-Century Spanish Poetry* (1994), Mayhew offered a sobering reading of Gil de Biedma's poetry, arguing that it was informed by a postmodern scepticism towards language. Mayhew pertinently pointed out that readers tend to disregard the closely knit patterns of "Apología y petición" and thus to understand it restrictively as "a prosaic statement of political ideas" (101). However, Mayhew reasoned, the sestina, if taken as the "fixed form of Provençal origin" that it in fact is, becomes a "generative device that actually produces the content of the poem," whose effect is one of Brechtian estrangement likely to provoke "a questioning of conventional modes of thought that more natural seeming literary forms often reinforce," as well as "an interrogation of the conventional position between politically committed poetry and aestheticism" (*The Poetics* 101–3). Mayhew went on to provocatively propose, among other approaches to the poem, a parodic reading as "a critique of the tautological and formulaic discourse of Marxist discourse itself" (*The Poetics* 102).

Mayhew was also careful to remind readers that Gil de Biedma was, like Luis Cernuda, whom he admired, well versed in Anglo-American poetry, as he had translated poems by W.H. Auden and T.S. Eliot (*The Poetics* 97). He also stressed that the sestina is not an uncommon form in Auden's poetry (100). When read alongside the ongoing debates about historical memory in Spain, Mayhew's analysis shows the need to pay close attention to elements of poetic memory – in this case, the highly patterned texture generated by a fixed form like the sestina, and the specific border crossings, non-chronologies, intertextual, plurivocal, and plurilingual threads traceable in a poem written within the particular cultural and political environment of Spain in the 1950s. One does not need to fully agree with Mayhew's suggestive readings to see that these elements take on critical value in discussions about the problematic links between national politics and the conventions of literary form. Even more important for our study, such elements highlight the tension between the specific modes of memory folded into a tightly structured poem about history such as "Apología y petición" and the modes of historical memory plotted into Cercas's investigative story about the presumed secret to Spain's recent history (including his narrative use of verses by Machado and Gil de Biedma as throwaway lines). As mentioned earlier, this secret is presented in *Soldados de Salamina* through a memory moulded by poetry.

Despite Mayhew's compelling analysis, Gil de Biedma's lines are still being read in twenty-first-century Spain as the straightforward, "prosaic statement of political ideas" that Mayhew characterizes as reductive. In a 2013 op-ed for the *New York Times* titled "When We Were Poor Before," Almudena Grandes also quoted Gil de Biedma's postwar poem in reference to the ongoing effects of the 2008 financial meltdown on Spanish society: "To us children, the war was the mysterious conflict nobody dared speak of ... We children learned not to ask, even before we read the terrible and poignant verses by Jaime Gil de Biedma: 'Of all the stories in history, the saddest is undoubtedly Spain's, because it has an unhappy ending.' Even today, Spaniards don't want to remember" (n. pag.). The categorical and dramatic rhetoric shaping Grandes's sweeping statement about what Spaniards did not want to remember in 2013 is reinforced by her use of Gil de Biedma's subtly terse verses.

But the last lines of Grandes's article about Spain's history are, conceivably, as sternly categorical and essentialist ("Because Spaniards, who for centuries knew how to be poor with dignity, never knew how to be docile. Never. Until now.") as Gil de Biedma's last lines are ironically playful and open-ended ("que la pobreza suba hasta el gobierno / que el hombre sea el dueño de su historia" [that poverty rise all the way to the government / that man be the master of his story/history] (*Las personas* 80). Grandes's use of Gil de Biedma's lines, then, invites reflection on the suitability of poetry as a critical tool for questioning, even parodying, "conventional modes of thought that more natural seeming literary forms often reinforce," including certain formulaic political discourses (Mayhew, *The Poetics* 101–3).

Also in question would be the possibility of exploring the ways in which the production of national identity during the Spanish Civil War is read today, in a historical period marked by the narrativization of collective memory. Neither Javier Cercas's narrator in *Soldados de Salamina* nor Almudena Grandes in her op-ed seemed to have second thoughts about the specific value and function of poetry as cultural memory before quoting Gil de Biedma's lines in their respective reflections on the historical memory of the war. Since we are also remembering Gil de Biedma's poetry here, quoting some memorable lines about poetic form by W.H. Auden, whom he translated, may offer an apposite opportunity to dwell on such value and function: "Blessed be all metrical rules that forbid automatic responses / force us to have second thoughts, free from the fetters of Self" (857). Ironically enough, one possible function of poetry in current debates about the historical memory of the civil war in Spain would be to remind narrators – whether of national literary history like Gracia or of national history understood as storytelling like Cercas and Grandes – that the definitions of nation may be bound by similar identitarian fetters.[39]

Examinations of the value and function of poetry in debates about historical memory become particularly fraught when one considers the ways in which exilic poetry is remembered today. Recent reconsiderations of Republican exile in relation to turn-of-the-century Spain have questioned the recuperative paradigm fostered by today's hegemonic nationalist emplotment of Spanish literary history. Indeed, several cultural historians have made the case that the Republican exile holds an extrinsic position vis-à-vis the nation. Thus Mari Paz Balibrea's challenge to discourses of integration and recuperation goes hand-in-hand with her vision of Republican exile cultures as determined by a "multiplication of difference in time and space" ("Rethinking" 7). From this angle, Republican exile cultures constitute a "vanishing point on the national map" and an "exterior ... to the Spanish modernity rooted in Francoism and later continued in democracy" ("Rethinking" 11). Antonio Gómez López-Quiñones has similarly argued that "this critical inassimilable exteriority" of exile "gestures toward a political break, toward the possibility of a different type of (radically emancipatory and equalitarian) modernity" ("A Secret" 111). What reading practices would assess the value of seeing exile as a "vanishing point on the national map," and to appreciate the "gestures" of its presumed "inassimilable exteriority"?

For one, in 2014, cultural historian Luisa-Elena Delgado noted that sometimes returning to one's homeland after being exiled from it is simply not possible, and when it is, one should not try to "normalizar la ruptura temporal, geográfica y espiritual que el exilio supuso" [normalize the spiritual, geographic, and temporal rupture that exile brought about] (*La nación* 127). This claim epitomizes yet another critical position towards institutional attempts to recover the cultural legacy of Republican exiles. Questioning the normalization of rupture implies, for Delgado, a recuperation of exilic culture but only, again, as an "exterior irredimible" [irredeemable exterior]. This recuperation would thus entail allowing "que el gesto de exclusión hable por sí mismo de una historia que fue como fue, y no como querríamos que hubiera sido" [that the gesture of exclusion may speak for itself of a history which was what it was, and not as we would have liked it to be] (*La nación* 127). At play in proposals that would let such a gesture of exteriority speak for itself is precisely the critical potential of reading practices sceptical of an institutional recuperative paradigm grounded on the temporality of national literary history. If a gesture of exteriority went unchallenged, so, perhaps, would the recuperative gesture intent on normalizing it, as though all reading practices – including critical practices – had to be bracketed for some reason.

Delgado's proposal pertains to a wider critical current intent on seeking a reading practice premised on a new recuperative paradigm, one that, as Carla Kaplan proposed in 1996 from the field of women's studies, "both complicates recuperation and takes it in a new direction" (28). But Kaplan advanced this critical complication as she questioned "a sentimentalization of the marginal, the oppositional, and the subversive" (52), and challenged, in a poststructuralist vein, problematic categories used in previous recuperative paradigms, such as "experience," "identity," and "voice" (26–7). In critiques of institutional attempts to recover the cultural legacy of Republican exiles, the potential dangers of normalizing spatiotemporal ruptures and of sentimentalizing the marginal – and perhaps, also, of bracketing critical readings of it – could be eschewed by means of reading practices sensitive to both the claim-subverting textual elements in, and the critical potential of, exilic poetic discourse. Indeed, as Terry Eagleton explained in *How to Read a Poem* (2007), discourse implies "attending to language in all of its material density, whereas most approaches to poetic language tend to disembody it" (2). This sort of attention to the textual and verbal materiality of poems would make it hard to simply hear a gesture of exteriority speak "por sí mismo," as Luisa-Elena Delgado flatly contends. Eagleton was conclusive in this regard: "Nobody has ever heard language pure and simple" (*How to Read* 2).

In *The Poetics of Unremembered Acts: Reading, Lyric, Pedagogy* (2013), Brian McGrath also took issue with the interpretive strategy adopted in recent decades in historicist or cultural approaches to literature, in that it assumes "that one can move from the literary text to history and culture unproblematically, as if literary texts do not pose questions about themselves as 'objects'" (4). Thus, readers often take a literary text as an object that enables them to think critically about history and culture at the cost of reading the text uncritically. In McGrath's deconstructive framework, literary texts like poems name "a particular form of attention," and hence they "expose readers to a certain not-knowing about how to proceed with reading; they expose readers to the impossibility of reading, an impossibility that is, of course, the very chance to begin" (6).

Exilic poems also name particular modes of attention. Beyond – or rather than – speaking for themselves, they pose questions about themselves, and thus they offer the possibility of rereading their relation with cultural and literary history in a new critical light. Among the Spanish critics who have thrown critical light on the questions that poems pose about themselves and on the modes of attention they demand are Miguel Casado and Julián Jiménez Heffernan. In 2005, the same year that Mari Paz Balibrea urged a theoretical, political, and critical rethinking of the Republican exile, Casado decried the tendency, among historians and critics of poetry in Spain, to keep lists of names, topics, and labels in constant circulation for the sake of continuity and universality. As Casado saw it, such historians and critics forgot the critical analysis of "los problemas concretos del lenguaje" [the concrete problems of language] (*Artículos* 135).

Tradicionalismo [traditionalism], as Casado called this tendency, was a form of oblivion, as it subsumed all textual conflicts and resistances under a diachronic narrative: "Su mecanismo es amnésico: necesita olvidar la naturaleza conflictiva, la diversidad de las contradicciones que distinguen cualquier corte sincrónico, cualquier *presente,* y aboca a que este, al convertirse en pasado, ingrese en la conciliación" [its mechanism is amnesiac: it needs to forget the conflictive nature, the diversity of contradictions distinguishing any synchronic cut, any *present*, and leads the latter, when it becomes past, to join in conciliation] (*Artículos* 197). To counter the critical inadequacy resulting from the linear, consecutive temporality of traditionalist literary history, Casado suggested shifting the reader's attention to a "historia malla," that is, a history understood as a discontinuous, multidirectional, transversal mesh of linguistic tensions (*Artículos* 137).[40] A critical reading practice attuned to the temporality specific to each poem, and to the traces of historical conflict and upheaval distinctively threaded into its texture, would be at odds with a national history centred on supporting and strengthening catalogues, trends, and traditions, and therefore on reinforcing a sense of national unity and continuity (Casado, "Sobre historia" 14–15).

The sense of national unity and continuity fostered by traditionalist literary history is likely to make invisible not only the textual traces of a historical conflict and upheaval, such as civil war and exile, but also those traces of cultural diversity woven into the poem through translation or other means of linguistic exchange. A reading practice in line with Casado's vision of poetic history as a mesh of linguistic tensions, and also, indirectly, with Balibrea's notion of Republican exile cultures as determined by a "multiplication of difference in time and space," would be alert, for instance, to the spectral traces of French, British, and American poetic textualities haunting Spanish literary history, but also, beyond modern national and linguistic labels, to a plurality of age-old echoes from the stockroom of biblical, classical, and modernist topoi of banishment. This reading practice would be profoundly historical. Indeed, one of the historian's responsibilities may be, as Reinhart Koselleck underscored in differentiating between history writing and historical research, "to represent conflicts in their actual plurality and not to seek out identity," thus cautioning against the idealistic form of history writing that presumes to control or produce political identities through its narratives: "historical research has the duty to represent conflicts in their actual plurality and not to seek out identity ... [I]t requires a kind of reading against the grain" (*Sediments* 262).

A complementary critical approach to Casado's questioning of traditionalist poetic history can be found, within the cultural field of Spanish poetry, in Julián Jiménez Heffernan's *Los papeles rotos: ensayos de poesía española contemporánea* (2004), a collection of essays devoted to individual poets and poems from Spain and Latin America. Jiménez Heffernan drew on Ernst Blochs's notion of *ungleichzeitkeit*, or nonsynchronism, to propose critical readings receptive to the specific time signatures of "cierta escritura poética" [a certain poetic writing] (9). In Jiménez Heffernan's understanding, if a poem's temporality is not simultaneous with that of historical narratives, it is also resistant to its plotted articulations.[41] Thus, a poem can be seen as being fashioned in untimely, haphazard, and uneven ways by figurations emerging, beyond authorial intention and national affiliation, from the textual immanence of other poems through "una supervivencia tan pertinaz como inasible" [a dogged and ungraspable survival] (9). Certain poetic figurations drift and persist in a "materialidad tenaz" [tenacious materiality], and their "anamnesis discontinua" [discontinuous anamnesis] informs the "extrañeza" [strangeness] produced by the poem (10). In a sense, this "extrañeza" can be regarded as historical to the extent that the poem's texture is in a tense dialectical interplay with chronological narratives.[42]

As Ernst Bloch had it in "Ungleichzeitigkeit und Pflicht zu ihrer Dialektik" [Nonsynchronism and the Obligation to Its Dialectics] (1932), poems can be read, in line with Jiménez Heffernan's notion of the temporality of poetry, as carrying "earlier things with them, things which are intricately involved" (22). Folded into poems are times "older than the present [that] continue to effect older strata ... [and] contradict the Now in a very peculiar way, awry, from the rear" (22). Thus what makes poems historical is the sheer untimeliness of their layered texture, contradicting or interrupting the Now – i.e., the time of their reading – thematically, rhetorically, or prosodically. Bloch's concept of the simultaneity of the non-simultaneous, which "represents histories and temporal strata that coexist at the same synchronic moment yet do not correspond" (Blake Ewing 418), was similarly used by Reinhart Koselleck. Koselleck's geologic metaphor, *Zeitschichten* – sediments or layers of time –, encapsulated his understanding of the plurality of historical times as a "synchronic layering of diachronic times" (Blake Ewing 418).[43]

It is in a similar tropological light that Jiménez Heffernan argues for the existence of at least two histories of poetry in Spanish. *External* history is the developmental chronology as canonically arranged by philology and literary history. By contrast, *internal* history is anachronistic – it is, in fact, a non-history, or at least, a ghostly history: a conflicting non-sequential "cúmulo verbal," that is, a verbal accumulation or mound of sedimented poetic lines spectrally surviving in poets' and readers' memories in a sort of persistent non-contemporaneity (79). In

Jiménez Heffernan's view, this "cúmulo verbal" cannot be contained by national and generational spatiotemporal boundaries.[44] The "cúmulo verbal" of poems would diverge from conventional literary history in manifold ways. Far from contributing to "a continuous and progressive incorporation of the past," its temporality would follow, as Christoph Cox observed in his critical discussion of Hegelian conceptions of the end of history, an "errant movement whose present is troubled by a retrace that it never articulates once and for all" (130).

In keeping with Walter Benjamin's notion of history, poetic memory would then conform an image of the past not as it actually was, but rather as a constellation of linguistic remnants and traces dramatizing spatiotemporal disruptions: "while the relation of the present to the past is a purely temporal one, continuous one, the relation of what-has-been to the now is dialectical: is not progression but image, suddenly emergent. Only dialectical images are genuine images (that is, not archaic); and the place where one encounters them is language" (*Arcades* 462–3). In brief, the time signature of poetic memory would be non-teleological with regard to literary history. The non-history of Jiménez Heffernan's "cúmulo verbal," like Casado's notion of history as mesh, would also skirt the risk of reducing the connections between exilic culture and national culture to clear-cut dichotomies like before/after, progress/decline, centre/margin, individual/collective, or inside/outside. It would likewise skirt the risk of sentimentalizing "the marginal, the oppositional, and the subversive" (Kaplan 52).

Jiménez Heffernan's and Casado's approaches suggest provocative critical models for examining the historiographical quandaries that the study of exilic poetry raises. James Valender's remarks in this regard are noteworthy. In his introduction to *Poetas del exilio español: una antología*, an ambitious collection of Republican exilic poetry in Spanish co-edited with Gabriel Rojo-Leyva and published in Mexico in 2006, Valender emphatically asked how the history of exilic poetry was supposed to be written (25). Among the problems involved in this task Valender identified the use of national frameworks: "la obra de los poetas exiliados pertenece no sólo a la historia de la literatura española, sino también a la de la literatura hispanoamericana" [the work of exiled poets belongs not only to the history of Spanish literature, but also to the history of Hispanic American poetry] (*Poetas* 27). Accordingly, Valender reminded readers of Max Aub's heterodox decision to include several Spanish exiled poets in his anthology *Poesía mexicana (1950–1960)*, published in Mexico in 1960. In Valender's view, Aub's anthology was a telling example of "cuán en serio tomaban algunos su posible integración al mundo latinoamericano" [how seriously some of them took their possible integration in the Latin American world] (*Poetas* 28). It also showed how deeply transnational Aub's critical approach was.[45]

As Aub claimed in the foreword to his anthology, an overview of Mexican poetry produced in the 1950s would be incomplete without a sample of "tantos poetas extranjeros trasterrados" [so many foreign poets in exile/trans-terred]

(*Poesía mexicana* 20). Thus Aub chose to include "unos cuantos poemas de poetas españoles y americanos, mexicanos de hecho y pecho. No sería justa, ni para ellos ni para México, su ausencia" [some poems by Spanish and American poets, Mexicans in fact and in heart. Their absence would be unfair both for them and for Mexico] (20).[46] Although Valender left unaddressed other possible overlaps beyond cultural and linguistic commonality among Spanish and American poets, he did warn that the inscription of Republican exilic poetry in such an "espacio fronterizo" [frontier space] may nonetheless still be an inadequate critical and methodological model for the historical study of exilic poetry: "los desterrados debieron de sentirse, muy a menudo, no tanto ciudadanos de ambos mundos, cuanto nómadas sin arraigo en ninguno ... [E]l criterio generacional, que sigue dictando el curso tomado por la historiografía española, resulta del todo inadecuado para el caso del exilio" [exiles must have also felt, quite often, not so much citizens of both worlds as nomads without any rootedness in either ... The generational criterion, which still dictates the course taken by Spanish historiography, is rendered totally inadequate for exile] (*Poetas* 29). Valender's warning emphatically pointed to the need to attend critically to the sheer spatiotemporal complexity specifically inscribed in exilic poetry.

This complexity is enigmatic, but historically situated, as signally evidenced by Tomás Segovia's rootless nomadic figures who, in their wanderings through a nameless landscape of spectres, destabilize the reader's deictic orientation. Conventional historiographical methodologies grounded in national and generational boundaries tend to confine such complexity and therefore, paradoxically, to dehistoricize it. Poetic memory casts into relief the ghostly anachronistic temporality of exilic poetry in relation to the recuperative paradigm that, as we have seen, undergirds the hegemonic nationalist emplotment of Spanish literary history. Critical considerations of this ghostly temporality are especially germane inasmuch as poetry was generally understood as a pre-eminent form of national discourse in the historical context of the Spanish Civil War and its aftermath. It is to this context we now turn.

CHAPTER THREE

Writing the War, Re-writing the Nation, Embodying the Voice of the People

A ghostly understanding of history connotes a dynamic, multidirectional, discontinuous process marked by the returns and doublings-up of voices from the past (Labanyi, "Introduction" 12). From this angle, every successive utterance of a poem foregrounds the uncanny forms in which voices appear, disappear, and reappear in its verbal fabric, partly as a result of each reader's horizon of expectations. The question of poetic voice is all the more relevant within the framework of exilic poetry when one considers that the internecine conflict in Spain was idealized as a poet's war by numerous participating and observing intellectuals of very different political orientations, Spanish nationals or not. Indeed, the thousands of poems composed, recited, and sung about the conflict, both in Spain and abroad, by amateur and established authors are memorable evidence of the high, even pre-eminent, symbolic, cultural, and political value accorded to poetry at that particular historical conjuncture.[1] This value was emphasized in *The Last Great Cause: The Intellectuals and the Spanish Civil War* (1968), Stanley Weintraub's classic study about the "platoon of poets" who flocked to Spain in 1936 from English-speaking countries: "never since has a cause so captured the moral and physical influence of so many makers and molders of the language," Weintraub proclaimed (2).

For many intellectuals, the murder of internationally acclaimed poet Federico García Lorca in 1936 meant, symbolically, that "Franco y sus aliados fascistas representaban el repudio y el silenciamiento de la poesía" [Franco and his Fascist allies represented the repudiation and the silencing of poetry] (Binns 21). W.H. Auden's widely published and quoted lines from his 1937 poem "Spain" made unforgettable the figure of the poet as possessing not only considerable political capital, but also a certain capacity for decisive deadly action: "To-morrow for the young the poets exploding like bombs, // ... // To-day the deliberate increase in the chances of death, / The conscious acceptance of guilt in the necessary murder" (Spender and Lehman 58).[2] A disturbingly different perspective was later offered in Pablo Neruda's memoirs *Confieso que he vivido* [I Confess that I Have Lived] (1974), in which war was organically depicted as fruitful soil for poetry's transnational productivity: "No ha habido en la historia intelectual una esencia tan fértil para los poetas como la guerra española ... [La Segunda Guerra Mundial] no alcanzó nunca a embargar como la española el corazón colectivo de la poesía" (*Confieso* 177) [In intellectual history there has not been a subject as fertile for poets as the Spanish war ... The Second World War did not ever manage to grip the collective heart of poetry as the one in Spain did (*Memoirs* 177–8; translation modified)].

In *La poesía de la guerra de España* (1985), Serge Salaün focused instead on the poetic production by Spanish authors and gave an estimate of 3,400 published poets during the war (158).[3] According to Jo Labanyi, "1,376 Republican wartime magazines publishing poetry have been counted, and some 8,500 poems survive, mostly signed but by unknown individuals, a few by women and children" (*Short* 116–7). Even more than novels and plays, verses cast in a nationalist and neo-populist rhetoric became "armas de combate" [combat weapons] (Alvar, Mainer, and Navarro 621). Jorge Urrutia argued in 2006 that the Republicans may not have been a united people in arms, but at least they were a united people in poetry (19). But, if poetry's high symbolic, cultural, and political value enabled soldiers and civilians to "write the war" (Labanyi, *A Short* 117), it also allowed them to rewrite the nation in that poems were fashioned through a rhetoric of orality and performativity premised on the notion that people, language, and nation could be articulated and embodied by poetic voice in times of crisis.[4]

Poetry was massively widespread during the war largely because it was thought to emerge from the voice of the people. As César Vallejo wrote in "Himno a los voluntarios de la República" [Hymn to the Volunteers of the Republic] from *España, aparta de mí este cáliz* [Spain, Take This Cup from Me], his major 1937 volume of poems about the war: "Todo acto o voz genial viene del pueblo / y va hacia él" (249) [Every act or voice of genius comes from the people / and goes towards them (*Complete* 571)].[5] "Voz" is a loaded signifier here, given the added value that the performative and oral aspects of poetry, particularly in popular *romances* or ballads, took on under these historical conditions.[6] Poetry was obviously not only spoken, it was also presented in written form, although predominantly as a public and popular mode of expression. As Michael Iarocci explained in 2007, "it was shouted across trench lines; printed on postcards, leaflets, and posters; painted on walls; sung at battles; and declaimed on loudspeakers at political rallies" ("War" 186). The voice of the people was then both presented and represented in poetry, as Vallejo's lines make explicit.

In fact, poetry was perceived as embodying the voice of the people to such an extent that it seemed able to accommodate cultural dichotomies and differences beyond its modes of production and its contexts of enunciation and reception, irrespective of whether the immediacy of orality was presented or represented in poems. Serge Salaün has argued that both popular and cultivated expressions preserved strong vocal elements during the civil war. The conflict "da a las tradiciones orales un impulso nuevo insuflándoles un carácter de cultura de masa y de cultura oficial que reconcilia todas las modalidades expresivas, locales o nacionales, literarias o políticas ... Con la voz y el sonido, la palabra se vuelve contacto y carne" [gives oral traditions new momentum, breathing into them a character of mass and official culture which reconciles all modes of expression, local or national, literary or political ... With voice and sound the word becomes touch and flesh] (111).

This reconciliation of all modes of expression, including popular and high-culture modes, materializes, for instance, in "Vientos del pueblo," a *romance* written in 1937 by the revered poet Miguel Hernández:

Vientos del pueblo me llevan,
vientos del pueblo me arrastran,
me esparcen el corazón
y me aventan la garganta.
...
No soy de un pueblo de bueyes,
...
Nunca medraron los bueyes
en los páramos de España.
¿Quién habló de echar un yugo
sobre el cuello de esta raza?
...
Cantando espero a la muerte,
que hay ruiseñores que cantan
encima de los fusiles
y en medio de las batallas. (311–12)[7]

People, land, and nation come together here through the poet's singing voice, which in turn comes from the nation, the land, and the people.[8] "Pueblo" was, of course, a highly ambivalent signifier in the war context, as it could refer, among other things, to a national people and/or to an international people, whether within the boundaries of the Spanish state or not.[9] In Hernández's poem the Spanish "raza" encompasses other "razas," which become a collective of singularities as the speaker calls each one of them to arms by means of a long unifying apostrophic address informed by a rhetoric of heroic epithets and figures of land work and manual labour.[10] This sort of rhetoric is in line with Hernández's communist affiliation in 1937 but also with his persona as a nature and war poet.

Pablo Neruda dubbed Hernández a "poeta de cabras" [poet of goats] (*Confieso* 164, *Memoirs* 117). He also explained how the nature poet became a war poet: "de pastor de cabras se había transformado en verbo militante. Con uniforme de soldado recitaba sus versos en primera línea de fuego" (*Confieso* 174) [had been transformed from a goatherd into a fighting word. In soldier's uniform, he read his poems on the front lines] (*Memoirs* 125). Neruda identified the figure of the poet with the Spanish *tierra*: "Miguel era tan campesino que llevaba un aura de tierra en torno a él. Tenía una cara de terrón o de papa que se saca de entre las raíces ... Me contaba cuentos terrestres de animales y pájaros. Era ese escritor salido de la naturaleza como una piedra intacta ... Su rostro era el rostro de España" (164–5) [Miguel was a peasant with an aura of earthiness about him. He had a face like a clod of earth or a potato that has just been pulled up from among the roots ... He told me earthy stories about animals and birds. He was the kind of writer who emerges from nature like an uncut stone ... His face was the face of Spain (*Memoirs* 117–18)]. The Chilean poet's figuration is prosopopoeic: Hernández's face or persona is that of the Spanish land incarnate. The next link in Neruda's metonymic chain of Christian reconfiguration is, predictably enough, Hernández's "verbo," made flesh as a war poet for Spain. Indeed, Hernández's "voz" and "sonido" have become "verbo," and consequently, in Salaün's terms, "la palabra se vuelve contacto y carne" (111). Through Neruda's rhetoric of telluric organicism, the people and nation of Spain are hypostatized through Hernández's poetic persona turned "verbo."

In a poem as deftly modulated by dynamics of address as "Vientos del pueblo," the undecidability between readership and audience and between voice and voicing goes further in answering the question about the textual production of the nation than the poem's purported political affiliation. This consideration is important in the context of the Spanish Civil War, when the idea that national unity could be embodied by the oral force of poetic voice was often taken for granted, regardless of the speaker's specific political or national affiliation. As Walter J. Ong argued in *Orality and Literacy*, "To think of readers as a united group, we have to fall back on calling them an 'audience', as though they were in fact listeners. The spoken word forms unities on a large scale, too: countries with two or more different spoken languages are likely to have major problems in establishing or maintaining national unity" (78). Vocal tension in apostrophic poems like "Vientos del pueblo" may be read from this perspective: despite the conceit of an audience, Hernández is addressing the difficult question of how to unify the different voices – and implicitly, the different languages – heard in Spain by writing Romantic tropes of natural, phonic voicing like "vientos" and "ruiseñores" in Spanish.

In Hernández's poem, voice becomes, simultaneously, presentation and representation, *phone* and *logos*, voice and voicing, even human and non-human. At issue, then, in the relation established in "Vientos del pueblo" between the natural but collective voicings of "vientos" and "ruiseñores" and the also natural but singular voice of the poet of *tierra* is the status of the national voice of Spain "en medio de las batallas." The abstract notion of national voice is cast, on the one hand, in elusive, airy Romantic tropes; and, on the other, in a set of particular, albeit abstract, "razas," formulaically characterized by heroic epithets.[11] Either way, a long-standing memory of cross-boundary topoi of lyric voicing complicates Hernández's rewriting of national races and voices, whether Spanish or not, even as notions of people and nation are hypostatized through poetic voice.[12]

The dynamics of address in Vallejo's "Himno a los voluntarios de la República" also hints at the vocal complexity of the signifier "pueblo" thematically, when the speaker contrasts the world and Spain in the line "El mundo exclama: '¡Cosas de españoles!' Y es verdad" [The world exclaims: "Spanish things!" And it's true] (*Complete* 571) and then apostrophizes the Spanish worker hyperbolically so as to emphasize his ecumenical passion: "Proletario que mueres de universo" [Proletarian who dies of universe] (*Complete* 571).[13] However, the speaker has already undermined the suasory force of his own vocative abilities. The verbless first line of the poem is an authoritative call: "Voluntario de España, miliciano" [Volunteer from Spain, militiaman]. As in Hernández's poem, its effect is also constitutively apostrophic, since the verse evokes what Jonathan Culler has called "poetic power": "Apostrophe treats the subject's relation to the world as a specular relationship, a relation between subjects, and it has a highly optative character, expressing wishes, requests, demands and whatever that is addressed do something for you or refrain from doing what it usually does" (*Theory* 229). In this light, the speaker in Vallejo's poem conjures the volunteer into presence by means of a self-empowering speech act.

As Barbara Johnson contended, by means of apostrophe "[t]he absent, dead, or inanimate entity addressed is ... made present, animate, and anthropomorphic" (*A World* 185). Thus, Vallejo's volunteer is animated as a hero, as the poem's title and the heroic epithet in the second line announce – "de huesos fidedignos" [of trustworthy bones] – and a later verse confirms – "héroes a la redonda" [heroes all around]. But then, ironically, once the volunteer is made present as a hero bound to kill and be killed, the very speaker who conjured him so authoritatively through poetic enunciation turns to himself and ironically questions his own speech act or, indeed, all his acts: "no sé verdaderamente / qué hacer, dónde ponerme; corro, escribo, aplaudo, / lloro, atisbo, destrozo, apagan, digo / a mi pecho que acabe, al bien, que venga, / y quiero desgraciarme." (247) [I don't know truly / what to do, where to place myself; I run, write, applaud, / weep, glimpse, destroy, they extinguish, I say / to my chest that it should end, to the good, that it should come, / and I want to ruin myself] (*Complete* 569).

And yet, if attention is shifted from thematics and modes of address to the poem's prosodic and tonal fabric, Vallejo's line reveals an undecidable vocal tension within voice itself. The first line of the poem is also a melodic hendecasyllable, conventionally stressed on the third, sixth, and tenth syllables. Each stress falls on the open vowel "a" – "Voluntário de Espáña, miliciáno" – phonically prompting an authoritative and declamatory voicing of the line by the reader. In light of the thematic reading, the phonic animation of both the volunteer and the reader in the first lines should be followed by the reader's phonic deanimation. But the lines that thematically asserted the speaker's loss of vocal power phonically dynamize reading, if only by the sheer kinetic variety of stressed vowels in the richly toned sequence of action verbs: "corro, escribo, aplaudo, / lloro, atisbo, destrozo, apagan, digo."[14] Thus, the thematic self-questioning as to the speaker's vocative abilities is not necessarily transferred to the reader voicing the poem.

Additionally, in the lines "Todo acto o voz genial viene del pueblo / y va hacia él," the conjunction "o" in "acto o voz" can be parsed as conjunctive – to the point that it can be elided with the previous vowel – but also as disjunctive. Vallejo's line performs a "genial" speech act ("acto o voz"), while at the same time inviting the undoing of that very speech act by delaying the voicing of "voz" until after the seemingly genius-ridden "acto." Voice becomes here, as in Hernández's "Vientos del pueblo," both continuous and discontinuous, utterance and representation, *phone* and *logos*, voicing and voice. Indeed, following Michelle Clayton's illuminating reading of Vallejo's poem "Telúrica y magnética," voice in "Himno a los voluntarios de la República" can be construed dialectically with regard to the Marxist teleological temporality underpinning *España, aparta de mí esta cáliz*: "If prose walks alongside history, poetry attempts to interrupt it – resisting the march of history, yet still consciously inscribed within it" (15). The people's voice in Vallejo's poetic speech act both marches with history and interrupts it. Furthermore, voice can also be construed dialectically with regard to the temporality of national history: profoundly folded into the verbal texture of the poem as both voice and voicing, the people's voice is simultaneously marching with Spanish history and breaching it: it is both conjunction and disjunction.

A rewriting of the Spanish nation as the embodiment of popular voice was also what two canonically established, high-culture poets, Antonio Machado and Juan Ramón Jiménez, carried out during the war, before each of them went into exile. In a 1937 newspaper article titled "Voces de calidad" [Quality Voices], Machado – arguably the most emblematic poet living in Spain during the war after the death of Federico García Lorca in August 1936 – extolled the words written in America by Jiménez, "nuestro gran lírico" [our great lyric poet] about "la gran experiencia trágica de la España actual" [the great tragic experience of present-day Spain] (Jiménez, *Guerra* 7). With the "ojos excepcionales" [exceptional eyes] of a "verdadero poeta" [true poet], Jiménez had seen the naked truth, and shared it with "su pueblo" [his people]. The "pueblo español" [Spanish people] had effected, in Jiménez's words, a "violenta unión" [violent union] with "la verdad" [truth] through the war experience (*Guerra* 7).

Weintraub closed *The Last Great Cause* by concluding that, although the Spanish conflict had been, in effect, a poets' war, it had also "drained – or claimed – its poets" (303). But he was referring mostly to international poets. Many Spanish poets were far from drained. Some went into exile and continued writing. Machado's life, however, would be claimed on 22 February 1939, almost immediately after he crossed the border to France. Jiménez, who left in 1936, never returned to Spain and died in 1959 in Puerto Rico. In line with Machado's articulation of a "verdad española" [Spanish truth] as embodied by the conjoining of "poeta" and "pueblo," among Jiménez's stated goals as an exiled writer was the incorporation of his poetic voice into the "corazón" [heart] of popular poetry (*Guerra* 7). As we shall see in chapter 4, this symbolic incorporation into the collective voice of the Spanish people would result, however, in *Guerra en España*, Jiménez's transnational assemblage of heterogeneous verbal and visual materials.

(Re)Distributing Poetic Voices

León Felipe's "Reparto," one the most emblematic poems produced in exile by a Republican, dramatizes a similar rewriting of the nation by way of a seemingly unifying poetic voice.[15] Felipe was widely regarded among Republicans as a "symbol of opposition to the Franco dictatorship" (Bou 560). "Reparto" was inserted in Felipe's collection *Español del éxodo y el llanto: doctrinas, elegías y canciones* [Spaniard of Exodus and Weeping: Doctrines, Elegies, and Songs], published by La Casa de España en México in 1939, only a few months after the poet went into exile. Significantly, after the Republican defeat on 1 April, Franco had declared 1939 to be "el año de la Victoria" [the year of Victory]. Later retitled to "Hay dos Españas" [There are Two Spains], the poem is prefaced by a prose statement where a first-person speaker claims that, in a "reparto injusto, desigual y forzoso" [unfair, unequal and forced distribution], poets fell "del lado del éxodo" [on the side of exodus] (24–5).

But then the speaker goes on to assert that without poets keeping "vivo el fuego prometeico" [the Promethean fire alive] no "pueblo" will be able to exist, nor will Spain (25). "Reparto" is cast as an apostrophe to the victorious dictator and his army. After the speaker enjoins Franco to heed the poet's admonitory song – "que lo oiga Franco" [let Franco hear it] –, the poem reads:

> Tuya es la hacienda,
> la casa,
> el caballo
> y la pistola.
> Mía es la voz antigua de la tierra.
> Tú te quedas con todo
> y me dejas desnudo y errante por el mundo ...
> mas yo te dejo mudo ... ¡Mudo!
> ¿Y cómo vas a recoger el trigo
> y a alimentar el fuego
> si yo me llevo la canción? (*Español* 25–6)[16]

"Reparto" showcases a vehement rhetoric of orality and performativity premised on the notion that poetic voice could bring together person, people, land, language, and nation. Apostrophically enough, Felipe's boldly and baldly declamatory poem invites, almost compels voicing.

"Reparto" not only became one of the most oft-quoted poems among exiles: it would also emerge later, in poetry anthologies published in Spain, as the main symbol of the Republican cultural legacy.[17] In *Inmigración y exilio: reflexiones sobre el caso español* [Immigration and Exile: Reflections on the Spanish Case] (1997), a historiographical survey of the various forms that displacement took among Spanish Republicans in the Americas, Argentinian historian Clara Lida linked the exile's collective voice with Felipe's "canción" to explain that the largest loss of exile had been suffered by Spain itself: "en primerísimo lugar, la verdadera y mayor pobreza del destierro recayó sobre la propia España, que década tras década silenció la voz del expatriado, aquel que se llevó la canción" [first and foremost, the true and greatest poverty of exile befell Spain itself, which decade after decade silenced the voice of the expatriate, the one who took the song away] (122). Almost fifty years earlier, in 1949, another distinguished historian, Vicente Llorens, had similarly claimed that poetry constituted one of the most valuable cultural assets of the Spanish Republican exile (*Estudios* 131).[18]

In his Mexican exile, Max Aub reasserted the unique cultural and political value that poetry took on among Republicans during the war. In *Poesía española contemporánea*, his 1969 historical overview of twentieth-century Spanish poetry, Aub referred to the armed conflict in agonistic albeit enigmatic terms, calling attention to national poetry by means of a hyperbolic personification: "La poesía española era, tal vez, lo único que estaba preparado para ella, y toda de un solo lado, el de la España que había cobrado con la República cierta esperanza – esperanza cierta – de un renuevo" [Spanish poetry was, perhaps, the only thing that was ready for it, and all of it on one side: that of the Spain that had cherished, with the Republic, certain hope – a hope that was certain – of renewal] (135). In spite (or maybe because) of Franco's victory and the repression that followed, numerous exiled Republicans resolutely relied on the symbolic agency of poetry to uphold a certain sense of national continuity. Thus, canonical Republican poets such as Federico García Lorca, Antonio Machado, and León Felipe came to embody both Spanish cultural identity and modernity.

Felipe died in Mexico City in September 1968, after almost three decades of exile. A few weeks later, in December 1968, Aub published a tribute in the Spanish literary journal *Ínsula* to commemorate the cultural depth of Felipe's legacy and uphold the potency of his poetic voice for posterity:

> Fue carne de profeta desde que nació ... la Biblia, en su base; Job y el Eclesiastés. No los románticos, él vino de más lejos, de la oscuridad del desierto que creó el monoteísmo, porque su poesía clama en él. Y el mundo ... es desierto. No ve, no oye a nadie, sino la honda caracola del desierto, en la que sólo resuena la voz del hombre solo ... León Felipe fue el último profeta, el que se mete en la piel de todos, hurgando a ver si le sientan bien las abarcas de Job, las de Jonás, las de Shakespeare,

las de Whitman, a ver cómo se le oye mejor ... Después de esa voz, o a través de ella, ¿cómo oír las otras? Todas resultan blandas y apagadas. El dolor será el mismo, pero el arranque, el clamor, no ... También los muertos escriben; tal vez la tierra no es más que residuos de manuscritos ("León Felipe" 3, 15)

[His flesh was that of a prophet since he was born ... at its basis is the Bible; Job and Ecclesiastes. Not the Romantics, he came from farther away, from the darkness of the desert that created monotheism, because his poetry cries out there. And the world ... is the desert. He does not see, he does not hear anyone, but the deep shell of the desert, in which only the voice of man alone resounds ... León Felipe was the last prophet, the one who slips into everyone's skin, poking around to see if Job's sandals, or Jonah's, or Shakespeare's, or Whitman's will fit him, to see how he will be heard best ... After that voice, or through it, how are the other voices supposed to be heard? All of them seem soft and muted. The pain will be the same, but the outburst, the cry, will not ... The dead also write; perhaps the earth is nothing but remains of manuscripts]

Interestingly, Aub underscored here the ghostly cross-boundary, non-chronological, and plurivocal repertoires shaping Felipe's poetry. A critical element in Aub's reading is a time-honoured topos from scripture: *vox clamantis in deserto*, the voice of one crying out in the desert – a memorable reference to John the Baptist. Attention to the various textual threads entwined into poetic voice enabled Aub to read into Felipe's poetry yet another discursive space of continuity and discontinuity between living, writing, and reading, but also between voice and nation, especially the modern Spanish nation invented by Romantic historians.

If historians still find in Felipe's "Reparto" an organic, intrinsic nexus between the individual voice of the poet and the collective voice of the Spanish land, people, and nation, they often do so without addressing the concrete material ways in which such a nexus was and still is possible between the poem and "cada lector" – for instance, the ways in which the verbal texture of the poem compels its potential voicings. In addition to the ghosts configured in each reader's horizon of expectations, such voicings involve, among other elements, the poem's singular intertextual patterns, as Aub graphically and movingly explained in his tribute. Felipe's poetic memory is intermeshed with various textual motifs, most notably from the Bible and *Leaves of Grass*.[19] The plaintive yet defiant, declamatory, and self-affirming litany-like memorability of *Español del éxodo y el llanto*, whereby singular and collective voices join in unison, can be traced back to the Psalms – as explicitly prefigured in the volume's title. The title "Reparto" and the solemn preface to the poem itself are reminiscent of Pliny the Younger's dialogic letters.[20]

More generally, the anaphoric force driving Felipe's poetry also harks back to the ways in which he ventriloquized Walt Whitman's vibrantly manifold voices in his translation of "Song of Myself" – titled *Canto a mí mismo* – but also to previous Latin American readings and misreadings of the likewise psalmodic *Leaves of Grass* in assertively toned texts by Nicaraguan Rubén Darío and Cuban José

Martí.[21] Cross-boundary, plurivocal, and plurilingual threads from other texts, particularly Darío's and Whitman's, are thus thickly bundled into Felipe's poetic memory. The rhetorical, topical, tonal, translational, and intertextual forces animating "Reparto" resist the claim made by the first-person speaker about the potential rearticulation of the Spanish *tierra* in exile – whether Republican or not: "Mía es la voz antigua de la tierra." This resistance emerges from within its verbal fabric, reminding the reader of a spatiotemporal discontinuity vis-à-vis the form of national continuity that the poet's "canción" may conceivably bring about.

This resistance becomes stronger if the reader remembers the specific textual ways in which Felipe composed this self-affirming first-person speaker. His foreword to *Canto a mí mismo*, titled "Habla el prólogo" [The Prologue Speaks], is indeed an uncanny form of poetic ventriloquism: "No sé si será peligroso, / pero no es inoportuno. / ¿Es inoportuna esta canción? / 'Con estrépitos de músicas vengo'" [I do not know whether it is dangerous, / but it is not inopportune. / Is this music inopportune? / "With music strong, I come"] (10). The personified paratext takes a leaf from Whitman's book both tonally and typographically (*Canto* 9). Moreover, interspersed as it is with words taken from Felipe's Spanish translation of Whitman's poem – "music strong" – the foreword rhetorically asks about the spatiotemporal coordinates of the song and translation. The foreword is thus haunted by Whitman's absent (albeit robust) voice, which is variously folded into Felipe's Spanish words as both *imitatio* and translation.

This form of haunting adds a distinctly border-crossing and cross-historical dimension to Felipe's foreword: "es un gran poema polifónico. Es una sinfonía donde no falta ningún instrumento, ninguna voz, ningún paisaje ... ¿Falta algún personaje? ¿Falta alguna escena donde la vida y la muerte levanten su tinglado? ... ¡Pues a empezar! Porque de todos, de cada uno y de todos, y de mí mismo, sale esta canción ..." [it is a great polyphonic poem. It's a symphony where no instrument, no voice, no landscape is missing ... Are we missing some character? Are we missing some scene where life and death set up their stage? ... Let's start then. For this song comes out of everyone, out of each and every one, out of myself ...] (*Canto* 24). Through Whitman's haunting, Felipe posits a cosmic vocal identity, simultaneously individual and collective, of song, poet, instrument, voice, people, earth, drama, and book, among other elements.

"Reparto" is likewise traversed by the cross-boundary and cross-historical dimensions of Whitman's translated voice. The poem may be read and voiced as a borrowing from Whitman's source text; the self-affirming, declamatory first-person speaker was trying to distribute instruments, voices, songs, and landscapes in Felipe's new poetic polyphony of exile. But "Reparto" is also a misreading of Whitman's poetry in that it borrows from his wide-ranging polyphony of voices and then disavows at least one of them: the voice of the victorious dictator. Felipe denies this voice because he needs to contain the other Spain, represented by Franco, and prevent it from infiltrating the exiled Spanish people embodied by the first-person voice of the national poet. This is one of the implications of the poem's title: a *reparto* or distribution of national voices. But then, if intertextuality designates, as Barbara Johnson succinctly and perspicaciously argued, "the multitude of ways a text has of not being self-contained, of being traversed by otherness" (*A World* 116), Felipe's intertextual misreading of Whitman's democratic voices also necessarily animates the voice of the dictatorial other and thus lets its otherness traverse the poem's texture, despite claims otherwise. The crucial act of animation in "Reparto" is a rhetorical one: an apostrophe to Franco. Consequently, the *reparto* or distribution operating in Felipe's poem is indeed differently reanimated by the other Spain, as the later title, "Hay dos Españas," makes explicit.[22]

"Reparto" is thus intertextually and rhetorically "traversed by forces and desires that are invisible or unreadable to those who see it as an independent, homogeneous message unit" (Johnson, *A World*, 117), including Felipe himself, with his forceful rhetoric of national containment. The inscription of Franco's voice in the poem presents a paradox for the reader as he or she voices the text: even if the poem's claim and aim is to render the victorious dictator mute, the speaker still addresses him. Franco's voice is thus reanimated, if only as a ghostly voice, and national containment is textually defeated. But even if one fails or refuses to read the voice of this seemingly almost omnipotent figure, "Reparto" keeps defeating containment beyond a national rhetoric associated to the spatiotemporal coordinates of the Spanish Civil War, since the poem already contains at least one other voice different from the "voz antigua" of the earth or land embodied by the exiled first person: this voice is Whitman's own haunting, polyphonic voice, which Felipe has incorporated and expanded through translation. Thus, an intertextual, translational, and rhetorical reading and voicing of "Reparto" shows that Felipe's iconic poem cannot be contained within national boundaries, whether exilic or not.

No one's nation – neither Felipe's, nor Franco's, nor even a hypothetical nation distributed differently as a rearticulated nation – can avoid being traversed by voices or scenes "donde la vida y la muerte levant[a]n su tinglado" as Felipe's translation *Canto a mí mismo* histrionically but persuasively asserts (24). Along intertextual patterns, the dynamics of address generated by the deictic, rhetorical, tonal, topical, translational, and prosodic strands woven into the lines of "Reparto" also complicate its authoritatively commanding claim to national unison in the here and now of every reading and voicing. The shifting personal deictics at work in the poem – "yo," "tú," "mía," "tuya" – typify the apostrophic rhetoric informing much exilic poetry – that is, the rhetoric of addressing an absent entity or prosopopoeia. Felipe's famous central lines of vocal self-affirmation – "Mía es la voz antigua de la tierra. / Tú te quedas con todo / y me dejas desnudo y errante por el mundo ... / mas yo te dejo mudo ... ¡mudo!" – showcase this rhetoric at its most vehemently monitory and homiletic.

Such claim-making didacticism is conceivably one of the reasons why the poem and the poet became so famous among Republican desterrados. But it is also conceivably one of the reasons why some readers may now feel ill at ease – somehow out of place and out of time – in voicing a nationalistic verse like "Mía es la voz antigua de la tierra." Prosodically, this emphatic hendecasyllable solemnly and authoritatively reasserts the presence of the first-person voice, particularly since it starts with a possessive pronoun stressing the agency of voice. The main stress falls on "voz," and the secondary stresses fall on "mía" and "tierra." Also, the rhythmic pattern activated by the pairing of a hendecasyllable and a heptasyllable can be heard as vaguely – and arguably also anachronistically – reminiscent of a certain "voz antigua" of Spanish poetry, since the Italianate silva (which combines eleven-syllable lines with seven-syllable lines) harks back to lines by Spanish Golden-Age poets such as Lope de Vega and Góngora. And yet, in its hyperbolic, almost extravagant, contrast between the personal shifters "yo" and "tú," vocal self-affirmation is also disclaimed: "tú te quedas con todo." The first-person voice admits total defeat.

Additionally, in apostrophizing Franco, this poetic voice rhetorically foregrounds the victor. Thus the speaker throws, in Barbara Johnson's words, "voice, life, and human form into the addressee, turning its silence into mute responsiveness" (*A World* 185). The speaker in Felipe's poem throws Franco "into mute responsiveness" explicitly and categorically, but he also performatively apostrophizes him into presence, somehow assenting to the dictator's victory. The first person is then both self-affirming and self-defeating. As such, the relationship between claim-making and claim-subverting elements in the poem becomes, in a sense, undecidable. Furthermore, the first-person voice performatively reclaims *tierra* in the midst of *destierro,* while apostrophically surrendering the land to the victor: "tú te quedas con todo." The speaker's – and also, deictically, the reader's – voice both belongs and does not belong to *tierra.* If national voice is prosodically reasserted by the poet in exile, it is also ruptured from within the poem as rhetorically unstable. Rhetorical uncertainty runs counter to prosodic certainty. But then if rhetorical and prosodic deployments of poetic voice necessarily go together in poems (Nowell Smith 2), "Reparto" disclaims "voz" at the same time that it seeks to claim it.[23] Interestingly, in Spanish "reparto" means distribution, but also cast, as in cast of characters. In a way, Felipe's poem is not just a distribution of voices, but a cast of different voicings for his Whitmanesquely polyphonic "tinglado."

Whether through a wistful or hopeful rhetoric of attachment to the nation, or alternately through a defiant or indifferent rhetoric of detachment from it, a voice – such as the one figured into the first-person speaker understood as the voice of the people in Felipe's "Reparto" – can make various claims in an exilic poem about the ways in which the nation should be rewritten and its voices redistributed. Some of those claims may refer to the time and place from which the voice went originally into exile.[24] Conversely, historical readings of exilic Republican literature have persistently focused on the idea of a lost, impoverished, or broken nation, and thus on its potential cultural recuperation and restoration, as though the symbolic return of a poet's voice to the Spanish fatherland would suture and even overwrite the lost or torn thread of national history. Any claims in this respect made in poems, including those about national origins, are nonetheless complicated and even contradicted by the closely knit texture in which the voice of the people is presumably embodied.

As we have seen, the prevalent discourse during the Spanish Civil War and its aftermath was poetry, and it was poetry itself and poetry as the other (the *other* of narration) that introduced a potentially resistant uncanny temporality into the production of the nation.[25] Poetry as the voice of the people – whether embodied by amateur poets, established poets, or both – was pedagogical and performative, both a sign of a past national origin and a sign of a national contemporaneity in times of internecine conflict.[26] In the historical conditions under discussion, the nation's people may productively be thought of in the multiple temporalities of poetry, rather than narration, or even within poetry itself – in the multiple temporalities of *narrative* poetry – as in the epic tales constructed in myriad *romances* during the war.[27] Yet the claim-subverting elements in a poem's texture can also be read as interrupting the temporalities of poetry understood as the prevalent discourse of the nation.

In her perceptive study of César Vallejo's poetry, Michelle Clayton has reflected on the choices of genre made by academics in their treatment of nation: "as a genre that theoretically speaks for the individual and exhausts itself in its enunciation, poetry has often been deemed incapable of engaging with a collectivity and generating either immediate or lingering effects. Academic literary studies have for the most part clung to the relation between nation and narration – not nation and lyric – as the place where reflection on history happens" (26). Clayton's reflections point to a reductive notion of poetry in academic discourse, a notion that the relevance of Vallejo's and Felipe's poems, among those of others, in the context of the Spanish Civil War disclaims and undercuts. In the face of recent debates about the centrality of narrative in international literary history, Clayton has also persuasively reflected on the "continuing marginality" of poetry and on its function "as a mad discourse that interrupts and punctuates but remains outside narrative, theatrical, or theoretical inquiries into history and the human" (306). During the Spanish Civil War, poetry was far from marginal – it was indeed central to the production of notions of voice, people, and nation. However, as we saw earlier in the case of Javier Cercas and Almudena Grandes, the memory of such historical centrality now seems largely marginal.

A Politics of Exilic Poetry?

In *Theory of the Lyric* (2015), Jonathan Culler was leery of granting poetry much political potential. Culler approached this matter in a discussion of Theodor W. Adorno's and Jacques Rancière's argument that poetry maintains a negative, or oppositional, relation to society: "Not belonging in a realm one inhabits, ignoring or resisting its customs, and scattering or dispersing the words that organize life and social value certainly make possible social engagement but scarcely insure social and political effects" (*Theory* 296–7). It could also be argued, however, that it is actually the undecidable position of poetry's language vis-à-vis society's language that may render its effects political. Jacques Rancière's comparative description of the poet's position in the realm of politics, "the poet belongs to politics as one who does not belong there" (qtd. in Culler, *Theory* 296), could then be rephrased as "poetry belongs to politics insofar as it does not belong there." In other words, what makes poetry's language political is its undecidable position in politics.[28] This premise is in line with Barbara Johnson's claim that the political potential of a poem largely depends on our reading – and, arguably, voicing – the aporetic elements its verbal texture reveals (*A World* 194). As Judith Butler maintained in her detailed commentary of Johnson's claim, without undecidability, "there would be no open-ended debate, and no field of the political" (xxiii).

In this light, among the political effects of reading critically the concept of poetic voice in this context may be an open-ended debate about the fraught relations between the notions of person, people, land, language, and nation in historical conditions as politically disastrous as those of the Spanish Civil War. If one of the reasons why a poetic text has political potential is the undecidability between claim-making and claim-subverting elements in it, then the elucidation of the intentional, representational, and referential meanings in a poem like León Felipe's "Reparto" – as ascertained in narrative articulations of exilic cultural productions – does not constitute by itself an adequate criterion for gauging the extent of its political thrust. Such critical discriminations are consequential. After all, what happens if critical focus is centred onto the "conspicuously foregrounded statements" in "Reparto," and these are read "solely in function of intentionality and representativity" (Johnson, *A World* 18)? Emphasis on contextual reference and representativity reveals that the divisive statements in "Reparto" – or "Hay dos Españas" – echo the polarizing rhetoric endemic to civil war and exile.[29] But Felipe's poem harks even further back to the inflammatory sectarian speeches delivered in 1933 by José Antonio Primo de Rivera, the Spanish lawyer and nobleman who, inspired by Benito Mussolini, founded the fascistic party Falange Española [Spanish Phalanx] (Payne 104).[30] At stake in Primo de Rivera's charged rhetoric is, precisely, the position of "poesía" in relation to familiar notions such as "tierra," "España," "pueblo," and "voz," whether mute or not.

In "Orientaciones hacia un Nuevo Estado" [Guidance towards a New State], published on 16 March 1933 in the only issue ever published by the journal *El Fascio*, Primo de Rivera scathingly denounced the liberal state in Spain. As he saw it, among the consequences of the rule of the majority in the democratic system of the Second Republic were division and hatred: "El patrio solar se convierte en mero campo de lucha, donde procuran desplazarse dos –o muchos– bandos contendientes, cada uno de los cuales recibe la consigna de una voz sectaria, mientras la voz entrañable de la tierra común, que debiera llamarlos a todos, parece haber enmudecido" (*Obras* 40) [The fatherland is reduced to the state of a battlefield, where two – or several – contending factions seek to gain ground, each heeding a different sectarian voice, while the dear voice of the common land, which ought to make all of them brothers, seems to have fallen silent (*Selected* 44)].

Another crucial text at this historical intersection is the founding speech of Falange Española, delivered on 29 October 1933 – less than three years before the coup against the Republican government – in which Primo de Rivera explained his revolutionary program to bring together "una España dividida por todos los odios y por todas las pugnas" [a Spain divided by all manner of hatreds and conflicts (*Selected* 53)]:

> Yo creo que está alzada la bandera. Ahora vamos a defenderla alegremente, poéticamente. Porque hay algunos que frente a la marcha de la revolución creen que para aunar voluntades conviene ofrecer las soluciones más tibias; creen que se debe ocultar en la propaganda todo lo que pueda despertar una emoción o señalar una actitud enérgica y extrema. ¡Qué equivocación! A los pueblos no los han movido nunca más que los poetas, y ¡ay del que no sepa levantar, frente a la poesía que destruye, la poesía que promete! En un movimiento poético, nosotros levantaremos este fervoroso afán de España; nosotros nos sacrificaremos; nosotros renunciaremos, y de nosotros será el triunfo (*Obras* 69).
>
> [I believe that the flag is well and truly hoisted. Now let us defend it cheerfully, poetically. For there are some who, faced with the onslaught of revolution, believe that unity of purpose can best be achieved by proposing the most lukewarm solutions; they believe that anything which might arouse an emotion or prompt any vigorous and extremist attitude should be kept out of propaganda. What a misjudgment! None but the poets have ever moved a people, and woe to those who know not how to counter the poetry of destruction with the poetry of promise! In a poetic movement we shall raise high that fervent concern about Spain; we will sacrifice ourselves, we will renounce, and ours will be the victory (*Selected* 57)]

According to Primo de Rivera's confrontational rhetoric of political mobilization, then, a suitable tool for compelling people to seek unity of purpose in the battle for the Spanish *patrio solar* was the perlocutionary force of poetry. Primo de Rivera's fascistic belief in a revolutionary poetic movement resonates loudly with Mussolini's notion of the social function of poetry.

Paul de Man quoted Mussolini in a disturbing 1941 review of a survey of Italian poetry. In de Man's analysis, Italian poetry seemed to "réaliser avec le plus grand bonheur, le souhait exprimé par Mussolini lorsqu'il déclara que 'C'est surtout dans les temps presents que la poésie est nécessaire à la vie des peuples'" (*Wartime* 32) [realize most felicitously the hope expressed by Mussolini when he declared that 'It is especially at the present time that poetry is necessary to the life of a people'].

Fulfilling hope may then be among the political effects of poetic voice, according to Primo de Rivera's claims in his categorical speeches on the eve of the Spanish Civil War: "la voz entrañable de la tierra común, que debiera llamarlos a todos, parece haber enmudecido," "[a] los pueblos no los han movido nunca más que los poetas," "frente a la poesía que destruye, la poesía que promete." Poets were endowed with the power to bring about radical political change, as their voices were capable of awakening the muted voice of the land and the people. It should come now as no surprise that Felipe's discordant rhetoric against Franco – "Mía es la voz antigua de la tierra. / Tú te quedas con todo / y me dejas desnudo y errante por el mundo ... / mas yo te dejo mudo ... ¡mudo!" – may be eerily reminiscent of Primo de Rivera's factious rhetoric against the Spain legitimately represented by the Second Republic.

Establishing such similarities is, however, the outcome of reading apparently dissimilar political texts – poems and speeches – as analogous claim-making statements or narratives. This is arguably one of the reasons why Antonio Machado's poetic legacy, for instance, was up for grabs by both belligerent sides when he died in exile after the war. And yet the critical practice of finding similar claims between apparently dissimilar political texts may be faulted for giving them what Jo Labanyi called "an appearance of continuity" through "a kind of trick continuity editing" ("Introduction" 3). But historians may be hard-pressed to edit much "messy heterogeneity" – in Labanyi's terms – out of the similarities that emerge in this case, at least inasmuch as Felipe and Primo de Rivera belong to a historical intersection in which, as we saw, poetic voice was often presumed to be able to seamlessly articulate, even embody, notions of person, people, language, land, and nation ("Introduction" 3). Beyond party affiliations, both writers were drawing on similar notions of nation as imagined or invented by Romantic historians and philosophers (Appiah, *The Lies* 81–102). Following such presumption, the discordant rhetoric Felipe stages in "Reparto" could indeed be construed, in Sebastiaan Faber's terms, as a crack in the utopian "dream of a harmonious, unified, and glorious national community" that nonetheless the "dos Españas" somehow shared (*Exile* xi).[31]

And yet, from a historical perspective, what kind of reading practice would be more generative for a critical methodology focused on re-examining the specific political position that poetry in particular was made to occupy in a cultural field shaped by the extreme socio-political and ideological polarization brought about by civil war and exile? Perhaps not so much the establishment of intentional, representational, and referential similarities between poems and speeches as the pursuit of differences *within* each one of them; that is, in the case of "Reparto," the pursuit of those specific claim-subverting elements that tend to be overlooked and silenced when a poem is solely understood as a claim-making narrative. In other words, such reading practice would avoid critical methodologies that condemn as "noise" those elements in a poem that do not seem to fit "a signified-based theory of meaning" (Johnson, *A World* 18). Such claim-subverting elements would at least undermine the apparent similarities between Primo de Rivera's and Felipe's respective forms of discourse: elements like the non-chronological and cross-boundary verbal and textual patterns that "Reparto" makes available for the reader. These claim-subverting elements are quite remarkable: as Derrida submits to our "auditory grasp" in "The Law of Genre," such elements "resonate all by themselves," and thus they audibly demarcate "Reparto" as a poem: they mark it and remark it when we read it as listeners able to voice the text with an ear to its tightly knit verbal fabric (55).

Following a reading practice based on poetic memory, the position of Felipe's poem may then become less easy to pinpoint: it may be unquestionably continuous but also uncannily discontinuous with regard to the fascistic nationalist politics proclaimed in Primo de Rivera's speeches about the battlefield of the Spanish fatherland. Felipe's poem suggests a different sense of the political insofar as it is haunted by a ghostly undecidability as to its – intended or unintended – vocal, spatiotemporal, and therefore national affiliation. This undecidability would extend to the sense of national affiliation fostered by the conventionally referential readings of "Reparto" characteristic of Spanish literary history. Remarkably, Felipe rewrote the poem years later, and the only word he took out was the dictator's name: Franco. The apostrophe he wrote instead was less explicitly and immediately tied to the political circumstances of the Spanish Civil War: "hermano" [brother] (Castellet, *Veinte* 125).[32]

It behooves readers of exilic poetry to be alert not only to the presumptively intentional, referential and representational meanings of a text understood as an expressive medium – whereby land, language, nation, and poetic voice may be somehow conjoined in unison – but also to how the intertwining of its verbal fabric generates an undecidability between claim-making and claim-subverting elements. Such intertwining – for instance, the potential incompatibility between voices and voicings in the here and now of reading a powerfully declamatory text such as "Reparto" – raises the question of what hinges on the relationship between history and memory in a poem.[33] Indeed, one possible answer to this question is that such undecidability is inextricably bound up with history. That is, following a reading practice based on poetic memory, a political reading of an exilic poem lies in the enigmatic, ghostly shadows enveloping its presumptively intentional, referential and representational meanings. These meanings are shadowy because, as Theodor W. Adorno argued about artworks in general, it is through history that poems become an "enigma": "it is history that ever and again makes them such ... Through form, [poems] gain their resemblance to language, seeming at every point to say just this and only this, and at the same time whatever it is slips away" (*Aesthetic* 120). Indeed, Adorno's ideas about the enigmatic nature of artworks may be extrapolated to the specific modes of undecidability generated, as Barbara Johnson contended, by a poem's verbal fabric.[34]

Consequently, history is not only the past to which the poem may be referring (or intending to refer) but also the experience of a tense dialectical interplay between that past and each reader's present, as reading practices based on poetic memory suggest. From this standpoint, a poem only resembles society's language to the extent that, just as it may seem to yield a political meaning, "whatever it is" – in Adorno's words – enigmatically "slips away" through the specific "form" of memory provided by the multifaceted verbal texture that activates, and is activated by, every iterated reading of it.[35] This type of slippage yields a historical experience in that it establishes a non-chronological relation between what-has-been and now. This dialectical tension is all the more significant in that, as Niall Binns has argued, poetry was the most important literary genre in the Spanish Civil War because it retained "un prestigio que resulta en nuestros días inconcebible" [a prestige that in our times becomes inconceivable] (21). Thus, negotiating the ties between history and memory in a critical re-examination of poems written by Spanish Republican *desterrados* may require us as readers to shift our attention to the potentially undecidable elements of a text.

This shift would entail examining, in Johnson's terms, its "contradictions, obscurities, ambiguities, incoherences, discontinuities, ellipses, interruptions, repetitions, and plays of the signifier" (*A World* 18) – and thus reading a poem as a discursive space that may not produce political effects, as Culler claimed, but should certainly spur historical and political reflection. Terry Eagleton's spirited defence of the politics of close reading is helpful for this discussion, as it relates to textual ambiguity and dissonance in poetry: "[A]lertness to poetic ambiguities [is] also an openness to conflicting kinds of cultural meaning" (9). An apposite historical and political reflection in this regard may be inferred from a widely quoted paragraph in Adorno's exilic writings about the twofold exile that exiled authors may experience: if indeed authors who no longer have a homeland are, in the end, "not even allowed to be home in their writing," perhaps a productive reading strategy for exilic poems would be to shift the critical focus onto such twofold unhomeliness and its corresponding untimeliness. Perhaps such a reading strategy would reflect on the modes of otherness – including modes of political uncanniness, as can be traced in Felipe's "Reparto" – between writing and homeland, and between writing and home text, where "authors settle ... like home-dwellers" (*Minima* 51).[36]

The textual specificity of poetry must be emphasized in this respect, not just because poetry was a prevalent discursive form during the Spanish Civil War and its aftermath, but also because, as a verbal mode of memory, it was perceived at the time as generically distinct from other discursive forms. A dialectical reading of the modes of historicity specifically inscribed in exilic poems may then delve into spatiotemporal overlaps and departures between the individual and the collective, objectivity and subjectivity, the historical and the cross-temporal. Michelle Clayton has offered an Adornian description of the lyric from this perspective:

"Poetry's codes are structured in large measure by the possibilities of a historical moment, injected by a sense of local urgencies; but the lyric also aims to reach beyond them, opening itself up to interpretations that go beyond the purely local or contemporary, unfurling through history" (27). Such a dialectical reading extends to the relation between, for instance, the circumscribed here and now of pressing political necessity and the there and then of commemorative necessity in times of war. The tension between these two modes of necessity shapes the intricate rhetoric that articulates one of the most memorably arresting poems written about the Spanish Civil War: Pablo Neruda's manifesto-like "Explico algunas cosas" [I Explain a Few Things].

"Explico algunas cosas" was first published in Madrid in 1937 and later the same year in Chile as part of the illustrated volume *España en el corazón: himno a las glorias del pueblo en la guerra* [Spain in the Heart: Hymn to the Glories of the People in the War]. The poem focuses on Franco's siege of the Spanish capital, which started in November 1936. In dramatic counterpoint to the artful deictic play of pressingly hortatory apostrophes in the often-quoted anaphoric lines "Venid a ver la sangre por las calles, / venid a ver / ... / venid a ver la sangre" (*España* 14) [Come and see the blood in the streets, / come and see / ... / come and see the blood] stands the powerful animating prosopopoeia that precedes them: "Federico, te acuerdas / debajo de la tierra, / te acuerdas de mi casa con balcones en donde / la luz de junio ahogaba flores en tu boca?" [Federico, do you remember / under the ground, / do you remember my house with balconies where / the June light drowned flowers in your mouth?] (12). Through epideictic rhetoric suggestive of funeral ceremony, the first-person voice beseechingly invokes the ghost of Federico García Lorca, who was murdered by Franco supporters in Granada in August 1936, shortly before the siege of Madrid. The subsequent poetic voice's vehement call to testimonial, political, and military action is thus mediated by the commemorative speech act whereby the living poet enjoins the dead poet to remember. Prosopopoeia stirs the dead poet back to life and to action.

Prosopopoeia depends here on imagination-based deixis or *deixis am phantasma*. Each reader can somehow experience the impact of the poem's phantasmal uncanniness and therefore its commemorative force through the personal shifters that enable him or her to imagine the absent persons ("te acuerdas," "mi casa," "tu boca") who were present in Madrid from December 1934 to July 1936, a set of spatiotemporal coordinates that are obviously different from those of every successive reading.[37] If "cada lector" occupies the present site and time of enunciation of the first-person deictic marker, the tension between continuity and discontinuity created by a present-tense reference to memory ("te acuerdas") is hyperbolically reinforced not only by the fact that the prosopopoeic question is urgently posed by a now-dead individual (Neruda) to a then-dead individual (Lorca), but also by the contrast with the subsequent present-tense individual command to take urgent collective action. At stake in the seeming opposition between the rhetorically pressing temporalities of a historical moment of witnessed homicide and a long-term duration of commemorative invocation is the mnemonic value of the poem's texture in successive readings.

This testimonial poem is rendered all the more unforgettable by the deictic spatiotemporal tension between the forceful ring of sheer historical situatedness and the border-crossing, long-standing textual patterns woven into the text. Conventional testimonial rhetoric – the persistent urgency behind, for instance, discursive attempts at bridging the distance between the reading and the witness's need to mark in writing his or her presence – stands in contraposition to the emphatic deployment of rhetorical tropes like apostrophe and prosopopoeia. Neruda's commanding and deceptively simple run-on lines – all the more commanding for being economical – are indeed memorable because of the momentous historical occasion – Madrid's heroic resistance, against all odds, against Fascism, as trumpeted in Rafael Alberti's 1936 volume of poems *Capital de la gloria* [Capital of Glory]. They are also made resonant by various threads of intertextual density harking back to other poems by Neruda – for instance, the similarly parallelistic and dialogic "Barcarola" [Barcarole] – and, beyond them, to the Bible, especially the Book of Exodus and the Psalms.[38]

For the poem's verbal fabric to be perceived and remembered in its specific historical materiality, the reader needs to retain, as Clayton suggests, "a sense of the tensed relation between poetry and history, which we can trace in its forms and tones even more than in its contents" (27). Indeed, the historical force of "Explico algunas cosas" is largely quickened by the effective ways in which Neruda resignifies the topoi of blood, death, and resurrection through deixis, tone, anaphora, apostrophe, and prosopopoeia. Yet, the tensed relation between poetry and history goes beyond the synchronous lines of different discursive forms, as it is once and again intersected by the diachronous lines of successive readings. The patterns spun into the text animate each reader into voicing the text, animating the deanimated: dead Federico García Lorca and dead Pablo Neruda, but also, metonymically, the dead anonymous victims who shed their blood in the streets of Madrid in 1936.

However, by making the dead speak, the living reader is, in Paul de Man's view of the symmetrical structure of prosopopoeia, "struck dumb, frozen in [his or her] own death" (*The Rhetoric* 78). Thus, ghostly textual animation in Neruda's poem somehow brings about the deanimation of the reader in an eerie exercise of historical memory. The semblance of continuity that poetic commemoration through *deixis am phantasma* provides is therefore also a reminder of unbridgeable spatiotemporal discontinuity. To use Max Aub's language again, a rupture appears between the past of "lo vivo" and the present of "cada lector" but also between the manifold temporalities of "lo vivo," animated through the poem's texture: for instance, the temporalities of those who may now be living and reading the poem are discontinuous with the temporalities of those who wrote (a good example of which is the sheer temporal immediacy of Neruda's insistent "venid a ver"), those who read the poem in 1937, those who were murdered and prevented from writing and reading, and those who were murdered without leaving traces of a voice there and then. It is also in this sense that Neruda's "Explico algunas cosas" becomes historical material and historical experience.

Exilic poetry brings these tensions into sharper relief, as catastrophic historical conditions destabilize the presumed continuity of notions of voice, person, people, land, language, and nation. In an exploration of the discursive space between "lo vivo," "lo escrito," and "cada lector," poems must be read dialectically, in intergeneric dialogue with their discursive "others." If, following Barbara Johnson, a reading strikes one as "strong" inasmuch as it "encounters and propagates the surprise of otherness" (*A World* 15), then genre may be conceived as a "historically evolving set of possibilities with potential for surprise" (Culler, *Theory* 90).[39] In *Poetry and Its Others*, Jahan Ramazani showed how modern Western poetry is in intergeneric dialogue with kindred discourses such as the novel, theory, the law, the news, prayer, and song (15). When a text is studied from the standpoint of genre, it also opens up to transnational perspectives: "If you analyze a text without reference to its cross-border generic cousins, you ironically preclude an understanding of its specificity" (Ramazani, *A Transnational* 71).[40] At the same time, critical readings that privilege historical reference over prosodic patterns and repertoires of rhetorical, tonal, topical, translational, and intertextual elements may reproduce a conventionally restricted understanding of poetry as a genre, without being sensitive to how sociopolitical determinations affect writing practices.

A primarily referential approach would risk rendering invisible and silent the peculiar poetic memory of exile traceable not only in Juan Ramón Jiménez's unfinished cross-generic project *Guerra en España* but also in his poem "Espacio," written both in verse and in prose. In this dialogue with its others, poetry's movement "with potential for surprise" unfolds on a temporal plane as well. When a text is studied generically, it moves between contrasting time signatures. But, as Barbara Johnson also argued, differences between discourses are inescapably tied to differences within entities, including poems. A key difference within poetry is, as we saw earlier, that of narrative, especially historical narrative. Jonathan Culler has examined at length how neglecting the contrast within a poem between what he calls "poetic event" and narrative time – "a temporality of discourse" vis-à-vis "a referential temporality" – has crucial implications for reading strategies focused on differentiating the varieties of historical temporality (*Theory* 226–7). Forgetting the poetic event's specific time signature affects not only theoretical, critical, or methodological approaches, but also the exploration of the poem's potential political effects in "the real world" (Johnson, *A World* 2–3), as the undecidability within a poem may also allow for open-ended debate (Butler xxiii).

If debates about the conflicting narratives of history and memory concerning the war and its aftermath overlook poems' undecidability, context-specific political examinations of the notions of people, person, and nation may suffer. Edward Said's dialectical approach to exilic writing and nationalism is pertinent in this respect: "Nationalism is an assertion of belonging in and to a place, a people, a heritage. It affirms the home created by a community of language, culture, and customs; and by doing so, it fends off exile. Indeed, the interplay between nationalism and exile is like Hegel's dialectic of servant and master, opposites informing and constituting each other" (176). Said's dialectical approach to exilic writing, Johnson's contention that the political quality of a text lies in its undecidability, and Adorno's reflections on the enigmatic character of the work of art come together in a constellation of ideas to address the relation between history and memory in exilic poems. Viewed in this framework, some of the challenging political questions concerning a poetic line as enigmatic as the last verse Antonio Machado presumably wrote before he died in exile – "Estos días azules y este sol de la infancia" – may lie *within* the difference between memory and history. As we shall see in the coda to this book, such political questions would be about the memory of history and the history of memory, emerging in various ways through that line's verbal fabric.[41]

It is in this political sense – that of the specific historical experience ("lo vivo") Republican exiles endured and the hermeneutic distance between the loss of life folded into an exilic poem and its posterity in each new reading – that this analysis evokes again Paul Ricoeur's reflection on the enigmas of memory. Ricoeur pointed to testimony as the discursive form that gives rise to crucial questions about the complex relationship between memory and history: "we must not forget that everything starts, not from the archives, but from testimony" (*Memory* 147).[42] It is no surprise, then, that *This Ghostly Poetry* asks how we should approach the testimonial rhetoric that exiled poets often resort to when their poems revolve around loss and death. After all, Aub noted a fundamental connection between testimony and transience when he claimed that only his dead and surviving comrades would grasp what he pointed out in *Diario de Djelfa* (*Obras completas: Vol. I* 94). Indeed, much exilic poetry thematizes a preoccupation with death and posterity, closely associated to a sense of the impossibility of return and the inevitability of loss, as Francisco Caudet meticulously showed in *El exilio republicano de 1939* (2005).[43] This is, perhaps, the main reason why much exilic poetry should be approached through ghosts. As the poet Angelina Muñiz-Huberman – daughter of Spanish Republican exiles – declared in 1999, "Partir al exilio es partir a la muerte. Quien abandona el claustro materno inicia, en ese momento, su propia muerte: el viaje de tumba en tumba" [To depart for exile is to depart for death. Those who leave the mother's womb initiate, at that moment, their own death: the journey from tomb to tomb] (*El canto* 66).[44]

Muñiz-Huberman's arresting metaphor of exile as birth and a journey towards death underscores the complex, even contradictory, spatiotemporal interplay between political and existential belongings in exilic writings. The philosopher

María Zambrano similarly reflected on the spatiotemporal "contradicción" [contradiction] of her exilic experience (778).[45] In "Amo mi exilio" [I Love My Exile], an article published in Madrid in 1989, she saw exile as "una dimensión esencial de la vida humana" [an essential dimension of human life] (778). Five years after returning to Spain, Zambrano seemed unable to give up this necessary quality of exile: "Yo no concibo mi vida sin el exilio que he vivido. El exilio ha sido como mi patria, o como una dimensión de una patria desconocida, pero que una vez que se conoce, es irrenunciable" [I don't conceive of my life without the exile I have lived. Exile has been like my fatherland, or like a dimension of an unknown fatherland, but one that, once it is known, it becomes irrenounceable] (778). Returning to her *patria* may have meant "renunciar a mis cuarenta años de exilio" [renouncing my forty years of exile], but this renunciation also necessarily implied remembrance, as forgetting that exilic past would have been like "negar una parte de nuestra historia y de mi historia" [denying a part of our history and of my history] (778).

This sense of loss, experienced as both collective and individual, placed Zambrano in a contradictory position: it implied the loss of the Republic, experienced forty years earlier, when she left Spain; the loss of political exile, experienced now, when she returned to Spain; but also the impossibility of forgetting, experienced in her exilic memory as an irrenounceable *patria*. Zambrano resorted to a rhetoric of incomprehensibility to figure her painfully contradictory experience of exile: "una sensación como de ser despellejado, como San Bartolomé, una sensación ininteligible" [a sensation like being flayed, like Saint Bartholomew, an unintelligible sensation] (778). Exile contains something "inefable" [ineffable] that, from a historical perspective, may not be grasped by the young in the present: "no le pido ni le deseo a ningún joven que lo entienda, porque para entenderlo tendría que padecerlo, y yo no puedo desear a nadie que sea crucificado" [I do not ask or wish any young person to understand it, because to understand it they would have to suffer it, and I cannot wish anyone to be crucified] (778). Thus, folded into Zambrano's figuration of exile through a rhetoric of passion – of flaying and crucifixion – is a spectral understanding of loss that hovers tensely between past and present, historicity and trans-historicity, the individual and the collective, one's *patria* and another, life and death.

Exilic poetry's ultimate *other* – the most enigmatically uncanny discontinuity within it, the difference most adamantly resistant to dialectical articulation and narrative recuperation – might then be death itself. Perhaps this preoccupation with transience and mortality should inform any study of the testimonial rhetoric that tends to shape exilic poems. Exilic poetry's often necrological, epitaphic, and elegiac tenor – and elegy is a paradigmatically transnational genre, as Jahan Ramazani showed in 2009 (*A Transnational* xi) – invites readers to engage with the non-chronological temporality of death beyond the scope of national literary history.[46] The thematic exploration of this temporality in exilic poems necessarily entails close attention to their verbal fabric. Exiled writers often couch their concern with death in delicately elaborate, self-cancelling rhetoric. An eloquent example of this rhetoric is the impersonal circumlocution that closes Rosa Chacel's finely wrought poem "La ventana que da sobre la muerte" [The Window That Overlooks Death], published in 1942 in Argentina's foremost cultural journal *Sur*: "Vela sin viento en lago sin distancia, / cáscara del adiós, piel del olvido, / vigía sin vigilia, la ventana / calla, sin aldabón, sobre la muerte" [Candle without wind on a lake without distance, / husk of farewell, skin of forgetting, / watch without watchfulness, the window / keeps quiet, without knocker, over death] (*Poesía* 66). These four alliteratively interwoven hendecasyllables are subtly organized as a paratactic set of negative metaphorical substitutions ending in a performative contradiction: after reflectively employing a figurative opening on extinction, the poem emphatically closes in upon itself with a tightly knit periphrasis about ultimate silence, as though preventing physical and verbal communication.[47]

Relatedly, the concern *desterrados* often exhibited with spatiotemporal alienation, with transience and uprootedness, may explain their recourse to epitaphic addresses to posterity. Karen Mills-Courts's insightful examination of the spectral relation between the presentational and the representational workings of language in poetry is helpful for approaching the various forms in which poetic memory and epitaphic rhetoric relate to experiences of loss: "The death of presence leaves a ghost-like trace that is not quite nothingness ... Through writing one can construct oneself at least as a recollection and make good use of the fact that the recalling is always *epitaphic*" (13, 201). So, by obfuscating the boundary between life and death, epitaphic address can often appear hyperbolic, particularly as it invites consideration on the conditions of possibility for voicing. For instance, in "Canción lejana" [Faraway Song], a poem written in Mexico by Jomí García Ascot, we read: "Cántame, voz de lo muerto / agolpado en el caliente nido / de mi cuello" [Sing me, voice of what is dead / thronging in the hot nest / of my neck] (qtd. in Rivera 89).[48] The fact that such hyperbole may be characteristic of the lyric genre invites analysis (Culler, *Theory* 258–62), as many exiled Republican poets, including those discussed here, penned hauntingly memorable epitaphic lines. Needless to say, for exiled poets, epitaphic addresses to posterity activated unique modes of textual memory by which future readers might remember historically specific experiences of loss and perhaps even reflect on the irretrievable dimensions of such experiences.

Exploring the continuous and discontinuous poetic space between life and death can also provide grounds for political debate. In Judith Butler's moving posthumous reading of Barbara Johnson's re-examination of apostrophe, lyric poetry "engages the questions of what lives and what dies, what is animated and what is not. But instead of giving us fine and fast distinctions between life and death, it articulates another intermediate zone, one in which the sure distinction between the two cannot hold" (xxiv). And indeed, political urgency pervades the question of how poems by writers who died in exile address the presumed incompatibility of life and death. Adorno claimed that death in the concentration camps needed to be dialectical: "that ... it was no longer an individual who died, but a specimen – this is a fact bound to affect the dying of those who escaped the administrative measure" (*Negative* 362). Through Adorno's argument, the metaphysical question of an afterlife became, as Lisa Yun Lee has argued, a "critique of material suffering," in light of historically situated "systematic efforts to obliterate any contradiction, antagonism and forms of 'Otherness'" (141). Adorno's dialectical thinking on death illuminates the political potential of cultural production by Republican authors who, like Max Aub, were forced into exile after surviving the ravages of war and concentration camps. Many of them never returned to their homeland and died as expatriates or *desterrados*. Some of the poems these writers produced muster various forms of epitaphic, self-elegiac, and mythopoetic rhetoric, whereby the destruction of the poetic persona yields its disturbingly phantasmal survival – its textual afterlife. These formal qualities are conceivably one of the reasons why such poems, as historical materials, lend themselves to political readings.[49]

As such, exilic poems may animate figures of otherness, contradiction, and difference amid potentially nefarious fixed identities – including those shaped by representative voices in times of national war – and thus transfigure voices and voicings into hauntingly plural materializations of critical memory. If, according to Adorno, it was through history that poetry became an enigma, perhaps what lies behind the alterity of poetic memory is the loss of "lo vivo," as Aub suggested in his foreword to *Diario de Djelfa*. Perhaps it is also this inaudible, irretrievable dimension of past experience that underlies the question that Aub himself asked almost twenty-five years later in his 1968 necrological tribute to León Felipe's protean persona and its cross-boundary poems: "León Felipe fue el último profeta, el que se mete en la piel de todos ... Después de esa voz, o a través de ella, ¿cómo oír las otras?" [León Felipe was the last prophet, the one who slips into everyone's skin ... After that voice, or through it, how are the other voices supposed to be heard?]" ("León Felipe" 15). Perhaps readers could begin to answer Aub's question by trying to remember how to slip into the phantasmal personae of exilic poems. Thus, through their voices, "los fantasmas de cada lector" may be animated into recognizing, spectrally enough, the sheer enigmatic loss of exile.

PART TWO

Exiles in Poetic Memory

CHAPTER FOUR

Juan Ramón Jiménez: "Photography Is Death Itself"– Visionary Poetics, Ruins, and the Testimony of Antonio Machado

Portraits of Francisco Franco, Adolf Hitler, Benito Mussolini, Lluís Companys, and Dolores Ibárruri, a.k.a. *La Pasionaria*. Lines from the popular song "Anda jaleo, jaleo" [C'mon, Raise a Ruckus]. A quotation from a 1292 "espejo de príncipes" or manual of princely conduct. A newspaper clipping with a photograph of Federico García Lorca and a caption condemning the "inconcebible ... crimen de los fascistas de Granada [que] fusil[aron] al glorioso poeta" [inconceivable crime committed by the fascists from Granada who shot the glorious poet]. Anonymous verses from medieval *romances*. An untitled photograph of a street in ruins (figure 4.1). A copy of the review "Poetas en la España leal" [Poets in Loyal Spain], written by Luis Cernuda in 1937 for the wartime cultural magazine *Hora de España* [Spain's Hour]. A safe conduct pass. Letters, articles, lectures, forewords, and reviews written in Cuba between 1937 and 1939. Translations of poems by Charles Baudelaire, George William Russell, and W.B. Yeats. Another clipping with a photograph of Antonio Machado, news of his death in France after fleeing Barcelona with the Spanish government, and a handwritten annotation: "N[ueva] Y[ork]: 39" [N[ew] Y[ork]: 39]. A portrait captioned "¡Niña española en México!" [little Spanish girl in Mexico!]. Several close-ups of apparently dead children. His own original poems.[1]

These are only a few of the many heterogeneous materials that Juan Ramón Jiménez collected under the title of *Guerra en España* during his more than twenty years of exile. After leaving Madrid on 22 August 1936 – slightly over two months after the coup against the Republican government – Jiménez and his wife Zenobia Camprubí spent a few months in Puerto Rico and then went to Cuba, where they stayed for almost three years. Camprubí's diary details their activities in support of the Second Republic and records Jiménez's practical dependence on her (209). It also makes clear that the poet "was by no means an apolitical bystander and that the loss of his country affected him very deeply" (Ciplijauskaité, "Diary" 312). In January 1939, Jiménez and Camprubí moved to the United States, which became their residence until 1951, when they moved to Puerto Rico for good. Jiménez's

4.1 Untitled photograph of a street in ruins, from Juan Ramón Jiménez's archive *Guerra en España*. Reprinted by permission of Editorial Point de Lunettes.

project, initially called *Español con su España (Política poética)* [Spaniard with His Spain (Poetic Politics)] and *Desterrado, diario poético* [Exiled, A Poetic Journal], remained unfinished at his death in 1958. Jiménez aimed to leave a comprehensive record of his contribution "de hombre y poeta" [as a man and a poet] to the Republican cause both during the civil war and in exile, both his social and political activity as – in his terms – an "hombre de la realidad cotidiana" [man of quotidian reality], and his "trabajo normal" [normal work] as an "hombre vocativo" [vocational man] during this period (qtd. in Crespo 10). The materials gathered in *Guerra en España* documented what could be called his "biography" and his "bibliography" – the two writerly registers that created the tension animating Jiménez's exilic production.

Given its volume and heterogeneity, *Guerra en España* is exceptional among published testimonies about the Spanish Civil War and the Republican exile. Its prologue is "Voces de calidad" [Quality Voices], an article written by Antonio Machado in September 1937 for the Servicio Español de Información [Spanish

Information Service] of the Republic and published both in Valencia and in Havana (Crespo 22). As we saw earlier, in "Voces de calidad" Machado extolled Jiménez, "nuestro gran lírico" [our great lyric poet], for the texts he had written in America about the war. But Machado also praised the singular testimonial quality of Jiménez's writings. To him, Jiménez was not only a "testigo presencial" [eyewitness] to "la gran experiencia trágica de la España actual" [the great tragic experience of present-day Spain]; he was also a "verdadero poeta" [true poet] gifted with "ojos excepcionales" [exceptional eyes] that "ven en lo profundo" [see in the depths] (7–8). Here Machado underscored what could be termed Jimenez's *visionary* poetics. Understood as a visionary form of testimony, *Guerra en España* began two years later, in 1939, when Jiménez, exiled in Florida, learned that Machado had just died in exile, shortly after leaving Barcelona and crossing the French border at the end of the war.

This knowledge constitutes the emotional and symbolic core of the project that would occupy Jiménez until his death. He spent almost twenty years writing memoirs and journalistic pieces about that important moment of crisis, and creating an archive to help him remember – and be remembered – as both "hombre de la realidad cotidiana" and "hombre vocativo." This chapter takes this provenance of Jiménez's project as a starting point to examine Machado's symbolic status as a ghostly witness in *Guerra en España*. First, it explores and analyses possible links between materials associated with the commemorated poet: the article "Voces de calidad," the photograph that accompanies the news of his death, and an obituary of Machado that Jiménez wrote in exile. Then, the analysis focuses on the type of poetic testimony that these links permit – that of a "poeta" – and approaches Jiménez's project not just as a documentary or biographical repository, but as a literary or bibliographical project. In the last section, the chapter assesses the value that this poetic form of testimony has today in a field of cultural production defined by public and academic interest in recent Spanish history generally, and the debate over historical memory in particular.

Although unfinished, *Guerra en España* can be studied as a testimony in that it lets the reader draw connections between the various materials that attest to Jiménez as both a writer committed to his poetry and an intellectual committed to the Spanish Republic. Jiménez described himself as a "metamorfoseador sucesivo" [successive metamorphoser] (qtd. in Crespo 6). In keeping with this perception, this analysis not only explains the inclusion and, indeed, the metamorphosis of the materials in Jiménez project; it also suggests border-crossing, non-chronological, intertextual, plurivocal, and plurilingual ties between them. This constellation of materials and resonances foregrounds the manifold aspects of the poet's experience of crisis as a Republican exile in the Americas. Yet its discursive heterogeneity also points to a profound homogeneity – a homogeneity associated with the memory of death as it is shaped by poetic writing. This mode of memory becomes most salient when, after Machado's death in France, his iconic status as the poet of the people is put to what Jiménez condemns as an illegitimate political use. For Jiménez, this reductive reading of Machado's poetry serves as a warning that, if he too were to die in exile, his biography and bibliography would be similarly distorted. This necrological perspective is key to understanding how Jiménez experienced crisis as a *desterrado*.[2]

Through an allegorical recovery of Machado as a ghostlike poet who gives testimony to the tragedy of the Spanish people beyond the immediate political exigencies of the war, Jiménez seeks to protect his own work from circumstantial readings. In doing so, he attempts to ensure a symbolic return to Spain as a poet for posterity. The changes in perspective that Jiménez introduces in his project by shifting and intertwining his materials with Machado's speak to an ongoing reflection about the textual and material history of the witness and his testimony – a reflection about the writer as both "hombre de la realidad cotidiana" and "hombre vocativo," shaping his biography and bibliography for future readers. This specular play of authors and materials reveals the multifaceted textual history of Jiménez's work. According to Andrés Trapiello, Jiménez's textual history is "laberíntica" [labyrinthine], as his poems and books "cambiaban de orden, título, fecha y contenido de la noche a la mañana con milagrosa versatilidad" [would change order, title, date, and content overnight with miraculous versatility] ("Una imprenta" 530). Perhaps more important, this intertwining of authors and materials dramatically distills the exiled poet's continuous musings on the relationship between writing and death.

A significant step in Jiménez's symbolic return to Spain came twenty-seven years after his death, when *Guerra en España* was published for the first time in Barcelona in 1985. The Spanish poet and translator Ángel Crespo (1926–1995), who had himself gone into exile in Puerto Rico in 1967, edited the volume for the prestigious literary press Seix Barral. Crespo's edition – the outcome of his investigation in the "Sala Zenobia-Juan Ramón Jiménez" [Zenobia-Juan Ramón Jiménez Room] at the Universidad de Puerto Rico, Recinto de Río Piedras – amounts to a partial reconstruction of Jiménez's project, one that includes a very small portion of an archive that contained original poems, translations, aphorisms, anonymous verses from *romances*, lectures, interviews, letters, newspaper articles, propaganda posters, and photographs, among other things (Crespo 7). Almost a quarter of a century later, in 2009, Jiménez's symbolic return seemed to move forward again when a revised and expanded version of Crespo's edition, now with some 763 pages and more than 159 illustrations, was published in Granada, Spain. Soledad González Ródenas, who undertook the revision, found the assembly of materials to be an "auténtico fárrago" [a real hodgepodge] (X).

Hodgepodge or not, in 1984 Crespo claimed that, by its very nature, the book possessed "valor histórico y literario" [historical and literary value] (qtd. in González Ródenas X).[3] In addition to their value as documents covering more than twenty years of Francoism and Republican exile, the two editions appeared at two key moments for the cultural production about the memory of the Spanish Civil War and the ensuing dictatorship. In 1985, Spain signed the Treaty of Accession to the European Economic Community. In 2009, the United Nations Human Rights Committee suggested that Spain commission a panel of experts to establish the truth about human rights violations during the conflict. As such, 1985 and 2009 mark, respectively, the end of the transition from Francoism to democracy and the beginning of international intervention in the debate over the so-called historical memory of war and postwar repression in Spain. The enlarged edition of *Guerra en España* thus furthered a recuperation of the historical value of Jiménez's work that had already advanced in 1999 with the publication of *Lírica de una Atlántida* [Lyric of an Atlantis], his collected poems written in exile. Testimonies about the Spanish Civil War and its aftermath become particularly relevant in light of their multiplicity, variety, and discursive complexity (Hardcastle 155). Jiménez's project exhibits these characteristics in abundance – albeit in an idiosyncratically visionary manner. Approaching it as a literary testimony of exile is thus all the more germane in a context marked by controversies about the role of memory in coming to terms with a traumatic past.

Machado's Exceptional Testimony

Antonio Machado's name is cited far more than any other in *Guerra en España*. The author of the widely quoted war sonnet "Si mi pluma valiera tu pistola" [If my pen were worth as much as your gun] becomes the project's protagonist (*Poesía* 826). This is not only because of the high-culture associations and political symbolism that Machado's name took on right after his death in exile in 1939, but also as a reaction against what Jiménez believed was a reductive political reading of that symbolism in José Bergamín's prologue to *Obras*, his edition of Machado's collected works, published in Mexico in 1940.[4] Responding to Bergamín, Jiménez underscored the overlap between what he called the vocational man and the man of quotidian reality: "[p]oner a una obra poética de paz un prólogo de guerra, porque las circunstancias hayan convertido en 'guerrerosa' la última parte del libro, es relegar la obra verdadera a un segundo plano, como queda relegada nuestra vida en toda circunstancia trájica [*sic*]" [to put a prologue about war on a poetic work of peace, because circumstances have made the last part of the book 'warlike,' is to relegate the true work to the background, as our life is relegated in every tragic circumstance] (126).

Accordingly, Jiménez first defines Machado's "obra verdadera" [true work], and then uses it to transform him into an allegory of the people, understood as the collective victim of the "gran experiencia trágica de la España actual" [major tragic experience of today's Spain] (7). To Jiménez, Machado's symbolic value as allegory transcends the political value that Bergamín assigns him. In the obituary that Jiménez writes upon learning of Machado's death at the end of the war, Machado appears as a ghost, "vivo para siempre en presencia invisible" [alive forever as an invisible presence] (445). This ghost can cross "los montes altos de la frontera helada" [the tall mountains of the frozen border] because the "pueblo" also crossed them; "conocedor de los vericuetos estrechos de la muerte" [an expert on death's narrow byways], Machado can also return to Spain "por el cielo de debajo de tierra" [through the sky below the ground] (445–6). This spectral Machado figure encapsulates the idea of artistic posterity that Jiménez advanced. The notion of the "póstuma" [posthumous] consideration of his works as a "ruina secular de pasado y futuro" [secular ruin of the past and future] is key to his vision of the spectral exile and, more broadly, to his visionary poetics (*Metamórfosis* 415).

Jiménez maintained that certain "popular" works "de intemperie" [out in the open, exposed to the elements] like those of the "ya duradero" [already long-lasting] Machado, possess "una calidad particular que las hace ya parecer en el presente lo que serán en el futuro, con lo que toman aspecto de pasado" [a particular quality that makes them, in the present, already seem like what they will be in the future, so that they look like works from the past] (*Metamórfosis* 415). Time not only brings these works closer to "naturaleza" [nature], but also leaves them in "un estado más permanente, más eterno" [a more permanent, more eternal state] (415). In the peculiar temporality of "popular" poetry, the "obra verdadera" of dead writers like Miguel de Unamuno or Federico García Lorca can be protected from circumstantial uses arising from "una realidad espantosa, pero ocasional, accidental" [a frightful, but accidental, occasional, reality] such as war (126). An example of Machado's "popular" poetry is the *romance* "Iris de la noche" [Iris at Night], a poem that Jiménez praises as "hondo" [deep] and "eterno" [eternal] (446).

But Jiménez's similar view of his own work as a "ruina secular de pasado y futuro" does not necessarily correspond to a nostalgic search for suprahistorical origins or a historical *telos* (*Metamórfosis* 415). In the context of the controversial reception of Machado's work after his death in exile, Jiménez's reflections on ruins evinces a modern belief in authenticity that contrasts with the danger of falsehood that is most acutely experienced in periods of profound historical upheaval. As Andreas Huyssen argued in 2010 with respect to the authenticity of ruins in modernity, "[g]enuineness as naturalness in opposition to artificiality and the fake ... is an empirically verifiable criterion of the ruin" ("Authentic" 21). To Jiménez, ruins prevent artificiality in times of extreme change. In the case of *Guerra de España*, the authenticity of the memory of death, the *memento mori* inscribed in a posthumous work like Machado's poetry, is a response to what Jiménez sees as Bergamín's "falsía" [falsehood] (446–7).

This goal of defining the "verdad" of one's own work as protection from falsehood explains, for instance, Jiménez's decision to include in his project "A un amigo cuya obra quedó en nada," his prose translation of "To a Friend Whose Work Has Come to Nothing," a poem written by W.B. Yeats to offer artistic comfort and confirmation in the face of the lies and destructiveness of a fool (133). The apostrophic first paragraph of Jiménez's prose translation already affords several perspectives: "Ahora que la verdad se sabe, calla, y acepta de cualquier dura garganta tu derrota; porque ¿cómo puedes tú, criado en el honor, competir con ese que, si se probara que miente, no se avergonzaría ante sus propios ojos ni ante los de los demás?" (133) [Now all the truth is out, / Be secret and take defeat / From any brazen throat, / For how can you compete, / Being honour bred, with one / Who were it proved he lies / Were neither shamed in his own / Nor in his neighbors' eyes (Yeats 109)]. The shifts in genre, language, and spatiotemporal and personal deictics reflect biographically on the poet's personal circumstances as an "hombre de la realidad cotidiana." But, at the same time, they also bibliographically refract those very circumstances through translation.

The next paragraph in Jiménez's rendition confirms this shift in textual direction: "Hecho a cosa más dura que el triunfo, apártate; y como una cuerda riente que dedos locos están pulsando en un lugar de piedra, calla y regocíjate, que esta es la más difícil de todas las cosas conocidas" (133) [Bred to a harder thing / Than Triumph, turn away / And like a laughing string / Whereon mad fingers play / Amid a place of stone, / Be secret and exult, / Because of all things known / That is most difficult"] (Yeats 109). The now nameless poet has been asked to turn away: despite – or maybe because of – the fact that his work has come to nothing, he's compared to a string in a place of stone. But instead of being "secret," as in Yeats's poem, he keeps quiet. In parallel to Jiménez's defence of the "obra verdadera" of now-dead poets like Unamuno, García Lorca, and Machado, the anonymous poet's silent voice in this translation resonates as a ghostly voice. Moreover, the apostrophic "calla" inscribed in Jiménez's rendition extends to the here and now of enunciation and thus creates a spatiotemporal gap between the living reader and the poem, seen as "ruina secular de pasado y futuro."

But translation is just one of the ways in which Jiménez defended the specific "verdad" of poetic works exposed to the elements, "aunque se nos vuelva todo el mundo falso en contra con calumnia, mentira y basura" [even though the whole false world may turn against us with slander, lies and garbage] (126–7). In *Guerra de España*, the "ruinoso" [ruinous] aspect of poetic work viewed posthumously, its supposedly popular, eternal quality, is highlighted by a tense juxtaposition with documents that testify to the concrete circumstances that Jiménez and his wife Zenobia lived through. A snapshot of children outside a shrapnel-hit house in a ruinous street of Madrid, taken in late 1936 by the war photographer Robert Capa, is a memorable instance of such documents (figure 4.2).[5] Its biographical resonance is particularly strong, given that in 1936, only a few weeks before they went into exile, Jiménez and Camprubí provided care and accommodation to orphaned children of war.

A similar interplay emerges in the contrasting perspectives in *Guerra en España* between a lecture in which Jiménez claimed that he saw the "loca fiesta

4.2 A photograph with simply "Madrid" written under it is included in Juan Ramón Jiménez's archive *Guerra en España*. This is a slightly cropped version of one of the most internationally renowned images of the Spanish Civil War by Robert Capa. In 2017, the picture acquired renewed fame amidst ongoing debates about the historical memory of the conflict in Madrid. Reprinted by permission of Editorial Point de Lunettes.

trájica [*sic*]" [insane tragic party] that Madrid was during the war (194) and a poem in which the first-person speaker synesthetically claims to have seen birds singing their colours for him all night long: "cantándome los colores" (82–3). In particular, this tension between documentary evidence, testimony, and poetic vision recalls the dialectic between history and Unamunian *intrahistoria* peculiar to the Krausist institutionalism that deeply informed Jiménez's understanding of popular art. The protagonist of intrahistory is the silent, anonymous people.[6] This is one of the reasons why Jiménez juxtaposed materials from his biography as an "hombre de la realidad cotidiana" (documents from his political activism in wartime and exile) to popular materials from his bibliography as an "hombre vocativo" (documents from his "trabajo normal" as a poet, but also, for instance, from Machado's work) (XV; Crespo 10).

Jiménez's goal is to incorporate his own work, like Machado's "obra verdadera," into that of the "verdadero, milagroso poeta colectivo" [true, miraculous, collective poet]: "su pueblo" [his people] – in Machado's terms – whose tragedy transcends the specific circumstances of the war without diminishing the "realidad espantosa" [frightening reality] that he lived and witnessed (7). For this reason, Jiménez places popular verses, as an epigraph in *Guerra en España* ("En la calle de los Muros / mataron una paloma, / yo cortaré con mis manos / las flores de tu corona" [On the street of Walls / A dove has been killed / I will cut with my own hands / The flowers for your wreath]), next to his own popular-sounding verses, such as "En mi boca te aguarda tu sed, / tu sed que es la mía. / Entra, no soy seco, paloma ofendida" [In my mouth your thirst awaits you, / Your thirst that is mine. / Come in, I am not dry, offended dove] (12, 83). According to Jiménez's 1936 collection of essays *Política poética* [Poetic Politics], the fact that Federico García Lorca collected and harmonized these verses, titled "Anda, jaleo, jaleo" would be an instance of how the "popular y verdadera" [popular and true] work of dead writers like García Lorca or Machado would "naturalizarse" [become naturalized] through the anonymous work of the collective poet that is the people (409) (figure 4.3).[7]

Jiménez thus adds his verses to a collection of popular poems that keep alive the voice of the people, understood in the Krausist sense as an intrahistorical victim. The poet denounces the ability of words to injure, echoing the warning of Sancho el Bravo, King of Castile, León, and Galicia from 1284 to 1295, that is placed in *Guerra en España* right after Machado's prologue: "sanan las cuchilladas, mas non las malas palabras" [stab wounds heal, but bad words do not] (11–12). This vague, cross-historical denunciation of the deleterious power of words does not, however, stop Jiménez from condemning a concrete historical wound a few pages earlier, which he calls the trauma of the "gran experiencia trágica de la España actual" (7). Although the "ferida" [wound] is the result of José Bergamín's "falsía," it also somehow evokes a former, intrahistorical "mancilla" [blemish] inflicted by an undefined but "terrible guerra de tres siglos" [terrible three-century war] that Machado was able to witness as an allegorical "paloma de linde" [border dove] (446). Machado thus becomes the witness *par excellence* to the "tragedia" [tragedy] of the Spanish "pueblo."

Guerra en España opens with Machado's article "Voces de calidad," a historical document that Jiménez used to present himself, like Machado, as a witness (figure 4.4). This is a crucial decision, as Jiménez repeatedly stated that he wanted this article to be the prologue of his project (Crespo 22).[8] Through Machado's words the reader is introduced to the words of Jiménez, a "testigo presencial" to the "loca fiesta trájica" of Madrid in 1936 (7). In 1937, in Valencia, Machado takes these words from "Comprensión y justicia" [Understanding and Justice], a talk that Jiménez gave in New York one year earlier, in which he defended the Republic and explained his reasons for leaving Spain. In 1939, exiled in Florida, Jiménez wrote upon learning of Machado's death that Machado was a victim of the death suffered by the "pueblo" in exile, that the poet died "colectivamente,

Es tan inconcebible el crimen de los fascistas de Granada fusilando al glorioso poeta Federico García Lorca, que, a pesar de la confirmación que por fuente, al parecer fidedigna, llega de Granada, nos resistimos a negar resquicio a la esperanza de una inexactitud. García Lorca estaba en Granada, veraneando en una finca de sus padres, y según un evadido de la ciudad de la Alhambra, amigo del poeta, fué encarcelado por los fascistas y fusilado al día siguiente. También fué [illegible]nado el hermano político del gran escritor, señor Fernández Montesinos, alcalde de Granada

4.3 "Pedir la caricatura del *Heraldo*." Newspaper clipping with a photograph of Federico García Lorca and a caption condemning the "crime committed by the fascists from Granada who shot the glorious poet," from Juan Ramón Jiménez's archive *Guerra en España*. Reprinted by permission of Editorial Point de Lunettes.

JUAN RAMON JIMENEZ

Juan Ramón Jiménez, visto por David

SIEMPRE pensé que Juan Ramón Jiménez, en España o fuera de España, allí donde se encontrase, estaría con nosotros, con los amantes del pueblo español, del lado de nuestra gloriosa República. Y deseaba —porque nunca faltan malsines que gustan de enturbiar la opinión sobre la conducta de los excelentes— que esta convicción mía ganase la conciencia de todos.

Bien hizo el SERVICIO ESPAÑOL DE INFORMACION en publicar, hace ya muchos días, las palabras de nuestro gran lírico, a su llegada a América.

"Madrid ha sido —dice Juan Ramón Jiménez—, durante este primer mes de guerra, yo lo he visto, una loca fiesta trágica. La alegría, la extraña alegría de una fe ensangrentada rebosaba por todas partes; alegría de convencimiento, alegría de voluntad, alegría de destino, favorable o adverso. Y este frenesí entusiasta, esta violenta unión con la verdad, habrían decidido desde el primer momento el triunfo justo del pueblo, si la rebelión militar no hubiese sido amparada por codiciosos poderes extraños. Y España, la República española, democrática y legal, estaría hoy reorganizándose, completando su firme ejemplo ante el mundo".

Palabras son estas de testigo presencial, algo más, de quien hizo suya y vivió con el pueblo, con su pueblo, la gran experiencia trágica de la España actual. "Yo lo he visto", dice Juan Ramón Jiménez, aludiendo sin la menor jactancia a ojos excepcionales, los [illegible] en lo [illegible] verdad", nos define Juan Ramón aquel ímpetu popular que realizó el milagro del Guadarrama y obró, luego, tantas hazañas portentosas, que son hoy el asombro del mundo. En efecto nuestro pueblo ha necesitado siempre la violencia del frenesí entusiasta para unirse con la verdad; tantos son entre nosotros los poderes sombríos que contra ella militan, tantos los enemigos de la más humilde como de la más egregia verdad española. Por suerte, abundan ya los ojos que la han visto desnuda. Tal ha sido para muchos, para los mejores, la gran revelación de la guerra: la verdad española está en el corazón del pueblo como un arco tendido hacia el mañana, y es hoy una consciente voluntad de vivir en el sentido esencial de la historia.

* *

Cuando Juan Ramón escribió las palabras transcritas, eran los días en que la contienda que ensangrienta a España nos parecía con vagos caracteres de guerra civil entre dos categorías de españoles, o, si queréis, entre dos Españas: la España popular, ávida de nuevas experiencias humanas, España viva y, por ende, incapaz de vivir a retrotiempo, y la España desmayada y sombría tantas veces cobarde ante la historia, que invoca vanamente una tradición de cultura que ella nunca hubiera contribuido a crear, y cuya tradición verdadera está hecha de renuncias, fracasos y traiciones; una España triste que alguien, no yo, llamará burguesa, con objetivo sobradamente holgado para su mezquindad, una España de viejas infecundas, que compró al hambre africana los brazos que habían de defenderla.

* *

La guerra civil, tan desigual éticamente, pero, al fin, entre españoles, ha terminado hace muchos meses. España ha sido vendida al extranjero por hombres que no pueden llamarse españoles; quien vende a su patria se desnaturaliza y ha de sobreentenderse que renuncia a su patria para buscar cobijo en la patria del comprador. De suerte que ya no hay más que una España invadida, como otras veces por la codicia extranjera y, como otras veces, a solas con su pueblo y con su destino, quiero decir con su razón de ser en lo futuro, para luchar sin tregua ni desmayo por su propia existencia, contra dos potencias criminales, tan fuertes como viles, que le han salido al paso en la más peligrosa encrucijada de su historia.

Mucho alienta escuchar las voces de los buenos —su claro timbre español—, en los momentos más trágicos, que han de ser también los más fecundos, de esta magnífica soledad española.

ANTONIO MACHADO

4.4 "Voces de calidad," Antonio Machado's article extolling Juan Ramón Jiménez was published in Valencia on 12 September 1937. This clipping of the article, published in Havana in 1937, was added to his archive for *Guerra en España*. Reprinted by permission of Editorial Point de Lunettes.

res mayor de un rebaño humano perseguido, echado de España" [collectively, the leading head in a persecuted human herd, cast out from Spain] (445). Thus, as a victim of a collective death, Machado allows Jiménez to reframe his own testimony of the tragedy of the Spanish people: "'Como una violenta unión con la verdad,' nos define Juan Ramón aquel ímpetu popular" ['Like a violent union with the truth,' Juan Ramón defines that popular force for us] (8).

In other words, the deceased poet, Machado, places the testimony of the living poet, Jiménez, in the biographical register by citing his words: "yo lo he visto" [I have seen it] (7). As Paul Ricoeur argued, these words, "I have seen it," constitute the self-definition of the witness (164). Machado's text therefore becomes exceptional testimony; not only has he been a constant eyewitness to the war, but he has also defined the testimonial act and noted the existence of an anonymous collective of witnesses: "abundan ya los ojos que ... han visto desnuda [la verdad]" [there now abound eyes that ... have seen the naked [truth]] (8). This abundance of eyes is reinscribed in the heterogeneous materials that make up *Guerra en España*: Jiménez's testimonial words from his 1936 lecture reappear in Machado's 1937 article that, significantly, precedes the series of anonymous *romances* that Jiménez places at the beginning of his project. If, as handwritten notes in the writer's archive indicate, the same "escritos tienen un sentido distinto" [writings have a different meaning] in different places, then as a prologue, Machado's article sanctions not only Jiménez's cited testimony, but his project as a whole, including all of the "voces de calidad" that resound within it (Crespo 2).

In his capacity of the witness par excellence, Machado's testimony confers an authoritative testimonial value on *Guerra en España* in both the biographical and bibliographical registers. Jiménez's testimony, however, is not just that of a mere "testigo presencial"; it is the testimony of a "poeta" (7). In other words, his voice is interwoven with the collective of those who are able to see "en lo profundo" with "ojos excepcionales" – it is one of the "voces de los buenos" [voices of the good] (9). Jiménez, not only as an eyewitness to the tragedy but as an exile as well, seeks to add his voice to the anonymous "rebaño humano perseguido, echado de España" that Machado embodies; and to do so, he needs the authoritative words of that collective witness who has died in exile. Jiménez's testimony is thus joined to those of two crucial poets: Machado, the "verdadero poeta nacional" [true national poet] and the people, the "verdadero, milagroso poeta colectivo" (232; *Política* 409).

Together, Machado's and Jiménez's texts evoke for the reader different places and moments: New York in 1936, Valencia in 1937, Florida in 1939, Mexico in 1940, and posthumously, with the different editions of *Guerra en España*, Puerto Rico and Barcelona in 1985, and Granada in 2009. The play of mirrors between these locations and times is consistent with the visionary poetics and montage of perspectives of the metamorphosing "hombre vocativo." The definitional speech act of testimonial discourse – "I have seen it" – effectively changes meaning when it changes time and location. The first-person testimony that Jiménez gives in a lecture in New York is a call for justice read to an audience by a witness who hopes to provoke a reaction against the policy of non-intervention at the beginning of the Spanish Civil War. That same lecture, included in *Guerra en España*, takes on the value of the memory of that action, as well as, retrospectively, the memory of the international community's failure to react to the poet's words. In parallel, in "Voces de calidad" Machado's eyes and words channel Jiménez's first-person testimony. Thus, Jiménez's text, in which we read that eyes and voices (i.e., witnesses and testimonies) "abundan ya" [now abound], is built on a poet's testimony of various injustices, spanning time and space: the injustices that Jiménez denounced in his 1936 lecture (framed by Machado, the paradigmatic witness who will unjustly die in exile), and the injustice that is committed when his testimony and defence of the Republic fall into oblivion.

Jiménez's Visions of Posterity

Jiménez wanted to ensure his work's survival. Indeed, one aim of his project is to counter an image other writers have created of him: that of ghostlike poet – an image opposite, in a sense, to that of the dead Machado. For one, it is the image of the poet locked in his ivory tower (X, 42). But in the postwar years, Jiménez became known as not only an isolated poet, but a moribund one or a member of the living dead. In 1945, the Falangist writer Gaspar Gómez de la Serna compared Jiménez's isolation with "la fría paz de los sepulcros" [the cold peace of the tombs] in "Responso a Juan Ramón" [Funeral Oration for Juan Ramón], an article published by the pro-Nazi Spanish newspaper *Informaciones*. Jiménez added to *Guerra en España* a clipping of this article where he scribbled a bitterly sardonic response: "¡Y con salú!" [And with health!] (qtd. in Naharro-Calderón, *Entre el exilio* 244).

But Jiménez also received attacks from other prominent exiled poets. In 1953, José Moreno Villa taunted him from Mexico: "Grande obra ha dejado, pero gran vida ha perdido" [He has created great work, but he has lost a great life] (XCVIII). Attesting to the tense correspondence between biography and bibliography in *Guerra en España*, this image of the ghostly poet is inverted in the obituary of Machado that Jiménez included in his project, in which the dead poet is depicted as a spectre. Similarly, Jiménez composed an apocryphal epitaph announcing his own death in terms that closely recall Machado's: "Murió y fue enterrado en Font Romeu, Francia / el 18 de julio de 1936 / a los 48 años" [He died and was buried in Font Romeu, France / July 18, 1936 / at the age of 48] (717). In this epitaphic spirit, Jiménez fulfilled an old desire, inherited from his Romantic and Symbolist predecessors, and already expressed between 1897 and 1909: to view his works *sub specie aeternitatis*, as true ruins, "como si ya nos hubiéramos muerto y nos acordásemos de nosotros" [as if we were already dead, and were remembering ourselves] (*Metamórfosis* 48). This commemorative desire resurfaces in a note that Jiménez wrote more than thirty years later, on a date close to the war: "¡Si yo pudiera sobrevivir a mi muerte, sólo para definir lo acabado por ella!" [If only I could survive my death, just to define what it ended!] (*Metamórfosis* 496). Imagined by other writers as a member of the living dead, Jiménez yearns for posthumous activity as a ghostlike poet.

But moving writings around and intertwining them with other writers' work are far from the only ways in which tensions between biography and bibliography inform Jiménez's forward-looking poetic self-conception. The metamorphic and commemorative possibilities of *Guerra en España* also multiply through the juxtaposition of texts and images. In particular, the contrasting perspectives of the poetic witness's abundant "ojos exceptionales" articulate a play of gazes suggested by one specific image: a photograph added to a newspaper clipping that Jiménez received in 1939 (figure 4.5).[9] The newspaper article, signed in "Colliure, Francia, febrero 23," announced: "Murió el poeta español Antonio Machado" [The Spanish poet Antonio Machado has died]. If Jiménez presents himself as a witness

Antonio Machado

Murió en Francia el poeta español Antonio Machado

Sufrió mucho en la evacuación de Cataluña, junto con el gobierno de España

COLLIURE, Francia, febrero 23. (AP)—Antonio Machado y Ruiz, notable poeta español, falleció ayer, después de penosa enfermedad, a la edad de 63 años. Sus amigos declararon que Machado había sufrido mucho en la huida de Cataluña, con el Gobierno español.

4.5 Newspaper clipping of the article about Antonio Machado's death. Juan Ramón Jiménez kept the clipping in his archive for *Guerra en España*. It bears Jiménez's handwritten annotation: "N[ueva] Y[ork]: 39." Reprinted by permission of Editorial Point de Lunettes.

through a montage of his and others' materials that invite the reader to see "en lo profundo," then the photograph of Machado invites the reader to an "entrever" [glimpsing] that is "más que ver" [more than seeing]. It is "verlo todo" [seeing it all], going beyond the mere image (*Metamórfosis* 639).

Here, Jiménez's vision entails moving the photograph and its viewer imaginatively through time and space to commemorate events that would otherwise be absent from the witness's experience. Indeed, shifting perspectives is a central element in Jiménez's visionary poetics: "Yo quiero parar, clavar los ojos en las cosas, verlas a ellas; pero las traspaso sin querer, son sólo un cristal para mí, les veo lo de detrás ¡ay! a través de ellas" [I want to set, to fix my eyes on things, see them; but I move through them without meaning to, they are only glass for me, I see what is behind them, alas!, through them] (*Metamórfosis* 336). When Jiménez fixed his eyes on the photograph in the clipping, he would see a doubly absent Machado: absent because dead and absent because depicted. But if to Jiménez "entrever es más que ver" [glimpsing is more than seeing] because "es ver sin peligro de muerte de lo visto" [it is seeing without the danger of the death of what is seen], then his eyes would also move through the photograph, and he would imagine Machado "vivo" [alive]; behind the photograph, he would glimpse the poet he knew before the war.

Yet, changing perspective, Jiménez might also see Machado as dead not only because of his knowledge of Machado's death but precisely because of the photographic medium in which he was depicted. Indeed, Jiménez considered photography "la misma muerte" [death itself]: "Jamás he visto dos fotografías de una persona que se parezcan entre sí, lo que quiere decir que ninguna se parece a la persona" [I have never seen two photographs of a person that look the same, which is to say that no photograph looks like the person] (*Metamórfosis* 379). Following Jiménez's logic, if the Machado in the photograph died in 1939, Jiménez would not "reconocer" [recognize] him as Machado. What he might recognize instead is an image of the young poet. Although undated, the photograph in the newspaper clipping recalls another, almost identical, photograph that Machado dedicated to Jiménez a quarter of a century earlier, in 1913 (figure 4.6). This photograph was not included in *Guerra en España*. But when Jiménez saw the photograph from the 1939 clipping, he probably "entrev[ió]" [glimpsed] the young man in 1913. Yet Jiménez would have glimpsed him as a dead man. And thus the photograph dedicated in 1913 would have been for him "la misma muerte," since, ultimately, no photograph "se parece a la persona." The resulting tension between the news and the photograph would deepen the experience of absence and, with it, the memory of death.

That memory of death could have even deeper consequences for Jiménez. If the photograph in the 1939 clipping reminded him of a spectral 1913 photograph dedicated to him, then Jiménez, too, would turn ghostly. Photography presupposes the end of experience: closeness to the image is proportionate to distance

4.6 Portrait of Antonio Machado in 1913. Source: http://www.abelmartin.com/album/imag/06.html.

from what was lived, from "lo vivo." As Roland Barthes argued, photography offers testimony that "bears not on the object but on time" (*Camera* 88). That is, the photograph of Machado, identified by Jiménez with "la misma muerte," offers "a glimpse of a history to which we no longer belong" (Cadava xxviii). In a Barthesian *punctum* that would pierce or wound Jiménez as he considered the photograph from his exile in New York, he would see the ghostlike image of two histories that belong irremediably to the past: Machado's and his own. This spectralization would be magnified across space, because the poet was in exile, and across time, because he had met Machado in 1913. Looking at the photograph, Jiménez would glimpse a twofold historical gap: he would realize that the past of Machado's 1939 exile in France was out of reach, as was the past of Spain's relative peace in 1913, when the two friends saw each other.

Furthermore, as Barthes had it, Jiménez would experience a "microvision" of his future death; photography is a *memento mori* in that it already announces our absence (Barthes, *Camera* 14; Cadava 8). Thus, reaching into the past and future, spectralization allows viewers to peek into "lo profundo" of a history to which they do not belong. This dynamic parallels Max Aub's warning about the ghostly character of his exilic poetry: the way in which photographic commemoration provides a semblance of continuity through the image's piercing *deixis am phantasma* is also a reminder of the spatiotemporal discontinuity between the past of "lo vivo" and the present of viewers and readers. It is in this eerie space of continuity and discontinuity that Jiménez's use of photography takes on historical density.[10] This density increases with *Guerra en España*'s merging of photographs with verbal materials in dialectical images – that is, in Walter Benjamin's terms, non-chronological relations between what-has-been and now. It is therefore unsurprising that Jiménez should favour posthumous works like Machado's aforementioned ruins "de pasado y futuro" [of the past and future], with their "calidad particular que las hace ya parecer en el presente lo que serán en el futuro, con lo que toman aspecto de pasado" (*Metamórfosis* 415). Past and future are both out of the poet's reach, unless he can resort to the fiction of a poetic project capable of testifying "en lo profundo" to his and Machado's complex, ghostly vision.

This necrological framework for Jiménez's poetic memory explains the seemingly odd inclusion in *Guerra en España* of Spanish renditions of texts by George William Russell and Yeats about transience and (im)mortality. Translation was integral to Jiménez's endless re-examination of his visionary poetics amid personal and political uncertainty. Between 1936 and 1938 Jiménez translated several poems from *The Oxford Book of Modern Verse: 1892–1935*, edited by W.B. Yeats. The anthology was originally published in 1936, the year the Spanish Civil War broke out. This choice was hardly arbitrary. Jiménez's library had remained in his apartment in Madrid. As his translator Christopher Maurer explains, "[i]n his Madrid apartment, exposed to destruction and theft, he had left the entire 'rough draft' of his *Obra;* thousands of pages of poetry, personal correspondence, and notes" (12). Ransacked in June 1939, the library became a source of deep concern for Jiménez. *Guerra en España* records his anguished efforts to salvage it. Yeats's anthology had been a Christmas present to Jiménez – with his past bibliography at risk, the poet resorted to translating poems from *The Oxford Book of Modern Verse.*

Many of Jiménez's translations from English are the outcome of a collaborative effort with Zenobia Camprubí, who was fluent in English and who assisted him with his English readings. Jiménez and Cambrubí met in 1913 and were married in New York in 1916. As John Wilcox has argued, "Jiménez's exposure to English (and American) poetry is certainly one of the contributing factors to the stunning change that overcomes his work after 1913" (236). In a manner reminiscent of Paul Valery and W.B. Yeats, Jiménez often strove to adopt a poetic persona oblivious to temporal flow. The construction of this persona seems to be inseparable from a struggle to overcome his fear of death. Significantly, the translated poems included in *Guerra en España* are largely about transience. Thus, within the overall testimonial project, translation became another means of reflection on the relationship between writing and death in times of crisis. Particularly, it shows how closely bound up Jiménez's activities as "hombre de la realidad cotidiana" and "hombre vocativo" became as soon as he and Camprubí went into exile, as it was then that the dialectic between transcendence and immanence traceable in Jiménez's writings became more explicitly anchored in sociopolitical concerns.[11]

Salient among the texts selected for translation is Yeats's versification of a prose fragment by Walter Pater. Jiménez's Spanish rendition, in which Mona Lisa is described as "muerta varias veces" [dead several times over] and the holder of "los secretos de la tumba" [the secrets of the tomb] (137), finds two uncanny echoes: one in Jiménez's Machadian apocryphal epitaph and another in the obituary he writes for Machado, which depicts him as both dead in his prewar life and a ghost that, once buried in exile, can come and go between different times and spaces. Here, Jiménez wants to see beyond the photographic evidence of "la misma muerte," and "entrever" a Machado capable of the "natural milagro poético" [natural poetic miracle] of resurrection, across space and time. Accordingly, he invokes the prewar Machado, a ghostlike poet who "tuvo siempre tanto de muerto como de vivo" [always was as dead as he was living] (444).

Then, to protect – and free – Machado's true "voz" from what he sees as an illegitimate appropriation in José Bergamín's Mexican edition of his poetry, Jiménez employs the dominant trope of epitaphic discourse: prosopopoeia, the figure that enables voices to speak from beyond the grave (446; de Man 78). Literalizing this fiction, Jiménez's obituary commemorates Machado as a ghost who bridged the gap between "vivi[r] y m[o]ri[r], la distancia de las dos únicas existencias conocidas" [living and dying, the distance of the only two known existences] (444). Jiménez, the surviving poet in exile, tries to "resucitar" [revive] Machado, the dead poet, endowing him now with an eternal "voz de calidad" that would secure his posthumous life. This would, in turn, free him from both his biographical death in France and what he calls his bibliographical "sobremuerte" [sur-death], that is, the "falsía" of "aprovechadores de cadáveres y de famas" [exploiters of dead bodies and fame] like Bergamín (126).

Jiménez's attempt to undo a "falsía" of deleterious words again recalls the quotation from Sancho el Bravo that follows Machado's prologue to *Guerra en España*. Here, the "falsía" is twofold: on the one hand, it makes Machado's poetry exclusively a function of his political activity, erasing his authentic "popular" literary work; but on the other, it makes Jiménez's poetry exclusively a function of his literary work, erasing his authentic political activity on behalf of the "pueblo" and the Republic (447). In his capacity as the paradigmatic witness, Jiménez responds to this simplification by seeking a way to "verlo todo," to "ver sin peligro de muerte de lo visto," to see beyond, but without excluding, the "realidad cotidiana" of war and exile (*Metamórfosis* 639). Jiménez's poetic memory is crucial in this regard. Machado was able to equate life and death because he saw everything, just like the airman sees everything in "Un aviador irlandés prevé su muerte," Jiménez's prose translation of Yeats's poem "An Irish Airman Foresees His Death," also included in *Guerra en España*: "Todo lo sopesé, todo lo vi de golpe: los años venideros serían un desperdicio de afán, un malbarato de afán los años caídos, puestos contra esta vida, esta muerte" (133) [I balanced all, brought all to mind, / The years to come seemed waste of breath, / A waste of breath the years behind / In balance with this life, this death (Yeats 135)]. The existential symmetry that Jiménez finds between himself as "hombre vocativo" and spectral poetic figures like Machado, Yeats's airman, and Pater's Mona Lisa, fits prosopopeia's chiastic parallelism (Riffaterre 112).

In this sense, the spectralization of the poetic figure that fashions the voices from beyond the grave in Jiménez's translations in *Guerra en España* recalls the photographic *memento mori* in the newspaper clipping about Machado's death. Just as Jiménez can imagine Machado "amortajado" [shrouded] in life, he can also imagine himself dead: "No soy más que un sepulcro lleno de todos mis cadáveres" [I am nothing more than a sepulcher filled with all of my corpses] (*Metamórfosis* 319).[12] But imagining Machado's symbolic revival also allows Jiménez to imagine his own: "¿Morir? 'Yo' no he de ser enterrado. A la tierra no irá más que mi cáscara" [Die? 'I' do not have to be buried. To the ground will go no more than my shell] (443). Consequently, Jiménez's obituary of Machado serves a twofold commemorative function: the living poet prevents the death of the dead poet's voice as he ensures that his own voice will survive his death. The latter was important for Jiménez, who – perhaps suffering from a certain "necrophiliac anxiety" – also meditated on his own spectralization in exile when he wrote dramatically of himself as a dead man: "soñé que estaba muerto en Washington, y que, muerto, soñaba que resucitaba en España, y que no podía" [I dreamt that I was dead in Washington, and that, dead, I was dreaming that I resurrected in Spain, but that I was unable to] (qtd. in Naharro-Calderón, *Entre en el exilio* 308).[13]

Presciently, between 1900 and 1909 Jiménez had already apostrophized an anonymous "tú" that he calls "el muerto" [the dead man]: "ya no tengo más vida que la que me des tú. ¡Acuérdate de mí!" [Now I have no life other than the one you give me. Remember me!] (*Metamórfosis* 119). The rhetorical power of his prosopopoeic words would later allow the exiled poet to animate his posthumous "tú" so that his poetic "yo" could be remembered (de Man 78). Likewise, Jiménez would reanimate Machado with necrological words, picturing him as a ghost "conocedor de los vericuetos estrechos de la muerte," and thus ending his exile: "ha podido pasar a España por el cielo de debajo de tierra" [he has been able to enter Spain through the sky below the ground] (446). The symmetries embedded in the figure of prosopopoeia would also allow the exiled poet to "entrever" a possible spectral return to Spain through his work. Thus, Jiménez's visionary poetic voice was also among the "voces de calidad" framing his project. Juan Ramón Jiménez would die "todo en figura" [entirely as a figure] like Machado, who now lied "podrido en la tierra" [rotten in the ground] (446). And yet, although his "cáscara" might disappear, *Guerra en España* would function discursively as a death mask through which his "yo" would not be buried and the voice of his "obra verdadera" would survive – even in Spain and beyond what he called "los montes altos de la frontera helada."

In brief, to oppose the "falsías" spread by other writers about him and Machado, Jiménez assembled two testimonies of Machado's death and "sobremuerte" in *Guerra en España*: a documentary testimony of his death and later politicization of his work, and a poetic testimony of his spectralization and the posthumous recuperation of his work for "verdadera" poetry, the collective poetry of the "pueblo." From this angle, the "voces de calidad" are those of the "testigo presencial" in two senses: the witness as activist (the "hombre de la realidad cotidiana" who saw the tragedy of Madrid) and the witness as poet (the "hombre vocativo" who sees death "en lo profundo"). Other materials in *Guerra en España* credit both testimonies. Most obvious are the biographical documents pertaining to the first kind of testimony. Reflecting Jiménez's political activities, these materials include lectures, photographs, political statements and interviews, and a safe-conduct pass.

Less evident are those of the second kind: the outcome of his "trabajo normal" as a poet. These bibliographical documents not only attest to Jiménez's sense of approaching death, but also enable readers to imagine a testimony of how Machado "resucitaba cada día ante los que lo vimos" [was revived every day in front of those who saw him] (444). For in what was effectively a "milagro poético," Jiménez would claim that he saw Machado's ghost. Examples of such materials include Jiménez's spectral obituary for Machado, his translations of elegiac texts by Walter Pater, George William Russell, and Yeats, and the anonymous verses of "Anda jaleo, jaleo" ("las flores de tu corona" are funeral wreath flowers). Each of the materials Jiménez gathered as "hombre vocativo" in *Guerra en España* suggested yet another, perhaps less "popular," voice for posterity. They configure the manifold prosopopoeia – the death mask – that would allow the exiled poet to speak from his posthumous life. Among the most significant of these materials is Jiménez's extensive poem "Espacio." As we saw earlier, the same writings had for Jiménez "un sentido distinto" in *Guerra en España* (Crespo 2); in the specific context of his *destierro*, "Espacio" became an exiled poet's compelling reflection on a life viewed epitaphically as written in stone – as a "ruina que persiste" [persistent ruin], but also as a "muerte en movimiento" [shifting death] between America and Spain (135, 111). The rhetoric of spatiotemporal expansiveness that marks "Espacio" as one of Jiménez's most memorable pieces of writing is deeply grounded in his first years of exile.[14]

In 1939, three years after leaving Spain, Jiménez and Camprubí moved to Florida, where they learned about Machado's death. It was also in Florida where Jiménez started writing poetry after a long writer's block in the anxiety-ridden wake of the Spanish Civil War (de Albornoz, "Juan Ramón" 79). In a 1943 letter addressed to Enrique Díez-Canedo, another Republican poet and critic exiled in Mexico, Jiménez explained the close connection between his life – or rather, his revival – as "hombre de la realidad cotidiana," and his important decisions as "hombre vocativo" in exile:

> Una madrugada me encontré escribiendo unos romances y unas canciones que eran un retorno a mi primera juventud, una inocencia última, un final lójico de mi última escritura sucesiva en España. La Florida es ... un arrecife completamente llano y, por lo tanto, su espacio atmosférico es y se siente inmensamente inmenso. Pues en 1941,

saliendo yo, casi nuevo, resucitado casi, del hospital de la Universidad de Miami ... una embriaguez rapsódica, una fuga incontenible empezó a dictarme un poema de espacio, en una sola interminable estrofa de verso mayor. Y al lado de este poema y paralelo a él, como me ocurre siempre, vino a mi lápiz un interminable párrafo en prosa, dictado por la estensión lisa de La Florida, y que es una escritura de tiempo, fusión memorial de ideología y anécdota, sin orden cronológico: como una tira sin fin desliada hacia atrás en mi vida. Estos libros se titulan, el primero, "Espacio"; el segundo "Tiempo," y se subtitulan "Estrofa" y "Párrafo." (*Cartas* 374–5)

[One early morning I found myself writing some *romances* and songs which were a return to my first youth, a final innocence, a logical end to my last successive writing in Spain. Florida ... is a completely flat reef, and therefore its atmospheric space is, and feels, immensely immense. In 1941, as I was leaving, almost as good as new, almost resurrected, the University of Miami hospital ... a rhapsodic intoxication, an uncontrollable flight began to dictate to me a poem of space in one endless stanza of long lines. And next to this poem, and parallel to it, as always happens to me, came to my pencil an endless paragraph in prose, dictated by the smooth expanse of Florida, and which is a writing of time, a memorial fusion of ideology and anecdote, without any chronological order, like a never-ending strip untied backward along my life. These books are titled, the first Space, and the second Time, and their subtitles are "Stanza" and "Paragraph."]

Some of the short *romances* and songs Jiménez wrote in the early forties in Florida were couched in a lyrical language of return and nostalgia for his prewar childhood and his *patria chica* in the small Andalusian town of Moguer, where the poet was born in 1881.[15] These poems also implied a rhetoric of detachment vis-à-vis the uncertain here and now of his exile sixty years later, in 1941.

By contrast, "Espacio" enabled Jiménez to construct, in what he saw as the "inmensamente inmenso" scope of his American exile, a form of writing capacious and pliable enough to let the "I" move to and fro in space and time, unfolding along expansive syntactical units punctuated by reflections on chronotopes of continuity and discontinuity, attachment and detachment: "una tira sin fin desliada."[16] This cross-boundary and non-chronological perspective helps to elucidate the "sentido distinto" that "Espacio" acquires in the heterogeneous context of *Guerra en España*. In 1983, Howard T. Young underscored the various connections between Jiménez's formal explorations and his personal circumstances during his exile in America in the early forties. Moreover, Young stressed the need to read "Espacio" in the wider context of the great Latin American modernist long poems – like José Gorostiza's *Muerte sin fin* (1939) and Pablo Neruda's *Alturas de Macchu Picchu* (1946) – as Octavio Paz urged Juan Marichal to do in their 1967 debate about the place of Spanish letters in modernity (Marichal and Paz, *Las cosas* 50).[17]

Jiménez had become, in Aurora de Albornoz's words, "un ser alucinado" [an hallucinated being] in search of "palabras interminables, como la llanura, que reflejen un presente: su presente total, lleno de fantasmas que vienen de diversos lugares del tiempo y del espacio" [endless words, like the plain, that could reflect a present: his total present, full of ghosts that come from various places in time and space] ("Juan Ramón" 80). The poet's search would be endless indeed. Jiménez rewrote the verses of "Espacio" into prose form, but was unable to finish his two-book project by the time of his death more than fifteen years later. His remains and Zenobia's were moved to and buried in 1958 in Moguer.[18] But the memory of death had already become memory of life in "Espacio": "'Y para recordar por qué he vivido', vengo a ti, río Hudson de mi mar. 'Dulce como esta luz era el amor ... Y por debajo de Washington Bridge (el puente más con más de esta New York) pasa el campo amarillo de mi infancia'. Infancia, niño vuelvo a ser y soy, perdido, tan mayor, en lo más grande ... Y esta Nueva York es igual que Moguer" ['To remember why I have lived,' I come to you, Hudson River of my sea. 'As sweet as this light was love ... And under the Washington Bridge (the greatest bridge of this New York) the yellow field of my childhood flows.' Childhood, I become a child again, and am, lost, now so grown up, in the vastness ... And this New York is the same as Moguer] (107). Returning to the old topoi of the river and the sea as memory places for reworking (the end of) life's journey, the "I" is able to bridge his late years in exile with his early years in Spain.

Yet this "I" is also ringingly evocative of Walt Whitman's apostrophic rhetoric in his poem "Crossing Brooklyn Ferry," most markedly in the expansive amplifications and addresses leading to "the similitudes of the past and those of the future" (308). Through apostrophe – whereby "[t]he absent, dead, or inanimate entity addressed is ... made present, animate, and anthropomorphic" (Johnson, *A World* 185) – the Hudson River is animated in "Espacio." The yellow field of the "I"'s childhood is likewise reanimated, and so is the child in the non-chronological, ghostly "now" of lyric articulation (Culler, *Theory* 226): "Infancia, niño vuelvo a ser y soy." The grown-up "I" becomes a child again in the time of poetic discourse. In line with other spectral poetic figures such as Yeats's airman, Pater's Mona Lisa, and the ghostly Machado – who right before dying in France also seemed to bridge his time in exile with his childhood days: "Estos días azules y este sol de la infancia" – the poet sees life as "muerte en movimiento," crossing space and time, as though it were possible to interrupt exile.

But if *Guerra en España* is read through the lens of Jiménez's visionary poetics, the materials of the "hombre vocativo" can hardly be separated from those of the "hombre de la realidad cotidiana." Thus the interruption of exile through poetic animation is only possible within the historical time of Jiménez's exile in Florida. The *deixis am phantasma* provided by the poet's image – "vengo a ti, río Hudson de mi mar" – is also a reminder of the unbridgeable spatiotemporal gap between the past of the Jiménez's life – "lo vivo," in Max Aub's terms – and the present of "cada lector" of his exilic writings. This gap is most noticeable if "Espacio" is read out loud. As Christopher Maurer has argued, in his later years, Jiménez "transcribed hundreds of pages of his verse into prose, 'with all the sound at the center' rather than at the end of the line. 'The word,' he wrote, 'was made for the ear, and not the eye'" ("Introduction" 42).

In *Guerra en España* Jiménez chose to include the prose version of "Espacio." Interestingly, in exile Jiménez also developed an acute sense of linguistic difference: "if I want to remember, think, criticize the Spanish of Spaniards I no longer know what I read or what I speak or what I write" (qtd. in Maurer, "Introduction" 21). His tongue "was, and wasn't, his own," Maurer persuasively concludes (21). Although still shaped by a preoccupation with the survival of his work, Jiménez's visionary testimony here seems at odds with his desire to see his poetry inscribed in the anonymous work of the "verdadero, milagroso poeta colectivo" that for him was the Spanish people, as though he were now struggling to glimpse, or rather voice, a gap in language. Linguistic difference at the suprasegmental level is rendered acutely perceptible in precisely "the special 'now' of lyric articulation" (Culler, *Theory* 226), if the reader voices, for instance, an emphatic hendecasyllable like "Dulce como esta luz era el amor." The proximal demonstrative "esta" brings the "luz" close to the reader. But spatial deixis also implies a question: how is the consonance between "dulce" and "luz" supposed to be pronounced in successive readings? In whose tongue should one utter it? Here proximity also serves to foreground exilic distance.[19]

If the reader's voicing of Jiménez's hendecasyllable is prosodically and phonically animated by, among other elements, its tight vowel and consonant patterning, the somatic transaction between line and reader becomes an experience of otherness. On the one hand, this otherness subverts expressive approaches to "Espacio" as a mere depiction of the poet's historical experience of exile. On the other, it is precisely the somatic mode of disruption brought about by poetic memory – what John Vernon called "the resistance of form" (9) – that renders historical the form of otherness that the reader temporarily experiences every time he or she voices Jiménez's text. In this sense, one could hardly take positional deixis – the use of the proximal demonstrative "esta" in "Dulce como esta luz era el amor" – as only representative of the poet's voice in exile, as though voicing the poem could bring the reader closer to it.[20] Jiménez's concern that his tongue "was, and wasn't, his own" – in Maurer's words – is not solely an exile's presumable anxiety over losing his mother tongue, his identity, or even his national or "popular" origins. It is also a reminder of the different ways in which poetry can bring about a transitory suspension of representation.

Readers seeking to comprehend what "Espacio" represented there and then, in the specific circumstances of the poem's production, will face the resistant otherness of the poetic text in its sheer bodily materiality. At least this is what Jiménez implied in the early thirties, when he wrote: "la poesía debe tener apariencia comprensible, como los fenómenos naturales. La tormenta, por ejemplo; pero, como en ellos, su hierro interior debe poder resistir, en una gradación interminable de relativas concesiones, al inquisidor más vocativo" [poetry must have a comprehensible appearance, like natural phenomena. The storm, for example. But, as in their case, their inner iron must be able to resist, in an endless gradation of relative concessions, the most vocational inquisitor] (*Metamórfosis* 372). Grappling with the material dynamics involved in voicing exilic poetry brings out this experience of otherness at its most historically embodied.

Writing out of War and Exile

Just before his death in exile in Puerto Rico, Jiménez called the various books he wanted to write and the work that remained for him to accomplish a "calidoscopio" [kaleidoscope] and a "metamórfosis [*sic*] constante" [constant metamorphosis] (*Metamórfosis* 701–2). The miscellaneous discursive "calidoscopio" of *Guerra en España* is partly driven by the political thrust of the historical avant-gardes. Far from the rigid conventions of the epic and the lyric that define many testimonial poems written about Spain during the internecine conflict and the decades immediately following, Jiménez's multifaceted project instead recalls other heterogeneous works of difficult generic definition to come out of times of war, persecution, and exile (Siles 230–3).[21] The testimonial impulse informing these works stems from a challenging goal. For the witness who seeks a way to "verlo todo," as Jiménez put it, testimony must be multiperspectival – hence the use of various kinds of documents to attest as copiously as possible to the multiple personal, literary, and political crises the witness lived through (*Metamórfosis* 639).

Composed between 1934 and 1955, Bertolt Brecht's *Arbeitsjournal* [Work Journal] provides another example of this kaleidoscopic form of testimony: it includes notes, poems, quotes, photographs, and newspaper clippings. Moreover, both Jiménez's and Brecht's journals reveal an avant-garde ancestry. They are montages assembled as an immediate response to extreme historical circumstances that required the activation of multiple discursive practices. The materials that both poets respectively collected and assembled in times of exile transformed their ambitious works in progress, which were already informed by an aesthetic characterized by Georges Didi-Huberman as "exploratoria y prismática" [exploratory and prismatic] (*Cuando las imágenes* 15). Jiménez and Brecht sought to satisfy certain "exigencias formales" [formal demands] while also seeking to intervene "en el terreno de los análisis y de las tomas de posición" [in the field of the analyses and taking of positions] that the political moment demanded (29, 31). In Brecht's case, those "exigencias formales" would be satisfied in another text, *Kriegsfibel* (1955) [War Primer], a montage that combines media images with four-verse epigrams of his own writing. In similar exploratory fashion, Jiménez "recorta y pega, aquí y allá, en el cuerpo o el flujo de su pensamiento asociativo" [cuts and pastes, here and there, in the body or flow of his associative thinking] (31).[22]

Yet *Guerra en España* would remain unfinished. Although Jiménez wanted to define his work for posterity, his testimony of war and exile is built on a pile of tentatively assembled fragments. This is not a paradox, however. Jiménez, the "metamorfoseador sucesivo," saw his writings as mere "borradores" [drafts] of what he ultimately wanted to accomplish (*Metamórfosis* 95). Christopher Maurer has lucidly explained this openness in terms reminiscent of the biographical and bibliographical registers animating Jiménez's writing: "'To live is to create, and re-create, ourselves,' he wrote. No final solution is possible, no identity definitive. It would be harder to imagine an artist of greater integrity. But the notion of identity – of remaining 'the very same' person – was alien to him" ("Introduction" 21). From this twofold perspective, Jiménez's project becomes – much like Machado's work – a "ruina secular de pasado y futuro." Unfinished, it delineates the formal demands posed by the idea of "entrever." Through *Guerra en España*'s materials from different moments and places, Jiménez's visionary poetics invites the reader to peer "en lo profundo" of both his biographical and bibliographical documents, but also to look between them: to contemplate the photograph and fragmentary obituary of Machado, as well as the relationship between them. The photographs of and poems about ruins included in *Guerra en España* make this invitation all the more arresting.[23]

Understood as a posthumous ruin, Jiménez's project demands a visionary poetics allowing him to intervene critically in the cultural politics of Republican exile. To exploit – as he believes José Bergamín does – that "las circunstancias hayan convertido en 'guerrerosa'" the last part of Machado's *Obras* is to take a political position to the detriment of the poet's "obra verdadera." In fact, the discursive multiplicity of *Guerra en España* suggests a critical position similar to what Didi-Huberman has argued montage indicates in Walter Benjamin's work: "ahí donde el partido impone la condición pre-eminente de una parte en detrimento de otras, la posición supone una co-presencia eficaz y conflictiva, una dialéctica de las multiplicidades entre ellas" [here where the party confers a pre-eminent status on one part to the detriment of others, position presupposes an effective and conflictive co-presence, a dialectic of multiplicities among them] (*Cuando las imágenes* 145). Thus, while Bergamín takes sides, Jiménez takes a position. Bergamín's fragmentation is reductive, homogeneous, and partisan. Jiménez's is multiple, heterogeneous, and multifaceted.

The various dialectical connections between poems, photographs, lectures, translations, and quotations that *Guerra en España* makes possible respond to a broad idea of artistic autonomy. This idea poses political questions. It is telling that the poet initially subtitled his project *Política poética*. To paraphrase Jacques Rancière, Jiménez put forward a democratic equality of materials that echoes the egalitarianism of the "everything speak" that has defined the modern aesthetic since Gustave Flaubert: a dehierarchization of the relationship between form and content that contrasts with the conventional understanding of a relationship of necessity between one and the other (*Politics* 53–7). In mid-twentieth-century Spain, this conventional understanding fueled a dichotomous debate over art's autonomy from – or submission to – politics, a debate that extended to the "ímpetu popular" behind politics, to use Machado's terms (8). Jiménez found himself involved in this polarizing debate despite his exile in America. However, articulating the "equality of materials" gathered in *Guerra en España* requires the reader to constantly change perspective between them, and therefore to look beyond the dichotomy of form and content. The reader is thus able to adopt a critical position that lets him or her "ver" the ruins that war and exile left behind and "entrever" the death that surrounded them.

In the context of the present debate over historical memory in Spain, Jiménez's "calidoscopio" of materials redistributes the perceptions and expressions that are visible, sayable, and possible in reference to the Spanish Civil War and Francoism and consequently shapes how and what to remember about them (Rancière, "Art" 2). In *Unearthing Franco's Legacy*, a collection of essays from 2010 on the war's impact on today's Spanish society, Carlos Jerez-Farrán and Samuel Amago argued that Spain must "revise its past and publicly confront Franco's legacy" (5). Within this framework, the discursive heterogeneity of Jiménez's biographical and bibliographical materials makes a unique contribution to the public debate about the memory of the dead. From a historically situated perspective, the visionary poetics that underpins *Guerra en España* reveals "the power of the dead to speak beyond language as they mutely but eloquently remind the nation of the crimes perpetrated against its own people during and after the Civil War" (Jerez-Farrán and Amago 1).[24] Although right after Jiménez's death in 1958 important Spanish critics like José María Castellet faulted his poetry because it lacked "vigencia histórica" [historical relevance] when compared with Machado's work, which was seen as exemplary of ethical and political commitment in the context of postwar poetry in Spain (29), *Guerra en España*'s recent reception in Spain seems to have secured Jiménez a central place in twentieth-century Spanish cultural history.[25]

Studies by notable public intellectuals such as Jordi Gracia, Ian Gibson, and Andrés Trapiello are only among the most significant to have appeared in recent years on the relationship between culture and politics during the civil war and under Franco. Each arguably seems to mark a decisive step in the symbolic return to Spain that Jiménez sought. In *Las armas y las letras: literatura y Guerra Civil (1936–1939)* [Arms and Letters: Literature and Civil War] (1996, 2010, 2019), Jiménez serves as a key reference in Trapiello's elucidation of the relationship between literature and politics during the war. Trapiello calls *Guerra en España* one of Jiménez's crucial works, placing it among "los testimonios más lúcidos e impresionantes que se hayan escrito sobre la guerra" [the most lucid and impressive testimonies that have been written about the war] (100). Jiménez also figures prominently in *La resistencia silenciosa* [The Silent Resistance] (2004), Gracia's essay on Spanish culture during Francoism. Trapiello and Gracia use materials from *Guerra en España* to support their vindication of Jiménez as a public figure, portraying the poet, respectively, as an exemplary writer loyal to the Republic and as an enemy of Francoism from exile. The two essayists also highlight the combination of ethics and aesthetics that characterizes Jiménez's intellectual work.

Significantly, *Las armas y las letras* and *La resistencia silenciosa* have been both commercially successful and the recipients of important prizes, since the cultural field of historical memory in Spain is marked, as Germán Labrador argued in 2010, by the need to "explicar de una manera no mitológica las condiciones de visibilidad e invisibilidad de las representaciones del pasado franquista y de su violencia fundacional" [explain, in a way that is not mythological, the conditions of visibility and invisibility of the representations of the Francoist past and its foundational violence] (381).[26] In this context, the value of reissuing *Guerra en España* derives not only from the aforementioned circumstances of its 1985 and 2009 publications, but also from its contribution to recuperating, along with the aforementioned essays, the exiled Jiménez after his near invisibility in the late twentieth century. Thus, the biographical aspects of the poet's commitment to the Republican cause – most notably his denunciation of the horrors of war and his opposition to Francoism – gain visibility. So, too, do the disputes about the ideological appropriation of Machado's legacy as a witness to the Republican tragedy and, consequently, Jiménez's place in relation to Machado.

In particular, *Guerra en España* gives prominence to Machado and Jiménez in the memory of representations of Francoism and exile and places them alongside Federico García Lorca and Miguel Hernández. Evidence of this is found in *Cuatro poetas en guerra* [Four Poets at War], the biographical study that Ian Gibson dedicates to these poets and loyal Republicans. Yet Gibson, Gracia, and Trapiello are interested in this "valiosísimo" [highly valuable] collection of materials primarily for its documentary character regarding Jiménez's personal role in Spanish political and cultural history from the war to his death (Trapiello, *Las armas* 99). For these authors, the appeal of *Guerra en España* does not seem to lie in its significance as part of Jiménez's literary – or bibliographical – work, but in its archival function as a storehouse of information about the poet's ethics and politics in times of war and exile.[27] Nor do these authors explore the formal ties between these materials and Jiménez's exploratory work as an "hombre vocativo" – as a writer, reader, translator, and editor. As Trapiello has explained, "la óptica de la guerra, y su desenlace ... trocó no pocas de las visiones sobre obras y personas, desenfocándolas, de suerte que cuando se habla de poesía y literatura en realidad se habla de política" [the perspective of the war, and its outcome ... transformed many visions of works and people, blurring them, such that when one talks of poetry and literature, one really talks about politics] (16–17). Ironically, Trapiello's explanation echoes Jiménez's criticism of Bergamín's political reading of Machado's work.[28]

The debate between Bergamín and Jiménez over the value of Machado's work can be read as a warning of the danger of looking at *Guerra en España* with blurry vision: a vision that renders it valuable only as documentary evidence of Jiménez's political intervention. This vision would risk losing sight of the different ways in which Jiménez's poetics themselves inflect the representation of his political activities, and vice versa. Tomás Segovia did not seem to lose sight of Jiménez's singular poetics. In an article published in Spain in 2003, "Juan Ramón Jiménez: la otra fidelidad" [the other faithfulness], he pithily explained the reasons why the exploratory ways in which Jiménez's unwaveringly "fiel" [faithful] poetic gaze and highly personal and coherent sense of "desarraigo" [rootlessness] were inscribed in his poetry would complicate efforts at institutional reintegration. Segovia concluded: "Así como no militó nunca en el exilio instituido y sin embargo podría decirse que, en un sentido menos instituido, es un paradigma del 'verdadero' exilio; así estuvo lejos también de militar en ninguna vanguardia, y sin embargo podría ser paradigma de muchos vanguardismos [Just as he never militated in the instituted exile and yet it could be said that, in a less instituted sense, he is a paradigm of 'true' exile; thus he was also far from militating in any avant-garde, and yet he could be a paradigm of many avant-gardisms] (*Sobre exiliados* 73–5). From Segovia's standpoint, restricting critical focus on the documentary aspect of *Guerra en España* blurs Jiménez's specific sense of exile.

In 1984, when Ángel Crespo found the envelopes containing the materials for *Guerra en España* in Puerto Rico and decided to turn them into a book, he conveyed his enthusiasm to Jiménez's nephew, Francisco Hernández-Pinzón: "su valor histórico y literario unidos hacen de él una joya" [its historical and literary value together make it a jewel] (qtd. in González Ródenas X). Thus, decades before debates over the historical memory of the civil war began in Spain, an exiled poet was able to fully credit another exile's complex but coherent "intervención de hombre y poeta en la política de su España" [intervention as a person/man and a poet in the politics of his Spain] and accordingly offer an insightful, clear-sighted perspective for the future commemoration of its historical importance (qtd. in Crespo 10). In line with Crespo's assessment, our vision of *Guerra en España* some fifty years after Jiménez's death would be short-sighted if it failed to take into account the visionary poetics that he devised to ensure his ghost a long life and thus be remembered: "¿Morir? 'Yo' no he de ser enterrado. A la tierra no irá más que mi cáscara" (*Metamórfosis* 443).

Staring at History?

Photograph 57 of the second edition of *Guerra en España*, titled "El resultado" [The outcome], shows an open-eyed, open-mouthed girl (figure 4.7). Like Machado's ghost as Jiménez portrays him in his obituary, the girl's face seems "tanto de muerto como de vivo" [as much dead as alive] (444). In the framework of Jiménez's project, the photograph can be seen as the death mask of a civil war victim; in a sense, it brings to mind what Walter Benjamin called the *facies hippocratica* of history, the face that appears before the viewer's eyes as "a petrified, primordial landscape" (*The Origin* 166). In *Guerra en España*, this landscape is suggested by

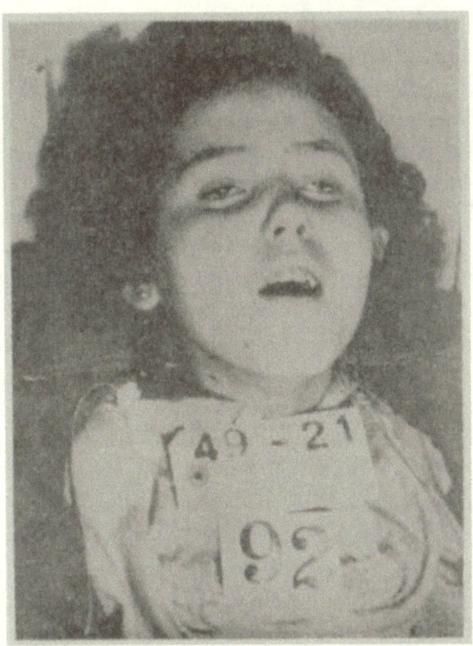

4.7 Juan Ramón Jiménez kept this photograph in his archive for *Guerra en España*. The manuscript note reads "El resultado." Reprinted by permission of Editorial Point de Lunettes.

"los montes altos de la frontera helada" that Machado's ghost crosses in the obituary that Jiménez wrote for him. Accompanied by the "poeta de la muerte" [poet of death], these primordial "montes" reach Jiménez in his exile on the other side of the Atlantic, "reflejados" [reflected] in the "espejo melancólico" [melancholic mirror] of the moon (444–6). If photography was "la misma muerte" to Jiménez, then this portrait – included in an unfinished project that sought to shape his self-image for posterity – likely brought to mind his own death. Indeed, the photograph, like the obituary of Machado, constitutes an allegory that confronts the viewer with his or her own transience.[29]

As Benjamin noted in his reading of Baudelaire, allegory's structure is based on the correspondence of a set of time signatures: eternal and temporal, spiritual and secular, long-lasting and perishable (Löwy 63–8). The same structure underpins Jiménez's vision of certain popular works as ruins: time spiritualizes these works, absorbing them into "la naturaleza," leaving them in "un estado más permanente, más eterno" (*Metamórfosis* 415).[30] Consistent with this allegorical vision, the landscape of ruins that *Guerra en España* suggests is dialectical, the function of a regime of doubles. These correspondences emerge between Jiménez's "duradera" [long-lasting] and "perecedera" [perishable] work – that is, between the posthumous life he seeks for the "eternos" materials of his bibliography (like the popular *romances*) and the "perecederos" materials of his biography (historical documents like war photographs). Indeed, according to Jiménez's visionary poetics, the "hierro interior" of *Guerra en España* was meant to resist "al inquisidor más vocativo." The simile underlying Jiménez's poetics – "como los fenómenos naturales" – can be read dialectically as possessing a solidly historical tenor: *Guerra en España* must resist eternally, "en una gradación interminable de relativas concesiones," because its materials are historical objects (372). If they failed to resist "al inquisidor más vocativo," their sheer historicity would be undermined.

Benjamin argued that a death mask not only raises the enigmatic question of "the nature of human existence as such, but also of the biographical historicity of the individual" (*The Origin* 166). To overlook the tense dialectical interplay between Jiménez's biography and bibliography animating *Guerra en España* is tantamount to looking at only the "cáscara" of his corpse, without attending to the work's prosopopoeia, the vision of the beyond that the "máscara" [mask] created in his historically situated exile uncannily intimates. Also, disregarding this visionary quality could entail focusing on Jiménez's pre-exile past as the main premise for approaching his later writings. This would threaten to make his melancholic reflections on death appear unrelated to the creative possibilities offered by exile's new spatiotemporal coordinates, which are unavoidably different from those conventionally established by national narratives, whether recuperative or not. The open eyes of the girl in "El resultado" stare straight ahead, but they do not look directly at us. As Machado wrote about the anonymous collective of war witnesses, these eyes may see "desnuda la verdad": they seem to glimpse beyond past and future, witnessing and reminding us of a history "en lo profundo," a history that transcends our own biographical historicity, a history to which we, the living, ultimately also belong.

CHAPTER FIVE

Luis Cernuda: "Remember Him and Remember Him to Others" – Historical Memory, Self-Elegy, and Mythopoetic Figuration

The arresting verse "Recuérdalo tú y recuérdalo a otros" [Remember It/Him and Remember It/Him to Others] seems to have accomplished what Luis Cernuda stated when he penned it. Written between December 1961 and April 1962 in the United States – roughly three years after Jiménez's death in Puerto Rico – the words serve as the opening line of the poem "1936":

> Recuérdalo tú y recuérdalo a otros,
> Cuando asqueados de la bajeza humana,
> Cuando iracundos de la dureza humana:
> Este hombre solo, este acto solo, esta fe sola.
> Recuérdalo tú y recuérdalo a otros.
>
> En 1961 y en ciudad extraña,
> Más de un cuarto de siglo
> Después. Trivial la circunstancia,
> Forzado tú a pública lectura,
> Por ella con aquel hombre conversaste:
> Un antiguo soldado
> En la Brigada Lincoln.
>
> Veinticinco años hace, este hombre,
> Sin conocer tu tierra, para él lejana
> Y extraña toda, escogió ir a ella
> Y en ella, si la ocasión llegaba, decidió apostar su vida,
> Juzgando que la causa allá puesta al tablero
> Entonces, digna era
> De luchar por la fe que su vida llenaba.
> Que aquella causa aparezca perdida,
> Nada importa;

Que tantos otros, pretendiendo fe en ella
Sólo atendieran a ellos mismos,
Importa menos.
Lo que importa y nos basta es la fe de uno.

Por eso otra vez hoy la causa te aparece
Como en aquellos días:
Noble y tan digna de luchar por ella.
Y su fe, la fe aquella, él la ha mantenido
A través de los años, la derrota,
Cuando todo parece traicionarla.
Mas esa fe, te dices, es lo que sólo importa.

Gracias, compañero, gracias
Por el ejemplo. Gracias porque me dices
Que el hombre es noble.
Nada importa que tan pocos lo sean:
Uno, uno tan sólo basta
Como testigo irrefutable
De toda la nobleza humana. (*Obra I* 544–5)[1]

"1936" was published in *Desolación de la Quimera* [Desolation of the Chimera] (1962), Cernuda's last book before his death in Mexico City in 1963: thirty-five years after he left the Andalusian capital of Seville, where he was born in 1902, and twenty-five years after he left Spain as a consequence of the Spanish Civil War. After a brief stay in Paris, Cernuda arrived in England in February 1938 to begin his long exile in the United Kingdom, the United States, and Mexico. In 1939 he taught Spanish at Glasgow University. In 1947 he moved to Massachusetts to take up a position as professor of Spanish at Mount Holyoke College. He remained in the United States until 1952, when he decided to become a permanent resident of Mexico. Although he had to earn his living by teaching in California, his time in Mexico City allowed him to return to a milieu that reminded him of his youth in Seville before the war.[2] Cernuda never returned to Spain.

More than fifty years after its initial publication, Spanish readers continue to repeat "Recuérdalo tú y recuérdalo a otros" as an authoritative exhortation. In doing so, they remember Cernuda and remember Cernuda to others, carrying out what this statement couched in verse demands, over and over again. And yet, is this all that Cernuda's insistently imperative line demands? Apart from its author, whom or what does "Recuérdalo tú y recuérdalo a otros" ask the reader to remember? Nineteen-thirty-six was, of course, the year that a military uprising challenged the legitimate Spanish Republican government, resulting in civil war. Cernuda's poem evokes a meeting some twenty-five years later in Los Angeles, California.

The other party to that meeting is an "antiguo soldado," an anonymous former member of the Abraham Lincoln Brigade, the group of international volunteers who went to Spain in 1937 to fight Franco's rebel forces.

The soldier is referred to as an "hombre" three times in "1936." This man chose to "apostar su vida" in the speaker's "tierra," which was "lejana / [y] extraña" to him. The poem seems to demand that the reader preserve the memory of "este hombre solo," who was unlike "tantos otros" who "[s]ólo atendier[o]n a ellos mismos." The soldier's singularity is underscored by the persistently anaphoric demonstrative deictics that situate and isolate objects of remembrance: "Este hombre solo, este acto solo, esta fe sola." The "antiguo soldado," who has been referred to in the third person, with varying degrees of distance, as "este hombre" and "aquel hombre," is then made discursively present through the use of the second person in the apostrophic address "compañero." Yet the last stanza generalizes this apostrophe, making the "compañero" an exemplary representative of a certain human collective, turning him into a universal signifier for human nobility. "1936" ends gnomically, establishing this solitary witness's individuality as fundamental: "Uno, uno tan sólo basta / Como testigo irrefutable / De toda la naturaleza humana" (*Obra I* 544–5). What modes of memory, then, did Cernuda enlist in writing "1936"? How do these modes of memory mould the figure of the irrefutable witness? To what extent do these modes of memory inflect the historical readings that "1936" seems to encourage today, in a moment of debate over the value of collective memory in Spain?

Immediately following "1936" is the last poem of *Desolación de la Quimera*, "A sus paisanos" [To His Fellow Countrymen]. In it, the first-person speaker, an exiled writer, worries that he may be forgotten in Franco's dictatorial Spain: "soy, sin tierra y sin gente, / Escritor bien extraño; sujeto quedo aún más que otros / Al viento del olvido que, cuando sopla, mata" [I'm, without land and without people, / quite a strange writer; even more than others I remain subject / to the wind of oblivion that, in blowing, kills] (*Obra I* 547). "A sus paisanos" addresses the potential "testigos" [witnesses] of the speaker's "existencia y su trabajo" [existence and his work] the fellow countrymen who could cast him and his work "afuera / [d]e la memoria" [outside / of memory] in their "corazón" [heart] and "mente" [mind] (547). Both "1936" and "A sus paisanos" depict a solitary stranger who risks his life in a strange land, but they stage the tensions between memory and history and between individuality and collectivity from different angles, bringing *Desolación de la Quimera* and Cernuda's poetic oeuvre to a decidedly memorable close.

Historical Memory and the Commemorative Value of "1936"

The statement "Recuérdalo tú y recuérdalo a otros" has had tangible social effects as a speech act. Its felicitous status as an illocutionary utterance, joining words to actions, is evidenced by its numerous public readings since Franco died in 1975 and

Spain transitioned from dictatorship to democracy. This act of remembrance lets readers bring the poem's speaker to life as a cognitive, affective, and ethical subject, confirming the links between memory and history and individuality and collectivity that Cernuda's last poems encourage to seek (Gaylord, "The Romance" 8). "Recuérdalo tú y recuérdalo a otros" thus promotes the collective memorialization of Spain's solitary poet par excellence, fulfilling the desire expressed by Cernuda's poetic persona in "A sus paisanos," an exiled poet deeply concerned about the future of "su trabajo" (Harris, *Luis Cernuda* 10–14). As Cernuda's fellow countrymen recite his poetry, they keep him and "su trabajo" in their "corazón" and "mente" and become "testigos" to his "existencia" as a poet (*Obra I* 547). But "1936" also asks the reader to remember at least another figure: the anonymous soldier and so-called testigo irrefutable who gave evidence of "toda la nobleza humana" through his "fe" and the "acto" of fighting for a "causa" worth dying for.

Unlike Cernuda's poetic persona, this figure is hardly remembered in Spain nowadays. Both the poem and a letter that Cernuda addressed to his friend Carlos Otero in December 1961 describing the encounter in Los Angeles extol the faith that drove the former soldier to fight for a noble cause. Yet references to the specific historical circumstances are relatively vague: "No importa cómo veamos hoy todo aquello; lo único que cuenta es el valor y la fe que algunos, como este hombre, pusieron en España entonces" [it does not matter how we see all that today; the only thing that counts is the courage and the faith some, like this man, put into Spain back then] (*Epistolario* 982–3).[3] Referential vagueness is not uncommon in Cernuda's poetry, even in explicitly historically oriented pieces such as the elegies that he wrote between 1937 and 1940 in war-torn Spain and his uncertain first years of exile in Great Britain. This contextual imprecision extends to the way "Recuérdalo tú y recuérdalo a otros" is publicly repeated and remembered in twenty-first-century Spain, complicating an interpretation of the modes of memory it can activate. Especially when the line is excerpted and recast as a standalone exhortation in a different historical framework, the former soldier seems to disappear behind the relatively depersonalized figure of a collective representative.

This anonymizing recontextualization is most noteworthy in *Recuérdalo tú y recuérdalo a otros*, the Spanish translation of *Blood of Spain*, the landmark oral history of the civil war put together by British historian Ronald Fraser. The book contains the testimonies of more than 300 survivors of the armed conflict, which Fraser collected between 1973 and 1975. When *Blood of Spain* was published in Spain and Great Britain in 1979, four years after Franco's death, the book was promoted as a "systematic oral history by eyewitness participants on both sides" (Fraser, *Blood* n. pag.).[4] Although the entire first stanza of "1936" (including the phrase "este hombre solo") was quoted as an epigraph, Fraser's book never mentioned the soldier. The 1997, 2001, and 2007 Spanish-language editions quoted only the first line of the poem, anonymizing the soldier even further. The first pages of all these editions, however, contained Cernuda's name, as well as the titles of his poem and his last book. As a result, the line from "1936" became a public yet somewhat abstract injunction to remember the war in general.[5]

Fraser's book was lavishly reissued in 2016 by the prestigious press Crítica, owned by the Spanish media group Planeta, one of the largest publishers in the world. The eye-catching red, black, and white cover is dramatically illustrated with a snapshot by war photographer Robert Capa, showing Republicans as they walk towards exile in France in 1939. The front cover of the 2016 reissue is headed by a superlative description by historian Julián Casanova: "la mejor guía para descubrir las historias escondidas de la guerra civil española" [the best guide to discover the hidden stories of the Spanish Civil War]. The description seems counterintuitive in light of the fact that this was the fourth reissue of Fraser's book by a distinguished publisher, and consequently the stories collected by Fraser could hardly be called "escondidas" in Spain in 2016, thirty-seven years after its first edition. Ironically enough, Cernuda's lines were printed for the first time on the back cover, but no reference to the soldier was included, and thus his "historia" did remain hidden.

Some thirty years after the publication of Fraser's collection of testimonies, "Recuérdalo tú y recuérdalo a otros" was frequently quoted amid the debates over the Law of Historical Memory that took place in Spain between 2004 and 2007 (Richards 353).[6] In 2006, the writer, neurologist, and psychiatrist Carlos Castilla del Pino published an op-ed titled "El uso moral de la memoria" [The Moral Use of Memory] in *El País*, the most widely read Spanish newspaper at the time. Castilla del Pino was an eyewitness to killings committed by both sides of the conflict – as he recounted in his self-reflective 1997 memoir *Pretérito imperfecto* [Imperfect Past] – and a highly respected therapist of war survivors during Franco's dictatorship. In "El uso moral de la memoria" Castilla del Pino advocated the recovery of the so-called historical memory of those who had been forced to silence their experience of Francoist repression. He emphatically argued that these victims needed to be remembered so that they would not die twice: "ser recordado es una forma de existencia, en vida pero también después de haber vivido. Sólo cuando se es olvidado por aquellos que nos recordaban, o cuando éstos han perecido, se puede afirmar que inexistimos" [being remembered is a form of existence, in life but also after having lived. Only when we are forgotten by those who remembered us, or when they have passed away, can we claim that we cease to exist] (n. pag.).

In defining identity and existence in terms of memory, Castilla del Pino echoed the fear conveyed by the speaker in Cernuda's "A sus paisanos" that the "viento del olvido" would kill him once the "testigos" to his "existencia" cast him and his work "afuera de la memoria" (*Obra I* 547). According to the psychiatrist, the moral basis for the recovery of historical memory in Spain was the "constancia ¡cuando menos! de los nombres y apellidos de los que vivieron el drama" [evidence – at least! – of the names and last names of those who lived the tragedy] (n. pag.). To emphasize the social value of both the "derecho a la memoria" [right to memory] and the "deber de recordar" [duty to remember], Castilla del Pino quoted Cernuda's line, "Recuérdalo tú y recuérdalo a otros." Although the author of *Pretérito imperfecto* did not mention the "antiguo soldado" – let alone by name – that the verse seemingly demands the reader to remember, he nonetheless highlighted the capacity of Cernuda's line to remind readers of their duty to remember.

Seemingly confirming such mnemonic power, the words "Recuérdalo tú y recuérdalo a otros" were inscribed on the "Memorial a las víctimas de la violencia franquista" [Memorial to the Victims of Francoist Violence], designed by Miguel Angel Arrudi and Fernando Bayo (figure 5.1). This bright red geometric monument was erected in 2010 in the municipal Torrero Cemetery of Zaragoza with unanimous support from all political parties in the city council. The memorial, which honours 3,543 Republican victims of Francoist violence between 1936 and 1946 in Zaragoza, was the first in Spain to commemorate such victims individually (Valero n. pag.).[7] Cernuda's name appears under the first line of "1936," and 3,543 separate plaques surrounding the geometric monument list every victim's name and execution date, when known (Valero n. pag.). This specificity brings the anonymity of the unmentioned "antiguo soldado" into relief. Significantly, Julián Casanova – the historian at the University of Zaragoza commissioned to establish the victims' identities and the circumstances of their deaths – rephrased Cernuda's line in his 2012 obituary of Ronald Fraser in *El País*: "Yo lo recordaré y se lo recordaré a otros" [I will remember him and I will remember him to others] (n. pag.). Other renowned Spanish writers have also leaned on "1936" to make general statements about the political value of memory in important Spanish newspapers such as *El País* and *El Mundo*. In 2012 Antonio Muñoz Molina, a writer who is publicly committed to promoting the cultural productions of exiled writers, stressed the "justeza del mandato" [justness of the command] stated in Cernuda's line: "Porque la manipulación política se sustenta muchas veces en la manipulación del pasado, es importante que los que han vivido una época se esfuercen en recordar y en contar cómo fue" [because political manipulation is often upheld by the manipulation of the past, it is important that those who lived in a certain age strive to remember and tell what it was like] ("Lazos" n. pag.). In this case, rather than attempting to remember the Spanish Republican exile, Muñoz Molina sought to denounce what he perceived as the recent "políticas oficiales de la memoria" [official politics of memory] for distorting the cultural ties between Spain and Catalonia (n. pag.).

In 2000, Luis García Montero, a left-wing politician, university professor, literary critic, and bestselling poet who has supported efforts to publicly remember the history of repression in Spain, described "el ejemplo moral de un antiguo soldado de la Brigada Lincoln" [the moral example of a former soldier from the Lincoln Brigade] in Cernuda's poem as an instance of the "fuerza de la escritura para conservar la memoria histórica" [the power of writing to preserve historical memory] (*Sexto* 253–4). Thirteen years later García Montero stressed that "1936"

5.1 Zaragoza Memorial. Source: Chamarasca, Wikimedia Commons, CC BY-SA 4.0, https://commons.wikimedia.org/w/index.php?curid=48468975.

was "dedicado a un luchador republicano" [dedicated to a Republican fighter], and concluded that it was a reminder that "la dignidad de la conciencia individual es imprescindible" [the dignity of individual conscience is indispensable] ("Luis Cernuda" n. pag.). To García Montero, this reminder was especially necessary in 2013, when in his opinion capitalism had become one of the "enemigos más poderosos" [most powerful enemies] of individual conscience (n. pag.).[8] Thus, in early twenty-first century Spain, "Recuérdalo tú y recuérdalo a otros" tends to be dehistoricized or, rather, rehistoricized, serving whoever quotes it as a placeholder for whatever readers need to remember in their own historical context – including that of debates about historical memory itself. Even sporadic references to the anonymous "antiguo soldado" seem to serve this purpose.[9]

This kind of discursive anachronism appears to be the unavoidable fate of any literary text that manages to outlast its original context, particularly when, as Antoine Compagnon argues, "[t]he answer brought by the text depends on the question we pose it from our historical vantage point" (10, 27). Nonetheless, it is a striking development for a poem so deeply grounded in specific historical circumstances. After all, the questions we ask of the text also depend "on our capacity to reconstruct the question to which the text is responding, for the text is equally in dialogue with its own history" (Compagnon 42).[10] To what extent, then, does the mnemonic power exerted by "1936" run against the grain of its historical underpinnings? What modes of historical time does it elicit if readers remember the line today, more than fifty years after it was written, while keeping in mind Cernuda's warning that the "viento del olvido" may kill his poetic speaker? What should readers remember to keep Cernuda's "existencia" and "su trabajo" from being cast out of "la memoria," to become "testigos" not just to his own history but also to that of his poetic persona? (*Obra I* 547). In short, what remembrance does Cernuda's poem encourage if it is read as both history and poetic memory?

Prominent critics have read "1936" as a dramatic monologue – that is, as a mimesis of the thoughts and affects of a persona created in the text by the poet. Luis García Montero, for instance, has written about the poem's "construcción de un personaje moral que toma postura ante las anécdotas de la realidad" [construction of a moral character that takes a stand before the anecdotes of reality] (*Sexto* 248). As a dramatic monologue, Cernuda's poem invites the reader to remember the singular moral example of the anonymous "antiguo soldado" that the narrator describes.[11] But "1936" – especially its frequently quoted opening line – also contains elements that complicate an understanding of the poem as the simple representation of an anecdote recounted by a narrator. For instance, the poem's commemorative speech act pivots on the contrast between an opening expression of disgust and anger at the "bajeza humana" and a closing expression of appreciation and gratitude for "toda la nobleza humana": "Gracias, compañero, gracias / Por el ejemplo. Gracias porque me dices / Que el hombre es noble. / Nada importa que tan pocos lo sean: / Uno, uno tan sólo basta / Como testigo irrefutable / De toda la nobleza humana" (*Obra I* 544–5). Cernuda's poem thus deploys a topical, semantic, and phonic opposition between nobleness and baseness.

A song of praise and thanksgiving, "1936" seems an unambiguous example of classical oratory in articulating a moral opposition between virtue and vice, which Aristotle considered the main topics of invention in epideictic rhetoric (book 1, chap. 9). Jonathan Culler has suggested that epideictic rhetoric enables us to see lyric not as "a world-creating fiction," or dramatic monologue, but rather as a "real-world utterance" (*Theory* 127). Aside from praise or blame, this epideictic component in lyric involves "language as action" and comprises multiple statements of value about the world at large (Culler, *Theory* 128). In this light, "1936" is not just a morality tale conveyed through a dramatic monologue, but a lyric utterance that makes a real-world statement of value about the general need or duty to remember.[12] The effectiveness – or, in J.L. Austin's terms, perlocutionary force – of Cernuda's poem as a speech act is amply evidenced by the fact that its opening line has been used as a capacious placeholder in different contexts and for various purposes. Even those readers who interpret "1936" as a dramatic monologue about specific historical circumstances arguably tend to remember the poem for its singularity as a lyric utterance. When "1936" is read, and voiced, as the latter, its epideictic force is bolstered by those elements that a conventional mimetic explanation would often neglect: the intertextuality of its references, its use of the present tense, and the materiality of its language (Culler, *Theory* 118–19).[13] As we will see, these are central elements of the statement of value that "1936" asks the reader to share: the need or duty to remember a noble (but lost) life-or-death cause and the faith that a single person placed in that cause.

In recurring, self-reflexive fashion, "1936," and most prominently its opening verses, use the lyric's mnemonic devices to persuade the addressed reader of the value of its own remembrance. The line "Recuérdalo tú y recuérdalo a otros" can refer to the "ejemplo" of the soldier's "fe," which the speaker gives as the reason for his gratitude. "Fe," appearing seven times in "1936," is the most reiterated noun in the poem, and perhaps, therefore, the most likely to be remembered. The soldier – who "decidió apostar su vida" because of "la fe que su vida llenaba" – has kept "su fe, la fe aquella ... / A través de los años, la derrota, / Cuando todo parece traicionarla." And that "fe" is "lo que sólo importa," concludes the speaker before thanking the "antiguo soldado" for his "ejemplo." "Esta fe sola" is not only one of the objects of remembrance singled out in the exhortative opening stanza; given the specificity accorded by the demonstrative and qualifying adjectives "esta" and "solo," it is also the very thing worth remembering (García Montero, *Sexto* 254–5).

Now, the epideictic force of "1936" as a statement of value rather than the narrative mimesis of a past anecdote requires the reader to remember similar utterances and Cernuda's poetry intertextually, albeit incompletely or disjointedly. That is, the poem's mnemonic power relies largely on each reader's poetic memory. Indeed, Cernuda built his poetic persona around a solitary individual who keeps his faith in a righteous, although lost, cause. This sort of faith is thematized in another explicitly historically oriented poem from *Desolación de la Quimera*, "Díptico español" [Spanish Diptych]. That poem's speaker emphasizes his sense of alienation from his "tierra" [land] and his individual experience as a human being. Having learned "[e]l oficio de hombre duramente" [man's trade harshly] and putting his own "fe" in "él," he refuses to return to his homeland, "cuya fe, si una tiene, dejó de ser mía" [whose faith, if it has one at all, ceased to be mine] (*Obra II* 503).[14] This "fe" resonates some pages later in "1936" (*Obra II* 544). In *Ocnos*, Cernuda's mythopoetic autobiography written between 1940 and 1961, the poet also resorts to "fe" to establish a similar contrast, this time through an opposition between the poet and the Christian: "cuando el poeta adquiere o recobra la fe, lo que el cristiano quiera decir, como cristiano, acaso no interese al poeta, como poeta" (*Obra II* 607) [when the poet acquires or regains faith, what the Christian wants to say as a Christian may not be of interest to the poet, as a poet (*Written* 89–90)]. Cernuda's "fe" is, from this angle, largely the faith of a poet.[15]

The earlier poem "Vereda del cuco" [Cuckoo's Lane] highlights Cernuda's commitment to his poetic "fe," as well as the intertextual and self-referential strands woven into his poetry. "Vereda del cuco" appeared in 1947 as part of *Como quien espera el alba* [Like Someone Awaiting Dawn] a book that, like *Desolación de la Quimera,* is profoundly marked by the experience of exile.[16] Octavio Paz, in "La palabra edificante" [The Edifying Word] – the widely influential obituary of Cernuda published in Mexico in 1964 – called this poem's meditation on erotic love a decisive step towards a rhetoric of self-reflectivity in Cernuda's poetry: "en la conciencia ajena no ve sino su propio rostro interrogante" (12) [in the conscience of the other person he sees nothing but his own questioning face ("The Edifying" xxxiv)]. In "Vereda del cuco" the poet rehearses a series of signature rhetorical modes, moods, and motifs. As a ruminative second-person dramatic monologue, the poem is structured as a fictional representation of a past event – in this case, a solitary summer stroll down a dark lane to a fountain.

But the monologue in "Vereda del cuco" also includes the present-tense utterance of real-world statements of value. The poem is a reflection on the life-risking experience of love, or "a contemplation of daemonic eroticism," in Derek Harris's description ("La poesía" 87), which the solitary traveller perceives as existential exile as he engages in a never-ending dialectic of life and death (and, correlatively, of memory and oblivion). By the end of "Vereda del cuco," the individual speaker has merged with both a collective that knows the "fuego originario" [original fire] and the phoenix, in an allegory of love's deadly but transcendent power: "Sin ceniza no hay llama, / Ni sin muerte es el cuerpo / Testigo del amor, fe del amor eterno" [without ash there is no flame, / Nor without death is the body / Witness to love, faith in eternal love] (*Obra I* 375–9). As we shall see, these are only some of the mythopoetic strands that Cernuda subtly weaves into "1936," and more widely into his long-standing meditation on the exiled individual.

Cernuda's Exiles and Daemonic Figurations

The figure of the exiled solitary traveller engaged in an endless dialectic of life-and-death and memory-and-oblivion is emblematic of Cernuda's self-perceived otherness, of what another gay poet, Jaime Gil de Biedma, called the poet's Romantic identity as an "hijo unigénito" [only-begotten son] ("Como en sí mismo" 342). The singularity of Cernuda's "diferencia" [difference], his experience as a unique "hijo de dios" [son of god] in contrast to everyone else's "experiencia común" [common experience], is linked to his self-understanding "en tanto que homosexual y en tanto que poeta" [as a homosexual and as a poet], a twofold condition that found its crucial confirmation in the experience of the civil war and exile (Gil de Biedma, "Como en sí mismo" 342). This twofold exile is explicitly referenced in "Escándalo" [Scandal], a prose poem from the 1942 edition of *Ocnos* in which the poet recalls a moment as a boy in his native Seville when he noticed some "maricas" [fairies] who behaved "[c]on dignidad de alto personaje en destierro" (*Obra I* 563) [with the dignity of lofty personages in exile (*Written* 17)].

In this sense, Cernuda's "irrevocable compromiso interior" [irrevocable inner commitment], as Gil de Biedma called the poet's faith in his self-perceived otherness, predated his experience of war and political exile ("Como en sí mismo" 342).

Indeed Cernuda's "diferencia" was already thematized in his pre-exilic poetry, particularly in *Un río, un amor* [A River, a Love] (1929) and *Los placeres prohibidos* [Forbidden Pleasures] (1931), where his homosexuality becomes defiantly manifest. Written in 1929 while he worked as a teaching assistant in Spanish at the École Normale in Toulouse, the significantly titled "Destierro" features a ghostly third-person figure who bears "su destino a solas" and feels the "[f]atiga de estar vivo, de estar muerto" (*Obra I* 146) [his lot alone ... a weariness of living and dying (*Selected* 33)]. Cernuda's poetic persona is here banished not just from society but from life itself. Interestingly, this self-image of a solitary and uncompromising individual is introduced in "Destierro" by a song on the threshold between life and death: "Ante las puertas bien cerradas / Sobre un río de olvido, va la canción antigua" (*Obra I* 146) [Past all the shuttered doors / Along a river of oblivion, the old song runs (*Selected* 33)]. In intertextually evoking the Orphic myth recreated in Garcilaso de la Vega's famous third eclogue – "y aquel sonido hará parar las aguas del olvido" [and that sound will stop the waters of oblivion] – Cernuda constructs a self-elegy out of an age-old figure of the exiled poet.

Numerous critics have claimed that Cernuda saw himself as an exiled poet long before his political exile.[17] In his 2003 introduction to *Poesía del exilio*, an anthology of Cernuda's poetry after 1937, Antonio Carreira contended that the poet felt exiled "no de un país, sino de su familia, del ambiente sevillano, de toda la sociedad, por su condición de homosexual y de poeta, así como por su personalidad insobornable" [not from a country, but from his family, his Sevillian environment, from all society, because he was a homosexual and a poet, and also because of his incorruptible personality] (7). The literary topos of exile shapes much of Cernuda's poetry before and after the war.[18] As Michael Ugarte noted in 1986, desire – one of two terms in the dialectical title of Cernuda's collected poems, *La realidad y el deseo* – is "both a motif and the force which sets his life and poetry into exile, an eternal movement away from a secure home" ("Luis Cernuda" 329). In a similar vein, Angelina Muñiz-Huberman foregrounded in 2009 the strong plurilingual elements informing Cernuda's poetics of exile as a result of his cross-border readings and translations: "Cernuda se apartó y se encerró en sí. Necesariamente. Eligió poetas de otras lenguas, francesa, inglesa, alemana ... A partir de su infancia encarnó en sí todos los grados del exilio, aun antes de padecerlo" [Cernuda stepped away and shut himself in. Necessarily. He chose poets from other languages: French, English, German ... From his childhood on, he embodied all degrees of exile, even before he suffered it] ("Luis Cernuda" 90). As Muñiz-Huberman suggests, translation encapsulates Cernuda's sense of self-exile, even before he left Spain on account of the war.

As it is well known, Cernuda translated Paul Éluard and Gérard de Nerval in the twenties, when he lived in Seville, Toulouse, and Madrid, and was becoming conversant with French poets like Louis Aragon, André Breton, Charles Baudelaire, René Crevel, Comte de Lautréamont, Stephane Mallarmé, Pierre Reverdy, and Arthur Rimbaud. It was later, during his exile in English-speaking countries in the late thirties and forties, that Cernuda familiarized himself with British and Irish literature, and started translating extensively, as evidenced by his published Spanish renditions of works by William Blake, Robert Browning, John Keats, Andrew Marvell, William Wordsworth, and W.B. Yeats.[19] Octavio Paz went further in considering the various ways in which Cernuda's poetic self-figuration was animated by an intertextual dialectic between the self-absorbed, isolated individual and a cosmopolitan multifaceted collectivity:

> errante en los cinco continentes, vive siempre en el mismo cuarto, habla con las mismas gentes y su exilio es el de todos. Esto no lo supo Cernuda – estaba demasiado inclinado sobre sí mismo, demasiado abstraído en su propia singularidad – pero su obra es uno de los testimonios más impresionantes de esta situación, verdaderamente única, del hombre moderno: estamos condenados a una soledad promiscua y nuestra prisión es tan grande como el planeta. No hay salida ni entrada. Vamos de lo mismo a lo mismo. Sevilla, Madrid, Toulouse, Glasgow, Londres, Nueva York, México, San Francisco: ¿Cernuda estuvo de veras en esas ciudades?, ¿en dónde están realmente esos sitios?" ("La palabra" 8)
>
> [wandering the five continents, he always lives in the same room, talks to the same people, and his exile is everybody's. Cernuda did not know this – he was too intent upon himself, too abstracted in his uniqueness – but his work is one of the most impressive personal testimonies to this truly unique situation of modern man: we are condemned to a promiscuous solitude and our prison is as large as the planet itself. There is no exit or entrance. We move from the same to the same. Seville, Madrid, Toulouse, Glasgow, London, New York, Mexico, San Francisco: was Cernuda really in those places? Where are those places in fact? ("The Edifying" xvi)]

In Paz's generalizing, universalist perspective, exile becomes Cernuda's founding myth as a modern poet, without which the layered dialectic between reality and desire that underpins his poetics would be hard to elucidate. Nevertheless, the different types of exile traceable in Cernuda's postwar poetry are also inextricably interwoven with the confrontational rhetoric of his particular critique of conservative mores in early twentieth-century Spanish provincial society.

Evidence of this is found in "La familia" [The Family], a poem written in 1941 and included in the exilic collection *Como quien espera el alba.*[20] Yet another solitary traveller engaged in a dialectic of life-and-death and memory-and-oblivion appears in this poem. The family, referred to as a "fantasmal conclave" [ghostly conclave], is evoked by a "tú" intent on magically making "a los idos visibles un momento" (*Obra I* 337) [those lost ones visible for a moment (*Forbidden* 297)]. This spectral setting parallels a strong sense of social and existential alienation, marked by a personification of death: "Te dieron todo, sí: vida que no pedías, / y con ella la muerte de dura compañera" (*Obra I* 336) [They gave you everything, a life you never asked for / And with it death as a hard companion (*Forbidden* 295)]. Yet for the indeterminate "tú" apostrophized by the first-person speaker, freedom from tyranny entails a life of loneliness, homelessness, and oblivion: "El tiempo que pasó, desvaneciéndolos / Como burbuja sobre la haz del agua, / Rompió la pobre tiranía que levantaron, / Y libre al fin quedaste, a solas con tu vida, / Entre tantos de aquellos que, sin hogar ni gente, / Dueños en vida son del ancho olvido" [Time went by, undoing them / Like bubbles on the surface of a stream, / Dismantling the poor tyranny they'd built, / And leaving you free at last, alone with your life, / Like all the others with neither home nor kin, / Masters in life of wide oblivion (297)].[21]

Notably, the "tú" "sin hogar ni gente" who in "La familia" seems to master the "ancho olvido" is implicitly requesting the reader to hark back to an earlier point in poetic memory: the insistent apostrophic hendecasyllable that opens the poem: "Recuerdas tú, recuerdas aún la escena" (*Obra I* 334) [Do you remember, do you still remember the scene (*Forbidden* 295)].[22] "Recuérdalo tú y recuérdalo a otros" brings echoes of this reiterative form of interpellation to the ears of readers alert to Cernuda's poetic memory. This ghostly interplay with Cernuda's earlier poems does not detract from the specific historicity of exile inscribed in "1936," composed twenty years later. On the contrary, it lends it historical density and singularity: it characterizes Cernuda's highly particularized memory of exile as an intricate textual mesh of non-chronological, cross-historical voices, including – but not limited to – those that resonate with the concrete conditions of the armed conflict. Indeed, a decisive factor behind the lives of loneliness, homelessness, and oblivion of Cernuda's various poetic personae was his increasing sense of alienation as the war drew on (Rivero Taravillo, *Años españoles* 380–93). In James Valender's words, "[i]ndependientemente de que volviera o no, su país ya se le había vuelto del todo ajeno [regardless of whether he returned or not, his country had already become completely alien to him] (*Luis Cernuda* 285).

Among the reasons for Cernuda's sharp break with Spain – but also for the fact that his commitment to the Republican side during the war became somewhat eroded – may be his being "openly homosexual in his life and in his writing" (Kessler, "Translator's Prologue: Exile" 10). Here political exile may be productively queered as gender politics in various transnational and transatlantic terms. Enrique Álvarez has perceptively read Cernuda's queer desire in exile as a form of discontinuity in continuity, disrupting the homophobic rhetoric of official discourses of Spanishness and Hispanicity: "Cernuda's Mexican reimagining of Spain builds on a queer affective narrative that replicates but at the same time undermines the Spanish nationalist principles it ostensibly articulates" (194). This queering of Cernuda's political exile may also be framed within a dialectic between metropolis and periphery: his exile may be everybody's, and everywhere, as Paz claimed in his reflections about the spatiotemporal coordinates of modernism.

And yet Cernuda's exile is also, in a strong sense, historically unique within modernism in general and within Spanish modernism in particular.[23] In line with Octavio Paz, Raymond Williams perceptively argued in "When Was Modernism?" for the need to explore the "City of Strangers" as the most appropriate location for a modernist art "made by the restlessly mobile emigré or exile, the internationally anti-bourgeois artist," and for the "intense, singular narrative of unsettlement, homelessness, solitude and impoverished independence: the lonely writer gazing down on the unknowable city from his shabby apartment" (34). But in his critique of universal spatiotemporal perspectives on modernism, Williams also stressed that this exploration should involve looking "from outside the metropolis: from the deprived hinterlands, where different forces are moving, and from the poor world which has always been peripheral to the metropolitan systems" (47). Cernuda's exilic writings are a testimony to these different sociocultural forces from the southern periphery of Spain.

Consequently, when, as an exile not just from his hometown but from his country, Cernuda wrote about his memory of seeing "maricas" in Seville and depicted them as having the dignity of an "alto personaje en destierro," the poet was hardly moving "de lo mismo a lo mismo," as Paz contended. Cernuda was also engaging, from the specific perspective of a Sevillian "marica" exiled in Great Britain, in a differential dialectic between one and many, sameness and diversity, periphery and metropolis, inside and outside, overtness and covertness: he was exiling and queering himself as irrepressibly, uncontainably *other* in the context of mid-twentieth-century modernism. In Williams's description of the modernist émigré, Cernuda was simultaneously "the lonely writer gazing down" from his balcony, but also one of the "misteriosas criaturas" [mysterious creatures] who, as depicted in *Ocnos*, "levantaban la mirada a un balcón, donde los curiosos se asomaban al ruido, y había en sus descarados ojos juveniles esa burla mayor, un desprecio más real que en quienes con morbosa curiosidad les iban persiguiendo" (*Obra I* 563) [would look up to a balcony, where the curious stuck their heads out at the noise, and in their brazen youthful eyes shone an even greater mockery, a more authentic contempt than that of the sick busybodies pestering them (*Written* 17)]. But Cernuda's exilic twofold gaze is not simply spatial: it is also temporal, as it extends backward in time. His poetic memory of *destierro* as a result of the war is inescapably interlaced with previous, and hence historically different, strands of exile. To leave this element of spatiotemporal disruption unaddressed would be to dehistoricize Cernuda's uniquely cast modes of memory.[24]

Gil de Biedma read Cernuda's use of dramatic monologues as a way of dealing with this self-image of a poet exiled from himself. Cernuda claimed that Robert Browning's poetry taught him to project his emotional experiences onto "una situación dramática, histórica o legendaria" [a legendary, historical, or dramatic situation], whether that situation be that of a volunteer for the International Brigades, as in "1936," or that of a biblical character, as in "Lázaro" (*Prosa II* 647). In other dramatic monologues, Cernuda builds the situation on his own biographical circumstances; in other words, the speaking voice impersonates the author. In Gil de Biedma's terms, the "protagonista" [protagonist] is "el mismo autor" [the author himself]: "La voz que habla en un poema, aunque sea la del poeta, no es nunca una voz real, es sólo una voz posible, no siempre imaginaria, pero siempre imaginada" [the voice that speaks in a poem, even if it is the poet's voice, is never a real voice, but only a possible voice, not always imaginary, but always imagined] ("Como en sí mismo" 348). Cernuda's dramatic monologues thus perform Rimbaud's deictic dislocation "Je es un autre" [I is someone else], discursively exiling the first-person speaker from him- or herself (374–5).

As Gil de Biedma explained, this "someone else" is Cernuda's "doble" [double], his "persona poética" [poetic persona]; but it can also be, as in "Vereda del cuco," his "daimon" [daemon] ("Como en sí mismo" 353). In 2002, Harold Bloom read Cernuda's dramatic monologue "Lázaro" as a poet's daemonic struggle with himself, in the Romantic heroic tradition of Hölderlin, Nerval, Novalis, Blake, Goethe, Browning, and Machado: "Perhaps Cernuda can be understood best as one of Browning's obsessed monologists" (615). Indeed, the life-and-death dialectic that inflects the poet's self-perceived otherness in Cernuda's poetry is often dramatized by daemonic figures endowed with destructive and self-destructive powers. According to Christopher Soufas, daemonic power in Cernuda's poetry "motivate[s] men to act even in spite of themselves" (168). Like Eros, it is "an energizing, a shocking of our normal existence" (Soufas 169). Although seemingly devoid of mythic qualities, the former soldier's heroic action in "1936" has the same purpose as any action driven by daemonic power in Cernuda's poetry: to exemplify human nobility against all odds. Among the consequences of such heroic actions are isolation, exile from daemonic paradise, and a return to ordinary reality (Soufas 171). But Cernuda's personae have another outlet for this daemonic power: poetry.

In *Ocnos*, Cernuda used the praise-and-blame rhetoric of "1936" to connect daemonic power and poetry through the striking characterization of a panther as a destructive force: "¿Qué poeta o qué demonio odió tanto y tan bien la vulgaridad humana circundante?" (*Obra II 593*) [What poet or demon ever hated so much or so well the encircling vulgarity of man? (*Written* 66)]. Here, the poet predicates his mythical self-creation as a noble creature in exile from ordinary human life. Indeed, Cernuda's essays about Ancient Greek mythology and about British and German Romantic poetry are evidence that this destructive daemonic force behind human nobility plays a key role in his poetics. A few months before the Spanish Civil War began, Cernuda wrote "Hölderlin," in which he contemplated a definition of solitary poetic genius through regenerative death by fire: "¿Quién ignora cómo lo mejor, lo más noble que la humanidad puede ofrecer, ha sido realizado por genios aislados y a pesar de los otros hombres? Una demoníaca fuerza aniquilaba a Hölderlin por el fuego, fuego que al propio tiempo lo salvaba" [Who is not aware that the best, the most noble that humanity can offer has been carried out by isolated geniuses and despite other men? A daemonic force annihilated Hölderlin by fire, a fire that at the same time saved him] (*Obra II* 105). It was in 1936 that Cernuda's translations of Hölderlin's selected poems were published in Spain.

Similarly, in "Marsias" (1941), Cernuda musters the eponymous mythological figure of the young satyr and musician as an allegory for his poetics. The contest between Marsyas and Apollo demonstrates that the poet must know "cómo tiene frente de sí toda la creación, tanto en su aspecto divino como en el humano, enemistad bien desigual en la que el poeta, si lo es verdaderamente, ha de quedar vencido o muerto" [how all of creation lies before him, both in its divine and its human aspects, this enmity being so unequal that the poet, if he truly is a poet, ought to be vanquished or dead] (*Obra II* 800). When Marsyas defies his "limitación mortal" [mortal limitation] and challenges Apollo, he is skinned alive. The young satyr has nonetheless been able to use his flute to convey "un afán sobrehumano" [superhuman eagerness] (*Obra II* 799).[25] Cernuda's depiction of John Keats – whose "Ode to Autumn" he translated and published in Mexico in 1940 – also echoes this mythical self-construction of the poet. In an eponymous essay from 1958, Keats becomes for him a solitary writer committed to "una experiencia humana y poética en la cual todo se arriesga" [a human and poetic experience in which everything is at stake] (350, 339). Keats's life thus serves as an "ejemplo de un poder bien raro" [example of a very rare power]: "experimentar lo que es morir y resucitar una y otra vez antes de la hora final" [to experience what it is like to die and be resurrected again and again before the final hour] (337). Cernuda summarizes his idea of poetry as a deadly but transcendent force by quoting one of Keats's letters from 1888: "el genio de la poesía debe procurar en el hombre su salvación propia" (341) [The Genius of Poetry must work out its own salvation in a man] (Keats 286).

These protean variations on the motif of the agonizing poet are long-standing, boundary-crossing figurations of self-exile embedded in Cernuda's poetic memory. Their spatiotemporal flexibility becomes all the more moving and memorable when rehearsed under traumatic historical circumstances, such as those the poet experienced during and after the Spanish Civil War. Often, the memory of these figurations is stored in topoi made available by another poet who endured painful political conditions: Ovid, one of the paradigmatic exiled poets in the Western literary archive. In 2011, Jennifer Ingleheart fleshed out the ways in which Ovid was able to transmute his personal situation as he appropriated the parts of a wide host of archetypes of suffering. Significant among these archetypal figures are "the unremitting target of the vindictive revenge of a piqued, all-powerful deity; the artist and/or parent destroyed by their own creation; the lover bemoaning their separation from their beloved; the agonized, isolated individual unable to articulate and share the burden of his suffering; the wanderer doomed to eternal separation from his homeland" (19). Cernuda's Ovidian memory of exile traverses his poems, essays, and translations. It is closely bound to the apostrophic rhetoric that characterizes his mythical self-construction of the solitary poet driven by daemonic forces. In its emphasis on total dedication to one's cause, this self-construction foreshadows and shapes the depiction of the "antiguo soldado" in the strongly apostrophic poem "1936."

In a 1935 essay titled "Palabras antes de una lectura," Cernuda described his introduction to poetry in terms that reiterate this seemingly inexhaustible reality-and-desire, life-and-death dialectic:

> El instinto poético se despertó en mí gracias a una percepción más aguda de la realidad, experimentando, con un eco más hondo, la hermosura y la atracción del mundo circundante. Su efecto era, como en cierto modo ocurre con el deseo que provoca el amor, la exigencia, dolorosa a fuerza de intensidad, de salir de mí mismo, anegándome en aquel vasto cuerpo de la creación. Y lo que hacía aún más agónico aquel deseo era el reconocimiento tácito de su imposible satisfacción. (*Obra II* 602)
>
> [The poetic instinct was awakened in me thanks to a more acute perception of reality – experiencing with a deeper echo the beauty and attraction of the surrounding world. Its effect, as in some way, occurs with that desire which provokes love, was the necessity – painful because of its intensity – of getting outside myself, negating myself in the vast body of creation. And what made that desire even more agonizing was the tacit recognition that it was impossible to satisfy it] ("Words" 43)

Cernuda also allegorized this form of destructive engagement with a daemonic power in "Lázaro." As mentioned earlier, the first-person speaker in this self-elegy is "un muerto / Andando entre los muertos" (*Obra I* 293). Feeling "el desconsuelo del hombre que está solo," the speaker asks for the strength to "llevar la vida nuevamente" (*Obra I* 292–3) [the dejection of the lonely ... the strength to bear life again (*Selected* 103)]. Cernuda wrote the poem during the war and his early exile, when, as C.B. Morris maintained in 1971, he felt "besieged and threatened by death" (239). This life-death imagery spans most of Cernuda's poetic production. It was already salient in *Los placeres prohibidos*, a book published in 1931, five years before the civil war broke out.

Cernuda's dialectically driven mythopoetic self-fashioning also shapes his more prosaic late poems (Valender, *Luis Cernuda* 446). In the words of his translator Stephen Kessler, these writings also "manifest his belief in the poem as ... a matter of life and death, a deadly serious act of self-realization against both human and cosmic odds against social ostracism and oblivion itself" ("Translator's Prologue: A Timeless" 17). More than twenty-five years after *Los placeres prohibidos*, in "Díptico español," Cernuda unforgettably described Spain as "la tierra de los muertos, / Adonde ahora todo nace muerto, / Vive muerto y muere muerto" [the land of the dead / Where now everything is born dead, / lives dead and dies dead]. In this ominous setting, the speaker explains that he has learned the "oficio de hombre duramente," and has put "su fe" in "él" (*Obra I* 239). The explicit historical referentiality of "Díptico español" reinforces the myth of a solitary traveller who must endure a life-or-death ordeal to survive as a poet and persuasively address posterity.[26]

Self-Exile and Self-Elegy

Cernuda's resolution to be "faithful to himself" and to his "love of solitude" gives the late poems of *Desolación de la Quimera* a "predominantly elegiac mood," as C.B. Morris put it (238). Some of Cernuda's most memorable exilic compositions are explicitly predicated on the consequences of war. This is most evident in the 1937 "Elegías españolas" [Spanish Elegies], including the melancholy-toned "Elegía a la luna de España" [Elegy to the Moon of Spain] and "A un poeta muerto (F.G.L.)" [To a Dead Poet (F.G.L.)], which were republished three years later in *Las nubes*. In this referential sense at least, as Edgardo Dobry has argued, the Spanish Civil War "arroja a Cernuda a la historia de España" [throws Cernuda into Spain's history], making the poet "contemporáneo de su tierra y del mundo" [contemporaneous with his land and with the world] (n. pag.). Two decades after *Las nubes*, *Desolación de la Quimera* also foregrounded a historically oriented mimesis: among its thematic pivots is the speaker's conflicted, even confrontational approach to political exile from Spain. Cernuda's memory of the consequences of the internecine conflict would lend a narrative framework to compositions such as "Díptico español," "Otra vez, con sentimiento" [Once More, with Feeling] and "A sus paisanos." This narrative framework lends special interest to those poems in *Desolación de la Quimera* that do not favour a historically oriented mimesis, particularly if they are read as dialectical counterpoints complicating Cernuda's temporality of exile.

A revealing example is "J.R.J. contempla el crepúsculo" [J.R.J. Contemplates the Twilight]. This poem was written in 1960 and published in Bogotá a year later, only a couple of years after Juan Ramón Jiménez passed away in Puerto Rico. Despite the title, its first stanza does not depict Jiménez contemplating the twilight, but John Ruskin going out into a garden. For a moment the reader is invited to imagine both poets in the act of contemplating the twilight. Garden and twilight configure a Romantico-Symbolist spatiotemporal axis of poetic creation. Jiménez can thus be seen as transmuted into the mythical poetic figure of Ruskin, whose work became known in Spain in 1903 through none other than Jiménez's *modernista* magazine *Helios*. "J.R.J. contempla el crepúsculo" then becomes an elegy to Jiménez, who is mentioned by his initials in the second title – "A J.R.J." – inserted before the second stanza. The phoenix, "ave fabulosa" [fabulous bird], departs at twilight, allegorizing a cyclical poetic recreation from the ashes, leaving behind "[d]e su retorno una costumbre" [a habit of its return]. "La noche ancestral" [the ancestral night] follows, but "J.R.J." will not be able to contemplate it anymore.

And yet "J.R.J." has already been recreated, mythopoetically, as the archetypal poet John Ruskin, enabling "J.R.J" to contemplate the twilight once and again in the absolute present tense of the poem's title: "contempla el crepúsculo." This present tense, "contempla," is simultaneously gnomic, durative, historical, and future. The largely cross-temporal dimension of this poetic present interrupts the temporality of historical extinction in exile, enabling a single empirical person to become part of a collective poetic persona.

The chronotope of the garden at twilight is reconstructed through poetic memory, complicating the spatiotemporal coordinates of historical exile, and allowing, in the midst of extinction, for the epitaphic commemoration of the poet. Yet this commemoration is only possible as prosopopoeia or *máscara*, as both Juan Ramón Jiménez and Octavio Paz argued. In the context of both Jimenéz's and Cernuda's long exiles, "J.R.J. contempla el crepúsculo" can also be read intertextually as a self-elegy in the larger framework of Cernuda's mythopoetic thematics. The poem is inserted in *Desolación de la Quimera* right after another elegy, "Amigos: Enrique Asúnsolo" [Friends: Enrique Asúnsolo], which articulates a meditation on friendship, but also on loneliness in the face of death. The poetic speaker wonders how to help a sick friend "ante el final que afrontaremos solos" (*Obra I* 508) [up against the end we face alone (*Desolation* 173)]. From this dialogic angle, both poems, "Amigos: Enrique Asúnsolo" and "J.R.J contempla el crepúsculo," become melancholic variations on the elegiac theme that marks Cernuda's modernist figurations of the solitary poet in exile, particularly since they are both preceded by a powerful death-ridden meditation on exile in "Díptico español."[27] With Cernuda's poetic memory in mind, the "testigo irrefutable" remembered in "1936" can therefore be read as both representing an empirical person – the former member of the Lincoln Brigade – and as constructing a new avatar of Cernuda's lyric persona. In the poet's myth of self-creation, this figure must endure a life-or-death ordeal to recreate himself for posterity.

Octavio Paz suggested that readers can only know whether Cernuda's lyric persona is crafted as a historical exile or a figure from myth and poetry if they are familiar with his poetic memory ("La palabra" 14). At least in the immediate context of Cernuda's late exilic poems – those written from 1950 to 1962 and included in *Con las horas contadas* [With Time Running Out] and *Desolación de la Quimera* – the figure of the "antiguo soldado" takes on a profound cross-boundary and cross-historical mythical dimension in the close company of other heroic figures like El Greco, Mozart, Keats, Titian, and Ruskin. The lives and works of these exemplars of nobility are depicted, in Stephen Kessler's reading, "as measures of humanity's potential despite the bad faith, cruelties and pettiness of politics, war and commerce" ("Translator's Prologue: Exile" 11). Albeit indirectly, then, "1936" calls upon the reader to also remember those other figures that haunt Cernuda's oeuvre as daemonic characters. It is telling that individuality is deictically complicated and multiplied in the poem. "Tú" is the speaker, and thus "forzado tú a pública lectura" accomplishes a form of pronominal self-distancing that surfaces elsewhere in Cernuda's postwar poetry (Monegal 73). But later in "1936" "tú" also refers to the "antiguo soldado" ("gracias, compañero"), shifting the speaker (and the reader) from the second-person ("te dices") to a first-person position of utterance and listening ("me dices"). The protagonist of "1936" is then both "el hombre," a sort of indeterminate, universal everyman, and "un hombre solo," a particular man who serves as the "testigo irrefutable / de toda la nobleza humana" under the particular conditions of the Spanish Civil War.

Deictic fluctuation between identification and alterity makes "1936" yet another example of what Gil de Biedma called Cernuda's "irrevocable compromiso interior" to the various modes of otherness traceable in his poetic personae ("Como en sí mismo" 342). The soldier, the man alone, is the poet as other and as himself in poems from *Como quien espera el alba* such as "Elegía anticipada" [Elegy in Advance] and "Noche del hombre y su demonio" [Night of Man and his Demon] (*Obra I* 356, 366). Furthermore, the complex personal deictics in "1936" allow the "tú" of the speaker to become the "tú" of the soldier, and both to become the "tú" of the reader. When the reader remembers the poem – above all, its insistently reiterated first line "Recuérdalo tú y recuérdalo a otros" – the "tú" has retrospectively come to refer not only to the objectified I (following the conventions of dramatic monologue) but also to that reader (following the conventions of lyric utterance).[28] Reading and voicing the poem not only as the narrative of a specific encounter in Los Angeles in 1961 but also as a lyric utterance makes possible this deictic shifting.

As Jonathan Culler has argued, the reader of lyric poems can "occupy the position of the speaker, ritualistically performing ... lines" ("Language" 162). In this regard, Cernuda's "tú" remains ambiguous and/or indeterminate, an example of what Culler calls a "blurred you," which "gestures toward the reader but is also plausibly taken as either the poet himself or someone else" (*Theory* 194). This "blurred you" emphasizes the non-fictional nature of the first line of "1936." While the poem may be narrative in the sense that it offers the mimesis of a situation that can be recreated, the agent addressed in its first line nonetheless remains undecided. When "you" can be construed to refer to the reader, apostrophe revolves around the communicative situation (192). Octavio Paz also emphasized the ghostliness, intertextuality, self-reflexivity, and present temporality that shape such communication in Cernuda's poetry:

> Al hablar con las criaturas del mito, Cernuda habla para sí pero de esta manera habla con nosotros. Es un diálogo destinado a provocar indirectamente nuestra respuesta. El tiempo real no es el cotidiano de la conversación mundana sino el de la comunicación poética: el instante de la lectura, un ahora en el cual, como en un espejo, el diálogo entre el poeta y su visitante imaginario se desdobla en el del lector con el poeta. El lector se ve en Cernuda que se ve en un fantasma. Y cada uno busca en

el personaje imaginario su propia realidad, su verdad. Su demonio, en el sentido socrático. Cernuda también evoca personas históricas: Góngora, Larra, Tiberio. Son rebeldes, seres al margen, desterrados por la estupidez de sus contemporáneos o por la fatalidad de sus pasiones. Máscaras, *personae* ("La palabra" 14)

[When he addresses myth creatures, Cernuda speaks for his own benefit, but in this way he talks to us. It is a dialogue which aims obliquely to elicit our response. The real time is not the quotidian one of mundane conversation but that of poetic communication: the moment of reading is a now in which, as in a mirror, the dialogue between the poet and his imaginary visitor is reflected in the dialogue between the reader and the poet. The reader sees himself in Cernuda who sees himself in a phantom. And each seeks in the imaginary character his own reality, his truth: his daemon, in the Socratic sense. Besides figures from myth and poetry, there are historical persons: Góngora, Larra, Tiberius. Rebels, marginalized beings, exiled by the stupidity of their contemporaries or by the fatal course of their own passions, are also masks, *personae*] ("The Edifying" xxxix)[29]

Paz here references poetic memory, attuned to both the rhetorical force embedded in the now of apostrophic address and Cernuda's mythopoetic self-fashioning. This same self-fashioning is also at work in the markedly political and narrative poem "1936." Dramatic dialogue, understood as novelization, dominates Cernuda's later work.

Yet, as we have seen, "1936" is not just the representation of a biographical situation or "la construcción de un artificio capaz de elaborar un personaje significativo" [the construction of an artifice able to produce a significant/meaningful character], as Luis García Montero argued in 2000 (*Sexto* 264). Lyric utterance disrupts the poem's plotted construction. Herbert Tucker has called the eruption of a "lyrical interlude" within dramatic monologues a "paratactic pocket": "an insulated deviation from the syntax of narrative line" (234–5). Thus, as in Robert Browning's dramatic monologues, "1936" features "an interference effect between opposed yet mutually informative discourses: between an historical, narrative, metonymic text and a symbolic, lyrical, metaphoric text that adjoins it and jockeys with it for authority" (Tucker 229).[30] From this standpoint, the first five lines of "1936" can be approached not as an interlude but as a lyrical *prelude* that modulates the narrative from the outset. The voice of this mode of remembering, even if it is a "historical, narrative" poem about a solitary figure like the soldier, is also and simultaneously an archetypal mesh of poetic voices that recalls those of Cernuda's multiple mythopoetic personae, such as Keats, Marsyas, Lazarus, and even Juan Ramón Jiménez. In this light, the line "Recuérdalo tú y recuérdalo a otros" is an apostrophic address that seeks to foster remembrance of poetic voices themselves.

Discussions of Cernuda's poems of and about exile often neglect this lyrical element. As a result, the mythopoetic, epitaphic memory of the isolated protagonist who dies and, phoenix-like, is resurrected as a poet, tends to be silenced, forgotten and dehistoricized. But such poetic memory is essential. In a way, it keeps the recollection of dead poets alive; poets die over and over again to live on.[31] If lyric time is the time of remembrance, as Culler has claimed, it is also the time of the present and of presence: "the special 'now' of lyric articulation," which belongs in "a time of discourse rather than of story" (*Theory* 226). This claim may be debatable, but it nonetheless helps to understand Cernuda's specific use of apostrophe. For example, in the poem "Qué más da" [What Does it Matter] from *Los placeres prohibidos*, apostrophe is used to evoke an absent, adored "prodigio rubio" [blond prodigy], and thus brings him into the now of reading as a ghostly presence: "Porque aun siendo brillante, efímero, inaccesible, / Tu recuerdo ... / Basta para iluminar, tú ausente, toda esta niebla que me envuelve" [Because even though it is bright, ephemeral, inaccessible, / Your memory ... / is enough to illuminate, absent you, all this fog enveloping me] (188). "Qué más da" is also an elegy in that it substitutes "an irreversible temporal disjunction, the movement from life to death, with a reversible alternation between mourning and consolation" (227). The supposedly irretrievable past is temporarily retrieved in the discursive now of lyric. The reading, voicing, and remembering of the apostrophic "tú ausente" constitutes not only an elegy but a self-elegy for the continually resurrected poet.

Likewise, in "1936," the speaker asks himself and the reader to remember a former soldier, but he also asks them to remember the mythical poet so that he can be reborn again and again in the iterative now of lyrical time. The irrefutable witness is the soldier, but he is also Cernuda's poetic persona, apostrophizing posterity and demanding, in epitaphic fashion, to be remembered and kept alive in the reversible temporality of the poem. Thus, self-elegy is arguably Cernuda's generic response to a poetics of self-exile.[32] The dialectical play of absence and presence complicates the temporality of "1936," as the time signature of poetic memory alters that of narrative history by bringing 1936 and 1961 to the present. Poetic memory enables the reader to reanimate Cernuda's absent voice, and, through it, the figured – ghostly – voice of the "antiguo soldado." This triangulated act of remembrance recalls poems like "Destierro" and the strongly spectral "Lázaro" in that they ask the reader to evoke and re-evoke the poet's masks or personae, discursively revoking his death. As self-elegies, these poems enable a reiterative and ritualistic performance of death and resurrection.

Vocal Animation and Ghostly Memory

But other crucial modes of poetic memory are embedded in the untimely and unhomely construction of the "viejo soldado" as a ghostly mesh of mythopoetic personae. Intricate linguistic patterns render "1936" memorable as well. This occurs most perceptibly in its first lines, but also in the uncannily Shakespearean oratorical intonations running through the poem's concluding stanzas. These patterns are built on variations in rhythm and rhyme – the unpredictable syncopated stresses, the shifts between internal and external resonances, the percussive deictic drives – and on the hyperbolic deployment of rhetorical devices – apostrophe, amplification, anaphora, parataxis, parallelism – that make the prosaic diction of "1936" all the more haunting. This "ritual dimension" – as Roland Greene has referred to the "patterns that organize ... sounds in the reader-auditor's experience" (4–5) – equips every reader occupying the "I" position in the text with the material resources for a performative voicing every time he or she utters "Recuérdalo tú y recuérdalo a otros." "1936" is rendered memorable, then, by its sheer verbal texture and specifically by its opening stanza's sententious, earnest, propulsive prosodic pattern. It is worth paying detailed attention to the layered sonic fabric of its first lines. Two coordinated hemistichs join the apostrophized "tú" to "otros" both thematically and prosodically. The commemoration is therefore both constative and performative. Remembrance occurs and recurs, but with a difference – the consonant stress on the second syllable of each half-line ("é"-"é") is both reinforced and countervailed by the assonant stress on the pronouns ("tú"-"otros"). The phonemic and syllabic cadence created by the rising vowel pattern ("e"-"é"-"e"-"é") combined with the repetition of diphtongs ("ué"-"ué") also animates the sequence. Since the main stresses in the verse fall squarely on the second and sixth syllables, Cernuda's demand to remember resounds as a straight heroic eleven-syllable line. Additionally, "tú" further activates the rhetorical force of "Recuérdalo tú y recuérdalo a otros" as an apostrophe.

But the heavily accentuated second-person singular pronoun in the fifth syllable turns the heroic hendecasyllable into a *galaico antiguo*. This old Galician eleven-syllable line, conventionally stressed on the fifth syllable, may strike readers as an odd verse form unless they hear echoes of modernist experiments such as "Balada laudatoria a Don Ramón María del Valle-Inclán" ["Laudatory Ballad to Don Ramón María del Valle-Inclán"], written by Rubén Darío in Madrid in 1912 (1055).[33] The poetic memory specific to this line harks back to the Nicaraguan poet's free-ranging metrical explorations. Darío's seemingly anachronistic hendecasyllables in his poem in praise of a writer famous for his highly idiosyncratic Galician-inflected Spanish are also acts of poetic enunciation. They call into existence, through the invocation of another poet's enunciative powers, a freshly imagined cultural location, destabilizing and denaturalizing fixed local and national histories, be they Galician, Spanish, or Nicaraguan.[34] Thus, the poetic memory woven into Cernuda's "1936" runs along a tacit but very material plurality of temporal, spatial, and vocal lines.[35]

Accordingly, in "1936," interwoven linguistic patterns emerge not only at the level of the sentence – the sentence of intersubjective communication, of self-expression – but also at the prosodic and phonic levels (Nowell Smith 12). That is, vocal multiplicity is both semantically motivated by references – no matter how implicit – to Cernuda's personae, and enabled by the specific prosodic and sonic patterns of successive voicings. As Nowell Smith contends, "the rhythms in which we think always precede us, and exceed us – the subjectivity shaped by the prosodics of language is both internally plural and given over to external collectivity (87). Thus, beyond the expressive, grave evocation of figures of an ideal, mythopoetic interiority, plurivocality in "1936" results from the performative voicings of prosodic features like stress and intonation that take place in the transaction between poem and reader.

By the time the first line's two-step commemoration reappears four lines later in "1936," the three intervening lines have filled the first verse with ethical import. "Este hombre solo, este acto solo, esta fe sola" gains rhythmic and appositional strength from the syntactical and phonological parallelism of the two previous lines ("Cuando asqueados de la bajeza humana, / Cuando iracundos de la dureza humana"). Together, these verses foreground collective reactions to reprehensible human behaviours, as well as the contrast between collectivity and individuality. The fifth line both repeats this contrast and recasts it to prevent forgetting. Thus, remembrance is both requested and rhetorically activated as self-expression in a circuit of intersubjective communication. But perhaps more important, remembrance is animated through tonal and prosodic energy. The rhythmic dynamism in "1936" serves not only to bring into presence – and into the present – an absent entity from the past, but also to enable readers to enliven their own voices through the kinetics of its thick verbal fabric.

Functioning as a direct object in "Recuérdalo tú y recuérdalo a otros," the repeated pronoun "lo" has, nevertheless, a broad potential. It could conceivably refer not only to the "antiguo soldado," but also to meanings of the year 1936 that are not made explicit. Additionally, "Recuérdalo" can involve any of the three elements of the fourth line's appositional phrase ("[e]ste hombre solo, este acto solo, esta fe sola"), as well as the example of the soldier's faith and/or the solemn figure of the irrefutable witness of all human nobility that concludes the poem. "Recuérdalo" may even be read to allude to the entire poem as an emblem of the values it epideictically commemorates – nobleness, dignity, and faithfulness. Moreover, the urgency of the duplicated command to remember grammatically underscores the importance of "1936" as an act of shared memory and commitment in the present of reading. The appositional phrase evokes specific past events involving a historical individual. But the earnest command also constitutes a vehement series of deictic pointers that (re)iterates Cernuda's poetic project in the here and now of enunciation – a project that consists of an embodied act of remembrance in the present. The present tense of the poetic apostrophe evokes both something that happened in the past and a real-world utterance happening now, at the moment of reading. Every time the reader reads and repeats the first line, this immediacy highlights the "present of the past" (Ricoeur 101).

As an iterable speech act, Cernuda's line recasts memory for the reader, who remembers now and again. The poem is not just a narrative representation of things past remembered, but also the poetic event of remembering things present. Self-reflexively, "1936" relies on the contrast between the time signature of narrative and the time signature of lyric: if story is "about what happened next," Cernuda's poetic enunciation is "about what happens now" (Culler, *Theory* 226). To understand "1936" as simply the mimesis of a historical anecdote is to neglect its considerable rhetorical, prosodic, tonal, and intertextual mnemonic force. As we have seen, readers are most likely to remember the poem for its singularity as a lyric utterance. This is because the speech act of memory that opens "1936" relies heavily on its verbal texture: its self-reflexivity, refrain-like quality, and metre. Its mnemonic qualities invite the reader to remember its opening stanza, particularly its first and fifth lines. When the poem's first lines are read today, and "[e]ste hombre solo, este acto solo, esta fe sola" are remembered again, the anecdote about the speaker's encounter with "aquel hombre" is largely left behind in the past of representation and thus dialectically brought into historical relief.

Here, the notion of lyric as a paratactic pocket within a dramatic monologue echoes Theodor W. Adorno's robust critique of Martin Heidegger's content-oriented, "realistic" interpretation of Hölderlin's poetry: "Heidegger glorifies the poet supra-aesthetically, as a founder, without reflecting concretely on the agency of form" ("Parataxis" 114). More recently, in 2015, Caroline Levine likewise considered the ways in which between lyric forms and social forms interact. She proposed new approaches to connecting literature and politics in the face of historicism's hegemony in critical discourse: "literary forms can lay claim to an efficacy of their own. They do not simply reflect or contain prior political realities" (16). Indeed, the narrative structure of "1936" would hardly be remembered without at least some awareness of its richly textured lyric form. Voices of a historical and poetic past can somehow be animated through those of the lyric present. The sociopolitical efficacy of "1936" is inescapably mediated by the lyric force animating its potential voicings.

Sebastiaan Faber pointed out in 2013 that Cernuda paid his debt of gratitude to his American hosts "como solo lo puede hacer un poeta" [as only a poet can pay it] ("Español" n. pag.). Indeed, if "1936" resonates in Faber's ears as "el mejor poema que hay" [the best poem there is] about the 2,800 Americans who fought in the International Brigades, it is largely because the poem becomes memorably arresting in its sheer textual specificity ("Español" n. pag.). Whatever the combination of the terms history and memory may evoke today, the *historical memory* of the Spanish Civil War and its tragic aftermath can hardly be a productive critical category without an understanding of the complex modes of remembrance woven into the poems of Republican exiles like Cernuda. Examining the patterns of poetic memory inscribed in "1936" lets readers give Cernuda and the "antiguo soldado" another, paradoxical form of historical existence, "también después de haber vivido," in Castillo del Pino's poignant words (n. pag.).

Poetic Voice, Oblivion, Life

Max Aub remembered Cernuda's life as an exile in "Al volver del entierro de Cernuda" [On Returning from Cernuda's Burial], an obituary note signed in Mexico on 6 November 1963, a day after Cernuda's demise in Mexico City:

> Aun en España, hace treinta años, se sintió desterrado, por eso vivió casi siempre en el extranjero, a ver si daba con su patria ... Tímido, solitario, tuvo que escribir cuanto no dijo; la palabra viva sólo muerta le salía. Condenado "a gozar y a sufrir en silencio la amarga y divina embriaguez, incomunicable e inefable," dijo ese mal como nadie de su tiempo, porque para él nunca hubo diferencia entre la vida y la muerte. ¡Qué solos se quedan los vivos!, pudo haber escrito ... [E]xtraño entre extraños murió en casa amiga – mas no en la suya – ; en tierra extranjera, extranjero. (31)
>
> [Even in Spain, thirty years ago, he felt *desterrado*, that's why he almost always lived in foreign places, to see if he found his fatherland ... Shy, solitary, he had to write whatever he did not say; the living word only dead came out of him. Condemned "to enjoy and to suffer in silence the bitter and divine intoxication, incommunicable and ineffable," he spoke that ill like no one else in his time, because for him there was never a difference between life and death. The living are left so lonely! he could have written ... A stranger among strangers, he died in a friendly home – albeit not in his – in a foreign land, a foreigner.]

Striking a baroquely epitaphic note, Aub underscored the multiple lines – timelines, borderlines, even vocal lines – that the various senses of exile threaded into Cernuda's speaking and writing uncannily crossed even before the civil war broke out in Spain. Almost presciently, Cernuda penned the explicitly historically oriented poem "Díptico español" only a few months before writing "1936" and with just two years of life ahead of him.

Using the present tense of lyric address, the speaker in this poem hauntingly instructs himself and his readers to listen to the diverse plurivocal, non-chronological music of poetic memory: "Hablan en el poeta voces varias: / Escuchemos su coro concertado / Adonde la creída dominante / Es tan solo una voz entre las otras" [Various voices speak in the poet: / Let's listen to their concerted choir / Where the one believed to be dominant / Is just one voice among many] (*Obra II* 501). When "1936" is read today, past and present voices seem to fleetingly constellate together to conjure a self-elegiac image of history where at least two ghosts, "aquel hombre" and "este hombre," approach each other in the here and now of remembrance (Benjamin, *The Arcades* 463). In this way, without being deprived of his "dignidad de alto personaje en destierro," Cernuda gains a new "forma de existencia" (Castilla del Pino n. pag.). If only incompletely and disjointedly, the "voces varias" of the poet's personae, as well as his "voz entre las otras," can also be remembered through the verbal fabric of a single line. Thus,

Cernuda invites us to reanimate his various "forma[s] de existencia" by means of poetic memory.

And yet his poetry is also shot through with obscurity, ignorance, and oblivion. As the "I" in "A un poeta futuro" [To a Future Poet] defiantly tells the reader:

Tú no conocerás cómo domo mi miedo
Para hacer de mi voz mi valentía,
Dando al olvido inútiles desastres
Que pululan en torno y pisotean
Nuestra vida con estúpido gozo,
La vida que serás y que yo casi he sido. (*Obra II* 341–2)[36]

Cernuda wrote "A un poeta futuro" in 1947, during his early exile in Great Britain, five years before he moved to Mexico City. The poem is profoundly informed by his reading of *Four Quartets*: its moods and motifs vividly echo T.S. Eliot's own concerted choir regarding the inextricable meshes of time, memory, and knowledge.[37] The obscure form of remembrance specific to "A un poeta futuro" both hinders and haunts reading and voicing. On the one hand, the poem exposes readers, as Brian McGrath has argued, "to a certain not-knowing about how to proceed with reading," while, on the other, it also invites its own animation through the reader (7). This difficulty is deictically foregrounded when the "I" addressing the future poet refers to "mi voz," and contrasts it to "olvido." The future poet is told that it is not possible to know the ways in which the "I" differentiated between "mi voz" and "olvido," since all the reader will know about the "I"'s enigmatic "vida" when he or she voices the poem will be – in Aub's terms – "lo escrito."

To Cernuda, then, a reader cannot fully know "lo vivo" of the "I" in the simple present or the simple past, but only in the future perfect tense that closes this poem: "Y habré vivido" (*Obra II* 343) [And I'll have lived (*Forbidden* 307)]. This future perfect is a ghostly tense whereby the poetic "I" is able to live in posterity, in another time and in another place, beyond the chronology of history, whether national or not – "sin tierra y sin gente, / Escritor bien extraño" – and be remembered as "una sombra" [a shadow] in "lo escrito." The future perfect is, at least in this case, the tense of poetic memory, whereby the dead poet can be remembered, as a textual form of survival, when the reader begins voicing "habré vivido," and yet somehow feels that voice coming from "el fondo vivo en tu entraña" (*Obra II* 342–3) [the living / Depths of your being] (307)]. This half-remembered life may also be, enigmatically enough, "nuestra vida."

CHAPTER SIX

Max Aub

I. "ENCLOSED INTO MYSELF, PURBLIND, MUTE" – MARGINS OF THE POETIC "I" AND TESTIMONIAL MEMORY

Max Aub Mohrenwitz occupies an eccentric, even exceptional position in twentieth-century Spanish political and cultural history. Throughout the twists and turns of the historical circumstances that he experienced from his birth in Paris in 1903 to his death in Mexico City in 1972, Aub was, in a sense, always an exile. The combination of his specific ethnic, geographic, and linguistic conditions contributed to a relative estrangement or instability of his identity. In 1967, Octavio Paz stressed the inadequacy of nationality as a framework for approaching Aub's exilic writings: Aub was not just "un ejemplo de español hispanoamericano" [an example of a Hispanic-American Spaniard], but also "uno de los pocos escritores verdaderamente europeos de España" [one of the few truly European writers in Spain]; therefore, Paz concluded, "también es un escritor mexicano" [he is also a Mexican writer] (Marichal and Paz 43). Extrapolating from Paul Gilroy's idea that some identities can be more appropriately approached in terms not only of roots but, primarily, of routes, Aub's multifaceted figure may be characterized as one of other-rootedness and other-routedness (19). From this standpoint and given that poetic memory moves irrepressibly across spatiotemporal boundaries (Ramazani, "Lines" 310–11), Aub's exilic writings, and particularly his poetry, provide an enticing invitation to study the tensions between poetry and national identity in the framework of Republican cultural productions.

Max Aub was born to a German sales agent, Friedrich Aub, and the French-born Susanne Mohrenwitz. His father's family can be traced back to an eighteenth-century Jewish community in German Franconia (Zepp 170). At the outbreak of the First World War, Aub's family moved to Valencia, Spain, where he, aged eleven and a speaker of French and German, learned Spanish.[1] About a year later, in 1915, he reportedly wrote his first poem, in Spanish; when he turned twenty, he decided to become a Spanish citizen (*Cuerpos* 275). Aub visited Madrid for the first time in 1923, where he met the authors that he would later identify as "mi generación" [my generation] (276). The cultural field of prewar Madrid was broadly defined by the members and associates of the renowned *generación del 27* with whom Aub became acquainted in those years, such as Rafael Alberti, José Bergamín, Luis Buñuel, Federico García Lorca, Jorge Guillén, María Teresa León, José Moreno Villa, Emilio Prados, or María Zambrano. Yet, in a poem titled "Nosotros, entonces" [Us, Then], published in Mexico in 1968, Aub detailed, line by line, different positions in this lively community, such as Luis Cernuda's relative standoffishness and his own constant marginality: "La verdad es que fuimos buenas gentes / en general, Cernuda un poco aparte. / (Dalí entra en cuenta por la Residencia) / Yo no contaba, siempre tan de viaje" [The truth is that we were good folks / in general, Cernuda somewhat apart. / (Dalí is taken into the account because of the *Residencia*) / I did not count, always travelling so much] (268).[2]

A few months after the outbreak of the Spanish Civil War, Aub moved to Paris to serve as the cultural attaché for the Spanish Republican government's embassy. Back in Spain in 1937, he was appointed general secretary of the National Theater Council directed by Antonio Machado. In 1938–9 he worked with André Malraux on the film *Espoir: Sierra de Teruel* – the script was based on Malraux's novel *L'Espoir*, which Aub would later translate into Spanish. In February 1939, when Franco's troops occupied Barcelona, Aub returned again to Paris. About a year later, on the eve of the Nazi occupation of the French capital, he was anonymously and falsely denounced as a "sujeto peligroso," "hebreo de nacionalidad alemana," "nacionalizado español," "comunista y revolucionario de acción" [dangerous subject, Hebrew of German nationality, nationalized Spaniard, communist involved in revolutionary action] (*Diarios* 45). After his arrest, Aub spent more than two years imprisoned in jails and camps. In 1940, he was taken to the Roland Garros internment camp, in Paris. Shortly after, he was confined in Le Vernet, one of the camps set up in southern France for refugees from the Spanish Civil War. In 1941, he was sent to the Djelfa concentration camp in Algeria. When he was finally released in 1942, Aub fled to Mexico, where he lived for the remainder of his life.

On 2 August 1945, only a few days after the Potsdam Declaration – when Republican exiles still hoped that the Allied forces would put an end to Franco's repressive regime and enable them to return to Spain – Aub recorded in his diary an agonized description of his fate. Emphatically, he underscored the dangers of nationalism:

> ¡Qué daño no me ha hecho, en nuestro mundo cerrado, el no ser de ninguna parte! El llamarme como me llamo, con nombre y apellido que lo mismo pueden ser de un país que de otro ... En estas horas de nacionalismo cerrado el haber nacido en París, y ser español, tener padre español nacido en Alemania, madre parisina, pero de origen también alemán, pero de apellido eslavo, y hablar con ese acento francés que desgarra mi castellano, ¡qué daño no me ha hecho! (*Diarios* 128–9)

[It has been so painful to me, in our closed-minded world, to be from nowhere! To have the name I have, with a first name and a last name which could be from any country ... In these times of narrow-minded nationalism, to have been born in Paris, and to be Spanish, to have a Spanish father who was born in Germany, and a Parisian mother, also of German origin, but with a Slavic last name, and to speak with a French accent that tears my Castilian Spanish apart – all this has caused me much pain!]

Aub's self-description points to his indeterminate national and linguistic identity in the tragic sociopolitical and cultural circumstances of mid-twentieth-century Europe, and by extension, to his eccentricity in the twenty-first-century Spanish cultural landscape. Aub felt the effects of alienation and uprootedness on his life, work, and political activism.[3]

Aub wrote and published prolifically during his long exile. A large part of his literary production after 1939 was devoted to the Spanish Civil War and the various forms of repression, internment, banishment, death, and oblivion that resulted from it. In Mexico, Aub published, over a period of about twenty-five years, the six instalments of *El laberinto mágico* [The Magic Labyrinth], his vast cycle of testimonial fictions about the internecine conflict.[4] *El laberinto mágico* pivots around the polysemous term "campo," as the titles of the main texts make clear: *Campo cerrado* [Closed Field/Camp] (1943), *Campo de sangre* [Field/Camp of Blood] (1945), *Campo abierto* [Open Field/Camp] (1951), *Campo del Moro* [The Moor's Field/Camp] (1963), *Campo francés* [French Field/Camp] (1965), and *Campo de los almendros* [Field/Camp of Almond Trees] (1967).[5] Aub also produced extensive criticism of Mexican and transatlantic letters.[6] In 1955, he became a Mexican citizen.

In *Las vueltas* [The Returns], a play published in Mexico in 1965, Aub prefigured the problems that an exile may face in going back to the country he or she had to flee after the war: "lo terrible no es el exilio ... sino volver" [the terrible thing is not exile ... but returning] (*Obras completas: Vol. VII* 219). Four years later, in 1969, Aub was finally able to visit Spain, but for less than three months. In *La gallina ciega* [The Blind Hen], a diaristic text rewritten and published in Mexico in 1971, he further reflected on the seemingly insurmountable conflicts of returning: "Vengo – digo – no vuelvo ... Regresé y me voy. En ningún momento tuve la sensación de formar parte de este nuevo país que ha usurpado su lugar al que estuvo aquí antes" [I'm coming – I say – not coming back ... I returned and I'm leaving. At no time did I have the sense that I was part of this new country that has usurped the place of the one that was here before] (220, 595). Aub passed away in Mexico a few months later, on 22 July 1972.

Among Aub's many personal reflections on his multifaceted and indeterminate identity, there is a diary entry from 1956 about his recently granted Mexican citizenship which eloquently exemplifies his tendency to shift between positions of enunciation in his self-reflective writings: "¿Qué soy? ¿Alemán, francés, español, mexicano? ¿Qué soy? Nada ... Quise ser escritor. ¿Qué soy? ¿Novelista, dramaturgo, poeta, crítico? No soy nada ... si fueses poeta, novelista, lo que fuera, serías español, mexicano, francés o alemán. Como no lo eres, no eres nada, nada, nada: ni judío siquiera" [What am I? German, French, Spanish, Mexican? What am I? Nothing ... I wanted to be a writer. What am I? A novelist, a playwright, a poet, a critic? I am nothing ... if you were a poet, a novelist, anything whatsoever, you would be Spanish, Mexican, French, or German. Since you're none of these things, you are nothing, nothing, nothing, not even Jewish] (*Diarios* 273). Aub shifts from the first to the second person, disconcertingly relativizing his perspective on himself to the point of self-erasure.

Aub's tortuous rhetoric also points to a problematic association between nation and literary identity, as the denunciation of "nacionalismo cerrado" also implies. Indeed, this association was among the key issues Aub had to grapple with in the dramatic historical circumstances in which he lived. The questions of identity Aub lists in his diary entry were compounded, in his case, not just by his ethnic, geographic, and linguistic conditions but also by his long experience of exile. It should come as no surprise, then, that exiles in Aub's writings tend to be, as Sebastiaan Faber indicated in 2002, "creatures lost in time and space, out of sync with history. If they survive, it is at the cost of their most sincere convictions" (*Exile* 226). Among these undermined convictions is that of a stable national identity. Indeed, the intensely transnational and cross-historical voices folded into Aub's poetry reveal a uniquely shifting constellation of perspectives on belonging. Yet they do so tangentially, bringing into relief the eccentricity of Aub's testimonial rhetoric concerning the Spanish Civil War and its aftermath of repression, exile, and forgetfulness.

Poetry and Testimonial Fiction

What is the connection between poetry and testimonial rhetoric in Aub's exilic writings? This question is relevant inasmuch as the self-proclaimed "autor" [author] of *Campo de los almendros* (1967), arguably one of the most important testimonial narratives about the Spanish Civil War, mentions that it should have been "escrito en verso" [written in verse] (559).[7] This contention, which reads like a marginal note, is inserted in "Páginas azules" [Blue Pages], a ten-page excursus of meta-literary reflection on the conditions of possibility for narrating the experience of thousands of Republicans held in Francoist concentration camps in Valencia and Alicante as the conflict came to an end in March and April of 1939 (*Campo de los almendros* 566).[8] "Páginas azules" precedes the third and final section of *Campo de los almendros*, which depicts initial reactions to the insurrectionist victory and the tragic final hours of numerous characters, including inmates of the concentration camp named in the title.[9] The excursus suspends the narration at a key moment, just as the reader is about to reach the fatal denouement. This suspension is arresting, since *Campo de los almendros* is the sixth and final instalment of *El laberinto mágico.*[10] Why would "el autor" affirm poetry's value at a decisive moment in a narrative project consisting of more than 1,000 prose-dominated pages, centred on the disturbing notion of "campo"?

Aub himself characterized the six texts of *El laberinto mágico* as chronicles and testimonies (*Diarios* 236). In his view, the category of testimony included narrative and dramatic texts, but also poetic ones: "Mis *Campos* ... no son novelas sino crónicas ... Y en eso *San Juan*, *No*, *De algún tiempo a esta parte*, el *Diario de Djelfa* y tantas cosas más no son, no quieren ser otra cosa que un testimonio" [My *Campos* ... are not novels, but chronicles ... And in that sense *Saint John*, *No*, *For Some Time Now*, *Diary of Djelfa* and so many other things are not, and do not want to be, anything but testimony] (*Diarios* 236). Although Aub had been a first-hand witness to some of the events narrated in *El laberinto mágico* (Caudet, "Introducción" 49), his knowledge of the fatal events in Alicante and Valencia – the city he considered his hometown – was indirect, compiled from the testimonies of eyewitnesses (Caudet, *Galdós* 402).[11] Crucially, at the very moment that "Páginas azules" reasserts the importance of poetry in Aub's testimonial production, the text relativizes the narrator's site of poetic enunciation. At the end of the excursus, the "autor" cites one of the most important volumes of testimonial poetry about the war, César Vallejo's *España, aparta de mí este cáliz*: "Padre polvo que subes de España / Dios te salve, libere y corone, / padre polvo que asciendes del alma" [Father dust who rises from Spain / God save, free, and crown you, / father dust who rises from the soul] (*Campo de los almendros* 569). These verses, excerpted from the 1937 poem "Redoble funeral por los escombros de Durango" [Funeral Drumroll for the Rubble of Durango], are an epitaph for the memory and salvation of a Spain that at the time seemed in its death throes.

Aub first places himself behind an authorial figure; then, quietly remaining at the margin, he lets the major Peruvian poet have the last words of the excursus suspending the narration. Using the third person to distance himself even further, the "autor" has both already dwelled on the difficult relationship between words and truth in the face of death and further remarked that he considers himself a lesser poet: "si [él] acertara a inventar veinte [palabras] daría lo que siempre busca en vano" [if he managed to invent twenty words he would give what he has always searched for in vain] (*Campo de los almendros* 562). But, as he sceptically adds, "la verdad sólo es la poesía" [the truth is only poetry], "la poesía sólo son las palabras" [poetry is only words], and "la verdad poco tiene que ver con ellas" [the truth has little to do with them] (562). It is because poetry holds such truth value for the "autor" that he dismisses his own tentative poems as uninventive failures, and turns instead to the resonant funereal words of Vallejo's biblically inflected book of poems. Aub's self-reflective examination of the writer's ability to produce truthful poetry sheds light on the shifting perspectives between different poetic voices in

"Páginas azules." More generally, it illuminates the peculiar position that poetry occupies in his exilic production. Paradoxically, this position is both central and marginal.

The first half of this chapter examines Aub's idiosyncratic construction of poetic voices configuring the discourse of testimonial memory in his texts about the war. It does so by focusing on *Antología traducida*, the collection of apocryphal and semi-apocryphal poems that Aub published in Mexico in 1963, four years before *Campo de los almendros.*[12] Because *Antología traducida* contains only a few, tangential references to the Spanish Civil War, scholars tend to exclude it from Aub's historical and testimonial production.[13] This exclusion is also a product of the critical tendency to distinguish Aub's "serious" works from his "playful" ones. This dichotomous approach separates "crónicas" of the armed conflict and its consequences, like *El laberinto mágico* or *Diario de Djelfa*, from games of literary masks and apocrypha like the fictional biography *Jusep Torres Campalans* or *Antología traducida.*[14] It is precisely critical reductionism and thematic tangentiality that make *Antología traducida* a suitably marginal place to explore poetry's paradoxical position in Aub's exilic writings, as well as his rhetoric of testimonial memory.[15] This exploration demonstrates the productivity of delving into Aub's exilic production beyond merely thematic references to the war. The second half of this chapter analyses Antonio Muñoz Molina's efforts to encourage institutional and public recognition in Spain of Aub's testimonial writings about his experience of uprootedness in France, Algeria, and Mexico. Muñoz Molina tellingly overlooks Aub's poetry.

Yet Aub's poetry provides a productive approach to his rhetoric of alterity, plurivocality, and opacity, as well as his eccentric position in Spanish culture today despite efforts such as Muñoz Molina's. *Antología traducida* presents a highly elaborate construction of the witness figure. It does so while developing the dramatic dialectic between presence and absence that poetic voice enables, deictically, in testimonial rhetoric. Moreover, the figure of the apocryphal poet and translator is key for understanding Aub's construction of the witness figure. Aub relies on lyric conventions to assemble a plurality of minor poets who bring into the present the absent and/or marginal voices that history has forgotten.[16] The discursive complexity of these voices constellates around the striking textual invention of a poet named Max Aub in a semi-apocryphal poem titled "Max Aub." Situated at the threshold between historical figure and fictional character, this elusive self-portrait is "Cerrado en mí, / Cegato, mudo" [Enclosed into myself, / Purblind, mute] (*Obras completas: Vol. I* 245).

An apocryphal text can be used strategically to evoke a testimonial author that may have faded into total oblivion. Etymologically, apocryphal connotes a secret, hidden text, one not approved for public reading. It also implies an obscure, hard-to-understand book, one of unknown authorship, not taken as genuine.[17] The poetic figure "Max Aub" is semi-apocryphal in this etymological sense, to the extent that the "I" paradoxically presents himself in the text as private, encrypted, hidden away, secret, somehow absent, and even half-forgotten. The poet – enclosed into himself, purblind, and mute – describes his eyesight and voice as respectively enfeebled and gone. Thus the semi-apocryphal figure rhetorically highlights the basic traits of the witness able to give testimony – someone who saw something and is now able to present him- or herself in public and speak out – by denying them. Through rhetorical preterition, "Max Aub" occupies a memorable site of enunciation by both claiming and disclaiming the possibility of testimony. These paradoxes raise challenging questions about the historical and testimonial importance of his exilic writings and about the feasibility of remembering and recovering minor voices from the past.

Relatedly, in the purportedly original poems assembled in *Antología traducida*, editorial figures mediate the traces of surviving voices. "Max Aub" stands not only for a semi-apocryphal and semi-forgotten writer but also for the anthologist and translator. These editorial figures complicate the sense of presence that the first-person speaker in a lyrical poem conventionally conveys to the reader (Brewster 35). The poems included in *Antología traducida*, which the anthologist has rescued, collected, and translated, are described as remnants of an uncertain textual and material history. The fragility and fleetingness of these fragments left behind by minor poets are evidence of the danger of extinction and oblivion that threatens every historical document. Consequently, the vestigial character of these poems reinforces the tension between an event described in Aub's foreword to *Diario de Djelfa* as "real sucedido" [real as what happened], and the historical and testimonial discourses informing his exilic writings (*Obras completas: Vol. I* 93). This sense of danger invites reading *Antología traducida* as a sort of vanishing point in the witness's vision and power of speech. Aub configures a dramatically heteroglossic discursive space where the voices of marginal, obscure poets become precarious. Each reader of Aub's anthology is for this reason all the more pressingly interpellated to remember and recover these voices from the oblivion to which history supposedly condemns them.

At the same time, the precarious and fragmentary articulation of these testimonies renders any speech act of recovery virtually self-defeating. After all, the poetic voices of these dead authors are apocryphal. Their absence is therefore twofold. Their intrinsic obscurity, secretiveness, and falsity underscore the irreparable absence of the dead. In this sense, Aub's seemingly playful poems aim at the serious, perhaps unavoidable, yet unfulfillable task of retrieving the irretrievable. *Antología traducida* can therefore be read as a series of epitaphs, in line with Aub's meditation on the relationship between death and writing in his necrological, ghostly tribute to León Felipe: "También los muertos escriben; tal vez la tierra no es más que residuos de manuscritos" [The dead also write; perhaps the earth is nothing but the remains of manuscripts] ("León Felipe" 15). As we saw earlier, lyric conventions allow the reader of a poem to occupy the place of the poetic speaker, enabling him or her to bring the voices of the past into the present. The spatio-temporal deixis in "Max Aub," for instance, brings to readers' minds not only their future absence but also their potential semi-apocryphal future: readers are likely to become obscure, hard-to-understand, half-forgotten entities as well. In this light, the apocryphal or semi-apocryphal quality of the poetic voices assembled and translated by Aub produces a general sense of historical disruption. It therefore becomes vitally important to study the different ways in which the play of voices staged in *Antología traducida* is linked to the narrative fiction that Aub conceived in exile as a testimony of the Spanish Civil War's tragedy.

Jorge Manrique's *Ubi Sunt*: Poetic Memory in Testimonial Fiction

In *Campo de los almendros*, historical and fictional characters embody the Republican victims of Francoist persecution. However, instead of analysing issues resulting from this combination of characters – for example, "los problemas de la novela y la historia; del arte y la realidad" [the problems of the novel and history/story; of art and reality] – the "autor" of "Páginas azules" wonders about the future existence of the "treinta mil posibles protagonistas" [30,000 possible protagonists] of the war (*Campo de los almendros* 564, 563). Although he also wants to record "lo sucedido" [what happened] in Alicante (565), the "autor" focuses on these figures because they are "algo más que historia" [something more than history/story] (561). He hopes that his testimonial work will allow them to persist beyond the strictly historical circumstances of their tragedy: "quisiera que sólo quedaran – desnudos – " [I would want them to just linger – naked –] (564–5). Only the written record of this undefined form of unveiling can provide posterity with "una idea de la realidad" [an idea of the reality] that these "posibles protagonistas" experienced (561).

However, after writing hundreds of pages of testimonial fiction, the "autor" acknowledges his inability to attest to the particular experiences that his all-too-numerous "protagonistas" lived through and goes on to vent his frustration through rhetorical questions: "¿qué hacen, qué piensan todos estos personajes, todos estos que son y fueron?" [what do they do, what do they think, all these characters, all of them who are and were?] (*Campo de los almendros* 564). In addition, the "autor" acknowledges that something else prevents his characters – fictional or historical, anonymous or named – from enduring: oblivion. People die for a second time as those who knew them, or knew of them, during their lifetimes gradually lose their memories: "la gente existe mientras vive. Luego empieza lentamente a morir en los demás. Desaparece, teñida de sombras, en el olvido" [people exist while they live. Then they slowly begin to die in others. They disappear, tinged by shadows, into oblivion] (565). Yet another hindrance, associated with this gradual loss of memory, is the shift in perspective brought about by the years that these "historias" [histories/stories] accumulate and by "la manera de contarlas" [the way of telling them] (565).

Similarly, the narrator of *Luis Buñuel, novela* [Luis Buñuel, a Novel] dwells on the intricate relationship between posterity, perspective, and memory: "no permanece uno como lo que es – como lo que fue – sino como lo ven – como le vieron – los demás" [one does not endure as one is – as one was – but rather as others see – as others saw – one] (26). Aub had not completed his novelized biography of Luis Buñuel when he died in 1972. Presciently, this text contrasts the oblivion of those left behind by history to the fragile permanence that elegiac poems allow readers to imagine: "Fuimos; no somos historia. La historia está hecha de ceniza. No somos viejos ni siquiera arrinconados; sencillamente la gente olvida. Desaparecemos y los trenos y las elegías solo quedan por caridad" [We were; we are not history. History is made of ash. We are not old or even set aside; people simply forget. We disappear and the lamentations and the elegies are only for charity] (*Luis Buñuel* 27).[18] To Aub, or at least to his narrative figures, the writing of history and testimony is moulded by memory and point of view – crucial elements in every account of the past – so much so that it requires the aid not only of fiction but also, and above all, of poetry.[19]

In *Campo de los almendros*, the excursus "Páginas azules" offers an authorial meditation on the difficulties involved in giving an account of the lived experiences of the war's multiple protagonists, but it does so by dramatically shifting back and forth between a first-person site of enunciation and a more distant third-person position, as if Aub wanted to deictically emphasize the relativity of the witness's perspective. The "autor" declares that he ought to "abrir miles de cráneos" [open up thousands of skulls] to narrate the "miles de pensamientos enrevesados" [thousands of convoluted thoughts] and explain "las torturas, las esperanzas, los desengaños" [the tortures, the hopes, the disillusions] (*Campo de los almendros* 561). To the "autor," the inner lives of his characters are surrounded by darkness. Indeed, shadows close in on *El laberinto mágico* from the very first words of the narration. Its densely baroque first instalment – titled, significantly, *Campo cerrado* – begins with an impersonal and/or reflexive action that produces darkness: "De pronto se apagan las luces" [Suddenly the lights go out] (15).

Moreover, in the author's remarks added to the back cover of *La gallina ciega* in 1971 – four years after *Campo de los almendros* – a punctuation mark gives the reader pause, as though the relativity of testimonial vision needed to be considered at the syntactic level: "Pero eso vi. Acaso, ciego (o sin coma)" [But I saw that. Perchance, blind (or without the comma)] (n. pag.). To remove the comma between "acaso" [perchance/chance] and "ciego" [blind] would be to further complicate the impression of blindness. The unforeseen, unmotivated causes darkening the vision of the past remain outside of the witness's purview, and therefore outside of the light that narrative testimony of "lo sucedido" could possibly shed. Indeed, *La gallina ciega* chronicles Aub's perception of the different forms of oblivion that many Spaniards suffered as a result of Franco's dictatorship. This diaristic text intensifies the tortuous play of light and shadows that characterizes the symbolic maze experienced by the civil war's victims, which Aub narrates in *El laberinto mágico* (Caudet, "Introduction" 28).

Aub inserts himself among these victims as an exile who, after temporarily returning to Spain thirty years after the war, issues a disconsolate judgment marked, once again, by blindness: "España con los ojos vendados, los brazos extendidos, buscando inútilmente a sus compañeros o hijos, dando manotazos al aire, perdida ... Tal vez los ciegos seamos sus hijos. Quizá la Gallina Ciega soy yo" [Spain blindfolded, arms outstretched, uselessly searching for her friends or children, smacking the air, lost ... Perhaps we her children are the blind ones. Maybe I am the Blind Hen] (n. pag.). Aub associates the relativity of point of view with blindness, and believes that every witness suffers the relative blindness of seeing only from a particular angle: "Nadie ve todo igual, es decir todos ciegos, y sin contar que no somos cíclopes y dos, cuatro, seis ojos ven más que uno, pero siempre desde ángulos distintos" [No one sees everything the same, so we are all blind; we are not cyclopes and two, four, six eyes see more than one, but always from different angles] (qtd. in Sánchez Zapatero 207). Paradoxically, that which the witness's vision can reveal is darkness.

In this vein, "Páginas azules" addresses the inability of the "autor" to gain access to the interiority of the historical and fictional characters in *Campo de los almendros*. It does so early in the excursus, through an anaphoric set of rhetorical questions: "¿Qué ha sido de Azaña, de Companys, de Negrín, de Prieto, de Miaja? ¿Qué fue de Salomar, de Cuartero, de Templado? ¿Qué de Pilar, de Asunción, de Teresa, de Tula?" [What has become of Azaña, Companys, Negrín, Prieto, and Miaja? What happened to Salomar, Cuartero, and Templado? What about Pilar, Asunción, Teresa, and Tula?] (*Campo de los almendros* 559). Confronting extinction and forgetting, the "autor" asks these questions in a memorably intertextual way, drawing on Jorge Manrique's widely quoted elegiac formula from his *Coplas a la muerte de su padre* [Verses on the Death of His Father]. One of the most unforgettable verses from the *Coplas*, the rhetorical question "¿Qué se hizo el rey don Juan?" [Whatever happened to King Don Juan?], is inserted in the text a few pages later (565).[20] The set of rhetorical questions that the "autor" asks at this moment amounts to a catalogue of absences. This is consistent with the *ubi sunt* topos – the medieval and Renaissance poetic motif reflecting on mortality and the transience of life (Hornsby, Brogan, and Warren 214).

By interweaving one of the most prominent instances of early modern elegiac poetry into the texture of his testimonial fiction, the "autor" of the narrative goes beyond recording a historically situated event. He relies on his cross-boundary and cross-historical poetic memory to invite a more general reflection on death, forgetting, and fleetingness.[21] By resorting to the *ubi sunt* topos, Aub broadens the scope of the commemorative effort in his narrative cycle.[22] Nevertheless, the use of this poetic motif also highlights the historical limitations of testimonial memory. As Susan Stewart argued in *Poetry and the Fate of the Senses*, the *ubi sunt* tradition speaks to "the farthest reaches of sensual apprehension, the point where such apprehension trails into unintelligibility and disappearance and so where memory turns to imagination" (216). The "autor" of "Páginas azules" is therefore also encouraging reflection on the future of his testimonial memory and – since this mode of memory is conventionally tied to sense-perception – on the sensorial dimensions of rhetoric. If *Campo de los almendros* is interpreted as testimonial fiction, in what forms will its future readers remember victims such as the last president of the Second Republic, Manuel Azaña, who died in exile in 1940, shortly after he fled to France when Barcelona fell to Francoist troops?

One possible answer to this question is poetic memory: the sheer materiality of the rhetorical questions asked by the now Manrique-like "autor" may invite readers to utter – albeit silently, under their breath – the names of the victims. This poetic animation of the reader brings absent, ghostly voices from the past into the present of enunciation. In fact, they are doubly absent, since the "autor" inscribes them in his fiction in epitaphic form. Immediately after the opening paragraph of the excursus (in which the "autor" asks the above-mentioned rhetorical questions), he explicitly underscores the epitaphic quality of his testimonial writing: "El autor no está seguro más que de los muertos; los entierra – los de verdad – con lápida y todo" [The author is only sure about the dead; he buries them – the true ones – with gravestone and all] (*Campo de los almendros* 559). The double absence of the voices from the past is further complicated by the presence of fictional characters like Julián Templado in the same set of rhetorical questions: "¿Qué ha sido de Azaña, de Companys, de Negrín, de Prieto, de Miaja? ¿Qué fue de Salomar, de Cuartero, de Templado?" (559).

Among the voices from the past is also the voice of the "autor" himself. Reflections on fleetingness, death, and the historical limits of testimonial memory built into Aub's fiction inflect the construction of this authorial "I." In 1968, a few months before he completed *El laberinto mágico*, Aub remarked on the connection between writing and his concern with posterity in his diary: "Escribo para seguir aquí cuando haya muerto" [I write to remain here after I have died] (*Diarios* 380–1). Aub's interest in the future remembrance of the protagonists of *Campo de los almendros* is refracted through a reflexive split between the "autor" and the "I."[23] The rhetorical questions inserted in the first paragraph of "Páginas azules" ask about the location of the "autor," but they do so with reference to the locations of people that he knew, who contributed to his testimonial fiction: "¿Dónde quedan Chabás, Sánchez Ventura, Hemingway, Paulino, yo, Medina, los centenares, los miles que me sirvieron?" [Where are Chabás, Sánchez Ventura, Hemingway, Paulino, I, Medina, the hundreds, the thousands that helped me?] (*Campo de los almendros* 559). Located in the grammatical first person, the "autor" inscribes himself in the *ubi sunt* site of enunciation and draws attention to his own transience in the present tense of his elegiac aside.

When he returns to prose a few lines later, the "autor" distances himself by using the third person. The poetic invocation of the "I" amid characters about whose future memory he enquires allows the "autor" to remember and (re)present, by means of the third person framing its spectral (re)appearance, his own absent "I" – presumably that of "Max Aub." Needless to say, this "I" is the personal marker *par excellence*, the deictic that grammatically situates the first person in the text. In Aub's poetry, this grammatical indication, shifting by definition, marks the discursive place in which the testimonial historical "I," the poetic "I," and – in the case of lyric – the "I" of the reader, both converge and diverge (Jakobson 388). As these different "I"s momentarily take over the first-person site of enunciation, they activate the dialectical play between presence and absence that characterizes testimonial memory in Aub's exilic narrative.

Some Notes on Testimony

Testimony is defined as much by the presence of the witness in the place and at the time of the event as by the witness's ability to perceive (see and/or hear) the event that he or she will later recall and tell as a story. Perception, memory, and narration therefore constitute the necessary conditions of testimony. However, these same conditions generate doubt as to whether testimony is able to tell the truth (Ricoeur 164). Far from contradicting this definition of testimony, the blindness and destabilization of the place of the "I" underscore it, highlighting the vanishing point in the field of vision that makes testimony possible. Further, as Paul Ricoeur explained, when a person designates him- or herself a witness, the "I" shows "the inextricable opacity of a personal history that itself has been 'enmeshed in stories'" (164). Aub not only saw that the failures of memory and the relativity of point of view complicated testimonial writing. He also remarked on the narrative density – and potential opacity – resulting from the discursive condition of the autobiographical "I": "las notas y los recuerdos que acumulé necesitarían cien años de vida para resolverse en libros" [it would take me 100 years to arrange my accumulated notes and memories into books] (*Cuerpos* 278). The narrator of *Luis Buñuel, novela* speculates on this discursive condition: "traslado, omito, remedo y – en caso extremo – retrato (lo cual es falsedad, cosa de la que huí en lo posible). ¿Cómo ajustar la copia a un original vivo?" [I shift things around, I omit, I imitate, and – in extreme cases – I portray (which is deceit, something I avoided whenever possible). How can I adjust the copy to a living original?] (25).

As Jacques Derrida contended, testimonial rhetoric implies the possibility of literature, or at least the possibility of "simulacra, dissimulation, lie, and perjury" ("Demeure" 29). The literary or fictional element in Aub's understanding of testimony is as crucial as it is complex: "Testimonié. Ahora cada día, creo que la ficción es el único medio posible (útil) de hollar, de dejar rastro, de testimoniar" [I gave testimony. Now every day, I believe that fiction is the only (useful) possible way to tread, to leave a trace, to give testimony] (*Nuevos* 209). Darkness, or, more precisely, the play of light and shadow – of presence and absence – traceable in testimonial writing accounts for the variety of lapses, distortions, and shifts of perspective that, to Aub, make it fiction: "la novela no es sino reducir a memoria lo olvidado o imaginado que viene a ser, para los demás, lo mismo pero siempre desde ángulos distintos" [the novel is nothing more than the reduction to memory of what has been forgotten or imagined that becomes, for others, the same thing, but always from different angles] (qtd. in Sánchez Zapatero 207).

Under conventional generic definitions, the marked literariness of poetry would seem to depart from the representational purpose of the discursive practices associated with testimony (Guyer 32). Nonetheless, it is precisely literariness that allows poetry to attest to situations of traumatic violence (Suleiman 135). Slavoj Žižek has argued that testimony about a deeply violent shock cannot be expected to tell factual truth clearly, but rather to convey a sense of truthfulness through unreliability, confusion, and inconsistency (5). Accordingly, indirect, oblique, even obscure discursive approaches to traumatic violence may be more suitable to giving "una idea de la realidad" that many Spanish Republicans suffered. Focusing on testimony about the concentration camps, Žižek has also maintained that where realistic prose fails, poetic evocation may succeed, since poetry always revolves around something that cannot be "addressed directly, only alluded to" (5). Likewise, Shoshana Felman and Dori Laub claimed in 1992 that the fragmentation that defines the poetry of Stéphane Mallarmé or Paul Celan makes it an apt form of testimony; unlike the closed coherence of factual truth, such poetic language "does not possess itself as a conclusion, as the contestation of a verdict or the self-transparency of knowledge" (5). As shall be seen, the fragmentation of the testimonial "I" and the poetic "I" in Aub's *Antología traducida* raises at least two important questions in this regard: First, is there an appropriate and definable site of enunciation for the witness? Second, what discursive practice can adequately attest to the disruptive memory of past violence in the here and now of reading?

Absence is constitutive of testimony. The witness is defined by personal presence in the past, according to the testimonial formula "I was there" (Ricoeur 163). A structural fissure then opens between the witness and each testimony: that witnesses were present at the event means that absence shapes their account every time they give testimony (LaCapra 61). As Derrida also argued, witnesses are no longer present to what they perceived: they constitutively remember their presence as an absence (*Sovereignities* 76). Aub tends to situate the witness in a secondary and/or marginal place (a form of discursive absence that creates a blind spot in the testimonial account) and the protagonists of the event in a central place. In fictions seemingly unrelated to his testimonial impulse like *Jusep Torres Campalans*, Aub offers a clear-cut definition of the narrator's displaced site of enunciation: "Escribí mi relación, valiéndome de otros, dejándome aparte" [I wrote my account, availing myself of others, leaving myself aside] (644).

All these elements – the dialectical play between presence and absence (or centre and margin), the marked sense of literariness, the indirect approach to violence, the staging of fragmentation and blindness, and the discursive destabilization of the first person's site of enunciation – are foregrounded in *Antología traducida.* The constellation of voices encountered in this collection of poems is thus deeply informed by Aub's rhetoric of testimonial memory.

Voices and Voicing in *Antología traducida*

Published in 1962, when Aub lived in Mexico, *Antología traducida* collects poems by seventy-nine apocryphal and semi-apocryphal authors like Teodoro Bar Adda (247–72) or Vladimiro Nabukov (1871–2). Each poem is preceded by a brief biographical sketch notable for its "abundante erudición ficticia" [abundant fictitious erudition] (Gracia and Ródenas 491). In the foreword to the collection, the anthologist and translator, Max Aub, warns that the assembled poets are "menores" [minor] and the chosen poems "segundones" [second-rate] works that he found "husmeando aquí y allá" [poking about here and there], "semiborrados de toda memoria" [partially erased from all memory] (*Obras completas: Vol. I* 166–7). Notwithstanding the marginal – even negligible – place of these poets and their poems in history, the collection so resembles a history of international poetry that it has been called "una antología lírica universal" [a universal anthology of the lyric] (Gracia and Ródenas 491).

Despite the poems' supposedly inferior status, the anthologist praises them, deems them "tan buenos como los mejores" [as good as the best], and describes his collection as having a representative and historical quality (*Obras completas: Vol. I* 167–8). A salient feature of *Antología traducida* is geographic heterogeneity and movement. Estelle Irizarry pointed out that Aub's collection offers a "vertiginosa mezcla de nacionalidades, países de residencia y viajes" [dizzying mix of nationalities, countries of residence, and travels] (114). Its linguistic and spatiotemporal scope is far-reaching. Historically, it covers poets from the fourteenth century BCE to the twentieth century CE. Aub collects works by poets from every continent except Australia and Antarctica; the sketches that precede the poems refer to more than thirty-five countries, ethnicities, and/or cultures. *Antología traducida* is therefore a sterling example of Aub's border-crossing, cross-historical, plurivocal, and multilingual writing.

The first-person-singular speaker predominates throughout *Antología traducida.* Of the 124 poems comprising the collection, fewer than fifteen dispense with the grammatical first or second person. As a result, in keeping with generic conventions, the anthology can be characterized as a collection of lyric poems (Jackson 833). Although it may seem hard to find a common denominator for such a diverse assortment of poets, a constellation of shared concerns nonetheless emerges: identity, alienation, persecution, exile, itinerancy, ephemerality, death, and oblivion, as well as the relationships between poetry and survival (or salvation), and lies and truth. The resulting composite figure recalls other, more personal texts by Aub where he offers a fragmentary and multifaceted portrait of himself as a marginal writer. "¿Por qué ando lejos de todos los convites?" Aub wondered in his diaries. "¿Por qué soy el 'raro'?" [Why am I left out of all the get-togethers? Why am I the "strange" one?] (*Diarios* 108).

Likewise, in a 1951 letter to French president Vincent Auriol, Aub summarized his feelings of insecurity, alienation, and personal estrangement resulting from exile. French authorities denied Aub a visa to visit his country of origin because he had been falsely denounced in 1940 and the collaborationist police of Vichy had him on file at the time:

> Que lo que diga la ficha sea verdad o no, [esto es] lo que importa, lo que entra en juego. Es decir, que yo, mi persona, lo que pienso, lo que siento, no es la verdad. La verdad es lo que está escrito. ... Es decir, que lo que vive de verdad son los personajes y no las personas ... Yo, Max Aub, no existo: el que vive es el peligroso comunista que un soplón denunció un día ... Ése soy yo, y no yo, Max Aub, ése que yo conozco y con quien estoy hablando. (*Hablo* 113–16)
>
> [Whether or not the file tells the truth is, [this is] what matters, what is at stake. That is to say, I, my person, what I think, what I feel, is not the truth. The truth is what is written ... That is to say, what truly lives is the characters and not the people ... I, Max Aub, do not exist: he who lives is the dangerous communist that a snitch denounced one day ... That is me, and not me, Max Aub, the one that I know and with whom I am speaking.]

In 2004, Sebastiaan Faber emphasized the ways in which this letter could be associated to the apocryphal biography *Jusep Torres Campalans*. He argued that it contains a meditation on the dialectic between lies and truth shaping the discourse of history in Aub's writings: "For Aub, the only way of getting to the truth, be it historical or personal, is not through serious, explicitly documentary texts that are invested with the authority of more or less repressive institutions" ("The Truth" 244).[24] Indeed, as one of the epigraphs in the opening pages of *Jusep Torres Campalans* reads, "¿Cómo puede haber verdad sin mentira?" [How can there be truth without lies?] (9).

Faber went on to argue that, to a monolithic State-supported truth founded on the risky assumption that texts can "represent or even replace reality itself," Aub opposes his own truth, which can only be reached through realist, ironic, and self-referential fiction ("The Truth" 244). "Páginas azules" exemplifies this approach. Yet, when its "autor" wants to talk about "la verdad," his self-referential voice turns to poetry. *Antología traducida* is laced with similar reflections on the relationship between truth and lies, history and fiction, and identity and alienation. These reflections reach the reader in refracted and fragmentary fashion, through the numerous and heterogeneous voices folded into its diverse poems. The dominant use of the first-person-singular position underscores Aub's characteristic, uncanny site of testimonial enunciation.

Together, the various voices conveyed by the translator of the anthology enable readers to piece together a portrait of Aub characterized by linguistic density, heterogeneity, and instability. In 1964 – two years after publishing *Antología Traducida* – Aub explained his own transnational linguistic singularity: "Ni alemán, ni francés, ni español, ni mexicano; o francés, alemán, español, mexicano ... Nacido en París, crecido en Valencia, hablando en español – que sé escribir – con acento francés, hablo francés – que no sé escribir – como si lo fuera y pronuncio perfectamente el alemán, qué no sé hablar" [Not German, not French, not Spanish, not Mexican; or French, German, Spanish, Mexican ... Born in Paris, raised in Valencia, speaking in Spanish – which I can write – with a French accent, I speak French – which I cannot write – as if I were French, and I pronounce German perfectly, though I cannot speak it] (*Diarios* 128–9).[25] Aub's linguistic singularity is dramatized by the different accents, languages, idiolects, linguistic codes, textual histories, and communication disorders that lend a family air to works as different from each other as "Manuscrito Cuervo: Historia de Jacobo" [Crow Manuscript: Jacobo's Story/History] (1952), *Las buenas intenciones* [Good Intentions] (1954), *Jusep Torres Campalans* (1958), "La verdadera historia de la muerte de Francisco Franco" [The True Story/History of the Death of Francisco Franco] (1960), *La calle de Valverde* [Valverde Street] (1961), and the unfinished *Luis Buñuel, novela.*[26]

As for *Antología traducida,* its title appropriately prefigures the rhetoric of multiplicity and alterity through which it dramatizes linguistic density, heterogeneity, and instability. In 1996, Antonio Carreño stressed the importance of this volume for any critical approach to Aub's self-representation as a writer when he called *Antología traducida* "un mágico retablo (a modo de epitafios) de las múltiples más/caras de Max Aub, lector de otros textos, como traductor, antólogo, crítico, biógrafo y poeta" [a magical tableau (by way of epitaphs) of the multiple faces/masks of Max Aub, reader of other texts, as a translator, anthologist, critic, biographer, and poet] ("Hacia una morfología" 143). Other critics have nonetheless downplayed the historical thrust of *Antología traducida* by emphasizing its comical tones.[27] Yet in the context of Aub's ethnic, geographic, and linguistic multifariousness after almost twenty-five years of exile, the fictitious translation of poems allegedly composed in dozens of different times, places, and languages points beyond a mere linguistic game. Humour in *Antología traducida* reads in this sense as a many-sided reflection on what James Valender referred to in 2006 as the "dolorosa historia" [painful history] of Aub's experience of cultural dislocation ("Max Aub" 278).[28] Additionally, other exilic texts cast indirect light on the historical situatedness of *Antología traducida*: in "Manuscrito Cuervo: Historia de Jacobo," for example, the complex relationship between biography and linguistic play, although analogous to that of the anthology, takes on a more sombre undertone.[29]

Rhetorically and thematically, the poems of *Antología traducida,* together with the biographical notes preceding them, can be examined as a multiperspectival sequence grappling with some of Aub's aforementioned concerns. The first, anonymous poem in the collection is prefaced by a short description stressing the likely ideological underpinnings of the composition, "sin duda de la época de Amenofis IV, en el que rezuma un curioso anticlericalismo, probable consecuencia de la perdida de las provincias sirias" [undoubtedly from the time of Amenhotep IV, in which a curious anticlericalism seeps out, probably a consequence of the loss of the Syrian provinces] (*Obras completas: Vol. I* 170). The poem is constructed as an apostrophic address to the Egyptian sun god Ra. It can thus be read as prosopopoeia – in Paul de Man's terms, "the fiction of an apostrophe to an absent, deceased, or voiceless entity, which posits the possibility of the latter's reply and confers upon it the power of speech" ("Autobiography" 926). But this anonymous poem not only enables the animation of the voiceless sun in the present of reading; it also introduces a trans-historical note on fleetingness in its denunciation of those priests who, uninterested in truth, forget that "la noche vence, y la muerte" [night wins, death too] (*Obras completas: Vol. I* 170).

A few pages later, the Chinese poet Cste Yuan Wu is given a single biographical line with only a few details recalling Aub's broader motifs: "vivió bajo la dinastía Ts'in, en el siglo III. Fue perseguido, murió joven" [he lived under the Ts'in dynasty, in the third century. He was persecuted, and died young] (*Obras completas: Vol. I* 174–5). The first of Cste Yuan Wu's three epigrammatic poems assertively dwells on movement and transience: "El hombre anda y vuelve, / pronto muere. / El árbol no se mueve, permanece" [Man walks away and returns, / he soon dies. The tree does not move, / it remains] (175). In a similar vein, banishment is an important feature of the biographical note for Julio Monega Brandão (1901–1936). This Portuguese poet was, remarkably, one of the few poets personally known to the anthologist, presumably because he was "desterrado largos años en Madrid, donde murió de mala manera" [exiled for many years in Madrid, where he died in a bad way] (240). Monega Brandão's three poems draw on the Book of Genesis to offer different takes on the origins of human death and its relationship to language. The first poem describes how Eve realized that Adam was dead: "Aulló nombrándolo. Adán fue el primer nombre verdadero de la muerte. / Abel fue otra cosa, murió asesinado y fue enterrado" [She howled naming him. Adam was the first true name of death. / Abel was a different thing, he was murdered and was buried]. Interestingly, Abel is later described as "aventurero" [adventurer], underscoring the relationship between itinerancy and death (240–1).

About the poet Guilhaume de Bourgogne nothing seems to be known but his name. Hence, his epitaphic poem "El cementerio" [The Cemetery] presents a dark meditation on loneliness couched in apostrophic rhetoric: "sólo te acompaña la indiferencia, la saciedad, el cansancio / para los que no existe campo santo" [only indifference, weariness, and fatigue accompany you / and there is no cemetery for them] (*Obras completas: Vol. I* 200–1). With regard to exile, Teodoro Lavren, a Polish poet, creates an effect of paradoxical enclosure through epanalepsis and prosodic emphasis: "tengo una patria / y no la tengo" [I have a fatherland / and I do not have it] (232). By shifting perspectives in this way, Aub's key motifs are subtly enmeshed throughout a multiplicity of poems and biographical sketches, configuring a constellation that, nevertheless, can only be established in piecemeal, fragmentary fashion. Only one record survives of the poetry of Simón Gómez, a Portuguese Jew marked – says the anthologist and translator – by "el tiempo y la raza" [time and race]: "le perdió en 1581 el Anschluss de Felipe II" [was destroyed by the Anschluss of Philip II in 1581] (209–10). The seeming anachronism introduced by the mention of "Anschluss" brings out an unsettling recurrence of tragic episodes of annexation and persecution in the context of Aub's more general meditation on the historical link between identity and nation.

This form of anachronism takes on a significant critical value in light of "Definición de la historia" [Definition of History/Story], a poem by Abbasid poet Ibn Abu Hakin in which history is defined through *accumulatio* as an inextricable linguistic tangle of "dudas" [doubts], "desengaños" [disillusions], "intrigas" [intrigues], "deslealtades" [disloyalties], "artificios" [artifices], "tratos dobles y aun triples" [double- and even triple-crosses], "mala fe" [bad faith], and "mentiras" [lies] (183).[30] Ibn Abu Hakin's voice is not the only one to explicitly complicate the relationship between lies and truth. The imprisoned Paduan poet Marco Bruto Crispo – who "tal vez tuviera que ver con el destierro" [may have had something to do with the exile] of Ovid – also dwells on this connection, and relates it, epitaphically, to the survival of the poet's inscribed voice. Thus, he leaves a message for Caesar on the walls of his cell: "Mientras yo viva, César, vivirás. / ... / Si me mandas asesinar acabaré contigo / haciendo de mentira verdad" [For as long as I live, Cesar, you will live. / ... / If you order me to kill I will kill you / Making truth out of a lie] (*Obras completas: Vol. I* 173–4). In a similar admonitory tone, the apostrophic verses of the Jewish writer Josef Ibn Zakkariya, a native of Zaragoza, develop the metaphor of darkness in order to reflect on truth: "Si estás decidido a la verdad, sólo puedes alzar / la tuya ... / ... // Porque para ti puede ser noche lo que sólo es un / eclipse. Nadie te lo probará y será tu verdad mentira" [If you are decided on the truth, the only truth that you can raise / is yours ... / ... // Because for you what is only an eclipse can be / night. No one will prove it to you and it will be your lying truth] (189).

Lack of information about the poet's past and the fleetingness of literary prestige are also important motifs in *Antología traducida*. About the Chinese poet Fu-Po, for instance, the anthologist writes: "no se sabe dónde ni cuándo murió" [it is not known where or when he died] (*Obras completas: Vol. I* 183). Hardly any trace is left of the Tibetan poet Ti Kappur Maitili, as "sólo queda el nombre sin que se sepa a ciencia cierta si corresponde al autor de lo que sigue" [only the name remains, without it being known for certain whether it corresponds to the author of the following] (184). Of the Maghrebin poet Abu Abd Al-Jatib Talik "poco se sabe, como no sean las fechas de su nacimiento y probable muerte" [little is known, except for the dates of his birth and likely death] (*Obras completas: Vol. I* 195). The terseness of biographical notes therefore highlights, with a tinge of wryness, the unreliability of written records. Besides, numerous poems in Aub's anthology offer readers the possibility of exploring the ties between knowledge and identity – particularly literary identity – through apostrophe. The Polish poet Josef Waskiewitz, author of *Diálogo con un poeta muerto* [Dialogue with a Dead Poet], deploys the emphatic dialogic structure afforded by apostrophic address to focus on the fragility of literary fame, the fragmentariness of representation, and the potential for marginalization: "Sólo os leen los que no os necesitan, roto el espejo – a trozos, a trozos no escogidos, a trozos recogidos – sólo esos solos, para mirar en sus espejos y no en el vuestro / ¿Qué creéis? ¿Ser alguien? ¿Quién es alguien? No lo sabéis. / Ninguno de vosotros sabe quién es alguien" [Only those who do not need you read you, the mirror broken – into fragments, unchosen fragments, collected fragments – only those alone, to look into their mirrors and not yours / What do you believe? To be someone? Who is someone? You do not know. / None of you knows who someone is] (224).

Among the most telling explorations of identity and knowledge through the rhetorical, tonal, and dramatic possibilities provided by apostrophe is a set of six kharjas by another Jew of Iberian origin, Mose Ibn Barun, a musician from Lucena, near Cordoba (*Obras completas: Vol. I* 192).[31] Conventionally sung by a girl about her beloved, kharjas have been described as a "quotation from vernacular songs otherwise lost" (Scheindlin and Barletta 28). One of Mose Ibn Barun's kharjas reads: "Tú no sabes quién soy / tampoco lo sé yo" [You do not know who I am / Neither do I] (193). The shifts in perspective between the first and the second persons are stressed by the assertive rhetoric and percussive consonant rhyme scheme. At the same time, they are complicated by the use of non-gendered deictic markers. These markers stand out prominently, as each of the other five kharjas in the set includes at least one female noun or pronoun. A reader may, then, rely on the spatiotemporal shifters that organize the site of enunciation in these two lines to position him- or herself in the text. Through *deixis am phantasma* (or imagination-based deixis), the reader is able to recreate an absent there and then different from the here and now of voicing, revealing an uncanny tension between discursive continuity and historical discontinuity.

Voicing these lines entails transitorily occupying the present site and time of enunciation of a singer that reaches the reader through, among other mediations, a "quotation from vernacular songs otherwise lost," Ibn Barun's "gran voz atenorada" [great tenor-like voice], and the language of the anthologist, who has translated the kharja from Andalusian Romance (*Obras completas: Vol. I* 192). As such, the singer's voice is rendered spectral by its undecidable language, accent, and gender, among other elements. Moreover, the inscription of this voice is apocryphal, becoming, by implication, a secret, hidden text, one not approved for public reading. Indeed, the voice's undefined identity – the sense that it resonates in a historical enclosure of sorts – both facilitates and complicates its voicing. The two lines' categorically conclusive tone seems to amplify their echo, as though they both sounded and resounded in a spatiotemporal vacuum. With a paradoxically memorable rhetorical force, voicing them implies in fact an act of remembrance and, therefore, an experience of continuity. Yet the reader can also remember, among other things, the impossibility of voicing the lost, forgotten voices of history, and may consequently be afforded an experience of discontinuity. Aub's poetic memory becomes an unsettling form of testimony: it bears witness to the historical *aporia* folded into the discursive space of the poem.

From this position, a reader's lending voice to Aub's apocryphal personae can become a historical event in the here and now of enunciation. Yet, Aub's catalogue of fragmentary voices is fashioned, first and foremost, by the idiosyncratic and unstable voice of its anthologist and translator. A "Nota preliminar" [preliminary note] on the process of translating the collection of poems into Spanish describes mediations that reinforce the tension between immediacy and strangeness informing *Antología traducida*. Although the dominant first-person lyric voice creates an impression of presence, the anthology also conveys an overall sense of absence and distance. Because each author contributes only a few compositions – usually only one, never more than six – to the volume, the lines come across as remote echoes of each poetic voice. The anthologist strengthens this rhetoric of distance when he argues that the poems "posiblemente tampoco tienen interés" [possibly hold no interest] (*Obras completas: Vol. I* 168). Consequently, the anthology undergoes a threefold decrease in value: the reader gets translated versions of a very limited selection of poems, the poems have been labelled "segundones," and the anthologist warns that they may lack redeeming qualities. Continuing to detract, and to detach himself, from his own collection of poems, the anthologist and translator also maintains that, when poetry is both poorly written and poorly translated, "peor es publicarlo" [to publish it is even worse] (168).

Furthermore, the edition is not bilingual: the "originals" are missing. "Originals" belongs in quotes here because a highly pronounced intertextuality is noticeable among several Spanish renditions, as we shall see. In addition, the anthologist alarmingly acknowledges that his skills as a translator are so limited that other translators had to help him render most of the poems in Spanish (*Obras completas: Vol. I* 53–7, 167–9). In fact, translation takes on deeply unsettling commemorative undertones when the anthologist compares it to death: "Las poesías, traducidas, pierden tanta sangre que no hay transfusión que valga" [Poems, when translated, lose so much blood that no transfusion in the world can save them] (168). In opposing translation to blood transfusion, the anthologist personifies his poems. Hence, a translation becomes one more ghost of an absent "original" composition. All these mediations make the poets' voices markedly spectral, especially since their poems have been "semiborrados de toda memoria" [half-erased from all memory] (167). This spectrality – the tension between presence and absence conveyed by the poets' translated voices – takes on a personal note of seeming despair when the anthologist prophetically and dogmatically concludes: "Dejando aparte que el que haya escrito un solo verso verdadero se salvará" [leaving aside that he who has written a single true verse will save himself] (168). But apparently the anthologist-translator has already found a degree of – ironic – comfort in the words of Bernal Díaz del Castillo, who called translators "verdaderas lenguas" [truthful tongues] (168).

As is well known in Mexico – where *Antología traducida* was first published in 1963 – Bernal Díaz del Castillo was one of the Spanish soldiers who took part in the conquest of the Aztecs under Hernán Cortés between 1519 and 1521. The anthologist's reference to him is then laced with sardonic, self-deprecating irony. This irony involves not only his allegedly underwhelming skills as a translator, but also the bloody consequences brought about by, among other aspects of the Spanish conquest, the translation of religious concepts, as chronicled by Díaz del Castillo himself.[32] The dark connotations of this reference from *La Historia Verdadera de la conquista de la Nueva España* did not escape Aub. After all, he played on the title of Díaz del Castillo's chronicle in yet another deeply ironic text: his short story "La verdadera historia de la muerte de Francisco Franco," where he dwelled on the violent elements of linguistic and cultural translation resulting from the arrival of Spanish exiles in Mexico.[33] Consequently, the allusion to Díaz del Castillo's "verdadera historia" in *Antología traducida* raises multiple questions in the broad context of the historical relationship between Mexico and Spain, specifically in the framework of the Republican exile in Mexico: is the anthologist, poet, and translator named Max Aub one of the "verdaderas lenguas" able to save themselves in the midst of death and oblivion? Or is he instead one of the less "verdaderas lenguas" whose voice will lose so much blood that it will also end up erased from all memory? (*Obras completas: Vol. I* 168).

In its emphasis on salvation, this introductory passage from *Antología traducida* strongly echoes the meta-literary excursus in *Campo de los almendros*. The "autor" of "Páginas azules" explains that his narration has proceeded to the point "donde la palabra laberinto cobra su significado" [where the word labyrinth finds its meaning]; having arrived there, his protagonists can only say "sálvese el que pueda" [every man for himself] (*Campo de los almendros* 567). As mentioned earlier, at this key moment of confusion in his chronicle about the end of war, the "autor" lends his testimonial voice to César Vallejo and his cross-temporal, biblically inflected apostrophe about the residual salvation of Spain: "Padre polvo que subes de España."[34] *Antología traducida* prefigures this concern with poetic salvation in lines by Nahum Bem Gamiel, a non-orthodox Jew condemned to "olvido por el odio de los talmudistas" [oblivion by the hatred of the Talmudists]: "Dice el Sanedrín, y miente. Porque yo te salvé" [The Sanhedrin speaks, and it lies.

Because I saved you]. The first-person speaker in this poem writes about saving an anonymous you that neither God nor the Jewish council managed to save (180). Likewise, Marco Bruto Crispo credits words with the power to save yet another you: "Sólo mi odio y mis versos son capaces de mantenerte vivo" [Only my hatred and my verses are able to keep you alive] (174).

Antología traducida includes two poems by Bruto Crispo; the second composition, eloquently titled "De la necesidad de la escritura" [On the Necessity of Writing], connects poetry to posterity: "Por no correr el riesgo de que alguno / de tus hijos tus restos encuentre, / órdenes doy de quemar esto conmigo" [So as not to run the risk that one / of your children might discover your remains, / I order that this be burned with me] (174). Aub's writings contain many such expressions of anguish at the prospect of death and oblivion. In 1968, around the time that he was seeking a publisher in Spain for *Antología traducida*, Aub claimed in his diary that only the voices of others could save his name: "Soy los demás. Lo que no quede de mí en los demás no servirá para mí. De mí sólo quedará lo que quede en los demás" [I am others. The part of me that may not remain in others will not help me. All that will remain of me is whatever remains in others] (407). In "A J.C. Becerra, muerto joven" [To J.C. Becerra, Dead in his Youth], a moving obituary for the outstanding Mexican poet José Carlos Becerra published two years later in 1970, Aub succinctly and unequivocally asserted the power of literature against extinction: "Edítese: única protesta posible contra la muerte" [Publish him, the only possible protest against death] (298).[35]

Aub's Semi-Apocryphal

The three-part poem attributed to "Max Aub" in *Antología traducida* indirectly dramatizes Aub's elaborate construction of the witness figure. More important, Aub's own protest at the prospect of extinction and forgetting shapes the verbal fabric of this poetic testimony. Biographical information, historical reference, personal deixis, and apostrophic address contribute to complicate the potential discursive retrieval of a minor poet called "Max Aub." This complication can be taken as Aub's telling reflection on the possibility of his textual survival, since his composition has been selected by an anthologist by the same name who belittles the publication of badly translated, second-rate poetry (*Obras completas: Vol. I* 168):

MAX AUB

Nació en París en 1903. Aunque sale su nombre con cierta periodicidad sospechosa en los libros y revistas, no se sabe dónde está. Lo único que consta es que escribió muchas películas mexicanas carentes de interés. Nada tienen que ver con su homónimo Leandro Fernández de Moratín.

Los que quieran ver en estas líneas una intención política: ella-España, están equivocados.

Si pudiéramos fechar estas sentencias tal vez pudiera ponerse en claro. No hay tal. Mientras tanto recomiéndase la abstención que es lo único que, con seguridad, da fruto.

I
Cerrado en mí,
Cegato, mudo,
en lo que ha sido me hundo
pagando lo que fui.

II
Eres lo que fue y será.

III
Te fuiste y fui,
Nada queda de mí. (*Obras completas: Vol. I* 244–5)[36]

The semi-fictional biographical note preceding the poem destabilizes the site of enunciation of the author "Max Aub." First the reader is told that information regarding his name is uncertain and then that the name is a homonym: the same in sound and spelling as that of Leandro Fernández de Moratín, a Spanish playwright and royal librarian who had to leave Spain after the Peninsular War in 1817 and died in Paris in 1828. In light of the subsequent statement about the historical record surrounding "Max Aub" – "Lo único que consta" – mentioning the divergence between the poet's unknown location and his published name – "Aunque sale su nombre con cierta periodicidad sospechosa en los libros y revistas, no se sabe dónde está" – is consequential for any analysis of the historical situatedness of this composition.

In "Max Aub," wordplay delineates a discursive space of continuity and discontinuity between two writers, but also, more important, between living – "lo vivo" – writing – "lo escrito" – and reading – "cada lector" (*Obras completas: Vol. I* 94). If read together, the note and the poem underscore relative sites of enunciation. The use of an uncertain common name highlights, on the one hand, the location of the anthologist and translator and, on the other, that of the author of the poem, as well as the relationship between each of these voices and the reader. The "I" in the biographical note also relativizes its site of enunciation through a plural of modesty: "si pudiéramos fechar estas sentencias tal vez pudiera ponerse en claro" [if we could date these statements/sentences perhaps this could be clarified] (244). This "I" approaches the reader by means of a *plural sociativo*, a use of the first-person plural that allows the speaker to involve the addressee emotionally – in this case, through the recognition of their shared ignorance. The note ends with another change of perspective, as the first-person plural shifts to the impersonal third-person instruction "recomiéndase."

As we saw earlier, the value of temporal and personal shifters in lyric poetry is, by generic convention, different from that of fiction (Culler, *Theory* 376). Yet rhetorical and thematic overlaps between the two texts in Aub's composition suggest a certain spatiotemporal convergence. The structure of apostrophic address, centred on the present time, and the difficulty in determining the whereabouts of both "Max Aub" and the speaker raise questions about the ways in which the site of enunciation is constructed (286). Both texts emphasize a play of presence and absence. Even though the form of address in the poem can be taken as prosopopoeia – and thus as making present and animating a voiceless entity – the anonymous addressee has disappeared: "te fuiste." The "I" follows the addressee and disappears as well: "fui / Nada queda de mí." But the past tense of "ir" [to go] also means "ser" [to be]: "fui." Thus, the "I" remains as a past being. As the last line concludes, "nada queda de mí." The "I" remains textually present, as a trace – written, attested to in the poem – at the same time as the reader is told that it is absent.

This play of presence and absence is critical for any understanding of Aub's poem as a testimonial form. The chiasmic structure of prosopopoeia, which according to Paul de Man crosses "the conditions of death and of life with the attributes of speech and of silence," permits the animation of the dead or absent in the present of each reading ("Autobiography" 928). But it also deanimates and depersonalizes the reader in the very speech act of animation enabled by the voicing of the text. In de Man's terms, "the living are struck dumb, frozen in their own death" (928). Thus, this poem's rhetorical structure could be read topically as a memento mori, a reflection on transience and mortality. Indeed, this effect would be retroactively reinforced by the biographical note, in which the reader is told that "estas sentencias" cannot be dated. The "abstención" that the anthologist and translator advocates entails a reluctance to determine their historical context. "Max Aub" seems, then, to belong in a timeless site of enunciation, as evoked in the poem.

However, this timeless site of enunciation becomes indirectly historicized with the mention of "ella-España" [she-Spain]. The anthologist discourages the reader from seeking political allusions in the "sentencias," but then opens the possibility of dating them and hence of shedding light on their "intención política." In denying the association "ella-España" [she-Spain], the anthologist rhetorically implies it. This ironic warning notwithstanding, the reference remains open for the reader to interpret, particularly in view of the historiographical language in the (auto)biographical note: "lo único que consta," "si pudiéramos fechar."[37] The anthologist's warning points to the poet's undecidable position in the realm of politics; or, in Jacques Rancière's terms, "the poet belongs to politics as one who does not belong there" (qtd. in Culler, *Theory* 296). And yet a reader could also retrospectively ascertain an implicit political intention in this poem, when he or she reaches the poems by Luis Romaña and Jean Louis Camard later in the anthology and is given the opportunity to dwell on their commemorative import with regard to the Spanish Civil War and the exile that followed.

In this sense, the anonymous, disappeared addressee in the poem by "Max Aub" could be a voiceless entity called "España." The apostrophe would animate it and make it present as a ghostly revenant. But as we saw earlier, the testimonial "I" – self-fashioned as enclosed into himself, purblind, and mute – describes his eyesight and voice as respectively enfeebled and gone. His testimony is thus undermined: "Nada queda de mí." Yet this line is a performative contradiction. Even though it says that nothing remains, the line remains nonetheless, including the personal pronoun "mí." A textual trace of the self-defeating "I" is left over. Moreover, other textual traces of this line can be easily found in *Antología traducida*. "Max Aub" is almost identical to another poem collected by the anthologist that is written by a fictional poet: the French Bertrand de Crenne (1501–47). Some lines are rendered by the translator as "Cerrado en mí, sin luz, olor o gusto, / sin un resquicio, / en lo que fue me hundo. // ... // nada queda de mí" [Enclosed into myself, without light, smell, or taste, / without a crack, / I sink into what was. // ... // Nothing remains of me] (*Obras completas: Vol. I* 205). The one poem by the poet Max Aub included in *Antología traducida* is then close to a plagiarism by the anthologist and translator Max Aub. To complicate textual matters even more, Julio Monega Brandão (known personally by the anthologist, says his biographical note), plagiarized another poem by Crenne (205, 241).

Consequently, "Max Aub" emerges as a maddeningly intricate intersection of textual and material voices. From this standpoint, although one of these voices may be mute, "Max Aub" requires various cross-boundary, cross-historical, and implicitly plurilingual voicings from the reader (Nowell Smith 4). The anthologist knits together different poems by multiple fictional authors. These poems then somehow refer back to him. His verbal existence relies on the precarious transmission of texts over the course of an apocryphal history across widely different languages, times, and spaces. It is important that these authors be fictional, since, as the narrator of *Luis Buñuel, novela* has it, fiction is closer to the truth: "La historia es semiinvención y viene con el tiempo a ser una verdad variable, según el presente" [History is semi-invention, and over time it becomes a variable truth, depending on the present] (27). In addition, Aub asserted that documents "mienten como los hombres" [lie just like men do] (qtd. in Sánchez Zapatero 199). In this context, *Antología traducida* offers a sustained reflection on the relationship between documentary evidence and truth. Indeed, the lack of clarity as to the historical and political conditions surrounding the production of the semi-apocryphal poem "Max Aub" foreshadows the images of the blindfolded Spain and the aforementioned "acaso, ciego (o sin coma)" [perchance/chance, blind (or without the comma)] that inform the testimonial vision in *La gallina ciega*.

But perhaps what makes "Max Aub" political is precisely its lack of clarity, its (relative) blindness to historical evidence, its textual undecidability. Again, as Judith Butler has it, "if there were no undecidability, there would be no open-ended debate, and no field of the political" (xxiii). Indeed, blindness takes on a prominent dimension in *Antología traducida*, beyond the speaker in "Max Aub"'s self-description as "cerrado en mí" and "cegato" (*Obras completas: Vol. I* 245). In the biographical sketch about Aub the poet, Aub the anthologist claims that "no se sabe dónde está" [his whereabouts are unknown], "sus fotografías son evidentes trucos" [his photographs are obvious hoaxes], and "nadie le conoce" [no one knows him], once again using the third person to emphasize distance (244). A number of other poets relativize their ability to see in *Antología traducida*. The Provençal poet Ramon de Perpiñá avers that, without "tú," a blind person cannot see: "Ay, ciego de ti, ciego, / a través de ti veo" [Oh, blind of you, blind, / through you I see] (188). Following Yehuda Halevi – a Jewish poet of Iberian origin – the Sephardic poet Yojana Ben Ezra Ibn Al-Zakkai defiantly apostrophizes an undefined you while linking vision to exile, oblivion, and death: "¿Qué ves, qué ves más allá / de lo que ves? // Sólo adivinas lo que quisieras ver. // ... Si te has olvidado de España / ¿por qué no te mueres de una vez?" [What do you see, what do you see beyond / what you see? // You glimpse only what you would want to see. // ... If you have forgotten Spain / why don't you die already?] (207).

Aub contended that his exilic production was markedly testimonial. Nonetheless, the characteristics that define his semi-apocryphal self-portrait – artifice, ignorance, muteness, and partial blindness – subvert the defining traits of the reliable witness. To paraphrase de Man's essay on autobiography, Aub's apparently translated poem presents a face that disfigures itself before the reader's eyes. This disfigured "I" also undermines the conventions of lyric. John Stuart Mill famously argued that poetry is overheard, but a mute poet cannot be heard at all, let alone overheard (Brewster 31). And while de Man argued that the lyric posits an aesthetic of presence that determines the hermeneutic of the "I" ("Lyrical" 55), Aub's disfigured "I" seems to sink into the past, absenting himself until nothing remains of him but a series of undecidable marks on the page. Yet this undermining of generic conventions highlights, by sheer contrast, the testimonial drive behind his exilic writings. The disfigurement of the lyric "I" in Aub's semi-apocryphal poem is translated into the figuration or phenomenalization of a marginal, sunken, undermined, and absent testimonial voice.[38] The disconcerting self-description of the "I" as "cerrado en mí, cegato, mudo" strongly prefigures the wavering witness that lends a haunting voice to important prose texts that Aub wrote in exile, such as *La gallina ciega* and, most important, *Campo de los almendros*.

Lyric, Remortalization, and the Ghost of a Ghost

Taken from Jorge Manrique's *Coplas a la muerte de su padre*, the rhetorical question "¿Qué se hizo el rey don Juan?" appears in *Campo de los almendros* right after a meditation on prose fiction's limitations for reminding posterity of *El laberinto mágico*'s thousands of historical and fictional protagonists: "lo que importa es que quede, aunque sea para uno solo en cada generación, lo que aconteció y lo sucedido en Alicante estos últimos días del mes de marzo de 1939. El autor cree que, si en vez de escribirlo en prosa, lo cantara en ferias y plazas, tendría éxito" [What matters is that what happened, the events that took place in Alicante in these last days of March 1939, should remain, if only for just one person in each generation. The author believes that if instead of writing in prose, he would sing it in town fairs and squares, he would succeed] (*Campo de los almendros* 565). Only song would seem to convey enough force to commemorate what the characters in Aub's vast cycle of testimonial fictions suffered. But, as we saw earlier, the "autor" of "Páginas azules" goes on to reflect that these people "existe mientras vive" [exist while they live], until they "empieza lentamente a morir en los demás" [they slowly begin to die in others] and finally disappear "teñida de sombras, en el olvido" [tinged by shadows, into oblivion] (565). What is the function of Manrique's elegiac line at this juncture in Aub's testimonial narrative? How can it hinder the rapid ravages of death and oblivion, and somehow reach posterity?

In "El caso Manrique" (1974), a moving essayistic meditation on the primacy of the particular over the generic in lyric poetry, Rafael Sánchez Ferlosio called the line "¿Qué se hizo el rey don Juan?" "el más arrebatado canto a lo perecedero" [the most rapturous song to the transitory] (357). In Sánchez Ferlosio's view, the use of the proper name in lyric has a unique mnemonic power to vividly evoke the absent person among those who still remember him or her. Thus, a proper name like "el rey don Juan" resembles a "conjuro" [incantation] in that it manages to reach "lo nombrado" [what it names], which – spectrally enough – continues to exist as "una imagen empírica y sensible" [an empirical and perceptible image] in the common memory of those present. The use of this proper name in Manrique's elegiac question becomes memorable precisely because it underlines the transitoriness of life: "No porque inmortalicen, sino precisamente porque logran mortalizar, o remortalizar, al rey don Juan ... es por lo que esos versos consiguen hacerlo ... revivir" [Not because they immortalize, but rather precisely because they manage to mortalize or re-mortalize King Don Juan ... these verses make him ... live again] (358–9). The "autor" of Aub's "Páginas azules" fleetingly evokes his characters by their proper names, re-mortalizing them, in Sánchez Ferlosio's terms, like "una imagen empírica y sensible" in his memory as a lyric poet. What happens when "el autor" places himself among those names in the lines from Manrique that he rewrites: "¿Dónde quedan Chabás, Sánchez Ventura, Hemingway, Paulino, yo, Medina, los centenares, los miles que me sirvieron?" (*Campo de los almendros* 559)? Is he also re-mortalized? Does his own absence become more present and alive to the reader?

The "autor," who has already placed himself behind the mask of an anonymous third person, does not use a proper name here ("Aub," for instance). Instead, "yo" eloquently occupies his and its place. So, following Sánchez Ferlosio's analysis, the "autor" would not manage to live again through lyric: deprived of his proper name, he would have yielded his place to the reader by means of the first-person deictic. This is an important difference as, right after quoting Manrique's line, the "autor" continues his meditation on death and memory, focusing on song: "¿Quién sabe quién fue ese rey don Juan? Los eruditos, los historiadores. Queda la música del verso, el sentido" [Who knows who that King don Juan was? Scholars, historians. What remains is the music of the verse, the sense] (565). Consequently, Aub's poetic memory – his memory of sound in poetry – would prompt each reader to voice lines and proper names such as: "¿Qué fue de Largo Caballero? ¿Qué de Besteiro? ¿Qué fue de Sanjurjo? ¿Qué de Azaña, de Juan Negrín? ¿Qué fue de Mola?" [Whatever happened to Largo Caballero? To Besteiro? Whatever happened to Sanjurjo? To Azaña, to Juan Negrín? Whatever happened to Mola?] (565). Driven by the anaphoric force of Manrique-like questions, the reader would be able to re-mortalize, and then to reanimate – "revivir" – key personalities of the civil war in that their names would remain as traces in the "música del verso."

However, the reader would also be reminded of the death of "yo," since the first-person pronoun would only act as a placeholder in such rhetorical music: "¿Dónde quedan Chabás, Sánchez Ventura, Hemingway, Paulino, yo?" More than just a personal deictic, here "yo" would act as a memento mori, a textual commonplace whereby the contrast between yesterday and today hauntingly reaches each living reader.[39] Barbara Johnson defined the use of the first person in poetry as "an act of animation": "the notion of 'person' has something to do with presence at the scene of speech and seems to inhere in the notion of *address*. 'I' and 'you' are persons because they can either address or be addressed, while 'he' can only be talked *about*" (*Persons* 6). This lyric speech act of animation drives both the epitaphic rhetoric and motifs in *Antología traducida* and the elegiac inscriptions in *Campo de los almendros*. As Johnson goes on to explain, what an epitaph accomplishes is "what all literature has to accomplish: to make poetry that convinces the reader that the poet speaks, that the poem gives access to his living voice ... This is the immortality of literature brought about by reading – to bring alive the voice of a dead author ... Prosopopoeia is thus *the* figure for reading" (14).[40]

Rhetoric is at the heart of Aub's preoccupation with death in "Páginas azules." As the "autor" of the excursus claims, "la muerte no pasa de ser un artificio retórico, como la palabra fin; no hay fin, no hay muerte" [death is nothing but a rhetorical artifice, like the word end; there's no end, there's no death] (*Campo de los almendros* 562). Guided by the first-person-singular deictic, when the reader encounters the rhetorical questions echoing Manrique's elegiac lines, he or she can make use of prosopopeia – the mask of "yo" in this case – to remember a past and a future death; in this sense, "yo" would act as a memento mori in the present of reading. This uncanny cross-temporal effect becomes all the more dramatically vivid alongside the multitude of marginal, nameless characters that populate *El laberinto mágico*. Every time a reader asks him- or herself Aub's elegiac questions, the absent voices of at least some of these dead witnesses to Republican Spain's disastrous end resound, epitaphically enough, in the here and now of reading; they may be, by extension, fleetingly re-mortalized – or even, following Johnson, immortalized: "¿Dónde quedan ... yo, Medina, los centenares, los miles que me sirvieron?" (559). However, following Sánchez Ferlosio's essay, deprived of their proper names as they are, these witnesses would not "live" again. Neither would "yo."[41]

The poem attributed to "Max Aub" in *Antología traducida* has a similar, although less explicitly historically situated, effect: "Cerrado en mí, / Cegato, mudo / en lo que ha sido me hundo" [Enclosed into myself, / Purblind, mute / I sink into what has been] (*Obras completas: Vol. I* 245). The more this ghostly voice reminds the reader that it sounded, and stopped sounding, in the past, the more it may resound in the present, albeit in this case through a displaced proper name. In constructing an eccentric, unstable figure of the witness, Aub productively disfigured what could be described as hybrid testimonies – that is, in Shoshana Felman's terms, texts produced by "second-degree" witnesses or witnesses of witnesses such as interviewers and translators (213). Aub used translation and poetry to foreground the complex discursive mediations inherent in testimonies produced by this kind of witnesses. His collection of apocryphal and semi-apocryphal poems contributes to emphasizing the uncanny multilayeredness of this site of enunciation, as it stages the difficulties involved in remembering the absent and/or marginal figures of history. To extrapolate from Walter Benjamin's reflections on history in *The Arcades Project*, *Antología traducida* depicts the past not as it actually was, but rather as a constellation of discursive remnants and traces that dramatize the ephemeral (re)presentation of spectral voices condemned to disappear from historical accounts: the relation between the now of every successive reading of Aub's poems and "lo que ha sido" is not continuous, but dialectical (462–3).

The cross-temporal historical reach of *Antología traducida* explains both Aub's recourse to lyric in "Páginas azules" and his preoccupation with textual and material survival in a work of testimonial fiction as historically situated as the final instalment of *El laberinto mágico*. The dramatically transient quality of the first-person-singular mask that the reader momentarily adopts in "Páginas azules" creates the conditions for a specific historical experience in the present. In other words, the lyric "yo" and each reader's "yo" meet only briefly behind this mask, registering a disjunction between past and present, a spatiotemporal heterogeneity unlike the sense of continuity provided by historical narrations that proceed in teleological order (Jay 238). Because the "autor" of *Antología traducida* also takes the proper name "Max Aub," the person so designated may be reanimated by the reader through *deixis am phantasma*. In the poem attributed to "Max Aub," however, this first-person speaker has been discursively displaced and disfigured into a spectral mask. Thus, his mute voice can somehow return to "life," but only, perhaps, to die again at the vanishing point where memory fades, following a fate similar to that which befell the marginal, nameless witnesses who died in Alicante in the last days of March 1939.

From this standpoint, Aub's poetic voice may possess a transformative temporal power. As his apocryphal *Jusep Torres Campalans* stated in an eponymously titled work of fiction: "La poesía, muda. (No habla: cambia, remueve, hace mayor, transforma, callada)" [Poetry, mute/sheds/turns. (It does not speak: it changes, it stirs, it makes older, it transforms, quiet)] (*Jusep* 238). The poetic mask's interpellation to the reader may then make the reader "mayor," as the apparent atemporality of the inanimate mask – like Juan Ramón Jiménez's *máscara* vis-à-vis his *cáscara* – does not age while the reader's face does, or at least its aging is different from the reader's. In the context of the testimonial literature of exile, this sense of temporal disjunction may generate an acute awareness of historical irretrievability. Aub staged apocryphal voices in *Antología traducida* to obliquely address events of the Spanish Civil War and its aftermath to which he was a direct or indirect witness. In doing so, he took the tension between an event's "real sucedido" and historical and testimonial discourses to a dramatic limit (*Obras completas: Vol. I* 93).

A case in point is the voice of Jean Louis Camard, a volunteer from the International Brigades. The anthologist states in his biographical note that Camard was "mi amigo en el campo de concentración de Vernet d'Ariège y luego en la raya del Sahara, donde murió de los malos tratos de sus casi compatriotas ... Publico estos poemas no por lo que valgan, sino en homenaje a su amistad y su recuerdo" [my friend in the concentration camp of Vernet d'Ariège and then at the border of the Sahara, where he died of physical abuse by his quasi-compatriots ... I publish these poems not for what they may be worth, but as tribute to his friendship and his memory] (*Obras completas: Vol. I* 245). Aub's poetic commemoration of, and homage to, a fictional victim like Camard highlights the anonymity surrounding the victims interned at the border of the Sahara between 1941 and 1942: the ghostly "compañeros muertos y enterrados," as he refers to them in his foreword to *Diario de Djelfa* (94). As if to emphasize the silence that also surrounded their suffering as "real sucedido," Aub's book of poems included an uncaptioned two-page photo spread of five apparent victims of physical abuse (figure 6.1).

As we saw in chapter 1, only the ghosts of Aub's absent comrades might be able to grasp or capture "lo que se apunta" [what is pointed out] in *Diario de*

6.1 Photograph inserted in *Diario de Djelfa*. Courtesy of Editorial Joaquín Mortiz S. A.

Djelfa (*Obras completas: Vol. I* 94). In this light, the apocryphal Camard is the ghost of a ghost, and Aub's poetic commemoration in *Antología traducida* takes his forewarning in *Diario de Djelfa* a step further: the discursive spatiotemporal gap between "lo vivo," "lo escrito," and "cada lector" has widened (93–4). Also, the possibility of reading a poem as a historical event has deepened. It is in this deeper historical sense that the set of poems that Aub collected in *Antología traducida* can be read as a uniquely personal testimony to the unavoidable yet unfulfillable task of retrieving the irretrievable. Although, unlike Manrique's "música del verso," little of the music in Aub's poetry might remain today, his use of poetic memory within prose can still, paradoxically, contribute to constructing a memorable testimony of what happened in Alicante in the last days of March 1939.

II - USURPING THE APOCRYPHAL: EXILIC TESTIMONY, COSMOPOLITAN MEMORY, AND NATIONAL CULTURE (THE CASE OF ANTONIO MUÑOZ MOLINA)

> Perhaps one day there will even emerge something like a global memory as the different parts of the world are drawn ever tighter together. But any such global memory will always be prismatic and heterogeneous rather than holistic or universal.
>
> Andreas Huyssen, "Presents" 35

Sepharad and Testimony

The intricate rhetoric of alterity, plurivocality, and opacity shaping Aub's exilic writings seems at odds with recuperative efforts driven by the teleological temporality underlying national-literary and cultural historicism. Yet Aub's multifaceted cultural legacy as a Republican exile appeared eminently recuperable in the context of the debates about the historical memory of the Spanish Civil War that gained traction at the turn of the twenty-first century.[42] As Aub's position in Spanish public culture is subject to debate even today, it is important to examine the critical framework for the reception of his legacy.[43] This critical framework has been largely informed by Antonio Muñoz Molina's worthy efforts as a public intellectual to bring to light neglected or forgotten testimonial accounts by Spanish Republican writers who became exiles as a result of the war ("Dos exilios" n. pag.). As Muñoz Molina put it in a 2002 newspaper interview, present-day Spain is the result of an irreparable "cataclismo," "[i]gual que lo que sucedió con la cultura centroeuropea después de la II Guerra Mundial" [cataclysm, the same as what happened to Central European culture after the Second World War] ("Muchos" n. pag.). In this statement Muñoz Molina likened the cultural consequences of the Spanish Civil War and Franco's dictatorship to those brought about by "irracionalidad" [irrationality] and "fascismo" [fascism] in continental Europe ("Caso" n. pag.). This dynamic of sweeping, clear-cut equivalences predominates in Muñoz Molina's writings on authors of testimonies.

The title of his partially fictionalized compilation of testimonial narratives, *Sefarad* (2001) equates the exile of Jews from Spain in the fifteenth century with the exile of Spanish Republicans fleeing Franco's repression in the twentieth century. For Muñoz Molina, *Sefarad* (the Sephardic name for the Iberian Peninsula) constitutes "a metaphor for destruction, expulsion, or loss ... the place one wants to come back to" ("Company" n. pag.). Consequently, as a trope "Sepharad" stretches beyond the imagined community of Spanish exiles persecuted since early modernity to encompass "secular and progressive" European Jewish authors who suffered the consequences of the "cataclismo único en la historia del mundo" [cataclysm unique in the history of the world] that shook twentieth century Europe

("Max" 120). Among these authors are Primo Levi and Jean Améry – two prominent Jewish survivors of Auschwitz whose writings have a strong bearing on current understandings of Holocaust testimony – along with "the great writers of the Civil War era," "the new Sephardim," "democrats" such as Max Aub ("Company" n. pag.). Muñoz Molina's book stretches the metaphor even further to include "people who are sick and are exiled by their illness" ("Dreaming," n. pag.). From this now trans-historical perspective, Muñoz Molina draws what may be considered a questionable global equivalence: "todo el mundo es judío o puede ser judío en cualquier momento ... Cualquiera puede tener su Sefarad. Todos somos posibles condenados" [anyone is or can be a Jew at any moment ... Anyone can have their Sepharad. We all are potentially condemned] ("Todos" n. pag.). "Sepharad," Muñoz Molina's master metaphor of destruction, expulsion, or loss, is therefore a trope that universalizes experiences of victimhood.

Read against the backdrop of Max Aub's testimonial writings, Muñoz Molina's texts about Europe's deadly twentieth century underscore the tensions involved in creating or promoting a cosmopolitan memory inflected by testimonies of the Holocaust. His discussions of the memory of victimhood are deeply shaped by his reading of Aub's testimonies of exile and loss, but they do not take into account his poetry, let alone the particular modes of memory inscribed in it. Muñoz Molina treats Aub as a key witness to both the Spanish Republican exile and "una especie de guerra civil europea" [a sort of European civil war] lasting more than thirty years ("Max" 121). Although Aub's life and works do belong to these two general contexts, Muñoz Molina tends to politically and rhetorically universalize Aub's specific historical position in both, to a point at which Aub comes to embody Sepharad. Thus remembered, Aub's complex experiences and testimonies lose their singularity. Muñoz Molina's reading downplays Aub's main tropes of testimony – what can schematically be called *the alias* and *the apocryphal*, characterized by a rhetoric of alterity, plurivocality, and obscurity. Muñoz Molina instead favours equivalence, univocality, and self-evidence and thereby turns Aub into a precursor whose place he tries to usurp symbolically. Thus Aub is made to occupy, along with other Jewish authors, a trans-historical topos that Muñoz Molina "wants to come back to" ("Company" n. pag.).

It is in this sense that contrasting Muñoz Molina's testimonial rhetoric with that of Max Aub becomes productive. As we shall see, these different rhetorics do not constitute a binary opposition but, rather, different textual strategies highlighting in varying degrees the uncanniness of testimonial discourse.[44] In exploring these textual strategies, I will address three relevant questions in contemporary memory studies: how the globalization of Holocaust memory can decontextualize and relativize testimony; how so-called cosmopolitan memory can be used to foster one's imagined national culture; and what kind of testimonial literature may best memorialize, in a transnational context, specific experiences of repression. These three questions foreground, among other things, the status of Aub's poetry as testimonial memory. Moreover, they hinge on the critical relevance of Aub's poetry in discussions about the relationship between cosmopolitan memory and efforts to retrieve and recuperate exilic texts with the aim of achieving what Muñoz Molina has called the "verdadera plenitud" [true plenitude] of Spanish culture ("Destierro" 117).

Antonio Muñoz Molina's Rhetoric of Equivalence, Univocality, and Self-Evidence

Muñoz Molina's gesture of multicultural assimilation intervenes in a Spanish cultural field marked by questions about a common European memory, insofar as the invocation of the Holocaust frames current debates about the historical memory of the Spanish Civil War (Muñoz Molina, "Destierro" 92). The existence of a Spanish literary archive about the Holocaust was still widely overlooked at the turn of the twenty-first century due to Spain's peripheral position with respect to the Final Solution (Gómez López-Quiñones, "El Holocausto" 59). As Dan Diner argued in 2010, although the Spanish Civil War is part of a "historical constellation of European crises," the Spanish conflict and the Holocaust belong to "different spaces" of historical reference (8). Yet, the rhetoric of the Holocaust has recently offered a significant set of criteria for representing and understanding repression during the Spanish war and the Francoist dictatorship (Moradiellos, "Revisión" 379).[45] The term *genocide* was loosely used during the so-called *guerra por la memoria* [war for memory] that took place in Spain during the first decade of the twenty-first century (Marco 27). The issues debated ranged from the commemoration of politically repressed victims buried in Spanish mass graves to the arrest of former Chilean dictator Augusto Pinochet on the principle of universal jurisdiction.

In this context, Paul Preston's 2011 *The Spanish Holocaust*, a painstaking investigation of the atrocities committed by Franco, stirred a heated debate about how to characterize and name Francoist repression. The term "Spanish Holocaust" relates to two recently developed concepts in sociological memory studies: cosmopolitan memory and multidirectional memory. These two perspectives take Holocaust memory as their "paradigmatic object of concern" (Rothberg 6). As Daniel Levy argues, the notion of "cosmopolitan memory" uses the Holocaust as a template for the "creation of a European cultural history" and thus helps to develop transnational memories that could serve as a basis "for global human rights politics" (Levy and Sznaider 87). Multidirectional memory shows how one's own identity can be "a borrowing or adaptation from a history that initially might seem foreign and distant" (Rothberg 5). According to Michael Rothberg, remembering the Holocaust can contribute to the "articulation of other histories" of victimhood (6).

In this sense, both Preston and Muñoz Molina would be loosely borrowing or adapting from the history of the Holocaust to rearticulate the memories of

Franco's repression.[46] However, Rothberg also insists that such borrowings be clearly drawn and that they recognize the uniqueness of historical circumstances and lived experiences. Thus, parallels between historical spaces of reference such as the Spanish Civil War and the Holocaust should be distinctly defined (Gómez López-Quiñones, "El Holocausto" 65). The use of the Holocaust as a paradigm in cosmopolitan memory faces criticism precisely because the Nazi extermination of the European Jews is taken to be "a particular event" and its mourning is grounded in "a specific place and cultural tradition" (Assmann and Conrad 8). Holocaust memory, therefore, "cannot be easily appropriated everywhere" (9), even when the Holocaust is used as a paradigm to lay the foundation for a universal understanding of human rights, based on notions such as a "commonly remembered barbarism" (Assmann 14).[47]

A key figure in this polemic is Holocaust survivor Jean Améry, considered by Muñoz Molina as a hero against "irrationality" and "fascism" ("Caso" n. pag.). Yet Améry not only decried the equating of Bolshevism and Nazism and the indiscriminate use of broad terms such as totalitarianism to refer to Hitler's Reich; he also predicted in 1966 how the term Holocaust would be immersed within a larger frame of reference such as "a general 'Century of Barbarism'" and would thus become progressively indistinguishable from the term genocide (79–80). As he knew, claims of universality can lead to fetishizing or trivializing trauma. Also, the indiscriminate use of master metaphors or broad terms such as "barbarism" to link specific traumatic events can misrepresent not only the particular circumstances of the Holocaust but also the idiosyncratic testimony and experiences of a writer like Max Aub. With a touch of dark humour, José María Naharro-Calderón has alluded to the inadequacy of such indiscriminate use of cosmopolitan memory by remembering Aub's internment at a concentration camp as "una especie de 'solución final' ma non troppo" [a sort of 'final solution' *ma non troppo*] ("Max Aub" 116). Thus, if Aub's rhetoric of testimony is to be understood in the light of cosmopolitan memory, as Muñoz Molina suggests, it would be pertinent to posit a cosmopolitanism able to address, as Kwame Anthony Appiah has argued, the challenge of reconciling "a kind of universalism with the legitimacy of some forms of partiality" (*Ethics* 223).

Aub – like Améry – is one of Muñoz Molina's "héroes civiles e íntimos de la palabra escrita" [civil and intimate heroes of the written word] ("Destierro" 99). Muñoz Molina has published several texts about his formative connection to Aub. An early instance is "Recuerdo de Max Aub" [Memory of Max Aub], an article published in 1993 by the widely-circulated newspaper *El País*, where Muñoz Molina stressed Aub's desire to be Spanish, and claimed that Aub had been forgotten in Spain for a long while: "A Max Aub no lo lee nadie, o casi nadie, por la triste y cruda razón de que perdió la guerra" [No one reads Max Aub, or almost no one, for the sad and harsh reason that he lost the war] (34). One of Muñoz Molina's most culturally significant texts in this respect is his 1996 official speech accepting his induction into the Royal Spanish Academy. In this markedly institutional context, Muñoz

Molina presents himself as an "involuntario usurpador" [involuntary usurper] of Aub's place in the Academy: "Usurpamos el lugar ... de quienes podrían haber obtenido con más mérito lo que el azar reservó para nosotros" [we usurp the place ... of those who more deservedly could have achieved what chance reserved for us] ("Destierro" 93).

The "usurpación" is justified in that Muñoz Molina's real speech revolves around the apocryphal speech Aub prepared in exile accepting an imaginary 1956 induction into the Royal Spanish Academy, "El teatro español sacado a la luz de las tinieblas de nuestro tiempo" [Spanish Drama Brought to Light Out of the Shadows of Our Time].[48] Muñoz Molina contends that Aub is a political and a literary exile "sin patria y sin lectores" [without fatherland and without readers] who has to be rehabilitated because he legitimately belonged in the Spanish Academy ("Destierro" 93). Muñoz Molina concludes his official speech by granting Aub's work a key role in the cultural resurgence of Spain from the "cataclismo" that the civil war brought on: "yo no creo que la cultura española pueda lograr su verdadera plenitud si no recobra la tradición abolida en 1939" [I don't believe Spanish culture can reach its true plenitude if it does not recover the tradition abolished in 1939] (117). Thus, without addressing the sheer historical and discursive complexity of concepts such as culture and tradition in frameworks of nation-building (and -breaking), Muñoz Molina becomes the "lector" that Aub supposedly needed to return to his presumptive cultural "patria." By supplementing Aub's absence from the Academy with his own presence and testimony, Muñoz Molina can, presumably, claim and represent the theoretical "verdadera plenitud" of Spanish culture.

Here, however, the "plenitud" of national culture depends on the paradoxical assimilation of a writer who, as Muñoz Molina himself acknowledges, seemed difficult to define in terms of national belonging, as he was "[j]udío, alemán, francés, valenciano, apátrida, mexicano, peregrino en su patria, regresado al destierro y muerto en él" [Jewish, German, French, Valencian, stateless, Mexican, a pilgrim in his *patria* who went back into exile and died in it] ("Destierro" 114). Although this constellation of qualifiers may be quite rare in characterizations of the twentieth-century Spanish cultural field, Muñoz Molina depicts Aub as a literary and political archetype, a "leyenda ... del escritor republicano exiliado" [legend ... of the Republican exile writer] (100). More important, Muñoz Molina claims that Aub seemed to be able to rebel against the fate of a "porvenir obligatorio" [obligatory future], and to overcome his exceptionality: "decidió ser español, un español demócrata y de izquierdas, sin más raíces que las elegidas por él mismo" [he decided to be Spanish, a Spanish left-wing democrat, with no roots other than the ones he chose] (105, 107, 114). However, Aub's experience of exile was very different from that of other exiled Spanish Republican writers whom Muñoz Molina admires, such as Antonio Machado or Manuel Azaña. Aub also had other roots and followed other routes – roots and routes that he could not possibly choose to own or disown in the specific historical circumstances in which he lived.

Indeed, Aub's literature largely testifies to this singular experience of alienation. More precisely, it testifies to the perhaps irresolvable tension between the concrete reality of being, as he claimed, "de ninguna parte" [from nowhere] and what Muñoz Molina calls his desire to be Spanish (*Diarios* 128; "Destierro" 114). At least Aub's own paradoxically eloquent rhetoric of irresolution and tentativeness about his sense of belonging during his visit to Spain in 1969 should caution against final conclusions regarding his national identity: "Estaba cogido en esa trampa del decir y del decidir. ¿Era España esta oscura neblina que iba tiñéndose de no sé qué colorcillo rosado? No sabía qué pensar, no sabía ni qué pensar" [I was caught in that trap of saying and deciding. Was Spain this dark mist that was becoming I do not know what pinkish colour? I did not know what to think, I did not know what to think at all] (*La gallina* 310). From this cautionary perspective, Muñoz Molina's institutional attempt at restoring Aub's standing in the Spanish cultural field brings out more dramatically Aub's exceptionality and, with it, the tensions involved in promoting a national cultural memory from a cosmopolitan perspective. Muñoz Molina's symbolic usurpation of Aub's place poses a paradox because, by turning him into a central paradigm – a "leyenda" – of the Spanish Republican exile, he disregards Aub's experience of other-rootedness – the very experience that Aub could not possibly choose to disregard. In this paradox, both writers can be rooted or re-rooted in Muñoz Molina's imagined community of an ideal, full-fledged progressive Spanish culture. By the same token, Muñoz Molina can claim the distinguished intellectual legacy of an alienated victim, while being safely ensconced in today's Spanish cultural field.

Premised on a notion of history as progress, Muñoz Molina's gesture of cultural recovery echoes Nietzsche's idea of goal-oriented, "monumental" history. As Nietzsche claimed in *Untimely Meditations*, this type of history consists of "the great moments in the struggle of the human individuals [which] constitute a chain," and this chain "unites mankind across the millennia like a range of human mountain peaks" (68). As we shall see, Muñoz Molina's gesture prefigures a key rhetorical move the narrator of his book *Sefarad* makes: that of identifying himself with a prestigious literary community of victims such as Primo Levi or Jean Améry.[49] The narrator can belong to this monumental community only if their particular experiences of repression are universalized by way of a unifying narrative voice (Gómez López-Quiñones, "El Holocausto" 64–5). Likewise, in Muñoz Molina's reading of Aub's legacy, exile from space and time is somehow suspended, so that, to him, Aub's imaginary speech feels real and his own real speech feels "maxaubianamente imaginario" [Maxaubianly imaginary] ("Destierro" 117–18). In this and other depictions of Aub, Muñoz Molina tends to abstract the historical context of the Spanish Civil War so as to illustrate a certain trans-historical Spanishness across millennia (106).[50] Aub embodies one of the "great moments" in Nietzsche's monumental history in that he is "un ejemplo ... de esa clase de ciudadanía y de inteligencia españolas ... que para nuestra desgracia acabó demasiadas veces en el infortunio y el exilio" [an example of ... that sort of Spanish civility and intelligence ... that, to our misfortune, ended up too many times in adversity and exile] (114).

Muñoz Molina has tied the experience of reading Aub's novels during the last years of Franco's dictatorship to a "nostalgia doble del porvenir y del pasado, del mañana en el que podríamos respirar y vivir en libertad y del lejano ayer en el que la libertad existió brevemente" [double nostalgia for the future and the past, for a tomorrow when we would be able to breathe and live freely and for a distant yesterday when freedom briefly existed] ("Notas" n. pag.). The destroyed Spanish Second Republic thus becomes part of Sepharad, the imagined cultural community that Muñoz Molina can only desire to "go back to" because it is, historically speaking, unattainable: "I am a grandchild of the generation of García Lorca, of the great writers of the Civil War era. These artists are like the new Sephardim in the sense that they have been expelled from their country. And they have preserved the best of Spanish culture" ("Company" n. pag.). If Sepharad is Muñoz Molina's master metaphor for destruction, expulsion, or loss, Aub is, for him, the epitome of the Sephardic exile – one who witnessed and gave testimony to the loss of the various communities from which Muñoz Molina feels exiled and to which he desires to return. As the exemplary Sephardic witness, Aub is behind Muñoz Molina's perception of what he calls the "apocalipsis" [apocalypse] of twentieth-century Europe ("Destierro" 100).

By invoking Aub's name, Muñoz Molina wishes to connect his imagined Spanish culture with the European culture of progressive intellectuals represented in *Sefarad*, such as Jean Améry, Walter Benjamin, Margarete Buber-Neumann, Eugenia Ginzburg, Willy Haas, Milena Jesenská, Franz Kafka, Arthur Koestler, Victor Klemperer, Primo Levi, Nadezhda Mandelstam, or Willi Münzenberg. In a 1997 lecture titled "Max Aub: una mirada española y judía sobre las ruinas de Europa" [Max Aub: A Spanish and Jewish Gaze on Europe's Ruins], Muñoz Molina tentatively claims that, as a Jew, Aub was able to look into the past and into the future, since he "casi heredaba la tradición de lealtad y destierro de los sefardíes" [almost inherited the tradition of loyalty and exile of the Sephardim] (127). Furthermore, Aub's Jewishness helped him to be "consciente, con clarividencia precoz, de la forma particular y definitiva del cataclismo europeo que iba a culminar en los campos de exterminio" [aware, with precocious second sight, of the particular and definitive shape of the European cataclysm that was going to culminate in the extermination camps] ("Max" 127). Thus, Aub is depicted as moving beyond the concrete historical circumstances in which he lived and wrote to become a sort of Virgilian guide in Muñoz Molina's trans-historical journey to Sepharad.[51]

Moreover, Muñoz Molina claims that the Spanish Civil War is part of a European disaster which he describes as "un cataclismo único en la historia del mundo, tanto en la escala de su destrucción como en la cualidad planificada y sistemática de la saña con que ésta se llevó a cabo" [a cataclysm unique in the history of the world, both in the scale of destruction and in the planned and systematic quality of the viciousness with which it was carried out] ("Max" 120). By defining "cataclismo único" in general terms, without further historical qualification, Muñoz Molina suggests there is an equivalence between violence during the Spanish Civil War and the destruction of national, racial, religious, or political groups during the Second World War. His frame of reference is arguably the definition of *genocide* as intentional coordinated destruction used at the Nuremberg trials.[52] The war in Spain is thus metonymically conflated with the Holocaust. This metonymic relationship is strengthened by Muñoz Molina's use of generic expressions borrowed from Aub's writings: "el totalitarismo aspira a anegar la vida individual en una masa unánime ... Nadie está a salvo" [totalitarianism aspires to drown individual life in a uniform mass ... No one is safe] ("Max" 135). "Nadie está a salvo" is a key leitmotif in Muñoz Molina's reading of Aub's work.

Likewise, the phrase "Noche de Europa" is taken from Aub's play *El rapto de Europa* [The Rape/Kidnapping of Europa/Europe]: "Entre la riada de fugitivos de la noche de Europa ... están casi todas las inteligencias mayores del siglo XX" [Amid the flow of fugitives from the night of Europe ... are almost all of the greatest intelligences of the twentieth century] ("Max" 126). Channeled through the narrator's voice, these generic leitmotifs find their way into *Sefarad*, linking some of the disparate testimonial stories that make up the text and allowing Muñoz Molina to offer a panoramic view of "un cataclismo único, [donde] la gran noche de Europa está cruzada de largos trenes siniestros" and "nadie ... está a salvo" (*Sefarad* 49, 285) [a unique cataclysm [where] the great night of Europe is shot through with long, sinister trains [and] no one ... is safe (*Sepharad* 29)].[53] Some of these stories are about the Holocaust, while others seem less historically specific. Thus, Holocaust survivors Levi and Améry are not safe, but neither are "people who are sick" ("Dreaming" n. pag.). Not even the reader – or perhaps the narrator – addressed in the second person singular seems to be safe: "puedes entrar al café de todos los días creyendo que nada se ha modificado ni en ti ni en el mundo exterior y comprobar en el periódico que ya no eres quien creías que eras y no estás a salvo de la persecución y la infamia" (*Sefarad* 457) [you can go to your usual café believing that nothing has changed, and learn from the newspaper that you are no longer safe from shame and persecution (*Sepharad* 297)].

Muñoz Molina's perspective explains the relations of equivalence prevalent in his testimonial literature. His anti-fictional rhetoric draws on an idea of testimony as a self-evident account of an event, as if experience could be seamlessly narrated and plotted and there were no gaps between bearing witness and testimony: "Apenas hay detalles, y da pereza inventarlos, falsificarlos, profanar con la usurpación de un relato lo que fue parte dolorosa y real de la experiencia de alguien" (*Sefarad* 179) [If the details are lost, the easy thing is to invent them, falsify them, profane what was a painful part of another human being's experience by claiming it as your own (*Sepharad* 118)].[54] But, as Dominick LaCapra has shown, gaps between bearing witness and testimony do exist; in fact, testimony is largely characterized by such gaps ("Traumatropisms" 61).[55] In *Sefarad* there is a tension between the obvious artifice of the text and the earnest statements by both the narrator and the author about their anti-fictional textual strategies. According to the narrator, "[l]os hechos de la realidad dibujan tramas inesperadas a las que no puede atreverse la ficción" (214) [real events weave unexpected dramas that fiction would never dare (*Sepharad* 142)]. Later, in an author's note, Muñoz Molina writes: "He inventado muy poco en las historias y las voces que se cruzan en este libro" (*Sefarad* 597) [I have invented very little in the stories and voices that weave through this book (*Sepharad* 383)].[56] In his account of the lives of witnesses like Primo Levi, Muñoz Molina also claims that he didn't "really have to invent anything," since he felt as though *Sefarad* was "writing itself" ("Company," n. pag).

Symbolic usurpation occurs in *Sefarad* precisely for lack of invention – as Muñoz Molina would say – that is, for lack of a defamiliarizing distance between the narrator's account and the witness's testimony. This distance might have made it easier to acknowledge the singularity of the witness's experience. If defamiliarization is the literary technique whereby the reader sees common things in an uncommon way, in testimonies of an extreme experience defamiliarization can allow uncommon things to be seen in their singularity, strangeness, and even obscurity. Or rather, following LaCapra's distinction between bearing witness and giving testimony, testimony can be understood as the textual gap between experience and expression ("Traumatropisms" 61). Symbolic usurpation of the witness's testimony is most evident in Muñoz Molina's account of the experience of Jean Améry, of all people: "Eres Jean Améry viendo un paisaje de prados y árboles por la ventanilla del coche en el que lo llevan preso al cuartel de la Gestapo" (*Sefarad* 462) [You are Jean Améry seeing a landscape through the window of the car in which you are being taken to the barracks of the Gestapo (*Sepharad* 299)]. Here the narrator states straightforwardly that the reader is seeing what Améry saw, as if Améry's experience could be conveyed transparently.

However, this is precisely the moment chosen by Améry as an illustration of the discrepancy between witnessing and testimony, let alone between witnessing and the retelling of one's testimony by another writer. Améry claimed that even in "normal life" "reality is nothing but codified abstraction" and only exceptionally "do we truly stand face to face with the event" (26). In the case of "an event that places the most extreme demands on us, [there is] never an imaginative power that could even approach its reality. That someone is carried away shackled in a car by the Gestapo is 'self-evident' only when you read about it in the newspaper" (Améry 25–6). It is important to remember that Améry is the very witness who feared that the term *Holocaust* would be blurred into larger categories. Améry sharply criticized attempts to establish an unequivocal relationship between evidence and reality: "everything is self-evident, and nothing is self-evident as soon as we are thrust into a reality whose light blinds us and burns us to the bone" (26). The narrator of *Sefarad*, however, imagines himself unproblematically seeing what Améry saw, sharing it transparently – infallibly – with the reader, and even becoming Améry himself.

In a way, the narrator makes the experience of a Jewish survivor of the Holocaust seem familiar, turning it into an abstraction so that Améry's individual place can be symbolically usurped. As he explains elsewhere in the text: "Estoy muy dotado para intuir esa clase de angustia" (*Sefarad* 225) [I'm quite capable of sensing that sort of anguish (*Sepharad* 150)].[57] Using the second-person singular pronoun, he also invites the reader to imagine him or herself in Améry's situation. The addressed reader could reply with Susan Sontag's words from *Regarding the Pain of Others*: "'We' – this 'we' is everyone who has never experienced anything like what they went through – don't understand. We don't get it. We truly can't imagine what it was like" (125).[58] Sepharad understood as a metaphor of destruction, expulsion, or loss allows Muñoz Molina to "naturally identify with those who are left out": "When I was a child, the history of Spain that was taught was the official Catholic history: We were Catholics, we expelled the Jews. I naturally rebelled against all that. If traditional Spain expelled the Jews, I had to identify with the Jews" ("Dreaming" n. pag.). This identification allows for a narrowing of the gap between experience and expression.

Max Aub's Rhetoric of Alterity, Plurivocality, and Obscurity: The Spanish Nation and Poetic Animation in "Tres años"

Max Aub's rhetoric of testimony draws on a different premise: the necessity of a rhetoric of fiction and invention and thus the opening of the gap between experience and expression. As he maintained: "la ficción es el único medio posible (útil) de hollar, de dejar rastro, de testimoniar" [fiction is the only (useful) possible way to tread, to leave a trace, to give testimony] ("Nuevos" 209). That is, Muñoz Molina's defence of an anti-fictional rhetoric is at odds with Aub's decided defence of a rhetoric of fiction as a means for writing about his experience of alienation. Always already exiled, Aub's dominant testimonial tropes are, as we saw, the alias and the apocryphal. In Spanish, alias can mean both "nickname" and "otherwise." Etymologically, alias is a marker of difference. It also means "at another time," "in another place." Apocryphal can mean false, fictitious, of doubtful authenticity; it implies something secret and obscure. Aub's apocryphal figures, most notably in his exilic poems, also involve a plurivocal component requiring different voicings from the reader. These tropes resonate with the definition of exile suggested by Claudio Guillén as an experience of *destierro* and *destiempo* – an experience of linguistic, temporal, and spatial estrangement ("El sol" 83).[59] Aub's use of apocryphal voices and documents informs his exilic writings in various ways: a prime example is *Jusep Torres Campalans*, his biography of a fictitious Catalan painter, described as one of the co-founders of Cubism. The 1958 edition of this apocryphal biography included illustrations and photos created by Aub. Tellingly, *Jusep Torres Campalans* has sometimes been listed as a biography of a real painter (Aub, "El teatro" II).

As mentioned earlier, in the foreword to *Diario de Djelfa* Aub claimed that all that is narrated in the book was "real sucedido" (*Obras completas: Vol. I* 93). Yet, the testimony in "estos versos" is far from self-evident since, as he went on to explain, the poems are "inimaginados o inimaginables" [unimagined or unimaginable] (93). This defamiliarizing gesture, underscoring a certain fallibility of testimony, is compounded by a poem significantly titled "Alias" (146). "Alias" makes no direct reference to the Algerian concentration camp or any other historical events. It is a characteristically baroque meditation on the conflicts and tensions between language, accent, and identity.[60] The first stanza reads: "En este mundo todo son apodos, / alias, dichos y modos, / por mal nombre o por bueno / no valgo lo que soy, sí lo que sueno" [In this world all things are nicknames, / aliases, sayings, and modes, / by a bad name or a good one / I'm not worth what I am, but what I sound] (146). The poem ends on a sceptical note about the ambivalent power of language: words "llenan pliego tras pliego / dando en decir lo que no pueden dar" [fill up sheet after sheet / insisting on saying what they cannot give] (146).

As if to supplement the incapacity of words to name the witness and give an account of the witness's experiences, *Diario de Djelfa* incorporates six photographs. Self-reflexively, one of these photographs seems to reproduce the sheets of which the manuscript of the diary was made – and perhaps also the "pliegos" mentioned in "Alias." However, as critic Bernard Sicot has shown in a revealing essay titled "Max Aub en Djelfa: lo cierto y lo dudoso" [Max Aub at Djelfa: The True and the Doubtful], this image is that of a largely apocryphal manuscript (420–1). Aub went as far as to counterfeit at least part of the physical evidence of his own diary of the concentration camp, as though he were trying to impress upon the reader the obscurity of the words used in his testimony. Indeed, the handwriting reproduced in the photograph is "ilegible" [illegible] (Sicot, "Max" 421). Some of the lines are so blotted that they look censored (figure 6.2). Curiously enough, Aub warned the reader about this illegibility or fallibility in the foreword to the diary: "si de lo vivo a lo pintado piérdese una dimensión, ¡qué no perderá en lo escrito!" [if one dimension is lost from living to painting, so much more will be lost in writing!] (*Obras completas: Vol. I* 94) The lines are therefore "inimaginables" in another sense: we cannot picture them as such. Susan Sontag's words take here an added poignancy: "we truly can't imagine what it was like" at Djelfa because Aub's verses are uncannily obscure (125). Analogously, the "pliegos" in "Alias" are indeed distinct from the sheets reproduced in the photographic image, let alone the names and voices respectively inscribed in each of them. As Sicot concludes, the mysterious manuscript of *Diario de Djelfa* is an "artificio" [artifice] (421).

Obscurity, self-enclosure, and plurivocality are key to the short story that Aub inserted on the back cover of *Diario de Djelfa*, "Ver y creer" [Seeing is Believing],

6.2 Photograph of manuscript inserted by Max Aub in *Diario de Djelfa*. Courtesy of Editorial Joaquín Mortiz S.A.

as a deceptive blurb about his text. This fictional narrative is signed by the very real Guatemalan author Augusto Monterroso. According to this story, Aub is employing a ghostwriter, a Jew who fled Germany but is now hidden in the basement of his house in Mexico City, where "escribe y escribe, a oscuras casi" [he writes and writes, almost in the dark] (*Djelfa* n. pag.). "Ignorante de la realidad" [ignorant of reality], this ghostwriter comforts himself producing texts about the past. Aub publishes "esas producciones con su propio nombre, pero su prisionero no se entera" [these productions under his own name, but his prisoner is not aware of it] (*Djelfa* n. pag.). Yet the story is supposed to date back to 1929, thirteen years before Aub arrived in Mexico. By means of this fiction, Aub's authorship – the name that identifies him as a writer – is destabilized, and his writings take on an apocryphal tinge. The title of this short story, "Ver y creer," plays on a paradigmatic figure of witnessing in Christianity, the Doubting Thomas, throwing further into question the evidence supposedly provided by Aub's testimonial poetry.

Diario de Djelfa is thus already partly inflected by a ghostly authorial "Max Aub," similar to Aub's semi-apocryphal self-portrait in *Antología traducida* as a mute and purblind figure who, enclosed into himself, subverts the defining traits of the reliable witness through linguistic, spatial, and temporal estrangements. As we saw earlier, cross-boundary and cross-temporal patterns of poetic memory mould this authorial figure. From this angle, the most explicitly historically situated poems in *Diario de Djelfa* can be productively explored for traces of border crossings and non-chronologies, as well as plurivocal and plurilingual patterns. A good example is "Tres años" [Three Years], an agonized litany about the painful memory of Spain, seemingly intoned by an exiled prisoner interned in the Algerian camp. Offering one of the most notable thematizations of voice and nation in *Diario de Djelfa,* this poem lends itself to a highly detailed close analysis of the disruptive ways in which poetic memory interacts with national history in Aub's testimonial poetry:

TRES AÑOS

Tres años, tres años que las piedras, además de ser piedras,
son piedras francesas.
Tres años, tres años que los pájaros cantan en extraño.
Tres años que esperamos.
Tres años de Francos, tres años de noche, tres años,
y para otros hermanos tres años más, tres años.
Tres años de noche, tres años de campos, tres años de Francos.

Tres años que España está borrada del mapa.
Tres años que vivimos más abajo del mundo,
erramundos.

Tres años de Sahara
– todo el mundo es Sahara, menos España –,
Tres años de sangre, tres años de podredumbre, tres años
de muerte, tres años de hambre.
Tres años que muerden, tres años que roen.
Febrero del treinta y nueve.
Tres años de muerte.

España, voz y tierra,
tierra y palabra,
lengua y sierra.

Por mucho viento,
no hay quien nos borre.
Por mucho desierto,
no hay quien se nos ponga sobre.
A los tres años ya se empieza a hablar ...
España, mi agua. España, mi mar.

Te me subes a la garganta, España,
cada palabra regurgita sal ...
Tres años que estás borrada del mapa.
España, España, España, España ...
Febrero del treinta y nueve
Tres años de muerte.

(2-2-1942) (*Obras completas: Vol. I* 111–12)[61]

The apparently seamless articulation of land, language, nation, and poetic voice in this poem sutures the discontinuity of exile in the camp. This articulation is highlighted in the central lines, which are typographically set apart between two sets of stanzas: "España, voz y tierra, / tierra y palabra, / lengua y sierra."

Following Aub's claims in his foreword to *Diario de Djelfa* about the ways in which his poems relate to his personal experience in the camp, the grammatical voice in this and other poems in the collection – for example, the insistently apostrophic "¿Dónde estás España?" – can be examined deictically as an expressive poetic persona (*Obras completas: Vol. I* 135). Not only is the event narrated here "real sucedido," the prisoner may even owe his life to his compositions: "les debo quizá la vida" [I owe them perhaps my life] (93). Such prefatory claims are a compelling premise for taking *Diario de Djelfa* as a narrative form of testimony. The poems may then be read as recounting, in Noël Valis's words, "in verse form the novelist-critic's experiences as a Republican exile in the Saharan concentration camp" (129). Once his identity was stripped away, the poet framed his loss in collective terms by constructing a "memory of home" (Valis 131). This brief description illustrates a reading strategy grounded in an understanding of these poems as dramatic monologues. In other words, *Diario de Djelfa* may be interpreted as a series of episodes in a referential, claim-making narrative told through the voice of Max Aub, a writer who positions himself in the text as a representative witness, both as a first-person collective ("Tres años que esperamos," "no hay quien nos borre"), and as a first-person individual ("Te me subes a la garganta, España").[62]

The photographs inserted in the volume reinforce the strong sense of personal presence and proximity conveyed throughout the poems.[63] One of these images is a wide shot of Aub, seemingly as a prisoner (figure 6.3). Aub stands comfortably out in the open, his body centred at medium distance and framed by tents and deserted plains and hills. His face looks straight at the camera in such a way that the viewer can see his shaded eyes against a background washed in bright sunlight. However, the solid, almost monumental, sense of presence that the prisoner's body conveys contributes to making the absence of his person more sharply obvious to the reader. Likewise, the semblance of vocal presence created in "Tres años" by the deployment of testimonial rhetoric – such as the insertion of the toponym "Sahara" and the date "Febrero del treinta y nueve" – highlights the ghostliness that informs his poems. Hence, the sense of bodily and vocal presence in *Diario de Djelfa* underscores all the more starkly a spatiotemporal disruption vis-à-vis the here and now of reading. Indeed, geographic immediacy is brought into typographical relief in the three short lines from "Tres años" in which voice is thematized: "España, voz y tierra, / tierra y palabra, / lengua y sierra." These lines are grouped together in an an isolated stanza devoid of specific anaphoric and cataphoric pointers, complicating for the reader – if ever so briefly – the possibility of deictically framing any spatiotemporal coordinates beyond the proper name of "España."

"España" is here animated and personified to the extent that, as Barbara Johnson explained, apostrophic address enables the poet to "transform an 'I-it' relationship into an 'I-thou' relationship" (*Persons* 9). Before this isolated stanza, poetic voice has appeared as an embodiment of memory through a paradigmatically mnemonic topos: the biblical *vox clamantis in deserto*. Only now does the speaker's voice turn, in apostrophic fashion, to a third entity. In this rhetorical light, "España" is uncannily portrayed, via the mask of prosopopoeia, as a source of voice, word, and language, and therefore as giving the power of speech to the speaker that animated it in the first place. In this isolated stanza, poetic voice and nation are, if not one, at least at one with each other. These lines may then be taken as a sovereign act of self-referentiality, self-affirmation, and self-proclamation, as though sheer naming were tantamount to a speech act of presencing and self-presencing. The poetic voice claims back "tierra," making it both present and a presence and consequently cancelling out the spatiotemporal gap brought about by "destierro." In this speech act, then, national evocation plus poetic invocation equals revocation of exile. Three years of exile are erased beneath three lines of poetry; the first one "España,

6.3 Photograph of Max Aub inserted in *Diario de Djelfa*. Courtesy of Editorial Joaquín Mortiz S.A.

voz y tierra," seems to draw forth the next two, accumulating upon one another. Poetic voice and nation are performatively conjoined. In the face of separation and alterity, banishment is tersely reverted and identity reinstated through poetic address. A conventional set of stresses on the fourth and seventh syllables – enclosed in a semi-chiastic mesh of assonances and alliterations – underpins a cumulative prosodic pattern, confirming poetic self-presencing.

And yet the textual presence of "España" turns discontinuous as it diverges, iterated and reiterated along a syntactical chain. It follows a supplementary logic, along a set of paratactically arranged segments in which metaphoric and metonymic figurations become hard to tell apart from each other: "voz y tierra, / tierra y palabra." These simultaneous instances of self-deferral and self-distancing make "España," "voz," and "tierra" as absent and disconnected from one another as they were present and conjoined in the first act of self-proclamation. The very act of naming and self-naming entails, then, both continuity and discontinuity. Thus, the unifying power of poetic voice becomes a fleeting rhetorical illusion. If nation and voice are not intrinsically linked, whose voice is that of the first-person-singular speaker addressing Spain in the similarly apostrophic line "Te me subes a la garganta, España"? Whose voice is it that, while trying to invoke "España," makes explicit the phonetic materiality of this proper name – the "texture, weight and density" of the word (Labelle 33) – as it rises through his or her throat, almost blocking it and thus choking – if only for a brief moment – the voice that might conceivably convey its semantic weight?[64] Whose voice is it that, reverting the speech act of personification from an I-thou relationship to an I-it relationship, depersonifies and deanimates "España" in the process? Whose voice is struggling to utter the alliterative set of "r" and "g" sounds – "garganta," "regurgita" – as they come out of his or her throat? Whose struggle is this phonic struggle? Is this poetic line a reflection on its own production as sound, which self-referentially refracts the nationalistic claims that a reader may conventionally presume the poetic voice to make if he or she reads the poem as a dramatic monologue?

Now, "Tres años" is resolutely shaped by varying rhetorical projections and prosodic patternings, including a dialogue with old anaphoric forms of the Psalmist lament. Beyond the compelling recourse to the topos of *vox clamantis in deserto*, the implicit thematic – and linguistic – allusion to the biblical exodus in "Tres años que vivimos más abajo del mundo, erramundos," as well as to Elijah's prophesy of three years of dryness and death as recounted in the first book of Kings, may resound in the reader's mind's ear as the Psalm-like anaphoric incantation "tres años" becomes increasingly pervasive (Valis 130). These biblical references were quite frequent among Republican exiles, most distinctly – as we saw earlier – in their journal *España peregrina* and in León Felipe's iconic collection of poems *Español del éxodo y el llanto*. Such topical and rhetorical allusions necessarily hinder readings of poetic voice as the privileged embodiment of the Spanish nation in the specific historical circumstances of Republican exile. Although "Tres años" may be construed thematically as an exile's formulation of a desire for the recovery of an immediate geographic and linguistic presence and present of "España," the poem is also deeply mediated by the cross-boundary, cross-historical, and plurilingual elements embedded in its poetic memory. The most prominent of these elements is anaphora. Such prominence is perhaps the reason why this rhetorical scheme is routinely taken for granted and its radically transnational drive neglected. No other figure of speech travels across borders as lightly as anaphora does; no other pattern translates so speedily.

Indeed, "Tres años" can be read as a form of translation, whereby the Spanish "lengua" becomes spectrally plurilingual. Also, anaphora characteristically enacts – or offers the possibility to enact – temporal subversions, since it underscores poetic lines as "discrete units while simultaneously binding those lines together" (Weare 50). These temporal subversions occur most emphatically when time is thematized, as evidenced by the title "Tres años." Rendered continuous and discontinuous by way of anaphoric reiteration, time is also at once repeatedly invoked – the title refers to the three years that have passed since the end of the civil war – and persistently performative, as the years somehow pass in the present of reading. Insofar as anaphora is read as a paradigmatically pliable, protean, and polymorphic rhetorical figure – and hence as contributing to the subversion of spatiotemporal coordinates – Aub's insistent use of it renders this poem radically untimely and unhomely. It is in this sense that "Tres años" resists being neatly fit into a national narrative line. In particular, the wide-ranging effects that the rhetorical deployment of anaphora in the text can have on the reader's spatiotemporal imagination render it uncanny with regard to national coordinates. Although the first-person-singular deictic permits the invocation of "España" in every act of enunciation, this invocation is simultaneously revoked. The ghostly animation of voice and voicing available in the poem's verbal fabric invites readers to question the sense of national embodiment and presence underpinning the lines "España, voz y tierra, / tierra y palabra, / lengua y sierra."

In short, the claim-making voice of the father- or motherland, supposedly able to bridge the gaps between person, people, land, and nation dramatized in this eloquently exilic poem, is both continuous and discontinuous with respect to the claim-subverting voicing of what Joseph Brodsky memorably called "otherlands" (32).[65] "Tres años" is then a ghostly poem on account of its thick textual and verbal materiality, even beyond the unequivocal and conclusive reference to death in the last line – "Tres años de muerte" – and, more generally, to Aub's thematization of ghosts in his foreword to *Diario de Djelfa*. The somatic memory animated through interpellation is specific to the verbal dynamics inscribed in the text. While interrupting the temporal movement of narrative history – or, similarly, of an account "in verse form [of] the novelist-critic's experiences" (Valis 129) – this somatic memory also enables us to read the poem as deeply historical: it highlights a spectral disruption concerning what Aub lived – "lo vivo" – what he wrote – "lo escrito" – and what each reader – "cada lector" – enunciates in every here and now of reading.

Enunciation takes us back to the question about whose voice is that of the first-person speaker addressing "España" in the apostrophic line "Te me subes a la garganta." In a dramatic monologue narrating Aub's experiences, the speaker in "Tres años" would seem to be remembering a Spanish sea: "A los tres años ya se empieza a hablar ... / España, mi agua. España, mi mar. // Te me subes a la garganta, España, / cada palabra regurgita sal." On the other hand, the act of remembrance can also be read as the performative speech act of a phonic struggle. If it is the reader that struggles to utter obstruent and sonorant sounds like "r" and "g" in "garganta" and "regurgita" as they come out of his or her throat, who is the "I"? And what language is this first-person speaker using? If these lines are read in light of Aub's experience as a Spanish speaker in the 1940s, a case can again be made for interpreting "Tres años" as a referential, claim-making narrative about the poet having trouble with Spanish. As we saw earlier, Aub complained in his diaries about the tragic impact that the association of accent and nationalism had on him at the particular historical conjuncture to which he was a witness: "hablar con ese acento francés que desgarra mi castellano, ¡qué daño no me ha hecho" (*Diarios* 128–9). In this light, "Tres años" becomes a dramatic monologue uttered by the poet's voice about a concrete, biographically identifiable event.[66]

A fitting conclusion to this interpretation would be that Aub expressed in verse form the frustration that he felt when his French accent tore his Spanish apart, disrupting his evocation of Spain, and that this personal frustration was a historically specific symptom of his political frustration. Accordingly, a performance of linguistic frustration would be embedded in this dramatic monologue. Thus, the interruption in the temporal movement of narrative history could be interpreted within a dramatic framework as well. Favouring this interpretation of "Tres años" as a dramatic monologue brings into question the possibility of shifting attention to the discordant and discontinuous elements in the poem that would impede access to meanings based on an intentional reading. Such an interpretation would be at odds with Aub's forewarning against attempts to recover and comprehend in the present a loss that he deemed ungraspable. The loss was "lo vivo": in this case, how he lived out his linguistic frustration in "horas de nacionalismo cerrado" [times of narrow-minded nationalism] (*Diarios* 128–9). Consequently, Aub discouraged intentional readings of his poems, including "Tres años." From this perspective the previous interpretation of the poem – premised on potential access to its presumed meaning, on continuity between living, writing, and reading – would, in hindsight, become mediated by the very ghosts that should have hindered our reading to begin with. Thus, our explicitly referential reading would be rendered retrospectively spectral. This critical aporia could, however, in turn be read as providing the conditions for a historical experience to the extent that, in Walter Benjamin's terms, the relationship between present and past would not be continuous, but dialectical.

This aporia may alert readers to the value of attending not just to the claim-making structures within the text, but also to the claim-subverting ones;

that is, the ghostly elements of difference, disruption, and otherness inscribed in the poem. What sort of ghosts may be traceable in "Tres años"? The site of enunciation Aub creates in the quoted lines can indeed be seen – if we dwell again on the undecidability between constative and performative readings – as a site of national struggle, mediated by the political complications brought about by the use of different accents. If at age three Aub was living in France and was starting to speak French and German, and no Spanish water or sea was conceivably available to him, whose childhood is the poem speaking about? Is this salt sea salt or desert salt? What Spain is being remembered here? Poetic voice and nation seem, at least temporarily, discontinuous with each other. In this sense, poetic voice becomes ghostly. But then again, this arresting act of remembrance is perceptible in the here and now of enunciation, as though there was an excess of *phone* over *logos*, or at least a momentary precedence of one over the other, "when the sheer extravagance of sound becomes opaque to speech or semantics" (Nowell Smith 12). The strongly alliterative set of vowel and non-vowel echoes, complicated by the set of obstruent and sonorant consonants – "agua," "garganta," "regurgita" – physically animates and is animated by reading, since it becomes increasingly hard to enunciate fluently, due to the obstruction of airflow. The spatiotemporal coordinates of the objects or experiences that the poetic voice referentially evokes may then be deemed undecidable by a reader who dwells on the phonic struggle. Again, whose struggle is it? And again, who, and what, is the first person speaking?

The rhythmic dynamics activated by the characteristic hendecasyllabic pattern of "A los tres años ya se empieza a hablar ..." reinforce this impression. This pattern causes the next rhyming line, "España, mi agua. España, mi mar," to waver on the edge of metric undecidability – should one read ten or eleven syllables here? The effect is magnified when the two following rhyming lines pick up the hendesyllabic pattern, confirming the prosodic tendency that constrains one to keep one's mouth open as the vowel "a" is accentuated once and again. But then, right after the reader is told that "España" has been erased from the map, the phonic struggle seems to end, and the phonically problematic word – "España" – now detached from cartography, somewhat uprooted, is loosened in the speaker's throat. "España" then emerges as an incantatory apostrophic sound, sliding as a smooth octosyllabic line over four identical stressed vowels – "España, España, España, España ..." – only to begin, shortly after, closing down on the ominous "e" vowels guiding the poem to its presumed end in protracted death. As the epitaphic date signalled by the last line confirms, "Febrero del treinta y nueve / Tres años de muerte." In this sense, also, poetic voice becomes ghostly.

Significantly, in the second stanza, the first-person-plural speaker has evoked an absent "España" in the third person, which is the grammatical person of absence (Johnson, *Persons* 10): "Tres años que España está borrada del mapa." In the last stanza, however, the first-person-singular speaker reanimates "España" into presence, as we have seen, by recourse to the apostrophic second person. If the poem ends in an epitaphic refrain – "Tres años de muerte" – who is dying this time around? Perhaps it is the first-person-singular speaker that is dying after going through the above phonic struggle that now, retroactively, can be remembered as the sound of his or her death throes. In this sense, the last two lines can also be read epitaphically. But if "España" has been apostrophically reanimated by precisely that speaker, and that speaker dies, is his or her "España" – the "España" imagined and invoked from exile by that speaker – also dead? At issue in asking who or what dies at the end of the poem is the value of the poetic voice as embodiment of the nation. The tenor of this question is political inasmuch as the political potential of poetry may lie in reading its aporetic textuality as a premise for critical debate.

Along with the different vocal lines and attitudes laced into "Tres años," the contrasting voicings of the word "España" that the reader is compelled to enunciate can overwhelm any sense of determined or undetermined voice (namely, the dramatic monologue of Max Aub's persona, or that of a speaker situated in an undefined set of spatiotemporal coordinates). These contrasting voicings speak to the ghostly animation that the verbal texture of the poem generates.[67] Who, then, is the first-person-singular speaker? This "I" is obviously not Max Aub here and now. Maybe Aub is just another name for the poem's "I," just another possible holder of the first-person position. Voice stems animatedly from the text itself, but only as a possibility. The text does not just facilitate the mimesis – via the rhetorical figure of prosopopoeia or personification – of an apparently empirical, but now absent voice, nor does it simply rehearse a repertoire of vocal dynamics available for the reader's self-expression. Voices and voicings are enacted, embodied, in every space and time of enunciation. Combined, such voices and voicings are always somewhat different from those pertaining to the text itself. As David Nowell Smith argues, "animation does not only treat 'voice' as an object in poems, a material made use of by poems; its dynamics resides in the space between poem and any singular, provisional voicing of the poem" (12). There is, then, as Aub reminded his readers, a discontinuity between the voice in "lo escrito" and the voice of "cada lector" – an eerie in-between act of enunciation.

This act is discontinuous not just with the body of the text and the reader's body, but also with both the mimesis of the absent voice and the representation of the reader's self-expressive voice. It is as if, in Mladen Dolar's words, "the voice were the very principle of division into interior and exterior ... both the surplus of the body, a bodily excess, and the no-more-body, the end of the corporeal" (71). Remarkably, this uncanny act of enunciation can be singular, collective, and even plural. If the different modes of ghostly presence that the vocal performance of the poem entails may speak to its plurality, then they also invite us to reflect on the paradoxical possibility of a poem premised on various first-person-singular positions that could materialize as a twofold collective subject: a constative collective subject and a performative collective subject. In short, in "Tres años," both the referential singular "I" – historically and biographically positioned as Max

Aub – and the grammatical singular "I" – deictically positioned as the reader in every different here and now of enunciation – mediate, present, and represent different collectives. All these shifting subjects – collective and singular, historical and grammatical – follow contrasting temporalities: respectively, the temporality of "lo vivo," of "lo escrito," and of "cada lector." But every time the poem is read, all of these temporalities are inextricably intertwined in its uncanny textual and verbal materiality. Since the reader's "lo vivo" is discontinuous with Aub's "lo vivo," these temporalities make the poem alive in every new voicing of the poem.

Thus, on the one hand, "Tres años" can be understood as a constative speech act with recourse to a first-person singular position interpreted as that of Aub's poetic voice and a second-person collective position interpreted as "España" – regardless of the possibility that both positions may become conjoined. On the other, the poem can also be taken deictically as a performative speech act if uttered in the here and now of reading from both a singular and a plural position. This plural position does not necessarily have to be collective. In fact, in a poem as thematically and referentially overdetermined as "Tres años," the continuity of nation, *tierra*, voice, and poet is constatively dramatized as an experience of discontinuity. The discontinuity – that of exile – nonetheless ends after a protracted "muerte" by becoming a kind of historical survival, a kind of return to the "tierra" of "España," and thus a form of the unified nation's resurrection, resumption, and continuity: "no hay quien nos borre." Yet "Tres años" may also be performed as an intricately animated texture of spatio-temporal continuities and discontinuities where no voice lends itself to being pinned down as representing the nation – unless, of course, the reader forgets precisely those dynamics that enable him or her to voice it. In other words, unless the reader forgets the specific formal, verbal, and textual patterns that hinder interpreting "Tres años" exclusively as a narrative of the survival or resurrection of the Spanish nation.

The Uncanniness of Testimony and National Culture

The verbal complexity of Aub's testimonial rhetoric displayed in explicitly referential poems like "Tres años" is refracted by their narrative "others" in prose form. Many of Aub's works of narrative fiction tend to foreground textual and linguistic instability. The short story "El cementerio de Djelfa" [The Cemetery of Djelfa] (1965), for instance, provides a narrative counterpart to *Diario de Djelfa*, just as *Antología traducida* provides a lyrical counterpart to *Campo de los almendros*. The premise of "El cementerio de Djelfa" is the transcription of a letter from Algeria that an anonymous narrator receives in Mexico in a soiled and torn envelope. The sender, a survivor of the Djelfa concentration camp, casts doubt on the evidentiary value of words by underlining the artificiality of his account: "Las palabras son tan pobres frente a los sentimientos que hay que recurrir a mil trucos para dar con el reflejo de la realidad" [words are so poor in the face of feelings that one must resort to a thousand tricks to come up with a reflection of reality] (79).

Likewise, linguistic and existential alienation presides over one of Aub's most compelling stories about the experience of exile, the unequivocally fictional "La verdadera historia de la muerte de Francisco Franco," published in Mexico in 1960. Its ironic title patently poses the problem of truthfulness in storytelling. The main character – Nacho, a Mexican waiter – links his isolation to his frustration with the way Spanish Republican exiles jarringly and incessantly talk in a Mexican café: "De verdad, sólo se habla con uno mismo ... A mí me hubiera gustado mucho hablar. Por eso fui mesero; ya que no hablaba, por lo menos oía. Pero oír veinte años lo mismo y lo mismo y lo mismo, con aquellas ces" [the truth is that one only talks to oneself ... I would have very much liked to talk. That's why I was a waiter; since I did not talk, at least I could hear. But to hear the same again and again for twenty years, with those c's] (31–2). Nacho doubts that his interviewer – the narrator – is Mexican like him: "¿Usted no es mexicano, verdad?" [You are not Mexican, isn't that the truth?] (31). Yet despite his disparaging remark about the Castilian accent, Nacho does not identify the interviewer as Spanish.[68] The interviewer could then be seen as a fictionalized Aub, with his French accent.

But Nacho might also be an apocryphal Aub, talking to himself in Mexico and reflecting on the constant disputes of other Spanish exiles and on his own linguistic experiences. As Aub noted in his diaries: "Uno no sabrá nunca cómo habla la gente de otro país, aunque con la misma lengua" [one will never know how people from another country speak, even if they speak the same language] (*Diarios* 165). Characteristically, the highly individualized main character, Nacho, becomes a narrative vanishing point when he disappears from view at the end of the story: "Ignacio Jurado Martínez se hizo pequeño, pequeño, pequeño; hasta que un día no se le vio más" [Ignacio Jurado Martínez became small, so small that one day he was not seen anymore] (31). Nacho's "verdad" that "sólo se habla con uno mismo" casts a shadow over his testimony and, consequently, over the narrator's transcription. Much like the semi-apocryphal poem attributed to "Max Aub" in *Antología traducida*, the narrator plays here, self-reflectively, with the idea of an enclosed-in-himself, mute figure.[69] Also, the question about phonic struggle in "Tres años" can be productively refracted through "La verdadera historia de la muerte de Francisco Franco."

In other works of fiction, Aub relies on the Cervantean ruse of the found manuscript. His 1952 "Manuscrito Cuervo" is a Swiftian chronicle of dehumanization in the concentration camp of Le Vernet d'Ariège. With a nod to the series of fictional authors referred to in Cervantes's *Don Quixote*, the manuscript is presented as "traducido fielmente del idioma cuervo por Aben Máximo Albarrón" [faithfully translated from the corvine language by Aben Máximo Albarrón], and edited by a certain J.R. Bululú ("Manuscrito" 151). All these modes of mediation are further complicated by the fact that the purportedly true author of the manuscript is a conspicuously fictional crow named Jacobo, while the translator's name, Aben Máximo Albarrón, alludes to the name of the story's author, Max Aub. The crow's claim that "[t]odo cuanto describa o cuente ha sido visto y observado por mis ojos" [all the things I may describe or tell have been seen and observed by my eyes] underscores the artificiality of both the witness and the testimony – and also, by contrast, the blindness of human beings (156). Authorship and authenticity are thus subverted in the *mise en abîme* of one of Aub's favoured literary devices, the found manuscript. Aub seemed, then, to be well aware that, as LaCapra explains: "any account – representation, narrative, understanding, explanation, form of knowledge – is constitutively limited, notably when it addresses certain phenomena" ("Lanzmann" 242).

Among the "phenomena" addressed by Aub's accounts may be his own singular experiences of alienation and other-rootedness, including "the traumatic effects of limit-experiences" on a survivor of the Djelfa camp – but not of the Final Solution ("Lanzmann" 234). Thus, as Jean Améry has it in *At the Mind's Limits*, Aub's dubious witnesses could also claim that "nothing is self-evident as soon as we are thrust into a reality whose light blinds us" (26). His tropes of testimony, the alias and the apocryphal, entail a rhetoric of fiction and obscurity, precluding usurpation. In the fifth instalment of *El laberinto mágico*, titled *Campo francés* – a 1964 film script based on his experiences at the Roland Garros prison in Paris and the concentration camp at Le Vernet d'Ariège – Aub memorably stated: "fui ojo ... no me represento" [I was an eye ... I do not represent myself] (7). In this manner, for Aub, the act of seeing that defines witnessing implies a disappearing act, the elusive presence of a purblind individual giving obscure testimonies. In 1968, a few years before his death, Aub concluded: "El exiliado murió: lo que ha cambiado es España" [The exile died; it is Spain that has changed] ("Diarios" 413). That is, after almost thirty years in exile, the writer reiterated his sense of estrangement while pointing out the potential complications of attempts at rehabilitating him for what Muñoz Molina calls "cultura española" ("Destierro" 117).

Although Aub might embody the metaphor of Sepharad, his name is absent from Muñoz Molina's book of the same title. It could be argued that, responding to a deep anxiety of testimonial influence, Muñoz Molina's narrator has symbolically usurped Aub's place. Following Muñoz Molina's Bloomian notion that writers learn their trade by following a dialectic of treason and tradition, the narrator in *Sefarad* could be said to ventriloquize real victims, assuming their voices and subsuming them under his univocal persona ("Destierro" 99). In this sense, universality of experience equals univocality of expression. Muñoz Molina's misreading of Aub's diversity of fictional voices as a universal narrative voice may help answer a key question in memory studies regarding the dynamics of testimonial memory. When witnesses to a specific historical event die, how can future legatees of testimonies best memorialize the singularity of experience? As Susan Suleiman suggests, although sentiment can be shared even by "authors and readers who were not there," it is as personal, subjective expression that the experiences of survivors can "most memorably be communicated. The meaning of their experience remains, despite the collective nature of the historical event, and of its official commemoration, individual rather than collective" (183).

Muñoz Molina's model downplays the defamiliarizing effect that would indicate to readers that someone's experience may have happened at another time and in another place, in different ethnic, geographic, and linguistic conditions. If W.G. Sebald's testimonial novel *Austerlitz* – with which *Sefarad* has been compared – can be considered an example of "the power of imagination to construct the inner world of a child survivor" (Suleiman 212), then Muñoz Molina's "novela de novelas" [novel of novels] could be said to be an example of the power of imagination to construct the inner world of a reader of testimonial literature who was not there.[70] In this sense, Aub and Muñoz Molina suggest two contrasting models of literary testimony. Aub's plurivocal model posits the obscure specificity of individual experience, whereas Muñoz Molina's univocal model posits the transparent universality of shared sentiment.[71] These contrasting textual strategies highlight in varying degrees the uncanniness of testimony, thus problematizing oppositions such as individual/collective, fiction/fact, literature/history (Felman and Laub 7). As we have seen, Aub's recourse to artifice does not undermine his efforts to account for what he calls "real sucedido" (*Obras completas: Vol. I* 93). *Sefarad*, by contrast, reveals a tension between the artifice of the text and the anti-fictional rhetoric that the narrator and the author proclaim.

For Muñoz Molina, the recuperation of the literary memory of Europe's deadly twentieth century is linked to the denunciation of Spanish "provincianismo intelectual e histórico" [historical and intellectual provincialism] in the 1980s ("Obra" n. pag.). In his opinion, even a few years after Franco's death, Spain continued to be politically isolated, and Spaniards still believed that "cuestiones relativas al Gulag y al Holocausto" [matters related to the Gulag and the Holocaust] did not have much to do with them (n. pag.). In this manner, Muñoz Molina can commemorate not only European survivors whose works have been overlooked or disregarded in Spain, but also posthumously forgotten Spanish exile writers such as Manuel Chaves Nogales or Arturo Barea. According to Muñoz Molina, in the late thirties these figures opposed "dictaduras comunistas o fascistas" [communist or fascist dictatorships] and only belatedly "vuelven a ser leídos y ... reciben una consideración literaria y política de la que no disfrutaron en España mientras vivían" [are read again and ... receive the literary and political recognition that they did not enjoy in Spain when they were alive] ("Dos exilios" n. pag.).[72] If remembering the Holocaust can contribute to the "articulation of other histories" of victimhood, then Muñoz Molina rearticulates a Spanish history of isolation multi-directionally, in terms of a European cosmopolitan memory (Rothberg 6).

From this angle, the cultural importance of *Sefarad* cannot be underestimated. The book was canonized in 2013 by its inclusion in Cátedra Letras Hispánicas, a widely distributed series of annotated classics in Spanish. *Sefarad* has, to date, been translated into eleven languages. The backcover blurb of this edition advertises the word *Sefarad* as the embodiment of a universal symbol "de todas las víctimas que han conformado la memoria cultural europea compartida del Holocausto y del exilio republicano de 1939" [of all the victims that have shaped the

European cultural memory shared by the Holocaust and the 1939 Republican exile] (n. pag.). However, Muñoz Molina tends to undermine this symbolic scope in a statement from 2001 in which *Sefarad* is universalized even further: "Sefarad es una metáfora. Es el país que se añora, puede ser España, la infancia, incluso la salud" [Sepharad is a metaphor. It's the country one yearns for, it may be Spain, childhood, even health] (qtd. in Valdivia, "Introducción" 57). The metaphorical reach of Sepharad is extended beyond any historical specificity to a point at which it loses its representative and commemorative value.[73]

Muñoz Molina's efforts to break away from Franco's provincial Spain are nothing short of commendable. Yet, paradoxically, his championing of a supposedly "verdadera plenitud" of Spanish culture seems impervious to the "unsettling force" of exile understood as "nomadic, decentered, contrapuntal," to use Edward Said's words (186). As Aub's friend and exiled poet Tomás Segovia pointed out in a 2003 conference titled "Max Aub: testigo del siglo XX" [Max Aub: Witness to the Twentieth Century], institutional efforts to recover Aub's legacy could simplify his "ambigua y paradójica" [ambiguous and paradoxical] figure and neutralize the subversive potential of his exilic writings (254). When read against the trans-historical backdrop of Muñoz Molina's universalizing metaphor, Aub's literary testimonies of other-rootedness and other-routedness invite the reader not only to always historicize but also to always spatialize. Indeed, as Paul Jay has shown, current literary and cultural studies are partly defined by a spatial expansion away from national paradigms towards new transnational fields of research (16). Aub's particular experience as an exile is decentred because, at least in the framework of cosmopolitan memory, it goes beyond that of the Spanish Republic to point to an experience of the Holocaust to which it nevertheless cannot fully be assimilated. It thus signals an eccentric position towards the Spanish nation. It is in this sense that Aub's testimonial rhetoric posits the challenge of reconciling "a kind of universalism with the legitimacy of some forms of partiality" (Appiah, *Ethics* 223).

In "Entre España y América: en torno a la emigración republicana de 1939" [Between Spain and America: On the 1939 Republican Emigration], an essay published in Paris in 1967, the exiled literary historian Vicente Llorens also reflected on the cultural and historical decentredness of exiled Republicans. Twenty-seven years into exile, a political émigré was, in Llorens's view, "por naturaleza un ser descentrado" [a naturally decentred being] (*Estudios* 173). Llorens went on to explain that the difficult communication between a young Spanish poet and those who had gone into exile and were "sepultados ya ... en la historia" [already buried in history] was but one aspect of the cultural disruption caused by long banishment: "aunque ahora o más adelante se modifique totalmente la situación, quedará siempre un paréntesis, un largo vacío en la vida nacional, que no se cierra del todo cuando se llena a destiempo, parcial y anacrónicamente" [even if the situation totally changes now or later, there will always remain a gap, a long void in the national life, which does not entirely close when it is filled in an untimely fashion, partially and anachronistically] (*Estudios* 178–9). Efforts to recover the cultural legacy of poets already buried in history may then necessarily entail engaging with the untimeliness of ghosts, as Aub explained in his foreword to *Diario de Djelfa*. This form of "Maxaubian" engagement implies going beyond the form of imaginary usurpation suggested in *Sepharad*: it requires giving testimony to a spatiotemporal gap that the teleological history underpinning the idea of national cultural "plenitud" cannot possibly bridge.[74] No master metaphor can replace a legacy of displacement unless it heeds the ghostly voices that haunt and hinder the progressive movement of national monumental history.

Aub's Twofold Eccentricity

Aub's desire to return to Spain is well-known, and he was finally able to do so in 1969. Here again is how, in *La gallina ciega,* he recorded his bitter reflections while strolling by himself in Madrid in the small hours of the morning: "Sí: no era España, no era mi España ... Sí: te deshaces en deseos: te consume la furia del amor hacia un pasado que no fue, por un futuro imposible ... ¿A qué vienes? No lo sabía" [Yes: it was not Spain; it was not my Spain ... Yes: you're undone by desire: you're consumed the fury of a love for a past that never was, for an imposible future ... What have you come for? I did not know] (311). The reality of returning to Spain thirty years after the end of the war left much to be desired, at least in view of the shifting personal, spatial, and temporal deictics used in this passage.[75] For Aub, national cultural plenitude seemed certainly unattainable. In any case, cultural plenitude is a historical notion, and whatever cultural development Aub may have desired to see in Spain from the disorienting standpoint of his 1969 visit can hardly be the same as what Muñoz Molina understands by "verdadera plenitud" in the early twenty-first century. On a less speculative note, the spatiotemporal framework built into Aub's rhetorics of testimony brings out an eerie sense of continuity and discontinuity, one at odds with the spatiotemporal coordinates of developmental history underpinning the notion of cultural fulfillment that Muñoz Molina posits.

As we have seen, this textual uncanniness is most patently traceable in Aub's exilic poems. It is this seemingly irresolvable tension inscribed in Aub's highly self-reflective rhetoric as to his desire to return that would enable readers to align his writings with those of other exiled Spanish poets such as Antonio Machado and Luis Cernuda. As Brad Epps and Luis Fernández Cifuentes explained in 2005, "their poetry oscillates between a critical rhetoric of fragmentation and a lyrical rhetoric of attachment, between exclamations of political dissidence and avowals of irrepressible belonging" (38). Yet Aub's experience of exile was also different from that of Machado or Cernuda in that he had, as we have seen, other roots that he could not choose to own or disown. In this sense, his writings testify to a contrapuntal, uncanny tension between the concrete reality of being "de ninguna parte" and his unattainable desire to return to a certain idea of Spain (*Diarios* 128). It is in Aub's "marginal" poems, especially – but not exclusively – those of *Antología traducida*, where the conflicting personal, spatial, and temporal deictics used in his prose take on an unprecedented textual density. Those poems haunt *La gallina ciega*, and hinder claims of national belonging. Aub's self-apostrophic "te deshaces" is a strong indication of his shifting, labyrinthine rhetoric of identity, and therefore of his seemingly endless personal, temporal, and spatial undoing. From this standpoint, Aub's position towards the Spanish nation becomes eccentric twice over. Perhaps his testimonial rhetoric of alterity, plurivocality, and obscurity should also be remembered as doubly eccentric vis-à-vis the marginality or decentredness of other exiles.[76]

One of the goals of this chapter has been to encourage such remembrance and, thus, to suggest critical perspectives on attempts to attain the "verdadera plenitud" of national culture. One such critical perspective was offered by Octavio Paz in 1967 with regard to Aub's position in Spanish culture. In his response to Juan Marichal's "Apología de la literatura española, siglo XX," Paz found it necessary to remind the prestigious Harvard professor that a vast portion of Aub's work had been produced in America. As we saw earlier, Aub was for Paz not just "un ejemplo de español hispanoamericano" [an example of a Hispanic American Spaniard], but a primary exponent of the dialogic pluralism of modern literature in terms of language, form, style, and genre. Aub's oeuvre was thus characterized by a transnational discursive heterogeneity: "Los dialectos de Max Aub se resuelven en un tejido: un texto único. No es la recuperación de España – aunque este sea uno de sus temas – ni la preservación de la lengua española sino su reinserción en el lenguaje moderno" [Max Aub's dialects resolve themselves in a texture: a unique text. It is not the recovery of Spain – although this is one of his themes – nor is it the preservation of the Spanish tongue, but its reinsertion in the modern language] (Marichal and Paz 43–4). Although Paz focused primarily on Aub's work as a novelist, he was quick to underscore the interwoven texture of Aub's exilic production as a whole, which marked it as both Spanish and Mexican, and therefore as also European and American. This interwoven texture comes to the fore in the border-crossing and plurivocal complexity informing the play of identities in his poetry.

On this plurivocal note, it seems appropriate to end these reflections on Aub's shifting identities by turning to one of the ways in which the jocoserious author and translator of *Antología traducida* was publicly perceived in Mexico four years before he passed away. On 15 July 1968 – a few months after Paz's essay came out – the masterful Mexican political cartoonist and painter Abel Quezada published in the daily Mexico City newspaper *Excélsior* a cartoon about the "misterio" [mystery] behind Aub's elusive identity as a writer. Quezada's ironic take on the relationship between national belonging and literary output brings out Aub's linguistic, temporal, and spatial eccentricity. As the cartoon implies, central to Aub's prolific production is an irreducible multiplicity of writerly filiations and affiliations.[77]

Quezada was acutely attuned to this exhilarating irreducibility. In Maxaubian fashion, he highlighted the inextricable relationship between Aub's copious

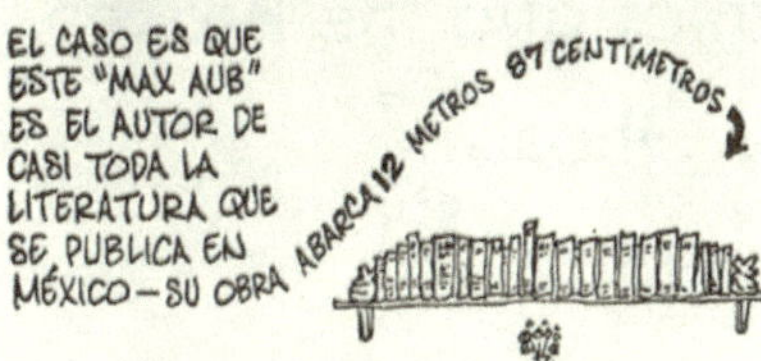

6.4 Abel Quezada's 1968 cartoon about Max Aub's elusive identity as a writer. (De Rojo, *Cara y cruz* 73). Reprinted by permission of Fundación Max Aub.

writings and his mysterious existence: "Algunos suponen que ese es el seudónimo de un escritor, de varios escritores, bueno, de todos los escritores ... 'Max Aub' es el autor de casi toda la literatura que se publica en México" [Some presume that this is the pseudonym of one writer, of several writers; well, of all writers ... "Max Aub" is the author of almost all of the literature that is published in Mexico] (figure 6.4).[78] One possibility implicit in the cartoonist's assertion is that *this* "Max Aub" may have also written texts by other Spanish Republican exiles living in Mexico at the time. But then again, Maxaubianly enough, one could also imagine Quezada paraphrasing Aub – or Jusep Torres Campalans, for that matter: "si de lo vivo a lo escrito piérdese una dimensión, ¡qué no perderá en lo dibujado!" [if one dimension is lost from living to writing, so much more will be lost in drawing!]. Quezada's also jocoserious cartoon provides a welcome critical counterpoint to certainties about cultural identity and national belonging.

CHAPTER SEVEN

Tomás Segovia: "In Exile from Exile" – Nomadic Ethics and the Broken Language of Ghosts

In 1978 Tomás Segovia suggested the paradox of "exiliarse del exilio" – to be in exile from exile – as a critical key to reading his poems ("Respuestas" 206). In his view, his poetry conveyed a sense of the condition of exile that goes beyond the "experiencia episódica" [episodic experience] of the "exilio español histórico" [historical Spanish exile] – the political exile that the thousands of Republicans who moved to Mexico around 1939 as a result of the Spanish Civil War lived through (205). Moreover, for Segovia, the "tema" [theme] of exile only acquired "valor poético" [poetic value] when it became a "horizonte de sí mismo" [its own horizon] and was never entirely explicit (215). Indeed, Segovia's poetry is to a great extent devoid of precise spatiotemporal references that would allow the reader to situate it in a particular historical context. The Spanish Republican exile in Mexico is barely thematized in his poems, and any allusions to it speak, according to the poet, about "otras cosas" [other things] ("Entretien" 236). Segovia claimed to have learned about the "vocación universalmente humana" [universally human vocation] of poetry from his own multifaceted experience as an exile, and this lesson may be useful in elucidating just what those "otras cosas" might be (*Digo* 173). Segovia further argued that, in order to "entender" [understand] his poetry, a Spanish exile does not need to recognize in it "su identidad de exiliado, sino su humanidad de exiliado" [his/her identity as an exile, but rather his/her humanity as an exile] (173). One of those "otras cosas," therefore, is the universalization of whatever circumstances would allow the reader to identify a particular exile and, perhaps, identify with it. In short, "exiliarse del exilio" is to universalize a particular experience.

The spatial formulation of this paradox, however, shows that, insofar as the exile's estrangement reproduces the discursive space that s/he would abandon, Segovia's critical suggestion is not feasible. The paradox "exiliarse del exilio" in thus an aporia: the poet moves towards a universal horizon that becomes unreachable, and the resulting impasse returns him/her to the particular theme of exile from which s/he had tried to exile him-/herself. From this angle, Segovia would be inviting the reader, albeit tangentially, to read his poetry differently: not necessarily from a universal perspective, but as the "experiencia episódica" of the historical exile of a particular Spanish Republican. Furthermore, in addition to the "valor poético" of a theme that is never entirely explicit, Segovia would be inviting the reader to look for traces of an implicit political value in his poetry ("Respuestas" 215). Indeed, this paradox in Segovia's suggestion foregrounds a set of dialectical tensions peculiar to exilic literatures between universal, trans-historical, and collective elements, and particular, historical, and personal ones (McClennen 3). In Edward Said's model for reading exilic writing, these dialectical tensions would unfold as a series of counterpoints, in a sort of reciprocal supplementation between opposites that constitute each other (176). Recent readings of cultural production by Spanish Republican exiles in Mexico nonetheless tend to reproduce the rigid binary logic between universal and local elements that Said's contrapuntal model would discourage (McClennen 31–2).

One such reading follows Segovia's notion of exile without pursuing the question of its inherent paradox, and thus suggests that exile in his poetry "no ha de ser abordado desde una clave histórico-política, ni siquiera como tema específico que se pueda delimitar dentro de su obra" [ought not to be approached in a historical-political key, nor even as a specific theme that can be defined within his work] (Tasis 774). Contrasting with this restrictive approach, Sebastiaan Faber's position disregards the possibility of separating "literature proper from the sociological and political context of its productions" (*Exile* x). Although it is not difficult to accept this critical premise, Faber does not address how exile connects the three domains that he mentions "in a very explicit way," or the ways in which, for an exiled author, the act of writing becomes "expressly political" (*Exile* x). The link between the sociopolitical context of Segovia's exile and the text of his poetry is far from obvious, especially when one considers that other poets who experienced a similar exile expressly filled their poems with overtly thematic references to Spain and/or the historical circumstances of their exiles (Sicot, *Ecos* 27). This critical disregard may explain why some scholars situate their readings of Segovia's poetry squarely within a strictly socio-historical and political frame of reference, so much so that, where a poem reads "tierra," one scholar believes it should be interpreted as "España" – without accounting for possible tensions and even paradoxes between text and context, or between claim-making and claim-subverting elements within the poem's verbal texture (Logan 740).

Although the pages that follow keep with Faber's general critical premise, they work in a different direction. Beginning from the socio-historical circumstances that largely define the theme of the Republican exile in Mexico, they investigate the implicit political sense in which the condition of exile can be traced in the verbal fabric of Segovia's poetry. This enquiry is made particularly relevant by the fact that, as mentioned earlier, in his poems Segovia avoids and even hides the socio-historical circumstances of its writing – a manoeuvre that complicates the sometimes reductive contextual and thematic readings favoured in contemporary Hispanism and especially within academic and political institutions both in Europe and in America. This chapter proposes a reading practice that accounts for the tension between particularist and universalist elements underlying Segovia's notion of exile and consequently moves beyond strictly anti-historicist or historicist models for reading.[1] In other words, extrapolating from the poet's spatial language, this chapter explores the horizon of political expectations that the dialectic between universality and particularity activated by Segovia's aporetic understanding of exile may open up for readers.

Kwame Anthony Appiah's understanding of cosmopolitanism addresses the challenge of reconciling "a kind of universalism with the legitimacy of at least some forms of partiality" (*Ethics* 223). The ethical component of this cosmopolitanism lies in combining respect for "particular human lives" with obligations that extend "beyond those to whom we are related by the ties of kith and kind, or even the more formal ties of a shared citizenship" (*Cosmopolitanism* XV). If Segovia's poetry points to a universal horizon that derives from a difference to which the exile cannot entirely cease to belong, the aporia "exiliarse del exilio" encapsulates the challenge of harmonizing universality and difference posed by Appiah's cosmopolitan ethics (XV). As shall be seen, Segovia's dialectic can be productively approached within Appiah's ethical framework, whereby the paradox "exiliarse del exilio" functions as a reformulation of the tension between cosmopolitanism and nationalism that often animates the writing of exile (McClennen 30–1).

My Land No Longer in the Land

Tomás Segovia was born in Valencia, Spain in 1927 – "my mother was in the city by chance, and I decided to join her," he would claim (qtd. in Fotheringham n. pag.). In 1940, when he was thirteen years old, he arrived in Mexico. From 1976 until his death in Mexico in 2011, Segovia lived alternately between Spain and Mexico. He is considered a distinguished representative of the Republican exile on both sides of the Atlantic.[2] The writer frequently downplayed this characterization, calling political exile only one of many exiles that shaped his life:

> A los dos años perdí a mi padre y me mandaron a Madrid a casa de unos tíos. A los nueve años a mi madre. Después salí con mis tías y abuela a Burdeos, de allí pasamos a Casablanca y posteriormente a México. Sin hablar de mis tres divorcios que son otros tantos exilios, a lo que hay que añadir diferentes estancias en diversos países. El exilio no hizo en mí sino reforzar una soledad de origen. Reforzada aún más por el precio que hay que pagar por no ser partidario. (Mateo Gambarte 241)[3]
>
> [At the age of two, I lost my father and I was sent to Madrid to the home of some aunts and uncles. At nine, I lost my mother. Then I went with my aunts and grandmother to Bordeaux; from there we went to Casablanca and then to Mexico. That is, without mentioning my three divorces, which are another set of exiles, and to

which must be added different amounts of time spent in various countries. Exile did nothing to me but reinforce an initial loneliness. Reinforced even more by the price one must pay for not being partisan to anyone.]

Significant among the studies and anthologies to explore and include Segovia's writings are those dedicated to authors who arrived in Mexico as exiles around 1940 as children and adolescents between three and fifteen years old (Sicot, *Ecos* 31). "Hispanic-Mexicans," one name for this group of writers, does not fully capture an experience its members have described as feeling neither Spanish nor Mexican.[4] Perhaps a better term for this group of writers and the exilic experience that defines them is the adjective *nepantla*, meaning "in the middle" in Nahuatl.[5] In 2002, one of these so-called *niños del exilio* [children of exile], Carlos Blanco Aguinaga, described the intermediate situation that *nepantla* represents in negative terms; as he saw it, the internationalism that characterized them was "una forma de sustraerse al conflicto de identidad" [a way of withdrawing oneself from the conflict of identity] and demonstrating that they were "ni aquí ni allá" [neither here nor there] (38–9). This vague internationalism distinguished these writers from older exiles like Manuel Altolaguirre, Max Aub, Agustí Bartra, or Emilio Prados, who had been, according to Blanco Aguinaga, "internacionalistas en función de transformar la realidad española y, ya en el exilio, seguían pensando en España como ámbito natural de su producción" [internationalists who worked to transform the Spanish reality and, once in exile, continued thinking about Spain as the natural environment for their production] (38–9).

Although Segovia did not dispute that he belonged to "una clase netamente particularizada" [a clearly particularized class] such as that of "los niños del exilio," he explained that circumstances made him feel "marginal y anómalo" [marginal and anomalous] and without a "patria" [fatherland] long before the exile brought about by the civil war ("Entretien" 235):

> Nací en Valencia por casualidad, pero cuando vinimos a Madrid me llamaban *pataqueta*, un panecillo valenciano. Luego, durante la guerra, nos marchamos a Valencia para huir de los bombardeos. Fue el primer lugar en el que me llamaron refugiado. Nos lo llamaban los niños valencianos a los de Madrid. Y nos tiraban piedras. Luego, en Francia, *petit réfugié*. Y en México, *refugacho*. ("El exilio no es" n. pag.)
>
> [I was born in Valencia by coincidence, but when we came to Madrid they called me *pataqueta*, a type of small Valencian bread. Later, during the war, we went to Valencia to flee the bombings. It was the first place where I was called a refugee. The children from Valencia called the children from Madrid refugees. And they threw rocks at us. Later, in France, *petit réfugié*. And in Mexico, *refugacho*.]

In this light, the particular socio-historical circumstances of Segovia's personal experience of uprootedness do not entirely overlap with those of the children of exile with whom he is usually associated (López Aguilar xviii–xxxv). The writer underscored this difference in 2008: "mi experiencia personal es distinta. Comprendo a aquellos que vivieron profundamente el exilio de sus padres, pero yo no lo viví así" [my personal experience is different. I understand those who experienced the exile of their parents in a profound way, but I did not experience it that way] (*Apalabrarse* 60). Segovia consequently tried to exile himself from both the exilic experience of his elders and the exilic awareness that his contemporaries – the "niños del exilio" – inherited from writers as emblematic as Aub or Cernuda ("Respuestas" 216).

Roberto Ruiz, another child of exile, noted in 1989 that when Segovia's contemporaries wanted to write about Spain, they had to "volverla a inventar" [reinvent it], since the place from which they had been exiled constituted "un ambiente difuso" [a vague environment] (2). But it was precisely in this exilic context, especially in the early 1940s, that, as Blanco Aguinaga maintained in 2008, Segovia was already making a point of his singularity as a poet: "era el poeta ... Por algo lo decía desde los 14 o 15 años. Y claro, aunque ha hecho otras cosas, Tomás es siempre poeta" [He was *the* poet ... He had said so since he was fourteen or fifteen for a reason. And, of course, although he has done other things, Tomás is always a poet] (qtd. in López Aguilar 56). To the extent that, as Faber argues, the cultural production of Republican writers exiled in Mexico is marked by the defence of an idealized Spanish nation, Segovia's poetry would, in principle, invite a political reading premised on its referential distance vis-à-vis his elders' expressly national rhetoric and his contemporaries' relatively indirect rhetoric (*Exile* X–XI, 10).

It could then be argued that Segovia sought to exile himself not only from his elders' exile from their "lived nation" – particularly as "invented" during the civil war – but also from what could be termed the twice-invented nation that the *nepantla* group wanted to write about (Hobsbawm, "Introduction" 13–14).[6] This distance would explain the absence from Segovia's work of explicit apostrophes or references like "¿Dónde estás, España? Donde sea te veo" [Where are you, Spain? I see you everywhere], written by Aub between 1941 and 1944, when he was nearly forty years old; the ironic "somos (nos lo dicen) / 'la España peregrina'" [we are (we are told) / 'the peregrine Spain'], published in 1959 by Nuria Parés, a "niña del exilio" [girl of exile] born in 1925, two years before Segovia; the melancholy "Catedral de León, tierra de España," "sólo vista en fotografía" [Cathedral of León, land of Spain, only seen in photography], which Enrique de Rivas, another child of exile, put to press in 1949, before he was twenty; or "España, sombra, España, / garganta en que me nacen las palabras," [Spain, shadow, Spain, / throat in which my words are born], penned by Jomi García Ascot, Segovia's exact contemporary, in 1964 (Aub 64; Sicot, *Ecos* 129, 305, 145).

In this sense, the referential distance between Segovia's poetic work and so-called exilic poetry is programmatic. Segovia stated his eccentric position eloquently: "yo ya estaba marginándome porque esa ha sido la vocación de toda mi vida, estar al margen siempre" [I was already marginalizing myself because that's been my calling all my life: to be always on the margin] ("Luz de aquí" 71). This distance comes as a result of the writer's decision to avoid in his poems what he called the "impronta" [stamp] of the historic Spanish exile, which he dismissed as a "tipo (menor) de patriotismo" [(minor) type of patriotism] and a "discurso de la opresión" [discourse of oppression] ("Respuestas" 215). Indeed, Segovia was very careful in his use of the term *patria*:

> Hay que tener muchísimo cuidado de no decir, por ejemplo, "Esto es mi patria, mi terruño, mi raíz", porque en seguida se vuelve peligrosísimo. Así empiezan todos los fascismos del mundo, empiezan con mi infancia y mi patria y mi mamá y mi papá ... No hay que olvidar que la palabra "patria" ya es un falseamiento. Porque empieza por convertir a la madre en padre, porque hace de la patria la tierra del padre pero no de la madre. ("Entretien" 234)
>
> [One must be very careful not to say, for example, "This is my fatherland, my native soil, my root," because at once it becomes very dangerous. This is how all fascisms in the world begin; they begin with my childhood and my fatherland and my mom and my dad ... Do not forget that the word "fatherland" is already a distortion. Because it begins by turning the mother into a father, because it makes the fatherland the land of the father but not of the mother.]

To Segovia, the very idea of identity was reprehensible, and he claimed to feel neither "nacional" [national] nor "identificado" [identified] (*Apalabrarse* 100). Thus, the seeming universalism of his poetry was a political gesture aimed at undermining the notion of national identity and belonging. Segovia saw it as an oppressive notion also among his contemporaries Rivas and García Ascot, even though they defended such national identity in a detached manner.

Despite his attempts to distance himself from "poesía 'exilista'" ["exilist" poetry], however, Segovia recognized with some resignation in 2002 that many of his readers' interest in his poetic work arose from a reductive view of exile linked to the idea of national identity. In his opinion, this was not the situation in Mexico, where most of his readers were located and the theme of exile was comparatively unimportant ("Entretien" 235).[7] Nevertheless, neither his warnings about the disparity between poetic and institutional language nor his attempts to discourage reductive readings of his poetry based on the theme of the historical Spanish exile have prevented the reception of his poetic work within a clearly and even exclusively national framework ("Márgenes" 58–72). Cervantes Institute Director Carmen Caffarel's 2011 statement on the occasion of the poet's death provides a significant example of this type of reception:

> las letras españolas pierden a uno de los grandes referentes de lo que se ha denominado la generación de poetas españoles en el exilio. Su escritura honda y reflexiva, al

margen de corrientes, auténtica y a veces difícilmente clasificable, lo hizo merecedor de premios de la talla del Juan Rulfo o el Octavio Paz. Aunque pasó más de media vida en el exilio, circunstancia que marcó toda su obra, supo mantener su vinculación con España sin rencor. (n. pag.)

[Spanish letters have lost one of the icons of what has been called the generation of Spanish poets in exile. His deep and reflective writing, at the margin of trends, authentic and sometimes difficult to classify, made him worthy of awards such as the Juan Rulfo Prize or the Octavio Paz Prize. Although he spent more than half his life in exile, a circumstance that marked all of his work, he was able to maintain his connection to Spain without ill will.]

This statement makes three direct references to Spain, but none to Mexico, the country where the poet lived and died and where the portion of his personal archive that had remained in Spain was transferred for storage shortly after his demise (Talavera n. pag.). Furthermore, the director of the Cervantes Institute suggests that Segovia is simply an exiled Spanish poet. Omitting or circumventing the biographical details that would complicate his purported national identity, she orients her reading of his poetry around the episode of the historic Spanish exile, and interprets this episode without regard for its cultural repercussions in Mexico. Devoid of context, her mention of the Juan Rulfo and Octavio Paz Prizes only serves to highlight the national (and nationalist) slant of this institutional homage.

Ironically, Christopher Domínguez Michael, the president of the jury of the Premio Juan Rulfo, announced the decision to award Segovia the prize in symmetrically nationalistic terms: "Segovia es un escritor mexicano" [Segovia is a Mexican writer] (Espinosa n. pag.).[8] The exclusive national identifications that both Caffarel and Domínguez Michael institutionalized contradict the poet's own idea of his *patria*. For Segovia, his *patria* was "intermitente" [intermittent] because "uno no es perpetuamente español o mexicano, uno lo es a ratos y nunca del todo, uno lo es un poco, a veces uno tiene algo de ... uno o la obra de uno" [one is not perpetually Spanish or Mexican, one is those things for a time and never entirely, one is those things a little bit, sometimes one has something of ... one or one's work] ("Entretien" 233). The anomaly and marginality that, to Segovia, shaped his biography are dialectically reinforced against a background of different homogenizing definitions assigned by political and cultural institutions.

These national identifications cast into relief precisely the difference that characterizes the universality advocated by the poet. But in doing so such identifications blur the dialectical interplay between universality and particularity articulated in Segovia's idea of exile: "Extranjero propiamente yo no me siento en ningún sitio, pero precisamente porque no me siento extranjero en ningún sitio es otra manera de sentirme extranjero en todas partes. En España me siento tan perteneciente como me siento en México, como me sentía en Uruguay cuando vivía en Uruguay" [I don't feel like a foreigner proper anywhere, but precisely because I don't feel like a foreigner anywhere it's another way of feeling like a foreigner everywhere. In Spain I feel like I belong as much as I feel like I belong in Mexico, as I felt in Uruguay when I lived in Uruguay] ("Luz de aquí" 76). Indeed, without taking into account his paradoxical marginal cosmopolitanism, Segovia's years of somewhat reluctant centrality in the inner circles of the Mexican literary intelligentsia would be hard to understand:

> Siempre he sido marginal aunque no marginado, que no es lo mismo ... Yo había seguido ... trabajando fuera de grupos [en la Facultad de Filosofía y Letras]. Pero en una época en que estaba muy desvalido, el que me ayudó a no quedarme totalmente aislado fue Xirau, y a través de Xirau me conecté con el grupo de la *Revista Mexicana de Literatura*, es decir, me conecté con Carlos Fuentes ... [Y]o no era parte, no formaba proyectos con ellos ni ellos conmigo ... Cuando disolvieron *Plural* yo no estaba en México y ya no estaba en *Plural*. Me sentí esa vez sí marginado porque de todos modos yo había sido muy cercano a *Plural* aunque no estaba ya en México y me dejaron completamente al margen. ("Luz de aquí" 71–2, 75)
>
> [I've always been marginal but not marginalized, which is not the same thing ... I kept ... working outside of groups [at the School of Philosophy and Literature]. But at a time when I felt I was quite helpless, Xirau helped me avoid ending up totally isolated, and through Xirau I got in touch with the *Revista Mexicana de Literatura* group – that is, I got in touch with Carlos Fuentes ... I was not part of it, I did not do projects with them, nor they with me ... When *Plural* was dissolved I was not in Mexico and I was not in *Plural* anymore. This time I did feel marginalized because in any case I had been very close to *Plural* even though I was not in Mexico anymore, and they left me completely on the margin.]

Segovia's self-fashioning as "marginal" and as not, or only intermittently, "identificado" – and therefore as resisting the sense of state and national control that the term "identificado" connotes – defines his public persona. More important, as Said's contrapuntal model and Appiah's redefinition of cosmopolitanism suggest, exclusive national identifications erase the ethical element subtending the dialectical interplay between particularity and universality that characterizes such self-fashioning.

The universalist distance that Segovia contrapuntally proposed, in contrast to any collective or institutional particularist reading, marks the horizon of expectations that becomes available to the reader who encounters the term *patria* in his poems. "Patria" appears devoid of geographical or historical characteristics that would permit its identification:

> Nunca dije nosotros sin que al punto
> Alguna voz en mí gritara ¡ellos!
> Tuve todas las patrias verdaderas

Las únicas que dejan a sus hijos
Dueños de todo su peligro
Las que no los protegen de otras patrias. (*Poesía: 1943–1997* 529)[9]

The plurality of identities of these "patrias" is prefigured by pronominal jumps in the first verses. Issuing from an undefined voice split between the first- and the third-person singular – "dije," "alguna voz" – pronouns shift from the first-person plural to the third-person plural, passing through the first-person singular. The "patrias" of this pronominally mobile voice are anonymous, different from other "patrias" by virtue of the fact that they are indifferent to their natives' fate and leave their "hijos" in the precarious situation of displacement or homelessness. In their relative anonymity or indistinctness, these "patrias" for the homeless constitute an aporia that recalls both the formulation "exiliarse del exilio," and the most overtly universalist verses that Segovia wrote on the condition of exile:

desde el comienzo ya no estaba en la casa mi casa
ni en la tierra mi tierra ni el amor en mi amor
la memoria estuvo siempre en otra parte
y de círculo en círculo todo fue exilio. (*Poesía: 1943–1997* 234)[10]

The metonymic transfer throughout these verses effects a series of figurative dislocations around possible identity modes: "ya no estaba en la casa mi casa / ni en la tierra mi tierra ni el amor en mi amor." But the totalizing "exilio" in which these dislocations conclude does not simply come as a result of a lack of particular characteristics that might allow a proper name, and an identity, to be given to "la casa," "la tierra," and "el amor." Even the possibility of refuge from a vague universality that the first-person possessive adjectives may suggest to the reader in relatively particularized phrases like "mi casa," "mi tierra," and "mi amor" is withheld by the difference introduced by the metonymic reiteration of identical nouns. This metonymic reiteration continues beyond the poem through the border-crossing intertextual echo of the verses "Yo ya no soy quien soy / ni mi casa es ya mi casa" [But I'm no longer I / and my house is no longer mine], from Federico García Lorca's famous 1928 "Romance sonámbulo" [Sleepwalking Ballad] (555). Notably, García Lorca's *romance* is, among other things, a fragmented narrative about an unfulfilled desire for refuge in someone else's house (Maurer, "Poetry" 29). Thus the nomad's memory also seems to be "siempre en otra parte" in that it is mediated by other verses about dislocation.

Within the spatial approach to his poetry that even Segovia resigned himself to accepting, these verses can be read as allusions to an experience of uprootedness that the poet publicly decried until shortly before his death: the experience of being trapped at the margin of history, having no name, no voice, and no say on the course of political events: "lo más triste del exilio ... es que nos exilia de la historia ... Ni Max [Aub] ni yo nos las veíamos con los protagonistas de la historia. Yo desde siempre; Max, ya no" [the saddest thing about exile ... is that it exiles us from history ... Neither Max [Aub] nor I dealt with the protagonists of history. I never have; Max no longer does] (*Exiliados* 262). Segovia's personal condemnation of the political marginality of uprootedness extends across space and time; for the poet, Spanish exiles in Mexico of every age shared this marginality "con todos los desarraigados del mundo, emigrantes, metecos, refugiados, desplazados" [with all the uprooted of the world, emigrants, metics, refugees, displaced persons] and with "[t]oda esa población de no ciudadanos o de ciudadanos de segunda, cada vez más numerosa en los países del primer mundo" [that whole population of non-citizens or second-class citizens, increasingly large in the countries of the first world] (*Digo* 162–3). And yet, it is because of this commonality that, in his view, Spanish Republican exiles should have discredited the idea of national identity: "Eso es lo que la gente del exilio olvidó, que formábamos parte de un exilio más vasto" [That is what the people in exile forgot, that we were part of a greater exile] (*Apalabrarse* 67).[11]

This border-crossing and cross-historical dimension of the exilic condition may explain why Segovia referred to his trips to Spain as a variation on Aub's rhetoric of exile, a variation that enabled him to take historical distance from Aub's explicit thematizations of nation while nonetheless paying homage to his critical legacy: "yo no he vuelto, voy y vengo" [I have not returned, I come and go] ("Reúne" n. pag.). Segovia resorted to an analogous idea of coming and going to describe his first visit to Madrid in 1976 after more than thirty-five years of absence, and only seven after Aub's visit: "Cuando me preguntan: '¿Por qué volviste?' Digo que yo no he vuelto. Como decía Max Aub, aunque en otro sentido, he venido, pero no he vuelto. Quería decir que volver no significaba que quisiera integrarse, sino asomarse. Yo no he vuelto porque no puedo volver. Sigo viviendo entre dos mundos" [When they ask me, 'Why did you return?' I say that I have not returned. As Max Aub said, although in another sense, I have come, but I have not returned. He meant that to return did not mean that he wanted to integrate himself, but rather to take a brief look. I have not returned because I cannot return. I continue to live between two worlds] ("El exilio no es" n. pag.). Segovia eschewed Aub's tense rhetoric of national belonging and alienation in that his return was not marked by the conventional political borders of Spain or Europe. At least in the specific circumstances of his visit right after Franco's death in 1975, his dialectic of exile was driven by an anthropological desire to return to his childhood, especially to a vaguely defined agricultural temporality closely linked to Mediterranean culture ("Entretien" 236).

Following Segovia's geographical comings and goings as a perpetual exile that outlines marginal spaces and times between understood and understated national identities, the reader can move dialectically among various discourses of exile: the exiles identified in the public intellectual's statements and the unidentified exiles configured again and again in the poet's verses. More specifically, the reader can attempt to track the different positions of the *pataqueta*, the *petit réfugié*, and the *refugacho* – historically and geographically situated in the 1930s and 1940s in Spain, France, and Mexico – and that of the anonymous "meteco" [metic] that populates his poetry, difficult to place because "perdur[a] / en el refugio enfermo de la amada ceguera" [he endures / in the sick refuge of beloved blindness] (*Poesía: 1943–1997* 733). Simultaneously or – in Edward Said's terms – contrapuntally, the reader can come and go "de círculo en círculo" [from circle to circle] in both the historical sense and in a cross-temporal anthropological sense: in the historical sense, the reader can move between Segovia's particular experience as a young boy who already felt marginal and anomalous and the universal experience of displacement that he decried; cross-temporally, the reader can move between the universal "la tierra" and the particular "mi tierra" of his verses (234). These relative shifts between particularity and universality reproduce the dialectic between nationalism and exile that Said identified as a relationship between opposites informing and constituting each other (176).

Segovia's explorations of the shifting "I" are already traceable in his earliest poetry. A case in point is "Navegante" [Seafarer], a poem included in *País del cielo: 1943–1946*. Segovia wrote it when he was sixteen to nineteen years old; that is, three to six years after his arrival in Mexico as a *refugacho*:

Por más que busco el rompiente
de mis olas, estoy siempre
más allá de mi horizonte;
mi espuma siempre alcanzando
más allá de lo que alcanza. (*Cuaderno I* 179)[12]

The search of oneself or, rather, of *yo mismo* in these lines materializes as the paradoxical movement within and beyond itself generated by the ever-recurring breaking foam of the waves. The self-fashioning of the "I" is compared through metaphor to – but also paradoxically carried through via metonymy and enjambment as – an unreachably dynamic horizon ("alcanzando / más allá de lo que alcanza"). Tropically and typographically, these verses keep coming and going. They converse with each other while diversifying themselves, figuring, disfiguring, and configuring, both constatively and performatively, the ceaseless foaming waves of a shifting, drifting self, distantly building on, and complicating, Paul Valéry's famous line "La mer, la mer, toujours recommencée!" [the sea, the sea, perpertually renewed!] (212–13). Focus on the "yo" in Segovia's lines throws into relief the deployment of personal deixis, bringing out the relative absence of the first person – apart from its trace in the self-defeating possessive adjectives designating elements like "olas," "horizonte," and "espuma" that cannot be possessed in the setting of the poem – and above all the absence of the first-person singular pronoun.

However, it could be argued that "yo" is spectrally re-presented as literally being beyond itself in the ending "est-oy." The instability of self, allegorized in the description of the endless breaking of the waves, is inscribed in the anagram "yo," which performs a dislocation whereby it becomes linguistically in exile from exile. This anagrammatic reading of the first-person-singular pronoun's uncanny presence in Segovia's early poetry is premised on his analysis, as a translator of Jacques Lacan's *Écrits* into Spanish, of the grammatical singularity of the French pronominal equivalent *je* at the most elementary linguistic level, vis-à-vis verbal endings in Spanish:

> *je* no es en realidad sino una especie de desinencia verbal, función que sólo tendría equivalente en nuestra lengua en la efectiva desinencia personal del verbo (la *o* de "amo"); pero mientras *je* tiene la autonomía, la identidad y la persistencia de una palabra, nuestras desinencias son sentidas como parte inseparable del verbo, una parte extremadamente cambiante y que puede llegar incluso a reducirse a cero. El hablante francés establece espontáneamente la relación entre un *moi* aislable y subsistente y un *je* puramente funcional. ("Nota" 16)
>
> [in fact, *je* is nothing other than a sort of verbal ending, a function which in our language would only be equivalent to the actual personal ending of the verb (the *o* in "amo"); but whereas *je* has the autonomy, identity, and persistence of a word, our endings are felt as an inseparable part of the verb, an extremely shifting part that can even be reduced to zero. The French speaker spontaneously establishes the relation between an isolatable and enduring *moi* and a purely functional *je*]

The relative shifts between the particularity and universality of an anonymous "yo" are here generated metaphorically – wave by wave, so to speak – but also through basic linguistic differences. The play of differences at the level of the signifier – foregrounded if the reader pays close attention to the verbal fabric of the poem, that is, the sort of close attention that translation requires – helps explain Segovia's paradoxical notion of exile.[13]

A Nomad's Historical Marginality

One of the most prominent circles of exile at the margins of history that Segovia outlined in his poetry figures in his collection "Cuaderno del nómada" [Nomad's Notebook], published in Mexico in 1982. The writer stated in 1986 that these poems allow readers to see his "impresiones" [impressions] of his 1976 visit to Spain, his first trip there since childhood ("Respuestas" 217). Significantly, a comparison of different editions of this notebook reveals that these impressions grow vaguer over time, as if Segovia tried to make it increasingly difficult to read the poems in a biographical or historical key. "Cuaderno del nómada" appeared in the last section of *Poesía 1943–1976*, the first edition of his collected poetry.

One year later, in 1983, it was included in the first part of the poetry collection *Partición: 1976–1982* [Partition]. The final version of "Cuaderno" appeared in 1998, in the expanded edition of his collected poetry, *Poesía 1943–1997*. Although Segovia did not usually include information to tell the reader the place and time of a poem's production, the title of the first edition of "Cuaderno" was accompanied by the year – 1976 – and the collection closed with the note "Madrid, invierno de 1976" [Madrid, winter of 1976]. While the "nómada" – the collection's protagonist – declares that he builds his "tienda siempre fuera de los muros" [tent always outside the walls], these spatiotemporal coordinates can also place the speaker of the poem within a city called Madrid in the year 1976 (*Poesía: 1943–1976* 421).

These coordinates disappear, however, from the 1983 and 1998 editions of "Cuaderno," so that only a reading based on prior knowledge of Segovia's particular historical and biographical circumstances would allow readers to locate the poem's production in Madrid in 1976 and thus contextualize the situation, attitude, and intention of the speaker. Such prior knowledge could furnish the reader with an experience of spatiotemporal disruption, but it could also conceivably justify the interpretation that "al llegar a España, el paso del Nómada acaricia y humaniza la tierra" [upon arriving in Spain, the Nomad's footsteps caress and humanize the land] or that Spain appears "indiferente ante el sufrimiento del Nómada" [indifferent to the Nomad's suffering] (Logan 740). This strictly referential reading presupposes a conception of the poem as a dramatic monologue or a narrative imitation of statements made in real life, allowing the reader to imagine the circumstances that lead a certain "I" to speak this way. Hence the speaker of "Cuaderno del nómada" could be, for example, an exile from the Spanish Civil War like Tomás Segovia, who returns to Spain, his country of origin, at the end of the Franco dictatorship. The spatiotemporal information, "Madrid, invierno de 1976," paratextually inserted after the poems in the first edition of "Cuaderno del nómada," provides clues that support such a reading – one that Segovia would dismissively call a thematic reading of "exilista" poetry ("Respuestas" 215).

Nonetheless, even before this information was stripped from the text in later editions, the poems of "Cuaderno del nómada" complicated thematic readings inspired by a mimetic model. When the nomad hyperbolically exclaims "¿Todo el viento fue mío?" [All the wind was mine?] while speaking to an "[i]nquieto Ángel de alas de borrasca" [[r]estless Angel with stormy wings] (*Poesía: 1943–1997* 425–6), it seems difficult to take the voice of the speaker as an imitation or fictional interpretation of a plausible historical and personal statement (Culler, "Changes" 38–41). This difficulty affects nearly all of Segovia's poetry. For example, it is problematic to identify and narratively reconstruct the situation, attitude, and intention of a speaker through a voice that apostrophizes: "Memoria, memoria desolada, / oh mal mío, la noche se prolonga. // Aún iremos por otras regiones desoladas" [Memory, desolate memory, / o my woe, the night grows long. // We shall still go through more desolate regions] (272). As Jonathan Culler has noted in his study of the function of apostrophes in lyric: "to ask when, why, and how one might say, for example, 'O lift me as a wave ...' is not guaranteed to yield pertinent replies" ("Changes" 40). What kind of voice constitutes an "I" about which it is difficult to ask when, why, and how that "I" speaks in its particular mode? The large majority of Segovia's poems seem characteristically lyrical in Culler's sense, insofar as it seems challenging to recreate a plausible context for them.

Segovia described a poetic "I" that resists mimetic readings of a biographical nature: "Si el poeta habla en primera persona es porque toda persona es necesariamente primera. Su 'yo' no es el de la psicología, es el del lenguaje" [If the poet speaks in the first person it is because every person is necessarily first. The 'I'of the poet is not that of psychology, it is that of language] ("Márgenes" 60). As a grammatical category, the "I" of lyric poetry gives the illusion of a live voice, since, as Mary Malcolm Gaylord has argued, "hace 'presente,' revistiéndola de la ilusión de realidad, a una *persona* (en el sentido radical etimológico de la palabra)" [it makes a *person* (in the radical etymological sense of the word) "present," investing that person with the illusion of reality] ("Imagen" 299). That is, unlike the "I" of epic poetry, narration, or dramatic monologue, to whom the reader listens, the "I" of lyric poetry functions as a personal deictic in such a way that the reader can speak with the voice of the poem. The meaning of the pronoun shifts according, in large part, to the reader's context, because the "I"'s main function is indicative. Thus the reader can temporarily become a first person that "habla por sí y de sí" [speaks for itself and about itself] (Sánchez Ferlosio 319). As we saw earlier, a lyric, unlike a novel, is also spoken by the reader: "When we read a lyric, aloud or silently, we utter the words, we temporarily occupy the position of the speaker" (Culler, *Pursuit* XXII). In this way, the performative function of the lyric "I" allows the reader to share, if only for a fleeting moment, a common voice (Quance 234).

The "I" of "Cuaderno del nómada" resists being reduced to a constative "I" whose statements constitute a true or false description of a given state of things (Culler, *Deconstruction* 112). Instead of an "I" that the reader listens to while imagining an external situation that plausibly corresponds to that "I," the poet constructs a performative "I" that the reader can use to speak in keeping with the situation that the poem creates. Specifically, "Cuaderno del nómada" constructs a marginal "I" in a precarious situation with respect to the voices of the city. The lack of precise spatiotemporal references to the nomad creates the linguistic conditions whereby anyone can occupy the speaker's site of enunciation in every here and now of reading, hence abandoning for a moment his or her original site of enunciation as well as the language of his or her particular *polis*. Thus, in the poem titled "Cuaderno del nómada," the "I" describes the experience of being about to utter a voice "quemada en los caminos" [burned on the roads] (*Poesía: 1943–1997* 424). This situation of marginality leads the nomad to speak an uncanny "lengua bárbara" [barbarous language], supposedly alien to the civilized language of the *polis* (420).

"Bandera" [Flag], a prose poem also included in "Cuaderno del nómada," performs the way in which the deictic "I" leaves the reader of that "I" in a situation of marginality, separated from the *polis*. Segovia creates this situation by grammatically banishing the "I" of the poem or, as Carlos Piera has it, "dispersándolo, desdibujándolo, haciéndolo imposible o accesible a cualquiera" [dispersing it, blurring it, making it impossible or accessible to anyone] (28). As we will see below, within the framework of readings oriented around the condition of exile, this banishment has ethical and political consequences:

BANDERA

> Mi tienda siempre fuera de los muros. Mi lengua aprendida siempre en otro sitio. Mi bandera perpetuamente blanca. Mi nostalgia vasta y caprichosa. Mi amor ingenuo y mi fidelidad irónica. Mis manos graves y en ellas un incesante rumor de pensamientos. Mi porvenir sin nombre. Mi memoria deslumbrada en el amor incurable del olvido. Lastrada en el desierto mi palabra. Y siempre desnudo el rostro donde sopla el tiempo. (*Poesía: 1943–1997* 424)[14]

"Bandera" resists the narrative reconstruction of the situation, attitude, and goals of an "I" that can be identified as an exile in Mexico who returned to Spain in 1976. In the poem's reiterative series of absolute clauses, the "I" only manages to identify itself in a series of predicates. This "I" does not even appear grammatically in the poem; it does not act, or at least does not assert itself as a subject that can take a verb. It is an absent "I," or, given the number of times it is indicated by a possessive pronoun, it is repeatedly displaced.

This passive "I" uses the "lengua aprendida siempre en otro sitio" to speak helplessly and in fragments, reiterating phrases in the passive voice that take a first-person possessive pronoun. The reiteration of the pronoun shifts syntactically in the penultimate phrase, where his or her "palabra" appears "[l]astrada en el desierto," evoking – as in Aub's poem "Tres años," but without any specific spatiotemporal reference – the biblical topos of the *vox clamantis in deserto*, as if the voice cried out but no one heard it. The reader who occupies the place of the "I" is thus grammatically and rhetorically displaced to the margin, at least with respect to the anonymous walls beyond which the suggested "I" sets up a tent. Any attempt to reinstate this marginal "I" is compromised by "el amor incurable del olvido" [the incurable love of forgetfulness] that obscures a view of memory. In Segovia's poetry, according to Piera's reading, "'Yo,' requisito de la condición moral de lo que digo, me hallo tan sin identidades y determinaciones que doy fácilmente en 'anti-yo' o en 'nadie,' inútil hasta como punto de referencia" ["I," that requirement of the moral condition of what "I" say, find myself so without identities and determinants that "I" easily turn into an "anti-I" or a "no one," useless even as a point of reference] (168).

The displacement performed in "Bandera" can be construed as universal in space and time: the poem points to both a permanent but temporary residence ("mi tienda") and a seemingly eternal temporality (the temporal adverbs "siempre" and "perpetuamente") which is situated in the marginal "I." All but one verb in the poem are participles. The exception is "sopla," the verb whose subject is, in fact, "tiempo." This situated time reads, in the context of Segovian nomadism, as the time of "vida" – a sort of continuous present with no turning back. As the poet explained, "la restauración de lo perdido sería una negación de nuestra vida más radical aún que su ausencia, porque es esa vida misma la que lo hizo perdido" [the restoration of what has been lost would be a denial of our life even more radical than its absence, because it is that very life that lost it] ("Respuestas" 209).

The first poem of "Cuaderno del nómada," titled "Retorno" [Return], already situates the reader in a cross-temporal now: "(Siempre viajo hacia ahora / Y nunca nada está más lejos / Que lo que queda atrás)" [(I always travel towards now / And nothing is ever farther away / Than that which stays behind)] (*Poesía: 1943–1997* 418). However, the fact of always returning to the now of the poem does not necessarily negate "that which stays behind" – indeed, the verse break makes for two possible readings: both the "ahora" [now] and "lo que queda atrás" could be distant – just as "lo perdido" does not disappear merely because its "restauración" is impossible. Another of Segovia's poems calls memory a "vasallaje alternativo / de donde voy y vengo" [alternative vassalage / from where I come and go] (113). Even in the time that blows in the present indicative in "Bandera," memory remains active, in spite or because of the fact that it is "deslumbrada en el amor incurable del olvido" [dazzled by the incurable love of forgetfulness] (424). Following Segovia's dialectic, it is possible to return to the past, but only to a past irreparably touched by the oblivion, the anonymity, and marginality shaping the "I," a past that the now of the poem brings into the present.

This marginal "I," available for the reader's use, has not abandoned all flags but rather flies a white one. Here, the white flag symbolizes the absence of weapons, surrender, or an end to hostilities, but it also allows the question of identity – and more precisely the national identity that a flag often signifies – to become permanently suspended or available. The symbol refers to the sense of identity, but its interpretation remains undecidable, irreducible. Memory is "deslumbrada," so the past offers no guarantees, and the future is "sin nombre"; the flag therefore serves only to demonstrate the extent to which, as Segovia stated, the nomadic poet "hace su casa en todas partes" [makes his house everywhere] (*Poesía: 1943–1997*

424; *Tiempo* 661). In other words, the white flag is a symbol of poetry, viewed as a place external or alien to the *polis*, a place of displaced enunciation where the reader becomes aware of "la creatividad todavía proteica, informe, del lenguaje" [the still-protean, unformed creativity of language] that has not yet been fixed, interpreted, or institutionalized as meaning ("Entretien" 244).[15]

In Segovia's terms, the poem, in this sense, is "entrando en nuestro mundo de significaciones pero todavía (o ya) no disuelta en él" [entering into our world of meanings but still (or already) not dissolved in it] (*Miradas* 50). The poetic language is, then, a barbarous language that consists of "el quebrantamiento de la ley de la lengua ... en el seno de la significación" [the breaking of the law of language ... in the heart of meaning] (38). The barbarous language of poetry lies at the margin of the Platonic *polis* but does not deny that Republic. After all, the nomad's language is, among other things, fundamentally intelligible to a Spanish speaker. Although the nomad cannot return to his particular past, language, or place of origin, he does not abandon them entirely. The space of universal marginality that the nomad inhabits is only possible as a result of the particular, differentiated exile that Segovia experienced. But only a displacement away from national and linguistic institutions offers the first person the possibility to differentiate itself as an "I."[16]

According to Segovia, exile acquires political weight when it allows the reader to "traspasar la idea de país y de idioma" [go beyond the idea of country and language], to arrive in a sort of linguistic no man's land that anyone can enter ("Respuestas" 206). This type of universality is based on a difference that is, after all, "liberada de su limitación de simple tema" [freed from its limitation as a simple theme] (206). The difference is defined per se, radically, as a marginal place where the speaker cannot recognize his/her own sovereignty, cannot locate or identify him-/herself spatially or temporally. This seeming freedom from limitation allows virtually any reader of Spanish to occupy the "I" position in the poem so as to frame – if only temporarily – his/her own episodic particularity in what Appiah calls cosmopolitan or universal terms (Sánchez Ferlosio 317; "Education" 88).[17] The almost complete lack of explicit historical and geographical references in Segovia's nomadic poetry can be taken as an invitation to consider the dimensions of a tragedy that belongs to every place and every era. Namely, it gestures towards the uprootedness of remaining at the margin of history and political geography that results when one lacks the protection of a legal *patria* and cannot be a protagonist of one's political history, as was experienced by Max Aub and Tomás Segovia. Does Segovia's poetry suggest a universality shaded by the multiple particularities and differences of marginality, a universality that is cross-temporal and that, in the poet's spatiotemporal terms, wanders through history as if it were a horizon of meaning? ("Márgenes" 68). And if we can read Segovia's formulation "exiliarse del exilio" this way, what ethical and political potential does this paradoxical suggestion imply?

Following Appiah, Homi Bhabha has described a modern cosmopolitanism characterized by marginality and located "on the liminal borders of the homogenizing discourses of nationality" ("Unsatisfied" 196). This cosmopolitan marginal community comprises "refugees, peoples of the diaspora, and migrants and exiles" (Breckenridge et al. 582). In an analogous way, Segovia drew from his particular condition as an exile to publicly denounce not only the oppressive discourse of patriotism but also the universal problem of the worldwide uprooting of "ciudadanos" [citizens] and "ciudadanos de segunda" [second-class citizens] (*Digo* 162–3). In his 2013 examination of the cross-border webs formed by Republican exiles after 1939 and by Spanish migrants in the 1970s, Benito del Pliego suggested that Segovia's writings could be productively mapped following critical categories such as "nacionalidades lábiles" [labile nationalities] (16).[18] In this light, Segovia's "exiliarse del exilio" would signal an easily redefinable textual space that, like a white flag, suspends but does not abolish national identity, insofar as it implicitly refers to a historical exile defined by a particular national identity while also pointing to a horizon of exile defined by a universal idea of humanity.

Whatever abstract universalism can be invoked in the name of a purportedly ahistorical humanity – or, in Bhabha's terms, whatever sovereignty a "'representative' human or world-subject authorized in its mastery of events" can possess – finds itself undermined by the incurable difference of a historically situated experience of marginality such as Segovia's ("Unsatisfied" 198). For Appiah, the ethics advocated by the cosmopolitan project depend on a particular form of rootedness (*Ethics* 232). For Segovia, rootedness refers to particular and differentiated human lives like those of the "nepantla" group and the singular marginal life that was his before, during, and after the Spanish Civil War ("Entretien" 235). Yet his rootedness is also universal, he argued, insofar as the roots are up in the air, suspended at the margin of oppressive discourses of patriotism: "las raíces se arrancan hacia arriba; el desarraigo es un grado más de universalidad" [the roots are pulled out upwards; uprootedness is a greater degree of universality] ("Dentro" 160). Thus, Segovia's ethics are built on a paradoxical rootedness in uprootedness. The cosmopolitan ethics that underlies his biography creates a tension between the particular marginality of his personal experience and the universal marginality of collective experiences.

This marginal cosmopolitanism affords a horizon of ethico-political expectations onto which the reader of Segovia's poetry can project his or her own historically situated particularities, but only if they are also situated at the margin at some moment of reading – in other words, only if the particularity of reading also paradoxically takes root in uprootedness. The poems of "Cuaderno del nómada" resist being fully situated or interpreted, preserving the openness of their meaning or, as José Luis Pardo has suggested, a meaning that is "implícito e irreductible" [implicit and irreducible] (14). From this angle, Segovia's suggested cosmopolitanism is of a self-limiting order. As it is read, his poetry opens up a very specific universe of exile: a constellation of *patrias* of the homeless creating the conditions for a nomadic ethics.

The Broken Language of Ghosts

Animated as it is by Appiah's cosmopolitan ethics, the approach to Segovia's notion of exile proposed in these pages may also be easily reduced to a thematic reading. After all, Segovia's denunciation of historical uprootings can only be read, it seems, as a specific linguistic dislocation in his poetry. As the poet claimed: "Podremos creernos cuanto queramos preservadores de un idioma nacional, incluso tal vez misioneros regeneradores de los extraviados hijos de ese idioma: la realidad es que con nosotros ese idioma deja de ser nacional, se pone fuera de sí y es roto y violado" [We can believe as much as we like that we are the preservers of a national language, or even restorative missionaries to the lost children of that language: the reality is that, with us, that language ceases to be national, it goes outside of itself and is broken and violated] ("Respuestas" 207). Yet the reader who searches Segovia's poetry for traces of national linguistic identity arrives sooner or later in a linguistic no man's land, marginal, anomalous, barbarous, and without the flag of any *polis*.

León Felipe's iconic lines about the site of enunciation of the Spanish poet in exile, which we analysed in chapter 3 ("Mía es la voz antigua de la tierra. / Tú te quedas con todo / y me dejas desnudo y errante por el mundo ... / mas yo te dejo mudo ... ¡mudo!" [*Español* 24–6]) could be read now, in historical hindsight, from somewhere in Segovia's no man's land. Felipe's lines would become a telling illustration of the rhetorical undoing of a certain Romantic notion of the continuity between nation, person, and people through poetic voice. As Max Aub claimed in 1968, Felipe was not a Romantic poet: "él vino de más lejos, de la oscuridad del desierto ... porque su poesía clama en él" [he came from farther away, from the darkness of the desert ... because his poetry cries out there] ("León Felipe" 3). Likewise, with their somewhat marginal perspective for readings of Spanish Republican exilic poetry, Segovia's post-exilic essayistic reflections ring a revealingly discordant note, as they open the possibility of reading a reversal of values in Felipe's claim-making oratory. They also open the possibility of re-examining interpretations of these and other exilic poems premised on claims of personal intentionality and national representativity, including Segovia's own poems. In this retrospective sense, Felipe's "voz antigua" belongs, epitaphically, as much to "tierra" as to any "patria," since, as Aub suggested, "[t]ambién los muertos escriben; tal vez la tierra no es más que residuos de manuscritos (15).

The dialectic between universality and particularity activated by Segovia's aporetic notion of exile is dramatized in his essayistic reflections. One of the "others" of Segovia's poetry is his essayistic voice as it assertively states: "con nosotros ese idioma deja de ser nacional, se pone fuera de sí y es roto y violado" ("Respuestas" 207). Segovia's use of the first-person-plural pronoun is arresting here: it activates a plural vocality that is empowered at the same time that it is disempowered. The passive voice, "es roto y violado," runs against the grain of this plurality; in doing so, it deactivates the agent of a disquieting linguistic rupture and violation. The modifier "con nosotros" [with us] is rendered richly ambivalent: in Spanish, the proposition "con" implies, among other things, by means of, in relation to, and accompanied by. In terms of medium, circumstance, and association, "nosotros" can be parsed as uncannily active and passive. Nonetheless, "nosotros" is not necessarily the active agent of Segovia's alluded-to linguistic rupture and violation. It is a claim-subverting pronoun, both textually present and absent, both exiled and otherwise. Within Segovia's cunningly irreducible syntax is a poetic politics critical of national and linguistic identity.

The undecidability of Segovia's reflection prompts political debate, as it troubles the mutually dependent binary of poetic voice and national language among exiled writers:

> La crítica de una idea de patria (tan criticable) mediante la idea de una "patria lingüística" es insuficiente y en cambio tranquiliza de una manera peligrosa. Hay que traspasar también el patriotismo lingüístico para encontrar la idea de Palabra ... Algunos españoles exiliados en Hispanoamérica creen por ejemplo que el idioma es suyo. Extraña obcecación, cuando los hechos les están mostrando tan claramente lo contrario. ("Respuestas" 207)
>
> [The criticism of an idea of fatherland (so criticizable) through the idea of a "linguistic fatherland" is insufficient and nonetheless dangerously reassuring. Linguistic patriotism also needs to be left behind in order to find the idea of Word ... Some Spanish exiles in Hispanic America believe, for instance, that the language is theirs. Strange stubbornness, when the facts clearly show them otherwise.]

Segovia's injunction to leave a linguistic fatherland to find what he calls "la idea de Palabra" takes us back to the question of how to go into exile from exile. This question evokes, and is here mediated by, Theodor W. Adorno's reflections on the dialectical quandary faced by the exiled writer: "Authors settle into their texts like home-dwellers ... To those who no longer have a homeland, writing becomes home ... In the end, authors are not even allowed to be home in their writing" (*Minima* 51). Adorno's *Minima Moralia* in turn mediated Edward Said's reflections on the nomadic, decentred, contrapuntal quality of exilic writing. What's at stake in dwelling on the mediatedness of such critical reflections on exile? Perhaps the different modes of "vida" animated in every here and now of reading and thus the potential modes of memory that readers – including historians and critics – may activate when they examine their readerly ghosts. Indeed, this dynamic unfolds on their singular albeit ever-shifting horizon of expectations vis-à-vis the uncanny relationship between "lo vivo" and "lo escrito," as Max Aub wrote in 1944. At least in 2002, Segovia's poetry was still haunted by the ghosts of exile, as he resignedly acknowledged in view of his readers' horizon of expectations.[19]

In fact, one of the figures visiting the nameless roads Segovia's nomad travels in a poem from "Cuaderno del nómada" called "El simún del tiempo" [The simoom of time] may be that of the exile's own ghost: "El viento ha hecho invisibles los caminos / Por los que vino a este lugar de espectros" [The wind has made invisible the roads / Whereby he came to this place of spectres] (*Poesía: 1943–1997* 423). Segovia's poetry thematizes exile, but at one or several uncanny removes from the particular exilic experiences to which he refers in his essays. In this sense – in "este lugar" at least – the third-person exilic figure is exiled from him- or herself. The poet leaves roads or channels open in which readers can travel and perhaps also run into a ghost, one that may remind them of a historical intersection at which the nomad was none other than Tomás Segovia, *el refugacho*. Yet these places of travel are not quite visible, or seem somehow split – bifurcated – within themselves; therefore readers will have to invoke their own historical ghosts – and let their reading and their voicing of the poem bifurcate themselves – to remember other times and other places – the irretrievable spatiotemporal coordinates at which such roads might have been clearly visible in "lo vivo." It is also in this sense that Segovia's poetry creates the conditions for a nomadic ethics.

One historical ghost of exile that may be intertextually invoked, reread, reanimated, and commemorated here and now is, again, that of Luis Cernuda's "Lázaro."[20] As the spectre in the poem is retracing his steps back from *tierra*, the sparse scenery becomes the inner landscape of the reborn body. Sound is somehow emitted, yet the *alma* crashes against the wall of bones and therefore cannot reach the mouth and become voice. It seems as though the soul internalizes the grave as it tries to move away from it. Thus, the *ánima* is both animated and deanimated in the very midst of leaving *tierra* and becoming reanimated. Interestingly, Segovia underscored how "despersonalizado" [depersonalized] the tone of Cernuda's poem is (*Sobre exiliados* 86). In "El simún del tiempo," Segovia depicted a similar allegorical fleshless landscape of endless travel: "Corre la leve arena / Sobre la vasta tierra descarnada" [Light sand runs / Over the vast discarnate earth] (*Poesía: 1943–1997* 424). In the next poem, "Cuaderno del nómada," significantly titled "Voz de nómada" [Nomad's Voice], the figurative overlap inscribed in "tierra descarnada" is further mediated and allegorized through the synesthetic thematization of vocal suspension. The nomad states: "Y un momento he sentido / Que iba a salir de mí como un deslumbramiento / Una voz que no esperan / quemada en los caminos" [And for a moment I have felt / About to come out of me like a dazzle / A voice they did not expect / Burnt on the roads] (424).

This allegorical thematization of the tensions between voice/voicing and land/flesh draws on the border-crossing, non-chronological allegory of the spiritual journey. This is largely a trans-historical master narrative. Yet exilic poems often describe an allegorical landscape that serves to construct a story about the seeming impossibility of storytelling. In other words, they present a ghostly absence.[21] The spatiotemporal discontinuities of bodily discarnation and vocal disarticulation in poems like Cernuda's and Segovia's are intertwined with the spatiotemporal continuities of writing and, presumably, of reading. Consequently, the historical articulation of the spatiotemporal absences and disruptions traceable in each successive here-and-now of reading is among the critical questions at issue in reading seemingly cross-historical poems written in the there-and-then of exile.

Much like Aub, Segovia distrusted attempts to restore what was lost in the experience of exile. Much like María Zambrano, he considered such restorations a denial of "vida" even more radical than its absence. In this sense, the contention that the work of both exiled intellectuals and those who remained in Spain should be seen as belonging to a "solo cauce" [single channel] defined by Spanish culture needs to be qualified (Gracia, *A la intemperie*, 19, 72). To restore the exile to a "solo cauce" of culture – whether Spanish, Mexican, Hispanic-Mexican, or that of any other national identification – risks denying a "vida" inescapably mediated by cultural diversity and linguistic dislocation. Moreover, such a restoration would distort the perception of a life that, in Segovia's writings, is moulded by complex historical comings and goings. This life takes shape in the oscillations between rootedness and uprootedness along the shifting margins of different national "cauces." Accordingly, Segovia's poetry resists the axis of inclusion and exclusion of homogenizing national filiations and affiliations to the extent that his writings complicate the definition of exile as a cultural and biographical phenomenon lying in the opposition between "ensimismamiento en la tragedia histórica" [self-absorption in the historical tragedy] and "reintegración estable" [stable reintegration] (Gracia, *A la intemperie*, 19).The paradoxical path of "exiliarse del exilio" that Segovia tracked in his writings acquires its political value by calling attention to the margins of the institutional discourses that define national cultural history. These margins are eloquently reinscribed in "Veinte rastreos por mis lindes" [Twenty Trackings Through My Boundaries], the series of poems that he wrote in 2010, shortly before passing away in Mexico City (*Cuaderno* II 466–504).

A Cross-Boundary Epitaph?

On 8 November 2011, one day after Segovia died at the age of eighty-four, the Ateneo Español de México [Spanish Athenaeum of Mexico] posted an epitaphic plaque to memorialize him on its website.[22] Part of the inscription read: "Tomás

Tomás Segovia acaba de morir.

Pero su voz permanece como una expresión fundamental, bella y conmovedora, de la poesía mexicano-española del exilio republicano.

El Ateneo Español de México
lamenta profundamente la partida del poeta y envía un abrazo solidario a su esposa, sus hijos, a toda su familia, amigos y colegas.

7.1 The Ateneo Español de México's 2011 plaque memorializing Tomás Segovia. Reprinted by permission of Ateneo Español en México.

Segovia acaba de morir. Pero su voz permanece como una expresión fundamental, bella y conmovedora, de la poesía mexicano-española del exilio republicano" [Tomás Segovia just died. But his voice endures as a fundamental, beautiful, and moving expression of the Mexican-Spanish poetry of Republican exile] (figure 7.1). Three years later the prestigious Mexican press Fondo de Cultura Económica published the first edition of Segovia's collected poems, titled *Cuaderno del nómada*. The charcoal cover of the beautifully printed two-volume box set features an eye-catching photograph by Isabel Ruiz Santillana, depicting a single footprint in dramatic high relief (figure 7.2).[23]

This footprint is an uncanny image in its blurring of boundaries and perspectives. Among other things, it may suggest one of Segovia's *nómadas* upside-down under sand – as though the readers were somehow on the sand looking down – but also right-side up, as though the readers were somehow buried underneath, looking up. The box could thus be viewed – simultaneously but perhaps only

7.2 Cover of *Cuaderno del nómada*, 2014 edition of Tomás Segovia's collected poems. Photography by Isabel Ruiz. Design by León Muñoz. Reprinted by permission of Fondo de Cultura Económica.

fleetingly – as a twofold tomb, and the poetry contained under the epitaphic title *Cuaderno de nómada* as an enigmatic form of prosopopoeia signalling a voice from beyond the grave. But whose voice would be speaking? The clearly defined spatio-temporal boundaries of the commemorative plaque are somehow troubled by the cover of this two-volume set, as though the expressive voice of the representative exile – "su voz permanece como una expresión fundamental, bella y conmovedora, de la poesía mexicano-española del exilio republicano" – could also go into exile from such strict national boundaries, like a ghost moving in and out of poems, animatedly moving the readers who voice them now and again.

Coda: Antonio Machado's Afterlives and Memories of Spanish Literary History

Rereading Machado's Poetry from Tomás Segovia's Another Shore

Among the events the Ateneo Español de México held in 1979 to celebrate both the thirtieth anniversary of its opening in Mexico City and the fortieth anniversary of the arrival of exiled Republican intellectuals in Mexico was a tribute to Antonio Machado, who had died in exile forty years earlier, in 1939.[1] Coinciding with another commemoration of Machado's demise in France, which included a "peregrinaje" [pilgrimage] by Spanish students to his place of death in Collioure, the Ateneo's tribute featured a reading of a selection of his poems by the actress Ofelia Guilmáin – born in Madrid in 1921 and exiled in Mexico since 1939 – as well as Tomás Segovia's remarks about the reading.[2] Segovia's trenchant reflections would be published a year later in the Spanish literary journal *Cuadernos hispanoamericanos* under the title "Machado desde otra orilla" [Machado From Another Shore]. Segovia took the opportunity of this threefold commemoration to reminisce about his childhood years in Republican Madrid in the early thirties, before he went into exile in 1937 at age nine, first to France and then to Mexico.

As the poet and translator hastened to make clear, among the aims of his remarks was to try to save Machado from the "institución machadiana" [Machadian institution] and the "culto a Machado" [Machado cult] ("Machado" 400). In Segovia's view, one of this cult's rituals was, ironically, listening to Machado's poems as a group. For this reason, the author of *Cuaderno del nómada* decided to quote poems that would not "perpetuar y automatizar" [perpetuate and automatize] such a cult, thus sidestepping "los lugares comunes del hispanismo y de la hispanidad, de la solemnidad y del academismo ... de las estatuas" [the commonplaces of Hispanism and Hispanicity, of solemnity and academicism ... of statues] (400).[3] Accordingly, the first poem chosen by Segovia was an early, lesser-known *romance* by Machado titled "Caballitos" [Little Horses]. This *romance* is devoid of explicit historical references: it evokes the happiness felt by the first-person speaker when as a child he went round and round on a wooden horse under a blue night sky filled with stars. Segovia explained that he memorized sections of this *romance* before he left Spain as a boy, without knowing who the author of the poem was.

But Segovia's main reason for quoting "Caballitos" in particular was not his resistance against official or institutional celebrations, let alone the potential audience for his personal evocations of childhood. What Segovia found especially worth considering on such a markedly commemorative occasion was the fact that he had had to memorize a *romance* like "Caballitos" in a very specific socio-historical setting: "la circunstancia de que yo lo supiera de memoria, en mi infancia, en España" [the circumstance that I should know it by heart, in my childhood, in Spain] ("Machado" 401). During the Second Spanish Republic – from 1931 to 1939 – children memorized poems, as Segovia went on to explain, written by celebrated living Spanish poets such as Antonio Machado, or younger ones like Rafael Alberti:

> Los niños de la República se aprendían a los poetas de la República. La poesía, oíamos repetir, se hacía popular; o más bien volvía a serlo; o todavía más bien, nos decía el consenso, lo fue siempre, por lo menos en España e incluso, si apurábamos la opinión recóndita de ese consenso, *sólo* en España. Lo que no nos decían tanto es que también se hacía o se volvía a hacer didáctica. ("Machado" 401)
>
> [The children of the Republic learned the poets of the Republic. Poetry, we repeatedly heard, was becoming popular; or rather, it was popular again; or rather still, consensus told us, it always was, at least in Spain, and even, if we puzzled out the recondite opinion of that consensus, *only* in Spain. We were less often told that it was also becoming or once again becoming didactic.]

The widespread assumption among Republicans in the 1930s that poetry had always been popular but – as Segovia wryly added – *only* in Spain was premised on the Romantic belief that Spain was uniquely characterized by its popular poetry and most prominently by its so-called *Romancero popular*.

When the Second Spanish Republic was proclaimed in 1931, this Romantic belief was restated and disseminated above all by reputed literary historian and philologist Ramón Menéndez Pidal, most notably in his *Flor nueva de romances viejos* [New Garland of Old Ballads]. This famous anthology appeared in Madrid in 1928, only a few months after Segovia was born in Valencia. At the very beginning of the foreword, Menéndez Pidal squarely addressed the purportedly inextricable and exclusive connection between Spanish identity and *romances*: "España es el país del Romancero, se ha dicho; pero, ¿es esto verdad?" [Spain is the country of the *romancero*, it has been said; but is this true?] (9). Menéndez Pidal traced the origin of this national singularity to the discovery of the *romancero* by English, German, and French Romantics and ascribed to Friedrich Schlegel the notion that *romances* forged a unique link between nation and people (38). In the historian's understanding, Schlegel extolled the "hondo espíritu nacional" [deep national spirit] of Spanish literature as "el primero en el mundo" [the first in the world] on account of the "prodigiosa y fecunda continuidad" [prodigious and fecund continuity] of historical themes that the *romancero* enabled (15).[4]

Perhaps more important – Menéndez Pidal continued – whereas in nations like France epic poems fell into oblivion by the fifteenth century, popular memory in Spain was able to preserve the epic tradition through the *romance* form: "el pueblo recordó persistentemente muchos de los fragmentos más famosos y los cantó aislados" [the people persistently remembered many of the most famous fragments and sang them separately] (11). The continuity of national history was possible, Menéndez Pidal argued, because the Spanish people had learned *romances* by heart and sang them. He underscored the vitality of the new *romancero* in the modern Spanish literature that poets like Federico García Lorca and Rafael Alberti represented. Through a rhetoric of cultural essentialism, the historian was conclusive in establishing the defining value of *romances* in the persistence of Spain's "espíritu nacional" across different historical periods, regardless of the specific social, political, economic, and cultural circumstances of each: "El Romancero en fin, por tradicionalismo, por la cantidad de vida histórica que representa y por la multitud de reflejos estéticos y morales, es quintesencia de características españolas" [the *Romancero*, in short, because of its traditionalism, because of the amount of historical life that it represents, and because of its myriad aesthetic and moral reflections, is the quintessence of Spanish characteristics] (38–40). Menéndez Pidal could thus confirm Spain's national identity: "España es el país del Romancero" (40).[5]

From this historical perspective, Tomás Segovia not only took issue with the cult of Machado as the national poet of Spain when he spoke about his *romance* "desde otra orilla": in reminiscing about his childhood years during the Second Republic in Spain, Segovia also disputed the well-established commonplace that the *romance* embodied, as Menéndez Pidal contended, the unbroken and unbreakable national spirit of the Spanish people. Segovia was critiquing a long-standing invented tradition whereby Machado's poems and the Machadian institution could be construed as capable of maintaining, in spite of violent historical disruptions like civil war and exile – or perhaps precisely because of them – a sense of deeply rooted continuity in Spanish national culture: "El Machado castellano y castellanista, becqueriano y manriquiano, antibarroco y folklorista" [the Castilian and Castilianist, Becquerian and Manriquean, anti-baroque and folklorist Machado] ("Machado" 404).[6] But then, next to this institutional construction of Machado, Segovia crucially placed "también el Machado modernista ... latinoamericano y 'galicista mental'" [also the modernist Machado ... Latin American and Gallicist-minded] (142). "Galicista mental" is a loaded phrase in Segovia's critical re-examination of Machado's poetry as a nationalist cultural phenomenon.

The label "galicismo mental" [mental Gallicism] was one of the criticisms the Nicaraguan poet Rubén Darío received in 1888 from Juan Valera y Alcalá Galiano, the novelist, critic, diplomat, and member of the Spanish Royal Academy who introduced Darío's *modernismo* in Spain after reading his first major collection of poems, *Azul* [Blue], published in Chile that same year.[7] Indeed, the *romance* chosen by Segovia, "Caballitos," was published in Machado's 1907 *Soledades. Galerías. Otros Poemas* [Solitudes. Galleries. Other Poems], a collection composed under the aegis of Darío's *modernismo,* as Machado explained in its foreword. Furthermore, in writing "Caballitos," the poet drew closely from "Les Chevaux de Bois," a poem from Paul Verlaine's 1874 *Romances sans Paroles.* The first lines of Machado's *romance* – "Pegasos, lindos pegasos / caballitos de madera" [Pegasi, beautiful Pegasi, / little wooden horses] – echo a line from Verlaine's *romance,* which is quoted in French as an epigraph: "Tournez, tournez, bons chevaux de bois." Verlaine was also famously eulogized in one of Darío's poems as "padre y maestro mágico, liróforo celeste" [father and magical master, celestial lyrophore] (*Poesías* 594).

From this angle, one facet of the undefined "otra orilla" from which Segovia remembered Machado's *romance* in 1979 harks back to the Latin American and "Gallicist-minded" shores of his personal experience of exile. Furthermore, it harks back to his cross-boundary, plurilingual poetic memory as a reader of *modernismo* and translator of poetry in French, among other languages. In the refracted light of Segovia's reading, Machado's mythological winged horses fly free from the nationalist and popular cultural practices promoted by institutions during the Second Spanish Republic – when, in Segovia's evocation, poetry was becoming didactic again. Moreover, they become discontinuous with Menéndez Pidal's 1928 neo-Romantic, traditionalist belief that the "vida histórica" that the *romancero* "representa" ensures the continuity of the Spanish national spirit throughout history. In his ironic reference to the notion in Spain in the early thirties that poetry was always – and only – popular there, Segovia was also implicitly undermining a basic tenet in modern Spanish literary history: a historical understanding of poetry premised on the continuity between people, nation, language, and voice.

Only a few years later, this historical understanding was distinctly favoured during the Spanish Civil War. In *Poetas de la España leal,* an anthology published in Madrid in 1937 as a gift for antifascist writers participating in the *II Congreso Internacional de Escritores en Defensa de la Cultura* [International Conference of Writers in Defence of Culture], writers such as Rafael Alberti, Manuel Altolaguirre, Luis Cernuda, Miguel Hernández, León Felipe, José Moreno Villa, and Emilio Prados were presented as "los poetas que encabezan el Romancero Popular, que ellos mismos han recitado ante su pueblo en los días más duros y hostiles de la contienda" [the poets leading the *Romancero Popular,* which they themselves have recited before their people in the hardest and most hostile days of the war] (in Machado et al. 11). As an exception to the alphabetical order in which the poets were listed, Antonio Machado opened the anthology on account of his high symbolic value as a cultural icon for the Republic under attack. Such prestige explains why, according to the editors, Machado "preside estas páginas" [presides over these pages] (155).

But Machado was not simply the most important poet among Republicans. He was also capable of reciting the *Romancero popular* – the Spanish people's distinctive body of poems – to the people themselves as their representative voice par excellence. In a review written that same year for the wartime cultural magazine *Hora de España,* Luis Cernuda made explicit this Romantic notion of the poet as the people's historical representative in times of national crisis: "Es probable que andando el tiempo el historiador que quiera dar voz expresa a la hazaña anónima del pueblo que ahora pelea acuda a los versos de un poeta" [Eventually, the historian wishing to give express voice to the anonymous feat of the people now fighting is likely to resort to a poet's verses] (qtd. in Aznar Soler, *República* 581).[8] Thus, Machado's individual voice came to embody the collective voice of the Spanish nation.

Exilic Memories of Spanish Literary History

Interestingly, Cernuda's prediction was foreshadowed by none other than Juan Valera's uncle, Antonio Alcalá Galiano, a liberal politician. Alcalá Galiano was arguably the first poet and historian in modern Spanish history to advance the Romantic notion that people, language, and nation could be articulated and embodied by poetic voice. His formulation surfaced in 1834, amid another national crisis. In 1823, in the wake of the restoration of absolute monarchy in Spain, Alcalá Galiano had exiled himself to England. From the lecture theatres of the University College of London, where he held a chair in Spanish, he enjoined Spanish poets to write mostly about Spain: "Their native history, their popular traditions, the face of their country, teem with the elements of poetry and romance. Let them then arise, and make their poetry ... national and natural ... let us hear their own popular traditions and superstitions" (453). Underpinning Alcalá Galiano's vindication of a "national and natural" link between people and poetry in Spain was a Romantic rhetoric of cultural uniqueness prefiguring Menéndez Pidal's traditionalist take on the *romancero.*

Alcalá Galiano made this resounding nationalistic claim in the concluding paragraphs of five essays written in English for the prestigious Victorian literary weekly *The Athenaeum.* Published under the title *Literature of the Nineteenth Century: Spain,* these essays presented an ambitious overview of the literature produced by Spanish authors in their native country or in exile from the late eighteenth century to 1833. Alcalá Galiano paid particular attention to the ways in which cultural production in Spain had been affected by the recent Peninsular War, which he dramatically characterized as a "revolution" that had "diverted the attention of the Spanish people from the pursuit of literature, to the chances of civil war" (292).[9] The exiled Republican and literary historian Vicente Llorens argued that, although written in English, *Literature of the Nineteenth Century: Spain* was the first history of Spanish literature "propiamente dicha" [strictly speaking] ("Introducción" 11). In Llorens's estimation, no other literary history before had aimed to situate works of literature squarely within their historical context. Llorens explained that such a contextualization was more than justified: in the historical period covered by Alcalá Galiano's essays, writers were forced to take political sides, as Spain was undergoing a "transición violenta" [violent transition] marked by "luchas intestinas y situaciones extremas ... persecuciones políticas y frecuentes emigraciones" [internecine struggles and extreme situations ... political persecutions and frequent emigrations] ("Introducción" 11).

Indeed, even before the start of the Napoleonic Wars in 1803, Spanish literature was, in Alcalá Galiano's terms, "denationalized by the dominance of French classicism," and as a result its language had become "adulterated" (290). In a way, the armed conflict in Spain was preceded by a cultural conflict over national and linguistic identity. Following contemporary Romantic notions of national literature, Alcalá Galiano prescribed that Spanish poets eschew copies of foreign models and instead "observe human nature in their own land, and draw after it" (*Literature* 453). Poets should also "pay less attention to style, more to matter" (453). If they "lay this to heart," poets will achieve "excellence," added the liberal historian (453). But literary excellence – which a prominent poet like Juan Meléndez Valdés had failed to attain in his misguided cultivation of *romances*, "the true national poetry of Spain" (370) – was now a historical necessity, as Alcalá Galiano's rousing words concluding *Literature of the Nineteenth Century: Spain* declared: "Spain requires a warning voice to stimulate her sons to retrieve their national character" (454).

When Vicente Llorens argued for the historical modernity of Alcalá Galiano's essays, he was an exiled literary historian teaching Spanish literature at Princeton University, where he had arrived through the offices of another prominent Republican exile, Américo Castro. There Llorens rendered *Literature of the Nineteenth Century: Spain* into Spanish. His translation and introductory critical study, *Literatura española siglo XIX: de Moratín a Rivas*, would be published in Spain in 1969, after Franco had been in power for thirty years.[10] Llorens's understanding of Alcalá Galiano's writings was somewhat analogous to Segovia's re-examination of Machado's poetry on the fortieth anniversary of the arrival of exiled Republican intellectuals in Mexico: it also came "desde otra orilla," at least to the extent that he had read Alcalá Galiano's exilic poetry as a form of disruption in Spanish national culture. In "El retorno del exiliado" – an essay published in the Mexican journal *Cuadernos americanos* more than twenty years earlier, in 1948 – Llorens focused on topical references to exile in poems by authors from different periods and origins such as Ovid, Dante, and Victor Hugo.

Most of the poets selected by Llorens were nonetheless from Spain: Alcalá Galiano, Rafael Alberti, Víctor Balaguer, Luis Cernuda, José de Espronceda, Ángel de Saavedra, Juan Meléndez Valdés, Emilio Prados, Juan Rejano, Miguel de Unamuno, Antonio Enríquez Gómez, and José Moreno Villa, among others. Above all, Llorens was interested in charting what he saw as the spectral, near-death existence of exilic figures in poems written primarily by Spanish authors: "La vida del desterrado apenas merece tal nombre. Rota, frustrada, vacía, fantasmal, está en realidad más cerca de la muerte que de la vida" [The exile's life is hardly worth such a name. Broken, frustrated, empty, ghostly, it is actually closer to death than to life] (*Estudios* 105). As Llorens saw them, exilic figures seemed to dwell on distant memories of their native land, but such memories were punctuated by mnemonic topoi of death, even when exilic figures were able to return to their place of origin. Thus, he concluded, the exile "vive muriendo, pero no deja de vivir" [lives dying, but does not stop living] (126). Llorens took this image from Ovid's rewriting of *non omnis moriar*, Horace's time-honoured motif of poetic posterity, as found in his odes: "I have finished a monument more lasting than bronze ... I shall not wholly die, and a large part of me will elude the Goddess of Death. I shall continue to grow, fresh with the praise of posterity" (217). Ovid is, of course, a paradigmatic exiled poet in the Western literary archive.

As we have seen, Juan Ramón Jiménez, Luis Cernuda, and Max Aub mustered various rhetorical strategies addressing the relationship between uprootedness and transience in their exilic writings. This concern with spatiotemporal alienation and posterity may explain, for instance, their recourse to poetic forms of epitaphic address. Indeed, Alcalá Galiano's 1834 apostrophic lines to his native country, quoted by Llorens in "El retorno del exiliado," foreshadowed the rhetoric of spatiotemporal and personal uncanniness Aub deployed in *La gallina ciega*, the diaristic account of his temporary return to Spain in 1967: "¿Qué vale que tu tierra conocida / mis años juveniles / recuerde ... / ... / si, alrededor de mí todo trocado, / hallo madrastra dura / la que madre dejé?" [What good is it that the land that you know / should remember / my youthful years / ... / if, all changed around me, / a hard stepmother I find / where I left my mother behind] (*Estudios* 122). When the first-person speaker in Alcalá Galiano's exilic poem personifies Spain as first a mother and then a stepmother, the present memory of his past youth deepens a sense of fleetingness. Returning to one's native land involves a spatiotemporal disruption informed by an acute intimation of mortality: "madrastra dura" is deeply echoed in "abierta sepultura" [open grave] (Alcalá Galiano 554).

In the examples of twentieth-century Spanish literary history that we have briefly considered in the last pages, Spanish exilic poetry is understood as a largely thematic account of national history. This is irrespective of whether the account is one of continuity – Menéndez Pidal's interpretation of the Cid ballads – or of discontinuity – Llorens's motif-driven analyses of poems as death-ridden meditations inflected by exiles' nostalgia for early life in their homeland. At play in these readings is the historical specificity of the spatiotemporal complexity shaping exilic poetry, a historical specificity left unaddressed by critical readings intent on interpreting poems solely as thematic accounts of national history. By contrast, Segovia's reading "desde otra orilla" highlights spatiotemporal complexity through non-thematic poetic memory, thus pointing to this specificity. In his commemoration of Machado, Segovia quoted a memorized *romance* about an evocation of childhood to foreground a temporal experience that speaks to a mode of historical disruption unbound by the referential framework of national culture.

Segovia went on to reflect on this form of historical disruption: "algo excepcional sucedía en aquellos tiempos, algo seguramente irrepetible; en todo caso inimaginable en estos días nuestros ... No hace falta renegar de la nostalgia, a mi entender legítima, de momentos como aquél, para estar convencido a la vez de que la tentativa de restaurarlos es insensata, y la renuncia a cambiarlos por otros, mortífera" [something exceptional happened in those times, something probably unrepeatable, at any rate unimaginable in our days ... There is no need to disown nostalgia, which is legitimate as I understand it, for moments like that one, to be convinced at the same time that attempting to restore them makes no sense and refusing to change them for others is deadly] (401). Far from circumventing the question of the historical situatedness of his evocation, Segovia dwelled on the conundrum posed by the seeming inextricability of memory and historical change from each other. The way he addressed this conundrum was through poetic memory. In Segovia's perception, poetic memory entails an experience of historical disruption that would withstand the sutures of national literary history's emplotments. His manner of returning to the past and laying history "to heart" – to use Alcalá Galiano's phrase – implies, among other things, remembering a past and acknowledging its uncanniness.

Thus, in Segovia's reading of Machado's poetry "desde otra orilla," poetic memory becomes, even in the grip of nostalgia, a form of resistance. This resistance pushes against monumental forms of national literary historicism that aim to recuperate and restore an irretrievable loss of life, as though the historical gap of exile could be retroactively closed. As Vicente Llorens warned, that gap cannot be entirely erased "cuando se llena a destiempo, parcial y anacrónicamente" [when it is filled in an untimely fashion, partially and anachronistically] (*Estudios* 178–9). But in attempting to trouble a recuperative narrative, Segovia may have gone even further than Llorens, since, as we saw, he believed that the historical gap of exile not only could not but should not be erased: "la restauración de lo perdido sería una negación de nuestra vida más radical aún que su ausencia" [the restoration of what has been lost would be a denial of our life even more radical than its absence] ("Respuestas" 209). In addition to the sense of temporal continuity that a nationalist suturing of exile may imply, Segovia also resisted the spatial impact of such a suturing – i.e., the erasure of the Latin American, Gallicist-minded, *modernista* Machado. Indeed, in Segovia's account, the memory of Machado's *romance* brought these resistant border crossings and non-chronologies to the fore. Segovia's memory of "Caballitos" also reminds us that Alcalá Galiano's apostrophic lines to Spain can be reread, along with Llorens's interpretation, as a performance of historical discontinuity in every here and now of voicing.

Spatiotemporal uncanniness is thematically and narratively arranged in Alcalá Galiano's poem, as Llorens suggested, yet this uncanniness is also woven into its verbal fabric by, among other elements, a paronomastic rhyme between "extraña" and "España" that performs strangeness between consonants just as it brings them together almost irresistibly (Llorens, *Estudios* 121). Moreover, Alcalá Galiano's address to Ángel de Saavedra – another liberal Spanish poet exiled in the early nineteenth century – extends to every future poet in posterity, beyond the referential framework of national culture. As we read in Alcalá Galiano's memoirs: "tú recordando los pasados días //... // tú oirás mi cuita con afecto fino" [you remembering past days // ... // you will hear my affliction with fine affection] (553). "Tú" becomes here, in Jonathan Culler's terms, a "place holder for indeterminate agency": the reader is interpellated by the first-person speaker and thus simultaneously invited into the poem and banished from it through *deixis am phantasma* ("Language" 164–5). Couched in the future tense, Alcalá Galiano's apostrophe "tú oirás" alerts the reader to the eerie historical gap between the present of reading – "recordando" – and the present of the first person's memory – "mi cuita." This form of triangulated address turns all people involved in the poem into ghosts of history or, rather, ghosts of historical exile. Likewise, Segovia's poetic memory will remind us that Machado's emblematic line "Estos cielos azules y este sol de la infancia" can be reread as yet another form of historical discontinuity.

Another child of Republican *destierro*, the literary historian and comparatist Claudio Guillén, returned to Spanish shores to re-examine, in a markedly institutional setting, the relationship between exile and cultural history. He did so in light of his correspondence and friendship with Llorens and Llorens's writings about exilic literature, including his 1975 memoirs *Memorias de una emigración. Santo Domingo, 1939–1945* [Memoirs of an Emigration. Santo Domingo, 1939–1945].[11] In "De la continuidad" [On Continuity], his 2003 speech accepting his induction into the Royal Spanish Academy, Guillén drew on Llorens's own words to assert that Republican exile created "un corte, una discontinuidad" [a cut, a discontinuity] in Spanish letters ("De la continuidad" 23). Drawing on the contrast between "juicio" [judgment] and "afectos" [affects] posited by José María Blanco White – another nineteenth-century Spanish exiled poet whose work Llorens unearthed and studied – Guillén also turned his critical focus towards poetic memory. As if his mind's ear somehow recalled Alcalá Galiano's line "tú oiras mi cuita con afecto fino," he championed a reading practice with an "oído" [ear] to the "cadencias" [cadences] of "la memoria poética hispánica" [Hispanic poetic memory] (30). What mattered in a poem to Guillén was not so much "el pensamiento" [the thought] as "el pensar ... que ocurre y que discurre a lo largo de su andadura" [the thinking ... that occurs and discourses along its course] (30–1). Avoiding a clear-cut binary opposition between form and content, Guillén instead underscored a manner of "pensar" [thinking] inseparable from the somatic experience of hearing and voicing the verbal texture of a poem as it unfolds in every reading.[12]

But then what did he mean exactly by "hispánica" when he mentioned poetic memory? Machado's poetic memory, for instance, could not simply be "hispánica," as Segovia argued in his anti-institutional reading, and as Llorens suggested when he traced the Ovidian motif informing ghostly figures in exilic poems. Analogously, Guillén stressed his view of history as "un contrapunto de continuidades y discontinuidades superpuestas" [a counterpoint of overlapping continuities and discontinuities] that complicated "la idea de continuidad y la de sincronía" [the idea of continuity and that of synchrony] in re-examinations of Spanish society (35). Republican exile constituted one such discontinuity or, in Guillén's terms, "una bifurcación entre el itinerario de las letras peninsulares y el de los escritores de la diáspora" [a bifurcation between the itinerary of Peninsular letters and that of diaspora writers] (23). Claudio Guillén's contrapuntal notion of cultural history and his suggestion that poetry should be approached with an "oído" to the "cadencias" of poetic memory forms a productive historical constellation with Tomás Segovia's and Vicente Llorens's re-examinations of exilic poetry. It also offers yet another invitation "desde otra orilla" to read the patterns of poetic memory inscribed in Machado's famous last verse in exile, "Estos días azules y este sol de la infancia," with an ear to the contrasting cross-boundary, non-chronological threads woven into its verbal texture.

Machado's Exile and His Afterlives

But – to paraphrase Segovia – the Machadian institution became quite strong shortly after the Spanish Civil War. Or rather, it became strong again, even in "Spain beyond Spain" – in Epps's and Fernández-Cifuentes's phrase – despite the historical gap opened by Republican exile. Right after Antonio Machado passed away in Collioure in 1939, his symbolic resurrection became a pressing need for both victorious Francoists and vanquished Republicans. Important editions of Machado's poetry were promptly issued by two highly prominent figures in Spanish letters intent on reimagining Machado as the potential re-embodiment of national cultural continuity.[13] *Obras* was published in Mexico in 1940 by José Bergamín, the co-founder of *España peregrina* who also ran the pro-Republican Editorial Séneca.[14] *Poesías completas* appeared in Madrid in 1941, with a foreword by none other than Franco's chief of propaganda, Dionisio Ridruejo.

From his Mexican exile, Bergamín depicted Machado in terms borrowed from Christian rhetoric. Thus, wrapped in its "mortal e inmortal empeño" [mortal and immortal resolve], Machado's voice revealed "la vida visible ... de un pueblo entero" [the visible life ... of a whole people] (10). Accordingly, when Machado chanted his song for the death of Federico García Lorca, his voice was able to attain the "plenitud de tantas voces vivas" [plenitude of so many living voices] in a baroque mystical union between poet and people: "Sin equívoco, con una sola y única, total y perfecta palabra verdadera. Pues como un solo hombre la multitud se revelaba en esa voz entera del poeta que al decirse, al hablar, lo hacía como un solo pueblo y como un hombre solo" [Unequivocal, with one and only, total and perfect true Word. For, as one man, the crowd was revealed in that whole voice of the poet who, in declaring himself/itself, in speaking, did it as one single people and as one man alone] (Bergamín 10–11). In the words of another Republican exile, Machado was reimagined as a Christ-like figure capable of bringing together person, people, land, and nation through poetic voice.

The struggle over Machado's life-after-death was to continue only a few months later in Madrid. The self-styled "escritor falangista" Dionisio Ridruejo proclaimed in his foreword "El poeta rescatado" [The Rescued Poet] that Falangists had to "rescatar" [rescue] Machado, "el poeta más grande de España desde el vencimiento del siglo XVII hasta la fecha" [the greatest poet in Spain since the end of the seventeenth century till today], to honour "la causa" [the cause] for which they had waged war against the Second Republic: "por conciliar en unidad toda la dispersión española y por poner todo lo español ... al servicio de un solo destino universal, de una sola poesía y de una sola historia" [to reconcile in unity all the Spanish dispersal and to put all things Spanish ... at the service of one single universal destiny, one single poetry, and one single history] (xii–xiii).[15] Bergamín's trope of resurrection also informed Ridruejo's vision of Machado's cultural role in the new postwar Spain: "Con su muerte moría la melancolía de España. La melancolía que pudo llevar a España y la llevó al error y a la muerte. Con su muerte, o con su vida, nacía la otra España, clara, la que va a merecer el alma de su verso" [With his death, Spanish melancholy also died. The melancholy that was able to lead Spain – and led it – to error and to death. With his death, or with his life, the other, clear Spain was born, the one soon to deserve the soul of his verse] (xv). The cultural politics pursued by both Bergamín and Ridruejo revolved around a similar identification of the dead Machado as an embodiment of poetic voice and national people. Moreover, both employed an analogous Christian rhetoric whereby Spain would be born again through the prosopopoeic invocation and resurrection of the exiled poet's voice.

Beyond Ridruejo's Spain and Bergamín's peregrine Spain, yet another land was imagined for Spain's rebirth after the war: the poet's own flesh in *destierro*. In his introduction to the first anthology dedicated exclusively to the poetry of Republican exiles, *Poetas en el destierro* [Poets in Exile], published in Chile in 1943, José Ricardo Morales – an exiled writer from Málaga – equated the land of the Spanish nation with the living flesh of exiled Spanish poets. If "el venero puro y eterno de la lírica española" [the pure and eternal spring of Spanish lyric] could not rise from the devastated land of Spain, then it would flow from "la otra tierra que es carne viva en sus mejores hijos, tierra o carne desolada y doliente" [the other land which is the living flesh of their best children, ravaged and grieving land or flesh] (10). If Spain was to speak and name itself – that is, if Spain was to regain its own voice as a means of self-naming, self-identification, and perhaps even self-unification – the voice of the Spanish exiled poets was, in Morales's understanding, essential: "A los desterrados corresponde levantar la voz con que nuestra malherida España, vueltas las tornas, se dirá a sí misma" [it behooves exiles to raise the voice with which, when the tables turn, badly wounded Spain will declare itself] (11). Morales exploited the semantic possibilities of *tierra* – country, land – so that the fate of the *enterrado* – buried – could be redeemed by the *desterrado* – exiled – and the dead voices of Federico García Lorca, Miguel Hernández, Antonio Machado, and Miguel de Unamuno could live again (10).

Thus, the idea of Spain beyond Spain – of a Spain exiled from its own native land – became hypostatized. It became a popular voice that flowed from that other land, now reimagined as the living flesh of poets. Notably, in selecting poems by Antonio Machado, Juan Ramón Jiménez, León Felipe, José Moreno Villa, Pedro Salinas, Jorge Guillén, Juan Larrea, Emilio Prados, Rafael Alberti, Luis Cernuda, and Manuel Altolaguirre, Morales drew heavily on Gerardo Diego's 1932 *Poesía española: antología 1915–1931*, which, as we saw in chapter 2, was and still is an eminently canonical text in the construction of modern Spanish cultural history.[16] No wonder, then, that Morales chose Machado's poems to open *Poetas en el destierro* – he considered his lyric poetry "expresión viva" [living expression] of the Spanish "pueblo" [people] (16). Once again, the invocation of Machado's voice was imagined to bind together organically the peoplehood and nationhood of the torn Spanish land. Morales's rhetoric of resurrection proposed to suture and reconstruct the Spanish nation's historical disruption.[17]

When Franco died in 1975, exiled poets resorted once more to the prosopopoeic invocation of Machado's voice as a rhetorical means of closing up historical discontinuity. Of the group of poets gathered in Gerardo Diego's anthology only Jorge Guillén and Rafael Alberti returned to Spain and stayed there. They both went back in 1977, two years after the dictator's death. Both of them were awarded the prestigious Cervantes literary award – Guillén in 1976 and Alberti in 1983. Alberti devoted a large part of his acceptance speech to commemorating dead and exiled poets. After reminiscing about his days with Federico García Lorca, José Bergamín, and Miguel Hernández before the war, he read lines by exiled poets such as Juan Ramón Jiménez, Emilio Prados, José Moreno Villa, Pedro Salinas, Luis Cernuda, and León Felipe, among others. Punctuating his speech with solemn, litany-like invocations of Spain, Alberti also claimed that the very first verse to be written in exile by a Spanish Republican was Machado's stand-alone alexandrine, "Estos días azules y este sol de la infancia." Framing his evocation with seemingly trans-historical references to Cervantes's exile and death, Alberti described Machado's line simply as "lleno ya de nostalgia y lejanía" [already full of nostalgia and distance] (4–7).

After evoking other Republican poets who died in exile, Alberti then struck a more personal, anaphoric chord. He explained that it was his good fortune to return and "recomponer de verdad las rotas raíces, cubriéndolas de nuevo con la tierra de España, del pueblo de España, España, con quien me uno a diario" [to truly put the broken roots back together, covering them again with the earth of Spain, with the people of Spain, Spain, with which I'm joined every day] (10). Here, Alberti leaned heavily on a lyrical rhetoric of homecoming and intimacy, of belonging and restoration, of telluric and national organicism. He presented himself as narrowing the distance from – and assuaging the presumed nostalgia in – Machado's exilic line, as though the Spanish people who were left disembodied after Machado's death could be re-embodied again through Alberti's prosopopoeic poetic voice.

Additionally, Alberti positioned his exilic voice as materializing the linguistic identity of *hispanismo* beyond historical differences among Spanish-speaking voices, while suggesting that exile characterized the Spanish language trans-historically: "es como centrar en mi sola voz la de más de 338 millones de seres que, con tantas diferentes modalidades, nos expresamos en la lengua, nunca mejor llamada peregrina, de Don Quijote" [it's like centring on my voice alone the voice of more than 338 million beings who, with so many different modalities, express ourselves in Don Quijote's language, never more fittingly called peregrine] (10). The institutional recognition of Alberti's return to Spain as a representative of the Republican exile allowed him to redeploy Alcalá Galiano's Romantic notion of poetic voice as a political metaphor for the (re-)embodiment of the Spanish people in times of national crisis. But Alberti's poetic voice not only hypostatized concepts of Spanish peoplehood and nationhood, rhetorically bridging the historical gap of *destierro*. In extolling pan-Hispanism, his voice as a representative exiled poet erased spatiotemporal discontinuities among different cultural shores.[18] It is in this sense of poetic voice that Tomás Segovia's critical commemoration of Machado's poetry as disruptive within Spanish history takes on political relevance.

Amid the early-twenty-first-century debates about the collective memory of the Spanish Civil War, "Estos días azules y este sol de la infancia" was also understood as a biographical mode of historical continuity. In his 2006 *Ligero de equipaje: la vida de Antonio Machado* [Travelling Light: The Life of Antonio Machado], historian and Hispanist Ian Gibson interpreted Machado's line found in Collioure as follows: "transido de dolor por el derrumbamiento de la República, e intuyendo que llegaba el final, se sintió una vez más transportado a la Sevilla de sus años primaverales, aquella Sevilla preñada de oro y azul que fue eterno presente en su corazón de poeta caminante" [racked with pain from the fall of the Republic, and sensing that the end was near, he felt once again transported back to the Seville of his spring years, that Seville pregnant with gold and blue that was eternally present in his wandering poet's heart] (629). Gibson forwent examining the alexandrine as a lyric line devoid of personal markers or even as a fragment from a dramatic monologue – that is, as a mimesis of the affects of a persona created by a writer renowned for creating apocryphal poets. Instead, Gibson chose to take it as an "emocionante documento" [moving document] that enabled him, as biographer, to *know* what Machado's actual feelings were right before he passed away in exile.[19]

Hence, in the biographer's estimation, the alexandrine became a primary historical source, apt for seamless incorporation as evidence into a claim-making historiographical emplotment.[20] Only if Gibson confined his explanation of Machado's line to its referential "content" as an expressive, reductively Romantic linguistic medium for the poet's feelings about his personal and public life could *Ligero de equipaje* be advertised as "Machado's life story – a passionate journey through the private life, philosophy and work of a man who is considered today one of the most read and loved Spanish poets of all times."[21] Yet "Estos días azules y este sol de la infancia" can also be productively read within the uncanny discursive space between "lo vivo," "lo escrito," and "cada lector" that Max Aub delineated. It is through the lens of poetic memory that Machado's enigmatic alexandrine points spectrally to "lo escrito" and thus resists claim-making narratives of national continuity. This resistance persists even as the line may invite readers to construct it and commemorate it as a historical record of the poet's experience of "lo vivo" at the very beginning of the Spanish Republican exile.[22]

It was in Puerto Rico that Aurora de Albornoz, another exiled Republican poet and literary critic, chose to read Machado's line not only as a genuine poem in and of itself, but also as Machado's last poem.[23] De Albornoz decided to insert it as a stand-alone composition at the end of her anthology *Poesías de guerra de Antonio Machado* [War Poems by Antonio Machado], published in Puerto Rico in 1961 ("Rubén" 252). But de Albornoz did not just acknowledge the potential cultural value of Machado's alexandrine for commemorating the Spanish Civil War and its aftermath of repression, exile, death, and oblivion. In her 1986 essay "Rubén Darío en el último verso de Antonio Machado," she broadened the spatiotemporal coordinates of her analysis. From her Puerto Rican shore, de Albornoz read "Estos días azules y este sol de la infancia" with an ear to the border-crossing, non-chronological elements of its verbal texture. For her, some of those elements struck a revealingly Latin American, *modernista* note, as they brought to mind Rubén Darío's 1898 sonnet "A Bolivia" and specifically its first line: "En los días de azul / de tu dorada infancia" [In the days of blue / of your golden childhood] (*Poesías* 1000).

Thus de Albornoz turned to what Claudio Guillén would later call "memoria poética hispánica" to trace in Machado's exilic line an intertextual borrowing reminiscent of a wider *modernista* cosmopolitanism. This cosmopolitanism was not limited to Darío's signature cross-boundary and cross-historical thematizations – for example, the spatiotemporal amplifications that chiastically pattern the subsequent lines of his sonnet, characteristically suggesting resonant Symbolist correspondences: "yo solía pensar en Grecia y en Bolivia: / en Grecia hallaba el néctar que la nostalgia alivia, / y en Bolivia encontraba una arcaica fragancia" [I used to think about Greece and about Bolivia: / in Greece I discovered the nectar that alleviates nostalgia, / and in Bolivia I found an archaic fragrance] (*Poesías* 1000). De Albornoz also argued that *azul* was a key signifier for the far-reaching aspirations of aesthetic modernity among Latin American *modernistas*, at least since 1877, when José Martí used the phrase "días azules" in a sketch of Curaçao ("Rubén" 252).[24] The universalist scope of such aspirations was confirmed less than twenty years later by an important *modernista* publication titled *Revista Azul* [Blue Review], published in Mexico from 1894 to 1896.[25] According to de Albornoz, the understanding of *azul* as a "símbolo epocal" [epochal symbol] in this circumscribed *modernista* context was not as prevalent in Spain as it was in Latin America.

Hence, in Machado's case, *azul* could simply be associated "a la nostalgia – a un pasado perdido – cuando, por ejemplo, evoca Soria desde la lejanía, y, sobre todo, cuando sueña una Sevilla infantil, ya sólo viva en el recuerdo" [to nostalgia – to a lost past – when, for instance, he evokes Soria from a distance, and, above all, when he dreams about a childhood Seville, now only alive in his memory] ("Rubén" 253). Yet, when it came to her analysis of Machado's exilic alexandrine, de Albornoz departed from biographical and national history and took a more decisive comparative approach within the broader cultural framework of *modernismo*.[26] In this light, Machado's phrase "días azules" could be read as "el Ideal imposible: es el Azul-Darío; el Azul-Martí" [the impossible Ideal: it's the Darío blue, the Martí blue] ("Rubén" 252). Significantly, in Martí's descriptive essay about Curaçao the phrase "días azules" derived directly from memory, "que se goza generosamente en volvernos a nuestros inmaculados días azules" [which takes generous pleasure in taking us back to our immaculate blue days] (qtd. in Schulman 258). De Albornoz failed to address this link. However, it may have bolstered her argument, at least in the sense that a rhetoric of remembrance built on the Romantic notion of an unsullied past may conceivably underpin defensive reactions among *modernistas* vis-à-vis the harsh sociopolitical realities of modernity – including, eventually, that of Machado's exile.

Interestingly, Darío's "A Bolivia" moves from the first-person speaker's brief memory of his or her personal past – "yo solía pensar" – to a cross-historical now of poetic enunciation ("El tirso griego rige la primitiva danza" [the Greek thyrsus rules the primitive dance]). The confident yet moderate tempo shaping Darío's alexandrines is reinforced by a concluding and conclusive rhyme: "nuestro Pegaso joven, mordiendo el freno, brinca / ... / con Sol y Luna triunfan los vástagos del Inca" [our young Pegasus, champing at the bit, springs / ... / with Sun and Moon the Inca's offsprings triumph] (*Poesías* 1000). The indicative mood conveys a sense of present factuality that leaves the past tense of the first stanza behind, and with it the individual past – "mi dorada infancia" – on which the self-reflective "yo" dwelled. The sonnet opens up to a plural poetic present – "nuestro Pegaso joven" – following a seemingly cyclical temporality that enables the speaker, and hence the reader, to weaken, without necessarily erasing, a sense of individual transience. The mythological temporality in "A Bolivia" is thus uniquely informed by a specific verbal texture. This verbal texture, in turn, is shaped by Darío's poetic memory – the poetic memory of a *modernista* closely attuned to the historical contingencies of fin-de-siècle cultural discourses. His non-chronological and border-crossing response to modernity's temporality – described by Charles Baudelaire in "The Painter of Modern Life" (1859) as partly transient, fleeting, and contingent (403) – is also folded into Machado's 1907 winged "Caballitos," and into the alexandrine that the exiled poet wrote down eighty years later in the face of ultimate transience.

In brief, "Estos días azules y este sol de la infancia" became deeply transnationalized in Aurora de Albornoz's reading. This is a significant critical gesture, as only three years earlier – in 1983 – Machado's last line had been institutionally characterized by Rafael Alberti – an officially sanctioned representative of Republican exile in post-Franco Spain – as one of the highest national symbols among Spanish *desterrados*. Nonetheless, in de Albornoz's approach "desde otra orilla," the cultural value of Machado's poetry would be difficult to assess adequately without taking into full account the profound transformation of Spanish culture brought about by Darío's cross-boundary and cross-historical poetry. The same holds more generally for what she considered the "renacimiento" [renaissance] of Spanish poetry in the first decades of the twentieth century – epitomized by writers of the "Edad de Plata" such as Federico García Lorca, Juan Ramón Jiménez, Luis Cernuda, and Rafael Alberti himself ("Rubén" 248).[27].

In re-examining the relationship between *modernismo* and Spanish poetry, de Albornoz addressed a controversial chapter for literary historians in Spain. This chapter is one with important counterproductive repercussions for any critical analysis of poetry as a cultural phenomenon during and after the Spanish Civil War, including the poetry produced by Republican exiles. Among the various historiographical problems posed by the hard-and-fast separation between *modernismo* and the cultural productions of the Spanish *generación del 98* were the critical limitations created by linking a generational approach to specific moments in Spanish history and, concomitantly, by understanding exilic poetry within a narrowly nationalistic framework.[28] In 1994, Andrew Debicki described in no uncertain terms the negative effects this approach had on the study of the poetry produced in Spain after the war: "critics classified poetry by first, second, and third postwar generations; both the fragmentation and the emphasis on an exclusively Spanish event and situation led to isolated judgments and to an ignorance of wider issues applicable to Western literature" (*Spanish* 3).

De Albornoz's Puerto Rican memory of Machado's line viewed through the lens of Darío's and Martí's *modernismo* resonates deeply with Segovia's Mexican reading of Machado as "modernista, latinoamericano y 'galicista mental'" – both exiled writers objected to the narrowly Castilian and Castilianist image of the poet associated with the *generación del 98* (404).[29] At the Ateneo Español de México, Segovia asserted his belief in "la plenitud y la inagotabilidad del sentido" [in the plenitude and inexhaustibility of meaning] and professed to distrust "todo reduccionismo" [all reductionism], particularly with regard to the poet "que los españoles insisten en llamar 'nuestro Machado'" [that Spaniards insist on calling 'our Machado'] (403–4). Mindful of the hermeneutic gap between texts from the past and their future readers, he refused to judge "a la Castilla gloriosa, contra Machado, con criterios de hoy e ignorando toda la distancia histórica que la separa de nosotros" because, he argued, "ayer no es literalmente hoy, pero tampoco es literalmente ayer ... [L]a historia es la no literalidad. Por eso la ambigüedad de Machado no la esgrimo contra él; la esgrimo contra nosotros: contra la literalidad del culto" [the glorious Castile, against Machado, with today's criteria and ignoring all the historical distance that separates it from us. ... [Y]esterday is not literally today, but neither is it literally yesterday ... [H]istory is non-literality. That is why I don't wield Machado's ambiguity against him; I wield it against ourselves: against the literality of the cult] (403).

As we saw earlier, Segovia was particularly wary of Hispanists' efforts to reinforce an "exilio instituido" that might weaken the exploratory, subversive, and paradoxical elements traceable, respectively, in Juan Ramón Jiménez's, Luis Cernuda's, and Max Aub's writings (*Sobre exiliados* 71–3). But in de Albornoz's claim that the traces of Darío's *modernismo* extended until "las últimas palabras escritas en verso por Antonio Machado, unos días antes de su muerte" [the last words written in verse by Antonio Machado, a few days before he died], she arguably went beyond Segovia's critical re-examination ("Rubén" 248). In "Machado desde otra orilla," Segovia quoted "Caballitos," which Machado wrote *before* becoming the exemplary poet of the Spanish Republic in war and in exile. As Segovia saw it, remembering this *romance* would not "automatizar" [automatize] the Machado cult established by the institution of Spanish national literary history (400). In its focus on an emblematic exilic line, de Albornoz's reading seemed even more resistant to such recuperative efforts, as it contributed to deautomatizing the tenaciously nationalistic Castilian (re)appropriation of Machado's poetry on both sides of the catastrophically polarized Spanish cultural field – signally represented by two key cultural players like José Bergamín and Dionisio Ridruejo – during and after the civil war.[30]

Epitaphic Memory Amid Histories of Modernity

In her emphasis on influences and inspiration – a critical approach quite prevalent in Spanish literary history (Faber, "Beyond" 428) – de Albornoz might nevertheless have reproduced a sense of historical and cultural continuity at a transatlantic level. Underlying the merely thematic disparities between Darío and Machado identified in her reading of "Estos días azules y este sol de la infancia" may be the problematic presupposition of a chronological seamlessness of *hispanismo*, or even *pan-hispanismo*. Her essay leaves this presupposition unaddressed.[31] Nevertheless, de Albornoz also teased out of Machado's last line a distinctive textual form of disruption, one with implications for historical readings of his famous alexandrine. Remarkably, she emphasized how the use of demonstratives such as "estos" or "este," a proximal type of demonstrative that she characterized as "lleno de temporalidad" [full of temporality], can "trastocar el tiempo cronológico" [disrupt chronological time], and turn the past into the present ("Rubén" 254). Darío does not use these demonstratives in "A Bolivia," and consequently, as de Albornoz points out, his evocation remains fixed in the past (254).

The cross-boundary and non-chronological operations made possible by proximal demonstratives may strike readers as quite memorable in an exilic verse like "Estos días azules y este sol de la infancia." Indeed, what de Albornoz calls "presentización del pasado" [presentization of the past] or "fusión de tiempos" [fusion of times] in Machado's line also brings about "tiempo discontinuo" [discontinuous time] in every here and now of successive readings ("Rubén" 253–4).[32] The poet's use of proximal demonstratives creates the textual conditions for the reader to experience a chronological disruption of his or her of frame of reference – in Aub's terms, "según los fantasmas de cada lector" [depending on each reader's ghosts] (*Obras completas: Vol I* 94). The frame of reference for "Estos días azules y este sol de la infancia" itself is largely undefined; the reader can use its two proximal demonstratives as discourse deixis and thus is able to occupy the present site and time of utterance as though hardly any gap between "lo vivo," "lo escrito," and "cada lector" needed to be taken into account – as though Machado's exilic line were a free-floating signifier for a trans-historical experience of present time.

But contrasting modes of historical and poetic memory – for instance, the memory of Machado's historical circumstances at the end of the war and the memory of his line's various intertextual echoes – can potentially mediate and disrupt this apparent sense of continuity and immediacy – this "fusión de tiempos." In fact, the unbridgeable spatiotemporal gap between the past of "lo vivo" and the present of "cada lector" is brought more starkly into relief by the sense of continuity or immediacy that deixis facilitates. From this perspective, the absence of personal deictic markers in the alexandrine can render discontinuous time ghostly for each reader. It is in this light that the "tiempo discontinuo" folded into "Estos días azules y este sol de la infancia" can afford readers a historical experience. In keeping with Walter Benjamin's theorization of historical experience, the two proximal demonstratives in Machado's last line delineate the uncanny boundaries of a dialectical image between what-has-been – the poet's "presentización del pasado" then – and each now of reading and voicing – the reader's current "presentización del pasado" – a suddenly emergent image made up of a constellation of linguistic traces dramatizing a spatiotemporal disruption (*Arcades* 462–3).

This historical experience is not simply constative or referential – despite interpretive efforts in this direction by historians and biographers – but performative. In addition to historical and intertextual references, deictic insistence and reiterative sound patterning help animate each new voicing of Machado's alexandrine (Nowell Smith 84). While the verse may become indelible for readers attending to its referential signs, it is also potentially responsive to the voicings that its distinctively memorable verbal texture offers, traversed as it is by, among other elements, deictic, tonal, topical, gestural, prosodic, rhetorical, and rhythmical strands from and beyond Darío's sonnet "A Bolivia."[33] Thus, on the one hand, the commemorative character of Machado's last verse may become retrospectively evident in light of his death in exile after the Spanish Civil War: indeed, de Albornoz foregrounded this character in her anthology *Poesías de guerra de Antonio Machado*. Yet, on the other hand, the spectral trace that characterizes textual elements such as "estos" and "este" is already implicitly epitaphic, as it signals "tiempo discontinuo" with regard to posterity. As Karen Mills-Courts maintained, "the death of presence leaves a ghost-like trace that is not quite nothingness. The act of representation bears the doubleness of an epitaphic gesture" (13).

Significantly, Max Aub meditated on this form of ghostliness in a short commemorative text dated in Paris in January 1940, less than a year after Machado's death. It was published in Mexico ten years later under the new title "Antonio Machado: en el décimo aniversario de su muerte" [Antonio Machado: On the Tenth Anniversary of His Death]. In it, Aub reflected on the time-memory relationship specific to Machado's poetry: "Todo en su poesía es presente, y todo escrito con el recuerdo. De ahí el retumbar (re-tumba) de sus versos. Poesía sin tiempo, luz sin sombra" [Everything in his poetry is present, and everything written from memory. Hence the resonance (re-sounding / re-entombing) of his verses. Poetry without time, light without shade] ("Antonio" 13–14).[34] Aub resorted here to paronomasia – "retumbar (re-tumba)" – to mark the echo of loss inscribed in the verbal fabric of his obituary rhetoric, and thus memorably underscore the haunting time signature of Machado's poems. Aub read the modes of memory folded into the dead poet's verses in terms of a specific poetic temporality: epitaphic present, a present rendered all the more eerie as it was invoked in the uncertain present of Aub's exile. Much like Cernuda's exilic poetry, Machado's verse can hardly be reduced to the narrative representation of things past remembered; it is, dialectically enough, the poetic event of remembering things present. In this sense too, "Estos días azules y este sol de la infancia" may keep sounding – and resounding – as an epitaph.[35] That echo of loss somehow "retumba" in the troubled words that Aub wrote a few years later, in 1944, to forewarn potential readers of the loss underlying his own poems: "¡qué no perderá en lo escrito!" (*Obras completas: Vol. I* 94).

Aub's forewarning also resonates in a question posed forty years later by Edward Said in his widely quoted essay "Reflections on Exile": "The achievements of exile are permanently undermined by the loss of something left behind forever. But if true exile is a condition of terminal loss, why has it been transformed so easily into a potent, even enriching, motif of modern culture?" (173). As we have seen, Aub claimed that only the dead victims and survivors of the Djelfa concentration camp would be able – if at all – to grasp what his writings pointed at. In doing so, Aub was foreshadowing Said's fine distinctions concerning both the inescapably historical character of exile and also the potential danger involved in disregarding the gap between the experience of exile and that of the reader of exilic literature in modern times: "On the twentieth-century scale, exile is neither aesthetically nor humanistically comprehensible: at most the literature about exile objectifies an anguish and a predicament most people rarely experience at first hand" (174). Both Aub and Said thus identified an arresting tension between the productivity of exilic literature – often associated with a deeply acute sense of transience and mortality – and the "terminal," possibly melancholy, loss suffered by actual exiles. *This Ghostly Poetry* has explored some of the ways in which exilic poems can be read as reminders of the paradoxical spatiotemporal disruption between "lo vivo" of exile and the here-and-now of reading, and, hence, as affording "cada lector" a historical experience.

From the retrospective vantage point of Said's critical caveats, the discontinuities between "lo vivo," "lo escrito," and "cada lector" that Aub underscored take on dramatic relief. This is especially so in that they can be traced in the larger context of the peculiar linguistic pluralism or "unhousedness" of much modern writing, characterized by George Steiner as "extraterritoriality" (120). In his 1990 articulation of *destierro* and *destiempo* – two key concepts in his panoramic overview of exilic literature – Claudio Guillén set out to survey the overwhelming scope of modern extraterritoriality and its connections to the different forms of exile and self-exile among modern writers in the West: "from Baudelaire to Rilke, Joyce, Cernuda, Celan, and so many others: wanderers, refugees, expatriates, nihilists, suicides" ("The Sun" 277).[36] It was in the framework of a wide-ranging overview of the interplay between "lo vivo" and "lo escrito" in modernity that Guillén quoted Arthur Rimbaud's famous assertion "La vraie vie est absente" [True life is absent] from his 1873 collection of poems *Une saison en enfer* [A Season in Hell] (278).[37]

In line with Said's preoccupations, part of Guillén's overview also involved exploring the historical tensions between the defamiliarizing rhetoric of exiled and self-exiled writers and modern experiences of absence, alienation, and uprootedness associated with nineteenth-century discourses of Romantic cultural nationalism such as poetry:

> Modern nationalism, the plurality of allegedly original and valid cultures, the growth of a voracious sense of regional difference that absorbs all – thought, social usage, literature, the arts – clearly exacerbate the tensions of exile. The nineteenth century marked the heyday of the appreciation of local roots and popular poetry, of the awareness of the singular as unique, of a particular language or culture as an untranslatable and irreplaceable condition. ("The Sun" 277)[38]

As we have seen with regard to Luis Cernuda's melancholy rhetoric of exile and self-exile, Raymond Williams urged critically re-examining the spatiotemporal coordinates of modernism in terms of "the changing cultural milieu of the metropolis" from the late nineteenth century on (44).[39] In Williams's view, the new metropolis was now the City of Strangers, where "new social and economic and cultural relations, beyond both city and nation in their older senses, were beginning to be formed" (44). Thus Williams saw the metropolis as the most appropriate location for a modernist art "made by the restlessly mobile emigré or exile, the internationally anti-bourgeois artist" (34).

But Williams also emphasized that the re-examination of this shifting cultural location beyond both city and nation involved looking "from time to time, from outside the metropolis ... and from the poor world which has always been peripheral to the metropolitan systems" (47). It is from this twofold perspective – cross-temporal and cross-boundary – that Williams's critical approach to the specificity – the "extraterritoriality" – of new linguistic forms produced by exiled modernists seems most productive:

> To the immigrants especially, with their new second common language, language was more evident as a medium – a medium that could be shaped and reshaped – than as a social custom ... The preoccupying visual images and styles of particular cultures did not disappear, any more than the native languages, native tales, the native styles of music and dance, but all were now passed through this crucible of the metropolis. (45)

This spatiotemporal perspective seems apt for analysing the textual modes of memory available in Spanish modernist writings by authors variously associated with the so-called Edad de Plata. Indeed, if Spanish modernity is understood to be at the relative periphery of European and American modernity, it is also important to stress that a considerable number of these authors – including many who would become exiles as a consequence of the war such as León Felipe, Juan Ramón Jiménez, Antonio Machado, Luis Cernuda, Max Aub, María Zambrano, and Tomás Segovia – moved to metropolitan centres like Madrid from peripheral regions in Spain.[40]

In *Historias de las dos Españas* [Histories/Stories of the Two Spains] (2004), a historical overview of the grand narratives that have shaped modern dichotomous understandings of the Spanish nation and people – the one liberal/progressive, the other reactionary/conservative (53) – historian Santos Juliá also dwelled on the tensions between nation and territory and between centre and periphery in the devastating circumstances at the end of the civil war. As Juliá argued, these tensions were already established in the early 1930s by intellectuals who would leave Spain for America as a result of the conflict, such as Aub and Ramón J. Sender. In the poetry of Federico García Lorca, Jorge Guillén, and Antonio Machado, among others, readers could find traces of a sense of spatiotemporal exile from origin in the fraught context of Spanish modernity's cultural production before Franco's coup in 1936:

> estos intelectuales son los últimos hijos de la tierra; en la mayoría de ellos perdura todavía fuerte la ligazón con sus orígenes, cuando se arrancaron del pueblo o de la aldea para iniciar una aventura incitante en la capital ... Y si la capital se vuelve hosca y amenazante, el poeta prefiere volver a su tierra, a buscar el refugio cerca de la madre, como le ocurrió a Lorca: "vuelvo a mi tierra" todavía quería decir en los años treinta volver realmente a la tierra, a la madre, a la infancia, por las que el tiempo no había

> pasado. Habían emigrado, habían salido del pueblo o de pequeñas ciudades con la ruralidad metida hasta los tuétanos ... "Estos días azules y este sol de la infancia," que Machado contempla poco antes de morir. (274)
>
> [these intellectuals are the last children of the land/earth; in most of them there remains a strong link to their origins, when they tore themselves from their small town or village to start an enticing adventure in the capital ... And if the capital turns forbidding and threatening, the poet prefers to return to his native land/earth, to seek refuge close to his mother, as Lorca did: "I return to my native land" still meant in the 1930s to actually return to the land, to mother, to childhood, where time had not passed. They had emigrated, they had left a village or small town with rurality deep in their very marrow ... "These blue days and this sun of childhood," contemplated by Machado before he died]

Indeed, Machado's last line also harks back to an image used in 1920 by León Felipe to dismiss the "glorias de la patria" [glories of fatherland]. In "¡Qué lastima! [What a Pity!], a poem included in his first book, *Versos y oraciones del caminante* [Verses and Prayers of the Wayfarer] (1920) and later inserted under the heading "Autorretrato" [Self-Portrait] in his 1947 exilic collection *Antología rota*, an ironic lament for the lack of *una patria* and even a *patria chica* leads to a specific but highly resonant memory of childhood: "pasé los días azules de mi infancia en Salamanca" (*Antología* 122–3) [I spent the blue days of my infancy in Salamanca] (Schwartz 217).[41]

If for many exiled poets "llorar a la Madre España, traicionada, vendida, desangrada, era llorar por un tiempo cercano que ya nunca más será" [to weep to Mother Spain, betrayed, bartered away, bled to death, was to weep for a near time that will never be again] (Juliá 274), folded into the melancholy, elegiac lament for the lost, Spanish motherland was also a multifaceted sense of spatiotemporal continuities and discontinuities, a complex experience of loss that can hardly be reduced to frameworks of national, let alone war, culture.[42] The historical and socio-biographical perspectives provided by Claudio Guillén, Raymond Williams, and Santos Juliá on the shifting cultural landscapes of modernity help elucidate the various ways in which the memory of exile inscribed, for instance, in Machado's emblematic last line evokes contexts beyond, and prior to, the civil war and its aftermath.[43]

Along with these perspectives, "Estos días azules y este sol de la infancia" can also be read for specific textual modes of *destierro* and *destiempo* vis-à-vis the spatiotemporal emplotments organizing national cultural history narratives. One such form would be the elegy.[44] Machado's last line is indeed elegiac across cultural and historical boundaries. It is in this sense as well that Machado's poetic language – a medium that, according to Raymond Williams, modernist writers "shaped and reshaped" (45) – may be productively re-examined in light of Guillén's understanding of history as a counterpoint of overlapping continuities and discontinuities. Fredric Jameson's reflections on historiographical periodization may be pertinent for a discussion of this mode of counterpoint: "In historiography – whether it is that of a form, a national population, or a single productive psyche – the decision about continuity or discontinuity is not an empirical one ... it is taken in advance, as a kind of absolute presupposition, which then determines your subsequent reading and interpretation of the materials (sometimes called 'the facts')" (3). Conventional literary history in Spain seems to presuppose continuity in the face of violent historical conditions like civil war, dictatorship, and exile.

Taking into account Guillén's examination of the textuality of *destierro* and *destiempo*, my emphasis on the resistance and disruption identifiable in poetic memory analogously entails modes of textual continuity, beyond nationally inflected spatiotemporal continuities. Some of the elements informing exilic poems – such as the patterns that shape their textual and verbal materiality – presuppose a certain constancy of memory. But, as I have argued in this book, this constancy emerges in largely multilayered, untimely, haphazard, and uneven ways, and thus may enable readers to explore, among other things, the various conflicting ways in which such poems are woven into, against, and beyond, linear literary history. At the concrete historical intersection of the Spanish Civil War, the production of those elements was still informed by the different senses of exile associated with the various cultural shifts of modernity – sketched, as we have seen, by Said, Steiner, Juliá, and Williams, among others – as well as by the long-standing Romantic presupposition that poetic voice could somehow embody a sense of continuity between person, people, land, and nation.

It is in this light that the proposed cross-boundary and cross-temporal constancy of poetic memory acquires political potential: its undecidable, thickly stratified, textual forms resist the presupposed teleological continuity of national culture in a particular historical setting.[45] Poetic memory's "sediments of time," the long-term patterns folded into each singular exilic poem, run against the grain of a "sequential unfolding" of history (Koselleck, *Sediments* 3). This way of reading poems is deeply historical. As Theodor W. Adorno contended, it is through history that a poem becomes an enigma (*Aesthetic* 120). Consequently, its political potential can only be said to be specific to the text: for an exilic poem to maintain its power to animate open-ended debate – and hence to provide a "profoundly historical perspective" on the field of the political (Morcillo 3) – it needs to be read and voiced with a careful ear to the distinctive ways in which its verbal texture provides a historical experience. Only thus may an exilic poem remain resistant to what Raymond Williams eloquently denounced as "a crude sociologism, which never really looked at the work at all but looked at elements which could be extracted from it and handled in other transferred ideological terms" (183).

Also, perhaps, only thus may exilic poetry complicate commemorative historical fictions such as Javier Cercas's *Soldados de Salamina*, in which Machado's "Estos días azules y este sol de la infancia" is handled in narrative form and presented as the key to a purported "secreto esencial" in Spain's tragic history. As we saw in chapter 2, that "secreto esencial" is only available through the narrator's memory of Machado's enigmatic poetic line. Given the strongly elegiac and prosopopoeic rhetoric informing much of exilic cultural productions, epitaphic addresses to posterity – whether explicit or not – can be fruitfully explored in a poem's elements of resistance and disruption. Thus, the deictic power of each proximal demonstrative – "estos," "este" – in Machado's alexandrine is to a certain degree epitaphic. It enigmatically animates us and future readers, who remember an irretrievable loss – Aub's "lo vivo" – in every iterative here and now of enunciation, thus haunting and hindering the textual encounter between the ghosts of the dead and the ghosts of the living. In this sense too, as Guillén's exilic memory of Rimbaud's *Une saison en enfer* may still remind us, true life may be absent.[46]

In the short text "Antonio Machado" – inserted in a volume of funereal reminiscences published posthumously in Spain in 2001, and significantly titled *Cuerpos presentes* [Present Bodies / Lying in State] – Aub not only paid tribute to the famous Republican poet who died in exile, but explored textual continuities and discontinuities between true life and an image of life after death. Aub attempted to bring Machado to the present of reading through deixis: "Éste es Antonio Machado ... dos días antes de morir in Collioure, del otro lado de su frontera" [This is Antonio Machado ... two days before dying in Collioure, on the other side of his border] (*Cuerpos* 173). The demonstrative pronoun "éste" referred in fact to the last photograph taken of Machado before he passed away in France in 1939. Although Aub called it "imagen verdadera" [true image], he described this photograph in increasingly defamiliarizing terms: "Parece otro. Es él, con la faz del 'otro' ... la muerte" [He seems other than himself. It's him, with the face of the "other" ... death] (173). Aub's depiction is a peculiar form of prosopopoeia in that the photograph of Machado's aged face is not only given voice by means of language but likewise blended with the face of death – "la faz del 'otro'" – whose otherness is marked by inverted commas (de Man, "Autobiography" 930). Indeed, the light in Machado's gaze is, according to Aub, already "muerta" [dead] (173).

Aub's text was originally titled "Mínimo homenaje" [Minimal Homage], and published in 1958 by the Mexican *Revista de la Universidad de México*, which, unlike *Cuerpos presentes*, did include the photographic portrait of an emaciated Machado, as well as a landscape of an apparently empty Collioure by Spanish painter Celso Lagar (figure C.1).[47] Under the portrait, readers could find six lines excerpted from one of Machado's sonnets glossing Pierre de Ronsard's internationally acclaimed poems about transience (*Poesía* 326). Striking a necrological note reminiscent of Juan Ramón Jiménez's visionary montage of images and texts in *Guerra en España*, Aub reduced the excerpt to an unfinished *vanitas*, reframing the first verse of Machado's gloss in epitaphic fashion, as both a caption and an apostrophe addressed to future readers: "Cuando veáis esta sumida boca" [When you see this sunken mouth]. Aub deictically foregrounded verbal mediation – or rather the poetic figuration of vocal obscurity ("esta sumida boca") – as though the

C.1 "Mínimo homenaje," Max Aub's epitaphic tribute to Antonio Machado, published in Mexico in 1958. Reprinted with permission of *Revista de la Universidad de México*.

MINIMO HOMENAJE

CUANDO *veáis esta sumida boca*
que ya la sed no inquieta, la mirada
tan desvalida (su mitad, guardada
en viejo estuche, es de cristal de roca),

la barba que platea, y el estrago
del tiempo en la mejilla . . .

Este es Antonio Machado, el profundo, el 20 de febrero de 1939, dos días antes de morir, en Collioure, del otro lado de su frontera. Salió de su patria, perdió pie, dio en tierra; desterrado.

Parece otro. Es él, con la faz del "otro". (¿Por qué la muerte no es, como el nacer, masculino?)

El cuello fofo, descarnado, agria la boca, vieja la barba, que ya no se afeitaría; muerta —ya— la luz de la mirada, calavera el gran ruedo de su frente; amarga caspa en sus hombros vencidos. Roto.

Imagen verdadera —alguna vez se ha publicado esta fotografía, retocada—, partida el alma en pena, "transparente, vacío, ciego, alado" víctima de la España "vieja y tahur" que le mató.

El crimen fue tras la frontera, para que no se viera. Ahora, a los diecinueve años, vence, en pie, como fue. Sé: olvidar, manda la ley. Viéndole así, ¿cómo? ¡Qué olviden otros!

M. A.

Celso Lagar— Paisaje de Collioure

eerie tension between presence and absence found in photography, and even more dramatically in epitaphic address, could only be performed by displacing figures of poetic voice ("Mínimo" 16).

This figural displacement is complicated and rendered enigmatic in several supplementary ways: ekphrasis – a trope of animation that means speaking out or calling an inanimate object by name – metonymy – whereby "esta sumida boca" repeatedly but variously displaces "voz" – and translation and intertextuality – the different ways in which Aub's text is traversed by other languages and voices (Ronsard's and Machado's). In a strictly rhetorical sense, Aub's text is a textual aporia in that prosopopoeia – the figure presumably capable of animating the dead in conferring a mask or persona to a voice – is at the same time disfigured by the othering mask of death – "con la faz del 'otro'" – and the othering masks of different discourses. "Antonio Machado" situates itself in the uncanny space between various personal voices – Ronsard's, Machado's, and Aub's supposedly absent voices, as well as the future readers' supposedly present voices – but also between said voices and a different "otro": seemingly impersonal, voiceless "muerte."

In the concluding paragraph of his tribute, Aub claimed that "el crimen" [the crime] – that is, Machado's death – took place on the other side of the border "para que no se viera" [so that it would not be seen] ("Mínimo"16). Playing on the rich polysemy of *tierra* with a characteristically baroque, paratactic style, Aub described Machado's exile as dramatically leading to the tomb: "Salió de su patria, perdió pie, dio en tierra; desterrado" [He left his fatherland, lost his footing, fell to earth/ground/land; exiled/dis-terred] (16). And yet, "ahora, a los diecinueve años" [now, nineteen years later], Machado "vence, de pie, como fue" [wins, standing up, as he was/went]. A reader may ask: how can Machado win "de pie" now? Aub supplied a photographic "imagen verdadera" of Machado "como fue" before he lost his footing and his life and fell into his grave as an exile. But Aub also supplemented this image through poetic memory, composing a new image of him now as a standing or walking ghost. In a way, Aub brought Machado back to life by evoking and reshaping Stéphane Mallarmé's "presentización del pasado" in his haunting epitaphic line "Tel qu'en Lui-même enfin l'éternité le change" [As into Himself at last eternity changes him] from the sonnet "Le tombeau d'Edgar Poe" [The Tomb of Edgar Poe] (50–1).

"Viéndole así" [seeing him this way] others may be able to forget Machado, Aub disparagingly added: "¡Que olviden otros!" But Aub also asked himself and his readers rhetorically: "¿cómo?" How could anyone forget Machado "así"? Readers are still being apostrophized by Machado's gloss "cuando veáis esta sumida boca." If "así" signals the way in which Aub's poetic memory fashioned Machado's ghostly image, his rhetorical question could be recalled and also recast now, in the present of this reading, as an apostrophe: "viéndole así," others may still be able forget him, but how will you forget? How is true life – "lo vivo" – absent for you here and now?

Pamplona and Cambridge, 2020

Notes

1 Introduction: On Forewords and Historical Ghosts

1 According to Bernard Sicot, Aub was interned in Djelfa from 28 November 1941 to 18 May 1942 ("Max Aub" 406). For other discussions of Aub's foreword, see "La imaginación concentracionaria: Testimonio visual y ficcionalidad en *Diario de Djelfa*," chapter 2 of Carlos Varón's *La retirada del poema: literatura hispánica e imaginación política moderna.*

2 In using the ghost as a trope to read unhomely and untimely dimensions resistant to historicist recovery, I loosely draw from what Freud called "aesthetic investigations" of the *unheimlich* – or uncanny – as a paradoxical hermeneutic category for the study of works of art (123). As Hugh Haughton suggests, Freud's understanding of the uncanny invites readers to engage in "a double commitment to interpretation and resistance to interpretation" (lx). Among significant Freudian concerns in these reading practices are: a) the "uncanny, enigmatic character" ['das unheimlichen und rätselhaften Charakter'] of textual and artistic materials understood as sites of thick spatiotemporal complexity where historical, cultural, and biographical conflicts are at play (Freud 87); b) the equivocal sense of "homely," when *heimlich* "becomes increasingly ambivalent, until it finally merges with its antonym *unheimlich*," and "[t] he uncanny (*das Unheimliche*, 'the unhomely') is in some way a species of the familiar (*das Heimliche*, 'the homely')" (Freud 134); c) the eerie sense of a simultaneity of linguistic foreignness and domesticity – unfamiliarity and familiarity – when reading a translation (Haughton xliv); d) the intellectual doubt as to whether "a lifeless object might not perhaps be animate" (Freud 135); and e) the uneasy connection between the desire to return to an upset home ["Die Heimlichkeit der Heimath zerstören, 'To destroy the tranquillity of the homeland'" (Freud 127)], and "anything to do with death, dead bodies, revenants, spirits and ghosts" (Freud 148).

3 In *The Spanish Holocaust* (2011), historian Paul Preston described some of the fatal consequences that the final victory of Franco's military forces at the end of March 1939 had for Republicans, "[m]ore than half a million refugees were forced into exile

and many were to die of disease in French concentration camps. Several thousand were worked to death in Nazi camps" (7). No fewer than 30,000 exiled Republicans ended up in Mexico (Moradiellos, *Historia* 286).

4 Here and elsewhere in this book, topical refers to motifs and topoi such as, for instance, the Biblical commonplace *vox clamantis in deserto*, as shall be discussed later with regard to Max Aub's poem "Tres años." Needless to say, these topoi tend to travel quite easily across generic and national determinations.

5 In *Untimely Meditations*, Nietzsche's dismissed developmental, goal-oriented history as "monumental": "That the great moments in the struggles of individuals form links in one single chain; that they combine to form a mountain range of humankind through the millennia; that for me the highest point of such a long-since-past moment is still alive, bright, and great – this is the fundamental thought in the belief in humanity that expresses itself in the demand for a *monumental* history. Precisely this demand that what is great be eternal sparks the most terrible struggle, however. For every other living thing cries out: 'No! The monumental shall not come into being'" (68). For connections between Nietzsche's *Untimely Meditations* and Walter Benjamin's "Theses on the Philosophy of History," see Löwy 48.

6 For the convergence of serious national and international conflicts in this period, see Eric Hobsbawm's classic *The Age of Extremes: The Short Twentieth Century, 1914–1991* (1994), especially pp. 142–63, and Enzo Traverso's *Fire and Blood: The European Civil War, 1914–1945* (2007). According to Traverso, in Spain "there was a civil war within the civil war," and both conflicts were in turn part of yet another European civil war (55).

7 For the use of Freud's formulation of the uncanny in recent approaches to the recovery of memory in Spain and exhumations of mass graves from the war, see Jennifer Sime's "Exhumations: The Search for the Dead and the Resurgence of the Uncanny in Contemporary Spain" (2013).

8 Antonio Gómez López-Quiñones pointed in 2012 to the multiplicity and variety of historical memories in this context: "Spanish historical memory should be better theorized as an unstable constellation of diversified positions and voices" ("A Secret" 90).

9 The hermeneutic problem presented by Aub obviously extends to the relation between "lo escrito" and "cada lector," and even further to the relation between "lo escrito" and Aub as "lector" of his own poems in his foreword. As Jonathan Mayhew contended in *Apocryphal Lorca* (2009), "there is no way of restoring the author's work to what it was before being subjected to the distorting lens of interpretation" (1). Even if there is arguably no such a thing as an undistorting hermeneutic lens, Mayhew's point is apposite here in that some canonical poets – most notably Federico García Lorca – have been considered as embodiments of Spanish culture and even of Spanish cultural exceptionalism in modernity (29). In the specific circumstances of the Spanish Republican exile, a similar case could be made regarding Antonio Machado, as shall be seen in the discussion about attempts by Spanish literary historians to recuperate and restore the work of exiled poets for national culture.

10 As Brad Epps and Luis Fernández-Cifuentes argue, among the outstanding examples of established Spanish literary historiography is Francisco Rico's *Historia y crítica de la literatura española* (1980–present) (16). In their view, Rico's "penchant for the canon," displayed in phrases like "las cimas y los grandes momentos" [high points and great moments] (16), as well as his "explicit and authoritative concern with coherence and consecutiveness" (17) reveal an understanding of literary history as Nietzschean monumental history. For the current canonical status of exiled poets such as Juan Ramón Jiménez and Luis Cernuda, see Mari Paz Balibrea, "El paradigma," 18. The interest of Max Aub's and Tomás Segovia's exilic poetry for examining questions of national canonicity will be discussed in their respective chapters.

11 See Paul Jay's *Global Matters: The Transnational Turn in Literary Studies* (2010) and, more recently, César Domínguez and Birgit Neumann's "Introduction: Delocalizing European Literatures" (2018).

12 See, for instance, Brad Epps and Luis Fernández Cifuentes's *Spain Beyond Spain* (2005). See also Joan Ramon Resina's *Iberian Modalities* (2013) and Fernando Cabo Aseguinolaza, Anxo Abuín González, and César Domínguez's *A Comparative History of Literatures in the Iberian Peninsula* (2010, 2016), as well as Ottmar Ette's consideration of transculturality in literature, *Writing-between-Worlds* (2016). Focusing on the charged relationship between Spanish imperialism and transatlantic studies, Alejandro Mejías-López outlined in 2015 some of the issues discussed by Brad Epps and Luis Fernández Cifuentes, Sebastiaan Faber, Mabel Moraña, Joan Ramon Resina, and Abril Trigo: "Peninsular studies have been losing ground vis-à-vis Latin American studies ... For these critics, transatlantic approaches have developed as a compensatory measure, a type of colonization of the field of Latin American studies by Peninsularists in order to stay relevant. Thus, as the term 'transatlantic' keeps gaining currency in our field, critics have raised voices of concern if not outright rejection, seeing it as the reincarnation of neo-Hispanism" (212).

13 See, for instance, Patricia M. Keller's *Ghostly Landscapes: Film, Photography, and the Aesthetics of Haunting in Contemporary Spanish Culture* (2016), Carlos Jerez-Farrán and Samuel Amago's edited volume *Unearthing Franco's Legacy* (2010), Mari Paz Balibrea's several studies of the fraught return of Republican exiles to collective memories of Spain, Jo Labanyi's edited volume *Constructing Identity in Twentieth-Century Spain* (2002), and Jessica A. Folkart's *Liminal Fiction at the Edge of the Millennium: The Ends of Spanish Identity* (2014).

14 Spanish historiographical overviews such as Jordi Gracia's *La resistencia silenciosa* (2004) and *A la intemperie* (2010), Andrés Trapiello's *Las armas y las letras: literatura y Guerra Civil (1936–1939)* (1994, revised and enlarged in 2010 and 2019), and *Historia de la literatura española* edited by José-Carlos Mainer (2010–13) have provided significant contextual material for this project. Other important references are Sebastiaan Faber's *Exile and Cultural Hegemony* (2002), Mari Paz Balibrea's *Tiempo de exilio* (2007), and her edited volume *Líneas de fuga: hacia otra historiografía cultural del exilio republicano español* (2017), which reconsider Spanish Republican exile from a cultural studies

perspective. See also Sebastiaan Faber's *Memory Battles of the Spanish Civil War* (2018). A multifaceted reflection on the political uses and abuses of the various Republican exiles in recent debates about the connections between historiographical discourses, memory discourses, and nationalist politics in Spain is José María Naharro-Calderón's *Entre alambradas y exilio: sangrías de las Españas y terapias de Vichy* (2017). See particularly chapter 1, "Falacias de exilios" (11–51). For a recent overview, and a reflection on the study of Spanish Republican exile as "deber de memoria" [duty of memory], see Juan Manuel Bonet's 2019 "Para un mapa del exilio republicano" (46).

15 Beyond scholarly studies, *This Ghostly Poetry* is also in dialogue with books for the general public about Spain's recent social and cultural history like Giles Tremlett's *Ghosts of Spain* (2006), Ian Gibson's *Cuatro poetas en guerra* (2008), and Jeremy Treglown's *Franco's Crypt* (2013).

16 Thus this book converses with a recent comparatist postnational approach. This approach is "linked to questioning the idea of 'nation' as an adequate framework for explaining and justifying literature insofar as a cultural phenomenon, needing to distance itself from 'monological' concepts of culture, emphasizing those of interference or transmission/convergence" (Cabo Aseguinolaza, González, and Domínguez, xii). Arguably, no cultural practice can be adequately studied through a predominantly national lens. In this sense I also believe in the critical value of exploring those liminal spaces where national and transnational cultural productions overlap. As Peter Giles contended in 2010, "the globalizing process is at its most illuminating precisely when it runs up against the sharp vested interests of local concerns. Indeed, many of the most crucial – and often the most heated – debates in social and political life are taking place at various boundaries where traditional allegiances of national identity are encountering the turbulence of the transnational" (12–13). Postnationalism, along with multinationalism, may serve, "within an increasingly anxious intellectual market, as a sign that sells" (Epps 133). Yet, while it now seems doubtful that nationalism will continue to be "out of sync with new material technologies, modes of information, and markets," certain nationalisms seem to have been largely out of sync with recent reading practices for poetry, at least as these have been channeled through literary history in Spain (Epps 133). One reason that nationalism is still a strong global cultural force, though, may be that not enough critical attention has been paid to the claim-subverting elements traceable in their canonical literary texts, especially poems. Cabo Aseguinolaza pointed in 2010 to a similar critical issue with regard to the entire Iberian Peninsula: "the model of an Iberian Peninsula with four literatures ... is the result of a complex discourse that is full of affiliate excisions and artificial overlaps, and which derives from limited and hierarchical access to the concept of nation ... In this realm, historiographical discourse, according to its habitual parameters, is a saturated and intimately conservative mode of discourse" (52). Instead of considering "canonical hunks" of "old disciplines" like foreign literatures and cultures as "floating in global fluidity" (Resina, "Iberian" 8), *This Ghostly Poetry* examines works by canonical poets as being historically situated, but also as activating specific cross-boundary, non-chronological, and plurivocal modes of memory. For a recent exploration of liminal spaces in – or next to – Spain where national and

transnational cultural productions overlap, see Sergio del Molino's journalistic travelogue *Lugares fuera de sitio: viaje por las fronteras insólitas de España* (2018).

17 See Fernández Cifuentes's "Discurso" (1995) for an incisive comparative approach to academic reading practices in Spain and in the United States at the end of the twentieth century.

18 A transnational perspective would at least encompass Mexico, in the case of Max Aub and Tomás Segovia; Mexico and the United States, in the case of Luis Cernuda; and Puerto Rico and the United States, in the case of Juan Ramón Jiménez. In the context of Spanish literary history, it is instructive to read Christopher Domínguez Michael's *Critical Dictionary of Mexican Literature (1955–2010)* (2007, 2012) on the subject of Aub's nationality: "before Spain was celebrating him, Aub was being included in Mexican dictionaries as a Mexican author, not just because of his passport but also because of his profound devotion to us over the course of thirty years" (33). Domínguez Michael's entry for Luis Cernuda is also inflected by a restrictive concept of national literary canon: "Mexican literature – in a rather unequal exchange – appropriated him entirely, consecrating a tomb for the poet in the national pantheon, seeing Cernuda as a body that germinated in foreign soil" (81). Nonetheless, in his reflections on the forms of exile traceable in Segovia's poetry, Domínguez Michael also makes significant border-crossing connections extending to other Republican poets like Juan Ramón Jiménez: "In Jiménez (and Ungaretti, and Gilberto Owen, and Pavese) Segovia found an exemplary form of rootlessness, not only historical and existential but also stylistic" (472).

19 In a similar vein, Jahan Ramazani argued in 2009 that poems keep "criss-crossing unequal and discrepant worlds" (*A Transnational* 8). In his study of the political complexities involved in Derek Walcott's use of the character Philoctete in his poem *Omeros*, for instance, Ramazani contended that a poem's reach can be so broad in geography and history that it "carves out" an interstitial cultural location; that is, a cultural location where, as Homi Bhabha argued in the context of colonial or postcolonial cultural productions, the "incommensurable differences" between global and national cultures are tensely negotiated (*Location* 312). The cultural differences found in exilic poems can be read along similar lines. Nonetheless, poems hardly "carve out" a cultural location, as Ramazani's sculptural metaphor seems to suggest, as though such a "third space" between the national and the transnational could be solidly inscribed in and circumscribed by a new set of fixed spatiotemporal coordinates ("Poetry" 294).

20 Prime Minister of Spain Pedro Sánchez visited Machado's grave in Collioure on 24 February 2019 to commemorate the anniversary of the poet's death in exile. In January 2019 Sánchez's government announced that it would play "a major role at the commemoration of the 80th anniversary of the republican exile." See http://www.lamoncloa.gob.es/lang/en/gobierno/news/Paginas/2019/20190124cultural-action.aspx (accessed 1 May 2019). See also, in this regard, Manuel Aznar Soler's and Idoia Murga Castro's wide-ranging exhibition catalogue *1939: Exilio republicano español* (2019).

21 *Breve historia de la literatura española* was published by the highly successful press Alianza Editorial, whose pocketbook collection "El libro de bolsillo" includes academic books at accessible prices. Although *Breve historia* was revised and expanded

in 2014, its historiographical framework remained the same. See Geraldine Cleary Nichols for a critique of its theoretical bases (260).

22 In May 2016, the Madrid City Council, in keeping with the Law of Historical Memory passed in 2007 by the Spanish Congress of Deputies, set up a Comisionado para la Memoria Histórica [Committee for Historical Memory] and tasked it to rename the streets and squares of Madrid. In March 2017 the Comisionado proposed a list of forty-seven new names, including that of Max Aub. While this was happening, Aub was also at the centre of a public controversy over the use of his name in the Matadero Madrid arts centre. The *terminus ad quem* of the cultural consequences of the civil war would then be hard to set, insofar as the question about the conditions of possibility for the symbolic return of exiles to Spain – that is, the cultural and political recovery of their legacy – remains open. For a critical reflection about the committee's proposal, see José María Naharro-Calderón's "Monos de la desfachatez: la Montaña in-civil" in his *Entre alambradas y exilio: sangrías de las Españas y terapias de Vichy* (363–422). Already in 1991, Naharro-Calderón addressed the charged relationship between the Spanish literary canon and the oblivion of exile in Spain. See the introduction to his commemorative edited volume *El exilio de las Españas de 1939 en las Américas: "¿Adónde fue la canción?"* ("Des-lindes" 17).

23 Many descriptions and samples of these efforts can be found online (accessed 1 November 2017): http://www.cervantesvirtual.com/bib/portal/exilio/index-2.html; http://www.residencia.csic.es/cernuda/edaddeplata/publicaciones/inicio.htm;http://www.residencia.csic.es/jramon/img/prensa/dossier.pdf; http://www.museoreinasofia.es/exposiciones/jusep-torres-campalans-ingenio-vanguardia-espanola; https://www.ibercampus.es/un-congreso-internacional-analizara-la-obra-literaria-y-la-experiencia-vital-10152.htm; http://www.elconfidencial.com/archivo/2009/09/18/2_espana_otros_paises_buscan_recuperar_memoria.html; http://www.publico.es/actualidad/rescatan-poemario-editado-motivo-del.html; http://www.abc.es/hemeroteca/historico-26-08-2002/abc/Cultura/sociedad-estatal-de-conmemoraciones-culturales_123920.html; http://www.abc.es/hemeroteca/historico-18-01-2003/abc/Cultura/el-centenario-de-max-aub-limpia-de-cliches-al-escritor-que-supo-hacer-del-exilio-un-paradigma_156321.html.

24 Epps and Fernández-Cifuentes also explained that these entities "have returned, sometimes in a scattered, spectral guise and sometimes with a vengeance" (14). Much the same could be said of poetry as a genre (Ramazani, "To Get the News"), and of genre in general (Duff 1). These issues are discussed later in this chapter.

25 Ugarte's insights into the specific problems involved in his study of exilic cultural productions are helpful in this regard: "Exile is both a phenomenon and a person, and the tension between these two categories is the tension of this book" (*Shifting* 5). As Andrew Debicki observed somewhat resignedly about the theoretical problem of analysing the individuality of specific poetic works: "we continue to seek, in some fashion, ways of setting literary texts in their contexts and organizational schemes that relate individual poems and books to each other and to currents of life and thought" (*Spanish* 1).

26 For an approach to the so-called exilio republicano within a larger historical framework of displacement and migration into and out of modern and contemporary Spain, see Raquel Vega-Durán's *Emigrant Dreams, Immigrant Borders: Migrants, Transnational Encounters, and Identity in Spain* (2016).

27 Francisca Montiel Rayo explained in 2017 that the most widely used terms among Republican expatriates were *destierro* and *desterrado*. *Exilio* and *exiliado* were not common terms until the 1960s. *Desterrado* also described Republicans condemned by Franco's regime to displacement within Spain. Important literary uses of the term are the *Cantar de mio Cid* and Miguel de Unamuno's *Romancero del destierro* (Montiel Rayo 37–40). José María Naharro-Calderón has written numerous insightful pages about the terminological and typological many-sidedness of *exilio*. See, above all, his seminal 1994 book *Entre el exilio y el interior: el "entresiglo" y Juan Ramón Jiménez*. For *transterrado* see, in particular, pp. 25–7. In his 2017 analysis of the vocabulary of exile, historian Peter Burke recognized the conceptual productivity of the term *transtierro*: "The traditional Spanish term, *destierro*, 'uprooting,' is vividly concrete in its reference to the loss of one's native land. One relatively optimistic exile, the Spanish philosopher José Gaos, who took refuge in Mexico after the civil war, preferred the neologism *transtierro*, declaring that he 'felt not uprooted in Mexico but ... transplanted' ... Unlike 'one-sided concepts' such as acculturation or assimilation, *transculturación* and *transtierro* imply that change takes place for both parties in the encounter" (2–3). For an illuminating, historically situated study of the relation between *destierro* and *transtierro* in the Mexican context, with a particular emphasis on exilic poetry, see "Del destierro al transtierro" (2000) in *A tiempo y destiempo* (2003) by exiled poet and philosopher Adolfo Sánchez Vázquez (590–605). The discussion about the various meanings of *tierra* will be picked up again in the book's coda.

28 For poetry as prevalent form of discourse, see Maryse Bertrand de Muñoz 10–12.

29 In *A vueltas con el exilio: de Juan José Domenchina a Gerardo Deniz* (2015), a largely thematic overview of Republican exiled poets, Antonio Carreira pointedly underscored the need to be alert to the complex geopolitical coordinates encompassed under the umbrella of exilic poetry (9–10).

30 José Bergamín (Spain 1895–Spain 1983) was a poet, essayist, and playwright. During the war, he became president of the *Alianza de Intelectuales Antifascistas* [Alliance of Anti-Fascist Intellectuals], and was named cultural attaché for the Republican government-in-exile in Paris. In 1937, he was also president of the *II Congreso Internacional de Escritores en Defensa de la Cultura* [International Conference of Writers in Defense of Culture]. Exiled in Mexico, Bergamín ran the publishing house Editorial Séneca, which in 1940 would publish storied editions of Antonio Machado's collected works, Federico García Lorca's *Poeta en Nueva York*, and César Vallejo's *España, aparta de mí este cáliz*, as well as works by Rafael Alberti and Luis Cernuda, among others. Bergamín later went into exile in Venezuela, Uruguay, and France. He returned to Spain in 1958, exiled himself again in 1963, and returned for good in 1970.

31 In 2002, Teresa Ferriz Roure pointed out the utopian cultural value that *España Peregrina* had for the definition of nation among Republican exiles. In her view, Larrea and Bergamín represented "aquellos escritores españoles que, durante los años anteriores, habían intervenido activamente en la creación de esa 'utopía' cultural republicana ... La Cultura se confunde, aquí, con 'patria' en un proceso a través del cual se apropia de la esencia de España" [those Spanish writers that, during the previous years, had actively intervened in the creation of that republican cultural 'utopia' ... Culture is mixed up, here, with 'fatherland' in a process through which the essence of Spain is appropriated] (n. pag.). Also in 2002, Sebastiaan Faber explained the binary underpinnings of this essentialist concept of national culture, "[t]he modern appreciation of technique, reason, utilitarianism, power, efficiency, and secularism stands in marked contrast with the Spaniards' humanism, spiritualism, aestheticism, and transcendentalism" (*Exile* 44).

32 As Aub also wrote, "si me quedara, andaría por ahí ... fantasma de mí mismo, vuelto sombra de lo que fui sin que nadie se acordara del santo de mi nombre ni de una línea de mi figura, como no fuera yo, siendo mi sombra" [if I stayed, I would walk around ... a ghost of myself, turned into a shadow of what I used to be, without anyone remembering the saint of my name or a line of my shape, unless it was me, being my own shadow] (*La gallina* 560).

33 Cecilia Enjuto argues that *Las nubes* "conveys a nationalist, nostalgic idealization of Spain's glorious past, tainted with *melancholia* and pain, typical of his political exile" (275).

34 These topoi include allegorical landscapes like the one depicted in "Lázaro." Such landscapes should be added to the three largely referential types of landscape that Goretti Ramírez finds in Cernuda's poetry of exile: "urban landscapes, mostly in Anglo-Saxon settings (parks, cemeteries, and city ruins); Edenic landscapes, mostly in Hispanic settings (gardens, other cemeteries, and other ruins); and Spanish historic landscapes (Castile and the Escorial palace complex)" (192). Landscape as the allegorical space where a tense figurative interplay of *voz* and *tierra* is staged can be productively read along landscape as a representative space where the "ideological framework of Spanish modernity as a struggle for the definition of cultural signs" can be considered (Ramírez 192).

35 Nuria Parés was born in Barcelona in 1925. She was raised in Madrid, where she became a concert guitar player. After fleeing to France, she stayed in Piraeus, New York, and Havana. She arrived in Mexico in 1943, where she worked as a translator. *Romances de la voz sola* was her first volume of poems. It was published in Mexico with a foreword by León Felipe. She died in 2010.

36 Manuel Durán was born in Barcelona in 1925. He fled to southern France, to Casablanca, Morocco, and then to Mexico. His first books of poems, *Puente* [Bridge] and *Ciutat i figures* [City and figures], were published in Mexico in 1946 and in 1952, respectively. He moved to the United States in 1953, where he worked as an interpreter. He earned a doctorate degree at Princeton University in 1953 and became a professor

of Spanish and Latin American literature at Yale University. He has written poetry in Spanish and in Catalan.

37 Joan Ramon Resina has cogently argued for the specificity of Catalan exile in Mexico: "El exilio catalán de 1939 ni puede subsumirse sin más en el español, ni en la vaguedad de una abstracción que acaba siempre invocando otras expatriaciones, otras ausencias" [The 1939 Catalan exile cannot just be subsumed within the Spanish exile, nor within the vagueness of an abstraction which always ends up invoking other expatriations, other absences] (n. pag.). While it would be hard to fully disagree with this argument, it should be noted that, without textual reference to other exiles beyond reductively nationalistic frameworks, a poem would hardly be able to refer to the strict circumstances of a poet's exile.

38 According to a note included in the Buenos Aires edition of *Nabí*, this "poema bíblic" [biblical poem] was "concebut a Hendaia, continuat a Beirut, repres a Paris, no l'ha enllestit el seu autor fins que l'ensulsiament de Catalunya va portar-lo al forçat exili i al germanivol acolliment de la terra mexicana" [conceived in Hendaye, continued in Beirut, resumed in Paris, it was not completed by the author until the collapse of Catalonia sent him into forced exile, and on to the fraternal reception of the Mexican land] (qtd. in Cornudella 407).

39 In the foreword to his Spanish translation of *Nabí*, Carner addressed the spatiotemporal complexity inscribed in the Mexican edition of his poem, as well as its cultural and political implications: "En aquel otoño parisiense [1938], escribí prácticamente todo mi poema, fiel a mi nativa lengua catalana, contra la cual se encarniza hoy una Nínive pigmea. En 1939, ya entre estos nobles valedores mexicanos, vertí mi poema a lengua castellana, con fines como de más acercada plática. Siguen en el mundo la opresión del espíritu y los amagos soterraños, pero yo prefiero ser anacrónico" [In that Parisian fall, I wrote almost my entire poem, faithful to my native Catalan language, against which a pygmy Nineveh fights fiercely today. In 1939, already among these noble Mexican guardians, I rendered my poem into the Castilian language, so as to hold a closer talk. Oppression of the spirit and subterranean threats continue to exist in the world, but I prefer to be anachronistic] (7–8). *Nabí* may then be most productively studied if read transversally, along multiple interlaced discursive lines. Some of these lines intersect with the cultural field of Mexican *transterrados* and/or *transterrats*, particularly if we take into account Carner's involvement in the founding of a key institution for Republican exiles, the Colegio de México, where he taught from 1939 to 1945 and his friendship with and admiration for Alfonso Reyes, co-founder and president of the Colegio (Manent 18–19). Such discursive lines would extend beyond national filiations or affiliations – without necessarily disavowing them – through the wide-ranging cultural field of exilic poetry in that period. See also José María Naharro-Calderón ("Twentieth-Century" 623).

40 In 1992, the exiled Catalan poet and critic, Manuel Durán, stretched open these historiographical confines in the essay "Josep Carner in Mexico: As I Remember Him." Durán's essay detailed the multifaceted, border-crossing context of this cultural field,

and also the inadequacy of the umbrella term *nation* for any critical approach to its concrete historical circumstances (421).

41 In terms of the multidimensional discursive complexity of Carner's poetry, another Catalan poet Gabriel Ferrater penned in 1986 a perceptive foreword to *Nabí* where he stressed the different values accorded to poetry in the particular historical circumstances in which its author wrote: "Cuando, en el año 1941, Josep Carner publicó *Nabí,* un largo poema narrativo sobre la historia de Jonás, seguramente que se sorprendieron los muchos que le atribuian como destino, y casi le imponían por obligación, el papel de poeta local, de estilizador de manías de gentecilla. Pero casi no era preciso saber leer para ver lo poco que se vinculaba Carner a sus temas locales" [When, in 1941, Josep Carner published *Nabí,* a long narrative poem about the story of Jonah, it probably came as a surprise to the many who attributed to him as a fate, and almost imposed on him as an obligation, the role of local poet, of having to stylize the hangups of unimportant people. But it was almost not necessary to know how to read in order see how little Carner linked himself to their local themes] (9). See also Manent 20.

42 In *A New History of Spanish Writing:1939 to the 1990s* (2000), Chris Perriam, Michael Thompson, Susan Frenk, and Vanessa Knights took the perspective of exilic writing to explain the definition of Spain in the early years of Franco's dictatorship. Under the chapter heading "What is Spain?" they offered a strictly narrative reading of Cernuda's poetry to conclude that Spain was simply dead: "Early in the Franco years, nation was redefined as abstract entity above and beyond the people, and the meanings of Spain were altered, both by the immediate destructive past and by current politics, in a process bitterly recognized by writers such as Luis Cernuda in exile: '-¿España?', observes a guest at a gloomy tea party in grey springtime London in the famous and chilling poem of 1939 'Impresión de destierro' ('Exile's Impress'), 'Un nombre. / España ha muerto' ... ('Spain? ... A name; no more. / Spain has died')" (106).

43 Sebastiaan Faber's claim that "an exile who, from abroad, refers to '*el país*' or '*la patria*' may be invoking Spain; yet she may also well be invoking Catalonia, Galicia or the Basque Country" might have the unwanted effect of reinforcing a reductively identitarian nationalistic paradigm at a different level, with regard to a historical conjuncture in which other senses of cultural and territorial belonging and identification were also at play ("Beyond" 429). As Epps and Fernández Cifuentes contended, the present remains in Spain "strongly imprinted by a post-Westphalian concept of the sovereign nation-state" (12). This contention may be qualified by pointing out another imprint within the sovereign nation-state of Spain: that of a desire for other sovereign nation-states without it. From this angle, many of the reflections that this book proposes about Spanish literary history can be extended to other national literary histories that, even without a state, contribute to a program of nationalization. José-Carlos Mainer's claim quoted by Epps and Fernández-Cifuentes can be extrapolated in this regard: "un programa de estudios literarios es sustancialmente un programa de nacionalización del conocimiento" [a program of literary studies is substantially a program of nationalization of knowledge] (12). Luis Beltrán Almería has strongly argued against this

nationalistic tendency: "The attacks leveled at Spanish nationalism for the construction of a high and exclusive canon that subordinates literary creation to an idea of national unity and glory do not necessarily target the fraudulence of this construct; rather, they perpetrate a parallel fraud – at least insofar as literary creation is concerned – by playing the card of *another* nationalism against imperialist oppression" (275). See Santana for the institutional construction of identitarian histories of national and regional literatures within Spain vis-à-vis Spanish literary histories in the context of the internationalization of literature in the Spanish language. For an insightful critical analysis of the relationship between the new separatist drive in Catalonia and the erasure of key aspects of geographic and linguistic pluralism among Republican exiles, see José María Naharro-Calderón's "Entre campos y vueltas" in his *Entre alambradas y exilio* (53–110).

44 According to Soo, refugees would refer to themselves as Spanish Republicans "as it was a term that was palatable and intelligible to their ... hosts. There was also a nebulous though tangible sense of common belonging evident in the evocation of certain iconic figures ... such as Antonio Machado and Federico García Lorca ... The notion of a republican identity was certainly ambiguous and there was no consensual discourse of the Spanish Republic throughout the entire period of exile, but the Spanish Republic was nevertheless evoked and remembered within specific contexts" (8–9). In 2017, Mari Paz Balibrea and Sebastiaan Faber pointed out the aporia constituted by pairing the noun *exilio* and its qualifying adjective *español* within the category "exilio republicano español": "Sometido a la lógica espacio-temporal de la nación, el exilio y el exiliado están condenados a ser una incongruencia" [Subjected to the spatiotemporal logic of the nation, exile and exiled person are condemned to being incongruities] ("Hacia otra historiografía" 19). See Mario Martín Gijón's 2017 "España, español" for "interpretaciones sacrificiales" [sacrificial interpretations] and a "conceptualización de una España casi 'espiritual'" [conceptualization of an almost "spiritual" Spain] among exiled Republicans (63–4). Martín Gijón mentions two crucial poets in the construction of this image of Spain: León Felipe and Juan Larrea. Felipe's poetry is discussed later in this chapter. See also "Vencedores y vencidos: el coste humano de la guerra civil" in Enrique Moradiellos's *Historia mínima de la Guerra Civil española* for a brief discussion of "el llamado exilio republicano español de 1939" [the so-called Spanish Republican exile of 1939] (276).

45 In 1988 Andrew Debicki highlighted the benefits of poststructuralist critical approaches to – and of new historical perspectives on – Spanish modern poetry among United States Hispanists ("Criticism" 587). An example of these benefits was the possibility of accounting, beyond the critical constraints of positivistic stylistics, for "the enigmas, gaps, and irrationalities" of Claudio Rodríguez's poetry ("Criticism" 588).

46 Bühler graphically explains imagination-based deixis in terms of position: "One visualizes a contribution to a conversation, one hears it within oneself with the vocal quality of the acquaintance concerned and finds that it sounded as if he, the speaker of this word, had been standing here next to us at the desk and had spoken to us from that position" (151).

47 Johnson's most explicit reference to ghosts is: "Under the spell of shape-changing, anything can become anything at any moment, and the world around us may contain the ghosts of the stories that we no longer know. The relation between person and things grows more uncanny" (*Persons* 5). Johnson's suggestion that the linguistic relation between persons and things can be undecidable follows the spectral logic of Ernesto Laclau's Derridean take on the undecidability between flesh and spirit. See Laclau's essay "The Time Is Out of Joint" (1995).

48 I thank Simos Zenios for alerting me to this illuminating book.

49 In his attempt to open up the concept of "voice" for poetics and thus to explore how voice is produced by text rather than "transcribed into text," Nowell Smith proposed to distinguish between: "(a) different *voices* (personae or pre-personae, because disembodied or not yet determined as speaker), (b) different *vocal lines* (polyphony, syncopation, counterpoint, indeterminacy of phrasal ending), (c) different *vocal attitudes* (registers, address, epideictic versus deictic, embodied versus disembodied, moments of excess of *phone* over *logos*, when the sheer extravagance of sound becomes opaque to speech or semantics), and finally (d) different *voicings* (demanded of a reader, or of performance more generally)" (12). In the edited volume *The Sound of Poetry / The Poetry of Sound* (2009), Marjorie Perloff contended that "conventional prosodic studies cannot allow for the difference individual performance makes, much less for variants of individual and culturally determined reception" (2).

50 Interestingly, Stephen Greenblatt's famous New Historicist gesture was also premised on a trope of textual spectrality whereby voice could be figured as persona, as subjectivity, even as an individual or collective identity: "I began with the desire to speak with the dead ... It was true that I could hear only my own voice, but my own voice was the voice of the dead, for the dead had contrived to leave textual traces of themselves, and those traces make themselves heard in the voices of the living. Many of the traces have little resonance, though every one, even the most trivial or tedious, contains some fragment of lost life" (1). In this regard, at least, Greenblatt did not address the tensions between voice and voicing as just outlined.

2 Re-engaging with Ghosts in the Poetic Machine

1 The use of the ghost trope has also been very productive in recent cultural history books for the general public such as Giles Tremlett's 2006 *Ghosts of Spain: Travels Through Spain and Its Silent Past* and Jeremy Treglown's 2013 *Franco's Crypt: Spanish Culture and Memory Since 1936.* Jo Labanyi's "History and Hauntology; or, What Does One Do *with the* Ghosts of the Past? Reflections on Spanish Film and Fiction of the Post-Franco Period" (2002) was among the first critical approaches to the haunting effects of the civil war in Spanish culture. A recent contribution to this line of critical thinking is *Ghostly Landscapes: Film, Photography, and the Aesthetics of Haunting in Contemporary Spanish Culture* (2016), Patricia Keller's analysis of the aesthetics of haunting in images of and about the Spanish Civil War.

2 Two important pioneering studies in this field are *Memoria y olvido de la guerra civil española*, by Paloma Aguilar Fernández (1996) and *Víctimas de la guerra civil*, an edited volume coordinated by Santos Juliá (1999). The passing of the Law of Historical Memory in 2007 is a key factor in this context. For a recent account of debates about historical memory in Spain, see Paloma Aguilar and Leigh A. Payne's *Revealing New Truths about Spain's Violent Past: Perpetrators' Confessions and Victim Exhumations* (2016). See also Alberto Reig Tapia's brief but careful recapitulation "La maldita memoria histórica" in *La crítica de la crítica: inconsecuentes, insustanciales, impotentes, prepotentes y equidistantes* (2017).

3 This encouragement is often symptomatic of various nationalistic motivations. As Sebastiaan Faber has argued: "among a significant portion of the Republican exiles the experience of displacement spurred a newly intensified focus on their own national identity. In some, this fueled a resurgence of different forms of cultural nationalism and pan-nationalism whose tenets harkened back to the eighteenth and nineteenth centuries" ("Beyond" 429). A form of cultural pan-nationalism can be detected, most notably, in Rafael Alberti's emblematic acceptance speech for the 1983 Cervantes Literary Award. Alberti returned to Spain in 1977, after spending thirty eight years in exile, mostly in Latin America. His speech is discussed in the coda to this book.

4 For another example see Blanco Aguinaga, Rodríguez Puértolas, and Zavala 145. For the controversial reception of this famous literary history, see Bellón Aguilera. For a similar, more recent reading, see Alvar, Mainer, and Navarro 623.

5 As Chris Perriam, Michael Thompson, Susan Frenk, and Vanessa Knights wrote in 2000, for Felipe "there is the brave and challenging affirmation that the exiled poets had taken with them poetry, 'the song,' itself, thus leaving those behind in fact the marginalized and disempowered ones" (127). For recent content-based readings of Felipe's exilic poetry premised on the idea of cultural continuity, see for instance José-Carlos Mainer's 2014 *Historia mínima de la literatura española* (184).

6 The old debate about the content-form dualism seems very much alive in early-twenty-first-century literary studies. In his pedagogical *How to Read a Poem* (2007), Terry Eagleton took issue with two recent trends in literary criticism: "If most of its practitioners have become less sensitive to literary form, some of them also look with scepticism on the critic's social and political responsibilities. In our own time, much of this political enquiry has been offloaded on to cultural studies; but cultural studies, conversely, has too often ditched the traditional project of close formal analysis" (16). In *Memory Battles of the Spanish Civil War* (2018), Sebastiaan Faber reflected on the importance of artistic and literary form in cultural and memory studies of the conflict. Among the questions that, in Faber's view, cultural critics assuming "a more or less explicit ethical or social commitment," and willing to contribute to the debates about historical memory in Spain need to address are: "Do art or narrative fiction have formal qualities that allow them to contribute in some specific way to our understanding of the past? To what extent are those qualities activated or realized, and how does any particular text or work of art affect its readers or viewers?" (177–8).

7 In the introduction to their edited volume *Espectros: Ghostly Hauntings in Contemporary Transhispanic Narratives* (2016), Alberto Ribas-Casasayas and Amanda L. Petersen contrasted a ghostly idea of historiography to scatological visions that tend to see the past as a breach that needs to be overcome. If history has conventionally been viewed "either as a series of moments in coherent chronological succession, or as a causal process that brings to one necessary point," thus becoming "nothing but a collection of the stories of the victors, or about the progressive constitution of a nation or civilization," a spectral approach to historiography explores "the notion of a present that is out of joint, divided from itself by a rift that makes room for the conflictive overlap of the present, the future, and the past, and alternative presents, pasts, and futures" (13). This approach enables to examine the ways in which the present is interrupted by "undecidable, non-contemporaneous entities that fill the emptiness of modem time with inexhaustible meaning that makes moments break free of any teleological scheme" (14). Interestingly, in this characterization of the past as haunting the present, present readers also become spectral, as we view "ourselves as divided from our current moment, ourselves as the ghosts of our past and future" (14). Hauntings of non-narrative elements specific to poetry are left unexplored in *Espectros.*

8 This notion of the poem may also foster the sort of historical understanding that arises, as Michael Ugarte advocated in 2017 in the context of the ongoing debate about historical memory in Spain, "from insistent interrogation of the memory and articulation of the Other, a spirit of enquiry that comes out of cultural and post-colonial studies focusing on the subaltern, gender, and race" ("In Praise" 152). In the case of Republican *desterrados*, the Other is not necessarily the subaltern voice, but, arguably, the enigmatic sense of otherness generated by exilic poems in the haunted and haunting discursive space of continuity and discontinuity between living, writing, and reading.

9 Labanyi opposes objects of high culture to subaltern cultural forms. The poetry produced in exile by canonical exiled writers may generally not be seen as belonging to a subaltern cultural form. Yet it may be productively read from a subaltern angle, at least in the case of the poetry penned in exile by a gay (albeit canonical) writer like Luis Cernuda, or by a Jewish (albeit canonical or potentially canonical) writer like Max Aub.

10 As Roger Bartra – Mexican-born son of Barcelonian exiled Republicans – explained in 2003: "What is new in the world today is the fact that expatriates and émigrés are part of a massive tide of extraordinary dimensions, an enormous and heterogeneous torrent ... that spills out from the interstices of every culture and society" ("Allegories" 118). Philosopher Seyla Benhabib eloquently asserted in 2018: "In the early decades of the twenty-first century, exile, statelessness, and migration have emerged as universal experiences of humanity" (xv). In *Once within Borders* – a history of modern territoriality in the West published in 2016 – Charles Maier considered the reasons for the precariousness of the notion of territory in the early twentieth-first century: "All our customary homelands seem assailed by global trends that transgress once

reassuring borders and spatial stability – by threats of terrorist attacks, uprooted refugees, tidal flows of international capital, the scary spread of new diseases, and the threat of climate change oblivious to frontiers" (1).

11 Sebastiaan Faber outlined some of these challenges in 2017: "Literary histories published in Spain during and after the dictatorship ... tend to place the center of gravity and normality within the Iberian Peninsula. In the first couple of decades, mention of the exiles and the work were unlikely to pass the censor's muster; later, they were awkwardly relegated to appendices ... Since the late 1990s, research groups have formed – most prominently the Grupo de Estudios del Exilio Literario (GEXEL) at the Universitat Autonoma de Barcelona – whose main purpose has been to recover the intellectual legacy of Spanish Civil War exile for democratic Spain" ("Beyond" 434).

12 For recent perspectives on Américo Castro's contribution, see Claudio Guillén's 2003 "De la continuidad," Eduardo Subirats's 2003 *Memoria y Exilio*, and Francisco Márquez Villanueva's 2009 "Américo Castro: entonces y ahora." See also Julio Rodríguez Puértolas's "Presentación." The question of the structural importance of exile in Spanish history will be picked up in the coda to this book. For a study of the retreat into mystical elements of a supposed "ser de España" [Spanish being] among exiled members of the liberal-leaning Institución Libre de Enseñanza [Free Educational Institution] like Castro, see historian Jorge de Hoyos Puente's 2016 *¡Viva la inteligencia!: el legado de la cultura institucionista en el exilio republicano de 1939* (103). As de Hoyos argued in *La utopía del regreso: proyectos de estado y sueños de nación en el exilio republicano en México* (2012), "durante toda la dictadura franquista, los exiliados hicieron de España su obsesión y su principal preocupación. Muchos intelectuales: filósofos, poetas, historiadores, trataron de comprender el *ser* de España [during the entire Francoist dictatorship, exiles made Spain their obsession and main concern. Many intellectuals: philosophers, poets, historians, tried to understand Spain's *being*] (12, emphasis in the original).

13 Structural long-term pattern in the sense of Fernand Braudel's definition of *longue durée*: "a reality that persists through time" (6). See Luis Beltrán Almería's *¿Qué es la historia literaria?* (2007) for a defence of Braudel's framework in literary history (114). See also Franco Moretti's reading of Braudel's idea of temporary structure (13–14). For a critique of the anachronistic idea of a "naturaleza eterna" [eternal nature] of nation – and therefore, of constant or structural exile – that arguably underlies Kamen's *The Disinherited* and similar books such as José Luis Abellán's *El exilio como constante y categoría* [Exile as a constant and a category] (2001), see Jorge de Hoyos Puente's "El exilio republicano en la historia de los exilios políticos en España" (314–5).

14 This is precisely the idea of culture with which Jo Labanyi takes issue ("Introduction" 3).

15 I follow here Chris Lorenz's understanding of the connection between teleology and national history: "As the nation became the almost 'natural' spatial framework of academic history – replacing the older frameworks of the dynastical state and of religious history – history's temporal framework also changed fundamentally ... Instead of the past being authoritative for the present in the form of practical *exempla*, after the French Revolution, the future became the point of orientation – in the form of a

telos in the making, especially 'the nation-state' in the making – and therefore national history is intrinsically connected with the idea of a 'special mission' of each nation resulting in its 'special path' in history" (75). For a metahistorical approach to the idea of teleological continuity as regards national contruction and reconstruction, see Rüsen.

16 In *El exilio republicano de 1939*, Francisco Caudet offers a largely thematic and topical exploration of this twofold uncanniness in a short selection of poems written by canonical Republican exiles, but does not address its inscription in their textual and verbal materiality (404).

17 This form of literary history is often fostered by established agents of culture in the "economy of prestige" and cultural capital in Spain like state institutions such as the Spanish Academy, literary and cultural historians frequently contributing to widely read newspapers such as *El País* and *El Mundo*, and eminent publishers such as Crítica and Anagrama (see English 9–11).

18 Enric Bou has underscored the canonical status of the "Edad de Plata" as a cultural formation, since it was "an impressive convergence that brought together certain individuals and certain poetic modalities which produced publications and public events which had a strong impact on the formation of a literary canon" (555). For the canonizing force of Diego's *Poesía española: antología 1915–1931*, see, for instance, José Luis García Martín's *Poetas del novecientos: entre el modernismo y la vanguardia: antología* (2001) (x). Recent research and archival work in Spain has focused on non-canonical figures of the "Edad de Plata." According to its self-description, *Mnemosine: Biblioteca Digital de La otra Edad de Plata* [Mnemosyne: Digital Library of the Other Silver Age] "reúne un repertorio de textos y autores que han permanecido a la sombra de las grandes figuras literarias del primer tercio del siglo XX" [gathers a repertoire of texts and authors who have remained in the shadow of the great literary figures of the first third of the twentieth century]. See https://www.ucm.es/loep/mnemosine and http://repositorios.fdi.ucm.es/mnemosine/index.php. I thank Lucía Cotarelo Esteban for this information (accessed 1 November 2018).

19 In his essay "La actividad literaria de la emigración española," published in 1949, during his exile in the United States, Vicente Llorens explained the impact that this setback had on the poets included in Diego's anthology: "De los diecisiete poetas representados en una antología publicada en 1932 ... uno de ellos había fallecido poco antes; dos murieron en 1936 durante la guerra -asesinado el uno y poco menos que confinado el otro-; cuatro han quedado en España; los diez restantes ... viven en el destierro, con la excepción de Machado" [Of the seventeen poets represented in an anthology published in 1932 ... one had passed away a little earlier; two died in 1936 during the war – one was murdered, the other a little less than confined – ; four have remained in Spain; the remaining ten ... live in exile, except for Machado] (*Estudios* 131).

20 See also Gracia y Ródenas 500.

21 In the 1997 and 2014 editions of *Breve historia de la literatura española* Carlos Alvar, José-Carlos Mainer, and Rosa Navarro also saw unequivocal evidence of a "poética de

la continuidad" [poetics of continuity] in the poetry produced in exile and in Spain (630). As Roberta Johnson explained in her study of the "solitude" that philosopher and sometime poet María Zambrano's experienced in exile, Mainer's *La Edad de Plata* (1974) "revolutionized the way we study and view the greatest moment in Spanish letters since the Golden Age" in that he approached "hallowed authors from early twentieth century Spain ... within their sociological circumstances" (149). In Johnson's description of Mainer's thesis, the "Edad de Plata" ended in 1939, "when the victory of the Nationalist forces over the Republic radically changed the sociopolitical landscape in which the authors ... had flourished" (149). Johnson argued for a historical prolongation and complication of the "Edad de Plata" – which she described as "a male dominated intellectual milieu" – but expanding Mainer's paradigm from an exilic and gendered perspective: "the Silver Age ... lived on in exile work like that of María Zambrano. Perhaps precisely because the war did not interrupt a fully developed intellectual trajectory, Zambrano blossomed in exile; in fact, rather than a hindrance, exile may have been a liberation for Zambrano as a woman philosopher ... Importantly the gendered phase of her theory of the self coincides with her geographical displacement from Spain to Latin America, her geographical and finally her matrimonial separation from her husband, and her establishing herself as an independent woman in both her personal and professional life" (151–5). After returning to Spain, Zambrano published her reflections on the spatiotemporal contradiction of her exilic experience. I address these reflections later in this chapter.

22 Nevertheless, the teleological temporality of Spanish history has been questioned by non-Spanish literary historians. In the introduction to his 2004 edited volume *Cambridge History of Spanish Literature*, David T. Gies meditated critically on the functionality of such a temporality: "What determines what is 'Spanish' about 'Spanish' literature? Is it the place of birth of the author? Is it his/her native language, the language in which he/she writes, or the language in which he/she is known? Is language the main determinant for nationality? If nation and language are not organizing categories for Literary History (and many today reject such categories as reductive and/or imperialistic), what groupings can be made which avoid the reality or appearance of teleology?" (9).

23 In 1989, Michael Ugarte was already perceptively examining the tensions involved in the recuperative method followed by "the tireless compilers of the facts": "The familiar and unfamiliar names of those who left during or after the war as well as their itineraries have been the objects of much attention ... [Those] lives [were] dying to be written, hoping for a reincarnation through writing ... One wonders how many other lives ... have gone neglected due to the conventions of our discipline, so that we who contribute to the compilation of the list will never know of their existence" (*Shifting* 14–16). In 2002, Mari Paz Balibrea denounced the persistence of this historiographical "paradigma de recuperación" [paradigm of recuperation] ("El paradigma" 18). Balibrea's arguments are discussed later in this chapter.

24 Antonio Muñoz Molina is arguably one of the most prominent public intellectuals in Spain today. He publishes regularly in *El País*, one of the most widely read

newspapers in the Spanish-speaking world. He is a member of the Royal Spanish Academy. He has served as the director of the Cervantes Institute in New York and taught at New York University. He has received countless awards. In 2013, he won the prestigious Jerusalem Literary Prize – previously awarded to Milan Kundera, Octavio Paz, Jorge Semprún, and Susan Sontag.

25 Anagrama published *A la intemperie* as part of its "Argumentos" series, one of the most respected essay collections in Spain.

26 For a well-documented account of the complex circumstances surrounding the supposed continuities between exiled and non-exiled cultures, see Jordi Amat's *La primavera de Múnich* (2016), a cultural, intellectual, and political history of the contacts between intellectuals in Franco's Spain and "lo mejor de la Edad de Plata exiliada" [the best of the exiled Silver Age] (148). For a broad understanding of the "Edad de Plata," and its connections to culture among Republican exiles, see José María Naharro-Calderón's "Des-lindes de exilio" (12–13).

27 The discussion of the relationship between the notion of Spanish national cultural development and the temporality of modernity is examined in the coda to this book.

28 Faber has pointed out the connection between the "narrow disciplinary framework" inherited from the Spanish philological school and Mainer's failure to take into account "any of the critiques leveled at the field from Iberian or Trans-Atlantic Studies" ("Beyond" 435–6). Mainer's historiographical claims of integration and continuity would run counter to the premises established by Andrew Debicki in *Spanish Poetry of the Twentieth Century: Modernity and Beyond*. Debicki made explicit the methodological and critical need to address historical discontinuities between the poets who remained in Spain and those who went into exile: "[T]heir work needs to be considered separately from that produced by their compatriots in Spain, since they were completely isolated from life in their native land and since their works, in turn, did not circulate in that land until toward the end of this period (*Spanish* 89). See Larraz for segregative and integrative approaches to post-dictatorship historiography.

29 The much-trumpeted modernization, after two decades of isolation, depended primarily on the 1959 Stabilization Plan, which was premised on "the creation in Spain of a market economy where prices would control the allocation of resources, and the integration of that market into the capitalist economy of the West" (Carr 156).

30 Balibrea's position regarding categories like nation and recuperation is complex. In *Tiempo de exilio* (2007) Balibrea took issue with what she saw as a hegemonic linear temporality of Spanish modernity between the Second Republic and the transition to democracy after Franco's demise in 1975. In Balibrea's view, this continuous historical narrative was based exclusively on the literary, cultural, and political discourses that the anti-Francoist opposition produced in Spain during the dictatorship, thus relegating the multiple temporalities of modernity inscribed in exilic cultural productions to an irrecuperable past (13–14). Balibrea argued that Jordi Gracia's successful *La resistencia silenciosa* contributed greatly to the construction of this narrative (23). She countered with the idea that there is a complex ethical, political, and cultural legacy of

exiled Republicans, "que está por recuperar como herencia legítima y valorable de la modernidad española" [that still needs to be recuperated as a legitimate and valuable inheritance of Spanish modernity] (*Tiempo* 29–30). In moving beyond the national framework of Gracia's and Balibrea's cultural histories, *This Ghostly Poetry* expands and complicates their respective understandings of the temporality of modernity.

31 Balibrea does not mention Muñoz Molina's speech, despite her interest in the symbolic value of Aub as an exile.

32 In *Words in Time: A Plea for Historical Re-Thinking*, originally published in 2013, historian Francesco Benigno underscored the problems involved in a nostalgic reading of history in the context of what he called "memorial history" in "a time of reproduction of icons" (11). Benigno warned against the risk of becoming anachronistically familiar with the past: "[T]he past, rather than being a mere given, is something which is continually being updated and re-presented so as it can be remembered ... A rational and emotional circuit is created between the reconstruction of the past and memory where the former endlessly modifies and adjusts ... the latter to the demands and needs of the present" (12). In his 2012 essay "Inconsolable Memory," Ángel Loureiro meditated on the affective and spectacular aspects of memorial history in the specific context of the Spanish Civil War: "The persistence of the conceptual questions regarding 'historical memory,' the affective nature of memory as the predominant way of relating to the past, and the unmistakable commemorative nature of the vindications of historical memory, are clear signs that the issue of 'historical memory' will not go away ... because its concepts and rituals are displaced signs of a profound discontent with history's unrelieved horrors and unredeemable catastrophes" (118).

33 Jessica A. Folkart deems *Soldados de Salamina* "perhaps the most famous of Spain's millennial ghost stories" (59).

34 In her cogent study, Ribeiro de Menezes also resorts to a rhetoric of ghosts: "Machado's sad end is evoked in terms not just of cultural loss, but also as a classic symbol of the demise of the Republic itself. Such an emotive reading of history is reinforced throughout *Soldados* in the manner in which spaces, places, and material objects are deployed affectively to summon up the past as a ghostly presence in the novel" (125). Ribeiro de Menezes does not dwell on the ways in which Machado's verse may summon up the past beyond its symbolic value, nor does she reflect on the relation of this poetic object to historical narratives.

35 Some of the historiographical terms of this debate – including those of the cultural significance of poetry and the iconic value of Antonio Machado – are stated in *La voz de los vencidos* [The Voice of the Vanquished] (2005), an informative 500-page overview of the 1939 Republican exile – as the subtitle describes it – by historian Alicia Alted Vigil. Alted explained how, since the turn of the twenty-first century, the grandchildren of those involved in the war had become interested in the conflict and its aftermath, and that the primary goal of her book was to honour the memory of the anonymous survivors who had gone into exile, by writing "una historia integradora en la que se aúna el análisis del historiador con la memoria de los protagonistas" [an

inclusive history in which the historian's analysis and the protagonists' memory are brought together] (*La voz* 17–18). In "La memoria de la república y del franquismo en el exilio" [Memory of the Republic and Francoism in Exile] (2006), Alted drew on Jacques Le Goff's distinction between the history written by historians and the history of collective memory to reiterate her appraisal of Machado's discursive significance (262–3). Alted also evoked in both books how she and many other Spaniards had visited Machado's grave in Collioure to honour the memory of the poet (272–3).

36 David Trueba's film *Soldiers of Salamis* enjoyed a measure of success among critics. The movie was selected for the "Un Certain Regard" section of the 2003 Cannes Film Festival.

37 As Sarah Leggott explains in her 2015 *Memory, War, and Dictatorship in Recent Spanish Fiction by Women*, *El corazón helado* depicts the effects of the experience of exile on several generations of a particular Spanish family (112). Leggott stresses that Grandes situates her novel "in the context of attempts to foreground Republican memory and amend the historical record" (112). For Grandes, Machado takes on an emblematic value as an embodiment of the best Republican virtues (144). *El corazón helado* ends with another quote from Machado: "Para los estrategas, para los políticos, para los historiadores, todo está claro: hemos perdido la guerra. Pero humanamente no estoy tan seguro. Quizá la hemos ganado" [For the strategists, for the politicians, for the historians, it is is clear: we have lost the war. But in human terms, I'm not so sure. Perhaps we have won]. Cercas also quotes Machado's statement at the outset of *Soldados de Salamina* (24).

38 Gil de Biedma participated in a gathering of intellectuals from Spain and exiled republicans. They paid tribute to Antonio Machado as an iconic figure symbolizing a bridge between the "dos Españas," and the potential end of the "división entre 'interior y exterior'" [division between "inside and outside"] (Glondys 252–4). For internal exile, see Londero.

39 For a recent re-examination of the relationship between narrative fiction and historical memory in Spain, see Alfons Cervera's *Yo no voy a olvidar porque otros quieran* (2017). Cervera launches a scathing critique of the cultural industry built around "la literature mal llamada de la memoria histórica" [the ill-named historical-memory literature], represented, in his view, by authors such as Javier Cercas, Andrés Trapiello, Antonio Muñoz Molina, and Jordi Gracia (pp. 219–29). See also Naharro-Calderón's *Entre alambradas y exilios* and Faber's *Memory Battles of the Spanish Civil War.*

40 To Casado, an important example of this form of poetic history is Francisco Rico's highly influential *Historia y crítica de la literatura española.* Epps and Fernández Cifuentes also critiqued Rico's project: "Rico's explicit and authoritative concern with coherence and consecutiveness; his calculated selection of authors (and critics); his essentially pre-structuralist notion of 'text,' and his omission of any metacritical questioning of literary history itself, disqualify his *Historia* as an example, let alone a model, of more contestatory or unconventional histories" (17). See also Juan Malpartida's critique (134).

41 For an analysis of different time signatures in narrative fiction, see Wood 34–8.

42 The history of this poetic survival could analogously be called "phantasmal" in the sense that Georges Didi-Huberman reads Aby Warburg's history, where "the archive is treated as

a material vestige of the sounds of the dead" (*The Surviving* 20). According to Didi-Huberman, Warburg's aim was "'to restore the tone and timbre of those unheard voices' (*den unhörbaren Stimmen wieder Klangfarbe zu verleihen*) – voices of the deceased, yet voices that still lie waiting, coiled up, as it were, simply in the writing itself" (*The Surviving* 20). Yet, despite its restorative aim, this perspective is irreparably ghostly, since, as a result of "a dynamic process of anthropological sedimentation that has become partial, or virtual, having been largely destroyed by time," writing needs to be viewed – in a way similar to the one proposed by Max Aub – as "what survives of a population of ghosts" (*The Surviving* 20). Pursuing the connections between Nietzsche and Warburg, Didi-Huberman also considers "the thought of a *memory understood as material*, the material of things themselves": "But what kind of material? ... a material capable of every type of metamorphosis. The notion of *survival* has revealed ... the indestructibility of traces and remains; the notion of *metamorphosis* will reveal ... their relative effacement, their perpetual transformation" (94). Didi-Huberman draws on Nietzsche's *Untimely Meditations*, where, as we saw, Nietzsche decries monumental historicism. Jiménez Heffernan's materialist understanding of textual survival is premised on an analogous critique of historicism.

43 Koselleck's understanding of historical temporality was premised on his idea of the *Gleichzeitigkeit des ungleichzeitigen*, or contemporaneity of the non-contemporaneous (*Futures* 90).

44 Along a critical line similar to those of Casado and Jiménez Heffernan, Juan Malpartida has championed critical readings of poetry alive "el tejido del lenguaje," its "historia diacrónica y sincrónica," and its "vasta memoria," which can only be constrained by "la cicatería nacionalista" [the fabric of language ... diachronic and synchronic history ... vast memory ... the nationalist stinginess] (11).

45 As Eva Soler Sasera remarked in 2015 concerning the methodological discrepancies in Aub's criticism: "Aub se dedica a establecer filiaciones transnacionales entre generaciones y estéticas, próximas entre sí a pesar de las fronteras y los océanos" [Aub devotes himself to establishing transnational filiations between generations and aesthetics, close to each other despite borders and oceans] (239–240). For Aub's problematic foreword in the context of Mexican politics, see, for instance, Francisco Caudet's *El exilio republicano de 1939* (418–20).

46 The American exiled poets included by Aub in his anthology were Nicaraguans Salomón de la Selva and Ernesto Mejía Sánchez, and Costa Rican Alfredo Cardona Peña.

3 Writing the War, Re-writing the Nation, Embodying the Voice of the People

1 The phrase "a poet's war" was used by Stephen Spender in *The God that Failed* (1949), where he drew on the old Romantic Byronic myth about the passionate Spaniards to paint the picture of the new poet of action: "The peculiar Spanish passion, idealism and violence of temperament, and even the Spanish landscape, colored the struggle and gave it intensity and a kind of poetic purity which it scarcely had before or afterward ... It was in part an anarchist's war, a poet's war" (244). See also Valentine Cunningham's

"The Spanish Civil War," and his introduction to *The Penguin Book of Spanish Civil War Verse*, as well as Gayle Rogers's *Modernism and the New Spain: Britain, Cosmopolitan Europe, and Literary History* and Hugh Ford's *A Poet's War: British poets and the Spanish Civil War*. Cunningham underscored in 2009 how hyperbolic the idea of a poet's war was: "Most of its participants – including the majority of the 40,000–60,000 international volunteers, most of whom were with the communist-organized International Brigades – were not intellectuals or writers or artists. But the war certainly involved – and divided – the literary and cultural worlds as no war before it" ("The Spanish" 185). For the military side of poetry, see also Blanco Aguinaga, Rodríguez Puértolas, and Zavala 18–19.

2 Auden's lines were included – and only partially showcased – in the anthology *Poems for Spain*, edited by Stephen Spender and John Lehman and published in London in 1939. In his introduction, Spender explained the close connection between poetry and war at the time: "Poets and poetry have played a considerable part in the Spanish War, because to many people the struggle of the Republicans has seemed a struggle for the conditions without which the writing and reading of poetry are almost impossible in modern society ... Moreover, where the issues are so clear and direct in a world which has accustomed us to confusion and obscurity, action itself may seem to be a kind poetry to those who take part in it" (7–8).

3 See Salaün 32–3 for poems in Catalan, Basque, and Galician.

4 Urrutia contends that, unlike in the First World War, in the Spanish Civil War there was such a demand for poetry that "los poemas fabricaron a sus receptores" [poems produced their recipients] (18).

5 Translation modified.

6 Enric Bou summarized the ways in which poems, and *romances* in particular, became a key cultural formation in times of war, and explained the importance of orality for the propagandist use of poetry: "Orality marks the diffusion and great success of poetry during the war. Radio addresses and political meetings, along with many journals and newspapers provide the materials that were later re-collected in anthologies ... Several anthologies from the time are instrumental in the dissemination of this poetry through publications controlled by political groups and institutions ... Well-known writers publish side by side with anonymous ones" (567). For the international impact of the popular *romance* form, see Binns 21.

7 [Winds of the people carry me, / winds of the people sweep me, / they spread my heart / and they winnow my throat. // ... // I am not from any people of oxen, / ... / Oxen never throve / in the wastelands of Spain. // Who talked about throwing a chain / over the neck of this race? // ... // Singing I await death, /as there are nightingales that sing / above the rifles / and in the middle of the battles].

8 As Urrutia explains, while pro-Franco poetry always referred to Spain, Republican poetry solved the problem of national conflict by resorting to the term "el Pueblo" (29). In the poem "Recoged esta voz" [Gather this Voice] from the same 1937 *Vientos*

del pueblo: poesía en la guerra, Hernández opposes "pueblo" to barbarians (Spender and Lehman 22). Jorge de Hoyos Puente has studied the two main senses that the concept "pueblo" had for left-wing political cultures during the Second Republican. He differentiates between an "imaginario liberaldemocrático" [liberal-democratic imaginary] and an "imaginario obrerista" [labour imaginary] (*La utopía* 342).

9 Valentine Cunningham has outlined the international dimension of the Spanish Civil War for poets: "The Left had long been preaching the need for writers to take up history's challenge, commit their whole being ... to resisting fascism by 'going over' wholeheartedly to the side of 'the people' ... Writers and artists took sides: one hundred and twenty-seven authors declared themselves FOR the republican government in the 1937 *Left Review* ... published as *Authors Take Sides on the Spanish War* ... The survey unearthed only a handful of Franco supporters" ("The Spanish" 185–6).

10 "Asturianos de braveza, / vascos de piedra blindada, / valencianos de alegría / y castellanos de alma, / labrados como la tierra / y airosos como las alas; / andaluces de relámpagos, / nacidos entre guitarras / y forjados en los yunques / torrenciales de las lágrimas; / extremeños de centeno, / gallegos de lluvia y calma, / catalanes de firmeza, / aragoneses de casta, / murcianos de dinamita / frutalmente propagada, / leoneses, navarros, dueños / del hambre, el sudor y el hacha, / reyes de la minería, / señores de la labranza" (311–2) [Asturians of bravery, / Basques of armored stone, / Valencians of cheerfulness / and soulful Castilians, / worked as the land / and airy as wings; / Andalusians of lightning, / born among guitars / and forged in the torrential / anvils of tears; / Extremadurans of ryegrass, / Galicians of rain and calm, / Catalonians of firmness, / Aragonians of class, / Murcians of dynamite / fruitfully bred, / people of Leon, Navarre, owners / of hunger, sweat, and axe, / kings of mining, / sires of farm work].

11 This poetic memory goes back to pre-modern times, before modern ideas of nation, writing, print, reading, and voice, when the anonymous medieval *romance* presumably became "popular." See Gaylord, "Spain" 1334. See also Şizen Yiacoup's *Frontier Memory: Cultural Conflict and Exchange in the Romancero fronterizo* for a compelling critique of *romances* as cornerstones of "the great national edifice" of Spain (8).

12 "Vientos del pueblo" was also included in Spender and Lehmann's anthology *Poems for Spain* (1939). Hernández's poem was written in 1937, also the year when the *II Congreso Internacional de Escritores en Defensa de la Cultura* was held. Hernández, Neruda, and Spender attended the congress. Spender's remarks on it in his 1951 autobiography are worth quoting at length, as they exemplify not only Spender's idea of "a poet's war," but also his exoticizing gaze on Spanish poets in general and on Hernández in particular: "The Congress served the purpose of showing that there were intellectuals from many countries who went to shelled Madrid in order to show their opposition to Fascism. Moreover, it enabled writers from abroad to become acquainted with the varied, fantastic, paradoxical, subtle, and yet passionately simple Spanish poets and writers: men like the grandiose and rhetorical Rafael Alberti, a

kind of Baroque Communist, the paradoxical and sensitive José Bergamin, follower of Unamuno, with a mind at once whimsical and definite, a little like that of E.M. Forster, or the poet Machado, absorbed in his world of pure poetic values, recalling Walter de la Mare, or perhaps the most astonishing of all – the young soldier-poet of Madrid, Miguel Hernandez, by origin a peasant and shepherd from the village of Oricuela. (There was a legend that Miguel Hernandez had been taught to read and write by a priest who met him in the hills, and educated him on examples of sixteenth- and seventeenth-century writings. So that his own passionate and ecstatic poetry produced a reaction against the prevailing modernism, when he came to Madrid in 1934 ...). The Congress, with all its good qualities, had something about of a Spoiled Children's Party, something which brought out the worst in many delegates. The circus of intellectuals, treated like princes or ministers ... had something grotesque about it" (*World* 264). Hernández died of tuberculosis in a Francoist prison in 1942, at thirty-one years of age.

13 Translation modified.

14 See also Clayton's own illuminating reading of the slapstick self-fashioning of voice in "Himno a los voluntarios de la República": "The poet's voice presents itself here not in search of a form but raising itself in excitement" (243). Alain Badiou's reductively expressive and thematic reading of Vallejo's (and Neruda's) poems for Spain stresses the internationalist and popular impulse behind them: "[T]he communist poets had found major subjective reasons in the Spanish war for renewing epic poetry in the direction of a popular epic – one that was both that of the suffering of peoples and that of their internationalist heroism, organized and combative" (97–8).

15 León Felipe (Spain 1884 – Mexico 1968) published his first collection of poems, *Versos y oraciones del caminante* [*Verses and Prayers of a Travelling Man*] (1920) in Madrid. He worked for an extended period of time in Mexico and the United States. He studied at Columbia University with Federico de Onís – founder in 1916 of the Instituto de las Españas – and taught and Cornell University (1925–29). A second edition of his first volume of poems came out in New York in 1929. When the Spanish Civil War broke out, he returned to Spain to support the Republican government. After 1938 he lived in Mexico for the remainder of his life.

16 [Yours is the hacienda, / the house, / the horse / and the pistol. / Mine is the ancient voice of the earth. / You keep everything / and leave me naked and wandering across the world ... / but I leave you mute ... mute! / And how are you going to harvest the wheat / And to feed the fire / If I carry off the song?]. The poem was retitled to "Hay dos Españas" in Felipe's *Antología rota*. This collection of poems was published in 1942 by the Buenos Aires publisher Pleamar in its "Mirto" poetry series, edited by Rafael Alberti. Another important change was that "Franco" was added to the first line of the poem: "Franco, tuya es la hacienda" (*Antología rota: 1930–1947*, 207). The new, shorter preface in *Antología rota* reinforced the binary "reparto" between arms and letters: "Hay dos Españas: la del soldado y la del poeta" [There are two Spains: that of the soldier and that of the poet] (*Antología rota: 1930–1947* 207).

17 José María Castellet's *Veinte años de poesía española: 1939–1959* (1960), one of the most influential postwar anthologies of poetry published in Spain, opened with Felipe. The anthology included "Reparto," but with one significant modification in the opening apostrophe (125). This modification is discussed later in this chapter.

18 For how the iconic value that these lines still possess reflects the impact that the 1939 exile had on Spanish culture, see "El paradigma exilio," Mari Paz Balibrea's 2003 essay about the state of Spanish exile studies in twenty-first century cultural criticism and history. Felipe's poem also provides the subtitle for José María Naharro-Calderón's edited volume *El exilio de las Españas de 1939 en las Américas: "¿Adónde fue la canción?"* (1991).

19 Felipe became acquainted with Whitman's poetry in New York, where he arrived in 1923. Felipe, who, according to John K. Walsh, "had been obsessed with Whitman's work and was preparing a translation of parts of it" including "Song of Myself," introduced Federico García Lorca to Whitman's poetry in 1929 (258).

20 "En este reparto injusto, desigual y forzoso, del lado de las harcas cayeron los arzobispos y del lado del éxodo, los poetas" [in this unfair, unequal and forced distribution, the archbishops fell on the side of the rebel armies from Morocco, and the poets on the side of exodus] (24–5). Pliny's letter LXXXIX is at times cast as a dialogue: "'But,' it is objected, 'if this separation is made between those who vote for inflicting death, and those who are on the side of exile, the opinion for acquitting the prisoners must necessarily prevail" (see http://www.gutenberg.org/files/2811/2811-h/2811-h.htm#link2H_4_0089).

21 The reception of Whitman in Latin America is quite complex. As is well known, Darío's reading of Whitman was in turn shaped by his memory of José Martí's own reading: "Mi memoria se pierde en aquella montaña de imágenes, pero bien recuerdo un ... Walt Whitman patriarcal, prestigioso, líricamente augusto, antes, mucho antes de que Francia conociera por Sarrazin al bíblico autor de las *Hojas de yerba*" (*Los raros* 222) [My memory loses itself in that mountain of images, but I do recall ... a patriarchal, prestigious, lyrically august Walt Whitman long before the French learned through Sarrazin of that biblical author of Leaves of Grass" (*Selected* 450)]. As Jorge Salessi and José Quiroga explained in 1996, "Martí himself, Rubén Darío, Jorge Luis Borges, and Pablo Neruda all read, misread, desired, repressed, had to come to terms with Whitman" (124). See also Siskind for a reading of Walt Whitman and Rubén Darío as institutions in the discursive debates about "the meaning of the process of aesthetic modernization ... in Latin American and peninsular modernist literature" (157).

22 According to Mónica Jato, Felipe's polyphonic discourse derived from his use of biblical language. Thus Felipe's "yo poético" [poetic I] became a "receptáculo de voces" [receptacle of voices] able to keep alive the memory of a "*común* dolor humano ... que el discurso monológico de la Historia, instaurado por la dictadura franquista, trataba de borrar" [common human pain that the monologic discourse of History, established by the Francoist dictatorship, tried to erase] (232). Jato's analysis remains within a national framework.

23 As Nowell Smith has argued, "apostrophes rarely remain simply apostrophe, be it as they verge on interjection, or on paronomasia and anarchic sound-patterning, or as they are drawn into a far more extensive rhythmic texture into which deictic and prosodic time are intricately woven" (84).

24 For a personal testimony of the ways in which Felipe's "voz" situated Republican exile within a universal framework, and a Baudelairean reflection on how the exiled poet is "dos veces desterrado ... como ciudadano y también como poeta" [twice banished ... as citizen and also as poet], see exiled poet Manuel Durán's autobiographical essay "La calzada de los poetas: un paseo lírico por la Ciudad de México" (215–16).

25 Poetry lends itself to being read as the *other* of nation in exilic narrative forms such as Max Aub's *El laberinto mágico* – as shall be seen in chapter 6 – and María Teresa León's 1970 autobiography *Memoria de la melancolía* [Memory of Melancholy], where poetry lines are often cited as signs of the "memoria desterrada" [banished memory] of national culture (216). Among the multiple poets quoted by de León are Rafael Alberti, Luis Cernuda, Rubén Darío, Juan del Enzina, León Felipe, Oliverio Girondo, Juan Ramón Jiménez, Antonio Machado, Pablo Neruda, Francisco de Quevedo, Boris Pasternak, Miguel de Unamuno y Lope de Vega.

26 Jo Labanyi has explained this temporal dichotomy with regard to the popular ballad form (*romance*), which was "familiar to the unlettered": "The ballad form allowed recital at the front, often with guitar accompaniment, continuing for emancipatory purposes an oral tradition unbroken since the Middle Ages. The ballad's regular rhythms made this poetry 'memorable'" (*Short* 117). To dwell on the relation between the signifier *people* and the textual production of the nation, it is helpful to draw on Homi Bhabha's enquiry into the ambivalent temporalities of the modern nation: "The people are not simply historical events or parts of a patriotic body politic. They are also a complex rhetorical strategy of social reference: their claim to be representative provokes a crisis within the process of signification and discursive address. We then have a contested conceptual territory where the nation's people must be thought in double-time; the people are the historical 'objects' of a nationalist pedagogy, giving the origin *in the past;* the people are also the 'subjects' of a process of signification that must erase any prior or originary presence of the nation-people to demonstrate the prodigious, living principles of the people as contemporaneity: as that sign of the *present* through which national life is redeemed and iterated as a reproductive process ... In the production of the nation as narration there is a split between the continuist, accumulative temporality of the pedagogical, and the repetitious, recursive strategy of the performative. It is through this process of splitting that the conceptual ambivalence of modern society becomes the site of *writing the nation*" (*Location* 208–9). At issue in Bhabha's dichotomization of the temporality of nation between the continuous temporality of the pedagogical and the repetitious temporality of the performative is the status of narration – as opposed to, but also as folded into, non-narrative forms of discourse – as the pre-eminent discourse in the production of the nation.

27 For the complications of using the category of nation, and particularly of modern nation, in the study of *romances*, see Mary Gaylord's "Spain" and Samuel Armistead's "Epic and ballad in the Hispanic tradition." Gaylord has emphatically underscored the border-crossing dimension of *romances*: "The origins of poetry in Spain are neither national nor exclusively Spanish. It is telling that the first instances of Iberian Romance lyric should perform poetic crossings of lines of gender, race, language, and class" ("Spain" 1333).

28 Susan Stewart has also reflected on the paradoxical social impact that the somatic element woven into a poem's verbal fabric can have. In this light, the lyric's divergence "between a subject transforming him- or herself from the somatic both toward and against the social" is reminiscent of the uncanny space of continuity and discontinuity circumscribed by Max Aub (46–7).

29 In this sense, "Reparto" should be read along with Felipe's conference "Poesía e Hispanidad" [Poetry and Hispanicity], delivered in Bogotá in 1946. Felipe prophetically claimed that America would be "el continente del espíritu, de la luz y de la poesía" [the continent of the spirit, of light and poetry] (147). But, disturbingly enough, Felipe staked his own claim on this poetry despite the fact that America was already, in his view, "el continente de los poetas" [the continent of poets] (147). He then defined *Hispanidad* in terms of the spirit and poetry that, in his view, would emerge from the Christ-like Spain sacrificed in the Spanish Civil War: "este espíritu que saldrá de la sangre y de la tumba de España ... para escribir un Evangelio nuevo" [this spirit which will issue the blood and tomb of Spain ... to write a new Gospel] (152). Thus the new, resurrected poetic word would not be that of America, but, specifically, the word of Felipe as representative poet of "todos los poetas del destierro y todos los españoles del éxodo y del llanto" [all poets of exile, all Spaniards of exodus and weeping] (150), and therefore the word of Spain: "América es sangre y verbo de España ... Porque es una América hecha con mi palabra, con la palabra nacida en los surcos y en el costado abierto de la carne de España ... Es una América creada con la canción" [America is the blood and word of Spain ... Because it's an America made with my word, with the word born in the furrows and the open side of Spain's flesh ... [I]t's an America created with song] (152–3). Felipe's spiritual vision of America also explicitly left aside the historical question of "América material" [material America] as an accomplished, and hence incontestable, fact: that America was, as he told his Bogotan audience, "vuestra sin disputa" [yours beyond dispute]. Disturbingly again, what mattered now was "la América de la sangre" which was the blood of Spain, past and present (153). Sections of Felipe's conference were incorporated in "Salmo fugitivo" [Fugitive Psalm], a poem later included in *Antología rota*, along with "Hay dos Españas," under the heading "España e Hispanidad (México-Bogotá, 1942 y 1946)" (*Antología* 299–311).

30 For a terminological analysis of fascist, fascistic, and para-fascistic, see Kallis.

31 In *Las armas y las letras: literatura y guerra civil (1936–1939)*, Andrés Trapiello sought to show "la similitud de las retóricas y de la barbarie de los dos bandos, sobre todo

en la retaguardia" [the similarity of the rhetorics and the barbarism of both sides, especialy in the rearguard] ("El milagro" n. pag.). In *El lenguaje bíblico en la poesía de los exilios españoles de 1939* (2004), Mónica Jato analysed the use of biblical discourse by both Republican exiled poets and dissident poets within Franco's dictatorship. According to Jato, this shared discourse contributed to destabilizing the cultural and religious uniformity of Francoism while serving as a "mecanismo de integración que acorta distancias hacia la eventual reunión de estos poetas en un espacio literario común" [mechanism of integration that shortens distances towards the possible reunion of these poets in a common literary space] (8–12). The prophetic rhetoric in Felipe's poetry was deeply shaped by Juan Larrea's messianic understanding of *hispanismo*, as reflected in the essays compiled in *Rendición de Espíritu* [Surrender of Spirit] (1943) (Jato 131). In 2002 Sebastiaan Faber studied Larrea's exalted vision of Spanish cultural and political values: "the 'death' of the Republic and the sacrifice of the Spanish people, however tragic, inaugurated a new phase in history in which the cultural hegemony of Europe would be replaced by that of the Americas. In this historical transition, Larrea believed, the Spanish exiles were to play a crucial role" (*Exile* 131). Faber called Larrea's thesis "a particular brand of 'poetic' historiography, which combined Hegelian teleology with an exceptionalist reading of Spanish history" (132), and saw coincidences between exiled Republicans' and Francoists' respective brands of *hispanismo*: "Both Francoists and Republicans expressed a belief not only in the existence of an essentially Spanish identity, but also in Spain's providential role" (*Exile* 136).

32 As it is well known, Felipe's own "voz antigua" did not return to its *tierra*. Yet he somehow let poets living in Francoist Spain own that "voz," thus making it plural. In 1959, Felipe penned a famous retraction, "Palabras ..." [Words ...], to Ángela Figuera Aymerich, a Basque poet born in 1902 who after the war suffered reprisals in Spain for her Republican sympathies: "Esa voz ... esas voces ... los que os quedasteis en la casa paterna ... Vuestros son el salmo y la canción" [That voice ... those voices ... those of you who remained in the father's house ... The psalm and the song are yours] (136). See Felipe's 1957 enlarged edition of *Antología rota*, where the new apostrophe, "Hermano" replaces "Franco" (312). As mentioned earlier, José María Castellet's highly influential postwar *Veinte años de poesía española* covered Spanish poetry since the last year of the war until 1959. Felipe's apostrophe was seen a gesture of reconciliation in this Spanish anthology. See Sebastiaan Faber's *Exile and Hegemony* for the political implications of the poet's public rectification (151–3). According to Mónica Jato, Ángela Figuera, and other women poets such as Carmen Conde, Maria Beneyto, and Angelina Gatell, who wrote in Spain as inner exiles during Franco's dictatorship, used biblical language to turn a discourse of fratricidal fatherland into an antiwar discourse of motherland (231–3). As we shall see in more detail in chapter 7, Tomás Segovia was highly critical of notions of national identity, and therefore also of national linguistic identity: "da lo mismo que la canción sea de León Felipe o de Ángela Figuera mientras la Palabra no sea de ninguno de los dos. Es en efecto el poeta

el que pertenece a la Palabra y no al revés" [it does not matter if the song belongs to León Felipe or to Ángela Figuera as long as the Word does not belong to either of them. It is indeed the poet who belongs to the Word and not the other way around] ("Respuestas" 207).

33 In *Líneas de fuga* (2018), an extensive edited volume of essays exploring new ways of understanding the cultural historiography of Republican exiles, Mari Paz Balibrea argued for a political re-examination of the spatiotemporal relation between "la nación perdida" [the lost nation] and Spanish exile ("Temporalidad" 147–50): "el espacio-tiempo del ahora común en el que se encuentren exilio y nación abandonada es un producto histórico a construir, un territorio de lucha" [the spacetime of the common now in which exile and abandoned nation may find each other is a historical product to be constructed, a territory of struggle] ("Temporalidad" 148). Yet when historians understand this construction in terms of narrative (Balibrea, "Temporalidad" 147), they tend to neglect the historically significant emergence of other exilic discourses specifically addressing the cultural construction of the here and now of national struggle. One such discourse is poetic discourse, where the temporality of a purported "ahora común" between exile and nation is often intricately braided with various strands of verbal and textual patterns. Although attention to these patterns does not preclude narrative and intentional models of reading spatiotemporal continuities and commonalities between exile and nation, it certainly complicates them. A crucial instance of this mode of poetic discourse is León Felipe's "Reparto," where the staging of the struggle over national territory is both constructed and deconstructed in a persistent present tense of assertion and address.

34 In 2007, Michael Iarocci made a sensible case for reading and teaching war poetry within the frame of historical reference: "In the midst of the most harrowing of conditions, what did poetry mean and how did it matter? ... The war demanded a kind of engagement that put an end to the waning *vanguardista* aesthetics of the years leading up to the conflagration ... Against such a backdrop, the simple but profound meaning of the return of historical reference, that function of language that had so often been suspended, eschewed, or subverted by the modernist pursuit of aesthetic autonomy, might begin to be understood more deeply" ("War" 185–6). Indeed, historical conditions shaped war poetry in Spain. The binary opposition between historical reference and aesthetic autonomy raises precisely the question of the contextually distinct status of war poetry's "meaning." In these specific circumstances, how did the meaning of poetry differ from other forms of historical reference? Why did it "matter" more than other forms of discourse, especially narrative forms? Or rather, in Adornian terms, what was the historical specificity of poetry's form at that particular conjuncture? How does it relate to other historical conditions?

35 In 2007, Terry Eagleton pithily summarized a similar position about the politics of poetic form: "There is a politics of form as well as a politics of content. Form is not a distraction from history but a mode of access to it ... [A] deep enough crisis of cultural form is usually an historical crisis as well" (8). In *Forms: Whole, Rhythm,*

Hierarchy, Network (2015), Caroline Levine persuasively championed new political, social and historical ways of thinking about formalism in literary studies (16).

36 According to Naharro-Calderón, however, for Max Aub, Luis Cernuda, Juan Ramón Jiménez, and other exiled writers such as Jorge Semprún, Agustí Bartra or Francisco Garfias, the language of poetry and fiction became "un substituto de la inaprensible pero real patria desterrada" [a substitute for the ungraspable but real banished fatherland] (*Entre alambradas* 107).

37 For the dates of García Lorca's meetings with Neruda in Madrid, see http://www.centrofedericogarcialorca.es/en/fgl/bio-1933-1936 (accessed 1 November 2018).

38 For anaphora in the Psalms, see Marks.

39 At least in this sense, *This Ghostly Poetry* is also, to some extent, a work of genre criticism and a project in poetics – rather than hermeneutics – in that it asks "what sorts of things do these poems do, what are the parameters on which they vary? ... What are the conventions and reading practices that enable texts to have the meanings and effects that they do for readers?" (Culler, "Extending" 7).

40 Culler's and Ramazani's historical understandings of genre are akin to Moretti's definition of genres – specifically the novel – as temporary structures: "morphological arrangements that *last* in time, but always only for *some* time. Janus-like creatures, with one face turned to history and the other to form" (14).

41 See, however, Cecilia Enjuto's *Cities in Ruins: The Politics of Modern Poetics* (2010) for a reading of canonical poetry of the Spanish Civil War and the Republican exile premised on an understanding of the political in terms of the nation (151).

42 For a discussion of the differences between testimonial memory and academic memory in debates about the historical memory of the Spanish Civil War and its aftermath, see Sebastiaan Faber's "'¿Usted, qué sabe?' History, Memory, and the Witness" in *Memory Battles of the Spanish Civil War* (57–73).

43 See specifically "La otra orilla" (21–70).

44 Angelina Muñiz-Huberman (1936–) is a Mexican writer and poet. She was born in Hyères, France, in 1936. Her parents were exiled Republicans. After a brief period in Cuba, they moved to Mexico City in 1942, where she now lives. In 2007, Christopher Domínguez Michael described Angelina Múñiz-Huberman as a "Jewish Mexican" (*Dictionary* 343). Antonio Muñoz Molina has labelled her "escritora hispano-mexicana-sefardí" [Hispano-Mexican-Sephardic writer] ("Una lengua" n. pag.). As we shall see later, Muñoz Molina's reading of the Sephardic legacy in Aub's writing brings the significance of this label into relief.

45 María Zambrano (Spain 1904–Spain 1991) studied philosophy under José Ortega y Gasset and Xavier Zubiri, taught at the University of Madrid in the 1930s, and joined the Republican exile in 1939. She lived in France, México, Cuba, Puerto Rico, Italy, and Switzerland. Among her most important works is *La tumba de Antígona* [Antigone's Tomb] (1967), which Andrew Bush situates "in a suite of texts that define her trajectory from the late period of her long exile through her return to Spain in 1984 ... Each of these texts returns to the ancient conflict between poetry

and philosophy, long since thematized in her work, above all in the volume *Filosofía y poesía* [Philosophy and Poetry], written at the outset of her exile in the autumn of 1939" (94). Zambrano's meagre poetic production is barely known. One of her overtly border-crossing, cross-temporal poems is "Merci Bien," written in French between 1946 and 1948 (277–8).

46 Naharro-Calderón contended that the "dominant tone" in Republican exilic poetry is elegiac, as elegy can be taken as "the memory and mourning of lost origins or unavoidable turmoil" ("Twentieth-Century" 622).

47 Rosa Chacel was born in Valladolid, Spain, in 1898. She returned to Spain in the early 1970s. She died in 1994. In an obituary published by *The New York Times* in 1994, Eric Pace described her as "a Spanish writer of complex, intellectual novels and poetry, who was in exile during most of the Franco era." As Pace explained, "she left Spain largely because her husband, Timoteo Pérez Rubio, had been active on the Republican side, and her sympathies were also with the Republic. She spent her thirty-six years in exile mainly in Buenos Aires and Rio de Janeiro" (n. pag.).

48 Poet and filmmaker Jomí García Ascot was born in 1927 in Tunisia. Fleeing Spain with his parents, he arrived in Mexico in 1939 as an exile. He died in 1986 in Mexico City. "Canción lejana" was inserted in *Un otoño en el aire* [An Autumn in the Air], his first book of poems (1964).

49 In 2017, poetry critic Dan Chiasson highlighted the relationship between posterity and poetic memory in terms of a discursive space between living, writing, and reading akin to the ghostly space delineated by Aub: "Poets have always had an advantage over other mortals, in that their souls, verifiably present in language that predated them by years or centuries, could therefore be counted on to outlive them. If I got half of my mind and two thirds of my emotions from George Herbert, there's something like an afterlife for George Herbert; maybe I can be, for some midcareer poet of the twenty-fifth century, proof of his own potential immortality in the hearts of poets of the twenty-ninth century" (34). Inversely, it could be argued that readers are both present and absent in "language that predated them by years or centuries." Reading becomes historical in this sense as well.

4 Juan Ramón Jiménez

1 Unless otherwise noted, all references in this chapter are to *Guerra en España: prosa y verso (1936–1954)*. The images cited in this paragraph are all from the section "Album I."

2 For recent discussions of the possible connections between political exile and Jiménez's understanding of poetry as a generative discursive space for articulating what I have termed biography and bibliography, see Rosa García Gutiérrez's 2018 edited volume, *Juan Ramón Jiménez e Hispanoamérica: diálogos, exilios, resiliencia*, particularly her "Presentación" (15, 18), and Mercedes Juliá's "El destino de Juan Ramón en las Américas" (287, 293).

3 The 1985 edition contained only 335 pages and 27 images. In the context of the debates about the historical memory of the war, it is significant that the publisher, Seix Barral, insisted that Crespo trim and modify his edition in response to Spain's delicate political situation in the early 1980s. As a result, Crespo cut explicit references to the June 1939 ransacking of Jiménez's residence (XIX). But, as Crespo explained: "Ya vendrán otros investigadores profundizando mucho más, y tarde o temprano se conocerá toda la verdad" [Other researchers will dig much deeper, and sooner or later the whole truth will be known] (XIX). His prediction came true when González Ródenas dedicated an entire section, almost fifty pages long, to the ransacking, giving it the title that Crespo had chosen: "El allanamiento del piso de Madrid" [the ransacking of the apartment in Madrid]. González Ródenas included other documents that had been cut for political and editorial reasons, and also added new materials that she had collected herself. "Album 2" thus includes a number of newspaper clippings, photographs, letters by Jiménez, and even an image showing the arrival of his remains, along with those of his wife Zenobia Cambrubí, to Spain in 1958.

4 Bergamín's prologue is discussed in the coda to this book.

5 As Sam Jones explained in July 2017, this photograph appeared in the US, Swiss, and French press, and "encouraged international volunteers to travel to Spain to join the civil war to fight Franco's forces. Today, more than eight decades on, a campaign is under way to have the rundown building protected and declared part of the Spanish capital's heritage" (n. pag.). For the connection between the house, the photograph, and debates about historical memory in Spain, see the statements made in December 2017 by former director-general of UNESCO Federico Mayor Zaragoza in "La casa que fotografió Capa es un símbolo del horror, como Auschwitz" [The house that Capa photographed is a symbol of horror, like Auschwitz]. See Sebastiaan Faber's "Memory as Montage: Spanish Civil War Photography" for a study of the fraught relationship between photography, documentary evidence, propaganda, and artistic mediation. Faber examines this relationship in connection to "fundamental questions about history, memory, and truth" during the "ideological war of words and images" that took place as part of the Spanish conflict (*Memory* 8, 19, 11–32). He pays special attention to Robert Capa's photographs.

6 The contrast between history and intrahistory in Jiménez's work follows the ideas of Francisco Giner de los Ríos and Bartolomé Cossío of the Institución Libre de Enseñanza [Free Educational Institution] (López Castro 41). Rachel Schmidt explains that *intrahistoria* refers to Unamuno's notion that "true history arise from the daily lives and customs of the people" (167). Jean Claude Rabaté specifies that its object of study is "the anonymous people of the countryside, the lives of millions of ordinary people living silent, obscure lives" (16). Rabaté also explains that the central metaphor of *intrahistoria* – deep sea waters – allows "a passage between *intrahistoria* and *historia*," and hence avoids "simplistic binary opposites" (18).

7 Jiménez captioned these verses "Popular (Con permiso)" [Popular (with permission)] (12).

8 Although Jiménez considered arranging other collected materials in different orders, he was clear in his desire that Machado's text should open *Guerra en España*. Both

Crespo and González Ródenas chose to place "Voces de calidad" at the beginning of their respective editions. Crespo claimed to fulfill Jiménez's "voluntad" [will] in placing it as a foreword to his edition (22). González Ródenas argued that "Voces de calidad" was given prime of place in Jiménez's project (XVII). The importance of Machado and his article in Jiménez's construction of his self-image for posterity is confirmed in yet another of his unfinished projects: *Vida*. According to editors Mercedes Juliá y Mª Ángeles Sanz-Manzano, "Voces de calidad" was also chosen to open *Vida* (744). In addition, Jiménez wrote for this project a response to Machado's article in which he explained the thorny aspects of their relationship. *Vida* and *Guerra en España* are then complementary projects within what Juliá y Sanz-Manzano have called "el vasto *corpus* de la escritura autobiográfica de Juan Ramón Jiménez" [the vast *corpus* of Jiménez's autobiographical writing] (20). "Voces de calidad" is in this light a key text for analysing the ways in which Jiménez's testimony of the civil war relates to his forward-looking self-presentation as a poet (Juliá y Sanz-Manzano 18).

9 Crespo did not include this clipping in his edition.

10 Drawing on Georges Didi-Huberman's reflections on the opening or wounding of time by the image, Patricia Keller has dwelled on the uncanniness of photographic time: "[T]he image turns time not against itself but into a ghostly other ... In generating the alterity of time's passage, the image makes an otherwise straightforward understanding of time appear abstruse, or feel dense and laden" (4).

11 The transcendent immanence shaping lines like "los dioses no tuvieron más sustancia que la que tengo yo" [the gods had no more substance than what I have] from the long poem "Espacio" takes on a powerful historical tinge in *Guerra en España*. Also the border-crossing, cross-temporal scope of "Espacio" is closely linked to translation, not only on account of the Blakeian undertones palpable in the quoted line, but also because, as Charlotte Ward has shown, translations became for Jiménez and Camprubí "a crucial source of psychological and financial support during the long exile from Spain after the Civil War" (n. pag.). For Jiménez's and Camprubí's translations, see also Howard T. Young's "In Loving Translation: Zenobia and Juan Ramón" (1996), as well as his seminal *The Line in the Margin: Juan Ramón Jiménez and his Readings in Blake, Shelley, and Yeats* (1980).

12 Tellingly, on 27 February 1939, Zenobia Camprubí wrote in her diary: "Me parece que, a ratos, había algo de envidia en los pensamientos de J.R. en cuanto a su muerte" [It seems to me that, at times, there was some envy in J.R.'s thoughts about Machado's death] (*Diario* 21).

13 For "ansiedad necrofílica" [necrophiliac anxiety], see Naharro-Calderón's *Entre el exilio y el interior* (308).

14 As Ciplijauskaité adds, Camprubí's diary "reveals new aspects of the poet but above all confirms that, without Zenobia, [Jiménez's] work would not have been what it is; neither would he have had such a protected life" (312). Ciplijauskaité's verdict can be extended to other important aspects of Jiménez's work in exile, most notably his translations.

15 These poems would be later published in *Voces de mi copla* [Voices of My Song] (1945) and *Romances de Coral Gables* [Ballads of Coral Gables] (1948).

16 Following Edward Said's dialectical approach to exilic rhetoric, Mercedes Juliá read "Espacio" in 2018 as a contrapuntal interplay of past and present experiences whereby spatiotemporal disjunctions between America and Spain take place simultaneously in the poem ("El destino" 296–7)

17 As Howard T. Young argued in 1983, "Perhaps inspired in part by Eliot's solution of similar problems in *The Four Quartets*, Juan Ramón abandoned his *verso desnudo* for the pell mell openness of *Espacio*. Octavio Paz's admiration for Juan Ramón's willingness to turn discourse into an examination of the possibilities of language may be excessive, but one cannot fail to recognize *Espacio*'s experimental venture into the form of the long poem" ("Introduction" 109–10). In his reply to Marichal, Paz's reading of *Espacio* is in line with his historization of Latin American *modernismo* and the international avant-garde: "*Espacio* es un poema extenso y, al mismo tiempo, vuelto sobre sí mismo y esto lo une a la tradición hispanoamericana más que a la española ... *Espacio* es lo que está mas allá de la poesía de Jiménez: es la transfiguración del poeta español en un poeta de vanguardia, el *Altazor* de Huidobro – y su negación. Uno de los textos capitales de la poesía moderna" [*Espacio* is an extensive poem and, at the same time, turned upon itself, and this links it to the Hispanic American tradition more than to the Spanish ... *Espacio* is what is beyond Jimenezs' poetry: it is the transfiguration of the Spanish poet into an avant-guard poet, Huidobro's *Altazor* – and its negation. One of the capital texts of modern poetry] (Marichal and Paz *Las cosas* 50–1). See also Paz, *Obras completas II* 743.

18 According to Mercedes Juliá, "*Space* was first published in 1943, and it consisted of two stanzas, written in verses of eleven syllables. Later, Juan Ramón added a new stanza and rewrote the poem entirely in prose. The final version of *Space* was published in 1954. *Time*, on the other hand, was never published during Jimenez' life time" (4).

19 For the politics of accent in questions about poetic voice, see Nowell Smith 121.

20 See the coda to this book for the use of proximal demonstratives in Machado's "Estos días azules y este sol de la infancia."

21 In 1968, Johannes Lechner proposed using the generic framework of testimony to explore post-civil-war Spanish poetry. For a taxonomic study of this kind of poetry, see Siles.

22 In *Memory Battles of the Spanish Civil War: History, Fiction, Photography*, Sebastiaan Faber outlined the general cultural and sociopolitical context that prompted the activation of of such discursive practices: "Photomontage not only bridged art, commerce, and politics; it also provided a productive transition between the self-absorbed, formalist artistic movements of the early twentieth century and the newfound political commitment that shaped Western art and literature in the 1930s. Modernism and the avant-garde had ushered in radically new conceptions of artists' relationships with their work and the world ... Indeed, the urgency of the Spanish

conflict confronted writers and artist with a series of difficult questions. Should they compromise on matters of artistic or literary form for the sake of political effectiveness? Should artists give up part of their individual autonomy and integrity for the sake of a collective cause or organization? Do writers and artists have a duty to to represent thr truth? If so, what truth? ... Positions tended to be cast in terms of binary opposites: modernism vs. realism, truth vs. propaganda, objectivity vs. partisanship, elitist detachment vs. political commitment" (28). *Guerra en España* is evidence of Jiménez's uncompromising response to such dichotomous positions. For the use of photomontage in depictions of the Spanish Civil War, see also Valentine Cunningham, "The Spanish Civil War" 190.

23 See, for example, photograph 17 in Album I and "Parque de Coole, 1929," Jiménez's translation of Yeats's poem "Coole Park, 1929" (134).

24 From this angle, it is worth extrapolating the words of Germán Labrador in his review of this essay collection and arguing that Jiménez prevents us from "naturali[zar] nuestras condiciones de percepción y nuestro conocimiento de las culturas del pasado, de los archivos que de él disponemos y de las articulaciones que en ellos se han dado entre lo público, lo privado y lo íntimo" [naturalizing our conditions of perception and our knowledge of the cultures of the past, of the archives that we have of the past, and of the articulations that take place in those archives between the public, the private, and the intimate] (382). At least in this sense, Jiménez's exilic writings would not simply "exacerbate a reclusive and 'pure', anti-realist strain in Spanish poetry," and consequently would not just serve as an example of "disinterested introspection, aestheticism, or abstraction" (Perriam, Thompson, Frenk, and Knight 125).

25 For the critical reception of Jiménez's work in the 1950s, particularly after the publication of "Espacio" in Spain in 1954, see Mercedes Juliá, "El destino" 303.

26 *La resistencia silenciosa* was awarded the 2004 Anagrama essay prize; *Las armas y las letras*, the 1995 Don Juan de Borbón Prize.

27 See González Ródenas for other studies on Jiménez's political ideas and activities in exile (XI). In *Breve historia de la literatura española* Carlos Alvar, José-Carlos Mainer, and Rosa Navarro didn't trace any connection between Jiménez's poetry and *Guerra en España*. According to their description, *Guerra en España* simply "compilaba con ánimo testimonial, su visión del conflicto civil" [compiled, with a testimonial intent, his view of the civil conflict] (594).

28 In "La traición de los intelectuales," a 2014 review of *Las armas y las letras*, Sebastiaan Faber took issue with Trapiello's "moralizing" and "anecdotal perspective": "He identifies a particular text as either honest or propagandistic and, then, uses a disqualifying, gossipy passage from a personal letter to close his case ... In the end, Trapiello locks himself into a simplistic scheme ... Even 'decent' writers like Gaya, Juan Ramón Jiménez, or Luis Cernuda can't always avoid falling victim to the temptations of propaganda ... or letting their work be marred by the 'stain' of 'the rhetoric of war'" (*Memory* 129–32). Trapiello dismissed Faber's review as "una de las más tendenciosas y difamatorias que he leído sobre este libro" [one of the most tendentious and defamatory I have ever read

about this book] ("Ante un 'paseo'" 13). The general tenor of this exchange is arguably indicative of how fraught discussions about the war can still be in the cultural field of historical memory in Spain.

29 In 2005, Roger Bartra reflected on the relationship between exile and melancholy: "a phenomenology of exile is related to melancholia. For the artists and writers, it has to do with the lost or abandoned objects whose absence produces melancholia. But the possibility of finding them again exists ... The suffering of the artist is offered to the spectator as an object of contemplation and admiration" ("Interview" 127). Bartra also linked political exile to a pre-national sense of identity connected to an experience of transience that can be formulated by means of the *memento mori* topos: "In Western culture, identity and subjectivity are previous to the constitution of nations. But of course, they have always been associated to some type of territory" (132).

30 "Allegories are, in the realm of thoughts, what ruins are in the realm of things" (Benjamin, *The Origin* 178).

5 Luis Cernuda

1 ["Remember it|him and remember it|him to others, / When all disgusted by human baseness, / When all enraged by human hardness: / This man alone, this act alone, this faith alone. / Remember it|him and remember it|him to others. // In 1961 and in a strange city, / More than a quarter century / Later. Trivial the circumstance, / Forced you were to a public reading / And on account of it with that man you conversed: / A former soldier / in the Lincoln Brigade. // Twenty-five years ago, this man, / Without knowing your land, / to him distant / And strange in its entirety, chose to go there / And there, if the occasion arrived, decided to bet his life, / Judging that the cause at stake there / And then was worth / Fighting for, for the faith that filled his life. // That that cause seems lost / Matters not; / That so many others, hoping faith in it, / Cared only to themselves / Matters less. / What matters, and is enough for us, is the faith of one. // That is why today once again the cause seems to you / As it was in those days: / Noble and well worth fighting for. / And his faith, that faith, he has held it / Through the years, the defeat, / When everything seems to betray it. / But that faith, you tell yourself, is the one thing alone that matters. // Thanks, *compañero*, thanks / For the example. Thanks, for you tell me / That man is noble. / It matters not that so few are: / One, one man alone, is enough / As an irrefutable witness / To all human nobility"]. "Remember him and remember him to others," Stephen Kessler's translation, is less ambiguous than the original Spanish line (Cernuda, *Desolation* 203–5).

2 See Paul Stewart's bio-bibliographical sketch "Cernuda, Luis (1902–63)."

3 In his 2011 biography of Luis Cernuda, Antonio Rivero Taravillo simply quotes Cernuda's letter to Otero, without mentioning the soldier (*Años de exilio*, 317–8).

4 *Blood of Spain* was first published in Spain in 1979, the year that marked the beginning of the so-called *desencanto*, "the mood of political disenchantment/

disappointment which prevailed in Spain in the later years of the transition period (1979–1982)" to democracy (Labanyi and Graham 312). According to José Colmeiro, during this period, memory "came to occupy a residual space with a sense of nostalgia for a utopian future indefinitely postponed" (25).

5 *Blood of Spain* has been criticized for anonymizing the eyewitness accounts. Although the witnesses' names are listed under the heading "relación de personas entrevistadas" [roster of interviewees] in Fraser's "otherwise groundbreaking" oral history, Jo Labanyi has argued that, because of "its mingling of historical narrative and first-person accounts," the reader is "not sure who is speaking" ("Testimonies" 196). The English edition did not include Cernuda's lines, instead quoting ten lines from Bertolt Brecht's "Questions from a Worker Who Reads" (27). The subtitle of the prologue to the 1997 Spanish edition was "(Especialmente) para aquellos demasiado jóvenes como para recordar" [(Especially) for those too young to remember], underscoring the non-specific quality of its injunction to remember.

6 In *The Spanish Civil War: A Very Short Introduction* (2005), Helen Graham argued that the debate over the historical memory of the Spanish Civil War and Francoist period gathered momentum at the beginning of the twenty-first century: "there has been an explosion of Republican memory with the creation of civil pressure groups" (141). Significantly, the first epigraph to Graham's book is a translation of Cernuda's line: "You must remember this and see that others remember" (n. pag.)

7 For changes in the sociopolitical situation in Spain regarding memorials for Francoist victims, see Aguilar and Payne 90–3.

8 For more on García Montero's ideas about historical memory, see Cruz and Morgado.

9 In a 1996 *El País* article titled "¡Ya se fueron!" [They are gone now!], literary critic Miguel García Posada, paraphrasing "1936" and its first line, lamented that Spain had paid almost no "homenaje perdurable" [enduring homage] to the soldiers of the International Brigades.

10 See Timothy Bahti for an analysis of the impossibility of reading lyric poems without reading "their tradition, their constitution and handing-down through writing, re-writing, reading, and re-reading" (7).

11 See also Gracia and Ródenas, Faber ("Español"), and Blanco Aguinaga, Rodríguez Puértolas, and Zavala. García Montero's interpretation of the poem recalls Jaime Gil de Biedma's reading of Cernuda's personae, which is analysed below.

12 As Barbara Cassin explained in 2014, epideixis consists in performatively "making use of accepted values to propose new ones." To that end, epideixis involves "moving, not from being to speaking about being," but rather "from speech to its effect" (1038).

13 Culler has argued against reading lyric as dramatic monologue because "[t]his model ignores or reduces, with its normalizing novelizing, the characteristic extravagance of lyric on the one hand and its intertextual echoes on the other; and it neglects all those elements of lyric – including rhyme, metre, refrain – not imitated from ordinary speech acts" (*Theory* 118–19).

14 Chris Perriam, Michael Thompson, Susan Frenk, and Vanessa Knights read this poem as a two-fold dialectic of national and spiritual desire: "The destiny and task of the

poet is to register the effects of the paradoxical positioning both inevitably within and irremediably outside Spain; but not only Spain, since ... for Cernuda the personal circumstances of exile are subsumed into Romantic and proto-Platonic notions of the unattainability of and yet faith in a metaphorical place, a place of language or forms or images, where wholeness, purity, and belonging are sealed together by the fulfillment of spiritual desire" (126–7).

15 Important scholars of Cernuda's work have emphasized his fidelity to the poet's fate (Harris, *Luis Cernuda* 36, 164–5, 166; Sicot 41).

16 Another significant iteration of this poetic "fe" can be found in "Río vespertino" [Evening River], also from *Como quien espera el alba* (*Obra I* 373).

17 See Sahuquillo, Jiménez Fajardo, Baquero, and de Villena.

18 Tomás Segovia underscored the elegiac or nostalgic tone in Cernuda's poems, but sceptically asked to what extent his nostalgia for the gardens of Seville, for instance, was "el efecto del exilio" [the effect of exile] or "nostalgia de la adolescencia, que habría sentido igual si no hubiese vivido en el destierro" [nostalgia for adolescence, which he would have felt as well if he had not lived in exile] ("Respuestas" 200). Segovia added that Cernuda felt "una añoranza no menos punzante por México, de donde no estaba exiliado" [a longing no less poignant for Mexico, where he was not exiled from] ("Respuestas" 200).

19 In the early nineteen-forties, Cernuda also started doing occasional translations for the BBC World Service, including lines or entire poems by Robert Bridges, Emily Brönte, Lord Byron, Thomas Campion, Samuel Coleridge, Robert Herrick, A.E. Housman, Ben Jonson, Rudyard Kipling, P.B. Shelley, A.C. Swinburne, and Alfred Tennyson. He also translated Psalm 118 from the Bible, and scenes from Shakespeare's *Antony and Cleopatra*, *Midsummer Night's Dream*, *Romeo and Juliet*, *Othello*, *Troilus and Cressida*, and *Twelfth Night*. The complete translation of *Troilus and Cressida* was published in Spain in 1953. Cernuda also read very widely in English criticism, particularly Dr Johnson, Coleridge, Matthew Arnold, and Keats's letters, among others. He also read Goethe and Kierkegaard. When in 1947 Cernuda accepted a teaching position at Mount Holyoke, he delved into *Die Fragmente der Vorsokratiker* [The Fragments of the Presocratics] by Hermann Diels, with the help of an English translation. See Hernández Bautista, "Luis Cernuda, colaborador de la BBC: traducciones y otros trabajos perdidos."

20 Reginald Gibbons sketched the general context for this critique: "In the first decades of this century, intellectuals did oppose both political constriction and the conformism of Spanish society. Intellectual life, however, was characterized not only by an intense scrutiny of Spain's melancholy social history, a new interest in the ideas and attitudes of the rest of Europe, and a feverish though marginal avant-garde literature, but also by an almost total isolation from the centers of authority and power within the nation. Cernuda, born in Seville in 1902, certainly registered the sense of exclusion and ineffectualness" (1).

21 Translation modified.

22 Translation modified. See below for an approach to Cernuda's characteristic "tú" in terms of what Jonathan Culler calls "blurred you."

23 Gibbons also eloquently explained Cernuda's singularity in the sociopolitical circumstances of 1930s Spain: "Although in 1934 he joined, for a brief time, the Communist party, it was his rebelliousness that made him a temporary communist, not his political consciousness that made him rebel. When later he wrote of enduring the bombardment of Madrid's University City by Franco's forces, it was to recall that at that moment he had discovered Leopardi, whom he read as the shells were bursting nearby. Cernuda's temperament was resolutely antiauthoritarian, anti-institutional, and by the time he left Spain he had become in essence politically inactive ... Highly principled, unsociable, dandified, very much an autodidact, homosexual, both grateful and grudging towards his literary elders, certain of his poetic powers Cernuda became quite early in his own mind a *poète maudit*" (2–3). The dialectic between metropolis and periphery with regard to Spanish modernism is also discussed in the coda to this book.

24 It was also along a spatiotemporal axis that Williams arranged his critique of the misleading use of universals in cultural analyses of modernism: "The power of metropolitan development is not to be denied. The excitements and challenges of its intricate processes of liberation and alienation, contact and strangeness, stimulation and standardisation, are still powerfully available. But it should no longer be possible to present these specific and traceable processes as if they were universals, not only in history but as it were above and beyond it. The formulation of the modernist universals is in every case a productive but imperfect and in the end fallacious response to particular conditions of closure, breakdown, failure and frustration. From the necessary negations of these conditions, and from the stimulating strangeness of a new and (as it seemed) unbonded social form, the creative leap to the only available universality – of raw material, of medium, of process – was impressively and influentially made. At this level as at others – 'modernisation' for example – the supposed universals belong to a phase of history which was both creatively preceded and creatively succeeded" (47). Cernuda's twofold exilic gaze preceded the Spanish Civil War both in space and in time. It also transcended it without abolishing it.

25 For a more detailed examination of the life-and-death dialectic in "Marsias," see Aguirre Oteiza 120–2.

26 For an illuminating reflection on an analogous life-and-death dialectic in twentieth-century poetry, see Tomás Segovia's essay significantly titled "Marsias y Orfeo" [Marsyas and Orpheus] (1952). For Segovia's insightful reading of Cernuda's poetry, see "Dos veces Cernuda" (*Sobre exiliados* 85–120).

27 With regard to melancholia, Paul Stewart contends that throughout Cernuda's complete poems "there is an extraordinary consistency due to the development of a private mythology which is in perfect accord with a prevailing tone of melancholy, unsatisfied desire, and intermittent defiance" (n. pag.) See Derek Harris's classic *Luis Cernuda: A Study of the Poetry* for more specific analyses of melancholia in Cernuda's poetry. See Francisco Caudet's *El exilio republicano de 1939* for a reading of "Díptico

español" as a lyric in the context of Cernuda's various exiles (421–2). See also Luisa Elena Delgado's "Settled in Normal: Narratives of a Prozaic (Spanish) Nation" for a restrictively biographical reading of "Díptico español" in the framework of a so-called normal national narrative (130).

28 Culler sees the underlying structure of lyric as one of "triangulated address," where "an audience of readers is addressed through the act of address (implicit or explicit) to an imagined addressee." Thus "the lyrical *you* is at bottom characterized by the foregrounding of that indeterminate potential that makes *you* at once a specific other, the most general other, and *one*, a pure place holder for indeterminate agency" ("Language" 164–5).

29 Translation modified.

30 In her study of the experience of time in lyric poetry, Sharon Cameron has argued that "the contradiction between social and personal time is the lyric's generating impulse" (206). Personal time in Cernuda's lyrics would be hardly separable from the mythopoetic personae inscribed in his writings.

31 Ugarte cogently explored the tensions between sociopolitical history and poetic memory in Cernuda's poetry of exile: instead of striving for "accuracy," Cernuda's vision of Spanish history is "a self-critique, a rendition of his own life on, through, and away from the land," where "the language of social history is the language of poetry, and by the same token, the language of verse is the idiom of a fleeting personal history" ("Luis Cernuda" 340).

32 Ugarte saw Cernuda as a witness to poetry where poetry is understood as linguistic exile: "exile is a prerequisite for poetic writing ... In being other, the poet welcomes otherness and inconsistency both in himself and in his word, and Cernuda testifies to this linguistic concept of exile" ("Luis Cernuda" 341).

33 "Del país del sueño, tinieblas, brillos, / donde crecen plantas, flores extrañas, / entre los escombros de los castillos, / junto a las laderas de las montañas; / donde los pastores en sus cabañas / rezan, cuando al fuego dormita el can, / y donde las sombras antiguas van / por cuevas de lobos y raposas, / ha traído cosas muy misteriosas / don Ramón María del Valle-Inclán. // ... // Para él la palma con el laurel / que en manos de España listas están, / pues mil nobles lenguas diciendo van / que han sido ganadas en buena lid / por el otro manco que hay en Madrid, / don Ramón María del Valle-Inclán. / Señor, que en Galicia tuviste cuna, / mis dos manos estas flores te dan, / amadas de Apolo y de la Luna, / cuya sacra influencia siempre nos una, / don Ramón María del Valle-Inclán" (1039) [From the country of dreams, darkness, and sparkle, / where strange plants, flowers grow, / among the debris of the castles, / beside the slopes of the mountains; / where the shepherds in their cabins / pray, when their dogs sleep by the fire, / and where the old shadows go / through caves of wolves and foxes, / very mysterious things have been brought by / don Ramón María del Valle-Inclán. // ... // For him the palm with the laurel / that in Spanish hands are at the ready, / as thousands of noble voices keep saying / they have been won over honorably / by the other one-armed man there is in Madrid, / don Ramón María del Valle-Inclán.

/ Sir, that in Galicia had your cradle, / my two hands give you these flowers, / loved of Apollo and of the moon, / whose sacred influence always unites us, Don Ramón María del Valle-Inclán].

34 For Valle-Inclán's literary language, see, for instance, Ignacio Soldevila Durante's "El léxico de Valle Inclán."

35 Other important Latin American modernist poets like the Uruguayan Julio Herrera y Reissig and the Mexican Ruben Bonifaz Nuño produced similar experiments with the old Galician hendecasyllable. And yet Cernuda's line would be hard to classify, wavering as it does between a heroic and an old Galician hendecasyllable. The stress on the fifth syllable characterizing the *galaico antiguo*, unorthodox as it may have traditionally seemed, was not usually combined with stresses on the second and sixth syllables. Nonetheless, Galicia's foremost nineteenth-century poet both in Galician and Spanish, Rosalía de Castro, tried this combination in her verse "como los caminos muy transitados" [like the much-travelled roads] (Paraíso 288).

36 [You'll never know how I mastered my fear / So I could turn my voice into my courage, / Tossing into oblivion those disasters / Swarming all around us, pointlessly, / Happily trampling our life, / The life you'll be and that I almost was (Kessler, *Forbidden* 307)]

37 See Emilio Barón Palma's *T.S. Eliot en España* (37–60).

6 Max Aub

1 Later, in 1962, Aub would relate his boyhood in Valencia to his identity as a writer: "Lo de ser escritor valenciano, además de parecerme bien, es verdad" [About being a Valencian writer – not only does it seem right to me, it is true] (qtd. in Soldevila, *El compromiso* 18).

2 Aub worked, like his father, as a travelling salesman, particularly between 1920 and 1924. This job enabled him to visit "todas las ciudades y pueblos de cierta importancia" [all cities and towns of a certain importance] (*Cuerpos* 275). Many members of the *generación del 27* met and worked at the Residencia de Estudiantes between 1910 and the beginning of the war. For more information about the Residencia de Estudiantes as a centre of international cultural activity, see its current webpage http://www.residencia.csic.es/en/info/history.htm (accessed 1 November 2018).

3 See Sebastiaan Faber's "Max Aub: Exile as *Aporia*" in his *Exile and Cultural Hegemony* for a study of Aub's political dilemmas during his Mexican exile.

4 In 1989, Michael Ugarte highlighted Aub's determination to "bear witness" to his experience of the civil war. Aub's political and literary ideology before the conflict made, in Ugarte's terms, "his rendering of the historic event different from most eyewitness accounts" (*Shifting* 118). According to Jordi Gracia and Domingo Ródenas, *El laberinto mágico* has a "propósito testimonial" [testimonial purpose] and is the "mayor empeño narrativo de reconstrucción de la guerra y sus causas" [greatest narrative effort to reconstruct the war and its causes] (*Derrota* 377–8). Sebastiaan Faber has also argued

that the "centerpiece" of Aub's writings is *El laberinto mágico*, which he describes as "five novels, a film script and some forty short stories that weave a sprawling epic tapestry of the war in which hundreds of characters, both historical and fictional, try desperately to make sense of their violent and chaotic times" ("Max" n. pag.). Francisco Caudet has explained that both *La gallina ciega* and *Luis Buñuel, novela* [Luis Buñuel, a Novel] have been read as a continuation of the testimonial account offered in *El laberinto mágico* ("Introduction" 28). For the construction of the writer's self-image in Aub's exilic works and its connection to literary history and criticism, the book publishing market, and memory discourses, see Francisco Gerhardt's "El buen paño en el arca. Una lectura de los diarios de Max Aub."

5 Ottmar Ette claims that "at the centre" of Aub's literary production is "a single, ambiguous word that always ties back to his experience of internment: *campo*" (71). *Campo cerrado* has been translated into English as *Field of Honor* (2009).

6 In her 2015 study of Aub's work as a literary critic in Mexico, Eva Soler Sasera argued that Aub was "liberado de las restricciones que la historiografía literaria imponía en su recorrido cronológico y estético" [liberated from the restrictions that literary historiography imposed on its chronological and aesthetic itinerary] and had "un canon particular de la literatura española y europea" [a particular canon of Spanish and European literature] (22). But Aub was primarily interested in the cultural formation of the transatlantic literary field, as his journal *Los Sesenta* [The Sixties] shows. Aub edited this literary journal in Mexico between 1964 and 1965. Soler maintains that Aub's effort "demuestra hasta qué punto el autor se convirtió en un puente entre dos orillas: la europea y la americana" [proves to what extent the autor became a bridge between two shores: the European and the American] (186–8).

7 Gracia and Ródenas claim that *Campo de los almendros* is "la pieza maestra del ciclo" [the masterwork of the cycle] (*Derrota* 377–8).

8 In the first edition of *Campo de los almendros*, published in Mexico in 1968, "Páginas azules" runs from page 358 to page 366. It takes up fewer than ten pages in Francisco Caudet's critical edition.

9 Los Almendros was the makeshift concentration camp north of the port city of Alicante, on the southeastern coast of Spain.

10 Every instalment of *El laberinto mágico* is subtitled "novela" except *Campo francés* and *Campo de los almendros*, texts of unstable generic categorization, according to Aub. Sebastiaan Faber has traced Aub's determination to write a chronicle of the conflict: "in the 1930s he made the conscious decision to put his work at the service of a political cause. For him, this meant a commitment to realism: chronicling his times as faithfully as possible" ("Max" n. pag.). But Aub's "all-inclusive, chaotic war novel" ended with the "metafictional 'blue pages,' in which he confesses to the impossibility of this monstrous enterprise" (Faber, *Memory* 158–62).

11 Those witnesses include the well-known historian Manuel Tuñón de Lara, who was imprisoned in Los Almendros. Tuñón described Aub's cycle as a complex testimonial reconstruction: "el tema del *Laberinto* es historia reciente de la que el autor ha sido

testigo a veces, protagonista otras y coetáneo el resto, pudiendo utilizar una masa de testimonios directos" [the subject of the *Labyrinth* is recent history to which the author has been a witness sometimes, a protagonist at other times, and a contemporary the rest of the time, allowing him to use a massive amount of direct testimonies] (38). Because portions of the historian's testimony wound up nearly unchanged in Aub's story, *Campo de los almendros* can be called a testimony of testimonies (Caudet, *Galdós* 426).

12 Aub wrote two other collections of apocryphal poems: *Versiones y subversiones* [Versions and subversions] and *Imposible Sinaí* [Impossible Sinai].

13 Notable references to the war can be found in the texts devoted to two apocryphal poets: the Catalan Luis Romaña (1916–1954) and Jean Louis Camard (1916–1942), a volunteer in the International Brigades. According to the biographical note preceding this poem, Romaña did not leave Spain at the end of the war, but lived in hiding for several months. His collection of poems *Llengües vives* [Living Tongues], was published in 1943, but was not available for purchase "por estar entonces prohibida cualquier manifestacion en ese idioma" [because any expression in that language was forbidden back then] (*Obras completas: Vol. I* 247). One of his poems is an apostrophe to Antonio Machado in the context of his death as an exile in France (*Obras completas: Vol. I* 248). The importance of the poet Jean Louis Camard is discussed later in this chapter.

14 Cilleruelo, Durán, López Casanova, and Valender all demonstrate this tendency to divide Aub's work into two distinct types. However, in one of the earliest wide-ranging essays about Republican exilic poetry to be published in Spain, "Poesía de la España peregrina: crónica incompleta" [Poetry of Peregrine Spain: An Incomplete Chronicle] (1977), the exiled literary critic Aurora de Albornoz disregarded this dichotomy and claimed unequivocally that the main theme in *Antología traducida* is "destierro" ("Poesía" 68). An important critical contribution in this regard is Antonio Carreño's series of essays about Aub's anthology. Carreño eschewed binary approaches to explore a complex discursive "encrucijada" [crossroads]: "El juego es lírico, dramático, lúdico; es existencial, filosófico y, sobre todo, literario" [the game is lyrical, dramatic, ludic; it is an existential, philosophical and, above all, literary game] ("Las otras" 8). Carreño also traced the genealogy of imaginary biographies in *Antología traducida* and *Jusep Torres Campalans* ("Alegoría" 10).

15 In *Breve historia de la literatura española* Carlos Alvar, José-Carlos Mainer, and Rosa Navarro claimed that Aub was "testigo de su tiempo" [witness to his times], but they made no reference to his poetry (627).

16 For connections between the critical marginality of Aub's poetry and his use of apocryphal masks, see César Núñez's "Max Aub 'en el país del viento': algunos poemas del denominado *Ciclo de Djelfa* (1941–1942)."

17 See "apocrypha" in http://www.etymonline.com/index.php?allowed_in_frame=0&search=apocrypha (accessed 1 November 2018).

18 Francisco Gerhardt has studied the connection between memory, literature, and posterity in relation to the disappointment that, according to *La gallina ciega*, Aub

experienced when he realized that his writings were not known in Spain in 1969 ("Max Aub revisitado" 280).

19 As Aub explained in the foreword to his 1966 *Manual de historia de la literatura española,* "la historia es una reconstrucción atada al ingenio de quien la escribe, según datos, como es natural, no siempre fidedignos ... Cualquier historia es restablecimiento poético, aunque no se quiera" [History is a reconstruction tied to the ingenuity of those who write it following data which are, naturally, not always reliable ... Any history is a poetic restoration, even if one does not want it to be] (5).

20 See Sánchez Ferlosio 356–8.

21 According to Ugarte, *El laberinto mágico* represents "a labyrinth of loss, death, insanity, and absence; it is the story of hundreds of individuals who question not only the ultimate reasons for the war but their own places within it. The very notion of place is put into question" (*Shifting* 119). This sense of dislocation extends to the narrator's site of enunciation.

22 Mary Gaylord explained in 2012 some of the reasons why Manrique's poem is important as a mnemonic device as regards death: "The poem musters literary devices such as the *ubi sunt* (where are they?) topos and classic heroic examples, biblical language, and the medieval tradition of the *danza de la muerte* (dance of death), intertwining them with simple imagery (the soul waking from mortal sleep, life as a delta of rivers flowing to the sea), simple axioms, and direct, intimate address of the ethical and metaphysical dimensions of life and death" ("Spain" 1335).

23 Ugarte perceptively identified the spatiotemporal dilemma that the exilic perspective presented for Aub: "The recovery and ordering of the past from the time and place of exile leads to a variety of obstacles which in the end render the recovery impossible" (*Shifting* 122)

24 Ugarte claimed that the dramatic paradox in Aub's personal situation was of a textual nature: "Aub's defense is a discourse not on writing and reality but on the difficulty of articulating the defense itself, considering the impossible situation in which he was accused ... Ironically, the writer of fiction must resort to reality to combat the tools of his own trade. In a sense, Aub is pursued by the fruits of his own labor. The writing of Max Aub underscores the textuality of both life and politics" (*Shifting* 115).

25 Already in his first book of poems, *Poemas cotidianos* [Quotidian Poems], published in Barcelona in 1925, Aub's linguistic and geographic singularity renders his identity complex, plural, and uncertain. As Enrique Díez-Canedo explained in the introduction: "Max Aub me da la sensación de un hombre múltiple. Llega a verme, viniendo de Alemania o de Francia, de Levante o del Noroeste ... Son versos balbucientes, inseguros, como si temieran, afirmándose demasiado, dejar escapar su esencia sutil. Parece que su musa los ha pensado en un idioma y ella misma los ha traducido en otro" [Max Aub strikes me as a multiple man. He comes to see me, from Germany or France, from Levante or the Northeast ... These are stuttering, uncertain verses, as though they feared that, in asserting themselves too much, they would let their subtle essence go. It seems that their muse has thought them up in one language and she herself has translated them into a different one] (*Obras completas: Vol. I* 53).

26 In 2007, Gérard Malgat showed how Aub's pre-exilic linguistic alterity complicated his rhetoric of attachment to Spain (303). In "Un mapa de lecturas. La biblioteca de Max Aub en Valencia" (2008), Joan Oleza studied the library collection put together by Aub in Valencia from 1919 to 1938, when he went into exile, and emphasized his vast reading interests in terms of both genre and language. Aub was widely read in Catalan, French, Italian, German, Latin American, Spanish, and Russian literature.

27 According to Estelle Irizarry, "resulta muy difícil tomar en serio una antología tan llena de comicidad" [it is hard to take seriously such a comic anthology] (127). See also Carreira.

28 Valender cautiously distinguishes between a collection of poems like *Antología traducida*, which attracts readers interested in Aub's "inventiva vanguardista" [avant-garde inventiveness], and *Diario de Djelfa*, which attracts those interested in "la forma en que este escritor se inscribe" [the way that this writer inserts himself] in a tragic historical period ("Max Aub" 278).

29 Ottmar Ette has explained that, as a narrative ploy, the crow's random selection of index cards identifying prisoners of a concentration camp in southern France in 1940 is "typical of Aub's strategy to have characters pop up suddenly and then disappear. Aub's telegram-like prose sketches a handful of biographies and outlines the ever-different ways in which individual lives were disrupted" (73). Just as in "Manuscrito Cuervo" "human fates flare up briefly, in highly compressed imagery, before receding again into the darkness of history and of the story itself" (73), the human fates of the barely sketched poets gathered in *Antología traducida* are surrounded by the linguistic obscurity of apocryphal texts.

30 Carreño saw this poem as a paradoxical definition of the poetics subtending the entire anthology ("Hacia una morfología" 152)

31 A kharja is the final refrain of a muwashshah, a lyric genre of Al-Andalus written in Arabic or Ibero-Romance.

32 Díaz del Castillo wrote the chronicle *La Historia Verdadera de la conquista de la Nueva España* [*The True History of the Conquest of New Spain*] in 1576. The two "verdaderas lenguas" are Jerónimo de Aguilar and doña Marina o la Malinche. As Salvador de Madariaga – another Spanish Republican exile – wrote in his 1941 biography of Hernán Cortés: "We can but surmise the waves of incomprehension and misunderstanding that the sudden meeting of the two civilizations raised in both Indians and Europeans. Granted that Aguilar and doña Marina, gifted as they both were, succeeded in rendering a tolerably adequate transfiguration of the Christian faith and dogmas not merely into the language but into the idiom of the Tlaxcatecs, but how could these Indians' minds assimilate the dogma of the Virgin Birth" (202–3).

33 "La verdadera historia de la muerte de Francisco Franco" is discussed later in this chapter.

34 See "labyrinth" in http://www.etymonline.com/index.php?term=labyrinth (accessed 1 November 2018).

35 *Ensayos mexicanos,* published in Mexico in 1974, is Aub's posthumous collection of essays about Mexican literature.

36 [MAX AUB. He was born in Paris in 1903. Although his name appears with a suspicious regularity in books and magazines, his whereabouts are unknown. All that is known for a fact is that he wrote many Mexican screenplays devoid of any interest. They have nothing to do with his homonym, Leandro Fernández de Moratín. Those who want to find a political intention in these lines: she-Spain, are mistaken. If we could date these sentences perhaps this could be clarified. That is not possible. In the meantime, avoidance is recommended as the only certainly fruitful course. I. Enclosed into myself, / Purblind, mute, / I sink into what has been / paying for what I was. // II. You are what was and will be. // III. You left and I went, / Nothing remains of me.]

37 In *The Ethics of Autobiography* (2000), Ángel G. Loureiro asked "why the most searching autobiographies in nineteenth- and twentieth-century Spain have been written by exiles," and reflected that "[i]f the most compelling Spanish autobiographies have been written against the grain of the nation, against Spain's past and past Spains, the issue must be the national subject and its history" (184–5). *Antología traducida* lends itself to being read as an idiosyncratic autobiographical text obliquely but critically concerned with national subjects and their histories.

38 Carreño resorted to Nietzsche, Borges, de Man, and Derrida to frame the discursive complexity of the autobiographical "I" and the use of prosopopeia in *Antología traducida* ("Las otras" 9). See also his brief comparative analysis of the semi-apocryphal poem "Max Aub" ("Las otras" 10).

39 As Sanchez Ferlosio put it, "tan verdad como que sólo lo que vive muere es que tan sólo lo que muere vive. Y sólo porque era un ayer verdadero del poeta puede seguir sonando hoy – ¡todavía! –, también para nosotros, como un verdadero ayer" [just as it is true that only what lives dies, so it is true that only what dies lives. And only because it was a true yesterday for the poet, it can continue to resound today – still! – like a true yesterday for us, too] (358–9).

40 Johnson's take on the relationship between literature and death is premised on Paul de Man's rhetorical understanding of autobiography. In his analysis of William Wordsworth's "Essay on Epitaphs," the author of *Blindness and Insight* argued that autobiography is "a figure of reading or of understanding that occurs, to some degree, in all texts" (926). This figure is identified by de Man with prosopopoeia.

41 In his essay "El yo culpable" (1997), Rafael Chirbes examined the ways in which Aub's *Campo de los almendros* carried out a narrative project capable of escaping "la tiranía de yo" [the tyranny of the I] in modern fiction (192): "introspección y uso de la primera persona como única forma del narrador, desaparición del tema hasta dejar el punto de vista como objeto mismo" [introspection and use of the first person as the only type of narrator, disappearance of theme until point of view is left as the object itself] (185). In Chirbes's view, Aub's aim was the "reconstrucción del edificio público de un imaginario reducido a escombros por los vencedores de la guerra" [reconstruction of the public edifice of an imaginary reduced to rubble by the victors of the war] (186).

42 Luis Fernández Cifuentes made a similar case in 2005 with regard to another exiled writer, Jose María Blanco White, who left Spain for England in 1810. Fernández

Cifuentes critiqued how Blanco White had become "el modelo de 'lo recuperable"' [the model for "what may be recuperable"] ("Las autobiografías" 25). Among the problematic aspects of this model was Blanco White's "mirada" [gaze], which, Fernández Cifuentes argued, "parece haber supeditado el escrutinio del país a la figuración de su propia identidad en un laborioso ejercicio de mediatizaciones'" [seems to have subordinated the scrutiny of the country to the figuration of his own identity in a painstaking exercise of mediatizations] (27). Fernández Cifuentes's analysis of Blanco White's figuration of identity sheds light on a similar multiplicity of mediations in Aub's exilic self-fashionings and offers a helpful angle on a potential anxiety of cultural recovery among Spanish literary critics and historians. An anxiety-ridden framework for national reception of exilic works may foster a certain blindness to resistant figurations of identity in exilic productions as intricately self-reflective as Blanco White's and Aub's.

43 See the first chapter for recent debates in Madrid about the public use of Aub's name.

44 There is an ample bibliography on Antonio Muñoz Molina's and Max Aub's respective literary projects. For the specific connection between identity, memory, and modes of representation – and its possible relevance in discussions about testimonial rhetoric in Muñoz Molina's work – see Ferrán, Herzberger, Labanyi, Navajas, and Pérez-Simón. For Aub, see Caudet, Fernández, Mainer, Pérez Bowie, and Sánchez Zapatero.

45 José María Naharro-Calderón sees, for instance, a commonality in terms of fundamental human rights between camps such as Le Vernet, Djelfa and Dachau. In Naharro-Calderón's view, the study of the Francoist, Vichyist, Nazi, and Soviet concentration camp regimes shows that, "compartían en general el mismo desprecio por la humanidad de sus moradores" [they shared, in general, the same contempt for the humanity of their inhabitants] (*Entre alambradas* 87).

46 The title of Preston's book was faulted because the repression to which it referred "differed qualitatively as well as quantitatively from the cold-blooded planning and industrial-scale implementation of the Nazi Holocaust" (Treglown n. pag.). By contrast, Helen Graham, who in 2002 claimed that for the Francoist project of "national reordering" of the Spanish working classes became what the Jews were to the Nazi people's community (*The Spanish Republic* 123), praised the title of Preston's book for the "category shift" it may effect, suggesting "parallels and resonances" between the Spanish case and the Holocaust, as well as "a deeper understanding of Europe's dark mid-twentieth century as a whole" ("The Spanish Holocaust" n. pag.). This "category shift" was taken to reframe the Spanish Civil War "as in part an ethnic conflict" because, as Sebastiaan Faber argued, "Franco's reign of terror, like that of Hitler and Goebbels, was carefully planned and systematically executed" ("The Spanish Holocaust" n. pag.). For a layered summary of the controversy, see Helen Graham, Jo Labanyi, Jorge Marco, Paul Preston, and Michael Richards. For an unqualified use of the term Holocaust to describe Franco's repression, particularly in reference to the deaths of Federico García Lorca and Miguel Hernández, see Gibson, *Cuatro* 300, 336. For recent historical research on Franco's connivance in the deportation of

Spanish Republican exiles from France to Nazi concentration camps, see Diego Fonseca's 2019 article "What was Franco's role in the deportation of 10,000 Spaniards to Nazi camps?" This research is concurrent with institutional efforts to publicly honour victims: "In 2005, former Prime Minister José Luis Rodríguez Zapatero visited Mauthausen, six decades after its liberation, and officially honored Spanish republican victims ... [In February 2019] Prime Minister Pedro Sánchez paid tribute to exiles at a French concentration camp in Argèles-sur-Mer, where 450,000 Spaniards were detained" (Fonseca n. pag.). In April 2019, the Spanish Government established 5 May as the "Day of Tribute to Spaniards that were deported to and died in Mauthausen and other concentration camps, and to all victims of Nazism from Spain." See http://www.lamoncloa.gob.es/lang/en/gobierno/councilministers/Paginas/2019/260419-nationalhealthsyst.aspx (accessed 1 May 2019).

47 In his informative and enlightening "The Voids of Sepharad: The Memory of the Holocaust in Spain" (2011), Alejandro Baer examined the different ways in which the Holocaust, understood as "both universal imperative and symbolic resource" within a "cultural matrix for various forms of production, circulation, and consumption of traumatic memory," is related to the Spanish Civil War, Francoism and Spain's transition from dictatorship to democracy (95). Baer tackled with what he called Spain's "very peculiar situation" at the beginning of the twenty-first century: "The European culture of memory and the globalized discourse on the Holocaust introduces a foreign body of ideas into Spain, which are simultaneously rejected and appropriated. They are rejected because there is no immediate historical connection with the events that are to be remembered and because the prevailing logic in Spanish political culture has been alien to memory ... And they are appropriated in different ways by identification and comparison with the Spanish tragedy" (108). Baer analysed the rhetoric deployed in historical works about the Civil War and Franco's regime that resort to the Holocaust as "a bridging metaphor that establishes analogic connections to other events": "The use of these analogies is perhaps best understood in the context of an extremely polarized historiography that resorts to hyperbole insofar as there is no agreement on the facts and, more important, as to how they are to be interpreted. Equating Franco's violence to that of the Nazis makes it possible to emphasize the moral equivalence between the perpetrators" (108–9). Muñoz Molina would arguably posit an analogous moral equivalence.

48 In Aub's speech, the Spanish Civil War never happened. Thus, poets like Federico García Lorca and Miguel Hernández are alive and present. This fiction has a strong historical significance, as it brings out the very absence of those dead and/or exiled writers who could have been members of the academy and consequently presents an opportunity to vividly remember authors like Rafael Alberti, José Bergamín, Américo Castro, Luis Cernuda, Juan Ramón Jiménez, Juan Larrea, Vicente Llorens, Antonio Machado, and Aub himself.

49 Monumental history leads to analogical fallacies. According to Nietzsche, when monumental history prevails over other modes of history, "the past itself suffers harm: whole segments of it are forgotten, despised, and flow away in an uninterrupted

colourless flood, and only individual embellished facts rise out of it like islands ... Monumental history deceives by analogies" (71).

50 Muñoz Molina is here referencing Américo Castro's reflections on Spanish history.

51 In the introduction to the 2013 edition of *Sefarad*, Pablo Valdivia underlined the ways in which Max Aub enabled Muñoz Molina to connect what he saw as Spanish culture and European culture (23). Muñoz Molina's 1993 article "Recuerdo de Max Aub" summed up "todos los grandes temas que vertebran las páginas de *Sefarad*: el destierro, los totalitarismos europeos, el horror estalinista, el genocidio nazi, lo judío como metáfora de todos los exilios, la configuración de la identidad personal y colectiva, la incertidumbre de un continente devastado por la guerra y la infinita crueldad de la represión" [all of the big themes that provide the backbone for the pages of *Sefarad*: banishment, European totalitarianisms, Stalinist horror, Nazi genocide, Jewishness as a metaphor for all forms of exile, the configuration of personal and collective identity, the uncertainty of a continent devastated by war and the infinite cruelty of repression] (24).

52 See Julius Ruiz for the problems involved in calling Francoist repression genocidal (175). For a detailed analysis of the complex overlaps between the terms *genocide* and *Holocaust*, see Yehuda Bauer's "What Was the Holocaust?" (2001).

53 The second quotation is my translation, as this part is missing on page 188 of the English translation.

54 Translation modified.

55 "Giving testimony involves the attempt to address or give an account of the experience one has had oneself and through which one has lived. In a sense, one might understand giving testimony as the fallible attempt to verbalize or otherwise articulate bearing witness" (LaCapra, "Traumatropisms" 61)

56 Translation modified.

57 Translation modified.

58 Dominick LaCapra has warned that "any attentive secondary witness to, or acceptable account of, traumatic experiences must in some significant way be marked by trauma or allow trauma to register in its own procedures" ("Lanzmann" 244). In this sense, the "transparent" account of Améry's experience given by the narrator in *Sepharad* can be argued to fall into a certain "positivism" to the extent that it follows "the idea that an objectifying notational system can ideally represent, transparently render, or capture the essence of an object" (239).

59 Guillén translated *destierro* as unearthing, and explained the term as follows: "*Destierro* leads to *destiempo* – to a décalage in historical rhythms of development or, for many, to the most demanding of punishments: exile from the present and hence from the future – linguistic and cultural – of on's native country" ("The Sun" 277).

60 Aub wrote that in the almost three years that he spent in jails and concentration camps before he arrived in Mexico in 1942 he was able to hold on to a book of poetry by Quevedo and a dictionary (*Cuerpos* 278).

61 [Three years, three years and the stones, besides being stones, / are French stones. / Three years, three years and the birds sing strangely. / Three years we wait. / Three

years of Francos, three years of night, three years, / and for many brothers three more years, three years. / Three years of night, three years of camps, three years of Francos. // Three years and Spain is erased from the map. / Three years and we live lower than the world, / roving worlds. / Three years of Sahara / – the entire world is Sahara but Spain – . / Three years of blood, three years of rottenness, three years / of death, three years of hunger. / Three years that bite, three years that gnaw. / February of thirty nine. / Three years of death. // Spain, voice and earth [land] / earth and word, / tongue [language] and [mountain] range. // No matter how much wind, / there is no one to erase us. / No matter how much desert, / there is no one to stand above us. / At three years one starts to speak ... / Spain, my water. Spain, my sea. // You rise to my throat, Spain, / each word regurgitates salt ... / Three years and you are erased from the map. / Spain, Spain, Spain, Spain ... / February of thirty nine / Three years of death.]

62 For other readings of *Diario de Djelfa* as a narrative form of testimony see López Casanova (23) and Alted (*La voz* 135). In *Poetas del exilio español: una antología* [Poets of Spanish Exile: An Anthology], arguably the most important selection of poems by Spanish Republican exiles, James Valender reads *Diario de Djelfa* as a tale: "Aub elaboró un vívido relato del trato inhumano que había experimentado en los campos de concentración" [Aub developed a vivid tale of the inhuman treatment that he suffered in the concentration camps] (277). Valender also underscores the formal connections between personal experience and history (278). For a critique of narrative referentiality in *Diario de Djelfa*, see Naharro-Calderón's *Entre alambradas y exilios* (188).

63 These photographs are not included in the 2001 edition of Aub's complete works.

64 As Brandon LaBelle argues in *Lexicon of the Mouth: Poetics and Politics of Voice and the Oral Imaginary* (2014), choking "occurs not only when something foreign enters to block the throat, but also when something rises up from inside ... Such instances of ... choking profoundly demonstrate the degree to which language is *stuff* ... whose crafting requires so much phsycial as well as emotional energy" (33).

65 In using "otherlands," Brodsky performed the difference within the term "motherlands" that, in his view, the exilic condition may compel (32).

66 A sample of Aub's "acento francés" can be found on https://www.youtube.com/watch?v=cKp3tQT0JWw (accessed 1 February 2019). Aub recorded his own reading of "La verdadera historia de la muerte de Francisco Franco" for *Voz viva de México* [Living Voice of Mexico], a collection of readings produced by the Universidad Nacional Autónoma de México. The reading was issued in 1971 as an LP record. As we shall see, linguistic alienation is an important feature of the story.

67 Extrapolating from Jonathan Culler's reflections on the lyric, "Tres años" would give us "not mimesis of a voice but *voicing* ... vocal effects that tend to be inversely related to representation; the more voicing, the less mimesis of a voice, and the less plausible the dramatic monologue model" ("Extending" 9).

68 Along similar lines, Aub explored the problem of elucidating truth amid the excessive verbosity of Spanish intellectuals in *La calle de Valverde*, as Fernández Cifuentes has

shown ("Estudio" 41). In this novel Aub focused on public life among intellectuals in pre-war Madrid. *La calle de Valverde* was published in Mexico in 1961, shortly after "La verdadera historia de la muerte de Francisco Franco."

69 In 1982, the Spanish-born Mexican literary critic Arturo Souto Alabarce claimed that the plot of this story was premised on a narrative "desdoblamiento" [splitting] that enabled Aub to offer, from Nacho's perspective, a "juego de espejos" [play of mirrors] between Mexican and Spanish cultures. Arturo Souto Alabarce was born in Madrid in 1930. He left Spain in 1937 and settled in Mexico in 1942. He passed away in Mexico City in 2013 ("Letras" 427).

70 For possible links between *Austerlitz* and *Sefarad*, see Martín-Estudillo and Grohmann. "Novela de novelas" is the subtitle of *Sefarad*.

71 See Francisco Caudet's objections to what he sees as Muñoz Molina's "simple declaración afectiva" [simple affective statement] of identification with repressed groups such as Jews, heretics, or Republicans. Caudet sees in Muñoz Molina a problematic tendency towards melancholy and sweeping generalizations with regard to historically situated political problems (*El exilio* 385).

72 In 2018, on the occasion of a commemorative exhibition about Arturo Barea at the Institute Cervantes in Madrid, Muñoz Molina qualified his views about the extent to which it is possible to know what the lives of exiles were like: "Una guerra tan destructiva y una dictadura tan larga y cruenta como la española hacen muy difícil y hasta imposible el regreso de los que se fueron. Las vidas humanas son muy cortas y la ausencia crea zanjas de desconocimiento que luego son muy difíciles de remediar" [a war so destructive and a dictatorship so long and bloody as the Spanish one make it very difficult and even impossible for those who left to return. Human lives are short and absence creates pits of ignorance that, later, are very difficult to fix] (Llamazares, n. pag.).

73 Alejandro Baer posited that the weakness of the link between Spain and the memory of the Holocaust is not historical but cultural: "It is not due to a (relative) distance from historical events, but mainly due to their weak reception, from 1945 onward, in a country that has been practically *judenrein* for the past five centuries. To a large extent, it is the voids, the silences, and the abiding prejudices regarding Judaism (which were exacerbated during Franco's dictatorship but did not fade away after democracy was established) that shape in sociological terms the discursive activity on the Holocaust in contemporary Spain" (114). Baer proposed a specifically Spanish memory of the Holocaust, "the forgotten traces of Sepharad": "Remembering the Holocaust while keeping alive the memory of Sepharad (including the Inquisition's centuries long persecution of conversos) is not only an apt tribute to the victims of both tragedies but it may also help, as Benjamin suggests, to illuminate the present" (114). Muñoz Molina's *Sefarad* would contribute to this specific form of cultural memory, as opposed to forms of memory that imply direct involvement in historical events, institutional and official ceremonies, or identifications premised on analogies between acts of extreme violence.

74 Naharro-Calderón has studied the ways in which Aub is particularly relevant in current debates about historical memory of the war. In Naharro-Calderón's view, Aub's exilic

writings reveal a tension between the broken memory of the conflict and "la imposibilidad de restañar completamente dicho recuerdo mediante un discurso teleológico asumible y concluyente" [the impossibility of completely healing such a memory through an acceptable and conclusive teleological discourse] (*Entre alambradas*, 171).

75 For a study of Aub's experience of *destiempo* while he strolled around Madrid in 1969, see Naharro-Calderón's *Entre alambradas y exilios* (210–13).

76 In 2015, Mari Paz Balibrea made the case that the politics of recuperation of exilic testimonies produced by Spanish Republicans should preserve as a critical position the "marginality" of exile with regard to the nation ("Rethinking" 13).

77 Drawing on Edward Said's reflections on the forms of legitimacy adopted by modern literary critics, Cabo Aseguinolaza has critiqued the ways in which nationalist discourses have shaped the forms of legitimacy adopted by literary historians in Spain: "The dominant discourse of literary history has primarily been a discourse of affiliation, that is, of adhesion or adscription to a certain tale, to a certain ideological concept, to a certain process of institutionalization, and to a certain ideal monolingualism. However, it has also been a discourse that has drawn its strength from a filiate pretense, that of the naturalness attributed to genealogies and identity when associated to language and land. Affiliation has disguised itself as filiation" (52).

78 [As a rule of thumb, cultivated people believe that Max Aub does not exist. Some presume that this is the pseudonym of one writer, of several writers; well, of all writers ... "Max Aub" is the author of almost all of the literature that is published in Mexico – his work comprises 12 metres and 87 centimetres ... What man is capable of so much? Some among the cultivated suspect, however, that Aub is not a myth: he does exist and he is Mexican. Other people believe that he does exist and that he is Spanish, but they are wrong. (The proof is that Spaniards call him 'masáu.') And the mystery gets worse by the day: yesterday, he published his "Incomplete Works," today, his "Complete Theatrical Works," tomorrow ... [Image caption:] Max Aub with his nanas, Paris, 1905. (?)]

7 Tomás Segovia

1 As we will see, Jonathan Culler's conceptualization of the lyric departs from historicist and anti-historicist models, that is, for instance, "the decontextualized expression of the interiority of the poet" and "the drama of a lyric persona or character" ("Genre" 52).

2 In *Mil años de poesía española* [A Thousand Years of Spanish Poetry], an anthology compiled in 2009 by the renowned philologist and member of the Spanish Academy Francisco Rico, Segovia was described as "Mexicano de España y español de México" [a Mexican from Spain, a Spaniard from Mexico] and canonized in Spanish literary history as "sin duda el poeta en castellano más eminente entre los exiliados de su generación" [without a doubt, the most eminent poet in Castilian among the exiles of his generation] (1363).

3 In Spain, France, and Mexico, Segovia is widely considered an important representative of the Republican exile. See *Sobre exiliados*, a volume of Segovia's essays published by the Colegio de México in 2007 as part of its "Serie Literatura del Exilio Español,"

and *El exilio republicano de 1939 y la segunda generación*, a collective volume published in 2011 by Renacimiento de Sevilla as part of its "Biblioteca del Exilio." The latter volume includes eight of Segovia's essays in a chapter dedicated to the writer. As for France, the work of Bernard Sicot, a translator and scholar of Segovia's work, must be emphasized.

4 In her indispensable "Poesía de la España peregrina: crónica incompleta," Aurora de Albornoz addressed the historiographical problem of using national labels in this specific case (15). Arturo Souto characterized this group of poets "indefinido" [undefined], "proteico" [protean], and "mixto" [mixed] ("Max Aub" 265). According to Roberto Ruiz, the "condición normal" [normal condition] of this group was "extranjerismo perpetuo" [perpetual foreigness] (3). For a study of the political, generational, cultural, and economic diversity of Spanish exiles in Mexico, see Jorge de Hoyos Puente's *La utopía del regreso*, particularly chapter 3. See p. 168 and p. 252 for a discussion of the "generación nepantla" in this general context.

5 For a recent wide selection of these writers and their poetry, see Enrique López Aguilar's anthology *Los poetas hispanomexicanos: estudio y antología*, published in Mexico in 2012.

6 Regarding his elders, Segovia was nonetheless critical of attempts to canonize tutelary figures such as Max Aub and Emilio Prados as part of the "patrimonio nacional, institucional, colectivo o supuestamente colectivo" [collective, or supposedly collective, institutional, national heritage] (*Sobre exiliados* 248). In his opinion, this honour may undermine the subversive potential in their writings. Segovia considered Aub and Prados marginal figures, almost as though he was anxious that their canonical influence would neutralize the subversive potential in his own work (*Sobre exiliados* 258; "Luz" 71). James Valender contends that Segovia's devotion to the poetry of Juan Ramón Jiménez – also an important canonical exile – could entail the marginalization of his own work, as Jiménez's poetry did not overtly engage with national culture, class struggle, or social alienation, common topics in the dominant trend among modernist poets (66). Quoting exiled painter Ramón Gaya, Valender claims that, as a poet, Segovia was always "extemporáneo" [untimely] ("*La luz*" 72).

7 The latter claim was partly countered by Mexican critic Jacobo Sefamí, who in 2012 described Segovia as follows: "known for his erotic poetry in the surrealist vein, and for *Anagnorisis* (1967), a long poem ... that explores the ambience of the exile from different perspectives: memory, travel, and orphanhood." (882).

8 Eduardo Mateo Gambarte has noted that the jury of the Premio Juan Rulfo indicated that their reading was very different from the Spanish national one, above all in their focus on the "entronque" [link] of Segovia's work with "la tradición poética europea leída, digerida y traducida, concretamente con la francesa, alemana, española e italiana" [the European poetic tradition, read, digested, and translated, specifically the French, German, Spanish, and Italian tradition] (207). For an analysis of national identifications in Segovia's work, see Mateo Gambarte's *Diccionario*. For the canonical status attained by Segovia as a poet of Republican exile, see, for instance, http://www.elconfidencial.com/archivo/2009/09/18/2_espana_otros_paises_buscan_recuperar_memoria.html.

9 [I never said us without, at that point / Some voice in me yelling, them! / I had all the true fatherlands / The only ones that leave their children / In charge of all their danger / The ones that do not protect them from other fatherlands.]

10 [from the beginning my house was no longer in the house / or my land in the land or love in my love / memory was always somewhere else / and circle after circle everything was exile.]

11 In 2017, Mari Paz Balibrea and Sebastiaan Faber's argued for a transnational approach to the Republican exile that would acknowledge "el alcance geopolítico de su influencia en un momento – el de los años treinta y cuarenta – de intensa globalización de los conflictos políticos, marcado por grandes movimientos diaspóricos " [the geopolitical scope of its influence at a time – the 1930s and 40s – of intense globalization of political conflicts, a time marked by large diasporic movements] ("Hacia otra historiografía" 20).

12 [As much as I seek the shoals / of my waves, I'm always / beyond my horizon; / my foam always reaching / beyond what it reaches.]

13 As Alasdair Fotheringham explained in his obituary "Tomás Segovia: One of Spain's 'poets in exile' during the Franco dictatorship" on November 16, 2011: "Segovia was equally talented as a translator – Shakespeare, Foucault, Nerval and Ungaretti all profited from his clear, taut style – and was a gifted printer and carpenter, sometimes publishing his own books ... He also worked as a critic, essayist, diarist, and was, at the age of 80, a keen blogger" (n. pag.). Segovia also translated works by Giorgio Agamben, André Breton, Alain Borer, Victor Hugo, Mircea Eliade, Lucien Febvre, Roman Jakobson, Cesare Pavese, Rainer María Rilke, and Frances Yates, among others. Beyond the scope of this book is Segovia's vast work as an essayist, especially in linguistics. See in this regard Eugenia Houvenaghel's illuminating studies, such as "Cruzando fronteras nacionales. Hacia una 'cartografía' del ensayismo de Tomás Segovia" (2014), where she argues that "a spatial dimension is introduced into [Segovia's] essays through multiple and international co-enunciators. Various alliances and oppositions are established between these different co-enunciators, not in accordance with their nationalities or geographic positions, but as a result from their attitudes towards literature" (27).

14 [FLAG - My tent always outside the walls. My language always learned in another place. My flag perpetually white. My nostalgia vast and capricious. My love ingenuous and my fidelity ironic. My hands serious and in them an incessant whisper of thoughts. My future nameless. My memory dazed by the incurable love of forgetfulness. Ballasted in the desert my word. And my face always bare where time blows.]

15 See Pascual Gay for an instructive approach to "Bandera" following the dialectic between "Tierra" and "tierra" in Segovia's poetry (148). Bernard Sicot identifies in "Bandera" a voice that insists on claiming to belong to a generalized exile due to multiple causes ("La poésie" 145).

16 This return is also a return to Segovia's long-standing reflection on the relation between modernity, tradition, and poetic language which harks back to what he called the Romantic revolution (Gay 138–43).

17 This temporary "occupation" of the "I" position by a reader of Spanish could be approached in terms of a politics of accent. See Nowell Smith 121.

18 Del Pliego did not entirely shun nation as a critical category, but also made clear that Segovia's writings were irreducible to the conventional historiographical model of single nationalities with regard to cultural productions by Spanish exiles (16).

19 The question posed by Segovia's rhetoric of exile can also be approached in terms of what Leszek Kołakowski described in 1985 as the "uncertain status, the lack of a well-defined identity" among intellectuals exiled from collective exile. In "In Praise of Exile," the Polish philosopher exiled in England sought to answer the question of whether exile might offer to intellectuals "privileges unknown to those who are securely settled on their native soil" (56). He provocatively reflected on the unbearability of total homelessness and the unlikelihood of perfect cosmopolitanism in what he called an "age of refugees, of migrants, vagrants, nomads roaming about the continents and warming their souls with the memory of their – spiritual or ethnic, divine or geographical, real or imaginary – home" (59).

20 Segovia found Cernuda one of the most interesting exiled poets from Spain. As he stated in 1986: "utiliza esa experiencia para exiliarse de verdad de España, para romperla, no para reconstituir una 'little Spain'" [As for the Spanish exile, perhaps the only interesting case for me is that of Cernuda: he uses that experience to exile himself from Spain, to break it, not to reconstitute a "Little Spain"] ("Respuestas" 215).

21 Exilic poems can be read, then, as being largely prosopopeic: they directly or indirectly apostrophize, as Paul de Man argued with regard to prosopopeia, "an absent, deceased, or voiceless entity, which posits the possibility of the latter's reply and confers upon it the power of speech" ("Autobiography" 926). In this sense, exilic poems have ethical import. As Ángel G. Loureiro contends in his re-examination of de Man's notion, prosopopeia's "primary, 'forgotten' meaning has nothing to do with giving 'face,' but points instead to structures of address and response to the other that not only make it complementary to apostrophe, but also place prosopopeia, in this peculiar sense, in the terrain of the ethical" (*The Ethics* xii).

22 See http://www.ateneoesmex.com/inicio/1204/noticias (accessed 1 November 2018).

23 See https://www.elfondoenlinea.com/Detalle.aspx?ctit=018350R (accessed 1 November 2018).

Coda

1 The Ateneo Español de México was arguably the most important association of Spanish Republican exiles in Mexico. It was both a cultural and political centre where exiles would gather, in Patricia Fagen's words, "to keep alive the Spanish culture which they represented, and to do whatever possible to bring about a change of regime in Spain" (99).

2 For the "peregrinaje," see Cruz, "Colliure." Among the events of the homage in Collioure was the presentation of the First International Antonio Machado Prize.

As Jo Labanyi stressed in *Spanish Literature: A Very Short Introduction* (2010), Machado's grave in France remains "a pilgrimage site still today" (116). See also in this regard Debicki (*Spanish* 121) and Pavlovic (44), and the first chapter of this book.

3 For informative studies in cultural and intellectual history focusing on the vast cultural capital Machado has accrued as an iconic figure after his death in exile, see *Antonio Machado y el exilio republicano de 1939 en Francia*, a collection of essays edited by Monique Alonso and Manuel Aznar Soler in 2015. Of particular interest are Manuel Aznar Soler's "Morir de exilio: homenajes a la memoria de Antonio Machado por parte del exilio republicano en Francia (1940 y 1945)," and José Ramón López-García's "Antonio Machado y la poesía del exilio republicano: un camino por andar." For the commemoration of the 80th anniversary of the republican exile in February 2019, see also https://elpais.com/cultura/2019/02/15/babelia/1550257997_731560.html (accessed 15 February 2019). See also Iravedra.

4 Paloma Díaz-Mas has studied Menéndez Pidal's craftsmanship in composing his anthology, and its impact on the cultural field of literature in Spanish. The texts Menéndez Pidal gathered "are reconstructed somewhat artificially by the collector himself, though of course they are based on versions of old and traditional balladry. The book was widely distributed in Spain and Latin America in the 30s" (489). In 2004, Wadda Ríos Font examined the crucial role of tradition and language in the conceptualization of a national literary canon by influential historians like Menéndez Pidal, as well as the political and cultural implications of this conceptualization in twentieth-century Spain, including the civil war and its aftermath: "Altogether, the 'story' told by Spanish literary history is quite consistent and definitely consolidated by the late nineteenth century: Spanish literature expresses the glory of Spain, based on the strength of its language, its religion, and its brave character ... The legitimizing language of Menéndez y Pelayo and, later, Menéndez Pidal is plainly the crystallization of directions already present in the earliest Spanish literary history ... [I]t is obvious that the many national crises brought about by the Second Republic, the civil war, the Franco Regime, the transition to democracy, and the entrance into the European Union could only prove forceful challenges to the discourse of literary history" (34). In 2005, Elsa Martí-López stressed the enduring impact of Menéndez Pidal's ideas in recent disciplinary debates about the historical and critical validity of Hispanism as a historiographical category in literary and cultural studies (153).

5 See Luis Beltrán Almería's "Las formas simples del romancero hispano" (2015) for a developmental, non-thematic approach to the *romancero*, as opposed to Menéndez Pidal's traditionalist view. The examination of *einfache Formen* [simple forms] in the *romancero* allows Beltrán Almería to elucidate the different ways in which certain *romances* were able to "traspasar las fronteras nacionales de la tradición" [pass through the national borders of tradition] (39).

6 In 1992 Eric Hobsbawm referred to this sense of temporal continuity when he defined invented tradition as a set of practices "which seek to inculcate certain values and norms of behaviour by repetition, which automatically implies continuity with

the past. In fact, where possible, they normally attempt to establish continuity with a suitable historic past" (*The Invention* 1).

7 In 2006 Roberto González Echevarría summarized the reception of Darío's ground-breaking *Azul* in the cultural field of poetry in Spain: "The initial reactions to Darío were hostile ... Fortunately, Darío had the audacity to send *Azul* ... to the powerful Spanish critic Juan Valera. Valera wielded his considerable influence ... to launch the young poet's career with two 'letters' about the book, which were printed as prologue in later editions of *Azul* ... Though also critical of Darío's adoption of French ways, Valera recognized his genius and predicted a bright future for the Nicaraguan" (n. pag.). As Alejandro Mejías-López explained in 2009, Valera's letters nonetheless played an "unwitting role in the modernista reversal of colonial dynamics" between Spanish American and Spanish literary and cultural productions (*Inverted* 86).

8 As we saw, Cernuda's review was among the materials collected by Juan Ramón Jiménez for *Guerra en España.* According to the editors of the anthology, Jiménez was not part of it because they had been unable to contact him (in Machado et al., 155). Jiménez had gone into exile a few months before the publication, in August 1936. For a detailed study of cultural politics involved in the production of this important anthology, see the third section of Aznar Soler's *República literaria y revolución.*

9 Only later would Alcalá Galiano call the conflict "War of Independence" instead of "Peninsular War," "revolution, " or "civil war. " See Álvarez Junco, 98.

10 Without calling attention to any historical or political analogies between the liberal politician's circumstances and his own, Llorens remarked that Alcalá Galiano had written his essays from memory and underscored that the period covered in the essays had been little or ill-studied because many literary productions mentioned by Alcalá Galiano could only be found in scattered or hard-to-find Spanish publications, or in hard-to-access foreign ones ("Introducción" 10).

11 In 2011, Donald Fanger, Luis Fernández-Cifuentes, Francisco Márquez-Villanueva, and Susan Rubin Suleiman published a memorial minute for Guillén where they summed up his understanding of literary history: "For him, comparative literature was not just an academic field – it was a way of life ... He sought to chart literary history in time and space, questioning and reconstruing every term used by others and by himself. History with a capital 'H' had no small role in Claudio Guillén's personal history. At the outbreak of the Spanish Civil War in 1936, he and his sister were sent to live with their grandmother in Paris ... [I]n 1983, Claudio himself became the first Harry Levin Professor of Literature at Harvard ... Claudio Guillén died in his home in Madrid on January 27, 2007" (n. pag.).

12 For a critical discussion of Guillén's examination of exilic literature, see Sophia McClennen's welcome invitation to a dialectical reading of the binary oppositions – global vs. national, universal vs. local, creative vs. nostalgic – that have conventionally guided exile studies.

13 For a recent summary of the different uses to which both exiles and intellectuals in Francoist Spain subjected Antonio Machado's figure as a re-embodiment of national culture, see Javier Muñoz Soro's "Antonio Machado" (2017).

14 As we saw, Bergamín had also been cultural attaché for the Republican government-in-exile in Paris and president of the *II Congreso Internacional de Escritores en Defensa de la Cultura.*

15 Ridruejo would later dismiss this foreword as Manichean. See Carbajosa and Carbajosa for further details about Ridruejo's evolving assessment of Machado's cultural value for his definition of Spain after the war (178–9).

16 See Valender for the peculiarities of this anthology vis-à-vis later anthologies of exilic poetry (*Poetas* 12). As we saw earlier, in his 1949 essay "La actividad literaria de la emigración española" Llorens underscored the importance of Diego's anthology to exilic culture (*Estudios* 131).

17 Another early anthology of exilic poetry by Republicans, Francisco Giner de los Ríos's *Las cien mejores poesías españolas del destierro* [The Hundred Best Spanish Poems of Exile], published in Mexico in 1945, is dedicated to Antonio Machado. In 1977, Aurora de Albornoz stressed the important cultural value acquired by Machado's poetry among exiled Republican poets from early on ("Poesía" 32).

18 Sebastiaan Faber's *Exile and Hegemony: Spanish Intellectuals in Mexico, 1939–1975* (2002) is an important study of the close links between Spanish nationalism, pan-Hispanism, and Republican exile. As he explained in 2008, "*hispanismo* is regularly used as a synonym for Pan-Hispanism – that is, the movement or ideology that presumes, celebrates, or promotes the cultural (if not political and economic) unity of the Spanish-speaking world" (*Anglo-American* 9). In 2015, Alejandro Mejías-López summarized the connections between the inception of modern national literary history, *hispanismo*, Republican exile, and the end of Franco's dictatorship: "while the end of empire was behind the constitution of national literary histories, which for political and ideological reasons kept Spanish American and Spanish peninsular literatures apart, the end of empire was simultaneously responsible for generating a countercurrent that aimed to prevent that very separation and to understand the literatures written in Spanish on both sides of the Atlantic as parts of a larger entity, whose center remained in Spain ... Embraced first by conservatives from both sides of the Atlantic but soon enough by Spanish liberals as well, *hispanismo* would become consolidated in the second half of the nineteenth century, emerge as a central discourse during the long years of the Franco regime in Spain (permeating also ... much of Spanish intellectual discourse in exile), and then be incorporated seamlessly with some updates into the official discourse of post-Franco Spain" (207).

19 For the high symbolic value that literary historians still accord to Machado's last days in exile and his grave, see the intensely commemorative introductory pages to *El exilio republicano de 1939 y la segunda generación*, edited by Manuel Aznar Soler and José Ramón López García in 2011 (7–17), in which Machado is described as "un mito ejemplar para nuestro exilio republicano" [an exemplary myth for our Republican exile] (12). Some of these pages were read in front of Machado's grave in Collioure in 2009. For an illuminating study of the connections between Machado's creation of apocryphal poets and his understanding of "pueblo," see José Luis Abellán's "Antonio Machado: la elaboración de pueblo como categoría cultural desde su teoría de los apócrifos."

20 Gibson was aware of the risks involved in his reading Machado's poetry as autobiographical evidence: "sé que me van a criticar por analizarlos de forma autobiográfica" [I know I'm going to be criticized for analysing [his poems] in autobiographical form] ("Machado" n. pag.). In "Resistencia vital," his 2007 review of *Ligero de equipaje*, Luis Fernández Cifuentes took issue with Gibson's use of documentary evidence to shed light on Machado's life, and specifically on his last days: "es el final, su retirada desde Barcelona hasta Collioure, el pasaje más minuciosamente documentado de esta biografía ... El misterio, el desconocimiento de la intimidad, la insuficiencia de lo accidental, esa suerte de vacío que la documentación más prolija apenas disimula, constituyen sólo uno de los desafíos de la biografía de Machado" [it is the end, his retreat from Barcelona to Collioure, the most thoroughly documented passage in this biography ... Mystery, ignorance of intimacy, inadequacy of accidental detail, that sort of void that the most exhaustive documentation is barely able to conceal, constitute only one of the challenges posed by Machado's biography] (35). For connections between *Ligero de equipaje* and debates about historical memory, see Benítez Ariza.

21 This promotional description of Gibson's biography was accessed in October 2017: https://www.amazon.com/Ligero-Equipaje-Vida-Antonio-Machado/dp/8403096860. For a formalist reading of Machado's verse, see Issorel. Issorel also provides a detailed reconstruction of Machado's last days in France. In Aznar Soler and Idoia Murga Castro's 2019 exhibition catalogue *1939: Exilio republicano español*, Juan Ramón López-García reads Machado's line as shedding light on exilic memory: "Machado anticipaba el refugio interior luminoso de la memoria por el que optarían no pocos poetas exiliados" [Machado anticipated the luminous inner refuge of memory that not a few exiled poets would choose] (629).

22 In his 2010 *Las armas y las letras* – a crucial book for controversies about historical memory in Spain – Andrés Trapiello took a much more cautious reading of the famous line: "cierra admirable, enigmáticamente su obra y su vida" [it admirably and enigmatically closes his work and his life] (465).

23 Rigoberto González's biographical note about Aurora de Albornoz (Spain, 1926–Spain, 1990), published by *The Poetry Foundation* in 2007, foregrounded the connections between her family's history and her contributions to exile studies: "Her body of work is an important contribution to world letters because ... it gives voice to the experience of *los exiliados*, or Spanish exiles – one of the prominent women poets in a group dominated by men ... In 1944, de Albornoz and her family relocated to San Juan, Puerto Rico. There she began her academic education, eventually earning an M.A. from the University of Puerto Rico. At that time, she was studying under the tutelage of the future Nobel Laureate, Juan Ramón Jiménez" (n. pag.).

24 De Albornoz drew here from Ivan Schulman's essay "Génesis del azul modernista" ("Rubén" 252).

25 For Darío's sometimes contradictory position within the relative cosmopolitanism of *modernismo*, see Siskind 184–222. Siskind reads "A Bolivia" as one of Darío's "localist, particularistic poems affirming the autonomy of Latin American culture, cities, and state-apparatuses" (284). In Siskind's thematic analysis, these poems are part of

Darío's broader cultural production, "crucial texts that denounced US imperialism and its materialist culture in order to affirm the spiritual core of Latin culture" (283). John Morrow's likewise thematic reading of "A Bolivia" goes beyond localist frameworks to explore how the poem engages in allegorical fashion with European and Amerindian cultures, "expanding its scope from the paganism of the Old World to the paganism of the New World" (115).

26 For an informative intertextual reading of Machado's last verse and of the childhood theme in particular, see Esther Lázaro's essay, "Estos días azules y este sol de la infancia" (2015).

27 Darío's reception in Spain has been slanted by the nationalist bias of Spanish literary history. As Mejías-López maintains: "Only when the towering presence of a writer like Rubén Darío was impossible to hide did Spanish literary history acknowledge it, but only by naturalizing him – that is, by incorporating him into Spanish literature and turning his Spanish Americanness into a mere footnote" (209–10). In 2017, the Uruguayan poet and critic Roberto Echavarren qualified this assessment: "la relación entre la poesía latinoamericana y española se asemeja a un diálogo de sordos ... Esto no sucedía en la época de la generación del 27. La influencia principal sobre Lorca es Rubén Darío, también Julio Herrera y Reissig. Uno de sus mejores amigos [fue] Pablo Neruda" [the relationship between Spanish and Latin American poetry resembles a dialogue of the deaf. They follow very different trajectories and filiations. This did not happen in days of the generation of 27. The main influence on Lorca is Rubén Darío, also Julio Herrera y Reissig. One of his best friends [was] Pablo Neruda] (qtd. in Layna n. pag.). Albornoz studied Darío's impact on Spanish poets, and specifically on Machado, but made clear that he was not "el único responsible de la revolución modernista" [the sole responsible for the *modernista* revolution] ("Rubén" 248).

28 Debicki explained the reasons for these historiographical problems in terms of cultural isolation: "Spanish poetry of the twentieth century has generally been studied in isolation from other literatures and from its European contexts. This occurred, first of all, because critics defined and discussed two specific movements at the turn of the century: *modernismo,* an aesthetic renewal originating with Rubén Darío in Latin America around 1885 and ending by the early 1900s; and the activity of the Generation of 1898, comprising philosophic and thematic developments in Spanish letters after the disastrous war with the United States. Attempts to characterize, contrast, and relate these two movements led critics into narrow perspectives and kept them from investigating larger patterns, especially the issue of how Spanish letters fit into the development of European modernity" (*Spanish* 2).

29 And yet de Albornoz followed the so-called Spanish epochal view of *modernismo* very closely. As Mejías-López explained, this view was "developed and argued by Ricardo Gullón and traced in Spain to Juan Ramón Jiménez and Federico de Onís, who claimed that *modernismo* was the pan-Hispanic expression of a universal crisis. This approach exposed the provincial shortcomings of the Generation of '98 fallacy ... Nonetheless, it did so only by erasing the central role of Spanish American writers and by presenting modernismo as a *simultaneous* pan-Hispanic opening to 'European'

currents ... In this way, Jiménez and Gullón ultimately traced the pan-Hispanic epochal view back to Spain." (*Inverted* 115–6). Despite her closeness to Jiménez and Gullón, Albornoz's reading of the key signifier "azul" in Machado's last line nevertheless reinforced the central role of Latin American writers like Martí. See also José-Carlos Mainer's "The Dialogue of Iberian Literary Nationalisms" for Jiménez's broadening of the *modernista* linguistic palette to Catalan and Galician. Jiménez saw Jacinto Verdaguer and Rosalía de Castro as forerunners of *modernismo* within the Iberian Peninsula (650). But see also Mejías-López's critical re-examination of this debate.

30 According to Sebastiaan Faber, twenty-first-century Spanish literary history continues to reduce Latin American *modernismo* to a footnote. Regarding the sixth volume of José-Carlos Mainer's monumental *Historia de la literatura Española* (2011), Faber wrote in 2015: "Mainer's eight hundred pages, which centrally cover *modernismo* and the avant-garde, once again relegate Latin America to the margins of cultural history. The first chapter, on *modernismo*, does not mention Latin America once, although Rubén Darío is incorporated as a kind of honorary Spanish writer and cultural operator" ("Hispanism" 20).

31 For this potentially problematic presupposition, see, again, Mejías-López (*Inverted* 115–6).

32 De Albornoz also pointed out that César Vallejo had achieved similar effects of "tiempo discontinuo" in *Trilce* (1922) and that Juan Ramón Jiménez had created analogous "superposiciones temporales" [spatiotemporal superpositions] before 1925 ("Rubén" 254).

33 Extrapolating from Mariano Siskind's arguments about world literature's potential for discursive disruption in the context of *modernismo*, de Albornoz's recourse to poetic memory would enable readers of Machado's alexandrine to "alter the epistemic geographies of [Spanish] literary history to produce new, contingent (ephemeral or not) large-scale spatial assemblages, redrawing the boundaries of the world with each utterance" (61).

34 For the textual history of "Antonio Machado: en el décimo aniversario de su muerte," see Aznar Soler's "Morir" (69).

35 For the specific time signature of poetic events, see chapter 3, "Writing the War, Re-writing the Nation, Embodying the Voice of the People" above.

36 For Guillén's definition of *destierro* or unearthing, see "The Sun" 177.

37 See Rimbaud 280–1.

38 Guillén's ideas are echoed in more recent studies like *Theorizing Modernity* (2001), in which social and political theorist Peter Wagner discussed the notion of "generalized exile" in modernity vis-à-vis nationalism: "The experience of nineteenth-century nationalism was an attempt to recreate a sense of origins in the face of the disembedding effects of early modernity and capitalism, whereas the experience of the twentieth century demonstrated the violent failure of the first and created a stronger sense of loss than ever before" (103). See also Mihai Spariosu's *Modernism and Exile* (2015) – particularly the first part – for a study of the modern nation-state as a product of what Spariosu calls the "exilic-utopian imagination" (1–39).

39 In 2003, Roger Bartra analized the potential advantages of exile for creative artists in terms of melancholia and territoriality: "The mob of artists and writers who live in displacement, in voluntary or involuntary exile, has, in the midst of the din, certain advantages for survival and the creation of new forms of expression ... [T]hese hybrid and migrant creators are constructing disturbing vertical territories where traditional rules are altered. They build the highest of walls, where they nest like stray bees or, better, like a mutant species of melancholic bats clinging firmly to the cracks" (118). In 2005, Bartra explained the cultural productivity of Republican exiles along similar lines: "the sad labor or melancholic pain, in spite of their dangers, can strengthen the self of the artist and drive him or her to the production of art objects" ("Interview" 127). He also underscored a spatiotemporal disruption related to a sense modernization in this specific context: "Frequently the change of territory implies an arrival to more modern or developed, or more free and flexible, situations. The Spanish who were exiled in Mexico lived in conditions of liberty that were inaccessible to those left behind in the Peninsula at least for another three decades. In the exiled person, the subjective sensation that one advances quickly in time is accentuated because the image of the homeland remains static" ("Interview" 131). For conflicting senses of modernity in this context, see also Mari Paz Balibrea's "Temporalidad exílica" (150).

40 See Mejías-López's "Hispanic Studies and the Legacy of Empire" for the view that Spain had also become peripheral with regard to Latin America in the wake of *modernismo*.

41 The ironic lament – "¡Qué lástima / que yo no tenga una patria! / ... / ¡Qué lástima / que yo no tenga comarca, / patria chica, / tierra provinciana!" (*Antología* 122–3) [What a pity that I don't have no country! / ... / What a pity / that I have no region, / native hearth, / provincial land! (Schwartz 217–8)] – concludes in a dramatic self-description – "soy un paria" [I'm a pariah] – and the articulation of a new poetics: "venga, forzado, a cantar cosas de poca importancia!" [I am forced to sing of things of such slight importance (Schwartz 218)]. Tellingly, Felipe`s new poetics is a reaction to trends in modern poetry exalting one's fatherland. Felipe's lament is premised on the claim that the I cannot sing "a la usanza / de este tiempo lo mismo que los poetas de hoy cantan" (*Antología* 122) [in the fashion / of this time as the poets of today sing (Schwartz 218)].

42 For possible cultural continuities and discontinuities between fin-de-siècle melancholia among modernistas of the *generación del 98* included in the "Edad de Plata," and various melancholic attachments to Francoism – for instance, Aub's irony in exilic fictions like "La verdadera historia de la muerte de Francisco Franco," the notion of *desencanto* [disenchantment] in critical debates about failures in modernization and democratization in Spain after Franco's death, or the melancolía de izquierdas [left-winged melancholy] in films and narratives about historical memory – see Santiago Morales-Rivera's *Anatomía del desencanto: Humor, ficción y melancolía en España (1976–1998)*, particularly pages 18–34. In his revealing Freudian reading of melancholy in modern Spanish exile, Ángel G. Loureiro also traced a complex, multilayered sense of loss in, for instance, María Teresa León's 1970 *Memoria de la melancolía* [Memory of Melancholy]: "The stubbornness of the subject prevents mourning from performing

its normal function of gradually assuaging, and accepting, the loss, a failure that transforms the labor of mourning into the permanent process of grieving known as melancholy. Haunted by wrenching separations, Leon's written life fits this description; however, still left is the task of identifying the loss(es) she never accepted ... Such wholesale modification will start by altering the experience of time itself, melancholy being mainly about time and timing. Far from being the only episode of loss endured by León, the war is one more, albeit very important, experience of privation in a life story periodically punctured by ruptures and separations" (*The Ethics* 67–8). Loureiro's analysis could be easily applied to other cultural productions by Republican exiles.

43 In his 2013 critique of literary histories that tend to see these intellectuals as "excepciones que confirman la regla nacional" [exceptions that confirm the national rule], Benito del Pliego linked the different supranational "redes y trayectorias" [webs and trajectories] that could be found in 1920s Paris (where artists and writers like Juan Gris, Pablo Picasso, Vicente Huidobro, Juan Larrea, César Vallejo, Luis Cardoza y Aragón, Guillaume Apollinaire, Gertrude Stein, Tristan Tzara, and Jacques Lipchitz could cross paths) with those established by Republican exiles after 1939 and even by Spanish migrants in the 1970s (15–16).

44 Jahan Ramazani has studied the transnational bearings of elegy's affective content in generic terms: "wherever there are bonds of family and friendship, death produces grief, mourning, and melancholia. Psychological responses to death are also, of course, culturally and historically conditioned ... Yet whether magnifying or compacting grief, elegy's affectivity is recognizable by family resemblances across cultural and historical boundaries (*A Transnational* 72).

45 Roger Griffin offered in *Modernism and Fascism* (2007) a revealing overview of recent research into the different but interrelated forms of exile associated with modernity, notably exile from a temporality of progress: "'modern' human beings feel permanently exiled from some primordial existential 'home' that was available for earlier generations in a way that alienates them from official Christian and Enlightenment values as well as any overarching teleology of progress or redemption" (48). At least two temporalities would converge in the defeat of Republicans in 1939: the temporality of Spain during the "Edad de Plata" as a modernizing nation in relation to Europe and the temporality of modernity as embodied in Spain in 1936, since the fight against fascism was seen by many in the West as a defence of modern values. Defeat reinforced a modern sense of exile as alienation from a teleology of progress. For teleological continuity, see Rüsen.

46 In his contrapuntal understanding of mourning and exile, Carlos Piera suggests a continuity which is traversed by forms of loss, absence, and/or disruption. Thus, in his view, Tomás Segovia's poetry posits "no la continuidad de lo que existía, sino la continuidad *con* lo que existía, que como en toda tradición, es sobre todo continuidad con lo que ha dejado de existir" [not the continuity of what existed, but the continuity *with* what existed, which as in every tradition, is above all continuity with what has ceased to exist] (167).

47 For the textual history of *Cuerpos presentes*, see Mainer's "Estudio." Mainer does not mention the photograph inserted in "Mínimo homenaje."

Works Cited

Abellán, José Luis. "Antonio Machado: la elaboración de pueblo como categoría cultural desde su teoría de los apócrifos." *La Torre* (University of Puerto Rico) 6.23 (July–September, 1992): 349–64.

– *El exilio como constante y como categoría.* Madrid: Biblioteca Nueva, 2001.

Adorno, Theodor. *Aesthetic Theory*. Edited by Gretel Adorno and Rolf Tiedemann. Newly translated, edited with a translator's introduction by Robert Hullot-Kentor. Bloomsbury Revelations. Bloomsbury UK, 2013.

– *Minima Moralia: Reflections on a Damaged Life*. Translated by E.F.N. Jephcott. London: Verso, 1978.

– *Negative Dialectics*. Translated by E.B. Ashton. New York: Seabury Press, 1973.

– "Parataxis." *Notes to Literature*. Edited by Rolf Tiedemann. Translated by Shierry Weber Nicholsen, Vol. 2. New York: Columbia UP, 1992. 109–49.

Aguilar Fernández, Paloma. *Memoria y olvido de la guerra civil española*. Madrid: Alianza, 1996.

Aguilar, Paloma, and Leigh A. Payne. *Revealing New Truths about Spain's Violent Past: Perpetrators' Confessions and Victim Exhumations*. London: Palgrave Macmillan, 2016.

Aguirre-Oteiza, Daniel. *El salto a lo desconocido: yo lírico y negatividad dialéctica en la poesía de la modernidad.* Vigo: Editorial Academia del Hispanismo, 2013.

Alberti, Rafael. "Ceremonia de entrega del Premio Cervantes 1983: Discurso de Rafael Alberti." *Ministerio de Cultura y Deporte del Gobierno de España*, 1983. www.mecd.gob.es/servicios-al-ciudadano-mecd/catalogo/cultura/premios/cervantes/cervantes-presentacion.html. 1 Aug. 2018.

Alcalá Galiano, Antonio. *Literatura española siglo XIX; de Moratín a Rivas*. Translated, with an introduction and notes, by Vicente Llorens. Madrid: Alianza Editorial, 1969.

– *Memorias de D. Antonio Alcalá Galiano*. Vol I. Publicadas por su hijo. Madrid: Imprenta de E. Rubiños, 1886.

– "Literature of the Nineteenth Century: Spain." *The Athenaeum*. London. (April–June 1834).

Alonso, Cecilio, ed. *Actas del Congreso Internacional "Max Aub y el laberinto español."* Vol. 1. Valencia: Ayuntamiento de Valencia, 1996.

Alonso, Monique, and Manuel Aznar Soler, ed. *Antonio Machado y el exilio republicano de 1939 en Francia.* Sevilla: Renacimiento, Biblioteca del Exilio, 2015.

Alted Vigil, Alicia. "La memoria de la república y del franquismo en el exilio." Dir. Santos Juliá, *Memoria de la Guerra y del franquismo*, 2006. 247–78.

– *La voz de los vencidos: el exilio republicano de 1939.* Madrid: Aguilar, 2005.

Alvar, Carlos, José-Carlos Mainer, and Rosa Navarro. *Breve historia de la literatura española.* Madrid: Alianza Editorial, 1997 [rev. and exp.] 2014.

Álvarez Junco, José. *Spanish Identity in the Age of Nations.* Translated by Patricia Newey and Nigel Townson. Manchester, UK; New York: Manchester UP, 2011.

Amat, Jordi. *La primavera de Múnich: esperanza y fracaso de una transición democrática.* Barcelona: Tusquets Editores, 2016.

Améry, Jean. *At the Mind's Limits: Contemplations by a Survivor on Auschwitz and Its Realities.* Translated by Sidney Rosenfeld and Stella P. Rosenfeld. Bloomington: Indiana UP, 1980.

Appiah, Kwame Anthony. *Cosmopolitanism: Ethics in a World of Strangers.* New York: Norton, 2006.

– "Education for Global Citizenship." *Why Do We Educate?: Renewing the Conversation.* Edited by David L. Coulter, Gary Fenstermacher, and John R. Wiens. Malden, MA: Blackwell, 2008. 84–99. 1 Sept. 2017.

– *Ethics of Identity.* Princeton: Princeton UP, 2005.

– *The Lies that Bind: Rethinking Identity.* New York: Norton, 2018.

Aristotle. *Rhetoric.* Translated by W. Rhys Roberts. Compiled by Lee Honeycutt. 27 Sept. 2011. Accessed 1 Sept. 2017.

Armistead, Samuel. "Epic and Ballad in the Hispanic Tradition." Edited by Fernando Cabo Aseguinolaza, Anxo Abuín González, and César Domínguez. *A Comparative History of Literatures in the Iberian Peninsula.* 502–9.

Assmann, Aleida. "Europe: A Community of Memory?" *GHI Bulletin* 40 (2007): 11–25, 15 Nov. 2014.

Assmann, Aleida, and Sebastian Conrad. *Memory in a Global Age: Discourses, Practices and Trajectories.* Basingstoke: Palgrave Macmillan, 2010.

Auden, W.H. *Collected Poems.* Edited by Edward Mendelson. New York: Modern Library, 2007.

Aub, Max. "Antonio Machado." *Sala de espera* 18. Mexico City: Gráficos Guanajuato, 1950, 12–15.

– *Campo cerrado.* Mexico City: Tezontle, 1943.

– *Campo de los almendros.* Edited by Francisco Caudet. Madrid: Castalia, [1967] 2000.

– *Campo francés.* Paris: Ruedo Ibérico, 1965.

– "El cementerio de Djelfa." *Historias de la mala muerte.* Mexico City: Joaquín Mortiz, 1965. 73–84.

– *Cuerpos presentes.* Edited by José-Carlos Mainer. Segorbe: Fundación Max Aub, 2001.

– *Diario de Djelfa.* 1944. Mexico City: Mortiz, 1970.

– *Diarios (1939–1972).* Edited by Manual Aznar Soler. Barcelona: Alba Editorial, 1998.

– *Ensayos mexicanos.* Mexico City: Universidad Nacional Autónoma de México, 1974.

– *La gallina ciega. Diario español.* Edited by Manual Aznar Soler. Barcelona: Alba Editorial, 1995.
– *Hablo como hombre.* Edited by Gonzalo Sobejano. Segorbe: Fundación Max Aub, 2002.
– *Jusep Torres Campalans. Novelas escogidas.* Mexico City: Aguilar, 1970. 635–876.
– "León Felipe." *Ínsula* 265 (December 1968): 3, 15.
– *Luis Buñuel, novela.* Edited by Carmen Peire. Granada: Cuadernos del Vigía, 2013.
– *Manual de historia de la literatura española.* Mexico City: Pormaca, 1966.
– "Manuscrito Cuervo." *Últimos cuentos de la guerra de España.* Caracas: Monte Ávila, 1969. 145–214.
– "Mínimo homenaje." *Revista de la Universidad de México.* XII.6 (February 1958): 16.
– *Nuevos diarios inéditos: 1939–1972.* Edited by Manuel Aznar Soler. Sevilla: Renacimiento, 2003.
– *Obras completas: Vol. I.* Edited by Juan Oleza and Arcadio López-Casanova. Valencia: Biblioteca Valenciana-Institució Alfons el Magnànim, 2001.
– *Obras completas: Vol. VII.* Edited by Silvia Monti. Valencia: Biblioteca Valenciana-Institució Alfons el Magnànim, 2002.
– *Poesía mexicana: 1950–1960.* Mexico City: Aguilar, 1960.
– "El teatro español sacado a la luz de las tinieblas de nuestro tiempo" *Triunfo.* Año 27. vol. 507 (17 June 1972): 56–69 [I–XI].
– *La verdadera historia de la muerte de Francisco Franco y otros cuentos.* Mexico City: Libro Mex Editores, 1960.
– "Al volver del entierro de Cernuda." *Revista de la Universidad de México.* XIII.5 (January 1964): 31.
Aznar Soler, Manuel. *República literaria y revolución.* Prologue by José-Carlos Mainer. Sevilla: Renacimiento Editorial, 2010.
– "Morir de exilio: homenajes a la memoria de Antonio Machado por parte del exilio republicano en Francia (1940 y 1945)." Edited by Monique Alonso and Manuel Aznar Soler. *Antonio Machado y el exilio republicano de 1939 en Francia.* 62–76.
Aznar Soler, Manuel, and José Ramón López García, eds. *El exilio republicano de 1939 y la segunda generación.* Sevilla: Renacimiento, 2011.
Aznar Soler, Manuel, and Idoia Murga Castro. *1939: Exilio republicano español.* Madrid: Ministerio de Justicia, 2019.
Badiou, Alain. *The Age of the Poets and Other Writings.* Edited and translated by by Bruno Bosteels with an introduction by Emily Apter and Bruno Bosteels. London-New York: Verso, 2014.
Baer, Alejandro. "The Voids of Sepharad: The Memory of the Holocaust in Spain." *Journal* of *Spanish Cultural Studies* 12:1 (2011): 95–120.
Bahti, Timothy. *Ends of the Lyric: Direction and Consequence in Western Poetry.* Baltimore: Johns Hopkins UP, 1996.
Balibrea, Mari Paz. "El paradigma exilio." *Nuevo Texto Crítico.* 15.29–32 (2002):17–39.
– "Rethinking Spanish Republican Exile: An Introduction." *Journal* of *Spanish Cultural Studies* 6.1 (2005): 3–24.

– "Temporalidad exílica." Coord. Mari Paz Balibrea. *Líneas de fuga: hacia otra historiografía cultural del exilio republicano español.* 146–51.

– *Tiempo de exilio: una mirada crítica a la modernidad española desde el pensamiento republicano en el exilio.* Barcelona: Montesinos, 2007.

Balibrea, Mari Paz, coord. *Líneas de fuga: hacia otra historiografía cultural del exilio republicano español.* Tres Cantos, Madrid: Siglo XXI de España Editores, 2017.

Balibrea, Mari Paz, and Sebastiaan Faber. "Hacia otra historiografía cultural del exilio republicano español. Introducción a modo de manifiesto." Coord. Mari Paz Balibrea. *Líneas de fuga: hacia otra historiografía cultural del exilio republicano español:* 13–24.

Baquero, Gastón. *Darío, Cernuda y otros temas poéticos.* Madrid: Editora Nacional, 1969.

Barón Palma, Emilio. *T.S. Eliot en España.* Almería: Universidad de Almería, Servicio de Publicaciones, 1996.

Barthes, Roland. *Camera Lucida: Reflections on Photography.* Translated by Richard Howard. New York: Hill & Wang, 1981.

– *Image, Music, Text.* Essays selected and translated by Stephen Heath. London: Fontana Press, 1977.

Bartra, Roger. "Allegories of Creativity and Territory." *PMLA*118.1 (Jan. 2003): 114–19.

– "Interview by Mari Paz Balibrea". *Journal of Spanish Cultural Studies* 6.1 (2005): 123–31.

Baudelaire, Charles. *Selected Writings on Art and Literature.* Translated with an Introduction by P.E Charvet. London: Penguin Classics, 2006.

Bauer, Yehuda. "What Was the Holocaust?" *Rethinking the Holocaust.* New Haven: Yale UP, 2001. 1–13.

Bellón Aguilera, José Luis. "La Historia social de la literatura española. Recepción y Polémica." *Sociología histórica.* 2 (2013): 239–61.

Beltrán Almería, Luis. "Las formas simples del romancero hispano." *Revista de Filología Española* 95.1 (January–June 2015): 25–44.

– "Hispanism and New Historicism." Edited by Brad Epps and Luis Fernández Cifuentes. *Spain Beyond Spain: Modernity, Literary History and National Identity.* 270–81.

– *¿Qué es la historia literaria?* Madrid: Editorial Mare Nostrum, 2007.

Benigno, Francesco. *Words in Time: A Plea for Historical Re-thinking.* Abingdon, Oxon; New York, NY: Routledge, 2017.

Benhabib, Seyla. *Exile, Statelessness, and Migration: Playing Chess with History from Hannah Arendt to Isaiah Berlin.* Princeton: Princeton UP, 2018.

Benítez Ariza, José Manuel. "*Ligero de equipaje. La vida de Antonio Machado,* Ian Gibson." Review. *El Mundo.* 20 Apr. 2006. 1 Sept. 2017.

Benjamin, Walter. *The Arcades Project.* Edited by Rolf Tiedemann. Translated by Howard Eiland and Kevin McLaughlin. Cambridge: Belknap Press of Harvard UP, 2002.

– *Illuminations.* Edited and with an introduction by Hannah Arendt. Translated by Harry Zohn. New York: Harcourt, Brace & World, 1968.

– "Theses on the Philosophy of History." *Illuminations.* Edited and with an introduction by Hannah Arendt. Translated by Harry Zohn. New York, Harcourt, Brace & World, 1968. 253–64.

– *The Origin of German Tragic Drama*. Translated by John Osborne. London: NLB, 1977.

Bergamín, José. "Antonio Machado." Antonio Machado. *Obras*. Mexico City: Editorial Séneca, 1940. 9–21.

– "Volver." *Entregas de la Licorne*. Segunda época. 5.11. (Montevideo 1958): 59–60.

Bertrand de Muñoz, Maryse. *Romances populares y anónimos de la Guerra de España*. Madrid: Calambur Editorial, 2006.

Bhabha, Homi K. *The Location of Culture*. London; New York: Routledge, 2004.

– "Unsatisfied: Notes on Vernacular Cosmopolitanism." *Text and Nation: Cross-disciplinary Essays on Cultural and National Identities*. Edited by Laura García-Morena and Peter C. Pfeifer. Columbia, SC: Camden House, 1996. 191–207.

Binns, Niall. *Voluntarios con gafas: escritores extranjeros en la Guerra Civil española*. Madrid: Mare Nostrum Comunicación, 2009.

Blake Ewing, Alexander. "Conceptions of Reinhart Koselleck's Theory of Historical Time in the Thinking of Michael Oakeshott." *History of European Ideas*. 42.3 (2016): 412–29.

Blanco Aguinaga, Carlos. "La literatura del exilio en su historia." *Migraciones y Exilios. Cuadernos de AEMIC, UNED* 3 (2002): 23–42.

Blanco Aguinaga, Carlos, Julio Rodríguez Puértolas, and Iris M. Zavala. *Historia social de la literatura española (en lengua castellana)*. Vol. 2, 1978. Madrid: Akal, 2000.

Bloch, Ernst. "Nonsynchronism and the Obligation to Its Dialectics." Translated by Mark Ritter. *New German Critique* 11 (1 April 1977): 22–38.

Bloom, Harold. *Genius: A Mosaic of One Hundred Exemplary Creative Minds*. New York: Warner Books, 2002.

Bonet, Juan Manuel. "Para un mapa del exilio republicano." Edited by Manuel Aznar Soler and Idoia Murga Castro. *1939: Exilio republicano español*. 11–46.

Bou, Enric, "Poetry between 1920 and 1940." Edited by David T. Gies. *The Cambridge History of Spanish Literature*. 555–68.

Braudel, Fernand. "History and the Social Sciences: The Long Duration." Translated and abridged by Morton and Florence Kroll. *American Behavioral Scientist* 3.6 (1960): 3–13.

Breckenridge, Carol A., Sheldon Pollock, Homi K. Bhabha, and Dipesh Chakrabarty, eds. *Cosmopolitanism*. Durham: Duke UP, 2002.

Brewster, Scott. *Lyric*. New York: Routledge, 2009.

Brodsky, Joseph. *On Grief and Reason: Essays*. New York: Farrar, Straus and Giroux, 1995.

Bühler, Karl. *Theory of Language: The Representational Function of Language*. Translated by Donald Fraser Goodwin, in collaboration with Achim Eschbach. Amsterdam; Philadelphia: John Benjamins Pub. Co., 2011.

Burke, Peter. *Exiles and Expatriates in the History of Knowledge, 1500–2000*. Waltham, MA: Brandeis UP, 2017.

Buse, Peter, and Andrew Stott. "Introduction: A Future for Haunting." Edited by Peter Buse and Andrew Stott. *Ghosts: Deconstruction, Psychoanalysis, History*. Basingstoke: Macmillan; New York: St. Martin's Press, 1999. 1–20.

Butler, Judith. "Personhood and Other Objects: The Figural Dispute with Philosophy." Barbara Johnson. *The Barbara Johnson Reader: The Surprise of Otherness*. Edited by Melissa Feuerstein, Bill Johnson González, Lili Porten, Keja Valens. Durham: Duke UP, 2014. xvii–xxv.

Cabo Aseguinolaza, Fernando. "The European Horizon of Peninsular literary historiographical discourses." Edited by Fernando Cabo Aseguinolaza, Anxo Abuín González, and César Domínguez. *A Comparative History of Literatures in the Iberian Peninsula*. 1–52.

Cabo Aseguinolaza, Fernando, Anxo Abuín González, and César Domínguez, eds. *A Comparative History of Literatures in the Iberian Peninsula*. Amsterdam; Philadelphia: John Benjamins Pub. Co., 2010–2016.

Cadava, Eduardo. *Words of Light: Theses on the Photography of History*. Princeton: Princeton UP, 1997.

Caffarel, Carmen. "Declaraciones de Carmen Caffarel sobre el fallecimiento de Tomás Segovia." Cervantes.es. 8 Nov. 2011. 1 Sept. 2017.

Cameron, Sharon. *Lyric Time: Dickinson and the Limits of Genre*. Baltimore: Johns Hopkins UP, 1979.

Camprubí, Zenobia. *Diario. 1: Cuba (1937–1939)*. Edited and translated by Graciela Palau de Nemes. Madrid: Alianza Editorial; [Río Piedras, P.R.]: Editorial de la Universidad de Puerto Rico, 1991.

Carbajosa, Mónica, and Pablo Carbajosa. *La corte literaria de José Antonio: la primera generación cultural de la Falange*. Foreword by José-Carlos Mainer. Barcelona: Crítica, 2003.

Carner, Josep, *Nabi, poema*. Mexico City: Séneca, 1940.

Carr, Raymond. *Modern Spain: 1875–1980*. Oxford; New York: Oxford UP, 1980.

Carreira, Antonio. "Introduction." Luis Cernuda. *Poesía del exilio*. Edited by Antonio Carreira. Madrid: Fondo de Cultura Económica, 2003.

– "Rasgos formales en la poesía de Max Aub". Edited by James Valender and Gabriel Rojo. *Homenaje a Max Aub*. 183–96.

– *A vueltas con el exilio (de Juan José Domenchina a Gerardo Deniz)*. Mexico City: El Colegio de México, 2015.

Carreño, Antonio. "Antología traducida, de Max Aub: la alegoría de las máscaras múltiples." *Ínsula* 406 (September 1980): 1, 10.

– "Hacia una morfología de *Personae* y máscaras: el caso Max Aub." Edited by Cecilio Alonso. *Actas del Congreso Internacional "Max Aub y el laberinto español."* 137–55.

– "Las otras 'Más/caras' de Max Aub: 'Antología traducida' (II)." *Ínsula* 569 (May 1994): 8–10.

Casado, Miguel. *Los artículos de la polémica y otros textos sobre poesía*. Madrid: Biblioteca Nueva, 2005.

– *La experiencia de lo extranjero: ensayos sobre poesía*. Barcelona: Galaxia Gutenberg – Círculo de Lectores, 2009.

– "Sobre historia, crítica y poética en la poesía española contemporánea." *Hofstra Hispanic Review* 2.4, Spring (2007): 9–24.

Casanova, Julián. "Ronald Fraser, la elegancia narrativa." *El País*. 13 Feb. 2012. 1 Sept. 2017.

Cassin, Barbara, ed. *Dictionary of Untranslatables: A Philosophical Lexicon*. Translated and edited by Emily Apter, Jacques Lezra, and Michael Wood. Princeton: Princeton UP, 2014.

Castellet, J.M. *Un cuarto de siglo de poesía española, 1939–1964*. Barcelona: Seix Barral, 1966.

Castilla del Pino, Carlos. "El uso moral de la memoria." *El País*. 25 July 2006. 1 Sept. 2017.

– *Pretérito imperfecto*. Barcelona: Tusquets Editores, 1997.

Castro, Américo. *España en su historia; cristianos, moros y judíos*. Buenos Aires: Editorial Losada, 1948.

– *The Structure of Spanish History*. Princeton: Princeton UP, 1954.

Caudet, Francisco. *El exilio republicano de 1939*. Madrid: Cátedra, 2005.

– *Galdos y Max Aub: poéticas del realismo*. Alicante: Publicaciones de la Universidad de Alicante, 2011.

– "Introducción." Max Aub. *Campo de los almendros*. Edited by Francisco Caudet. Madrid: Castalia, 2000. 7–111.

– "Mediterrani y Senyera: Dos revistas del exilio valenciano." *El exilio valenciano en América: obra y memoria*. Albert Girona Albuixech and María Fernanda Mancebo, coord. Universitat de València: Diputación Provincial de Alicante, Instituto Alicantino de Cultura Juan Gil-Albert, 1995. 69–86.

Cercas, Javier. *Soldados de Salamina*. Barcelona: Tusquets Editores, 2001.

– *Soldiers of Salamis*. Translated by Anne McLean. New York: Bloomsbury, 2004.

Cernuda, Luis. *Desolation of the Chimera: Last Poems*. Translated by Stephen Kessler. Buffalo: White Pine, 2009.

– *Epistolario, 1924–1963*. Madrid: Publicaciones de la Residencia de Estudiantes, 2003.

– *Forbidden Pleasures: New Selected Poems, 1924–1949*. Translated by Stephen Kessler. Boston MA: Black Widow P, 2015.

– *Las nubes – Desolación de la Quimera*. Edited by Luis Antonio de Villena. Madrid: Cátedra, 1984.

– *Obra completa I: Poesía completa*. Edited by Derek Harris and Luis Maristany. Madrid: Siruela, 1993.

– *Obra completa II: Prosa I*. Edited by Derek Harris and Luis Maristany. Madrid: Siruela, 1994.

– *Obra completa III: Prosa II*. Edited by Derek Harris and Luis Maristany. Madrid: Siruela, 1994.

– *Poesía del exilio*. Edited with an introduction by Antonio Carreira. Madrid: Fondo de Cultura Económica, 2003.

– *Selected Poems*. Edited and translated by Reginald Gibbons. The Sheep Meadow P: Riverdale-On-Hudson, New York, 1999.

– "Words Before a Reading." *A Poet's Work: 29 Poets on the Origins and Practice of Their Art*. Edited and translated by Reginald Gibbons. Chicago: U of Chicago P. 42–8.

– *Written in Water: The Prose Poems of Luis Cernuda.* Translated by Stephen Kessler. San Francisco: City Lights Books, 2004.

Chacel, Rosa. *Poesía (1931–1991).* Edited by Antoni Marí. Barcelona: Tusquets Editores, 1992.

Chiasson, Dan. "Vanities & Regrets." *New York Review of Books.* 8 June 2017. 34–5.

Chirbes, Rafael. "El yo culpable." *El novelista perplejo.* Barcelona: Anagrama, 2004. 169–96.

Cilleruelo, José Ángel. "Comprometidos y apócrifos. Los poemas de Max Aub." *Quimera* 168 (April 1998): 57–61.

Ciplijauskaité, Biruté. "Diary." Review of Zenobia Camprubí. *Diario. 1: Cuba (1937-1939). World Literature Today* 66.2 (1992): 314.

– "Nationalization of Arcadia in Exilic poetry." *Books Abroad* 50.2 (1 Apr. 1976): 295–302.

Clayton, Michelle. *Body in Pieces.* Berkeley, CA: U of California P: 2011.

Cleary Nichols, Geraldine. "Blank Spaces: Literary History, Spain, and the Third Millennium." Edited by Brad Epps and Luis Fernández Cifuentes. *Spain Beyond Spain: Modernity, Literary History and National Identity.* 253–69.

Colmeiro, José F. "A Nation of Ghosts? Haunting, Historical Memory and Forgetting in Post-Franco Spain." *452°F: Journal of Literary Theory and Comparative Literature* 4 (2011): 17–34.

Compagnon, Antoine. *Literature, Theory, and Common Sense.* Translated by Carol Cosman. Princeton: Princeton UP, 2004.

Cornudella, Jordi. "Cinc textos sobre 'Nabí', de Josep Carner." *Llengua & Literatura.* 1 (Barcelona 1986): 407–49.

Cox, Christoph. "The (End of the) End of History." Edited by Jerry Herron. *The Ends of Theory.* Detroit: Wayne State UP, 1996.

Cox, Michael, and R. A. Gilbert. "Introduction." Edited by Michael Cox and R. A. Gilbert. *The Oxford Book of Victorian Ghost Stories.* Oxford: Oxford UP, 2003. IX–XX.

Crespo, Ángel. "Introducción." Juan Ramón Jiménez. *Guerra en España, 1936–1953.* Barcelona: Seix Barral, 1985. 5–18.

Cruz, Juan. "Colliure celebró el cuarenta aniversario de la muerte de Antonio Machado." *El País.* 28 Feb. 1979. 1 Sept. 2017.

– "García Lorca es todos los muertos." *El País.* 19 Sept. 2008. 1 Sept. 2017.

Cuenca, Luis Alberto. "Presentación." James Valender. *Luis Cernuda: Álbum.* Madrid: Publicaciones de la Residencia de Estudiantes, 2002. 10.

Culler, Jonathan. "Changes in the Study of the Lyric." Edited by Chaviva Hošek and Patricia Parker. *Lyric Poetry: Beyond New Criticism.* 38–54.

– "Extending the *Theory of the Lyric.*" *Diacritics* 45.4 (2017): 6–14.

– "Genre: Lyric." *The Work of Genre: Collected Essays from the English Institute. ACLS Humanities E-Book.* Edited by Robyn Warhol. English Institute, 2011: 21–60, https://quod.lib.umich.edu/cgi/t/text/text-idx?c=acls;cc=acls;view=text;idno=heb90055.0001.001;rgn=div3;node=heb90055.0001.001%3A5.1.2. 1 Sept. 2017.

– *On Deconstruction.* Ithaca: Cornell UP, 1982.

– "The Language of Lyric." *Thinking Verse* 4.1 (2014): 160–76.

– *The Pursuit of Signs: Semiotics, Literature, Deconstruction.* 1981. London: Routledge, 2001.

– *Theory of the Lyric.* Cambridge: Harvard UP, 2015.

Cunningham, Valentine. "Introduction." Edited by Valentine Cunningham. *The Penguin Book of Spanish Civil War Verse.* Harmondsworth; New York: Penguin Books, 1980.

– "The Spanish Civil War." Edited by Kate McLoughlin. *The Cambridge Companion to War Writing.* Cambridge, UK; New York: Cambridge UP, 2009, 185–96.

Darío, Rubén. *Poesías completas.* Edited with an introduction and notes by Alfonso Méndez Plancarte. Expanded by Antonio Oliver Belmás. Madrid: Aguilar, 1968.

– *Los raros.* Barcelona, Buenos Aires: Maucci, 1905.

– *Selected Writings.* Edited with an introduction by Ilan Stavans. Translated by Andrew Hurley, Greg Simon, and Steven F. White. New York: Penguin Books, 2005.

De Albornoz, Aurora. "Juan Ramón Jiménez o la poesía en sucesión." Juan Ramón Jiménez. *Nueva antolojía.* Estudio preliminar y selección de Aurora de Albornoz. Barcelona: Ediciones Península, 1973.

– "Poesía de la España peregrina: crónica incompleta." Dir. José Luis Abellán. *El exilio español de 1939 IV: cultura y literatura.* Madrid: Taurus, 1977. 11–108.

– "Rubén Darío en el último verso de Antonio Machado." *Anales de Literatura Hispanoamericana* 15 (1 Jan. 1986): 247–54.

Debicki, Andrew. "Criticism and Poetic Creation: United States Critics and Contemporary Spanish Poetry 1998." *Revista de Estudios Hispánicos* 32.3 (Oct. 1998): 587–95.

– *Spanish Poetry of the Twentieth Century: Modernity and Beyond.* Lexington, Ky.: UP of Kentucky, 1994.

De Hoyos Puente, Jorge. "El exilio republicano en la historia de los exilios políticos en España." Coord. Mari Paz Balibrea. *Líneas de fuga: hacia otra historiografía cultural del exilio republicano español.* 314–19.

– *La utopía del regreso: proyectos de estado y sueños de nación en el exilio republicano en México.* Mexico City: El Colegio de México; Santander, Universidad de Cantabria, 2012.

– *¡Viva la inteligencia!: el legado de la cultura institucionista en el exilio republicano de 1939.* Madrid: Biblioteca Nueva, 2016.

Delgado, Luisa Elena. *La nación singular: fantasías de la normalidad democrática española (1996–2011).* Madrid, España: Siglo XXI de España Editores, 2014.

– "Settled in Normal: Narratives of a Prozaic (Spanish) Nation." *Arizona Journal of Hispanic Cultural Studies* 7 (2003): 117–32.

Del Molino, Sergio. *Lugares fuera de sitio: viaje por las fronteras insólitas de España.* Madrid: Espasa, 2018.

Del Pliego, Benito. "La metáfora del desplazado. En torno a los poetas latinoamericanos en España." Edited by Benito del Pliego. *Extracomunitarios: nueve poetas latinoamericanos en España.* Madrid: Fondo de Cultura Económica, 2013: 11–38.

De Man, Paul. "Autobiography as De-Facement." *MLN* 94.5 (December 1979): 919–30.

– "Lyrical Voice in Contemporary Theory: Riffaterre and Jauss." Edited by Chaviva Hošek and Patricia A. Parker. *Lyric Poetry: Beyond New Criticism*: 55–72.

– *Wartime Journalism, 1939–1943*. Edited by Werner Hamacher, Neil Hertz, and Thomas Keenan. Lincoln: U of Nebraska P, 1988.

De Rojo, Alba C., ed. *Cara y cruz: Iconografía de Max Aub*. Segorbe: Fundación Max Aub, 2000.

Derrida, Jacques. "Demeure: Fiction and Testimony." Maurice Blanchot. *The Instant of My Death*. Translated by Elizabeth Rothenberg. Stanford: Stanford UP, 2000. 13–114.

– *A Derrida Reader: Between the Blinds*. Edited by Peggy Kamuf. New York: Columbia UP, 1991.

– "The Law of Genre." Translated by Avital Ronell. *Critical Inquiry* 7.1 (Autumn 1980): 55–81.

– *Sovereignities in Question: the Poetics of Paul Celan*. Edited by Thomas Dutoit and Outi Pasanen. New York: Fordham UP, 2005.

– *Specters of Marx: The State of the Debt, the Work of Mourning, and the New International*. New York: Routledge, 1994.

De Villena, Luis Antonio. "Luis Cernuda, entre el exilio y sus metáforas." Luis Cernuda. *Las nubes – Desolación de la Quimera*. Edited by Luis Antonio de Villena. Madrid: Cátedra, 1984. 11–57.

Díaz-Más, Paloma. "Comparativism and Orality: Critical Approaches to the Ballads of *La boda estorbada* (The Thwarted Marriage)." Edited by Fernando Cabo Aseguinolaza, Anxo Abuín González, and César Domínguez, *A Comparative History of Literatures in the Iberian Peninsula*. 478–501.

Didi-Huberman, Georges. *Cuando las imágenes toman posición*. Translated by Inés Bértolo. Madrid: Antonio Machado Libros, 2008.

– *The Surviving Image: Phantoms of Time and Time of Phantoms: Aby Warburg's History of Art*. Translated by Harvey Mendelsohn. Philadelphia: Pennsylvania State UP, 2017.

Diego, Gerardo, ed. *Poesía española: antología 1915–1931*. Madrid: Editorial Signo, 1932.

Diner, Dan. "Preface." Edited by Antonio Gómez López-Quiñones and Susanne Zepp. *The Holocaust in Spanish Memory: Historical Perceptions and Cultural Discourses*. 7–8.

Dobry, Edgardo. "Cernuda y *Las nubes* (1937–1940)." *Laboratorio de poesía*, http://laboratoriopoetico.blogspot.com/2011/01/cernuda-y-las-nubes-edgardo-dobry.html. 1 Sept. 2017.

Dolar, Mladen. *A Voice and Nothing More*. Cambridge: MIT P, 2006.

Domínguez, César, and Birgit Neumann. "Introduction: Delocalizing European Literatures." *Arcadia* 53.2 (2018): 201–20.

Domínguez Michael, Christopher. *Critical Dictionary of Mexican Literature* 1955–2010: Translated by Lisa Dillman. Champaign: Dalkey Archive Press, 2012.

Duff, David. *Modern Genre Theory*. Harlow, UK; New York: Longman, 2000.

Durán, Manuel. "La calzada de los poetas: un paseo lírico por la Ciudad de México." Edited by José María Naharro-Calderón. *El exilio de las Españas de 1939 en las Américas: "¿Adónde fue la canción?"*. 213–26.

– "Josep Carner in Mexico: As I Remember Him." *Catalan Review* 6.1–2 (Barcelona 1992): 421–8.

– "Max Aub, entre el humorismo y la ética." *Ínsula* 5 (July–Aug. 1973): 320–1.

Eagleton, Terry. *How to Read a Poem*. Malden, MA: Blackwell Pub., 2007.

English, James F. *The Economy of Prestige: Prizes, Awards, and the Circulation of Cultural Value*. Cambridge, MA: Harvard UP, 2005.

Enjuto Rangel, Cecilia. *Cities in Ruins: The Politics of Modern Poetics*. West Lafayette, IN.: Purdue UP, 2010.

Epps, Brad. "Before Postnationalism: Supernationalism, Modernisme, and Catalonia." *Arizona Journal of Hispanic Cultural Studies* 7 (2003): 133–60.

Epps, Brad, and Luis Fernández Cifuentes, eds. *Spain Beyond Spain: Modernity, Literary History and National Identity*. Lewisburg: Bucknell UP, 2005.

Espinosa, Jorge Luis. "Gana Tomás Segovia premio de Literatura Juan Rulfo 2005." *El Universal.mx*. 2 Aug. 2005. 10 Oct. 2015.

Ette, Ottmar. *Writing-between-Worlds: TransArea Studies and the Literatures-Without-a-Fixed-Abode*. Berlin; Boston: De Gruyter, 2016.

Faber, Sebastiaan. *Anglo-American Hispanists and the Spanish Civil War: Hispanophilia, Commitment, and Discipline*. New York: Palgrave Macmillan, 2008.

– "Beyond the Nation: Spanish Civil War Exile and the Problem of Iberian Cultural History." Edited by Javier Munoz, Laura Lonsdale and Manuel Delgado. *Routledge Companion to Iberian Studies*. 427–38.

– "Elogio del olvido." *FronteraD*. 16 Feb. 2012. 1 Sept. 2017.

– "Español sin ganas: 50 años sin Luis Cernuda." *La Marea*. 5 Nov. 2013. 1 Sept. 2017.

– *Exile and Cultural Hegemony: Spanish Intellectuals in Mexico, 1939–1975*. Nashville: Vanderbilt UP, 2002.

– "Hispanism, Transatlantic Studies, and the Problem of Cultural History." Edited by Akiko Tsuchiya and William G. Acree Jr. *Empire's End: Transnational Connections in the Hispanic World*. Nashville: Vanderbilt UP, 2015. 17–33.

– "Max Aub's Civil War in English." *The Volunteer*, 6 Mar. 2010, www.albavolunteer.org/2010/03/max-aub%E2%80%99s-civil-war-in-english/. 15 Aug. 2010.

– *Memory Battles of the Spanish Civil War: History, Fiction, Photography*. Nashville: Vanderbilt UP, 2018.

– "The Spanish Holocaust: Reframing the Civil War." *The Volunteer*. 13 June 2012. 15 Nov. 2014.

– "La traición de los intelectuales." Review of Andrés Trapiello, *Las armas y las letras*, 3rd ed. (Madrid: Destino, 2010). *Ínsula* 809 (May 2014): 10–12.

– "The Truth Behind Jusep Torres Campalans: Max Aub's Committed Postmodernism." *Hispania* 87.2 (2004): 237–46.

Fagen, Patricia W. *Exiles and Citizens: Spanish Republicans in Mexico.* Austin, Tex: U of Texas Press, 1973.

Fanger, Donald, Luis Fernández-Cifuentes, Francisco Márquez-Villanueva, and Susan Rubin Suleiman. "Claudio Guillén: Faculty of Arts and Sciences – Memorial Minute." *Harvard Gazette.* 17 Feb. 2011. 1 Sept. 2017.

Felipe, León. *Antología rota.* Edited by Miguel Galindo. Madrid: Cátedra, 2008.

– *Antología rota: 1930–1947.* Buenos Aires: Pleamar, 1947.

– *Español del éxodo y el llanto: Doctrina, elegías y canciones.* Mexico City: La Casa de España en México, 1939.

– "Habla el prólogo." Walt Whitman. *Canto a mí mismo.* Translated by León Felipe. Buenos Aires: Editorial Losada, 1941. 9–21.

– "Palabras ..." *Renacimiento* 27/30, "Las Literaturas del Exilio Republicano de 1939" (2000), 135–6.

– "Poesía e Hispanidad." *Revista de América* 7.20 (Aug. 1946): 145–53.

Felman, Shoshana. "Education and Crisis, or the Vicissitudes of Teaching." Shoshana Felman and Dori Laub. *Testimony: Crises of Witnessing in Literature, Psychoanalysis, and History.* New York: Routledge, 1992. 1–56.

Felman, Shoshana, and Dori Laub. *Testimony: Crises of Witnessing in Literature, Psychoanalysis, and History.* New York: Routledge, 1992.

Fernández Cifuentes, Luis. "Las autobiografias de Blanco White: tres divergencias." Edited by Eduardo Subirats. *José María Blanco White, crítica y exilio.* Rubí, Barcelona: Anthropos, 2005. 25–67.

– "Discursos del método." *Quimera* 139 (September 1995): 36–43.

– "Estudio introductorio." Max Aub. *Obras completas: Vol. VI.* Edited by Luis Fernández Cifuentes. Valencia: Biblioteca Valenciana-Institució Alfons el Magnànim, 2007. 11–47.

– "Resistencia vital." *Revista de libros* 122 (2007): 34–6.

Ferrán, Ofelia. *Working Through Memory: Writing and Remembrance in Contemporary Spanish Narrative.* Lewisburg: Bucknell UP, 2007.

Ferrater, Gabriel. "Prólogo." Josep Carner. *Nabí.* Edited and translated by José Agustin Goytisolo and Juan Ramon Masoliver. Barcelona: Edicions del Mall, 1986. 9–26.

Ferriz Roure, Teresa. "Estudio de España Peregrina (1940): Una revista para la continuación de la cultura española en el exilio mexicano." Alicante: Biblioteca Virtual Miguel de Cervantes, 2002. www.cervantesvirtual.com.

Folkart, Jessica A. *Liminal Fiction at the Edge of the Millennium: The Ends of Spanish Identity.* Lewisburg: Bucknell UP, 2014.

Fonseca, Diego. "What was Franco's role in the deportation of 10,000 Spaniards to Nazi camps?" *El País.* 26 Apr. 2019. 1 May 2019.

Ford, Hugh. *A Poet's War: British Poets and the Spanish Civil War.* Philadelphia: U of Pennsylvania Press, 1965.

Fotheringham, Alasdair. "Tomás Segovia: One of Spain's 'Poets in Exile' during the Franco Dictatorship." *The Independent* 17 Nov. 2011. 1 Sept. 2017.

Fraser, Ronald. *Blood of Spain: An Oral History of the Spanish Civil War*. New York: Pantheon, 1979.

– *Recuérdalo tú y recuérdalo a otros: historia oral de la guerra civil española*. Translated by Jordi Beltrán. Barcelona: Editorial Crítica, 1997.

– *Recuérdalo tú y recuérdalo a otros: historia oral de la guerra civil española*. Translated by Jordi Beltrán. Barcelona: Editorial Crítica, 2001.

– *Recuérdalo tú y recuérdalo a otros: historia oral de la guerra civil española*. Translated by Jordi Beltrán. Barcelona: Editorial Crítica, 2007.

– *Recuérdalo tú y recuérdalo a otros: historia oral de la guerra civil española*. Translated by Jordi Beltrán. Barcelona: Editorial Crítica, 2016.

Freud, Sigmund. *The Uncanny*. Translated by David McLintock; introduction by Hugh Haughton. New York: Penguin Books, 2003.

García Gutiérrez, Rosa, ed. *Juan Ramón Jiménez e Hispanoamérica: diálogos, exilios, resiliencia*. Biblioteca de estudios juanramonianos, 4. Huelva: Universidad de Huelva, Servicio de Publicaciones; Diputación de Huelva, Servicio de Publicaciones y Biblioteca, 2018.

– "Presentación." *Juan Ramón Jiménez e Hispanoamérica: diálogos, exilios, resiliencia*. Edited by Rosa García Gutiérrez. Biblioteca de estudios juanramonianos, 4. Huelva: Universidad de Huelva, Servicio de Publicaciones; Diputación de Huelva, Servicio de Publicaciones y Biblioteca, 2018. 15–18.

García Lorca, Federico. *Collected Poems*. Introduction by Christopher Maurer. Translated by Catherine Brown et al. New York: Farrar, Straus and Giroux, 2002.

García Martín, José Luis, ed. *Poetas del novecientos: entre el modernismo y la vanguardia: antología*. 2 vols. Colección Obra Fundamental. Madrid: Fundación Central Hispano, 2001.

García Montero, Luis. "Luis Cernuda: el futuro es hoy." *El País* 4 Nov. 2013. 1 Sept. 2017.

– *El sexto día*. Madrid: Debate, 2000.

García Posada, Miguel. "¡Ya se fueron!" *El País* 15 Nov. 1996. 1 Sept. 2017.

Gay, Juan Pascual. "'Cuaderno del nómada': una poesía de la intemperie." *Escritos: Revista del Centro de Ciencias del Lenguaje* 32 (July–Dec. 2005): 131–49.

Gaylord, Mary. "The Romance as Poetry Out Loud." *The Poetics of Hispanism / Poéticas del hispanismo*. Vanderbilt U, Nashville, Tennessee. February 2009. Conference presentation.

– "Spain, Poetry of." Ronald Greene, editor in chief; Stephen Cushman, general editor; Clare Cavanagh, Jahan Ramazani and Paul Rouzer, associate editors. *The Princeton Encyclopedia of Poetry and Poetics*. 4th ed: 1333–9.

Gerhardt, Federico. "El buen paño en el arca. Una lectura de los diarios de Max Aub." *Primer Congreso* Internacional de Literatura *y Cultura Españolas Contemporáneas*, Universidad Nacional de La Plata. Los siglos XX y XXI, 1 and 3 October 2008. 12 April 2014.

– "Max Aub revisitado: lugares en (torno a) *La gallina ciega*." *Olivar* 7.8 (2006): 275–90. https://www.olivar.fahce.unlp.edu.ar/article/view/3326. 12 April 2014.

Gibson, Ian. *Cuatro poetas en guerra*. Barcelona: Planeta, 2007.
– *Ligero de equipaje: la vida de Antonio Machado*. Madrid: Aguilar, 2006.
– "Machado era un libro abierto en sus versos." Entrevista con Jesús Ruiz Mantilla. *El País* 16 Apr. 2006. 1 Sept. 2017.
Gies, David T, ed. *The Cambridge History of Spanish Literature*. Cambridge, UK; New York: Cambridge UP, 2004.
– "The Funes Effect: Making Literary History." Edited by David T. Gies. *The Cambridge History of Spanish Literature*. 1–14.
Gil de Biedma, Jaime. "Como en sí mismo, al fin." *El pie de la página: ensayos 1955–1979*. Barcelona: Crítica, 1980. 331–47.
– *Las personas del verbo*. Barcelona: Seix-Barral, 2001.
Giles, Peter. *Transnationalism in Practice: Essays on American Studies, Literature and Religion*. Edinburgh: Edinburgh UP, 2010.
Gilroy, Paul. *The Black Atlantic: Modernity and Double Consciousness*. Cambridge, MA: Harvard UP, 1993.
Giner de los Ríos, Francisco, ed. *Las cien mejores poesías españolas del destierro*. Mexico City: Editorial Signo, 1945.
Glondys, Olga. *La guerra fría cultural y el exilio republicano español: "Cuadernos del Congreso por la Libertad de la Cultura" (1953–1965)*. Madrid: Consejo Superior de Investigaciones Científicas, 2012.
Gómez López-Quiñones, Antonio. "El Holocausto según Antonio Muñoz Molina: ética y escritura en *Sefarad*." *Ojáncano* 25 (2004): 59–76.
– "A Secret Agreement: The Historical Memory Debate and the Limits of Recognition." Edited by Luis Martín-Estudillo and Nicholas Spadaccini. *Memory and Its Discontents: Spanish Culture in the Early Twenty-First Century*. Hispanic Issues Online 11 (Fall 2012): 87–116.
Gómez López-Quiñones, Antonio, and Susanne Zepp, eds. *The Holocaust in Spanish Memory: Historical Perceptions and Cultural Discourses*. Leipzig: Leipzig UP, 2010.
González, Rigoberto. "Aurora de Albornoz (1926–1990)." *The Poetry Foundation*. 10 December 2007. 10 Oct. 2017.
González Echevarría, Roberto. "The Master of Modernismo." *The Nation*. 25 January 2006. 1 Sept. 2017. 29–33.
González Ródenas, Soledad. "Introducción". Juan Ramón Jiménez. *Guerra en España: prosa y verso (1936–1954)*. Edited by Ángel Crespo; revised and expanded by Soledad González Ródenas. Seville: Point de Lunettes, 2009. vii–cix.
Gracia, Jordi. *A la intemperie: exilio y cultura en España*. Barcelona: Anagrama, 2010.
– *La resistencia silenciosa*. Barcelona: Anagrama, 2004.
Gracia, Jordi, and Domingo Ródenas. *Historia de la literatura española. 7. Derrota y restitución de la modernidad: 1939–2010*. Barcelona: Crítica, 2011.
Graham, Helen. *The Spanish Civil War: A Very Short Introduction*. New York: Oxford UP, 2005.
– *The Spanish Republic at War, 1936–1939*. Cambridge: Cambridge UP, 2002.

– "The Spanish Holocaust: Inquisition and Extermination in Twentieth-Century Spain, By Paul Preston." *The Independent.* 2 March 2012. 15 Nov. 2014.

–, et al. "Review Forum: Paul Preston, *The Spanish Holocaust: Inquisition and Extermination in Twentieth-Century Spain.*" *Journal of Genocide Research*, vol. 16 no. 1 (2014): 139–68.

Grandes, Almudena. *El corazón helado.* Barcelona: Tusquets Editores, 2007.

– "When We Were Poor Before." *The New York Times.* 13 Dec. 2013. 1 Sept. 2017.

Greenblatt, Stephen. *Shakespearean Negotiations: The Circulation of Social Energy in Renaissance England.* Berkeley: U of California P, 1988.

Greene, Roland. *Post-Petrarchism: Origins and Innovations of the Western Lyric Sequence.* Princeton: Princeton UP, 1991.

Greene, Ronald, editor in chief; Stephen Cushman, general editor; Clare Cavanagh, Jahan Ramazani and Paul Rouzer, associate editors. *The Princeton Encyclopedia of Poetry and Poetics.* 4th ed. Princeton: Princeton UP, 2012.

Griffin, Roger. *Modernism and Fascism: The Sense of a Beginning under Mussolini and Hitler.* Basingstoke: Palgrave Macmillan, 2007.

Grohmann, Alexis. "Errant Text: *Sefarad*, by Antonio Muñoz Molina." *Journal of Iberian and Latin American Studies* 12.2–3 (August/December 2006): 233–46.

Guillén, Claudio. "De la continuidad: tiempos de historia y de cultura." Alicante: Biblioteca Virtual Miguel de Cervantes, 2003.

– "El sol de los desterrados." *Múltiples Moradas.* Barcelona: Tusquets, 1998. 29–97.

– "The Sun and the Self. Notes on Some Responses to Exile." Edited by François Jost. *Aesthetics and the Literature of Ideas: Essays in Honor of A. Owen Aldridge.* Newark: U of Delaware P, 1990. 261–82.

Guillory, John. *Cultural Capital: The Problem of Literary Canon Formation.* Chicago: U of Chicago P, 1993.

Guyer, Sara. "Before *The Human Race:* Robert Antelme's Anthropomorphic Poetry." *Critical Survey* 20.2 (2008): 31–4.

Hardcastle, Anne. "'El documental es un arma cargada de pasado': Representation in Documentary and Testimony." Edited by Carlos Jerez-Farrán and Samuel Amago. *Unearthing Franco's Legacy: Mass Graves and the Recovery of Historical Memory in Spain.* 148–55.

Harris, Derek. *Luis Cernuda: A Study of the Poetry.* London: Tamesis, 1973.

– "La poesía de Luis Cernuda." Luis Cernuda. *Obra completa I: Poesía completa.* Edited by Derek Harris and Luis Maristany. Madrid: Siruela, 2013. 45–96.

Haughton, Hugh. "Introduction." Sigmund Freud. *The Uncanny*: vii–lx.

Hernández Bautista, Bárbara. "Luis Cernuda, colaborador de la BBC: traducciones y otros trabajos perdidos." *1611: Revista de historia de la traducción* 10 (2016). 1 Sept. 2017.

Hernández, Miguel. *Obra poética completa.* Edited by Leopoldo de Luis and Jorge Urrutia. Bilbao: Zero, 1979.

Herzberger, David. "Experience into Storytelling: Antonio Muñoz Molina's *Sefarad.*" Edited by Antonio Gómez López-Quinones and Susanne Zepp. *The Holocaust in Spanish Memory: Historical Perceptions and Cultural Discourses.* 213–26.

– "Writing Without a Grain: Identity Formation in Three Works by Muñoz Molina." *Arizona Journal of Hispanic Cultural Studies* 2 (1998): 23–40.

Hobsbawm, Eric. *The Age of Extremes: The Short Twentieth Century, 1914–1991*. London: Abacus, 1994.

– "Introduction: Inventing Traditions." Edited by Eric Hobsbawm and Terence Ranger. *The Invention of Tradition*. Cambridge: Cambridge UP, 1992. 1–14.

Hodgkin Katharine, and Susannah Radstone, eds. *Memory Cultures: Memory, Subjectivity, and Recognition*. Somerset, NJ: Transaction, 2006.

Horace. *Odes and Epodes*. Edited and translated by Niall Rudd. Loeb Classical Library 33. Cambridge, MA: Harvard UP, 2004.

Hornsby, R.A., T.V.F. Brogan, and J.P. Warren. "Catalog." Ronald Greene, editor in chief; Stephen Cushman, general editor; Clare Cavanagh, Jahan Ramazani and Paul Rouzer, associate editors. *The Princeton Encyclopedia of Poetry and Poetics*. 4th ed. 214.

Hošek, Chaviva, and Patricia A. Parker (ed). *Lyric Poetry: Beyond New Criticism*. Ithaca: Cornell UP, 1985.

Houvenaghel, Eugenia M. "Cruzando fronteras nacionales. Hacia una 'cartografía' del ensayismo de Tomás Segovia." *Cuadernos del CILHA* 20.15 (2014): 27–42.

Huyssen, Andreas. "Authentic Ruins: Products of Modernity." Edited by Julia Hell and Andreas Schönle. *Ruins of Modernity*. Durham: Duke UP, 2010. 17–28.

– "Present Pasts: Media, Politics, Amnesia." *Public Culture* 12.1 (2000): 21–38.

Iarocci, Michael. "El exilio romántico y el sujeto de la modernidad." *España: ¿Laberinto de Exilios?* Newark: Juan de la Cuesta, 2005. 73–84.

– "War and the Work of Poetry: Issues in Teaching Spanish Poetry of the Civil War." Edited by Noël Valis. *Teaching Representations of the Spanish Civil War*. 184–95.

Ingleheart, Jennifer. "Introduction: Two Thousand Years of responses to Ovid's Exile." Edited by Jennifer Ingleheart. *Two Thousand Years of Solitude: Exile After Ovid*. Oxford; New York: Oxford UP, 2011.

Iravedra, Araceli. "Los poetas del cincuenta bajo el signo de Collioure." *Campo de Agramante* 11 (2009): 5–22.

Irizarry, Estelle. *La broma literaria en nuestros días: Max. Aub, Francisco Ayala, Ricardo Gullón, Carlos Ripoll, César Tiempo*. Nueva York: Eliseo Torres, 1979.

Issorel, Jacques. *Últimos días en Collioure, 1939, y otros estudios breves sobre Antonio Machado*. Sevilla: Centro de Estudios Andaluces. Editorial Renacimiento, 2016.

Jackson, Victoria. "Lyric." Ronald Greene, editor in chief; Stephen Cushman, general editor; Clare Cavanagh, Jahan Ramazani and Paul Rouzer, associate editors. *The Princeton Encyclopedia of Poetry and Poetics*. 4th ed. 826–34.

Jakobson, Roman. "Shifters and Verb Categories." *On Language*. Edited by Linda R. Waugh and Monique Monville-Burston. Cambridge, MA: Harvard UP, 1990. 386–92.

Jameson, Fredric. *Late Marxism: Adorno, or the Persistence of the Dialectic*. London; New York: Verso, 1990.

Jato, Mónica. *El lenguaje bíblico en la poesía de los exilios españoles de 1939*. Kassel: Edition Reichenberger, 2004.

Jay, Martin. "Against Consolation: Walter Benjamin and the Refusal to Mourn." Edited by Jay Winter and Emmanuel Sivan. *War and Remembrance in the Twentieth Century.* Cambridge: Cambridge UP, 1999. 221–39.

Jay, Paul. *Global Matters: The Transnational Turn in Literary Studies.* Ithaca: Cornell UP, 2010.

Jerez-Farrán, Carlos, and Samuel Amago, eds. *Unearthing Franco's Legacy: Mass Graves and the Recovery of Historical Memory in Spain.* Notre Dame: U of Notre Dame P, 2010.

Jiménez Fajardo, Salvador. "Introduction." *The Word and the Mirror: Critical Essays on the Poetry of Luis Cernuda.* Edited by Jiménez Fajardo. London: Associated UP, 1989. 11–43.

Jiménez, Juan Ramón. *Cartas: primera selección.* Compilation, selection, organization, and prologue by Francisco Garfias. Madrid: Aguilar, 1962.

– *Guerra en España, 1936–1953.* Edited by Ángel Crespo. Barcelona: Seix Barral, 1985.

– *Guerra en España: prosa y verso (1936–1954).* Edited by Ángel Crespo; revised and expanded by Soledad González Ródenas. Seville: Point de Lunettes, 2009.

– *Metamórfosis.* Edited by Antonio Sánchez Romeralo. Barcelona: Anthropos, 1990.

– *El modernismo: apuntes de curso, 1953.* Edited by Jorge Urrutia. Madrid: Visor, 1999.

– *Política poética.* Edited by Germán Bleiberg. Madrid: Alianza, 1982.

– *Vida I. Días de mi vida.* Reconstrucción, estudio y notas de Mercedes Juliá y Mª Ángeles Sanz-Manzano. Valencia: Pre-Textos, 2014.

Jiménez Heffernan, Julián. *Los papeles rotos: ensayos de poesía española contemporánea.* Madrid: Abada Editores, 2004.

Johnson, Barbara. *Persons and Things.* Cambridge MA: Harvard UP, 2008.

– *A World of Difference.* Baltimore: Johns Hopkins UP, 1987.

Johnson, Roberta. "María Zambrano's Solitude: The Silver Aged Continued." *Anales de la literatura española contemporánea* 38.1–2, *Studies in Honor of José-Carlos Mainer/ Homenaje a José-Carlos Mainer* (2013): 149–74.

Jones, Sam. "How a Capa Photo of Bombed Flats in Madrid Could Help Today's Residents." *The Guardian.* 1 Jul 2017. 10 Dec 2017.

Juliá, Mercedes. "El destino de Juan Ramón en las Américas." *Juan Ramón Jiménez e Hispanoamérica: diálogos, exilios, resiliencia.* Edited by Rosa García Gutiérrez. Biblioteca de estudios juanramonianos, 4. Huelva: Universidad de Huelva, Servicio de Publicaciones; Diputación de Huelva, Servicio de Publicaciones y Biblioteca (2018). 285–306.

Juliá, Santos. *Historias de las dos Españas.* Madrid: Taurus, 2004.

– *Memoria de la guerra y del franquismo.* Madrid: Taurus, 2006.

–, ed. *Víctimas de la guerra civil.* Madrid: Temas de Hoy, 1999.

Kamen, Henry. *The Disinherited: The Exiles who Created Spanish Culture.* London; New York: Allen Lane, 2007.

Kaplan, Carla. *The Erotics of Talk: Women's Writing and Feminist Paradigms.* New York: Oxford UP, 1996.

Keats, John. *Poetry and Prose.* New York: W.W. Norton, 2009.

Keller, Patricia. *Ghostly Landscapes: Film, Photography, and the Aesthetics of Haunting in Contemporary Spanish Culture.* Toronto: U of Toronto P, 2016.

Kessler, Stephen. "Translator's Prologue: Exile, Eros, and the Sublime." Luis Cernuda. *Desolation of the Chimera: Last Poems*. Translated by Stephen Kessler. Buffalo: White Pine, 2009. 9–12.

– "Translator's Prologue: A Timeless Contemporary." Luis Cernuda. *Forbidden Pleasures: New Selected Poems, 1924–1949*. Translated by Stephen Kessler. Boston MA: Black Widow Press, 2015. 13–19.

Kołakowski, Leszek. "In Praise of Exile." *Modernity on Endless Trial*. Chicago: U of Chicago P, 1990. 55–59.

Koselleck, Reinhart. *Futures Past: On the Semantics of Historical Time*. Translated and with an introduction by Keith Tribe. New York: Columbia UP, 2004.

– *Sediments of Time: On Possible Histories*. Translated and edited by Sean Franzel and Stefan-Ludwig Hoffmann. Stanford: Stanford UP, 2018.

Labanyi, Jo. "Introduction: Engaging with Ghosts; or, Theorizing Culture in Modern Spain." *Constructing Identity in Contemporary Spain: Theoretical Debates and Cultural Practice*. Edited by Jo Labanyi. New York: Oxford UP, 2002. 1–15.

–"History and Hauntology; or, What Does One Do with the Ghosts of the Past? Reflections on Spanish Film and Fiction of the Post-Franco Period." *Disremembering the Dictatorship: the Politics of Memory in the Spanish Transition to Democracy*. Edited by Joan Ramon Resina. Amsterdam; Atlanta, GA: Rodopi, 2000. 65–82.

– "Postmodernism and the Problem of Cultural Identity." *Spanish Cultural Studies: An Introduction. The Struggle for Modernity*. Eds. Jo Labanyi and Helen Graham. Oxford: Oxford UP, 1995. 396–406.

– "Testimonies of Repression: Methodological and Political Issues." Edited by Carlos Jerez-Farrán and Samuel Amago. *Unearthing Franco's Legacy: Mass Graves and the Recovery of Historical Memory in Spain*. 192–205.

– *Spanish literature: A Very Short Introduction*. Oxford: Oxford UP, 2010.

–, ed. *Constructing Identity in Contemporary Spain: Theoretical Debates and Cultural Practice*. Oxford: Oxford UP, 2002

Labanyi, Jo, and Helen Graham, eds. *Spanish Cultural Studies. An Introduction: The Struggle for Modernity*. Oxford: Oxford UP, 1995.

Labelle, Brandon. *Lexicon of the Mouth: Poetics and Politics of Voice and the Oral Imaginary*. New York: Bloomsbury, 2014.

Labrador, Germán. "Review of *Unearthing Franco's Legacy: Mass Graves and the Recovery of Historical Memory in Spain*. Edited by Carlos Jerez-Farrán and Samuel Amago." *Arizona Journal of Cultural Studies* 14, 2010. 379–83.

LaCapra, Dominick. "Lanzmann's 'Shoah': 'Here There Is No Why.'" *Critical Inquiry* 23.2 (Winter 1997): 231–69.

– "'Traumatropisms' From Trauma via Witnessing to the Sublime?" *History and Its Limits: Human, Animal, Violence*. Ithaca, NY: Cornell UP, 2009. 59–89.

Laclau, Ernesto. "Time Is Out of Joint." *Diacritics*. 25.2 (Summer 1995): 85–96.

Lakoff, George, and Mark Johnson. *Metaphors We Live By*. Chicago: U of Chicago P, 1980.

Lanz, Juan José. "La poesía." Edited by Santos Sanz Villanueva. *Historia y crítica de la literatura española: 1939–1975. Primer suplemento*. 70–156.

Larraz, Fernando. "El lugar del exilio." Coord. Mari Paz Balibrea. *Líneas de fuga: hacia otra historiografía cultural del exilio republicano español.* 523–32.

Layna Ranz, Francisco. "20 años de *Medusario.*" Interview with Roberto Echavarren, Jacobo Sefamí y Eduardo Espina. *Transtierros: escrituras, pensamiento, postliteratura, poéticas, transducciones y tuneos*. 10 Oct. 2017. https://transtierrosblog.wordpress.com/2017/10/10/20-anos-de-medusario-francisco-layna-ranz/. 15 Oct. 2017.

Lázaro, Esther. "Estos días azules y este sol de la infancia." Edited by Monique Alonso and Manuel Aznar Soler. *Antonio Machado y el exilio republicano de 1939 en Francia.* 118–26.

Lechner, Johannes. *El compromiso en la poesía española del siglo XX.* Leiden: Universitaire Pers Leiden, 1968.

Lee, Lisa Yun. *Dialectics of the Body: Corporeality in the Philosophy of T.W. Adorno.* New York: Routledge, 2005.

Leggott, Sarah. *Memory, War, and Dictatorship in Recent Spanish Fiction by Women.* Lewisburg: Bucknell UP, 2015.

León, María Teresa. *Memoria de la melancolía.* Edited, with an introduction and notes, by Gregorio Torres Nebrera. Madrid: Castalia, 1998.

Levine, Caroline. *Forms: Whole, Rhythm, Hierarchy, Network*. Princeton: Princeton UP, 2015.

Levy, Daniel, and Natan Sznaider. "Memory Unbound: The Holocaust and the Formation of Cosmopolitan Memory." *European Journal of Social Theory* 5 (2002): 87–106.

Lida, Clara. *Inmigración y exilio: reflexiones sobre el caso español.* Mexico City: Siglo Veintiuno Editores en coedición con el Colegio de México, 1997.

Llamazares, Julio. "Barea." *El País*. 6 Jan. 2018. 6 Jan. 2018.

Llorens, Vicente. *Estudios y ensayos sobre el exilio republicano de 1939*. Sevilla: Renacimiento, 2006.

– "Introducción." Antonio Alcalá Galiano. *Literatura española siglo XIX; de Moratín a Rivas*, 7–17.

Logan, Aileen. "'Ser de intemperie': la figura y la ética del nómada en 'Cuaderno del Nómada' de Tomás Segovia." Edited by Manuel Aznar Soler and José Ramón López García. *El exilio republicano de 1939 y la segunda generación*. 737–44.

Londero, Renata. "De viaje por el tiempo y el espacio: Jaime Gil de Biedma exiliado interior." *Les Ateliers du SAL* 5 (2014): 73–85.

López Aguilar, Enrique, ed *Los poetas hispanomexicanos: estudio y antología.* Mexico City: Universidad Autónoma Metropolitana Azcapotzalco: Ediciones EÓN, 2012.

López Casanova, Arcadio. "Estudio introductorio." Max Aub. *Obras completas: Vol. I.* Edited by Juan Oleza and Arcadio López Casanova. Valencia: Biblioteca Valenciana, 2001. 5–49.

López Castro, Armando. *El rostro en el espejo: lecturas de Unamuno*. Salamanca: Ediciones Universidad de Salamanca, 2010.

López-García, José Ramón. "Antonio Machado y la poesía del exilio republicano: un camino por andar." Edited by Monique Alonso and Manuel Aznar Soler. *Antonio Machado y el exilio republicano de 1939 en Francia*. 127–40.

– "Un cielo gris: la poesía del exilio republicano español en Francia." Edited by Manuel Aznar Soler and Idoia Murga Castro. *1939: Exilio republicano español.* 627–36.

Lorenz, Chris. "Unstuck in Time. Or: the Sudden Presence of the Past." Edited by Karin Tilmans, Frank van Vree, and Jay Winter. *Performing the Past: Memory, History, and Identity in Modern Europe.* Amsterdam: Amsterdam UP, 2010. 67–102.

Loureiro, Ángel. *The Ethics of Autobiography: Replacing the Subject in Modern Spain.* Nashville: Vanderbilt UP, 2000.

– "Inconsolable Memory." *Armed Resistance: Cultural Representations of the Anti-Francoist Guerrilla.* Edited by Antonio Gómez López-Quiñones and Carmen Moreno-Nuño. Hispanic Issues Online (Fall 2012): 100–22. 1 Sept. 2017.

Löwy, Michael. *Fire Alarm: Reading Walter Benjamin's "On the Concept of History."* Translated by Chris Turner. London: Verso, 2005.

Machado, Antonio. *Poesías de guerra.* Edited by Aurora de Albornoz. San Juan de Puerto Rico: Ediciones Asomante, 1961.

– *Poesía y prosa. Tomo II: Poesías completas.* Critical edition by Oreste Macrí and Gaetano Chiappini. Madrid: Espasa-Calpe-Fundación Antonio Machado, 1989.

Machado, Antonio, et al. *Poetas de la España leal.* Edited by Manuel Aznar Soler. Reprint of the 1937 ed. published by Ediciones Españoles, Madrid. Sevilla: Renacimiento / Sociedad Estatal de Conmemoraciones Culturales, 2017.

Madariaga, Salvador. *Hernán Cortés – Conqueror of Mexico.* New York: Macmillan Company, 1941.

Maier, Charles. *Once Within Borders: Territories of Power, Wealth, and Belonging since 1500.* Cambridge, Massachusetts: The Belknap Press of Harvard UP, 2016.

Mainer, José-Carlos. "The Dialogue of Iberian Literary Nationalisms." Edited by Fernando Cabo Aseguinolaza, Anxo Abuín González, and César Domínguez. *A Comparative History of Literatures in the Iberian Peninsula.* 641–52.

– "Estudio introductorio." Max Aub. *Cuerpos presentes.* Edited by José-Carlos Mainer. Segorbe: Fundación Max Aub, 2001. 9–37.

– "La ética del testigo: la vanguardia como moral en Max Aub." Edited by Cecilio Alonso. *Actas del Congreso Internacional "Max Aub y El laberinto español.".* 69–92.

– *Historia mínima de la literatura española.* Mexico City: El Colegio de México; Madrid: Turner, 2014.

– "Max Aub entre la antiespaña y la literatura universal." *Ínsula* 320–1 (July– Aug. 1973): 320–1.

Mainer, José-Carlos, gen ed. *Historia de la literatura española.* Barcelona: Crítica, 2010–13.

Malcolm Gaylord, Mary. "Imagen y voz en el *Cántico espiritual* de San Juan de la Cruz." Edited by Mary M. Gaylord and Francisco Márquez Villanueva. *Fray Luis de León and San Juan de la Cruz: A Commemorative Symposium.* Newark, DE: Juan de la Cuesta, 1998. 97–108.

Malgat, Gérard. *Max Aub y Francia o la esperanza traicionada.* Sevilla: Renacimiento, 2007.

Mallarmé, Stéphane. *Selected Poetry and Prose.* Edited by Mary Ann Caws. New York: New Directions Books, 1982.

Malpartida, Juan. *La perfección indefensa: ensayos sobre literatura en lengua española del siglo XX.* Mexico City: Fondo de Cultura Económica, 1998.

Manent, Albert. "Josep Carner y América." *Cuadernos hispanoamericanos* 412 (October 1984): 15–21.

Marco, Jorge. "Genocidio y 'Genocide Studies': Definiciones y debates." *Hispania Nova* 10 (2007): 1–39. 15 Nov. 2014.

Marichal, Juan, and Octavio Paz. *Las cosas en su sitio: sobre la literatura española del siglo XX.* Mexico City: Finisterre, 1971.

Marks, Herbert. "The Book of Psalms." *The English Bible: King James Version (V. 1. The Old Testament).* Edited by Herbert Marks. New York: Norton, 2012. 955–8.

Márquez Villanueva, Francisco. "Américo Castro: entonces y ahora." *El pensamiento de Américo Castro. La tradición corregida por la razón.* 1 Sept. 2017.

Martí-López, Elsa. "Autochthonous Conflicts, Foreign Fictions." Edited by Brad Epps and Luis Fernández Cifuentes. *Spain Beyond Spain: Modernity, Literary History and National Identity.* 148–67.

Martín-Estudillo, Luis. "Muñoz Molina, Sebald y la identidad desheredada de Europa." *Ínsula* 737 (May 2008): 8–10.

Martín Gijón, Mario. "España, español." Coord. Mari Paz Balibrea. *Líneas de fuga: hacia otra historiografía cultural del exilio republicano español.* 62–8.

Martiny, Erik, ed. *A Companion to Poetic Genre.* Chichester; Hoboken, NJ: Wiley-Blackwell, 2012.

Mateo Gambarte, Eduardo. *Diccionario del exilio español en México (de Carlos Blanco Aguinaga a Ramón Xirau).* Pamplona: Ediciones Eunate, 1997.

Maurer, Christopher. "Introduction." Juan Ramón Jiménez. *The Complete Perfectionist: a Poetics of Work.* Edited and translated by Christopher Maurer. Chicago: Swan Isle Press, 2011. 1–16.

–"Poetry." Edited by Federico Bonaddio. *A Companion to Federico García Lorca.* Woodbridge, UK; Rochester, NY: Tamesis/Boydell & Brewer, 2007. 16–38.

Mayhew, Jonathan. *Apocryphal Lorca.* Chicago: U of Chicago P, 2009.

– *The Poetics of Self-Consciousness: Twentieth-Century Spanish Poetry.* Lewisburg: Bucknell UP; London; Cranbury, NJ: Associated UP, 1994.

Mayor Zaragoza, Federico. "La casa que fotografió Capa es un símbolo del horror, como Auschwitz." Interview with Luca Constantini. *El País.* 10 Dec. 2017. 10 Dec. 2017.

McClennen, Sophia. *The Dialectics of Exile: Nation, Time, Language, and Space in Hispanic Literatures.* West Lafayette, IN: Purdue UP, 2004.

McGrath, Brian. *The Poetics of Unremembered Acts: Reading, Lyric, Pedagogy.* Evanston, IL: Northwestern UP, 2013.

McLoughlin, Kate, ed. *The Cambridge Companion to War Writing.* Cambridge, UK; New York: Cambridge UP, 2009.

Mejías-López, Alejandro. "Hispanic Studies and the Legacy of Empire." Edited by Akiko Tsuchiya and William G. Acree Jr. *Empire's End: Transnational Connections in the Hispanic World.* Nashville: Vanderbilt UP, 2015. 204–21.

– *The Inverted Conquest. The Myth of Modernity and the Transatlantic Onset of Modernism.* Nashville: Vanderbilt UP, 2009.

Menéndez Pidal, Ramón. "Proemio." Edited by Ramón Menéndez Pidal. *Flor nueva de romances viejos*. Madrid: Espasa-Calpe: 1975. 9–42.

Mills-Courts, Karen. *Poetry as Epitaph: Representation and Poetic Language*. Baton Rouge: Louisiana State UP, 1990.

Mnemosine: Biblioteca Digital de La otra Edad de Plata. http://repositorios.fdi.ucm.es/mnemosine/. 1 May 2018.

Monegal, Antonio. "Pre-texto e intertexto en 'Retrato de poeta', de Luis Cernuda." *Boletín de la Fundación Federico García Lorca* 9 (1991): 65–75.

Moradiellos, Enrique. *Historia mínima de la Guerra Civil española*. Mexico City: El Colegio de México; Madrid: Turner, 2016.

– "Revisión histórica crítica y revisionismo político presentista: el caso español." *Memorias históricas de España (siglo XX)*. Edited by Josefina Cuesta. Madrid: Fundación Francisco Largo Caballero, 2007. 372–88.

Morales, José Ricardo, ed. *Poetas en el destierro*. Santiago de Chile: Cruz del Sur, 1943.

Morales Rivera, Santiago. *Anatomía del desencanto: humor, ficción y melancolía en España, 1976–1998*. West Lafayette, Indiana: Purdue UP, 2017.

Morcillo, Aurora G., ed. *Memory and Cultural History of the Spanish Civil War: Realms of Oblivion*. Leiden; Boston: Brill, 2014.

Moretti, Franco. *Graphs, Maps, Trees: Abstract Models for a Literary History*. London: Verso, 2005.

Morgado, María. "Caballero Bonald, García Montero y Benítez Reyes recitan su memoria." *El País*. 31 Mar. 2007. 1 Sept. 2017.

Morris, C.B. *A Generation of Spanish Poets*, 1920–1936. London: Cambridge UP, 1971.

Morrow, John A. "Darío's 'A Bolivia': Cosmic Correspondences and Universal Analogies." *Romance Notes* 44.1 (Fall 2003): 113–15.

Muñiz-Huberman, Angelina. *El canto del peregrino. Hacia una poética del exilio*. Barcelona: Sinaia, 1999.

– "Luis Cernuda: una fotografía y el exilio del viento y el alma" *Revistas de la UNAM: La experiencia literaria* 16 (2009).

Muñoz-Basols, Javier, Laura Lonsdale, and Manuel Delgado, eds. *The Routledge Companion to Iberian Studies*. Abingdon, Oxon; New York, NY: Routledge, 2017.

Muñoz Molina, Antonio. "El caso Hackl." *Lateral* (Jul.–Aug. 2001): 79–80. 1 Dec. 2010.

– "In the Company of Strangers." Interview with Robin Cembalest. *Tablet* 11 Mar 2004. 1 Dec. 2010.

– "Destierro y destiempo de Max Aub." *Pura alegría*. 87–118.

– "Dos exilios ingleses." *El País*. 28 Aug. 2010. 1 Dec. 2012.

– "Dreaming of Something Better." Interview with Maya Sela. *Haaretz*. 21 Jan. 2011. 1 Dec. 2010.

– "Lazos catalanes." *El País* 22 Sept. 2012. 1 Sept. 2017.

– "Una lengua peregrina." *Antonio Muñoz Molina*. 5 Apr. 2012. 1 Sept. 2017.

– "Max Aub: una mirada española y judía sobre las ruinas de Europa." *Pura alegría.* 119–38.

– "Muchos no quieren correr el menor peligro de dejar de ser 'progres.'" Interview with Arcadi Espada. *El País* 25 Aug. 2002. 1 Dec. 2012.

– "Notas escépticas de un republicano." *El País* 25 Apr. 2006. 1 Dec. 2012.

– "Una obra maestra desconocida." *Revista Arcadia* 20 (Apr. 2010). 15 Nov. 2014.

– *Sefarad: una novela de novelas.* Madrid: Alfaguara, 2001.

– *Sepharad.* Trans. Margaret Sayers Peden. Orlando: Harcourt, 2003.

– "Todos somos posibles condenados." Interview with Rosa Mora. *El País* 10 Mar. 2001. 1 Dec 2010.

– *Pura alegría.* Madrid: Alfaguara, 1998.

– "Una vida en el siglo." Edited by Alba C. de Rojo. *Cara y cruz: Iconografía de Max Aub.* 14–18.

Muñoz Soro, Javier. "Antonio Machado." Coord. Mari Paz Balibrea. *Líneas de fuga: hacia otra historiografía cultural del exilio republicano español.* 440–6.

Naharro-Calderón, José María. "Des-lindes de exilio." Edited by José María Naharro-Calderón. *El exilio de las Españas de 1939 en las Américas: "¿Adónde fue la canción?".* 11–39.

– *Entre alambradas y exilio: sangrías de las Españas y terapias de Vichy.* Madrid: Biblioteca Nueva, 2017.

–, ed. *El exilio de las Españas de 1939 en las Américas: "¿Adónde fue la canción?"* Barcelona: Anthropos, 1991.

– "Twentieth-Century Literature in Exile." Edited by David T. Gies. *The Cambridge History of Spanish Literature.* 620–7.

Nathanson, Tenney. *Whitman's Presence: Body, Voice, and Writing in Leaves of Grass.* New York: NYUP, 1992.

Navajas, Gonzalo. "La historia como paradigma introspectivo: El modelo ético de Muñoz Molina." *Cuadernos de narrative* 2 (Dec. 1997): 37–54.

Neruda, Pablo. *Confieso que he vivido: memorias.* Barcelona: Editorial Seix Barral, 1974.

– *España en el corazón: himno a las glorias del pueblo en la guerra* (1936–1937). Santiago de Chile: Ediciones Ercilla, 1937.

– *Memoirs.* Translated from the Spanish by Hardie St. Martin. New York: Farrar, Straus and Giroux, 1977.

Nietzsche, Friedrich Wilhelm. *Untimely Meditations.* Edited by Daniel Breazeale. Translated by R.J. Hollingdale. New York: Cambridge UP, 1997.

Nowell Smith, David. *On Voice in Poetry: The Work of Animation.* Houndmills, Basingstoke, Hampshire; New York: Palgrave Macmillan, 2015.

Núñez, César. "Max Aub 'en el país del viento': algunos poemas del denominado Ciclo de Djelfa (1941–1942)." Edited by James Valender and Gabriel Rojo. *Homenaje a Max Aub.* 283–363.

Oleza, Joan. "Un mapa de lecturas. La biblioteca de Max Aub en Valencia." Edited by Salvador Albiñana. *Libros en el infierno. La biblioteca de la Universidad de Valencia. 1939.* València: Servei de Publicacions de la Univ. de València, 2008. 63–112.

Ong, Walter. *Orality and Literacy: The Technologizing of the Word.* London and New York: Routledge, 1982, 2002.

Pace, Eric. "Rosa Chacel, 96, A Spanish Novelist Exiled for 36 Years." *The New York Times*. 2 Aug. 1994. 15 Dec. 2017.

Paraíso, Isabel. "La audacia metrica de Rosalia de Castro (*En las Orillas del Sar*)." *Actas do Congreso lnternacional de Estudios sobre Rosalia de Castro e o Seu Tempo (Santiago, 15–20 de xullo de 1985). Tomo II*. Santiago de Compostela: Consello da Cultura Galega / Universidad de Santiago de Compostela, 1985. 285–93.

Pardo, José Luis. "Tomás, el claro." Tomás Segovia. *Miradas al lenguaje*. Mexico City: El Colegio de México, 2007. 9–18.

Pavlovic, Tatjana. *The Mobile Nation: España Cambia de Piel* (1954–1964). Bristol: Intellect, 2011.

Payne, Stanley G. "Fascist Italy and Spain, 1922–45." Edited by Rein Raanan. *Spain and the Mediterranean since 1898*. London: Routledge, 1999. 99–115.

Paz, Octavio. *Obras completas II: Excursiones/Incursiones. Dominio extranjero. Fundación y disidencia. Dominio hispánico*. Barcelona: Galaxia Gutenberg – Círculo de *Lectores*, 2000.

– "La palabra edificante." *Revista de la Universidad de México* XVIII.11 (July 1964): 7–15.

– "The Edifying Word." Luis Cernuda. *Selected Poems*. Edited and translated by Reginald Gibbons. The Sheep Meadow Press: Riverdale-On-Hudson, New York, 1999. xii–xli.

Penalva Candela, Gonzalo. *Tras las huellas de un fantasma: aproximación a la vida y obra de José Bergamín*. Madrid: Ediciones Turner, 1985.

Pérez Bowie, José Antonio. "En torno a la concepción aubiana de realismo." *El correo de Euclides: anuario científico de la Fundación Max Aub*1 (2006): 486–96.

– "Sobre el compromiso de Max Aub: la literatura como rebelión y como revelación." *Revista de Occidente* 265 (June, 2003): 39–52.

Pérez-Simón, Andrés. "La ficción difícil: la escritura memorialista de Antonio Muñoz Molina." *Romance Notes* 54.2 (2014): 253–61.

Perloff, Marjorie. "Introduction: The Sound of Poetry." *The Sound of Poetry / The Poetry of Sound*. Edited by Marjorie Perloff and Craig Dworkin. Chicago and London: The University of Chicago Press, 2009. 1–9.

Perriam, Chris, Michael Thompson, Susan Frenk, and Vanessa Knight. *A New History of Spanish Writing, 1939 to the 1990s*. Oxford: Oxford UP, 2000.

Piera, Carlos. *La moral del testigo: ensayos y homenajes*. Madrid: Antonio Machado Libros, 2012.

Preston, Paul. *The Spanish Holocaust: Inquisition and Extermination in Twentieth-Century Spain*. London: Harper Press, 2011.

Primo de Rivera, José Antonio. *Obras completas*. Madrid: Delegación Nacional de la Sección Femenina de F.E.T. y de las J.O.N.S., 1954.

– *Selected Writings*. Edited and introduced by Hugh Thomas. Translated by Gudie Lawaetz. London: Cape, 1972.

Quance, Roberta. "Speaking with the Other: Reading Lyric." *Poetics of Hispanism.* Edited by Cathy L. Jrade and Christina Karageorgou-Bastea. Madrid: Iberoamericana/ Vervuert, 2012. 227–37.

Rabaté, Jean-Claude. "Unamuno before 1902: Writing Nation, History and Politics." *A Companion to Miguel de Unamuno.* Edited by Julia Biggane and John Macklin Woodbridge. Suffolk: Tamesis, 2016.

Ramazani, Jahan. "'To Get the News from Poems': Poetry as Genre." Edited by Erik Martiny. *A Companion to Poetic Genre.* 3–16.

– "Lines and Circles: Transnationalizing American Poetry Studies." *American Literary History* 28.2 (2016): 308–14.

– *Poetry and its Others: News, Prayer, Song, and the Dialogue of Genres.* Chicago; London: U of Chicago P, 2014.

– "Poetry, Modernity, and Globalization." *The Oxford Handbook of Global Modernisms.* Edited by Mark Wollaeger and Matt Eatough. New York, Oxford: Oxford UP, 2012. 288–312.

– *A Transnational Poetics.* Chicago: U of Chicago P, 2009.

Ramírez, Goretti. "Cultural Landscapes: Luis Cernuda's Exiled Poetry" *Spectacle and Topophilia: Reading Early Modern and Postmodern Hispanic Cultures.* Edited by David R. Castillo and Bradley J. Nelson. Nashville: Vanderbilt UP, 2012. 191–211.

Rancière, Jacques. "Art of the Possible: Fulvia Carnevale and John Kelsey in Conversation with Jacques Rancière." *ArtForum.* Mar. 2007. 5 Aug. 2014.

– "Contemporary Art and the Politics of Aesthetics." *Communities of Sense: Rethinking Aesthetics and Politics.* Edited by Beth Hinderliter, et al. Durham: Duke UP, 2009. 31–50.

– *The Politics of Aesthetics.* Translated with introduction by Gabriel Rockhill. London: Continuum, 2004.

Reig Tapia, Alberto. "La maldita memoria histórica." *La crítica de la crítica: inconsecuentes, insustanciales, impotentes, prepotentes y equidistantes.* Madrid: Siglo XXI, 2017. 169–83.

Resina, Joan Ramón. "Iberian Modalities: The Logic of an Intercultural Field." *Iberian Modalities: A Relational Approach to the Study of Culture in the Iberian Peninsula.* Liverpool: Liverpool UP, 2013. 1–20.

– "Presentación." *Fractal* (2012): 66–7.

Ribas-Casasayas, Alberto, and Amanda L. Petersen, ed. *Espectros: Ghostly Hauntings in Contemporary Transhispanic Narratives.* Lewisburg: Bucknell UP, 2016.

Ribeiro de Menezes, Alison. *Embodying Memory in Contemporary Spain.* New York: Palgrave Macmillan, 2014.

Richards, Michael. *After the Civil War: Making Memory and Re-Making Spain since 1936.* Cambridge: Cambridge UP, 2013.

Rico, Francisco, comp. *Mil años de poesía española: antología comentada.* Barcelona: BackList, 2009.

Ricoeur, Paul. *Memory, History, Forgetting*. Translated by Kathleen Blamey and David Pellauer. Chicago: U of Chicago P, 2004.

Ridruejo, Dionisio. "Prólogo." Antonio Machado. *Poesías completas*. Madrid: Espasa-Calpe, s.a., 1941. V–XXV.

Riffaterre, Michael. "Prosopopeia." *The Lesson of Paul de Man*. Edited by Peter Brooks, J. Hillis Miller, and Shoshana Felman. Spec. issue of *Yale French Studies* 69 (1985): 107–23.

Rimbaud, Arthur. *Complete Works, Selected Letters: A Bilingual Edition*. Translated with an introduction and notes by Wallace Fowlie; updated, revised, and with a foreword by Seth Whidden. Chicago: U of Chicago P, 2005.

Ríos-Font, Wadda. "Literary History and Canon Formation." Edited by David T. Gies. *The Cambridge History of Spanish Literature*. 15–35.

Rivera, Susana, ed. *Última voz del exilio: el grupo poético hispano-mexicano*. Madrid: Hiperión, 1990.

Rivero Taravillo, Antonio. *Luis Cernuda: años de exilio (1938–1963)*. Barcelona: Tusquets Editores, 2011.

– *Luis Cernuda: años españoles (1902–1938)*. Barcelona: Tusquets Editores, 2008.

Rodríguez Puértolas, Julio. "Presentación." Edited by Julio Rodríguez Puértolas. *El pensamiento de Américo Castro. La tradición corregida por la razón*. Madrid: Sociedad Estatal de Conmemoraciones Culturales, 2009. 1 Sept. 2017.

Rogers, Gayle. *Modernism and the New Spain: Britain, Cosmopolitan Europe, and Literary History*. New York: Oxford UP, 2012.

Romero Tobar, Leonardo. "Extraterritoriality and Multilingualism in Spanish Literary Historiography." Edited by Brad Epps and Luis Fernández Cifuentes. *Spain Beyond Spain: Modernity, Literary History and National Identity*. 189–204.

Rothberg, Michael. *Multidirectional Memory: Remembering the Holocaust in the Age of Decolonization*. Stanford: Stanford UP, 2009.

Ruiz, Julius. "A Spanish Genocide? Reflections on the Francoist Repression after the Spanish Civil War." *Contemporary European History* 14.2 (May 2005): 171–91.

Ruiz, Roberto. "La segunda generación de escritores exiliados en México." *El exilio español*. Spec. Issue of *OMNIA: Revista de la Coordinación de Estudios de Posgrado* 5.17 (December 1989). 1 Sept. 2017.

Rüsen, Jörn. "How to Make Sense of the Past: Salient Issues of Metahistory." *Journal of Transdisciplinary Research in South Africa* 3.1 (2007): 169–221.

Sahuquillo, Ángel. *Federico García Lorca and the Culture of Male Homosexuality*. Translated by Erica Frouman-Smith. Jefferson: McFarland, 2007.

Said, Edward. *Reflections on Exile and Other Essays*. Cambridge, MA: Harvard UP, 2000.

Salaün, Serge. *La poesía de la guerra de España*. Madrid: Castalia, 1985.

Salessi, Jorge, and José Quiroga. "Errata sobre la erótica: The Elision of Whitman's Body." *Breaking Bounds: Whitman and American Cultural Studies*. Edited by Betsy Erkkila and Jay Grossman. Oxford and New York: Oxford UP, 1996.

Sánchez Ferlosio, Rafael. *Las semanas del jardín*. Madrid: Alianza, 1981.

Sánchez Vázquez, Adolfo. *A tiempo y destiempo: antología de ensayos*. Mexico City: Fondo de Cultura Económica, 2003.

Sánchez Zapatero, Javier. "Aub o el poder testimonial de la ficción." *Estudios Humanísticos: Filología* 32 (2010): 197–211.

Santana, Mario. "Mapping National Literatures: Some Observations on Contemporary Hispanism." Edited by Brad Epps and Luis Fernández Cifuentes. *Spain Beyond Spain: Modernity, Literary History and National Identity*. 109–24.

Sanz Villanueva, Santos. "La vida cultural (1939 to 1975)." Edited by Santos Sanz Villanueva. *Historia y crítica de la literatura española: 1939–1975. Primer suplemento*. Barcelona: Crítica Grijalbo Mondadori, 1999. 3–23.

Scheindlin, Raymond P., and Vincent Barletta. "Al-Andalus, Poetry of." Ronald Greene, editor in chief; Stephen Cushman, general editor; Clare Cavanagh, Jahan Ramazani and Paul Rouzer, associate editors. *The Princeton Encyclopedia of Poetry and Poetics*. 4th ed. 27–9.

Schmidt, Rachel. *Forms of Modernity: Don Quixote and Modern Theories of the Novel*. Toronto: U of Toronto P, 2011.

Schulman, Ivan A. "Génesis del azul modernista." *Revista Iberoamericana* XXV.50 (July–December 1960): 257–70.

Schwartz, Kessel, ed. *Introduction to Modern Spanish Literature: An Anthology of Fiction, Poetry, and Essay*. New York: Twayne Publishers, 1968.

Sefamí, Jacobo. "Mexico, Poetry of." Ronald Greene, editor in chief; Stephen Cushman, general editor; Clare Cavanagh, Jahan Ramazani and Paul Rouzer, associate editors. *The Princeton Encyclopedia of Poetry and Poetics*. 4th ed. 879–83.

Segovia, Tomás. *Apalabrarse*. Mexico City: Consejo Nacional para la Cultura y las Artes, Ediciones sin Nombre, 2012.

– *Cuaderno del Nómada. Poesía completa: I–II*. Mexico City: Fondo de Cultura Económica, 2014.

– *Digo yo: ensayos y notas*. Mexico City: Fondo de Cultura Económica, 2011.

– "Entretien avec Tomás Segovia." Interview by Bernard Sicot. *Caravelle* 78 (June 2002): 233–46.

– "El exilio no es un tema, es una condición." *El País* 5 Apr. 2003. 1 Sept. 2017.

– "Luz de aquí: Entrevista por Christopher Domínguez Michael." *Letras Libres* 56 (December 2011): 70–7. 15 Mar. 2016.

– "Machado desde otra orilla." *Cuadernos hispanoamericanos* 359 (May 1980): 397–412.

– "Márgenes de Octavio Paz." *Resistencia: ensayos y notas*. Mexico City: El Colegio de México, 2005. 54–73.

– "Marsias y Orfeo." *Revista de la Universidad de México* XI.12 (Agosto 1957): 17–19.

– *Miradas al lenguaje*. Mexico City: El Colegio de México, 2007.

– "Nota del traductor." Jacques Lacan. *Escritos 1*. French translation by Tomás Segovia and Armando Suárez; Jacques Lacan, Juan David Nasio and Armando Suárez (rev.). Madrid: Biblioteca Nueva, 2013. 15–20.

– *Partición: 1976–1982*. Valencia: Editorial Pre-textos, 1983.
– *Poesía: 1943–1976*. Mexico City: Fondo de Cultura Económica, 1982.
– *Poesía: 1943–1997*. Mexico City: Fondo de Cultura Económica, 1998.
– "*Resistencia: ensayos y notas*. Mexico City: El Colegio de México, 2005.
– "Respuestas del exilio." *Sextante: Ensayos III*. Mexico City: Universidad Autónoma Metropolitana, 1991. 199–219.
– *Sobre exiliados*. Mexico City: El Colegio de México, 2007.
– *El tiempo en los brazos: Cuadernos de notas (1950–1983)*. Valencia: Editorial Pre-Textos, 2009.
Sicot, Bernard. *Ecos del exilio: 13 poetas hispanomexicanos. Antología*. Sada: Ediciós de Castro, 2003.
– *Exilio, memoria e historia en la poesía de Luis Cernuda* (1938–1963). Madrid: Fondo de Cultura Económica, 2003.
– "Max Aub en Djelfa: lo cierto y lo dudoso." *Nueva revista de filología hispánica* 55.2 (2007): 397–434.
– "La poésie de Tomás Segovia, de la paratopie à la présence (1943–2011)." *Tomás Segovia: Par delà les frontières*. Edited by Thomas Barège. Valenciennes: Presses universitaires de Valenciennes, 2014. 135–50.
Siles, Jaime. "La guerra civil como referencia explícita." *Estados de conciencia. Ensayos sobre poesía española contemporánea*. Madrid: Abada, 2006. 227–45.
Sime, Jennifer. "Exhumations: The Search for the Dead and the Resurgence of the Uncanny in Contemporary Spain." *Anthropology and Humanism* 38.1 (2013): 36–53.
Siskind, Mariano. *Cosmopolitan Desires: Global Modernity and World Literature in Latin America*. Evanston, Illinois: Northwestern UP, 2014.
Soldevila Durante, Ignacio. *El compromiso de la imaginación: vida y obra de Max Aub*. Segorbe: Fundación Max Aub, 1999.
– "El léxico de Valle Inclán: estado de la investigación y contribución a su estudio." Alicante: Biblioteca Virtual Miguel de Cervantes, 2011. 1 Sept. 2017.
Soler Sasera, Eva. *Max Aub, crítico literario y teatral. Hacia una función de su crítica*. Barcelona: Editorial Anagnórisis, 2015.
Sontag, Susan. *Regarding the Pain of Others*. New York: Picador, 2003.
Soo, Scott. *The Routes to Exile: France and the Spanish Civil War Refugees, 1939–2009*. Manchester: New York: Manchester UP, 2013.
Soufas, Christopher. "Cernuda and Daimonic Power." *Hispania* 66.2 (May 1983): 167–75.
Souto Alabarce, Arturo. "Letras." AA. VV. *El exilio español en México, 1939–1982*. Mexico City: Salvat - Fondo de Cultura Económica, 1982. 362–408.
– "Max Aub como crítico de la generación 'Nepantla.'" Edición de James Valender y Gabriel Rojo. *Homenaje a Max Aub*. 261–68.
Spariosu, Mihai I. *Modernism and Exile: Play, Liminality, and the Exilic-Utopian Imagination*. Basingstoke: Palgrave Macmillan, 2015.

Spender, Stephen. "Stephen Spender." *The God that Failed: A Confession*. Edited by Richard Howard Stafford Crossman. New York: Harper & Brothers, 1949. 229–73.

– *World within World: The Autobiography of Stephen Spender*. Modern Library Classics. New York: Random House Inc., 2001.

Spender, Stephen, and John Lehman, eds. *Poems for Spain*. London: The Hogarth Press, 1939.

Steiner, George. "Extraterritorial." *Triquarterly* 17 (1970): 119–27.

Stewart, Paul. "Cernuda, Luis (1902–63)." *Columbia Dictionary of Modern European Literature*. Gen. Edited by Jean-Albert Bédé and William B. Edgerton. New York; Guildford: Columbia UP, 1980. 1 Sept. 2017.

Stewart, Susan. *Poetry and the Fate of the Senses*. Chicago: U of Chicago P, 2002.

Subirats, Eduardo. *Memoria y exilio: revisiones de las culturas hispánicas*. Madrid: Editorial Losada, 2003.

Suleiman, Susan Rubin. *Crises of Memory and the Second World War*. Cambridge, MA: Harvard UP, 2006.

Talavera, Juan Carlos. "Donan la biblioteca y el archivo de Tomás Segovia al Colegio de México." *Crónica.com.mx*. 29 Aug. 2012. 1 Sept. 2017.

Tasis, Eduardo. "El porqué de la importancia vital en Tomás Segovia." Edited by Manuel Aznar Soler and José Ramón López García. *El exilio republicano de 1939 y la segunda generación*: 774–82.

Trapiello, Andrés. "Ante un 'paseo' de Sebastiaan Faber por *Las armas y las letras*." *Ínsula* 809 (May 2014): 13–15.

– *Las armas y las letras: literatura y Guerra Civil (1936–1939)*. Barcelona: Destino, 2010.

– "Una imprenta con baño (a propósito del tipógrafo JRJ)." Edited by Javier Blasco and Antonio Piedra. *Juan Ramón Jiménez: Premio Nobel 1956*. 509–34.

– "El milagro de la literatura consiste en doblar la vida." Interview with Emma Rodríguez. *Lecturas sumergidas* 7. September 2013. 1 Sept. 2017.

Traverso, Enzo. *Fire and Blood: The European Civil War, 1914–1945*. London, New York: Verso Books, 2007, 2016.

Treglown, Jeremy. *Franco's Crypt: Spanish Culture And Memory Since 1936*. New York: Farrar, Straus and Giroux, 2013.

– "The Spanish Holocaust by Paul Preston: Review." *The Telegraph*. 28 Feb. 2012. 4 Aug. 2014.

Tremlett, Giles. *Ghosts of Spain: Travels Through A Country's Hidden Past*. London: Faber and Faber, 2006.

Tucker, Herbert. "Dramatic Monologue and the Overhearing of *Lyric*." Edited by Chaviva Hosek and Patricia Parker. *Lyric Poetry beyond New Criticism*. 226–43.

Ugarte, Michael. *Shifting Ground: Spanish Civil War Exile Literature*. Durham: Duke UP, 1989.

– "Luis Cernuda and the Poetics of Exile." *MLN* 101.2 (Mar. 1986): 325–41.

– "In Praise of Forgetting and the Historical Memory of the Spanish Civil War." *Historiografías* 13 (January–June, 2017): 146–55.

Urrutia, Jorge, ed. *Poesía de la Guerra Civil española: antología, 1936–1939*. Sevilla: Fundación José Manuel Lara, 2006.

Valender, James. "Introducción." *Poetas del exilio español: una antología*. Edited by James Valender and Gabriel Rojo Leyva. Mexico City: El Colegio de México, 2006. 9–30.

– "*La luz provisional*: notas sobre el primer poemario de Tomás Segovia." *Homenaje a Tomás Segovia: maestro, ensayista, traductor y sobre todo poeta*. Edited by Luz Elena Gutiérrez de Velasco. Mexico City: El Colegio de México, 2014. 57–74.

– *Luis Cernuda: Álbum*. Madrid: Publicaciones de la Residencia de Estudiantes, 2002.

–, ed. *Luis Cernuda en México*. Mexico City, Madrid: Fondo de Cultura Económica, 2002.

– "Max Aub (1903–1972)." *Poetas del exilio español: una antología*. 277–8.

Valender, James, and Gabriel Rojo, eds. *Homenaje a Max Aub*. México: El Colegio de México, 2005.

Valero, F. "In Memóriam." *El Periódico de Aragón*. 22 Oct. 2010. 1 Sept. 2017.

Valéry, Paul. *Collected Works of Paul Valéry. Volume1: Poems*. Edited by Jackson Matthews; translated by David Paul; selected and translated from the notebooks by James R. Lawler. Princeton, NJ: Princeton UP, 1971.

Valis, Noël. "Nostalgia and Exile." *Journal of Spanish Cultural Studies* 1.2 (1 Sept. 2000): 117–33.

–, ed. *Teaching Representations of the Spanish Civil War*. New York: The Modern Language Association of America, 2007.

Vallejo, César. *The Complete Poetry*. Translated and edited by Clayton Eshleman. Berkeley: U of California P, 2007.

– *Poemas en prosa. Poemas humanos. España, aparta de mí este caliz*. Edited by Julio Vélez. Madrid: Cátedra, 1988.

Varón, Carlos. *La retirada del poema: literatura hispánica e imaginación política moderna*. Madrid: Iberoamericana-Vervuert, 2020.

Vega-Durán, Raquel. *Emigrant Dreams, Immigrant Borders: Migrants, Transnational Encounters, and Identity* in Spain. Lewisburg: Bucknell UP, 2016.

Vernon, John. *Poetry and the Body*. Urbana: U of Illinois P, 1979.

Walsh, John K. "A Logic in Lorca's Ode to Walt Whitman." Edited by Emilie L. Bergmann and Paul Julian Smith. *Entiendes? Queer Readings, Hispanic Writings*. Durham: Duke UP, 1995. 257–78.

Walters D. Gareth. *The Cambridge Introduction to Spanish Poetry: Spain and Spanish America*. Cambridge: Cambridge UP, 2002.

Ward, Charlotte. *Studies in the Translations of Juan Ramón and Zenobia Jiménez*. New York: Peter Lang Inc., International Academic Publishers, 2017.

Weare, J. "Anaphora." Ronald Greene, editor in chief; Stephen Cushman, general editor; Clare Cavanagh, Jahan Ramazani and Paul Rouzer, associate editors. *The Princeton Encyclopedia of Poetry and Poetics*. 4th ed. 50.

Weintraub, Stanley. *The Last Great Cause: The Intellectuals and the Spanish Civil War*. New York: Weybright and Talley, 1968.

Whitman, Walt. *Poetry and Prose*. Edited by Justin Kaplan. New York: Library of America, 1996.

Wilcox, John. "Howard T. Young, The Line in the Margin: Juan Ramón Jiménez and His Readings in Blake, Shelley, and Yeats" (Book Review). *Blake* 16.4: 235–9.

Williams, Raymond. *Politics of Modernism: Against the New Conformists*. London: Verso, 1989, 2007.

Wolfreys, Julian. *Victorian Hauntings: Spectrality, Gothic, the Uncanny and Literature*. Houndmills, Basingstoke, Hampshire; New York: Palgrave, 2002.

Wood, James. *How Fiction Works*. New York: Farrar, Straus and Giroux, 2008.

Yeats, W.B. *The Collected Poems of W.B. Yeats*. Edited by Richard J. Finneran. New York: Scribner Paperback Poetry, 1996.

Yiacoup, Şizen. *Frontier Memory: Cultural Conflict and Exchange in the Romancero fronterizo*. London, England: Modern Humanities Research Association, 2013.

Young, Howard T. "Introduction: Juan Ramón Jiménez (1881–1958): A Perspective." *Studies in 20th & 21st Century Literature* 7.2 (Spring, 1983): 107–13.

– *The Line in the Margin: Juan Ramón Jiménez and his Readings in Blake, Shelley, and Yeats*. Madison: U of Wisconsin P, 1980.

– "In Loving Translation: Zenobia and Juan Ramón." *Revista Hispánica Moderna* 49.2 (1 Jan. 1996): 486–93.

Zambrano, María. *Obras completas VI: Escritos autobiográficos. Delirios. Poemas (1928–1990). Delirio y destino (1952)*. Barcelona: Galaxia Gutenberg-Círculo de Lectores, 2014.

Zepp, Susanne. "Early Writing – Max Aub's *San Juan*." Edited by Antonio Gómez López-Quiñones and Susanne Zepp. *The Holocaust in Spanish Memory: Historical Perceptions and Cultural Discourses*. 169–82.

Žižek, Slavoj. *Violence: Six Sideways Reflections*. New York: Picador, 2008.

Index

Note: Page numbers in italics indicate figures.

TORONTO IBERIC

1 Anthony J. Cascardi, *Cervantes, Literature, and the Discourse of Politics*
2 Jessica A. Boon, *The Mystical Science of the Soul: Medieval Cognition in Bernardino de Laredo's Recollection Method*
3 Susan Byrne, *Law and History in Cervantes' Don Quixote*
4 Mary E. Barnard and Frederick A. de Armas (eds), *Objects of Culture in the Literature of Imperial Spain*
5 Nil Santiáñez, *Topographies of Fascism: Habitus, Space, and Writing in Twentieth-Century Spain*
6 Nelson Orringer, *Lorca in Tune with Falla: Literary and Musical Interludes*
7 Ana M. Gómez-Bravo, *Textual Agency: Writing Culture and Social Networks in Fifteenth-Century Spain*
8 Javier Irigoyen-García, *The Spanish Arcadia: Sheep Herding, Pastoral Discourse, and Ethnicity in Early Modern Spain*
9 Stephanie Sieburth, *Survival Songs: Conchita Piquer's Coplas and Franco's Regime of Terror*
10 Christine Arkinstall, *Spanish Female Writers and the Freethinking Press, 1879–1926*
11 Margaret Boyle, *Unruly Women: Performance, Penitence, and Punishment in Early Modern Spain*
12 Evelina Gužauskytė, *Christopher Columbus's Naming in the diarios of the Four Voyages (1492–1504): A Discourse of Negotiation*
13 Mary E. Barnard, *Garcilaso de la Vega and the Material Culture of Renaissance Europe*
14 William Viestenz, *By the Grace of God: Francoist Spain and the Sacred Roots of Political Imagination*
15 Michael Scham, *Lector Ludens: The Representation of Games and Play in Cervantes*
16 Stephen Rupp, *Heroic Forms: Cervantes and the Literature of War*
17 Enrique Fernandez, *Anxieties of Interiority and Dissection in Early Modern Spain*
18 Susan Byrne, *Ficino in Spain*
19 Patricia M. Keller, *Ghostly Landscapes: Film, Photography, and the Aesthetics of Haunting in Contemporary Spanish Culture*

20 Carolyn A. Nadeau, *Food Matters: Alonso Quijano's Diet and the Discourse of Food in Early Modern Spain*

21 Cristian Berco, *From Body to Community: Venereal Disease and Society in Baroque Spain*

22 Elizabeth R. Wright, *The Epic of Juan Latino: Dilemmas of Race and Religion in Renaissance Spain*

23 Ryan D. Giles, *Inscribed Power: Amulets and Magic in Early Spanish Literature*

24 Jorge Pérez, *Confessional Cinema: Religion, Film, and Modernity in Spain's Development Years (1960–1975)*

25 Joan Ramon Resina, *Josep Pla: Seeing the World in the Form of Articles*

26 Javier Irigoyen-García, *"Moors Dressed as Moors": Clothing, Social Distinction, and Ethnicity in Early Modern Iberia*

27 Jean Dangler, *Edging toward Iberia*

28 Ryan D. Giles and Steven Wagschal (eds), *Beyond Sight: Engaging the Senses in Iberian Literatures and Cultures, 1200–1750*

29 Silvia Bermúdez, *Rocking the Boat: Migration and Race in Contemporary Spanish Music*

30 Hilaire Kallendorf, *Ambiguous Antidotes: Virtue as Vaccine for Vice in Early Modern Spain*

31 Leslie Harkema, *Spanish Modernism and the Poetics of Youth: From Miguel de Unamuno to La Joven Literatura*

32 Benjamin Fraser, *Cognitive Disability Aesthetics: Visual Culture, Disability Representations, and the (In)Visibility of Cognitive Difference*

33 Robert Patrick Newcomb, *Iberianism and Crisis: Spain and Portugal at the Turn of the Twentieth Century*

34 Sara J. Brenneis, *Spaniards in Mauthausen: Representations of a Nazi Concentration Camp, 1940–2015*

35 Silvia Bermúdez and Roberta Johnson (eds), *A New History of Iberian Feminisms*

36 Steven Wagschal, *Minding Animals In the Old and New Worlds: A Cognitive Historical Analysis*

37 Heather Bamford, *Cultures of the Fragment: Uses of the Iberian Manuscript, 1100–1600*

38 Enrique Garcia Santo-Tomás (ed), *Science on Stage in Early Modern Spain*

39 Marina Brownlee (ed), *Cervantes' Persiles and the Travails of Romance*

40 Sarah Thomas, *Inhabiting the In-Between: Childhood and Cinema in Spain's Long Transition*

41 David A. Wacks, *Medieval Iberian Crusade Fiction and the Mediterranean World*

42 Rosilie Hernández, *Immaculate Conceptions: The Power of the Religious Imagination in Early Modern Spain*

43 Mary Coffey and Margot Versteeg (eds), *Imagined Truths: Realism in Modern Spanish Literature and Culture*

44 Diana Aramburu, *Resisting Invisibility: Detecting the Female Body in Spanish Crime Fiction*

45 Samuel Amago and Matthew J. Marr (eds), *Consequential Art: Comics Culture in Contemporary Spain*

46 Richard P. Kinkade, *Dawn of a Dynasty: The Life and Times of Infante Manuel of Castile*

47 Jill Robbins, *Poetry and Crisis: Cultural Politics and Citizenship in the Wake of the Madrid Bombings*

48 Ana María Laguna and John Beusterien (eds), *Goodbye Eros: Recasting Forms and Norms of Love in the Age of Cervantes*

49 Sara J. Brenneis and Gina Herrmann (eds), *Spain, World War II, and the Holocaust: History and Representation*

50 Francisco Fernández de Alba, *Sex, Drugs, and Fashion in 1970s Madrid*

51 Daniel Aguirre-Oteiza, *This Ghostly Poetry: History and Memory of Exiled Spanish Republican Poets*

www.ingramcontent.com/pod-product-compliance
Lightning Source LLC
LaVergne TN
LVHW040153080826
844660LV00014B/946/J

* 9 7 8 1 4 8 7 5 0 3 8 1 9 *